MARK L. KNAPP UNIVERSITY OF TEXAS AT AUSTIN
ANITA L. VANGELISTI UNIVERSITY OF TEXAS AT AUSTIN
JOHN P. CAUGHLIN UNIVERSITY OF ILLINOIS AT URBANA-CHAMPAIGN

Kendall Hunt
publishing company

interpersonal
COMMUNICATION
AND HUMAN RELATIONSHIPS

eighth edition

Book Team
Chairman and Chief Executive Officer   Mark C. Falb
President and Chief Operating Officer   Chad M. Chandlee
Vice President, Higher Education   David L. Tart
Director of Publishing Partnerships   Paul B. Carty
Senior Development Editor   Angela Willenbring
Vice President, Operations   Timothy J. Beitzel
Rights and Permissions Specialist   Carrie Gehl
Cover Designer   Faith Walker

Cover image © Shutterstock.com

www.kendallhunt.com
Send all inquiries to:
4050 Westmark Drive
Dubuque, IA 52004-1840

BRIEF CONTENTS

Once a human being has arrived on this earth, communication is the largest single factor determining what kinds of relationships she or he makes with others and what happens to each in the world. *How we manage survival, how we develop intimacy, how productive we are, how we make sense, how we connect with our own divinity—all depend largely on our communication skills.*

—*Virginia Satir*
The New Peoplemaking

CONTENTS

PREFACE

This is a book about interpersonal communication—with all the standard topics like perception, conflict, verbal and nonverbal behavior, and so on covered. But there is one big difference in this book and most other books on interpersonal communication. All the processes and principles of interpersonal communication are discussed in the context of developing relationships. So it is also a book about the way people communicate in relationships as they come together and come apart. We adopted this approach for three reasons: (1) There seems to be a widespread concern in this country and abroad for understanding the forces that bring people together and keep them together and those that divide and separate them; (2) students of human communication find concepts and principles easier to learn when they can analyze and test them in the context of common experiences.; (3) there are few, if any, factors more important to individuals' well-being than their relationships with other people. Whether it is with our roommates, our romantic partners, or our parents, we are constantly experiencing how communication behavior affects our relationships. It is within the context of our relationships with others that abstract concepts like feedback, perception, and conflict resolution become increasingly relevant and important for students of communication.

The book is divided into six parts. The first part has two objectives: (1) to identify several important patterns of communication, and (2) to show how these patterns of communication manifest themselves at different stages of a relationship. Part II shows how the characteristics of each individual (e.g., gender, age, needs) and the characteristics of the environment where the relationship develops can affect the way we communicate. The three chapters constituting Part III discuss various communication patterns in the context of relationships that are moving toward increased intimacy or closeness. Part IV examines a number of communication patterns that partners perceive as crucial to the adequate maintenance of relationships. And Part V takes a look at communication patterns in the context of relationships that are moving toward less intimacy. Although the concept of effective communication behavior is implicit in the preceding chapters, the last part of the book explicitly examines the subject. We believe that any discussion of how to be an effective communicator makes more sense if preceded by chapters detailing the variety of communicative goals and activities that characterize our relationships.

The chapter order was designed to emphasize the developmental theme of the book rather than to suggest a rigid chronology to our communication behavior in relationship development. Greeting behavior, as Chapter 6 points out, takes place between friends *and* enemies even though the discussion of greeting behavior is placed in the section labeled "coming together." Similarly, lying is not a type of behavior found only in the maintenance of relationships, even though it is discussed in that section of the book. Further, it should be noted that the terms *growth* and *decay* are meant to be descriptive rather than evaluative. In other words, relationship "growth" is not inherently "good," and relationship "decay" inherently "bad." Positive and negative consequences can accrue from either process.

The concepts presented in this book were not originally designed for generalization beyond our contemporary North American culture, but future explorations may uncover some extensions to other cultural contexts.[1] It is clear that each culture imposes slightly different rules on the development and deterioration of relationships—parental selection of potential relational partners, prohibiting intimate same-sex relationships, severely sanctioning the termination of marriages, and so on. It is equally clear that specific behaviors utilized to accomplish interpersonal goals may differ greatly from culture to culture. Compare these greeting rituals with your own:

> An Ainu, meeting his sister, grasped her hands in his for a few seconds, suddenly released his hold, grasped her by both ears and gave the peculiar Ainu greeting cry; then they stroked one another down the face and shoulders. . . . Adamanese greet one another by one sitting down in the lap of the other, arms around each other's necks and weeping for a while. . . . At Matavai a full dress greeting after long absence requires scratching the head and temples with a shark's tooth, violently and with much bleeding.[2]

Or consider these friendship rituals:

> To celebrate friendship in other parts of western Africa, men throw excrement at each other and comment loudly on the genitals of their respective parents when they meet; this behavior, perhaps unnatural and obscene to us, is a proof of love to friends. In Tanzania, if a man meets a woman who is his special friend, he has the right to insult her and playfully pummel her like a punching bag.[3]

Obviously, such displays are not typical among friends in U.S. culture and likely would be considered abusive. Yet, although the behaviors used to achieve the goal of initiating contact or showing friendship with others may differ dramatically, the functions served by these behaviors and the ends sought may have some cultural overlap.

[1] See, for example, R. Goodwin, *Personal Relationships Across Cultures* (New York: Routledge, 1999) and S. O. Gaines, Jr. and J. H. Liu, "Multicultural/Multiracial Relationships." In C. Hendrick and S. S. Hendrick, eds., *Close Relationships: A Sourcebook* (Thousand Oaks, CA.: Sage, 2000), pp. 97–108.

[2] W. LaBarre, "Paralinguistics, Kinesics and Cultural Anthropology." In T. A. Sebeok, A. S. Hayes, and M. C. Bateson, eds., *Approaches to Semiotics* (The Hague, Mouton, 1964), p. 199.

[3] R. Brain, "Somebody Else Should Be Your Own Best Friend," *Psychology Today* 11 (1977, October): 83–84, 120, 123.

This book contains a preponderance of examples from male-female romantic relationships and relationships in which people "voluntarily" seek contact with, or disengagement from, one another. While such examples are common, the interaction stages outlined in the book are not limited to these applications. Romantic partners and tennis buddies have gone through the same stages; the romantic partners have simply gone further. Business partners and sorority sisters find different topics, but both engage in a lot of small talk. All people drawn into, or pulled out of, relationships by forces outside their control will like that occurrence or not like it and communicate accordingly. For instance, a child's relationship with his or her parent may, at some point, be very close and loving (Integrating Stage) and at another time be cold and distant (Stagnating Stage).

The "Dear Dr. Knapp," "Dear Dr. Vangelisti," and "Dear Dr. Caughlin" letters that precede each chapter are from actual letters written by students. The problems posed in these letters have been analyzed and discussed in a university class without the writer's identity being revealed. In this book the letters are used to forecast some of the issues treated in each chapter. The boxed inserts scattered through the text are designed to provide amusing and/or thought-provoking asides associated with the adjacent material. The "So You Want to Know About…" inserts provide focused information about specific topics of interest that are otherwise discussed in various places throughout the book.

This edition, like the last, was written with several expectations: (1) We hope that some readers will reflect on the ideas presented and compare them against what they have experienced and seen in others, but certainly not blindly accept everything. (2) We hope that some readers will not only reflect on the ideas in this book but will also find them challenging enough to actively initiate a lifelong process of analysis and reanalysis of their everyday communicative behavior and that of others. (3) We hope that still other readers will be stimulated to formulate testable hypotheses and submit some of the speculation and undocumented thoughts presented here to the rigors of social science research. The references at the end of each chapter will provide an appropriate initial step in determining what others have found.

New to This Edition

The most obvious addition to this version of *Interpersonal Communication and Human Relationships* is the switch to a new publisher, Kendall Hunt. The change in publisher has facilitated a new attractive design and the incorporation of new features that will aid student learning (e.g., running glossary terms). The switch in publishers also has allowed us to create new online resources for instructors, which we believe will benefit both students and instructors.

Beyond the aesthetic changes, there are more substantive changes to this edition as well. Some of these involve subtle updates that reflect the most recent scholarship, but there are also a number of new and important topics. Among others, these topics include:

- Greatly expanded coverage of social media, online dating, and new communication technologies;
- Changes recognizing the legal recognition of same sex marriage in the United States;
- Additional information on communication across the lifespan;
- Significant material reflecting the newest research on lying and deception detection;
- Updated information about intimate partner violence, reflecting the changing understanding of different forms of violence;
- More examples that apply to varying types of relationships.

ACKNOWLEDGMENTS

This book is the happy product of authors who think and work in a similar manner. Each has a profound respect for the diverse talents of the others. Each of us has drawn on our own research and our knowledge of the now vast body of research focused on personal relationships and tried to present it in an interesting and accessible manner for students. Inevitably, our own experiences in personal relationships (good and bad) are sometimes used to illustrate and interpret ideas in the text.

The team at Kendall Hunt has been outstanding in every way; they have been helpful, timely, and responsive. In particular, Paul Carty has been fantastic in helping set an exciting direction for this new version, and Angela Willenbring has been extraordinarily insightful and efficient throughout the process.

Rachel Lloyd did excellent work on the new instructional materials, for which we are very grateful. We are also grateful to our colleagues who reviewed earlier editions of this book: Timothy Ashmore, Morehead State University; Thomas Bovino, SUNY Suffolk County; Marcia D. Dixson, Indiana University–Purdue University Fort Wayne; Joanne Gilbert, Alma College; Robin Gilmour, University of California–Santa Barbara; Rona Leber, Bossier Parish Community College; Sally Lederer, Carlson School of Management, University of Minnesota; Claude H. Miller, University of Oklahoma; Narissra Maria Punyanunt-Carter, Texas Tech University; and Marilyn Shaw, University of Northern Iowa.

Mark L. Knapp

Anita L. Vangelisti

John P. Caughlin

ABOUT THE AUTHORS

Mark L. Knapp (PhD, Pennsylvania State University) is the Jesse H. Jones Centennial Professor Emeritus in Communication and Distinguished Teaching Professor Emeritus at The University of Texas at Austin. He co-edited the *Handbook of Interpersonal Communication* and *The Interplay of Truth and Deception*. In addition to authoring and then co-authoring *Lying and Deception in Human Interaction*, he co-authored *Nonverbal Communication in Human Interaction* and *Interpersonal Communication in Human Relationships*. He is past president and fellow of the International Communication Association and past president and distinguished scholar of the National Communication Association.

© Mark Knapp

Anita L. Vangelisti is the Jesse H. Jones Centennial Professor of Communication at the University of Texas at Austin. Her work focuses on communication and emotion in close, personal relationships. She has published numerous articles and chapters as well as several books including *The Routledge Handbook of Family Communication*, *The Cambridge Handbook of Personal Relationships*, and *Hurt Feelings in Close Relationships*. Vangelisti has served on the editorial boards of over a dozen scholarly journals. She is a Distinguished Scholar of the National Communication Association, a Fellow of the International Communication Association, and served as President of the International Association for Relationship Research. Vangelisti has received awards for her work from the National Communication Association, the International Society for the Study of Personal Relationships, and the International Association for Relationship Research.

© Anita Vangelisti

John P. Caughlin (Ph.D., University of Texas at Austin, 1997) is Professor and Head in the Department of Communication at the University of Illinois. His research focuses on effective face-to-face and mediated communication in relationship, family, and health contexts. He has co-authored or co-edited two books and more than 75 journal articles and book chapters. He has served as the Executive Officer of the Campus Research Board at Illinois. He is a past Associate Editor for the *Journal of Social and Personal Relationships*, has been a member of 14 editorial boards, and is currently one of the General Editors for a book series at Cambridge University Press. He is a Fellow of the International Association for Relationship Research, a Fellow of the International Communication Association, and he has received the Bernard Brommel Award for Outstanding Scholarship or Distinguished Service in Family Communication from the National Communication Association.

© John Caughlin

PART I

Human Communication in Developing Relationships

CHAPTER 1
Communication: The Lifeblood of Relationships

CHAPTER 2
Stages of Coming Together and Coming Apart

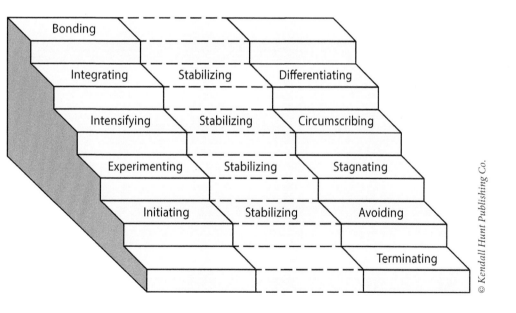

© Kendall Hunt Publishing Co.

CHAPTER 1

Communication: The Lifeblood of Relationships

Dear Dr. Knapp,

Why is it so difficult for people to express their true feelings to other people they are close to? My boyfriend drives me nuts sometimes because he can't seem to figure out how he feels about things. He'll say, "No, I don't think you're being too sensitive. . ." and think that he really believes what he's saying. But if I keep talking to him, I find that he's feeling something very different. . . which is what I thought in the first place! Even though he usually admits I was right not to believe what he says at first, I find this confusing and irritating. Why doesn't he know how he really feels about things? Why does he spout off and say things that aren't true? Is he afraid to express himself to me?

Bewildered and Bothered

Sometimes our communication with others is bewildering. It is the purpose of this chapter to explore some of the subtle and sometimes indirect, along with the more direct, ways we discuss the nature of our relationships with others. In general, then, this chapter is designed to provide the reader with some realistic expectations for the many ways we communicate with our relationship partners and how these patterns change when the relationship changes.

> *The study of everyday life quickly focuses on interpersonal communication—the sequencing of messages in conversations and the sequencing of conversations into relationships—as the primary activity in human sociation and has demonstrated that apparently simple acts of conversation are in fact incredibly complex feats which even social scientists can perform better than they can explain.*
>
> —W. Barnett Pearce

People meet and separate. But funny things happen in between. It's almost as if mysterious forces are pushing and pulling us—sometimes muddling our minds, sometimes captivating our souls. Abstract? Definitely. Poetry? Perhaps. The introduction to a scholarly textbook bent on demystifying human communication in developing relationships? Unlikely.

Fortunately, however, the foregoing introduction serves one rather important function. The abstract references to "things" and "mysterious forces" serve to remind all of us how frequently we avoid concrete and detailed descriptions of our own interpersonal relationships. For example, romantic partners may say: "What we have is so beautiful—to try to explain it, is to ruin it"; a divorcée might reflect: "I can't pinpoint anything specific . . . the relationship just wasn't making it for me anymore"; friends, too, may balk at detailed examination of their relationships: "I don't know. I just like him. Isn't that enough?"[1]

For those who study human communication, it is not enough. Such statements only raise questions: (1) Are there regular and systematic patterns of communication that suggest stages on the road to an intimate relationship? Are there similar patterns and stages that characterize the deterioration of relationships? (2) Can we identify communication strategies that attract and repel us at various stages in a relationship? Specifically, how do people talk to each other when they are building, maintaining, or tearing down a relationship? (3) What are these mysterious forces that propel us in and out of relationships? And what determines how quickly or slowly a relationship progresses or dissolves? It is the purpose of this book to seek answers to these questions.

One important issue that seems logically to precede tackling any of the aforementioned questions is the rationale for carefully scrutinizing the communication-relationship interface in the first place. Why devote an entire book to the communication behavior manifested at various stages of a relationship? Is it simply because this is a popular topic that reflects the climate of the times—surfacing in diverse sources such as the songs of Beyoncé and Katy Perry, the pages of the *Twilight* series, or the *Journal of Social and Personal Relationships*? If mere popularity were the sole justification for our concern, the idea would soon be stripped of any relevance to our daily lives. Instead, we are grappling with a phenomenon that has been, and always will be, with us—one that is inherent in everything we say and do and one that reflects the very nature of human communication itself.

Relationship Messages

It is difficult, if not impossible, to think of any message sent by one person to another that does not, in some way, also carry a commentary on the relationship between the two parties. In a sense, then, each message carries information at two levels. Watzlawick, Beavin, and Jackson call these the **content level** and the **relationship level**.[2] To illustrate this concept, consider the following example. When I say, "Come in. Have a seat," the content indicates some rather specific behaviors to follow. However, there may also be a relationship message that combines vocal, verbal, and nonverbal cues and says, "I don't know you very well; you probably want a lot from me but won't give much in return; let's keep this brief and formal; state your business and get out; I am in control of this situation, and this is just the first of several directives I'll be issuing in the next few minutes; because of my position, I expect you to follow my orders." In short, the relationship message tells us how to interpret the content. It should also be noted that message content may carry some important relationship information. In the phrase, "Get me a cup of coffee," the content itself involves one person doing something for the other and the form is a direct injunction. This may be taken by the recipient as a message indicative of a superior/subordinate relationship.[3] Regardless of their origin, relationship messages provide us with a good deal of information about how we see the other person, how we see ourselves, what kind of relationship the two of us have in this situation, what kind of relationship we have generally, or what kind of relationship is desired in the future.

What we are doing on the relationship level is sending a message about a message.[4] Sometimes we receive relationship information through the perception of nonverbal cues enacted during the verbal message—for example, a stern look, a curt voice, a warm handshake, a reduction of physical space separating the communicators. Sometimes messages are verbally altered and adapted to meet the demands of a specific relationship. A student may say, "Ok, uh, Professor Lipid. I can see you have some other students waiting to see you, so I guess I'll leave. Thanks so much for your help. I'll see you tomorrow in class." The same student would no doubt terminate his conversation with a close friend in a much different manner, "Yeah, right. Later." Sometimes we feel the necessity of metacommunicating verbally when we sense our nonverbal cues have not been sufficient. One partner in a dating pair says, "You think I'd watch an x-rated movie with *you*? You must be crazy!" This is followed by a smile, a friendly touch, and a laugh—all of which attempt to communicate, "We have such a warm and understanding relationship I can add a playful dimension and you will understand and accept it." However, if the nonverbal cues did not serve their intended purpose (either through sender or receiver error), it may be necessary for the speaker to metacommunicate by verbally stating that his or her

Content level: The specific information or references that a message conveys.

Relationship level: The message about the message, which tells us how to interpret the content and tells us what kind of relationship the two people have in this situation.

intentions were of a "kidding" nature. This example also illustrates the confusion that incongruous verbal and nonverbal cues can cause—for example, "Your words say you love me, but your behavior leaves considerable doubt."

Much of the time, we process relationship-level information without much conscious thought—almost automatically. On at least three occasions, though, we are keenly aware of relationship messages.

1. One such occasion occurs when the message seems to *drastically violate our expectations for the relationship* in a given situation—for example, being greeted by a stranger with a hello, a hug, and a kiss!

2. A second occasion occurs when we are involved in *relationships characterized by high levels of intensity*. Research by Knobloch, Solomon, and their colleagues, for example, shows that there are periods of *turbulence* in relationships, when reactions to relational messages are particularly strong (in both positive and negative ways). One time when a lot of couples experience a turbulent period is when they are deciding whether to transition from dating casually to more serious involvement.[5] Likewise, a couple battling the forces pulling their relationship apart will heighten their awareness for any information that threatens their two-person community. In these situations, we see a fusion of the content and relationship levels—both provide information pertaining to the relationship itself.

3. A third occasion occurs *when disagreement and conflict arise.* During such strife, the combatants may have several reactions: trying to become the sole "winner," planning strategies to "one-up" the other next time and thereby recoup losses incurred from not "winning," or simply enjoying the feeling of being whipped by the other's rhetorical superiority, and so on. The following dialogue, focusing on marital conflict, serves to summarize some of the concepts outlined in the preceding paragraphs:

WIFE: Honey, you really watch too much TV.	*Although the content addresses a specific behavior, the relationship level is saying: I wish you didn't have so many things that take time and attention away from me. TV is only one minor example that happened to strike me at the moment.*
HUSBAND: I do not.	*The relationship message has been ignored completely, and the husband prepares himself for the impending battle over TV watching.*
WIFE: C'mon, honey . . . you do too.	*The wife feels obligated to defend her initial statement. She cannot or will not verbalize the major problem with the relationship but tries not to be too argumentative at this point. She is still hoping her husband will respond to her cues that reveal the relationship message—sitting on the arm of his chair with her arm around his shoulders.*

HUSBAND: All right, then, I won't watch any TV for a whole week, damn it!

He is still trying to win on the content level. His kick-me-while-I'm-down strategy is clever because if she agrees, she is really a shrew—knowing what a sacrifice it would be. (The "damn it" dramatized the sacrifice.) Besides, if she agrees, he will still "win" because she will feel guilty for having caused him to be one-down—which of course puts him one-up.

WIFE: Oh, just forget it. Do what you want.

The wife sees the trap her husband has prepared on the content level. She gives up on the possibility of positive communication on the relationship level and removes herself from his chair and starts to leave the scene.

HUSBAND: Forget it! How can I forget it? You come in here and make a big deal out of my TV habits. Then, to satisfy you, I agree to cut it out completely and you say, "forget it"! What's wrong with you, anyway?

He realizes he has won on the content level and finally tunes into the relationship level—only to find negative cues. As if enjoying a relationship where he dominates, he tries to prolong his "winning" streak by urging continued argument—never realizing he is also prolonging his counterpart's losing streak.

Now the wife assesses her marital relationship. Her husband does not pay enough attention to her; he was insensitive to her meta-communication about their relationship; he enjoys dominating her; and now he has impugned her sanity for wishing to drop an issue she raised in the first place. The forecast for the immediate future is a long, miserable argument about TV watching. The long-range forecast is a frustrated and confused husband who can't understand why his wife is leaving him, especially since the only thing they fought about was so trivial—TV watching. For illustrative clarity, this dialogue focuses our attention on the husband's response to relationship messages. Obviously, this "interaction snapshot" distorts the dynamics of the husband-wife relationship and their mutual contribution to it. We might, for instance, find a link between the husband's desire to watch TV and the wife's previous orientation to *his* relationship messages.

© Jaroslav Moravcik/Shutterstock.com

Thus, human communication may be affected by the existing relationship, but it will also structure the nature of any future relationship. If you are in a serious relationship, you know you must communicate a great deal of affection to your partner because that is the nature of your commitment. In the process of making these messages of affection, however, you may do one of two things, depending on how effective you are at sending or how effective your partner is at receiving: (1) you may affirm the level of your relationship, or (2) you may change the level of your relationship to one of greater or lesser intimacy.

Up to this point, we have focused primarily on relationship messages communicated in the course of everyday conversation. But what about those times when people talk to each other (or third parties) directly and specifically about their relationship? What do they talk about? How do they talk in order to make sense of their relationship? Two studies that gathered information from people in a variety of relationships suggest the following:[6]

- People talk about relationships as *work*—the effort involved, the sacrifices, the energy needed, and so on.

- People talk about the *commitment* associated with relationships. This involves both the commitment necessary to begin a relationship and the commitment needed to sustain it.

- People talk about relationships as *involvement*. Involvement is reflected in such things as the time spent together, the quantity and quality of the talk, and sharing.

- People talk about their relationships as *unique* or *special*.

- People talk about relationships in terms of *manipulation*. Manipulation is the control of one's partner for one's own gains.

- People talk about relationships in terms of *consideration* and *respect*.

- People talk about their relationships as a developing *journey of discovery*.

- People talk about their relationships as a *game*.

- People talk about their relationships as *risky* and *potentially dangerous*.

- People talk about their relationships as *uncontrollable forces*.

- People talk about their relationships as a system of bargaining and *trade-offs*.

Obviously, different types of relationships will emphasize different themes. And sometimes the interaction will focus on the lack of these factors as well as their presence.

The *involvement* theme seems to be an overriding issue for relationships.[7] In one study of fifty-two married couples who were asked to discuss with each other a list of common problems facing married couples, the content of these conversations included *communal themes* (togetherness, interdependence), *individual themes* (emphasizing separate identities and roles), and *impersonal themes* (factors/forces outside the marriage that are believed responsible for shaping it). The couples who manifested more communal themes tended to report a greater satisfaction with their relationship than those who exhibited more individual themes.[8]

In addition to helping us understand the content of couples' talk about their relationships, this study identifies another important feature of interaction—namely, how the two partners combine their efforts as they discuss the content of their relationship. Thus, no matter what content was being discussed, the couples were also communicating a message about their relationship by *how* they interacted.

Five Important Misconceptions About Communication in Relationships

Even under the best conditions, communicating effectively in human relationships can be difficult. Even when we try very hard, effective communication may elude us. Sometimes these problems are associated with rigid and inappropriate assumptions about the nature of communication in relationships.

1. The Assumption of Consistency ("But that's not what you said yesterday.") Having *others* "be consistent" is highly valued in this society. It should be. It helps us make useful predictions about others so that we can adopt appropriate attitudes and behavior toward them. It is understandable, then, that seeming inconsistencies in others receive far less support than those we perceive in ourselves. On the other hand, we want to be able to change our *own* opinion or behavior, to be both independent and dependent, to be a person who is both stingy and generous, to be fully committed to cohabitation with somebody but also wanting time alone and to be a "take-charge" person in some things at some times and a willing "follower" on other occasions. And we really like people who understand this. Even though we value consistency in others, we rarely thank someone for pointing out a seeming inconsistency in our own behavior.

One of the reasons we aren't very receptive to another's accusations of inconsistency is that we may not perceive our behavior as inconsistent. Inconsistency and consistency are in the eye and ear of the beholder. For example, within fifteen minutes a wife makes these statements to her husband: "You spend too much money" and "You don't ever take me out to a nice restaurant anymore." The husband may perceive these as inconsistent—thinking he would have to spend money to take his wife out to dinner. The wife does not see the inconsistency because she is talking about his *personal* spending, not spending for their *mutual* benefit. In addition, to the wife the importance of going out together far supersedes the importance of spending money. Much of what we say omits important personal reservations that listeners would do well to explore before charging the person with inconsistency.

We should expect relationship messages to exhibit both consistency and inconsistency. The so-called "ideal" relationship does not manifest a continual stream of supportive messages. Ideal relationships are those in which the participants understand and appreciate the necessity of both positive and negative messages. Those with less tolerance for seemingly inconsistent behavior may have more trouble maintaining a wide variety of relationships. This intolerance for inconsistency may be especially troublesome in more enduring relationships because we often tend to emphasize our consistency first and reveal contrariety later.

Why do these seeming inconsistencies occur? Life situations and communication contexts change. You may want to be "wild and crazy" at the party and "quiet and conservative" at home; you may find frequent conversations on the topic of sex rewarding at one point in your life and boring at another. If we assume a person is "always like that" or "always will be like that," we run a high risk of being wrong. We may like somebody more than anyone we know but not want to marry him or her; we may love somebody more than anyone else but vehemently dislike something about him or her. While some may wish to view such behavior as "inconsistent," it is more productively viewed as natural—reflecting the continual unfolding and complexity of each human being. When it seems to occur, it may be a valuable opportunity for learning more about the other person and your relationship rather than a time for trying to straighten out what will never be straight.

2. The Assumption of Simple Meaning ("Well, you said it, so you must have meant it!") Most of us are taught to pay attention to what is said—the words. Words do provide us with some information, but meanings are derived from so many other sources that it would hinder our effectiveness as a partner in a relationship to rely too heavily on words alone. Words are used to describe only a small part of the many ideas we associate with any given message. Sometimes we can gain insight into some of those associations if we listen for more than words. We don't always say what we mean or mean what we say. Sometimes our words don't mean anything except "I'm letting off some steam. I don't really want you to pay close attention to what I'm saying. Just pay attention to what I'm feeling." Mostly we mean several things at once.

A woman says to the guy she's been dating, "I really like you, but I wish you weren't so messy. I couldn't live in a place that looks like your dorm room." The guy replies, "I've always been like this." Actually, he hasn't always been messy. When he lived at home, his parents wouldn't let him be messy, but the unspoken message is "I don't have a problem with my messiness. Why can't you be more accepting of how I am instead of trying to change me? Besides, who asked you to live with me?" The search for a more expansive view of meaning can be developed by examining a message in terms of *who* said it, *when* it occurred, the *related conditions* or situation, and *how* it was said.

The person *who* is making the message influences the meanings associated with it. If a parent says, "I see you have every season of *Sex in the City* on DVD" it may mean, "I don't approve of you watching this show. You should get rid of those DVDs." But if a friend says the same thing, it may suggest, "I wish I had those. Can I borrow them sometime?" When you have several different relationships with a single person (e.g., your teacher is also your friend), it is wise to consider the possibility of different meanings as you move from one type of relationship to another. Males and females may also say the same thing in different ways, or they interpret the same communication behaviors differently.[9]

When a message occurs can also reveal associated meaning. Let us assume two couples do exactly the same amount of kissing and arguing. But one couple always kisses after an argument and the other couple always argues after a kiss. The ordering of the behaviors may mean a great deal more than the frequency of the behavior. A friend's unusually docile behavior may only be understood by noting that it was preceded by situations that required an abnormal amount of assertiveness. Some responses may be directly linked to a developing pattern of responses and may defy logic. For example, a person who says "No!" to a series of charges such as "You're dumb," "You're lazy," and "You're dishonest" may also say "No!" and try to justify his or her response if the next statement is, "And you're good-looking."

The *related conditions* accompanying any given message are also influential factors in assessing the meaning of messages. For example, the meaning of "you're crazy" may vary greatly depending on whether it is said in the context of a psychiatric evaluation, a marital quarrel, or a playful gesture by a friend. "OK, let's step outside" may mean something very different to two men at a ski lodge wishing to determine the weather conditions or two men in a bar who are arguing intensely. It is also the analysis of the situation that informs us that the statement "It's cold in here" is not an observation but really a request to close the window.

We would do well to listen for *how* messages are presented. The words "It sure has been nice to have you over" can be said with emphasis and excitement or ritualistically. The phrase can be said once or repeated several times. And the meanings we associate with the phrase will change accordingly. Sometimes if we say something infrequently, it assumes more importance; sometimes the more we say something the less importance it assumes.

© mypokcik/Shutterstock.com

As if the factors in the preceding paragraphs did not complicate meaning enough, there are often multiple reasonable ways to interpret words, which is why people often have different perspectives, even on the same utterances or circumstances. There are, in short, many factors that affect the meanings we derive from interpersonal communication. In the interests of efficiency, we have learned to take a lot for granted as we speak and listen to others.[10] The recognition of this habit should make us especially careful about attributions of meaning when sending and attending to especially important messages in our lives.

3. The Assumption of Communicator Independence ("It wasn't my fault.") Many times we talk about our *relationships* with people as if we had no *relation* or connection to them—as if our behavior had nothing to do with what our partner said or did. In actuality, however, we have a lot more to do with our partner's responses than we may wish to acknowledge. The reason we often fail to acknowledge this interdependence is that it means we have to accept more of the responsibility for our communication problems. It is much easier to describe your partner's behavior as independent of your own—for example, "He never listens to me"; "She is never serious with me"; "He doesn't tell me the truth." Acknowledging interdependence forces you to ask yourself what you do to elicit such responses and what you can do to get the responses you desire. Communicators who recognize their interdependence also recognize that communication problems are the result of mutual contributions. One person can't be entirely clean and the other entirely dirty. Sometimes it is also hard to admit that our *success* in communicating with our partner may also be related to interdependence. We live in a society that reveres and rewards individual achievement, but whatever excellence in communication we achieve in relationships has to consider the role of our partner. For example, if your partner wasn't such a good audience for your humorous remarks, would you be as funny?

Communicative interdependence of relationship partners can manifest itself in many ways. One of these is called response matching. Sometimes **response matching** is performed almost unconsciously, but at other times it is well thought out. Studies reveal that people tend to match each other's length of utterance; interruptions and silences; the use of certain types of words; the extent to which one reveals information about himself or herself; and certain nonverbal signals such as nodding, smiling, posture, and voice loudness. In addition, certain types of responses are often matched. Cracking jokes, showing solidarity, giving opinions, disagreeing, and questioning often lead to more of the same from the other person.[11] Affectionate responses often follow affectionate responses; hostility often follows from hostile responses; distrust commonly leads to distrust. Sometimes one response will bring forth an almost opposite

Response matching: A tendency for people to react to others' communication behaviors with similar behaviors.

response. Dominance, for instance, often elicits submission, and submissive responses often elicit dominant reactions. To make matters more complex, sometimes we act on what we think a person thinks of us rather than how we see ourselves—for example, if you think of yourself as a rather conventional person and your friend thinks you are eccentric and expects you to behave that way, you may respond with eccentric behavior when you are with that person.

Matching and other manifestations of interdependent communication do not, of course, always occur. But they happen often enough so we know they play an important role in developing relationships. The longer a relationship endures, the more interdependence plays a role in each partner's behavior. Over time, each partner's behavior becomes so integrally bound up with the other partner's behavior that questions of what is interdependent and what isn't are no longer useful in analyzing the relationship. The knowledge that each partner's behavior has important effects on the other means we need to consider the important role our own behavior plays in how we feel our relationship partner treats us.

4. The Assumption of Obvious Causation ("You can't fool me. I know why you said that.") Sometimes people's motives are fairly clear, but often they aren't. Many times, people's behaviors and statements can be ascribed to more than one motivation. For example, imagine a classmate asks you, "Do you have big plans for the weekend?" It's possible that she wants to engage in small talk, but the same question could also indicate that she wants to invite you to do something but first wants to make sure you do not already have plans. Or, she may be hoping you'll invite her along if you have something fun planned. Whether people's motives are actually obvious or not, the motives we ascribe to them shape the meaning of the behaviors—we would probably respond quite differently to the question above if we think it is initiating small talk versus if we think it is an invitation to go on a date.[12]

Because people's intentions in conversations are not always obvious, it is important to be reflective about people's motives. We should approach this task with considerable tentativeness and humility. Too many of us jump too quickly to conclusions about the causes of another's responses. If these conclusions are the result of assuming such causes are simple and obvious, they may be incorrect and hinder communication. Even if you have correctly deduced your partner's motivation for saying or doing something, you may find he or she denies it and gets very defensive if you suggest that the behavior "was *obviously* caused by . . ."

Motivations and causes are usually complex and sometimes well hidden. As much as we try to be clear and certain about what we say, ambivalence is a common experience in today's world. Sometimes we honestly don't know why we say or do things.[13] And if it isn't clear to us, it is difficult to admit that another person might understand—although it is certainly possible. We enact many communication acts and routines at low levels of awareness. It's as if we follow certain unwritten and unknown *scripts* when confronted with the proper stimulus—for example, criticizing others when conditions signal that you need help solving a personal problem.[14] In short, the often-heard charge "You *knew* what you were saying (doing)" is something less of a truism than many people believe.

Your interpretation of your partner's behavior is inevitably filtered through your own needs and expectations. Your partner's perceptions of his or her own behavior are similarly affected, and sometimes the explanation of why something happened only becomes "clear" in retrospect. Each of our responses is overlaid with possible causations stemming from the specific encounter, the demands of the communicator's life stage, the relationship between the communicators, events and people outside the specific encounter, and many other sources. As listeners, we can only approach an understanding of some of these sources—and even then it may take an extended time.

Seven-eighths of everything can't be seen.

—*Anonymous*

5. The Assumption of Finality ("That settles it.") If something is "finished," it no longer requires the same effort, attention, and concern. As a result, we sometimes act *as if* something is finished in order to set other priorities for our available time and energy. This process will be functional until we begin to believe such things are *actually* finished. Then you are in for some surprises.

People can reach a compromise when they disagree, but the issue in some form may arise minutes, months, or years later. A person's trauma over a parent's untimely death may be temporarily concluded with "I'm over it," but the trauma may recur later. The partner to your relationship may be a person you "know well," but you will never be finished trying to know that person if you want to maintain a high degree of knowledge. The person changes from day to day. If you are mean to a person because you feel that your relationship will soon be "finished" and you'll never see the person again, you may be surprised to find that person in charge of something you want later in life. Divorce should not be expected to finalize your thoughts of the other person. And you should not assume that you have finished learning about certain communication situations just because you've faced them before.

All of these examples point out that both what we communicate about and the messages we make are constantly in process, ever-changing—a reality that prohibits the luxury of dismissing an issue, person, or behavior as forever finished. People who maintain effective relationships do not approach them passively. An understanding of process is just one factor that keeps people from assuming that the satisfying relationship they have today will continue without careful monitoring and adaptation.

Now we can return to one of our initial questions: How do people talk to each other when they are building, maintaining, or tearing down a relationship? A general understanding of this process can be gained by examining some broad dimensions of communication behavior in developing and deteriorating relationships.

How Communication Changes as Our Relationships Develop

Table 1.1 shows eight dimensions along which our communication with other people varies. Other communication dimensions may be important at certain times, but these eight allow us to discuss important differences in types of relationships and different stages in the development of a single relationship. Notice in Table 1.1 that relationships typically begin with communication characterized by the terms on the left-hand side of the table. We would predict that as relationships become closer, the communication behavior associated with the dimensions would move toward the right. When relationships are in trouble or when they are coming apart, we would expect to see communication behaviors increasingly associated with the terms on the left-hand side of the table. The terms used to describe these communication dimensions that vary as relationships change are explained next.

1. Narrow-Broad During the process of coming together, we would predict communication that shows a gradually increasing amount of talk and a gradually increasing variety in the topics explored. This has been called the "breadth" of interaction. **Breadth** just means the range of topics you discuss and how much information about those topics you reveal. You may choose to talk to

Breadth: The range of topics you discuss and how much of those topics you reveal.

Table 1.1	Eight Communication Dimensions That Change in Developing and Decaying Relationships

Growth Stages→
←Decay Stages

Narrow	___	___	___	___	___	Broad
Public	___	___	___	___	___	Personal
Stylized	___	___	___	___	___	Unique
Difficult	___	___	___	___	___	Efficient
Rigid	___	___	___	___	___	Flexible
Awkward	___	___	___	___	___	Smooth
Hesitant	___	___	___	___	___	Spontaneous
Over Judgement Suspended	___	___	___	___	___	Over Judgement Given

Adapted from I. Altman and D. A. Taylor, Social Penetration *(New York: Holt, Rinehart & Winston, 1973), pp. 129–135.*

another person about only two topics—college and sex (**Figure 1.1**). But within each of these two topics, many areas could be covered: facts, ideas, experiences, feelings about yourself or others, opinions, attitudes, and so on. These different areas within each topic are represented in Figure 1.1 by the smaller subdivisions on the outermost rim. Listed next are a few examples of people with different breadth profiles:

a. A person who talks about a few topic areas and reveals little within each area. For example, the person who wants to talk only about sports, and within that category only bowling, but won't reveal how he or she got started bowling or what score is usually bowled.

b. A person who talks about a few topic areas and reveals a lot within each area. For example, the person who limits conversation to job and sports categories, but will talk incessantly about both, freely divulging a wide range of nonintimate, superficial information.

c. A person who talks about many topic areas and reveals little within each area. For example, you may discuss sex, family, sports, religion, politics, child rearing, house construction, drugs, and school—all in the space of a short conversation—and come away with the feeling that you really don't know much about that person because as soon as you asked a probing question, the topic was changed.

d. A person who talks about many topic areas and reveals a great deal within each area. This person is probably perceived as a good conversationalist. Sometimes this person is also considered a very open person, willing to talk about a wide range of subjects and eager to reveal many items within each category. However, breadth of interaction is only one form of openness and should not be confused with depth or what we are referring to as the Public-Personal dimension (discussed later).

In the embryonic stages of developing relationships, our communicative options are often limited to a rather restricted range, which is usually determined by culturally accepted modes of exchange. When relationships begin to come apart, it is not unusual to note the need to circumscribe the breadth of communication topics and responses—"I just don't want to talk about that." When both parties are bent on destroying the relationship, they do not feel the need to broaden the scope of their interaction. But in attempts to save or

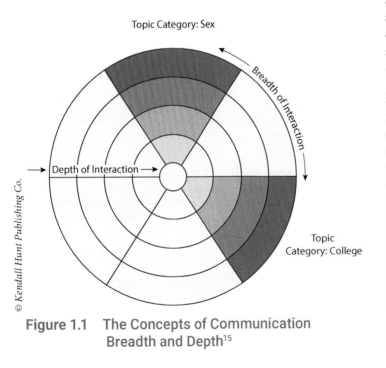

Figure 1.1 The Concepts of Communication Breadth and Depth[15]

rejuvenate a relationship, extending the breadth may be an effort to find other less sensitive areas in which nonthreatening interaction can take place and thereby increase the total rewards and offset increasing costs.

2. Public-Personal This dimension is also referred to as the **"depth" of social interaction.** When we first start talking to people, the things we say most likely reflect our public personality. Should the relationship move forward, we will increasingly uncover more and more of our private or personal selves. This is true for nonverbal as well as for verbal communication. In decaying relationships, we try to shut off valves that may release personal communication. To require someone to engage in more personal communication prior to the gradual establishment of a close and trusting relationship will sometimes induce frustration, resistance, rejection, or outright rebellion. Examples of this would be some welfare recipients who are required to hold almost nothing back from state agencies, prisoners who relinquish rights to privacy to their guards and lawyers, and nursing home residents whose dependent status often requires a list of immediate and personal disclosures to their caretakers.

Depth of social interaction: Describes the extent to which the conversation includes information that is private or personal.

You can visually observe the concept of depth by reexamining Figure 1.1. The concentric circles indicate the possibility of probing the depth of one's personality. The innermost circle represents the core, the most difficult to reach, a place that constitutes a last refuge for our most personal thoughts, feelings, and beliefs. The core and central layers of personality include information about our deepest fears, our most important needs, our basic values, and thoughts about our identity and self-worth. Once revealed, such information may make us very vulnerable. Hence, we often mask, hide, or generally make it difficult for most people to see these central layers. More often than not, the components found in the central layers are not common to many individuals but have an individual stamp of uniqueness attached to them. When changes occur in the central layers, there will be corresponding changes in the intermediate and outer layers. Once the foundation is changed, the outer structure changes accordingly. This interdependency helps explain some of our communication behavior. For instance, if a person has once penetrated into a central area and is familiar with a basic value held by another person, it is much easier to predict items that may be represented as attitudes in the intermediate area, and as personal history in the outer layer. This also helps explain why a pair, once having achieved penetration to a central layer in a given topic category, can move easily and swiftly in and out of preceding areas.

As we move outward from the central areas, we come to the intermediate layers. These may contain a wide range of attitudes and opinions on various issues that decrease in strength as outer layers are approached. The outermost circle represents the most easily accessible parts of an individual's personality and is often largely biographical in nature. The outer layer contains more items than the other layers, but these items will not tell us as much about who this person is as will the intermediate and core areas.

To summarize the concepts of both breadth and depth and to show their usefulness for examining communication at various stages of a relationship, look at **Figure 1.2**. Here we see the kind of social penetration taking place between a husband, his wife, his friend, and his new acquaintance.

Although the frequency of interaction is not visually illustrated, it is likely that greater breadth and depth will be associated with greater frequency. Several other observations can be made:

a. The wife has the most intimate relationship with her husband, achieving greater breadth and depth. She has penetrated more topic categories (all but two) and more items within every category. Some categories are special to her relationship and are revealed only to her.

b. The friend has had some breadth and some depth—less than the wife and more than the new acquaintance.

c. The new acquaintance has the most superficial relationship with the husband—little breadth and little depth.

d. The husband has one topic category that is not open to anyone at any level. He seems to be particularly comfortable with one topic category, since it has been penetrated by all persons. Should the relationship with the new acquaintance grow in breadth, we might predict the next category to be accessible would be the one already penetrated by both the wife and friend.

Stylized behavior: Communication practices or behaviors that are conventional and acceptable to many people.

3. *Stylized-Unique* The process of constructing a more intimate relationship eventually reaches a point at which we are interacting with the other person as a unique individual rather than as a member of a particular society. Uniqueness in communication simply suggests the adoption of a more idiosyncratic communication system adapted to the peculiar nature of the interacting parties. This is not to suggest adaptation is absent in early stages, but that it is adaptation to a more generalized other (an orientation toward another that makes sociological and cultural predictions rather than personal and individual ones) and involves a more **stylized behavior** acceptable to large groups of people. The handshake is one example of a stylized or conventional behavior that seems to fade away when people label themselves close friends. Actual handshakes or false starts may reappear, however, when close friends have been absent from each other for some time, if one party is unsure of his or her standing as a close friend, or when the content calls for great

© Kendall Hunt Publishing Co.

Wife
Friend
New Acquaintance

Figure 1.2 Multiple Relationships in the Social Penetration Process formality. In the deterioration process, it is not uncommon to see the formalities of stylized communication returning, as if to say, "I am no longer going to acknowledge the peculiar nature of our relationship and will treat you more like I would a large number of people."

4. Difficult-Efficient As a relationship grows and more of the other person is revealed to us, there will be increased accuracy, speed, and efficiency in our communication.[16] Early stages in a relationship hold greater possibilities for less accurate communication and slower progress because we rely so heavily on stereotyped behaviors and fewer channels of communication. There is less reliance on, and ability to interpret accurately, nonverbal cues. In short, sensitivity to sending and receiving increases with growing levels of intimacy even though a certain level of inaccuracy may be functional for all types of relationships.[17] Once familiarity with unique styles of communication is obtained, less energy is needed to communicate intended meanings. The decay process is often initiated when *less* energy is assumed to mean *no* energy, which of course precipitates more difficult communication and less efficiency.

5. Rigid-Flexible Flexibility simply refers to the number of different ways any given idea or feeling can be communicated. The more advanced the stage of growth, the greater the flexibility. For example, anger in long-married couples may take many forms—a frown, a long period of silence, a short, curt "yeah," a verbal statement, a grunt or growl, a flick of the wrist or arm, the use of the newspaper as a shield, or general fidgeting. In the early stages of growth and the later stages of decay, there is a greater demand for standardization of communication involving fewer channels.

6. Awkward-Smooth As knowledge of the other person increases, predictive ability also increases, which leads to greater synchronization of interaction. Each participant is well aware of mutual roles and plays them out in a smooth, complementary fashion. Some have called this phenomenon **meshing**. The comment "it was all very awkward" is most likely directed at an interaction with a stranger, new acquaintance, or a situation experiencing the strain of decay.

Meshing: When mutual knowledge results in smooth, complementary interaction.

7. Hesitant-Spontaneous Meeting new people is naturally accompanied by hesitancy. We can make some general predictions about how most people react in this situation, but caution is the byword when little information on a specific person is available. We can also assume that the forces that trigger the deterioration process are, at least in part, related to faulty predictions. When actively engaged in decay processes, we will see an increased hesitancy, whether the participants are trying to save the relationship or whether they both want to terminate it. In close relationships, on the other hand, we find a sort of communicative spontaneity—an informality, an ease of opening up oneself, a comfort in entering areas of the other person, a relationship that flows and changes direction easily. When talking to strangers, we seem to reflect caution by using a greater diversity of language choices than we use with friends. With friends we tend to fall back on more habitual verbal behavior.[18] Partners in intimate relationships are expected to grant each other a certain "latitude of understanding," which provides them with a freedom and relaxation that may not exist with newer acquaintances.

8. Overt Judgment Suspended–Overt Judgment Given Although our first impressions of another person probably involve a number of covert judgments, these evaluations are usually unspoken until the relationship reaches a more advanced stage. Large numbers of negative responses between strangers probably mean they have little interest, or opportunity for, developing the relationship further.[19] The closer the relationship, the greater the likelihood of freely giving and receiving positive and negative feedback. Both criticism and praise are much less inhibited in an intimate relationship. Naturally, judgments (usually negative) are an integral part of the initial decay process. Gradually, as the relationship continues to decay, the participants will move toward the suspension of overt evaluation again—for example, "I'd rather just not talk about it."

Now that we have a general understanding of these eight dimensions of communication and how they differ in intimate and nonintimate relationships, let's examine them in greater detail lest we be misled by the seeming simplicity of the process.

Dimensions of Communication: Patterns and Variations

As the arrows in **Figure 1.3** suggest, communication behavior typical of any of the eight dimensions moves from left to right (nonintimate to intimate) as people seek closer relationships; communication behavior on any of the dimensions may also move from right to left (intimate to nonintimate) as people become more distant from each other.

Stable and Varied Patterns of Communication

Figure 1.3 shows how one couple's communication behavior on each of the eight dimensions could be plotted. At any given time, the communication pattern may reflect deviations on some dimensions that are greater than the expected normal fluctuations. For example, in Figure 1.3, the difficulty and awkwardness of communication are greater than what we would have predicted, given the general similarity of the other dimensions. This configuration may reflect the beginning of communication at a less intimate level, or it may simply reflect the fact that all relationships are composed of coexisting forces that seem in opposition to one another. Intimate relationships have coldness, sadness, and difficulty to accompany the warmth, happiness, and ease. Thus, the behaviors that contribute to relationship decay are normally found in all relationships but in smaller doses. These "less-pleasant" behaviors may serve a useful function by creating the tension necessary to cause the participants to seek greater intimacy.

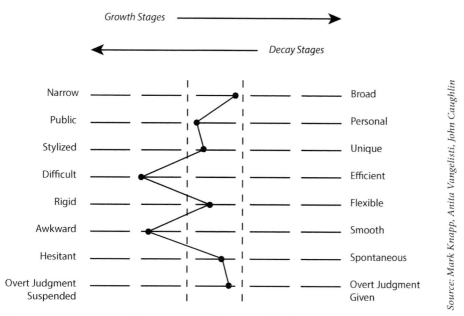

Figure 1.3 Plotting Patterns of Communication

Source: Mark Knapp, Anita Vangelisti, John Caughlin

These temporary fluctuations, however, take place within an overall pattern that reflects the relationship stage (see Chapter 2). Frequent fluctuations over time on many of the dimensions of communication rather than occasional variations on a few dimensions may indicate a period of change or turbulence.

It should also be noted that intimate relationships are not likely to sustain communication patterns that represent intimacy extremes. There are limits to which we can communicate uniquely, personally, smoothly, and so on. Empathic accuracy, for example, has been found to decline after the first year of marriage.[20] *Empathic accuracy* is the ability to accurately infer the specific content of a partner's thoughts and feelings. This skill gradually increases as a couple develops a close relationship, but there are limits to how accurately one can infer a partner's thoughts and feelings and limits to which it is functional for a satisfying relationship. Thus, at some point an optimum level for each dimension of communication will be reached and the couple will then fall back to a comfortable and functional level.

There are also limits or extremes for any type of communication that will vary with the preferences of the couple. One couple's "extreme" of personal communication may be much lower than another's. As relationships become increasingly intimate, some of these extremes may be reached, but then stabilize at lower levels. **Figure 1.4** illustrates this idea by showing how the pattern for public/personal communication may develop over time. Other dimensions probably show similar development. As Figure 1.4 shows, we do not continue to reveal more and more of ourselves to another forever. Not only are we limited in what we can and want to reveal, but our desire to know some aspects of our partner may change when we know we can.

Communication Patterns are Interdependent

Interdependent: Interdependency among the communication dimensions means that changes on one dimension will prompt changes on others.

The interdependency among the communication dimensions generally means that changes on one dimension will prompt changes on others—for example, if I am critical about the way you dress (overt judgment given), that conversation may be sufficiently unpleasant that we may decide to avoid the subject of your attire completely (decrease in breadth). This, in turn, may make me more cautious in other areas of appearance (increased hesitancy and further breadth reduction) and, in general, less likely to reveal my feelings (decreased depth revelation).

Quantity Versus Quality of Communication

The pattern shown in Figure 1.4 represents the quantity of personal disclosures as well as the quality. When relationships are reaching for more intimacy (during the establishment of a relationship or during periods when efforts are made to rejuvenate a troubled relationship), the quantity or frequency of behaviors is probably the best intimacy indicator.[21] When relationships have stabilized at a particular level of intimacy, the quality of the behavior (perceived sincerity, magnitude of expression, perfect timing, etc.) is more likely to be the best measure of intimacy. For example, many personal disclosures are necessary to establish an intimate relationship; thereafter, occasional disclosures are sufficient to sustain it. A single instance of **self-disclosure** may be perceived as the equivalent of many earlier disclosures, or it may simply serve as a reminder that when important disclosures need to be made, they will be. When intimates wish to recapture a lost level of intimacy, the frequency of personal messages is likely to increase.

Self-disclosure: Revealing personal or private information about oneself to another person.

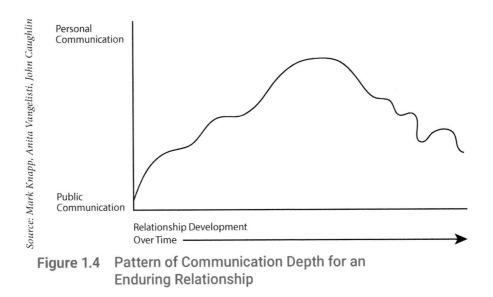

Figure 1.4 Pattern of Communication Depth for an Enduring Relationship

Diversity of Communication Characterizes Each Dimension

There are many ways of communicating at each point on each dimension. You may be operating at the lowest level of intimacy on the public/personal dimension with many people. Even though you communicate many different things in many different ways, the common characteristic is the extremely impersonal or public nature of this communication. The variety of possible communication patterns should increase as intimacy increases. Intimates may use unique and personal patterns, but they may also use patterns from earlier and less intimate stages of development that have less uniqueness and personalness. And, although people who are coming out of an intimate relationship should generally manifest more restricted patterns and patterns of less intimacy, we may occasionally observe a pattern developed during more intimate times.

Accounting for Communication Patterns of Both Relationship Partners

Thus far, we've been describing and plotting communication patterns as if both partners were communicating in the same general way. Partners will not communicate in exactly the same way, but if they are too far apart on these dimensions, they may not perceive the same type of relationship or degree of intimacy. Gross discrepancies will eventually have to be resolved, or the relationship probably has a limited life.

Testing the Model: Perceptions of Communication Behavior

In order to find out if people perceived relationships along the lines of these eight dimensions, we conducted a study.[22] We obtained ratings of communication behavior in various types of relationships (acquaintance, colleague, pal, friend, best friend, and lover) from more than a thousand people between ages 12 to 90 in eight states of the United States. Their responses revealed three things: (1) As the relationship rated became more intimate, they perceived communication behavior to become increasingly more personalized. **Personalized communication** included (a) telling another person things we don't tell most people—feelings, secrets, personal things—but not indiscriminately giving opinions of their behavior; (b) relying on a greater variety of channels for sending and receiving messages—including subtle nonverbal channels that may be considered a more specialized or personal domain; and (c) cultivating and using messages that are more personal to the interacting pair only. Personalized communication, then, encompasses some elements of the dimensions of public/personal, stylized/unique, rigid/flexible, and overt judgment suspended/overt judgment given. (2) As the relationship rated became more intimate, these people perceived communication behavior to become increasingly more synchronized. Synchronized communication included conversations that are smooth flowing, effortless, spontaneous, relaxed, informal, and well-coordinated. **Synchronized communication**, then, included some elements of the dimensions of difficult/efficient,

Personalized communication: Involves revealing information that most people do not know, the use of multiple channels for communication, and the exchange of unique or private meanings.

Synchronized communication: Involves conversations that are smooth flowing, effortless, spontaneous, relaxed, informal, and well coordinated.

awkward/smooth, and hesitant/spontaneous. (3) The last set of responses these people agreed upon as characterizing communication in relationship development concerned communication difficulty. Difficulty was not perceived to vary systematically across relationship types from nonintimate to intimate. This is understandable since both intimate and nonintimate relationships may have difficulties or "barriers" to effective communication. **Difficult communication**, for these respondents, reflected a general strain, difficulty, and awkwardness of interaction. But this difficulty did not necessarily mean greater inaccuracy in communication. The dimensions of difficult/efficient and awkward/smooth were represented in this factor. Thus, although people organize their perceptions somewhat differently, all but one of the dimensions described earlier are central to judgments of communication in different types of relationships.

Difficult communication: Involves interactions in which participants experience strain, difficulty, and awkwardness.

Subsequent studies focusing on perceptions of communication behavior at different points in relationship development add support to the communication dimensions we've identified. Baxter's study of relationship deterioration identified the following communication dimensions: *personalized communication, synchronized communication, smoothness of communication, flexibility of communication,* and *uniqueness of communication.*[23] Baxter and Wilmot's factor analysis of the eight dimensions of communication associated with relationship change outlined in this chapter found two central themes: a factor they called "effectiveness," which was a combination of *smoothness, efficiency,* and a second factor labeled "personalness," which was akin to the depth of communication. Diaries kept by university students indicated that these dimensions were associated with changes in relationship intimacy.[24] Tolhuizen studied eight stages in the evolution of friendships and found communication patterns could be identified along the following dimensions: *breadth of communication, depth of communication, flexibility of communication, ease of communication, and evaluation of communication.*[25] In a subsequent study that compared the perceptions of communication between friends to those of acquaintances and those in deteriorating relationships, friends reported significantly more *uniqueness* or other-orientation, more *depth* or personalness, and more ease and comfort (*efficiency and smoothness*).[26]

Other studies have focused on particular dimensions of perceived communication behavior—showing how people expect more breadth and depth in developing relationships.[27]

Testing the Model: Actual Communication Behavior

Even though people perceive communication to change along these dimensions at different points in relationship development, the question still remains: Does the *actual* communication behavior vary along the proposed dimensions? Two studies that compared samples of private conversations between acquaintances and between friends say yes.[28]

In one study, friends talked at a faster rate and were able to use "mutual knowledge" in their conversations—suggesting greater *efficiency*. This is not to suggest that mutual knowledge and speed of information exchange won't, on occasion, cause difficulties in communication as well. None of the characteristics of conversations that distinguish different points in a relationship are inevitably associated with a single outcome. This research does, however, support the contention that *difficult–efficient* is a useful dimension for examining differences in conversations between acquaintances and friends. This study also supports the use of other dimensions in our model. Intimacy and breadth of self-disclosure, identified more in conversations of friends, fits well with the *public–personal* and *narrow–broad* dimen-

© pixelheadphoto digital skillet/Shutterstock.com

sions. *Overt judgment suspended–overt judgment given* was reflected in several differences: friends offered more opinions and asked for more advice; friends offered more and higher quality feedback; friends expressed more negative judgments and argued more. Friends also seemed to be more *spontaneous*—laughing more and showing more overlaps and interruptions in their interaction. Acquaintances, on the other hand, were tentative. Friends showed *smoothness* in the transitions between topics, and their general style of interaction was judged more relaxed, casual, and friendly. There were few examples of extreme *uniqueness* (e.g., personal idioms) commonly seen in romantic intimates, but friends did use more informal language, jokes, repartee, and slang in contrast to the more *stylized*, polite, and formal communication of acquaintances. Even though the specific types of communication behavior used to characterize the dimensions proposed in this chapter may vary, the dimensions do seem to provide a useful framework for understanding the perceptions of relationship partners and for describing the differences observed in conversations associated with different stages or types of relationships.

In another study of actual conversations, Hornstein compared the structure of talk between friends and acquaintances.[29] Friends showed more *uniqueness* through their implicit ways of opening the conversation, more *breadth* in the form of a greater number of topics introduced, and *flexibility* in the greater complexity of conversational closings, and the greater number of questions asked (responsiveness) may have been a good measure of *spontaneity*.

Thus, in studies examining expectations for, perceptions of, and actual communication behavior, the dimensions outlined in this chapter provide useful yardsticks for measuring the manner of relating in changing relationships.

Summary

As in most introductory chapters, an effort has been made here to provide a framework for viewing the rest of the book. We started with the premise that most, if not all, messages contain information about the relationship. This, coupled with the fact that all of our communication takes place within the context of some type of relationship, provided the rationale for the focus of this book. Next we explored some common misconceptions about communication in relationships—misconceptions that often impede the understanding, analysis, and effective execution of communication in human relationships. We must be careful not to assume complete consistency in the communication behavior of others (or ourselves); we must be continually watchful for subtle sources of meaning in the messages exchanged; we must be willing to acknowledge our own role in structuring the responses of others to us; we must try to avoid making easy cause-effect attributions before a thorough analysis has been made; and we must learn to deal with people and things that are continually changing—a world in which closure is the exception rather than the rule. The last part of the chapter detailed eight broad dimensions of communication behavior that may help us understand how people communicate in relationships characterized by different levels of intimacy. It was proposed that as relationships reach for more intimacy, this will bring about corresponding communication behavior in the form of more breadth, depth, smoothness, uniqueness, efficiency, flexibility, spontaneity, and more overt judgments. The antonyms of these terms characterize communication in deteriorating relationships. This does not mean that even the most intimate relationships will not also experience difficulty, superficiality, awkwardness, and other patterns more typical of less intimate relationships at times. The model simply argues that such behavior will be less likely to *typify* the partners' communication. The chapter concluded with an examination of several different patterns and configurations possible within the eight dimensions outlined. The title of this chapter says that our communication behavior is the very lifeblood of our relationships. This chapter was designed to illustrate that.

Selected Readings

Interpersonal Communication

Berger, C. R., ed., *Interpersonal Communication: Handbooks of Communication Science: Vol 6.* Berlin, Germany: De Gruyter Mouton, 2014.

Berger, C. R., and Roloff, M. E., eds., *International Encyclopedia of Interpersonal Communication.* New York: Wiley-Blackwell., 2016.

Bochner, A. P. "Interpersonal Communication." In E. Barnouw, G. Gerbner, W. Schramm, T. L. Worth, and L. Gross, eds., *International Encyclopedia of Communications*, pp. 336–340. New York: Oxford University Press, 1989.

Dailey, R. M., and Le Poire, B. A. eds. *Applied Interpersonal Communication Matters: Family, Health, & Community Relations.* New York: Lang, 2006.

Daly, J. A., and Wiemann, J. M., eds. *Strategic Interpersonal Communication.* Hillsdale, NJ: Erlbaum, 1994.

Fisher, B. A. *Interpersonal Communication: Pragmatics of Human Relationships.* New York: Random House, 1987.

Goffman, E. *Behavior in Public Places.* New York: Free Press, 1963.

Knapp, M. L., and Daly, J. A., eds. *The SAGE Handbook of Interpersonal Communication.* 4th ed. Thousand Oaks, CA: Sage, 2011.

Smith, S. W., and Wilson, S. R., eds. *New Directions in Interpersonal Communication Research.* Thousand Oaks, CA: Sage, 2010.

Watzlawick, P., Beavin, J., and Jackson, D. D. *Pragmatics of Human Communication.* New York: W. W. Norton, 1967.

Wood, J. T. *Interpersonal Communication: Everyday Encounters.* 7th ed. Boston, MA: Cengage, 2013.

Relationships and Communication

Altman, I., and Taylor, D. A. *Social Penetration: The Development of Interpersonal Relationships.* New York: Holt, Rinehart and Winston, 1973.

Argyle, M., and Henderson, M. *The Anatomy of Relationships.* London: Heinemann, 1985.

Davis, M. S. *Intimate Relations.* New York: Free Press, 1973.

Duck, S., ed. *Handbook of Personal Relationships: Theory, Research and Interventions.* 2nd ed. New York: Wiley, 1997.

Fletcher, G. *The New Science of Intimate Relationships.* Malden, MA: Blackwell, 2002.

Galvin, K. M., Braithwaite, D. O., and Bylund, C. L.. *Family Communication: Cohesion and Change.* 9th ed. New York, NY: Pearson, 2015.

Guerrero, L, K., Andersen, P. A., and Afifi, W. A., *Close Encounters: Communication in Relationships.* 5th ed. Los Angeles, CA: Sage, 2018.

Kelly, H. H., Berscheid, E., Christensen, A., Harvey, J. H., Huston, T. L., Levinger, G., McClintock, E., Peplau, L. A., and Peterson, D. R. *Close Relationships.* New York: W. H. Freeman, 1983.

Miller, R. S. *Intimate Relationships.* 7th ed. New York: McGraw-Hill, 2015.

Sprecher, S., Wenzel, A., and Harvey, J. eds. *Handbook of Relationship Initiation.* New York: Psychology Press, 2008.

Sternberg, R. J., and Hojjat, M., eds. *Satisfaction in Close Relationships.* New York: Guilford, 1997.

Vangelisti, A. L. "Communication in Personal Relationships." In M. Mikulincer and P. R. Shaver, series eds., and J. A. Simpson and J. F. Dovidio, vol. eds., *The APA Handbook of Personality and Social Psychology: Interpersonal Relations and Group Processes: Vol. 2*, pp. 371–392. Washington, D. C.: American Psychological Association, 2015.

Vangelisti, A. L., and Perlman, D., eds., *The Cambridge Handbook of Personal Relationships.* 2nd ed. New York: Cambridge University Press, 2018.

Notes

[1] It isn't hard to see the benefits derived by omitting concrete referents. Lovers may wish to elevate their relationship to cosmic heights lest it become contaminated with the commonplace; the divorcée may derive comfort and protection by avoiding certain unpleasant realities associated with the broken relationship; friends may simply find that specifying what their relationship entails is a difficult and complex process to understand.

2 P. Watzlawick, J. Beavin, and D. D. Jackson, *Pragmatics of Human Communication* (New York: W. W. Norton, 1967). Other authors have commented on this same phenomenon. Ruesch and Bateson called it *the report and command aspects of messages*; Satir labeled the two levels as *denotative* and *metacommunicative*. See also J. Ruesch and G. Bateson, *Communication: The Social Matrix of Psychiatry* (New York: W. W. Norton, 1951), and V. Satir, *Conjoint Family Therapy* (Palo Alto, CA: Science & Behavior Books, 1967).

3 S W. King and K. K. Sereno, "Conversational Appropriateness as a Conversational Imperative," *Quarterly Journal of Speech* 70 (1984): 264–273.

4 C. M. Rossiter Jr., "Instruction in Metacommunication," *Central States Speech Journal* 25 (1974): 36–42. G. I. Nierenberg and H. Colero, *Meta-Talk* (New York: Simon & Schuster, 1974).

5 L. K. Knobloch and K. Carpenter-Theune, "Topic Avoidance in Developing Romantic Relationships: Associations with Intimacy and Relational Uncertainty," *Communication Research* 31 (2004): 173–205; D. H. Solomon, L. K. Knobloch, J. A. Theiss, and R. M. McLaren. "Relational Turbulence Theory: Explaining Variation in Subjective Experiences and Communication within Romantic Relationships." *Human Communication Research* 42 (2016): 507–532; D. H. Solomon and J. A. Theiss, "A Longitudinal Test of the Relational Turbulence Model of Romantic Relational Development," *Personal Relationships* 15 (2008): 339–357.

6 W. F. Owen, "Interpretive Themes in Relational Communication," *Quarterly Journal of Speech* 70 (1984): 274–287 and L. A. Baxter, "Root Metaphors in Accounts of Developing Relationships," *Journal of Personal and Social Relationships* 9 (1992): 253–275. Another effort to identify the substance of messages that relationship partners use to define their relationships can be found in J. K. Burgoon and J. L. Hale, "The Fundamental Topoi of Relational Communication," *Communication Monographs* 51 (1984): 193–214. Also see a follow-up study by Burgoon and Hale, "Validation and Measurement of the Fundamental Themes of Relational Communication," *Communication Monographs* 54 (1987): 19–41. The relationship themes identified by Burgoon and Hale are intimacy, dominance, emotional arousal, composure, similarity, formality, and a task-social orientation.

7 Involvement has been identified as a key dimension of relational communication across a wide variety of studies; for example, one study listed involvement as one of three basic dimensions in a taxonomy of relational speech events: D. J. Goldsmith and L. A. Baxter, "Constituting Relationships in Talk: A Taxonomy of Speech Events in Social and Personal Relationships," *Human Communication Research* 23 (1996): 87–114.

8 A. L. Sillars, J. Weisberg, C. S. Burggraf, and E. A. Wilson, "Content Themes in Marital Conversations," *Human Communication Research*, 13 (1987): 495–528; and A. L. Sillars, C. S. Burggraf, S. Yost, and P. H. Zietlow, "Conversational Themes and Marital Relationship Definitions: Quantitative and Qualitative Investigations," *Human Communication Research*, 19 (1992): 124–154.

9 A. Haas, "Male and Female Spoken Language Differences: Stereotypes and Evidence," *Psychological Bulletin* 86 (1979): 616–626. Also see T. D. Afifi, A. Joseph, and D. Aldeis, "The 'Standards of Openness Hypothesis': Why Women Find (Conflict) Avoidance More Dissatisfying than Men," *Journal of Social and Personal Relationships* 29 (2012): 102–125; J. C. Pearson, *Gender and Communication* (Dubuque, IA: W. C. Brown, 1985); R. D. Ashmore and F. K. DelBoca, *The Social Psychology of Female-Male Relations: A Critical Analysis of Central Concepts* (New York: Academic Press, 1986).

10 R. Hopper, "The Taken-for-Granted," *Human Communication Research* 7 (1981): 195–211.

11 For a summary of these findings, see M. Argyle, *Social Interaction* (New York: Atherton, 1969), 168–179; and J. N. Cappella, "Mutual Influence in Expressive Behavior: Adult-Adult and Infant-Adult Dyadic Interaction," *Psychological Bulletin* 89 (1981): 101–132.

12 J. P. Caughlin, "A Multiple Goals Theory of Personal Relationships: Conceptual Integration and Program Overview," *Journal of Social and Personal Relationships* 27 (2010): 824–848; S. R. Wilson, S. R. *Seeking and resisting compliance* (Thousand Oaks, CA: Sage, 2002).

13 A. Weigert, *Mixed Emotions: Certain Steps Toward Understanding Ambivalence* (Albany, NY: SUNY Press, 1991). C. R. Berger and M. E. Roloff, "Social Cognition, Self-Awareness, and Interpersonal Communication." In B. Dervin and M. J. Voight, eds., *Progress in Communication Sciences*, vol. 2 (Norwood, NJ: Ablex, 1980), 1–49.

14 S. Chen., G. M. Fitzsimons, and S. M. Andersen, "Automaticity in Close Relationships." In J. A. Bargh, ed., *Social Psychology and the Unconscious* (New York: Psychology Press, 2007), 133–172.

15 Adapted from "Analogue of Personality Structure." In I. Altman and D. A. Taylor, *Social Penetration* (New York: Holt, Rinehart & Winston, 1973), pp. 129–135.

16 J. M. Honeycutt, M. L. Knapp, and W. G. Powers, "On Knowing Others and Predicting What They Say," *Western*

Journal of Speech Communication 47 (1983): 157–174. W. Ickes, ed., *Empathic Accuracy* (New York: Guilford, 1997). W. Ickes, *Everyday Mind Reading: Understanding What Other People Think and Feel* (Amherst, NY: Prometheus Books, 2003).

[17] A. L. Sillars, "(Mis)understanding." In B. H. Spitzberg & W. R. Cupach, eds., *The Dark Side of Close Relationships* (Mahwah, NJ: Erlbaum, 1998), 73–102. S. L. Murray and J. G. Holmes "The Construction of Relationship Realities." In G. J. O. Fletcher and J. Fitness, eds., *Knowledge Structures in Close Relationships* (Hillsdale, NJ: Erlbaum, 1996), 91–120. J. L. Smith, W. Ickes, J. Hall, and S. Hodges, eds., *Managing Interpersonal Sensitivity: Knowing When—and When Not—to Understand Others* (Hauppauge, NY: Nova Science, 2011), 193–213.

[18] W. J. Jordan, R. L. Street Jr., and W. B. Putman, "The Effects of Relational and Physical Distance on Lexical Diversity," *Southern Speech Communication* Journal 49 (1983): 80–89.

[19] K. S. Aune, D. B. Buller, and R. K. Aune, "Display Rule Development in Romantic Relationships: Emotion Management and Perceived Appropriateness of Emotions Across Relationship Stages," *Human Communication Research* 23 (1996): 115–145.

[20] S. D. Kilpatrick, V. L. Bissonnette, and C. E. Rusbult, "Empathic Accuracy and Accommodative Behavior Among Newly Married Couples," *Personal Relationships* 9 (2002): 369–393.

[21] Perceived frequency of touching seems to follow a similar pattern. See T. M. Emmers and K. Dindia, "The Effect of Relational Stage and Intimacy on Touch: An Extension of Guerrero and Andersen," *Personal Relationships* 2 (1995): 225–236.

[22] M. L. Knapp, D. G. Ellis, and B. A. Williams, "Perceptions of Communication Behavior Associated with Relationship Terms," *Communication Monographs* 47 (1980): 262–278. A related study compared Japanese and North American perceptions of communication behavior. Both groups perceived relationships in terms of personalized, synchronized, and difficult communication, but cultural orientation played a major role in determining which kind of communication was associated with which kind of relationships. See W. B. Gudykunst and T. Nishida, "The Influence of Cultural Variability on Perceptions of Communication Behavior Associated with Relationship Terms," *Human Communication Research* 13 (1986): 147–166. Additional cross-cultural research on perceptions of relationships can be found in W. B. Gudykunst, S. Ting-Toomey, and T. Nishida, eds., *Communication in Personal Relationships across Cultures* (Thousand Oaks, CA: Sage, 1996).

[23] L. A. Baxter, "Relationship Disengagement: An Examination of the Reversal Hypothesis," *Western Journal of Speech Communication* 47 (1983): 85–98.

[24] L. Baxter, and W. W. Wilmot, "Communication Characteristics of Relationships with Differential Growth Rates," *Communication Monographs* 50 (1983): 264–272.

[25] J. H. Tolhuizen, "Perceived Communication Indicators of Evolutionary Changes in Friendship," *Southern Speech Communication Journal* 52 (1986): 69–91.

[26] J. H. Tolhuizen, "Affinity-Seeking in Developing Relationships," *Communication Reports* 2 (1989): 83–91.

[27] J. Ayres, "Relationship Stages and Sex as Factors in Topic-Dwell Time," *Western Journal of Speech Communication* 44 (1980): 253–260; and C. R. Berger, R. R. Gardner, G. W. Clatterbuck, and L. S. Schulman, "Perceptions of Information Sequencing in Relationship Development," *Human Communication Research* 3 (1976): 29–46.

[28] S. Planalp and A. Benson, "Friends' and Acquaintances' Conversations I: Perceived Differences," *Journal of Social and Personal Relationships* 9 (1992): 483–506. S. Planalp, "Friends' and Acquaintances' Conversations II: Coded Differences," *Journal of Social and Personal Relationships* 10 (1993): 339–354.

[29] G. A. Hornstein, "Intimacy in Conversational Style as a Function of the Degree of Closeness between Members of a Dyad," *Journal of Personality and Social Psychology* 49 (1985): 671–681.

CHAPTER 2

LEARNING OUTCOMES

Students will . . .

. . . know why expectations for relationships can be confusing and can change.

. . . be able to explain what constitutes a stage of relational development.

. . . know the interaction stages of coming together and coming apart.

. . . be able to describe movement in, out, and around the stages.

. . . be able to use dialectical theory and social exchange theories to explain movement within and across relationship stages.

KEY TERMS

avoiding	imitation
bases for prediction	initiating
bonding	integrating
circumscribing	intensifying
costs	need-based rule
coupling	norm of reciprocity
dialectical theory	on-again/off-again relationship
differentiating	rewards
disassociation	social exchange theories
distance	
emotional contagion	stages of relationship development
equality rule	
equity	stagnating
experimenting	terminating

Stages of Coming Together and Coming Apart

Dear Dr. Vangelisti,

My problem is that I recently broke up with a guy with whom I was previously very close and now he acts like he never even knew me. I've seen this happen with some of my friends too. Why can't people just be friends after they've been closer than that? How can people act so cold to those they've shared so much with? It's really an uncomfortable situation for me and I'd be a lot happier if we could just go back to being friends. Can we?

Not Wanting to Throw It All Away

The author of this letter is seeking an answer to why changing relationships follow the pattern they do. This chapter provides some answers to this question by first describing several possible stages that relationships may follow. These stages are based on the different patterns and changes in the eight dimensions of communication discussed in Chapter 1. When people want to move a relationship from one stage to another, it is probably because they desire to increase certain positive feelings, decrease certain negative feelings, or both. The couple described in the letter above probably perceive differing amounts of positive feelings expected from the proposed friendship and may have differing expectations at this time for the type of relationship people can have following a close romantic relationship.

In the development of a human communication system the purpose, function, or product is a relationship. The development of a relationship proceeds in rather uniform stages, though the time it takes to pass from the initial stage to a full relationship will vary greatly.

—*George A. Borden*

We describe our relationships in many ways. Sometimes we rely on conventional intimacy terms such as *stranger, acquaintance, buddy, close friend, lover;* sometimes role designations such as *neighbor, boss, hitchhiker, teacher,* or *pickup* are used; sometimes the nature of the relationship is linked to kinship terms such as *mother, sister, cousin,* or *husband.* Inferences about the nature of the relationship may be made from temporal descriptions—for example, "known him since high school," "going steady," or "just met her once"; or we may assume a reference to ethnicity or personal characteristics will be a sufficient relationship description—for example, "brothers" or "we think alike." A reference to joint activities or social organizations may provide the initial relationship description—for example, "we bowl together," "we're in the same sorority," "I work with him," or "I see her only in class."

Types of Relationships

The preceding relationship descriptions do very little to explain a multitude of personal and societal expectations attendant to these relationships. The type of relationship we develop with another person is heavily influenced by mutual and ongoing expectations for the relationship: What is it? What will it become? What should it be now? What should it become? What behavior is expected? What do most people do? Some *expectations for relationships* are held by many people in this culture—for example, that family members will most likely have close relationships, that male-female friendships are most likely to be romantic in nature, that same-gender relationships will most likely be limited to friendships (rather than romance), that marriage will most likely be the result of highly intimate feelings between the partners, and that participants in various role relationships (teacher-student; doctor-patient) will most likely behave according to those roles. The extent to which such expectations are shared and acted upon helps explain perceived similarities among relationships described as "friend" or "teacher" or "mother."

Sometimes expectations are not shared—with society or with one's relationship partner. Contrary to the expectations and/or wishes of many people, some family members develop distant relationships; some male-female pairs do not pursue romance; some same-gender pairs seek romantic relationships; some people get married who don't feel intense intimacy; and some people don't fulfill the expectations for their role as doctor, teacher, or mother. When we have difficulty establishing a relationship or in changing an established relationship to one of a different type, it is often linked to differing expectations for the relationship held by each party.[1]

© Bobex-73/Shutterstock.com

Sometimes relationship expectations are confusing because more than one relationship is involved. You may have several relationships with the same person and it is not always clear which relationship is being performed—for example, a teacher who is also your teammate in tennis. The tennis activity may suggest a new set of expectations for the relationship, but if you make a poor shot, you may hear a comment that sounds more likely to come from your teacher than from your teammate. Families also present a complex set of relationship expectations. An older parent living in his or her adult child's home may occasionally play parent and occasionally play dependent tenant to the adult son or daughter.

Expectations for relationships change with time and circumstances. The expectations for romantic relationships of today are quite different from the late 19th century, when courting typically involved a man "calling on" a prospective mate at her home so their interactions could be supervised. This calling system was gradually replaced by a dating system around the beginning of the 20th century. The dating system at that time had, among other features, the expectation that men needed to promise commitment if they wanted to have sex. In the 1960s, this expectation became less normative, and it was replaced by expectations of greater physical contact and also more expressions of both positive and negative emotions.[2]

Changes in expectations are not limited to romantic relationships. As a child reaches adolescence, he or she expects certain relationship changes with his or her parents. We found that people younger than age 22 expected more personalized and synchronized communication in all types of relationships than did those people older than age 41.[3] Similarly, a man and a woman may be assigned to work on a task in a corporate environment. The expectations for this relationship are formal, task oriented, and nonintimate. However, when the task relationship occurs for an extended period, when the pair works together several nights a week, and when they discuss various personal aspects of their lives during breaks, the relationship expectations may change.[4] Many of our relationship expectations are rooted in the activities we perform together.[5]

We don't always consciously pursue the relationships we have with others. Sometimes we're "thrown together" with people in certain circumstances. Similarly, we may not actively terminate a relationship, but changes in interests, priorities, or geographical location may contribute to a lack of initiative to keep the relationship going. So it fades away as a result of mindless inattention rather than planned avoidance.

The variety of relationships we have or could have seems quite diverse. There are, however, some basic principles that all types of relationships seem to have in common, such as the following:

1. Relationship expectations are often altered because of the way people communicate, and the way they communicate often helps to shape the expectations they have for a relationship. This principle establishes the central role of communication behavior in assessing the nature of relationships, but it also recognizes that overt communication behavior may tell only part of the relationship story.

2. Whether our relationships are actively sought or develop out of shared circumstances, each of them reveals fluctuations in closeness or intimacy. Superficial, task-oriented relationships and unfriendly relations can be viewed as less intimate while best friends and lovers are more intimate. In addition, we may see some more intimate behavior in less intimate relationships and some less intimate behavior in more intimate relationships.

With these foundation concepts in mind, we can return to our initial questions: Are there regular and systematic patterns of communication that suggest stages on the road to a more intimate relationship? Are there similar patterns and stages that characterize the deterioration of relationships?

A Model of Interaction Stages in Relationships

© TijanaM/Shutterstock.com

Stages of relationship development: Periods in which the communicative and perceptual changes associated with relational development become relatively stable.

Scientists are forever seeking to bring order to a seemingly chaotic world of overlapping, interdependent, dynamic, and intricate processes. Frequently, the process of systematizing our life and environment is discussed in terms of stages of growth, stages of deterioration, and the forces that shape and act on this movement through stages. For instance, developmental psychologists recount regularized patterns of behavior accompanying stages of infancy, childhood, adolescence, maturity, and old age. Anthropologists and geologists plot the evolutionary stages of human beings and human environments. Biologists note similarities in the life processes of such seemingly diverse organisms as trees and fish. Physical and social scientists talk about affinity and attraction, weak and strong interactions, friction, repulsion, and splitting up as basic forces acting on matter and people. Within these predictable patterns and so-called "steady states," there are always ongoing changes and deviations from the norm.[6] But it is when this variability is low that relatively stable patterns or stages are perceived. Are there patterns of human communication that suggest **stages of relationship development**?

Actually, the idea that there are stages in the development of relationships that are characterized by certain recurring patterns of communication is not new.[7] We tried to synthesize as well as expand on this previous work in the development of the model presented in **Table 2.1**. Many of the behaviors we use to describe each stage (see pages 40–50) are also used by relationship partners when they describe their relationship. As a result, Welch and Rubin were able to develop a way of determining a relationship stage by giving partners a list of behaviors and asking them to indicate the extent to which each one was characteristic of their relationship.[8]

Before each stage is described in greater detail, several preliminary remarks about the model are in order. First, we should resist the normal temptation to perceive the stages of coming together as "good" and those of coming apart as "bad."

Table 2.1	A Model of Interaction Stages	
Process	**Stage**	**Representative Dialogue**
	Initiating	"Hi, how ya doin'?"
		"Fine. You?"
	Experimenting	"Oh, so you like to ski . . . so do I."
		"You do?! Great. Where do you go?"
Coming Together	Intensifying	"I . . . I think I love you."
		"I love you too."
	Integrating	"I feel so much a part of you."
		"Yeah, we are like one person. What happens to you happens to me."
	Bonding	"I want to be with you always."
		"Let's get married."
	Differentiating	"I just don't like big social gatherings."
		"Sometimes I don't understand you. This is one area where I'm certainly not like you at all."
	Circumscribing	"Did you have a good time on your trip?"
		"What time will dinner be ready?"
Coming Apart	Stagnating	"What's there to talk about?"
		"Right. I know what you're going to say and you know what I'm going to say."
	Avoiding	"I'm so busy, I just don't know when I'll be able to see you."
		"If I'm not around when you try, you'll understand."
	Terminating	"I'm leaving you . . . and don't bother trying to contact me."
		"Don't worry."

Source: Mark Knapp, Anita Vangelisti, John Caughlin

It is not "bad" to terminate relationships nor is it necessarily "good" to become more intimate with someone. The model is descriptive of what seems to happen—not what should happen.

We should also remember that, in the interest of clarity, the model simplifies a complex process. For instance, the model shows each stage adjacent to the next—as if it was clear when a communicating couple left one stage and entered another. On the contrary, each stage contains some behavior from other stages. So *stage identification* becomes a matter of emphasis. Stages are identified by the proportion of one type of communication behavior to another. This proportion may be the frequency with which certain communication acts occur, or proportion may be determined by the relative weight given to certain acts by the participants. For example, a couple at the Intensifying Stage may exhibit behaviors that occur at any of the other stages, but their arrival at the Intensifying Stage occurs because (1) the most frequent communication exchanges are typical of the Intensifying Stage and/or (2) the exchanges that are crucial in defining the couple's relationship are statements of an intensifying nature. The act of sexual intercourse is commonly associated with male-female romantic couples at the Intensifying or Integrating Stages, but it may occur as an isolated or infrequent act for couples at the Experimenting Stage. Even when two people have sex regularly, it can still be the Experimenting Stage if the sex remains relatively unimportant for the couple in defining the closeness of their relationship. If sexual involvement is considered just a "hookup," for example, even regular sexual partners might not think of it as developing a close relationship.[9]

In short, interaction stages involve both overt behavior and the perceptions of behavior in the minds of the parties involved. During the formation of a romantic relationship, the couple's overt behavior (to each other and in front of others) may be a good marker of their developmental stage. During periods of attempted rejuvenation of a relationship, we may find that the overt behavior is an effective marker of the stage *desired*. However, in stable or long-established relationships, overt behavior may not be a very accurate indicator of closeness. Instead it is the occasional behavior or memories of past behaviors that are perceived by the couple as crucial in defining their relationship. For example, a couple married for fifteen years may spend much of their interaction time engaging in small talk—a behavior typical of an early developmental stage. And even though the small talk does play an important role in maintaining the relationship, it is the less frequent but more heavily weighted behavior that the couple uses to define their relationship as one that is at the Integrating Stage. Similarly, close friends may not engage in a lot of talk that outside observers would associate with closeness. In some cases, friends are separated for long periods of time and have little contact with one another. But through specific occasional acts and the memory of past acts, the intimacy of the friendship is maintained.

The dialogue in the model is heavily oriented toward mixed-gender pairs. This does not mean the model is irrelevant for same-gender pairs. Even at the highest level of commitment, the model may apply to same-gender pairs. Granted, in some American communities, cultural sanctions against the overt expression of high-level intimacy between same-sexed pairs may serve to inhibit, slow down, or stop the growth of relationships between same-sexed pairs. But when such relationships do develop, similar patterns are reported.[10]

The model (and the remainder of the book) also focuses primarily on relationships in which people voluntarily seek contact with, or disengagement from, each another. But the model is not limited to such relationships. All people drawn into, or pulled out of, relationships by forces seemingly outside their control will like or not like such an event and communicate accordingly. For instance, a child's relationship with his or her parent (involuntary) may, at some point, be very close and loving, at another time be cold and distant, and at another time be similar to relationships with other friends. The research by Welch and Rubin found the model to be useful in describing the development of task or business relationships as well as social relationships.

Our model of relationship development is primarily focused on the interaction patterns of the relationship partners. Nevertheless, we should not forget that these relationships are nested within a network of other social relationships that affect communication patterns manifested by the partners.[11] Friends, coworkers, and/or kin make up the larger social system that influences and is influenced by any single relationship. Sometimes these networks are small, sometimes large; sometimes they are influential on one issue or at one point in time and not so on other issues or at another point in time; sometimes these other relationships tend to serve one relationship partner, and at other times they serve both.

What role do social networks play as we develop and maintain a relationship? The people in our social networks shape our understanding of our relationships, sometimes providing information we do not have or making observations that are not obvious to us. The people who comprise these networks give us feedback, advice, and support; they act as a sounding board; they help mediate problems; they offer consultation and engage in persuasion. They may, of course, fail to provide these things when they are expected. In short, social networks are comprised of coaches who can dramatically affect our communicative performance as a relationship partner. In addition, they are sources of a social identity that extend beyond the pair bond (see boxed insert).

Finally, this model has a close association with the eight dimensions of communication outlined in Chapter 1. Although it is impossible to specify a precise configuration along the eight dimensions (see Table 1.1), we would expect the Initiating and Terminating Stages to be characterized by communication that is more narrow, stylized, difficult, rigid, awkward, public, hesitant, and with overt judgments suspended; the stages of Integrating and Bonding should show more breadth, uniqueness, efficiency, flexibility, smoothness, personalness, spontaneity, and overt judgments given. In short, it is proposed that we communicate within a prescribed range of content, style, and language at different levels of intimacy. Chapters 5 through 11 will further document behavior only briefly noted in the following pages.

So you want to know how others can affect the way you communicate with your relationship partner . . .

We often forget how much a couple's interaction is influenced by their communication with people in their social networks—coworkers, friends, neighbors, family, and in-laws. Communicating gossip, opinions, knowledge, support, and disagreement are some of the many transactions that characterize these relationships.

How much impact do social networks have on a couple? People in the social network help us make sense of our relationships, both providing information about it and providing a point of comparison (e.g., providing a model for how much affection is typical in relationships). The extent of the impact will vary depending on the strength of the ties a person has with relevant network members and that person's experience in "managing" those members. An example of managing a network would be the withholding of private information from certain people but giving these same people information you want many others to know. Another example of managing a network occurs when a spouse effectively edits information about how his or her parents feel about his or her spouse and vice versa in order to increase the quality of that in-law/spouse relationship. When the quality of the relationship between both spouses and their in-laws is good, it makes the quality of a couple's relationship better. Networks change over time and the amount of mutual influence that exists can change dramatically—for example, family support and approval may be influential at one point in time and less so at another.

What are the benefits of social networks? Social networks can help people understand and clarify aspects of their own relationship; they facilitate meeting new people and developing new contacts; and they are a source of information and social support. Diverse social networks are desirable, but a powerful predictor of whether a personal relationship develops productively is the level of support from these networks. Also, people's sense that their social network supports their relationship is related to greater relational satisfaction and more positive mental and physical well-being. The benefits of a supportive network are evident for both same-sexed and heterosexual couples.

How do people handle a friend of a friend they don't like? A disliked friend of a friend in your network is not all that unusual. Most people find ways to cope if the dislike for this person is not strong enough to jeopardize the relationship with the common friend. Coping may take the form of avoiding contact as much as possible, being pleasantly polite when contact occurs, and looking for positive aspects of the person. After all, you value your friend and your friend likes this person. But sometimes the dislike is so strong that it is explicitly addressed—with the target person, with the common friend, or some other member of the network.

How do networks influence the formation of relationships? Friends and romantic partners often meet as a result of actions taken by people in their social networks. These "helpers" often have large networks. They may "advertise" one person to another—telling good things about a person and what things he or she has in common with another; they may arrange a meeting in which they are present or not; and they may even act as a coach on what to say and what not to say.

How do networks influence the end of relationships? When a couple has a strongly integrated and supportive social network, it serves as a barrier to dissolving the relationship. But when relationships terminate, social networks will need rebuilding and restructuring. Couples who have been married for a long time may have an abundance of couples in their networks and their new status may require replacing some of these with single people. Many members of the couple's old networks will side with one partner or the other, and some will initially try to maintain ties to both. The dissolution of a relationship is also an opportunity for network members with weak ties to the couple to drop out of their network completely.

* * * * * * * * * * * * * * * * * * * *

There is much more to be learned about the way others affect your relationship communication. The preceding points are only a brief beginning. In various places throughout this book other aspects of this topic are treated. For those interested in more in-depth coverage, see Blair, K. L. and Holmberg, D. "Perceived Social Network Support and Well-Being in Same-Sex Versus Mixed-Sex Romantic Relationships," *Journal of Social and Personal Relationships* 25 (2008): 769–791; Felmlee, D. H. and Sinclair, H. C. "Social Networks and Personal Relationships." In A. L. Vangelisti and D. Perlman, eds., *The Cambridge Handbook of Personal Relationships* 2nd ed., pp. 467–480. New York, NY: Cambridge University Press, 2018; Morry, M. M., Chee, K. C., Penniston, T.L., and Sucharyna, T. A. "Relationship Social Comparisons: Comparison Interpretations and Attributions as Predictors of Relationship Quality," *Journal of Social and Personal Relationships* 36 (2019): 1069–1097; Parks, M. R. and Faw, M. H. "Relationships among Relationships: Interpersonal Communication and Social Networks." In Berger, C. R., ed.,

Interpersonal Communication: Handbooks of Communication Science: Vol 6 pp. 395–416. Berlin, Germany: De Gruyter Mouton, 2014; Serewicz, M. C. M. "The Difficulties of In-Law Relationships." In C. Kirkpatrick, S. Duck, and M. K. Foley (eds.), *Relating Difficulty: The Processes of Constructing and Managing Difficult Interaction* (pp. 101–118). Mahwah, NJ: Erlbaum, 2006.

Interaction Stages

Initiating

This stage incorporates all those processes enacted when we first come together with other people. It may be at a cocktail party or at the beach; it may be with a stranger or with a friend. It can also happen online or via a mobile app. As we scan the other person, we consider our own stereotypes, any prior knowledge of the other's reputation, previous interactions with this person, expectations for this situation, and so on. We are asking ourselves whether this person is "attractive" or "unattractive" and whether we should initiate communication. Next, we try to determine whether the other person is cleared for an encounter—is he or she busy, in a hurry, surrounded by others. Will she or he swipe right? Finally, we search for an appropriate opening line to engage the other's attention.

Initiating: The stage that incorporates all those processes enacted when we first come together with other people.

Typically, communicators at this stage are simply trying to display themselves as a person who is pleasant, likable, understanding, and socially adept. In essence, we are saying, "I see you. I am friendly, and I want to open channels for communication to take place." In addition, we are carefully observing the other to reduce any uncertainty we might have—hoping to gain clarification of mood, interest, orientation toward us, and aspects of the other's public personality. Our conscious awareness of these processes is sometimes very low: "Morning, Bob. How ya doin'?" "Morning, Clayton. Go to hell." "Fine, thanks."

Obviously, specific methods and messages used to initiate communication vary with:

1. The kind of relationship and whether the participants have been through this stage before. *Stranger:* "Hello. Nice to meet you." *Friend:* "Hey dude. What's up?"

2. The time allowed for interaction—passing each other on the street versus a formal appointment.

3. The time since last greeting—regreeting a person you saw just five minutes before versus greeting a relative at the airport who visits once a year.

4. The situational or normative constraints—meeting in the library versus meeting at a rock concert, or meeting in person versus meeting online.

5. The special codes of particular groups—fraternity handshake.

In spite of the possibility for considerable variance in initiating behaviors, people generally exercise a good deal of caution and communicate according to conventional formulas.

© Bobex-73/Shutterstock.com

Experimenting

Once communication has been initiated, we begin the process of experimenting—trying to discover the unknown. Even when we have never met the person before, we may have some information about him or her already, whether it comes from mutual acquaintances, the bio of a dating app, or a Google search.[12] Still, when entering the experimenting phase, we begin interacting with that person to find out more. Such interaction may happen online or in person, but either way interaction is essential for figuring out if this is a person with whom we want an ongoing relationship.

Experimenting: The stage during which we being interacting with another person to find out more.

Strangers trying to become acquaintances will be primarily interested in name, rank, and serial number—something akin to the sniffing ritual in animals. The exchange of demographic information is frequent and often seems controlled by a norm that says, "If you tell me your hometown, I'll tell you mine." Strangers at this stage are diligently searching for an integrating topic, an area of common interest or experience. Sometimes the strain of this search approaches the absurd: "Oh, you're from Oklahoma. Do you know . . . ?" Obviously, the degree to which a person assists another in finding this integrating topic shows the degree of interest in continuing the interaction and the willingness to pursue a relationship.

Miller and his colleagues have pointed out that we use three **bases for predictions** in interpersonal encounters.[13] With strangers we may have to rely primarily on *cultural information.* If one's partner is from this culture, he or she probably shares some predictable ways of behaving and thinking. You assume that person has knowledge of certain cultural happenings. It is a place to begin, but the potential sources of error are many.

Bases for prediction: Different levels of information from which people can make predictions about others in interpersonal encounters.

As we gain information about another person, we may begin to use *sociological information* as a basis for conversational strategies and adaptations. This knowledge of a person's reference and membership groups is frequently used in casual social gatherings. When we hear that a person is a feminist, a physician, or a Southern Baptist, we immediately begin scanning associations with these labels that may be useful to us in our conversational pursuits.

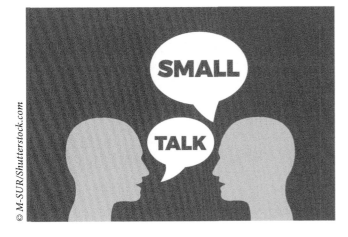

The third basis for predictions involves *psychological information.* This information recognizes the individual differences associated with one's conversational partner. It is more likely to occur with conversational partners who are better known to you. These sources of information are important because they will mark differences in the small talk of strangers, people from very different cultures, people who have a close relationship, and people whose relationship is close in name only.

It should be noted that people in established close relationships do spend a lot of time experimenting. It may be an effort to seek greater breadth and understanding of the relationship, to note any changes in current understandings, to pass the time, or to avoid some uncomfortable vibrations obtained at a more intense level of dialogue. Both strangers and friends are searching for possible similarities; both are trying to present a desirable "come-on self" ("If you like the label, you might like what's in the container"); both are concerned about setting up the next encounter in which consistency of behavior can be examined.

Small talk is the *sine qua non* of experimenting. It is like exercising; we may hate it, but we may also engage in large quantities of it every day. If we hate it, why do we do it? Probably because we are vaguely aware of several important functions served by small talk:

1. It is a useful process for uncovering integrating topics and openings for more penetrating conversation.
2. It can be an audition for a future friendship or a way of increasing the scope of a current relationship.
3. It provides a safe procedure for indicating who we are and how another can come to know us better (reduction of uncertainty).
4. It allows us to maintain a sense of community with our fellow human beings.

Relationships at this stage are generally pleasant, relaxed, overtly uncritical, and casual. Commitments are limited. And, like it or not, most of our relationships probably don't progress very far beyond this stage.

Intensifying

Intensifying: Stage of development in which partners have become "close friends" and the relationship becomes intensified.

When people achieve a relationship known as "close friends," indicators of the relationships are intensified. Active participation and greater awareness of the process typify this stage when it begins. Initial probes toward intensification of intimacy are often exercised with caution, awaiting confirmation before proceeding.[14] Sitting close, for instance, may precede hugging; holding hands will generally precede holding genitals. Connecting on social media and texting each other generally precedes talking to each other on mobile phones.[15]

The amount of personal disclosure increases at this stage, and we begin to get a glimpse of some previously withheld secrets—that my father was an alcoholic; that I masturbate; that I pretend I'm a rhino when I'm drunk; and other fears, frustrations, failures, imperfections, and prejudices. Disclosures may be related to any topic area, but those dealing most directly with the development of the relationship are crucial. These disclosures make the speaker vulnerable—almost like an animal baring its neck to an attacker.

Verbally, a lot of things may be happening in the intensifying stage:

1. Forms of address become more informal—first name, nickname, or some term of endearment.

2. Use of the first person plural becomes more common—"*We* should do this" or "*Let's* do this." One study of married couples found that the use of "we" was more likely to be associated with a relationship orientation, while the use of "I" was more likely to be associated with a task orientation or the functional requirements and accomplishments of marriage.[16]

3. Private symbols begin to develop, sometimes in the form of a special slang or jargon, sometimes using conventional language forms that have understood, private meanings. Places they've been together, events and times they've shared, and physical objects they've purchased or exchanged, all become important symbols in defining the nature of developing closeness.[17] Such items or memories may be especially devastating and repulsive reminders if the relationship begins to come apart unless the symbols are reinterpreted ("I like this diamond ring because it is beautiful, not because he gave it to me") or put in a different perspective ("It really was fun when we did _____, but in so many other ways he was a jerk").

4. Verbal shortcuts built on a backlog of accumulated and shared assumptions, expectations, interests, knowledge, interactions, and experiences appear more often; one may request a newspaper be passed by simply saying, "Paper."

5. More direct expressions of commitment may appear—"We really have a good thing going" or "I don't know who I'd talk to if you weren't around." Sometimes such expressions receive an echo—"I really like you a lot." "I really like you, too, Elmer."

6. Increasingly, one's partner will act as a helper in the daily process of understanding what you're all about—"In other words, you mean you're. . ." or "But yesterday, you said you were. . . ."

Sophistication in nonverbal message transmission also increases. A long verbalization may be replaced by a single touch; postural congruence may be seen; clothing styles may become more coordinated; possessions and personal space may be more permeable.

As the relationship intensifies, each person is unfolding his or her uniqueness while simultaneously blending his or her personality with the other's. It is not always easy to work through uncertainties associated with the blending process. This is true for both the relationship partners and for members of their social networks. As a result, there may be periods of turbulence as the relationship partners establish a more intensified relationship.[18]

Integrating

The relationship has now reached a point at which the two individual personalities fuse or coalesce more than at any previous stage. When romantic partners integrate, they try to develop a kind of interdependence that research tells us is crucial to satisfying close relationships.[19] The process Davis calls **coupling** is akin to what we call **integrating**. Coupling, says Davis, involves giving another person your self-symbols and/or bringing the other's self-symbols into alignment with your own.[20]

The experience of former Florida State Senator Bruce Smathers and his fiancée provides one example of movement toward this interpersonal fusion. He switched from Methodist to Presbyterian; she switched from Republican to Democrat. The wire service report indicated this was "a compromise they say will help pave the way for their wedding."

Verbal and nonverbal manifestations of integrating may take many forms:

1. Attitudes, opinions, interests, and tastes that clearly distinguish the pair from others are vigorously cultivated—"We have something special; we are unique."
2. Social circles merge and others begin to treat the two individuals as a common package—one present, one letter, one invitation.
3. Intimacy "trophies" are exchanged so each can "wear" the other's identity—pictures, pins, rings.
4. Social media profiles represent the coupling—social media profile pictures include the partners together, and the two people's depiction of the relationship online becomes similar.[21]
5. Similarities in manner, dress, and verbal behavior may also accentuate the oneness.
6. Actual physical penetration of various body parts contributes to the perceived unification.
7. Sometimes common property is designated—"our song," a joint bank account, or shared Netflix and Spotify accounts.[22]
8. Empathic processes seem to peak so that explanation and prediction of behavior are much easier.[23]
9. Body rhythms and routines achieve heightened synchrony.[24]
10. Sometimes the love of a third person or object will serve as glue for the relationship—"Love me, love my rhino collection."

Obviously, integration does not mean complete togetherness or complete loss of individuality. Maintenance of some separate and distinct selves is critical, and possible, due to the strength of the binding elements. Even dating partners who feel close enough and trust each other enough to share their social media passwords still often maintain their own accounts rather than merging them.[25] One married woman of ten years told us, "I still hold some of myself back from John because it's the only part of me I don't share, and it's important to have something that is uniquely mine."

Thus, we can see that as we participate in the integration process, we are intensifying and minimizing various aspects of our total person. Consequently, when we commit ourselves to integrating with another, we also agree to become another individual.

Bonding

Bonding is a public ritual that announces to the world that commitments have been formally contracted. It is the institutionalization of the relationship. There are many kinds of bonding rituals, and they characterize several stages of the relationship. In a romantic relationship, these may include going steady, engagement, and ultimately marriage. Until recently, there were fewer formal bonding rituals available to same-sexed romantic pairs, but a Supreme Court decision in 2015 meant that same-sexed marriages became legally recognized in all 50 U.S. states. Nonromantic relationships could also include the bonding stage; for example, the bonding ritual could be an act of becoming "blood brothers" by placing open wounds on each other to achieve oneness.

> **Bonding:** Stage in which a public ritual announces to the world that commitments have been formally contracted.

Since bonding is simply the contract for the union of the pair at any given stage of the relationship, one might question why it has been designated as a separate stage. It is because the act of bonding itself may be a powerful force in changing the nature of the relationship "for better or for worse." The institutionalization of the relationship hardens it, makes it more difficult to break out of, and probably changes the rhetoric that takes place without a contract. The contract becomes, either explicitly or implicitly, a topic of conversation. Communication strategies can now be based on interpretation and execution of the commitments contained in the contract. In short, the normal ebb and flow of the informal relationship can be, and often is, viewed differently.

When bonding is an extension of integrating, it is probably seen as a way to help stabilize one's newly formed individual and integrated selves. Our future is one of our most highly prized possessions so to commit it to another person is a gift of great value.[26]

Bonding is a way of gaining social or institutional support for the relationship. It enables the couple to rely on law or policy or precedent. Bonding also provides guidance for the relationship through specified rules and regulations.

The way up and the way down are the same.

—*Heraclitus*

Differentiating

Differentiating: Stage involving a process of disengaging or uncoupling.

Literally, to *differentiate* means to become distinct or different in character. Just as integrating is mainly a process of fusion, differentiating is mainly a process of disengaging or uncoupling. Even though individual differences are of some concern at any stage in the developing relationship, they are now the major focus and serve as a prelude to increased interpersonal distance. A great deal of time and energy is spent talking and thinking about "how different we really are."

Joint endeavors formerly described by "we" or "our" now assume a more "I" or "my" orientation. Previously designated joint possessions often become more individualized—"my friends," "my daughter," or "my bathroom." Communication is generally characterized by what distinguishes the two persons or how little they have in common. Differences may be related to attitudes, interests, personality, relatives, or friends or to a specific behavior such as sexual needs or personal hygiene. Individuals who persist in interaction at this stage perceive these differences as strongly linked to basic or core values. Hence, we would expect to see less conversation about certain central areas of personality that may reflect these basic values. Persons who move in and out of this stage develop a history of expectations for the manner in which such difficulties will be settled, even if it is simply an agreement to seal off the areas of potential conflict.

When an unusually intense siege of differentiating takes place following bonding, it may be because bonding took place before the relationship achieved sufficient breadth and depth. It may also be due to some unplanned individual or social changes that altered the data upon which the original commitment was made. Advocates of renewable-term marriage argue that couples would be more likely to face, discuss, and work out unexpected changes in their lives if the marriage bond was not a lifelong commitment—if "until death do us part" meant the death of the relationship rather than the death of the participants.

The most visible communication form of differentiating, or affirming individuality, is fighting or conflict, although it is possible to differentiate without conflict. The numerous interpersonal torture tests characteristic of some of this fighting will be more fully discussed in Chapter 11.

Circumscribing

Circumscribing: Stage in relationships during which information exchange markedly decreases in both breadth and depth.

At almost any stage of a relationship we can see some evidence of communication being constricted or circumscribed. In decaying relationships, however, information exchange qualitatively and quantitatively decreases. The main message strategy is to carefully control the areas of discussion, restricting communication to safe areas. Thus, we find less total communication in a number of interactions as well as depth of subjects discussed, and communications of shorter duration.

Communication restraint applies to both breadth and depth. As the number of touchy topics increases, almost any topic becomes dangerous because it is not clear whether the new topic may in some way be wired to a previous area of static. When communication does take place, superficiality and public aspects are increasingly the norm. Communications related to one's basic values and hidden secrets may have a history of unpleasantness surrounding them; hence, we see a lot less information exchanged about "who I am and what our relationship is like." A corresponding decrease in expressions of commitment may be seen. When one person ventures such an expression, the echo response may not be so prevalent: "In spite of our differences, I still like you a lot." (Silence)

Familiar phrases typical of this stage include "Don't ask me about that"; "Let's not talk about that anymore"; "It's none of your business"; "Just stick to the kind of work I'm doing and leave my religion out of it"; "You don't own me and you can't tell me what to think"; or "Can't we just be friends?" The last example is a suggestion that prescribes a whole new set of ground rules for permissible topics in the interaction.

When circumscribing characterizes the relationship, it may also have an impact on public social performances. Sometimes mutual social circles are also circumscribed. Sometimes the presence of others is the only time when communication seems to increase—an effort to avoid being seen as not getting along. The following routine is not at all uncommon for some couples at this stage: Driving to a party, the two people exhibit mutual silence, empty gazes, and a general feeling of exhaustion. While playing out their party roles we see smiling, witticisms, and an orientation for being the life of the party. The trip home becomes a replay of the pre-party behavior.

Stagnating

To stagnate is to remain motionless or inactive. Rather than orally communicate, participants often find themselves conducting covert dialogues and concluding that since they "know" how the interaction will go, it is not necessary to say anything. At this stage, many areas are closed off, and efforts to communicate effectively are at a standstill. Even superficial areas have become so infected by previous communicative poison that they are generally left untried. In a sense, the participants are just marking time.

Some of the messages that are sent reflect unpleasant feeling states through the medium of nonverbal behavior. Other messages are very carefully chosen and well thought out. Language choices and message strategies seem to come even closer to those used with strangers, and the subject of the relationship is nearly taboo. In the context related earlier in the discussion of Table 1.1, (page 15), communication is becoming more stylized, difficult, rigid, awkward, hesitant, and narrow. Although many covert judgments may be made, overt judgments are generally avoided.

Extended stagnating can be seen in many relationships: between alienated parents and children, just prior to divorce, just prior to the termination of a courtship, following unproductive small talk. The main theme characterizing this stage is, "There is little sense bringing anything up because I know what will happen, and it won't be particularly pleasant." Experimentation is

Stagnating: Stage at which relational counterparts stop trying to talk about many topics of conversation because they "know" how the interaction will go.

minimal because the unknown is thought to be known. It is during this time that each partner may engage in "imagined interactions."[27] These imagined dialogues will either take the form of narratives (e.g., "I'll say this and then she'll say this, and then. . .") or perceived actual dialogues (e.g., "I'll do it." "You don't have to." "OK." "OK, what?" "OK, I won't." "Your typical attitude." "And *your typical attitude!*").

You might legitimately question why people would linger at this stage with so many apparent costs accumulating. Most don't. But when persons continue interacting at this stage, they may be getting some rewards outside of the primary relationship, through increased attention to their work or in developing another relationship. They also avoid the pain of terminating the relationship, which they may anticipate will be stronger than the current pain. Others may have hope that they can still revive the relationship. Still others may spend time at this stage because of some perverse pleasures obtained in punishing the other person.

Avoiding

While stagnating, the participants are usually in the same physical environment and avoiding attempts to eliminate that condition. The rhetoric of avoidance is the antithesis of the rhetoric of initiation. Here, communication is specifically designed to avoid the possibility of face-to-face or voice-to-voice interaction. The overriding message seems to be, "I am not interested in seeing you; I am not interested in building a relationship; and I would like to close the communication channels between us." In this sense, then, avoiding suggests a much more permanent state of separation than that communicated by most people in their everyday leave-taking.

When the need to communicate avoidance results from an intimate relationship gone sour, the particular messages may contain overtones of antagonism or unfriendliness. They are more likely to be direct and to the point, "Please don't call me anymore. I just don't want to see or talk to you." This bluntness may naturally evolve from other conditions as well, such as when one person wants to pursue the relationship and ignores the subtler avoidance cues. These subtle or indirect cues may take the form of being consistently late for appointments or preceding each encounter with, "I can't stay long." Here the avoiding tactics are not motivated so much by dislike of the other as a lack of desire to expend time and energy pursuing a relationship. Sometimes an inordinate number of conflicting engagements can make the point: "I'm so busy I don't know when I'll be able to see you. Friday? I'm going home for the weekend. Monday? I have a sorority meeting. Tuesday? I have to study for a test," and so on.

Any of all forms of "distancing"[28] may occur at this stage:

1. Avoidance—preventing an interaction episode from happening and reducing interaction during an encounter.
2. Disengagement—hiding information about self, using a disengaged communication style, and interacting less personally.

3. Cognitive dissociation—disregarding messages, derogating the other person, showing cognitive and emotional detachment.

Cognitive dissociation occurs when physical separation cannot be achieved. It is a form of avoidance in the presence of the other. It is as if the other person doesn't exist. Not surprisingly under such conditions, we find the recipient of this behavior participating less in what interaction is available, not evaluating the other highly, and being less inclined to provide a reward to the other when an opportunity arises. The less obvious result of being ignored is the possibility of a lowered self-concept.[29]

Terminating

Relationships can terminate immediately after a greeting or after twenty years of intimacy. Sometimes they die slowly over a long period of time. The bonds that held the pair together wear thin and finally pull apart. The reasons behind such deterioration may be something obvious such as living in parts of the country separated by great distance, or termination may just be the end result of two people growing socially and psychologically at different rates and in different directions. At other times, the threads holding two people together may be abruptly cut. It may be the death of one partner, radically changed circumstances, or an effort by one person to spare both of them the anticipated agony of a prolonged termination period.

Naturally, the nature of the termination dialogue is dependent on many factors: the relative status held or perceived between the two communicators; the kind of relationship already established or desired in the future; the amount of time allowed; whether the dialogue is conducted via the telephone, through a letter or e-mail or face to face; and many other individual and environmental factors.

Generally, however, we would predict termination dialogue to be characterized by messages of distance and disassociation. **Distance** refers to an attempt to put psychological and physical barriers between the two communicators. This might take the form of actual physical separation, or it may be embedded in other nonverbal and verbal messages. **Disassociation** is found in messages that are essentially preparing one or both individuals for their continued life without the other—increasing concern for one's own self-interests, emphasizing differences. Obviously, the amount of distancing and disassociation will vary with the kind of relationship being dissolved, time available, and so on. Chapter 10 details the various phases in the process of terminating a relationship that are the result of messages signaling distance and disassociation.

We would also predict that the general dimensions of communicative behavior reviewed earlier in Chapter 1 would polarize more than ever around narrow, stylized, difficult, rigid, awkward, public, hesitant, and suspended judgments.

Finally, we would like to take a finding derived from the study of conversations and apply it to relationships. Thus, we would predict that termination dialogue would regularly manifest (1) a summary statement, (2) behaviors signaling the impending termination or decreased access, and (3) messages that indicate what

Terminating: Stage at which relational partners recognize that they are no longer part of a distinct relational unit.

Distance: A reflection of detachment, remoteness, or lack of intimacy.

Disassociation: An indication that individuals are preparing for their continued life without their partner – increasing concern for their own self-interests and emphasizing differences.

the future relationship (if any) will be like.[30] A summary statement reviews the relationship's history and provides the rationale for the imminent termination. Decreased-access messages clarify what is happening. Addressing the future avoids awkward interactions after parting. Even when dissolving a long-term relationship, the subject of being future friends or enemies must be addressed: "I'll always respect you, but I don't love you anymore" or "I don't ever want to see you again!" Saying good-bye to a long-term relationship may take longer, especially if one party does not want to end it and seeks to delay the final parting. These three functions of conversational leave-taking and their connection to the termination of relationships will be developed more fully in Chapter 10.

Movement: In, Out, and Around Stages

Let us now return to some of our original questions to explain more fully the stages just outlined: What are the forces that help us understand our movement in, out, and around the various stages? What directions for movement are possible at each stage? What is the likely rate of movement through the stages outlined in the model?

Directions Available for Movement Through Interaction Stages

The following propositions about movement possibilities can be derived from the staircase analogy presented in **Figure 2.1**:

Movement is generally systematic and sequential.

Movement may be forward.

Movement may be backward.

Movement occurs within stages.

Movement is always to a new place.

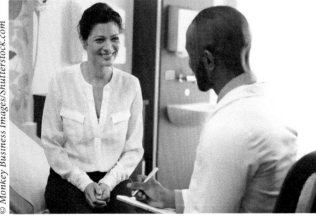

Movement Is Generally Systematic and Sequential Typically, when coming together, people follow a process of moving up the left side of the staircase in Figure 2.1; when coming apart, they commonly move down the right side. *This, however, does not suggest that the process is linear or that there is a fixed, unchangeable sequence of movement through stages.* We are dealing with a phenomenon that is never at rest, continually moving, and in flux.[31] Of course, the participants may perceive the development of a relationship as chaotic or "out of control," and moved by forces "bigger than either one of us." No doubt some relationships develop in a less orderly fashion than

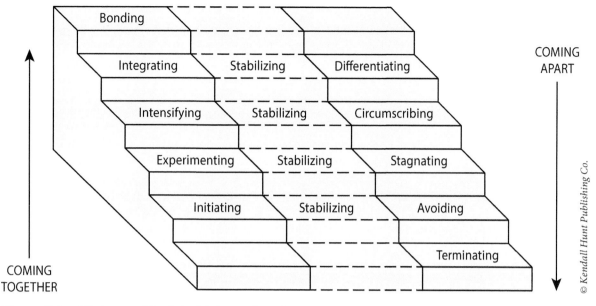

Figure 2.1 Staircase Model of Interaction Stages

others, but many people experience a general sequencing effect because (1) each stage contains important presuppositions for the following stage, (2) sequencing makes forecasting adjacent stages easier, and (3) skipping steps is a gamble on the uncertainties presented by the lack of information that could have been learned in the skipped step. Some social norms even help to inhibit skipping steps.

But, of course, sometimes people do skip steps. During growth processes, this may occur in the not unfamiliar pickup routine that moves from "Hi, what's your name?" (Initiating) to "Let's get out of this place and get to know each other better at my apartment" (Intensifying). Another familiar skip is for a couple to reach Intensifying and then move to Bonding—only to find out later that their major problem is the lack of integrating in their relationship. Each person "really loves" the other, but one or both are unwilling to move from a primarily "I" orientation to a "we" orientation—risking the merger of self with another.

The termination of relationships may also violate an orderly sequence, achieving sudden death rather than a slow decay. Sudden death is reflected when a couple is operating at the integration stage, making plans for marriage, and suddenly one party elopes with another person, never to be heard from again. Returning home to a house empty of furniture and finding divorce papers on the last remaining table is another example. As a general rule, movement is to adjacent stages (vertical or horizontal), but any final-state form can be approached from differing initial conditions and through a variety of paths.

Movement May Be Forward During phases of coming together, one evaluates the various rewards and costs associated with the relationship and may decide to advance the relationship to the next logical step upward. The decision might be one of formalizing one's commitments during integration by moving to the

Bonding Stage. It is, of course, possible to perform bonding rituals at earlier stages, thus having one foot on Intensifying and one on Bonding. During the phases of coming apart, forward movement means a movement from one of the stairs on the right to one on the left. For instance, a couple may be at the Circumscribing Stage and, after various efforts at rejuvenation, move back to Intensifying, and, in time, perhaps move toward Integrating. Any movement toward greater intimacy is considered *forward*.

Movement May Be Backward Having once achieved interaction at a level such as Intensifying, the relationship may not be able to stabilize and will slip back to a previous step, in this case, Experimenting. The parties may mutually agree that a more superficial relationship is more to their liking: "I like you a lot, Delbert. I still want to go out with you, but I would rather we didn't try to make something out of our relationship that isn't there right now. Maybe it will develop into something more intimate, but it takes time." Of course, backward movement in the deterioration process is a constant movement down the right-hand staircase from Differentiating to Terminating. Backward movement can also be lateral, moving from a stair on the left to one on the right. An example is meeting a person at a party and Experimenting, inviting the person over several times until Stagnating sets in, then Avoiding and eventually Terminating the relationship.

Movement Occurs Within Stages The central staircase represents the possibility of stabilizing relationships at a given level. As with any system, we are constantly fighting the law of nature, which says that all things move toward disorganization and death. We constantly try to arrest possible disintegration by achieving some steady state or equilibrium. This might involve brief forays into communication more characteristic of other stages, while generally maintaining the interaction within a given stage. When lovers quarrel, their disagreement can manifest characteristics more central to the deterioration process. Naturally, to maintain the relationship at the stage more appropriate to lovers, certain forces have to be enacted to counter this disruptive force. In some cases, such disruption may not be as harmful as it first appears. Those who study living systems argue that negative feedback is often needed to keep the system functioning. The absence of negative feedback can cause the steady state to vanish and terminate the system. This is probably why intimates are more apt to provide each other with evaluative judgments.

There will always be a certain degree of instability associated with any stable relationship. When we describe a relationship as stable, all we're saying is that the changes taking place are occurring at a slower rate or a lower level of intensity than would occur if a stage change were imminent. These within-stage changes during periods we think of as stable may, however, occur in regular almost predictable patterns—representing a kind of phase movement within a particular stage. To complicate things even more, it is likely that there are progressive steps within each stage—a beginning, middle, and end.

Movement Is Always to a New Place Once something has been worked through, it is different. Once communicators have achieved a certain level of interaction, they can never go back to "the way we were." They may, however, work through the same stages or even more intimate ones. Take, for example, a couple who spends considerable time in the Experimenting Stage. One person wants to move to the Intensifying Stage; the other doesn't. As a result, they gradually move toward Stagnating and, eventually, to Avoiding. Through chance, the couple is later put in adjoining rooms in a coed dorm. Should they choose to renew the relationship and start moving through the Experimenting Stage again, it will be colored by the previous experiences. It may mean some things can be worked through much more quickly, but others have to be handled with patience and sensitivity, perhaps because of the pain incurred in the original decay process.

As the dorm neighbor example suggests, sometimes the reason people who have broken up get back together is the situation changes, making the relationship seem more attractive again. "**On-again/off-again relationships**" can also result from the partners missing each other or simply trying harder to do nice things for each other. In other cases, people decide to go back to a relational partner because they've explored other options and learned that the original partner isn't so bad after all.[32] Of course, on and off are not the only two possible places a romantic relationship can go; sometimes couples redefine their relationship into one of friendship. The best predictor of who will be friends after an intimate relationship is whether they were friends prior to the romantic involvement. In addition, the extent to which a partner feels "taken advantage of" or manipulated is also an important factor in determining whether romantic partners can be "just friends" after romance.[33]

On-again/off-again relationships: Relationships in which the partners cycle between periods of being together and being broken up.

Now that we have some idea of the directions followed in developing relationships, a few comments about the rate of growth and deterioration are in order.

Rate of Movement Through Interaction Stages

Movement is usually rapid through stages already achieved or exposed. Intimates or close friends can more easily move through or dispense with small talk (characteristic of Experimenting) and move freely into more personal areas.

Movement is usually rapid through areas in which positive rewards have been achieved. Those married couples who avoid talking about "why don't you come to church with your family" may be agreeing not to disagree, which may be rewarding in itself. People interested in developing a positive relationship generally avoid conflict (which might elicit high costs or simply provide no reward) until their relationship has a sufficient reward reservoir to manage such conflict.

© Rawpixel.com/Shutterstock.com

Movement may be rapid where time is short—for example, summer romances. In a highly mobile society, many efforts are made to short-circuit a lengthy process for getting to know people.

Movement may be facilitated when proximity is high. Seeing someone on a daily basis allows more rapid assimilation of information used in determining whether movement will be forward or backward.

Movement may be facilitated by certain situational features, such as sensitivity groups, parents-without-partners groups, or a newcomer to a block party. In other situations, such as attending a church service, movement is inhibited by sanctions regarding what can be talked about and how much talk can occur.

Movement is generally faster during the early stages. Highly personal information, characteristic of more intimate stages, comes out slowly and acts as a governing agent. In addition, intimates are usually intimates because they have a backlog of rewards. Each reward is tempered by previous rewards, making it harder for dramatic movement to take place as a result of a new reward: "Sure Homer brought me flowers and I appreciate them, but he always does that."

Movement may be slow or rapid depending on individual needs. Two lonely, isolated people with few friends may move quickly; two popular people with a stable of friends may move more slowly.

Movement is bound to be slower if only one party to the relationship desires a change, whether it is to advance or retreat.

Movement during deterioration may be rapid if one person violates a particularly sacred part of their covenant. This is particularly true when (1) the offended person has repeatedly taken a strong stand on the issue and has forecast destruction of the relationship, should violation occur and (2) if the offended person sees no possibility for offsetting the violation.

Movement from courtship to marriage is accelerated by the time spent together in joint activities and the expression of strong feelings for the other. If the couple feels the reasons for their relationship growth are similar to what is generally expected, this also seems to promote faster movement from courtship to marriage.[34]

Sometimes movement is rapid when both parties agree that they have experienced a relationship "turning point." For example, the mutual expression of serious commitment, the energy each puts into making up after a bad fight, or the way each partner handles an external threat to the relationship can facilitate movement.[35] If one person thinks it is a turning point and the other does not, it is not as likely to stimulate rapid movement.

These are the major forces that determine how fast or how slow we move in and out of interaction stages and relationships in general. There are many other forces as well.

Two theories provide us with useful perspectives for explaining *change and movement within and across relationship stages:* (1) dialectical theory and (2) social exchange theories.

Dialectical Theory

From the perspective of dialectical theory, change takes place as the result of trying to resolve the inevitable tensions of relationship life. These tensions arise as we try to manage simultaneously two or more desirable, but contradictory, actions. For example, we want to maintain togetherness with our partner, but at any given point we may make autonomy and individual needs a priority. The tension we feel is rooted in the knowledge that we need to have both togetherness and separateness to sustain a relationship, while also recognizing that too much or too little of either (overall or at an inopportune time) can harm the relationship. The way a couple communicatively manages situations like this provides the measure of how and why their relationship changes.

What are the dialectical tensions facing those who are trying to build, maintain, or get out of a relationship? An important source of relevant contradictions is the type of relationship being undertaken.[36] A different set of contradictions, for example, may be at the heart of relationship-change processes for friends, coworkers, and coworkers who are friends. The most likely candidates for contradictions that cut across relationship types are probably similar to those found for other basic human responses to our social environment: involved/uninvolved, dominant/submissive, positive evaluation/negative evaluation (see pp. 74–79 and footnote 2, Chapter 3). Nevertheless, the most commonly identified dialectical tensions in the research to date are the following:

Integration-Separation Relationships require that each partner remain an individual while at the same time merging that self with his or her partner. Obviously, intimate relationships require more integration than those of casual friends, which, in turn, makes this an especially critical dimension for intimates. Too much or too little togetherness will create the tension that will initiate change. Questions about autonomy and connection occur at all relationship stages—whether it involves the decision to become a couple, the rules regarding freedom outside the relationship, or the process of deciding whether staying together is worse than terminating the relationship. Integration-separation tensions also exist for relationship partners and their extended social network as well. Partners want to blend effectively into the larger social system without losing their unique pair identity.

Expression-Nonexpression Even though beginning relationships are often characterized as efforts to seek information from another and provide information about yourself to this other, a counterforce cautions against revealing too much too soon. This kind of reveal-hide tension continues throughout various relationship stages. We know that on the one hand we need expression and openness to achieve intimacy; we also know that we make ourselves and our relationship more vulnerable by doing so. Similarly, there are contradictory demands regarding the expression of relationship information by one or both

Dialectical theory: Theory for which the primary tenet is relational change takes place as the result of trying to resolve the inevitable tensions of relationship life.

partners to members of their extended social network. As with the couple itself, the fluctuations associated with sharing relationship information and keeping secrets with members of the extended social network are key to the process of building, maintaining, strengthening, weakening, and terminating the relationships comprising that network.

Stability-Change In order to be comfortable with another person, a certain amount of predictability is necessary. Without predictable patterns, there is too much uncertainty and ambivalence for a long-term relationship—we need someone we know we can count on in certain predictable ways. But too much predictability (in certain areas or in general) may make the relationship seem stale and prompt a call for something "different." At the same time that partners are communicatively wrestling with stable, predictable actions versus changing, novel ones, they are also facing similar tensions as they consider how to relate to larger social systems they are part of. For example, couples may want to be associated with appropriate (and predictable) community relationship norms while simultaneously reaching for a degree of deviance from those norms that identifies *their* relationship as *their* relationship.

Each couple may react to the tensions created on these dimensions in different ways, but it can be a complicated process of negotiation. For example, partner A may want a great deal of autonomy and partner B may want only a little less. Partner A thinks that the survival of the relationship will require even more connectedness than partner B wants. But partner B thinks if partner A emphasized togetherness only a little more, they'd have a fine relationship. Both partner A and partner B were raised in families that emphasized togetherness as the key to satisfying and close relationships. At this point, we are less concerned with how this will be negotiated than we are in pointing out that change or movement in relationships involves (1) what one person wants for him- or herself, (2) what one person wants for the other person, (3) what both parties want for the relationship, and (4) what each party to the relationship wants as a result of past and current experiences with members of their social network. Often, the participants will not be nearly as clear about their wants as the preceding list suggests. In fact, sometimes people don't know what they want until they start talking.

Even though integration-separation, expression-nonexpression, and stability-change are frequently identified tensions associated with relationship change, the discussions that affect these contradictions may be on any topic. Suppose two intimates disagree about the need to recycle bottles, cans, and newspapers. They discuss it often and each maintains a position disagreeable to the other. Each realizes that the other's position is not likely to change by continued argument that creates unpleasant feelings for both of them. They develop a tacit agreement not to discuss the issue so often and, when they do, each subscribes to the rule that on this issue they will agree to disagree. The way this couple managed the issue of recycling affected all three tensions discussed earlier—that is, each can be separated on this issue but remain integrated in their relationship; each has agreed to a certain degree of expressiveness when discussing the issue, but each knows it is important to close down the number of times the topic is discussed; and there is a certain stability to their interaction on this issue, but this could change as each feels the need to change the current agreement.

Sometimes the responses of a couple to these tensions will produce dialogue that propels them toward greater intimacy, and sometimes toward less intimacy. It is important to remember that these tensions associated with building and maintaining a relationship are natural—part of what relating is all about. It is equally important to understand that one cannot "solve" relationship problems by seeking greater connectedness or openness or predictability, because the very act of moving toward these goals brings into focus the need for the polar opposite. The more you practice closed behavior, for example, the more salient openness becomes.

Social Exchange Theories

Social exchange theories have been used to explain changes in social behavior for many years.[37] These theories contend that (1) in social relationships, we are constantly exchanging resources (e.g., love, status, information, emotions, money, goods, services); (2) these resources are evaluated by us as rewarding or not; and (3) people have a tendency to seek those things that will be rewarding to them.

Given these assumptions, what are the rules or principles that govern productive exchange of these resources in developing relationships? One theory believes **equity** is at the heart of effective resource exchange in relationships. Partners in both happy and unhappy marriages pay attention to matters of equity in their relationships.[38] This theory predicts relationship partners will be most satisfied with their relationship when the ratio of benefits to contributions is similar for both of them. Inequity occurs when one partner is perceived as underbenefited relative to the other. When this happens, there are several ways equity can be restored by the underbenefited partner: (1) by obtaining increased benefits or rewards within the relationship; (2) by decreasing his or her contributions to the relationship; (3) by psychologically reinterpreting one's position so it no longer seems underbenefited—for example, "I'm getting a lot more than other people I know" or "Pat deserves more than I do anyway"; (4) by obtaining additional benefits or rewards outside the relationship; or (5) by terminating the relationship. Another theory maintains partners are most satisfied with their relationship when an **equality rule** operates—that is, when each partner is perceived as contributing equally and benefiting equally. A third theoretical perspective argues that the only thing that really matters to people is having the highest *reward level*. This theory is rooted in the belief that the more rewards people get, the happier they are. According to the **need-based rule**, people do not exchange resources because of a desire for equity or equality or for the most rewards possible. This theory says people exchange resources in response to their perceptions of their partner's needs. The more this is perceived as happening, the more satisfaction is felt for the relationship. All four of these exchange theories have received some support by researchers, but none seems

Social exchange theories: Theories contending that (1) in social relationships, we are constantly exchanging resources (e.g., love and status); (2) these resources are evaluated by us as rewarding or not; and (3) people have a tendency to seek those things that will be rewarding to them.

Equity: The notion that relationships progress in the most satisfying manner when the the ratio of benefits to contributions is similar for both of partners.

Equality rule: The idea that relational satisfaction is highest when each partner is perceived as contributing equally and benefiting equally.

Need-based rule: The idea that equity is not as important as exchanging resources according to the respective needs of the partners.

able to account for the entire range of complex responses associated with the exchange of resources in different types of developing and established relationships. Part of the problem is that some methods of social exchange (e.g., equity or equality) may not always be beneficial for both an individual relationship partner and the relationship itself. On the other hand, it is likely that one of these theories may be useful in explaining a particular episode or sequence of events in *your* relationship.

Rewards and Costs Each of the preceding theories is based on the premise that relationship partners make assessments of what they get and what they give. Has the exchange of resources been a rewarding one or a costly one? Should you be getting more rewards than you are? Will another relationship bring more rewards? In order to better understand this process of evaluating the exchange of resources, let's look more closely at the nature of what we've been calling rewards and costs.

> By rewards, we refer to the pleasures, satisfactions, and gratifications the person enjoys. The provision of a means whereby a drive is reduced or a need fulfilled constitutes a reward.

By costs, we refer to any factors that operate to inhibit or deter a performance of a sequence of behavior. The greater the deterrents to performing a given act—the greater the inhibition the individual has to overcome—the greater the cost of the act. Thus, cost is high when great physical or mental effort is required, when embarrassment or anxiety accompany the action, or when there are conflicting forces or competing response tendencies of any sort.[39]

Davis proposes an analogous concept when he discusses giving or not giving favors.[40] Favors may be physical or psychological. Although physical favors may certainly have psychological overtones, they include such behaviors as giving a monetary loan, satisfying sexual desires, having a person to dinner, protecting against physical harm, providing an extra hand when one person is incapacitated or lazy, or offering some expertise the other person lacks. Examples of psychological favors include feeling an integral part of the other's sorrows and joys, giving support for approved behavior, helping to offset or improve unapproved behavior while still communicating support, and helping the other to justify his or her problems (e.g., "You couldn't help it. Everybody goes through the same thing.").

> When favors are given, it may be because one participant in the relationship (1) is dependent on the other, (2) is returning a favor received, (3) wants to obligate the other in the future, or (4) is rewarded by seeing the other person enjoy the favor given.

> Withholding favors may occur when one person (1) doesn't think a similar favor will be needed in return, (2) feels the relationship will suffer by granting the favor, (3) doesn't think the favor can be returned, (4) doesn't have the time or resources to give the favor, or (5) doesn't think the other needs or will benefit from the favor.

Rewards: The pleasures, satisfactions, and gratifications that people enjoy due to their relationship.

Costs: Factors that reduce the enjoyment of being in a relationship and interacting with one's relational partner.

It would be a mistake to assume that we are constantly evaluating everything that happens to us as a reward or cost. On the contrary, much of the time we are not consciously processing the substance of our interactions as helping or hurting our relationship. Nevertheless, we are likely to make such evaluations as we try to explain why we *feel* especially good or bad. Emotions, then, often serve as reminders to consciously review the rewards and costs in our relationship.[41] We also pay particular attention to the reward/cost ratio when we have strong expectations for favorable or unfavorable outcomes. And our conscious awareness of rewards and costs is also likely to be higher with partners we have less experience with—that is, no historical record assures us rewards and costs will eventually reach a satisfactory state because they always have in the past.

When we do evaluate these rewards (or favors) and costs, we are, of course, relying on our own subjective view of reality. As such, our view of the distribution of rewards and costs may not be shared by our partner. The nature of the interaction between two partners who view the distribution of rewards and costs differently is when important changes occur. Communication about rewards and costs can itself be rewarding or costly. Sometimes the way people talk about rewards and costs in their relationship may be a more powerful reality than any actual exchange of resources. Even though we know the importance of this dialogue, we know very little about how partners to a relationship actually talk about rewards and costs. However, we do know that relationship partners review and weigh one or more of the following and how they affect the relationship as a whole: the current encounter, past encounters, and future encounters.

Analysis of the Current Encounter For any given encounter, you might assess the rewards and costs and ask yourself whether the rewards were greater than the costs. Naturally, the greater the ratio of rewards to costs, the more satisfied you are likely to be with the relationship. If your own investment is high, you may have to receive a proportionately high return to evaluate the experience favorably.

Sometimes we seek the highest rewards for ourselves with the least cost, a condition that may also increase the costs for the other person. While frequent application of this strategy sometimes works successfully for transient, short-term, or superficial relationships, it does not seem conducive to achieving greater intimacy because one party in the relationship is always "one down." Of course, you can try to keep the other person from knowing about your increased rewards—keeping the other from knowing that he or she is the "loser"—but daily interaction with intimates makes this chore especially difficult.

When a student tells a professor he or she is one of the best teachers in the school and receives a correspondingly high grade (deserved, of course), the situation could be described as rewarding to the student and the professor while incurring minimal costs for both.

Analysis of Past Encounters Our past experiences in a relationship influence how we think about new experiences with this person. In some ways our sense of rewards and costs can be thought of as a type of bank account.[42] If your relationship has been accumulating many rewards for you and not many costs, you will probably have a sense that your relationship is generally rewarding. In such instances, even if you have some encounters with your partner with high costs, you may not feel like these are a sufficient reason for slowing down the relationship. You might, for instance, willingly go see *The Magic Flute* with your partner (despite not enjoying opera) because you feel that the relationship has been rewarding enough that it more than offsets one less than enjoyable evening. Conversely, an extremely rewarding experience may not balance an interpersonal economy that has accumulated many costs. Close friends, lovers, and spouses are less likely to expect a constant balance of rewards and costs because they consider the past pattern of rewards and costs and anticipate that the favors given and received will average out during the course of their relationship. But as these relationships experience problems (and the bank account of rewards becomes depleted by costs), the demand for more immediate rewards may increase—particularly in newer relationships, with insecure partners. It is also worth noting that our perceptions of what is rewarding or costly can change over time. Sometimes we perceive something as a cost initially (an intense argument), but the long-term effects are rewarding (important issues for the relationship were openly discussed and mutually agreeable decisions were reached).

This analysis of the cumulative rewards and costs obtained in a relationship also provides valuable data for comparison with possible alternatives to the current relationship. For example, poor marriages often continue because the alternatives—divorce proceedings, living alone, division of the children, social criticism—offer potentially greater costs than those currently felt. Thus, not all the rewards and costs that affect the relationship are derived from the partners themselves. Other people in your social network, people you work with, relatives—all provide rewards and costs that may impact the two-person relationship.

Analysis of Future Encounters Finally, we may ask ourselves whether it will be rewarding to interact with this person in the future. What will be the relative rewards and costs derived from interacting at our current stage of the relationship? At a less intimate level? At a more intimate level? Such considerations have a definite impact on the movement through the various stages of growth and deterioration. When couples assess the current state of their relationship and conclude that they have made improvements over some dissatisfying episodes in the past, this gives them a basis for believing that future encounters will be satisfying.[43]

One important concept regarding expectations for future encounters concerns the norm of reciprocity.[44] Simply stated, the **norm of reciprocity** tells us that there is a strong tendency on the part of human beings to respond in kind to the behavior they receive. Are you willing to give another certain rewards today in the hope that the norm of reciprocity will be activated and you will be "done unto as you did unto them" sometime in the future?

Reciprocity does not have to be an immediate, unthinking response. It is often one that is conscious and planned. The return volley does not necessarily have to take place immediately following the other's serve—"they had

Norm of reciprocity: The strong tendency on the part of human beings to respond in kind to the behavior they receive.

us to dinner last month so we should have them over soon" or "they sent us a Christmas card last year, so maybe we'd better send them one this year." The reciprocated act may not be of exactly equivalent value. For example: A: "You're a great person." B: "I really admire your artistic talent." The exchange may concern two very different objects—trading access to one's genitals for access to the other's money. Or it may involve almost antithetical behavior—for example, dominance provoking submissiveness and vice versa.

A closely related phenomenon is known as **imitation**. Here, the reciprocated response usually follows soon after the initial response and is generally less conscious. The behavior is similar but still operates within a basic reward-cost framework. Have you ever noticed how jokes seem to lead to more jokes and strokes lead to more strokes? A: "You really did a good job." B: "So did you." Or A: "I love you." B: "I love you, too." Hostility may evoke hostility. I raise my voice and you counter by raising yours. Nonverbal cues such as smiling, nodding, and silence and structural dimensions such as interruptions or length of utterance are other examples of imitation that have been documented by research. The phenomenon known as **emotional contagion**, with which one person's feeling state is assumed and reflected by others present, would also seem to fall within the realm of imitation because it appears to be partly driven by a tendency to mimic the facial expressions of others when interacting with them.[45]

> **Imitation:** Specific type of reciprocated response that follows soon after the initial response and closely mimics the initial behaviour.

> **Emotional contagion:** Largely unconscious tendency for people who interact to be affected by each other's emotions in such a way that their emotions converge.

That a norm of reciprocity exists is evident. The exact manner in which it appears, however, is largely dependent on the nature of the relationship. For instance, some believe there is a reciprocity in disclosing information about oneself. Indeed, during Initiation and Experimentation Stages, the obligation for giving tit for tat is high: "I'll tell you my hometown if you'll tell me yours." Following the norm of reciprocating self-disclosures in initial interactions is associated with being liked, which may foster a closer relationship.[46] During Intensifying and Integrating, the parties to the relationship may feel that they can ask and expect greater reciprocity of more intimate information. It's almost like saying, "By revealing part of my inner self to you first, I'm showing my trust. This should give you sufficient reward and increase the possibility that you will trust me with an equivalent secret of yours. And if you do, our relationship will grow." Some, however, would argue that during the integrating process, the reciprocity norm becomes muddled because it is hard to analyze an exchange of intimate information between two people who see themselves so often as a single entity. It should be obvious that there are many relationships that do not demand reciprocation for a high degree of disclosure—you don't expect your physician, psychiatrist, or priest to exchange intimate information with you.

Rewards and Costs in Enduring Relationships. Several characteristics of more intimate, long-term relationships affect the way these participants deal with rewards and costs.

1. First, the value of both rewards and costs may increase as the relationship becomes more intimate. "I'd sure like to spend an evening just talking to you" may be much more powerful from an intimate than

an acquaintance; similarly, "You're too rigid in your beliefs" can be a great cost from an intimate and an unimportant opinion from an acquaintance.

2. Second, intimates exchange a greater variety of resources than do casual acquaintances. And seemingly inequitable resources may be equitably exchanged—for example, a special anniversary dinner is "paid back" by not going to play golf on Sunday. Intimates have had the time to negotiate the relative values of these different resources, but less intimate pairs have not. As a result, exchanges between acquaintances are often of the same type—for example, you had us over for dinner so we'll have you over for dinner.

3. Third, intimates are more likely than acquaintances to tolerate periods when costs exceed rewards. Since the relationship is expected to continue, the expectation is that losses can be recouped later.[47] In fact, sometimes people will incur considerable costs during the courtship period in order to win the other's approval for marriage. This may create an imbalance that is difficult to restore immediately and gets the marriage off to a rough start.

4. Fourth, some rewards and costs of intimates may need to be analyzed as a couple rather than as two individuals. The wife's career setback or the husband's success in losing weight may more appropriately be considered as costs or rewards for both people rather than the specific individual concerned. If one profits, both are rewarded; if one loses, both are hurt.

5. Fifth, since intimates in long-term relationships have many events over many years to consider in any assessment of overall rewards and costs, it is likely that intimates may find it more difficult to specifically account for an overall feeling of deficit or surplus in rewards and costs. After how much time does one stop expecting "payment" for something? To what extent can the time we spent together when dating be used to balance the time we are apart now?

Observers of people who have maintained a relationship over a long period of time may tend to believe that it is happiness or intimacy that has sustained the relationship over so many years. Some enduring relationships do manifest a high degree of intimacy over the years, but others are far less intimate. A married couple may stay together because the marriage provides needed security or because separation is perceived as more costly than a marriage with little intimacy. Sometimes the mutual commitment to the institution of marriage—rather than the marital partner—will sustain a marital partnership. In short, the rewards necessary to sustain a relationship over a long period of time may be derived from a variety of sources other than feelings of intimacy for one's partner.

An analysis of the rewards and costs in our everyday interpersonal relations can be very useful for understanding why we choose to pursue some relationships, remain at the same level with others, and terminate still others. Most resources we exchange have both a reward and a cost component to them. And some things are only rewarding because they aren't a cost. Some behaviors considered rewarding at one point in a relationship may be perceived as costs at another point. Just because we are rewarded by another person doesn't mean our relationship will continue to increase in intimacy. You may really like to play tennis with someone, but the rewards derived from this activity alone are not sufficient to bring the partners to a more intimate stage. And even if one partner believed the rewards were sufficient to move toward greater intimacy, the other partner may not.

Any analysis of human relationships in terms of an "economic model" of exchange inevitably causes some to think that the humanness has been taken out of relationships and that the possibility of behavior that is not self-serving has been eliminated. Do people help others without any desire for personal gain? Does altruistic behavior exist? We know that people run into blazing buildings and dive into freezing rivers to save strangers, and we know people donate blood and money to others without any hope of reciprocated gain. Examples such as these offer strong testimony to the existence of altruistic behavior. Still, there are questions. Is there something about the act of helping another person that, in itself, is a reward to the helper?

Batson's research shows that people experience one of two emotional responses (or some combination of the two) when they confront a distressed person: personal distress or empathic concern.[48] Personal distress involves getting upset, being worried, feeling troubled, and the like. Empathic concern means there is a real feeling of compassion and sympathy for the distressed person. When personal distress predominates, the helper's behavior is grounded in self-interest. When empathic concern predominates, the helper's behavior is designed to reduce the other's distress and qualifies as altruistic behavior. In addition, others have suggested that emotional attachment to another person may trigger altruistic motives even when that person is not suffering distress. Thus, even though we may be motivated by the accumulation of rewards for ourselves, this doesn't necessarily mean we will always act in a selfish manner. Maximizing our own gains may be achieved by maximizing our partner's.

Rewards and costs are determined by many things. We have touched on only a few. Chapters 3 and 4 will explore in more detail some of the situational, psychological, and societal forces that help structure the cost-reward process and, ultimately, our movement through relationships.

Summary

This chapter started with the idea that there are many different types of relationships, but all of them seem to have some characteristics in common. For example, relationship expectations change as a result of communication behavior, and communication behavior changes as a result of relationship expectations. In addition, each type of relationship appears to fluctuate along a continuum of intimacy or "closeness." With these features in mind, a model of interaction stages covering the growth and decay of relationships was proposed. The model was based on the idea that certain patterns of communication manifest themselves at different points in the life of a relationship. This evolutionary model of message making from greeting to good-bye included the following stages: Initiating, Experimenting, Intensifying, Integrating, Bonding, Differentiating, Circumscribing, Stagnating, Avoiding, and Terminating. An overview of the language, topics, and message strategies relevant to each stage was discussed. The model is closely linked to the eight dimensions of communication discussed in Chapter 1. In the last part of the chapter, the concepts of dialectical contradictions and rewards and costs (derived from social exchange theories) were introduced to help explain why, where, and how fast people move through interaction stages. In short, we have taken a quick trip via communication behavior through the birth, adolescence, maturity, sickness, isolation, and death of a relationship.

Relationship Development

Altman, I., and Taylor, D. A. *Social Penetration: The Development of Interpersonal Relationships*. New York: Holt, Rinehart and Winston, 1973.

Blieszner, R. "Close Relationships over Time." In A. L. Weber and H. H. Harvey, eds., *Perspectives on Close Relationships,* pp. 1–17. Boston: Allyn & Bacon, 1994.

Caughlin, J. P., and Huston, T. L. "The Affective Structure of Marriage over Time." In A. L. Vangelisti and D. Perlman, eds., *The Cambridge Handbook of Personal Relationships* 2nd ed., pp. 90–105. New York: Cambridge University Press, 2018.

Davis, M. S. *Intimate Relations.* New York: Free Press, 1973.

Duck, S. ed., *Handbook of Personal Relationships: Theory, Research, and Interventions.* 2nd ed. New York: Wiley, 1997.

Fox, J., Warber, K. M., and Makstaller, D. C. "The Role of Facebook in Romantic Relationship Development: An Exploration of Knapp's Relational Stage Model." *Journal of Social and Personal Relationships* 30 (2013): 771–794.

Goodwin, R. *Changing Relations: Achieving Intimacy in a Time of Social Transition.* New York: Cambridge University Press, 2009.

Hinde, R. A. *Toward Understanding Relationships.* New York: Academic Press, 1979.

Koerner, A. F. "Models of Relating—Not Relationship Models: Cognitive Representations of Relating Across Interpersonal Relationship Domains." *Journal of Social and Personal Relationships* 23 (2006): 629–653.

Levinger, G., and Rausch, H. L., eds. *Close Relationships: Perspectives on the Meaning of Intimacy.* Amherst, MA: University of Massachusetts Press, 1977.

Miller, R. S. *Intimate Relationships.* 7th ed. New York: McGraw-Hill, 2015.

Parks, M. R. *Personal Relationships and Personal Networks.* Mahwah, NJ: Erlbaum, 2007.

Pietromonaco, P. R., Lawrence, J. P., and Barrett, L. F. "Change in Relationship Knowledge Representations." In A. L. Vangelisti, H. T. Reis, and M. A. Fitzpatrick, eds., *Stability and Change in Relationships,* pp. 5–34. New York: Cambridge University Press, 2002.

Reis, H. T. Maniaci, M. R., Caprariello, P. A., Eastwick, P. W., and Finkel, E. J. "Familiarity Does Indeed Promote Attraction in Love Interaction" *Journal of Personality and Social Psychology* 101 (2011): 557–570.

Sharabi, L. L., and Caughlin, J. P. "Usage Patterns of Social Media across Stages of Romantic Relationships." In N. Punyanunt-Carter and J. S. Wrench, eds., *The Impact of Social Media in Modern Romantic Relationships,* pp. 15–29. Lanham, MD: Lexington Books, 2017.

Simmel, G. *The Sociology of George Simmel.* Translated by K. Wolff. New York: Free Press, 1950.

Solomon, D. H., and Roloff, M. E. "Relationship Initiation and Growth." In A. L. Vangelisti and D. Perlman, eds., *The Cambridge Handbook of Personal Relationships* 2nd ed., pp. 79–89. New York, NY: Cambridge University Press, 2018.

Solomon, D. H., and Vangelisti, A. L. "Relationship Development." In C. R. Berger, ed., *Interpersonal Communication: Handbooks of Communication Science: Vol 6,* pp. 347–369. Berlin, Germany: De Gruyter Mouton, 2014.

Sprecher, S., Wenzel, A., and Harvey, J. eds. *Handbook of Relationship Initiation.* New York: Psychology Press, 2008.

Welch, S. A., and Rubin, R. B. "Development of Relationship Stage Measures," *Communication Quarterly* 50 (2002): 24–40.

Social Exchange and Interdependence

Blau, P. *Exchange and Power in Social Life.* New York: Wiley, 1964.

Burgess, R. L., and Huston, T. L., eds. *Social Exchange in Developing Relationships.* New York: Academic Press, 1979.

Cook K. S., Cheshire C., Rice E. R. W., and Nakagawa S. "Social Exchange Theory." In J. DeLamater and A. Ward, eds. *Handbook of Social Psychology.* Dordrecht, Netherlands: Springer, 2013.

Foa, U. G., and Foa, E. B. "Resource Exchange: Toward a Structural Theory of Interpersonal Communication." In A. W. Siegman and B. Pope, eds., *Studies in Dyadic Communication.* New York: Pergamon Press, 1972.

Gouldner, A. W. "The Norm of Reciprocity: A Preliminary Statement." *American Sociological Review* 25 (1960): 161–178.

Homans, G. C. *Social Behavior: Its Elementary Forms.* New York: Harcourt Brace Jovanovich, 1961.

Kelley, H. H., Holmes, J. G., Kerr, N. L., Reis, H. T., Rusbult, C. E., and Van Lange, P. A. M. *An Atlas of Interpersonal Situations.* New York: Cambridge University Press, 2003.

Murray, S. L., Aloni, M., Holmes, J. G., Derrick, J. L., Stinson, D. A., and Leder, S. "Fostering Partner Dependence as Trust Insurance: The Implicit Contingencies of the Exchange Script in Close Relationships." *Journal of Personality and Social Psychology* 96 (2009): 324–348.

Roloff, M. E. *Interpersonal Communication: The Social Exchange Approach.* Beverly Hills, CA: Sage, 1981.

Stafford, L. "Social Exchange Theory: A Cost-Benefit Approach to Relationships." In D. O. Braithwaite, E. A. Suter, and K. Floyd, eds., *Engaging Theories in Family Communication: Multiple Perspectives,* 2nd. ed., pp. 279–289. New York: Routledge, 2018.

Stinson, D. A., Cameron, J. J., and Robinson, K. J. "The Good, the Bad, and the Risky: Self-esteem, Rewards and Costs, and Interpersonal Risk Regulation during Relationship Initiation." *Journal of Social and Personal Relationships* 32 (2015): 1109–1136.

Thibaut, J. W., and Kelley, H. H. *The Social Psychology of Groups.* New York: Wiley, 1959.

Tuggle, F. J., Kerpelman, J. L., and Pittman, J. F. "Parental Support, Psychological Control, and Early Adolescents' Relationships with Friends and Dating Partners." *Family Relations* 63 (2014): 496–512.

Walster, E., Walster, G. W., and Berscheid, E. *Equity: Theory and Research.* Boston: Allyn & Bacon, 1978.

Zhang, Y., and Epley, N. "Self-Centered Social Exchange: Differential Use of Costs and Benefits in Prosocial Reciprocity." *Journal of Personality and Social Psychology* 97 (2009): 796–810.

Dialectic Theory

Altman, I., Vinsel, A., and Brown, B. "Dialectic Conceptions in Social Psychology." In L. Berkowitz, ed., *Advances in Experimental Social Psychology*, pp. 107–160. New York: Academic Press, 1981.

Baxter, L. A. *Voicing Relationships: A Dialogic Perspective.* Thousand Oaks, CA: Sage, 2001.

Baxter, L. A. "A Tale of Two Voices: Relational Dialectics Theory." *Journal of Family Communication* 4 (2004): 181–192.

Baxter, L. A., and Montgomery, B. M. *Relating: Dialogues and Dialectics.* New York: Guilford, 1996.

Bochner, A. "The Functions of Human Communication in Interpersonal Bonding." In C. Arnold and J. Bowers, eds., *Handbook of Rhetorical and Communication Theory.* Boston: Allyn & Bacon, 1984.

Harrigan, M. M. "The Contradictions of Identity-Work for Parents of Visibly Adopted Children," *Journal of Social and Personal Relationships,* 26 (2009): 634–658.

Montgomery, B. M. "Relationship Maintenance Versus Relationship Change: A Dialectical Dilemma." *Journal of Social and Personal Relationship* 10 (1993): 205–223.

Petronio, S. *Boundaries of Privacy: Dialectics of Disclosure.* Albany, NY: State University of New York Press, 2002.

Sahlstein, E., Maguire, K. C., and Timmerman, L. "Contradictions and Praxis Contextualized by Wartime Deployment: Wives' Perspectives Revealed through Relational Dialectics." *Communication Monographs* (2009): 421–442.

Suter, E. A., and Seurer, L. M. "Relational Dialectics Theory: Realizing the Dialogic Potential of Family Communication." In D. O. Braithwaite, E. A. Suter, and K. Floyd, eds., Engaging Theories in Family Communication 2nd. ed. New York: Routledge, 2018.

Stamp, G. H. "The Appropriation of the Parental Role through Communication during the Transition to Parenthood." *Communication Monograph* 61 (1994): 89–112.

Notes

1. Relationship expectations have been examined from several different perspectives. See R. M. Sabatelli and J. Pearce, "Exploring Marital Expectations," *Journal of Social and Personal Relationships* 3 (1986): 307–321; J. H. Harvey, G. Agostinelli, and A. L. Weber, "Account-making and the Formation of Expectations About Close Relationships." In C. Hendrick, ed., *Close Relationships* (Newbury Park, CA: Sage, 1989). A. L. Vangelisti and J. A. Daly, "Gender Differences in Standards for Romantic Relationships," *Personal Relationships* 4 (1997): 203–219.

2. C. A. Bredow, R. M. Cate, and T. L. Huston, "Have We Met Before? A Conceptual Model of First Romantic Encounters," In S. Sprecher, A. Wenzel, and J. Harvey, eds., *Handbook of Relationship Initiation (New York: Psychology Press, 2008): 3–28;* M. Rands and G. Levinger, "Implicit Theories of Relationship: An Intergenerational Study," *Journal of Personality and Social Psychology* 37 (1979): 645–661.

3. M. L. Knapp, D. G. Ellis, and B. A. Williams, "Perceptions of Communication Behavior Associated with Relationship Terms," *Communication Monographs* 47 (1980): 262–278.

4. R. E. Quinn, "Coping with Cupid: The Formation, Impact and Management of Romantic Relationships in Organizations," *Administrative Science Quarterly* 22 (1977): 30–45; and J. P. Dillard, "Close Relationships at Work: Perceptions of the Motives and Performance of Relational Participants," *Journal of Social and Personal Relationships* 4 (1987): 179–193. For an analysis of non-romantic friendships between coworkers who differ in status, see T. E. Zorn, "Bosses and Buddies: Constructing and Performing Simultaneously Hierarchical and Close Friendship Relationships." In J. T. Wood and S. Duck, eds., *Under-studied Relationships*, pp. 122–147. (Thousand Oaks, CA: Sage, 1995).

5. J. G. Delia, "Some Tentative Thoughts Concerning the Study of Interpersonal Relationships and Their Development," *Western Journal of Speech Communication* 44 (1980): 97–103.

6. D. Weigel and C. Murray, "The Paradox of Stability and Change in Relationships: What Does Chaos Theory Offer for the Study of Romantic Relationships?" *Journal of Social and Personal Relationships* 17 (2000): 425–449.

7. Representative works include: F. Lacoursiere, *The Life Cycle of Groups* (New York: Human Sciences Press, 1980); R. Thornton and P. M. Nardi, "The Dynamics of Role Acquisition," *American Journal of Sociology* 80 (1975): 870–885; I. Altman and D. A. Taylor, *Social Penetration: The Development of Interpersonal Relationships* (New York: Holt, Rinehart and Winston, 1973); B. W. Tuckman, "Developmental Sequence in Small Groups," *Psychological Bulletin* 63 (1965): 384–399; S. W. Duck, *Personal Relationships and Personal Constructs: A Study of Friendship Formation* (New York: Wiley, 1973); M. S. Davis, *Intimate Relations* (New York: Free Press, 1973); T. M. Newcomb, *The Acquaintance Process* (New York: Holt, Rinehart and Winston, 1961); C. B. Broderick, "Predicting Friendship Behavior: A Study of the Determinants of Friendship Selection and Maintenance in a College Population" (Doctoral diss. Cornell University, 1956); G. M. Phillips and N. J. Metzger, *Intimate Communication* (Boston: Allyn & Bacon, 1976), pp. 401–403; C. R. Berger and R. J. Calabrese, "Some Explorations in Initial Interaction and Beyond: Toward a Developmental Theory of Interpersonal Communication," *Human Communication Research* 1 (1975): 99–112; C. R. Rogers, "A Process Conception of Psychotherapy," *American Psychologist* 13 (1958): 142–149; G. Simmel, *The Sociology of George Simmel*, trans. K. Wolff (New York: Free Press, 1950); K. Lewin, "Some Social Psychological Differences Between the United States and Germany," *Character and Personality* 4 (1936): 265–293; J. T. Wood, "Communication and Relational Culture: Bases for the Study of Human Relationships," *Communication Quarterly* 30 (1982): 75–83; D. P. McWhirter, and A. M. Mattison, *The Male Couple* (Englewood Cliffs, NJ: Prentice Hall, 1984); W. J. Dickens, and D. Perlman, "Friendship over the Life-Cycle." In S. Duck and R. Gilmour, eds., *Personal Relationships. 2: Developing Personal Relationships* (New York: Academic Press, 1981); C. A. VanLear Jr., and N. Trujillo, "On Becoming Acquainted: A Longitudinal Study of Social Judgment Processes," *Journal of Social and Personal Relationships* 3 (1986): 375–392; J. M. Honeycutt, J. G. Cantrill, and R. W. Greene, "Memory Structures for Relational Escalation: A Cognitive Test of the Sequencing of Relational Actions and Stages," *Human Communication Research* 16 (1989): 62–90; J. M. Honeycutt, J. G. Cantrill, and T. Allen, "Memory Structures for Relational Decay: A Cognitive Test of Sequencing of De-escalating Actions and Stages," *Human Communication Research* 18 (1992): 528–562; J. M. Honeycutt, "Memory Structures of the Rise and Fall of Personal Relationships." In S. Duck, ed., *Individuals in Relationships* (Newbury Park, CA: Sage, 1993); and J. C. B. Teboul and T. Cole, "Relationship Development and Workplace Integration: An Evolutionary Perspective," *Communication Theory,* 15 (2005): 389–413.

8   S. A. Welch and R. B. Rubin, "Development of Relationship Stage Measures," *Communication Quarterly* 50 (2002): 24–40.

9   A. Paik, "'Hookups,' Dating and Relationship Quality: Does the Type of Sexual Involvement Matter?" *Social Science Research* 39 (2010): 739–753.

10 McWhirter and Mattison, *The Male Couple;* S. M. Haas and L. Stafford, "An Initial Examination of Maintenance Behaviors in Gay and Lesbian Relationships," *Journal of Social and Personal Relationships* 15 (1998): 846–855; L. A. Peplau and L. R. Spalding, "The Close Relationships of Lesbians, Gay Men, and Bisexuals." In C. Hendrick and S. S. Hendrick, eds., *Close Relationships: A Sourcebook* (Thousand Oaks, CA: Sage, 2000), pp. 111–123.

11 T. L. Albrecht, M. B. Adelman, and Associates, *Communicating Social Support* (Newbury Park, CA: Sage, 1987). M. R. Parks and M. B. Adelman, "Communication Networks and the Development of Romantic Relationships: An Expansion of Uncertainty Reduction Theory," *Human Communication Research* 10 (1983): 55–79. S. Sprecher, D. Felmlee, T. L. Orbuch, and M. C. Willetts, "Social Networks and Change in Personal Relationships." In A. Vangelisti, H. T. Reis, and M. A. Fitzpatrick, eds., *Stability and Change in Relationships* (New York: Cambridge, 2002), pp. 257–284. R. M. Milardo and H. Helms-Erikson, "Network Overlap and Third-Party Influence in Close Relationships." In C. Hendrick and S. S. Hendrick, eds., *Close Relationships: A Sourcebook* (Thousand Oaks, CA: Sage, 2000) pp. 33–45. G. Allan, *Friendship: Developing a Sociological Perspective* (Boulder, CO: Westview, 1989). M. R. Parks, "Communication Networks and Relationship Life Cycles." In S. Duck, ed., *Handbook of Personal Relationships*, pp. 351–372. 2nd ed. (New York: Wiley, 1997). Parks, M. R. and Faw, M. H."Relationships among Relationships: Interpersonal Communication and Social Networks." In Berger, C. R., ed., *Interpersonal Communication: Handbooks of Communication Science: Vol 6* pp. 395–416. Berlin, Germany: De Gruyter Mouton, 2014; C. M. Proulx, H. M. Helms, R. M. Milardo, and C. C. Payne, "Relational Support from Friends and Wives' Family Relationships: The Role of Husbands' Interference," *Journal of Social and Personal Relationships* 26 (2009): 195–210.

12 L. E. LeFebvre "Swiping Me off My Feet: Explicating Relationship Initiation on Tinder." *Journal of Social and Personal Relationships* 35(2018): 1205–1229.

13 G. R. Miller, and M. Steinberg, *Between People: A New Analysis of Interpersonal Communication* (Chicago: Science Research Associates, 1975); G. R. Miller, and M. J. Sunnafrank, "All Is for One but One Is Not for All:

A Conceptual Perspective of Interpersonal Communication." In F. E. X. Dance, ed., *Human Communication Theory* (New York: Harper & Row, 1982).

14 M. R. Cunningham and A. K. Barbee, "Prelude to a Kiss: Nonverbal Flirting, Opening Gambits, and Other Communication Dynamics in the Initiation of Romantic Relationships." In S. Sprecher, A. Wenzel, and J. Harvey, eds., *Handbook of Relationship Initiation* (New York: Psychology Press, 2008).

15 L. L. Sharabi, and J. P. Caughlin, "Usage Patterns of Social Media across Stages of Romantic Relationships." In N. Punyanunt-Carter and J. S. Wrench, eds., *The Impact of Social Media in Modern Romantic Relationships*, (Lanham, MD: Lexington Books, 2017), pp. 15–29. C. B. Yang, B. B. Brown, and M. T. Braun. "From Facebook to Cell Calls: Layers of Electronic Intimacy in College Students' Interpersonal Relationships." *New Media and Society* 16 (2014): 5–23.

16 H. L. Rausch, K. A. Marshall, and J. M. Featherman, "Relations at Three Early Stages of Marriage as Reflected by the Use of Personal Pronouns," *Family Process* 9 (1970): 69–82.

17 L. A. Baxter, "Symbols of Relationship Identity in Relationship Cultures," *Journal of Social and Personal Relationships* 4 (1987): 261–280.

18 D. H. Solomon and L. K. Knobloch, "A Model of Relational Turbulence: The Role of Intimacy, Relational Uncertainty, and Interference from Partners in Appraisals of Irritations," *Journal of Social and Personal Relationships,* 21 (2004): 795–816. L. K. Knobloch, "Perceived Involvement of Network Members in Courtships: A Test of the Relational Turbulence Model," *Personal Relationships,* 13 (2006): 281–302. L. K. Knobloch, "Perceptions of Turmoil Within Courtship: Associations with Intimacy, Relational Uncertainty, and Interference from Partners," *Journal of Social and Personal Relationships* 24 (2007): 363–384.

19 Believing one's partner and relationship are unique appears to not only foster positive feelings in relationships, but also buffer against negative ones. People who believe their partner is uniquely suited to them, for example, are more likely than other people to respond constructively and forgive when a romantic partner engages in some transgression. M. R. Dillow, W. A. Afifi, and M. Matsunaga, "Perceived Partner Uniqueness and Communicative Behavioral Transgression Outcomes in Romantic Relationships," *Journal of Social and Personal Relationships* 29 (2012): 28–51. See also M.. R. Charania and W. Ickes, "Predicting Marital Satisfaction: Social Absorption and Individuation versus Attachment Anxiety and Avoidance," *Personal Relationships* 14 (2007): 187–208.

20. M. S. Davis, *Intimate Relations* (New York: The Free Press, 1973).

21. L. M. Papp, J. Danielewicz, and C. Cayernberg, "'Are We Facebook Official?' Implications of Dating Partners' Facebook Use and Profiles for Intimate Relationship Satisfaction," *Cyberpsychology, Behavior, and Social Networking* 15 (2012): 85–90.

22. Y. Noguchi (Producer). (2019, February 14). When Your Shared Netflix Account Outlasts the Relationship. Retrieved from https://www.npr.org/2019/02/14/693566073/when-your-shared-netflix-account-outlasts-the-relationship.

23. W. Ickes, ed., *Empathic Accuracy* (New York: Guilford, 1997). W. Ickes, *Everyday Mind Reading: Understanding What Other People Think and Feel* (Amherst, NY: Prometheus Books, 2003).

24. H. C. Davis, D. J. Haymaker, D. A. Hermecz, and D. G. Gilbert, "Marital Interaction: Affective Synchrony of Self-Reported Emotional Components," *Journal of Personality Assessment* 52 (1988): 48–57; and K. Grammar, K. B. Kruck, and M. S. Magnusson, "The Courtship Dance: Patterns of Nonverbal Synchronization in Opposite-Sex Encounters," *Journal of Nonverbal Behavior* 22 (1998): 3–29.

25. J. Van Ouytsel, E. Van Gool, M. Walrave, K. Ponnet, and F. Peeters, "Exploring the Role of Social Networking Sites within Adolescent Romantic Relationships and Dating Experiences." *Computers in Human Behavior* 55 (2016): 76–86.

26. See Davis, *Intimate Relations*, p. 195.

27. Imagined interactions may occur at other points in the relationship as well—and for different purposes. For example, a person may construct an imagined dialogue relative to a date or marriage proposal. See J. M. Honeycutt and J. G. Cantrill, *Cognition, Communication, and Romantic Relationships* (Mahwah, NJ: Erlbaum, 2001), pp. 62–81. Also, people considering whether to reveal a personal secret may imagine how the conversation would go before disclosing it. See A. S. Richards and A. L. Sillars, "Imagined Interactions as Predictors of Secret Revelation and Health," *Communication Research* 41 (2014): 236–256.

28. J. A. Hess, "Distance Regulation in Personal Relationships: The Development of a Conceptual Model and a Test of Representational Validity," *Journal of Social and Personal Relationships* 19 (2002): 663–683.

29. D. M. Geller, L. Goodstein, M. Silver, and W. C. Sternberg, "On Being Ignored: The Effects of the Violation of Implicit Rules of Social Interaction," *Sociometry* 37 (1974): 541–556.

30. M. L. Knapp, R. P. Hart, G. W. Friedrich, and G. M. Shulman, "The Rhetoric of Goodbye: Verbal and Nonverbal Correlates of Human Leave-Taking," *Speech Monographs* 40 (1973): 182–198.

31. Weigel and Murray, "The Paradox of Stability and Change."

32. R. M. Dailey, B. Jin, R. A. Pfiester, and G. Beck, G., "On-Again/Off-Again Relationships: What Keeps Partners Coming Back?" *Journal of Social Psychology* 151 (2011): 417–440; R. M. Dailey, K. R. Rossetto, R. A. Pfiester, and C. A. Surra, "A Qualitative Analysis of On-Again/Off-Again Romantic Relationships: 'It's Up, It's Down, All Around,'" *Journal of Social and Personal Relationships* 26 (2009): 443–466; R. M. Dailey, A. V. Middleton, and E. W. Green, "Perceived Relational Stability in On-Again/Off-Again Relationships," *Journal of Social and Personal Relationships* 29 (2012): 52–76.

33. S. Metts, W. R. Cupach, and R. A. Bejlovec, "'I Love You Too Much to Ever Start Liking You': Redefining Romantic Relationships," *Journal of Social and Personal Relationships* 6 (1989): 259–274. For an account of male-female nonromantic relationships, see K. Werking, *We're Just Good Friends: Women and Men in Nonromantic Relationships* (New York: Guilford, 1997).

34. T. L. Huston, C. A. Surra, N. M. Fitzgerald, and R. M. Cate, "From Courtship to Marriage: Mate Selection as an Interpersonal Process." In S. W. Duck and R. Gilmour, eds., *Personal Relationships. 2: Developing Personal Relationships*, pp. 53–88. (New York: Academic Press, 1981). Also see C. A. Surra, "Reasons for Changes in Commitment: Variations by Courtship Type," *Journal of Social and Personal Relationships* 4 (1987): 17–33.

35. L. A. Baxter and C. Bullis, "Turning Points in Developing Romantic Relationships," *Human Communication Research* 12 (1986): 469–493; and S. A. Lloyd and R. M. Cate, "Attributions Associated with Significant Turning Points in Premarital Relationship Development and Dissolution," *Journal of Social and Personal Relationships* 2 (1985): 419–436.

36. L. A. Baxter and B. M. Montgomery, *Relating: Dialogues & Dialectics* (New York: Guilford, 1996); L. A. Baxter and L. A. Erbert, "Perceptions of Dialectical Contradictions in Turning Points or Development in Heterosexual Romantic Relationships," *Journal of Social and Personal Relationships* 16 (1999): 547–569. R. L. Conville, *Relational Transitions: The Evolution of Personal Relationships* (New York: Praeger, 1991). W. R. Cupach, "Dialectical Processes in the Disengagement of Interpersonal Relationships." In T. L. Orbuch,

ed., *Close Relationship Loss: Theoretical Approaches* (New York: Springer-Verlag, 1993), pp. 128–141. B. M. Montgomery, "Relationship Maintenance versus Relationship Change: A Dialectical Dilemma," *Journal of Social and Personal Relationships* 10 (1993): 205–223. W. K. Rawlins, *Friendship Matters: Communication, Dialectics, and the Life Course* (New York: Aldine de Gruyter, 1992). G. H. Stamp, "The Appropriation of the Parental Role Through Communication During the Transition to Parenthood," *Communication Monographs* 61 (1994): 89–112. E. A. Suter, L. M. Seurer, S. Webb, B. Grewe Jr, and J. Koenig Kellas. "Motherhood as Contested Ideological Terrain: Essentialist and Queer Discourses of Motherhood at Play in Female–female Co-mothers' Talk," *Communication Monographs* 82 (2015): 458–483. C. M. Werner and L. A. Baxter, "Temporal Qualities of Relationships: Organismic, Transactional, and Dialectical Views." In M. L. Knapp and G. R. Miller, eds., *Handbook of Interpersonal Communication* (Thousand Oaks, CA: Sage, 1994), pp. 323–379.

[37] G. C. Homans, *Social Behavior: Its Elementary Forms* (New York: Harcourt Brace Jovanovich, 1961). M. Deutsch, "Equity, Equality and Need: What Determines Which Value Will Be Used as a Basis of Distributive Justice?" *Journal of Social Issues* 31 (1975): 137–149. E. Walster, G. W. Walster, and E. Berscheid, *Equity: Theory and Research* (Boston: Allyn & Bacon, 1978). J. M. Steil and B. A. Turetsky, "Is Equal Better?" In S. Oskamp, ed., *Family Processes and Problems: Social Psychological Aspects* (Newbury Park, CA: Sage, 1987), pp. 73–97. S. Sprecher, "Social Exchange Perspectives on the Dissolution of Close Relationships." In T. L. Orbuch, ed., *Close Relationship Loss: Theoretical Approaches* (New York: Springer-Verlag, 1993), pp. 47–66. J. G. Holmes, "The Exchange Process in Close Relationships: Microbehavior and Macromotives." In M. J. Lerner and S. C. Lerner, eds., *The Justice Motive in Social Behavior* (New York: Plenum, 1981), pp. 261–284. M. J. Lerner and G. Mikula, eds., *Entitlement and the Affectional Bond: Justice in Close Relationships* (New York: Plenum, 1994).

[38] D. Bellani, G. E. Andersen, and L. Pessin. "When Equity Matters for Marital Stability: Comparing German and U.S. Couples." *Journal of Social and Personal Relationships* 35 (2018): 1273–1298. A. DeMaris, "The Role of Relationship Inequity in Marital Disruption," *Journal of Social and Personal Relationships*, 24 (2007): 177–195.

[39] J. W. Thibaut and H. H. Kelley, *The Social Psychology of Groups* (New York: Wiley, 1959), pp. 12–13.

[40] Davis, *Intimate Relations,* pp. 131–168.

[41] S. Planalp, "The Unacknowledged Role of Emotion in Theories of Close Relationships: How Do Theories Feel?" *Communication Theory* 13 (2003): 78–99; N. K. Grote and M. S. Clark, "Perceiving Unfairness in the Family: Cause or Consequence of Marital Distress," *Journal of Personality and Social Psychology* 80 (2001): 281–293.

[42] B. C. Feeney and E. P. Lemay, Jr., "Surviving Relationship Threats: The Role of Emotional Capital." *Personality and Social Psychology Bulletin* 38 (2012): 1004–1017.

[43] B. R. Karney and N. E. Frye, "'But We've Been Getting Better Lately': Comparing Prospective and Retrospective Views of Relationship Development," *Journal of Personality and Social Psychology* 82 (2002): 222–238.

[44] A. W. Gouldner, "The Norm of Reciprocity: A Preliminary Statement," *American Sociological Review* 25 (1960): 161–178. J. K. Burgoon, L. A. Stern, and L. Dillman, *Interpersonal Adaptation: Dyadic Interaction Patterns* (New York: Cambridge University Press, 1995). S. Sprecher and S. Treger. "The Benefits of Turn-taking Reciprocal Self-disclosure in Get-acquainted Interactions." *Personal Relationships* 22 (2015): 460–475. T. Leary labeled a similar concept the *interpersonal reflex* in *Interpersonal Diagnosis of Personality* (New York: Ronald Press, 1957). W. J. Lederer and D. D. Jackson provide an interesting treatment of the reciprocity phenomenon in marriage in *Mirages of Marriage* (New York: W. W. Norton, 1968), pp. 177–186.

[45] E. Hatfield, J. T. Cacioppo, and R. L. Rapson, *Emotional Contagion* (New York: Cambridge University Press, 1994). E. Hatfield, L. Bensman, P. D. Thorton, and R. L. Rapson, "New Perspectives on Emotional Contagion: A Review of Classic and Recent Research on Facial Mimicry and Contagion," *Interpersona: An International Journal on Personal Relationships* 8 (2014): 159–179.

[46] S. Sprecher, S. Treger, J. D. Wondra, N. Hilaire, and K. Wallpe, "Taking Turns: Reciprocal Self-Disclosure Promotes Liking in Initial Interactions," *Journal of Experimental Social Psychology* 49 (2013): 860–866.

[47] A. R. Berger and R. Janoff-Bulman, "Costs and Satisfaction in Close Relationships: The Role of Loss-Gain Framing," *Personal Relationships*, 13 (2006): 53–68.

[48] C. D. Batson, *The Altruism Question: Toward a Social-Psychological Answer* (Hillsdale, NJ: Erlbaum, 1991). Also see D. L. Krebs, "Empathy and Altruism," *Journal of Personality and Social Psychology* 32 (1975): 1134–1146.

PART II

Factors Affecting Human Communication Behavior in Relationships

CHAPTER 3
The Nature of the Communicators

CHAPTER 4
The Communication Environment: Cultural and Physical

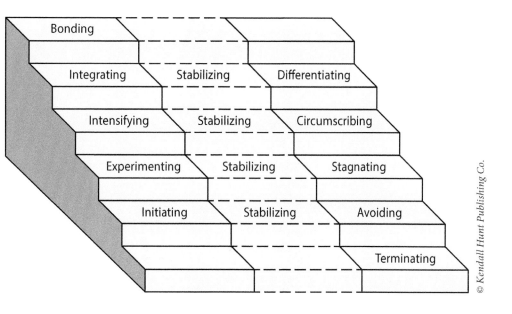

CHAPTER 3

Students will . . .

. . . define the three interpersonal needs that are widely discussed by researchers and describe their influence on interpersonal communication.

. . . explain the difference between symmetrical and complementary relationships.

. . . recognize how their own needs affect the way they communicate with others and explain why it is difficult for people to analyze their own needs.

. . . know the four barriers to accurate perceptions of others' needs.

. . . identify differences in interpersonal needs across the lifespan.

. . . explain possible differences in interpersonal needs of women and men.

KEY TERMS

acceptance

affection

challenge

complementary relationships

control

immediacy

inclusion

self-fulfilling prophecy

symmetrical relationships

The Nature of the Communicators

Dear Dr. Caughlin,

I am currently in a relationship with someone who refuses to take any responsibility for making decisions. She goes along with whatever I want to do, which is fine with me, but I never know what she wants to do or how she feels. I'm the one who is expected to make all the decisions. The problem is that I sometimes come off sounding like an authoritarian and I don't like that. I've tried being silent, hoping that this would force her into initiating action, but instead we end up doing nothing. Why won't she take charge sometimes? What can I do so I don't have to do everything?

The Boss

One of the factors that affects the way we communicate with our relationship partners involves communicator needs—needs to give and receive control (or dominance), affection, and inclusion. These needs change depending on with whom we are communicating and what other events are occurring in our lives. In the case presented here, the writer may have encountered several people who had strong needs to give control at this time in their lives. In addition, the writer may have been a relationship partner whose communication behavior expressed a need to control others. This chapter explores these interpersonal needs as they affect the way we communicate and the development of our relationships.

Throughout the life cycle, the developing individual undergoes qualitative change. Both the inner world and the outer world of the individual transform over time. Communication with others is central to the process.

—Lois M. Tamir

Relationships are created, sustained, moved, and dissolved by messages. People make and send those messages. But there may be a lot of variance in how individual personalities—each with his or her own special needs, skills, and motivations—choose to make these messages. Individual communicators differ in many ways, but their interpersonal needs are an especially important factor for understanding communication in developing and deteriorating relationships.[1]

The Influence of Interpersonal Needs

A vast body of literature consistently supports the idea that each of us needs (1) to include others in our activities and to be included in theirs, (2) to exert control over others and have them control us, and (3) to give affection to others and receive it from them.[2] While other needs do exist, most of our *interpersonal* behavior can be directly tied to inclusion, control, and affection.

In many respects, interpersonal needs are like biological needs; they help maintain a satisfactory relationship between ourselves and our environment. Sometimes it is difficult to know exactly how much inclusion, control, or affection we need in order to maintain that satisfactory balance. You can eat or drink too much; similarly, you can give or receive too much inclusion, control, or affection. Too little biological or interpersonal sustenance can cause physical or mental illness. Sometimes, however, we get by without needs being met.

For example, we can go without water for a time just as we can adapt to periods when we don't receive all the affection we feel we need.

For most of us, our interpersonal needs do not remain static; their strength or importance varies with the circumstances. For instance, giving and receiving affection may be far more important than inclusion or control needs when a relationship has just reached the Integrating stage; inclusion needs may be strongest during early growth stages or during the deterioration process.

© fizkes/Shutterstock.com

Our conscious awareness of our own needs and the needs of others also varies with the stage of the relationship, the timing, the context, and so forth. A husband may only become aware of his need for excessive control over others when his wife suggests she can no longer live under such tyranny. With this brief introduction, let's look more carefully at each of these interpersonal needs.

Inclusion It has been said that abandonment or isolation is the most potent of all interpersonal fears. In order to avoid such situations, we need to construct our lives so that others will include us in their activities. Sometimes we accomplish this goal by asking others to share our social environment, banking on the possibility that they will reciprocate. Frankly, we think it is hard for a person with a satisfying number of contacts to fully understand and empathize with a person who has few or no friends. Most of us try to maintain a balance between being together and being alone—between giving inclusion to others and being included by others.

> **Inclusion:** The state or condition of being part of a whole.

We tend to associate extroverted behavior with people who have strong inclusion needs. Exhibitionistic tendencies in this frame of reference, then, may be attempts to enhance the possibilities of togetherness and, eventually, acceptance. Extroverts tend to be socially active and have relatively strong social support networks.[3] They usually are seen as cheerful and enthusiastic; they tend to express satisfaction, agree with others, and seek out areas of commonality with their conversational partners.[4] Extroverts tend to experience more pleasant emotions than do introverts.[5] They are fairly confident of their ability to manage interactions.[6] They may use less spatial distance and more eye contact when they converse with others.

In the same stereotypical fashion, we tend to associate the opposite pattern of behavior, introversion, with low inclusion needs. People reflecting this pattern generally are seen as reserved and serious[7] and will tend to withdraw from or avoid verbal interaction with others. When in the presence of others, several behaviors may appear: (1) silence, (2) speech errors, (3) rapid and short statements, (4) initiating conversation with "I'm sorry, I can't stay long," (5) hedging ("Well, I'd sort of like to go"), and (6) presenting an inordinate number of conflicting engagements that prohibit inclusion in the activities of others. In short, there seems to be an inability, unwillingness, or apprehension about communicating with others.

Although we typically associate extroversion with strong inclusion needs and introversion with weak inclusion needs, it is important to note that these associations do not accurately reflect every situation. In some circumstances, extroverted behavior may mask a need to be alone, and introverted behavior may be exhibited by a person who secretly needs and desires a lot of inclusion. In fact, a number of studies have demonstrated that people who are not very expressive tend to be more physiologically reactive to emotional stimuli than those who are highly expressive.[8] It may be that less expressive people sometimes suppress their emotional expression as a way to cope with fairly strong inclusion needs. Research also has shown that people who have high inclusion needs tend to be particularly attentive to, and accurate in, decoding social cues.[9] Because these individuals attend closely to others' behavior, they may appear to be less talkative and extroverted than people who do not pay as much attention to others' behavior.

Dealing with inclusion needs is not limited to nonintimate relationships. The following situation is not unusual for a married couple with one person leaving the home to work and the other working at home. The partner who leaves the home may obtain satisfaction of inclusion needs at work. Hence, when this spouse returns home in the evening, he or she may need some solitude. The other spouse, however, having spent most of the day alone—not being included—wants to socialize and interact.

It should be clear that we are talking about normal patterns of behavior, not pathologies. Each of us moves along a continuum of high and low inclusion needs. Sometimes we manifest a particular pattern long enough so that others label us—"he's a loner" or "she's a social butterfly." Oftentimes the expectations created by these labels make it difficult for the loner to become a joiner and the butterfly to become a caterpillar. Should it reach a point at which one's perceived interpersonal needs cannot be satisfied through everyday social interaction, pathologies may develop.

Include me out.

—Sam Goldwyn

At least one physician believes the prolonged absence of inclusion can even be fatal.[10] He documents his contention with statistics that show that single, widowed, and divorced people not only die sooner than married people but have significantly higher death rates for every cause of death. Even though many people have been involved in marriages (or other relationships) that seem to cause more tension and unhappiness than they alleviate, having a network of social ties often provides us with emotional caring and a sense of personal control over our environment. Studies repeatedly show that social support is vital for coping with mental and physical illness, crises, transitions, and various other sorts of life stress.[11]

To some extent, social ties are probably made by those who are already physically and mentally healthy. Individuals who have problems forging social ties with others may engage in patterns of thought and behavior that undermine their ability to initiate and maintain social relationships. For example, people who are chronically lonely have been said to close off their own access to social support because they see themselves as relationally incompetent[12] and believe others will see them in similarly negative ways.[13] Not surprisingly, those who interact with or observe lonely people also see them as fairly poor communicators.[14] In such cases, the key to fulfilling inclusion needs may be reciprocity.[15] If we receive a great deal of support from others but are never able or willing to give support in return, our inclusion needs (and needs for support) may just continue to grow. Likewise, becoming overly involved in giving support to others may prevent us from receiving help when we need it most.[16] In fact, research suggests that people who focus on others to the detriment of themselves tend to experience psychological distress and poor physical health.[17]

Control Each of us needs the feeling that sometimes we're in charge of a situation; at other times, we want others to be in charge and don't mind assuming a more submissive posture. Most people want to achieve a balance, controlling some situations and topics and being controlled in others.

Control: The power to direct other people's behavior or the course of actions.

Sometimes we show an excessive need for dominance or control. The need for dominance may spring from many sources—possibly even a nagging fear or insecurity that we can't control others or that they will take advantage of us if we don't dominate them. Ironically, people who seem to have an extremely high need for control (e.g., spouses in abusive relationships) often see themselves as victims of their partners' verbal aggression.[18] Verbally, a person may attempt to gain control of an interaction by speaking sooner and more often; discussing a wide variety of topics; engaging in name dropping, startling comments, or exaggerations; and using an abundance of self-references.[19] Dominance also might be manifested in interruptions, speaking louder, or holding the floor longer.[20] Mehrabian's research on the nonverbal signals associated with power or status suggests looking for such signals as vast personal territory, arms akimbo, postural relaxation, dress ornamented by status symbols, greater height, and expansive movements.[21] Eye contact may be less since the high-status or powerful person does not feel the need to demonstrate attentiveness and may not be as worried about impression management or feedback. However, when speaking, dominant persons will sometimes use prolonged eye contact as a signal of their strength, trying to create anxiety in the other.[22]

Don't be misled by this partial listing of behaviors. Control, once achieved, can be maintained in many subtle ways while giving the illusion of low control and freedom for the other. For example, the statement "Sure, go ahead and go out with other guys; I don't mind" may actually represent (or be perceived as representing) a form of permission or indulgence from the person in control. Similarly, when individuals "help" others in the right situations, in front of the right people, they have access to a great deal of influence. Researchers note that a pattern of behavior called *overhelping* occurs when individuals explicitly help another person achieve some goal so that observers will attribute the person's success to the help he or she was given.[23] In this way, those who are helping get credit for the success. For instance, some parents give their adult children financial help even though the children are capable of getting along without it. By always being a financial resource, the parents maintain a degree of control over their grown children and may even undermine the children's confidence in their ability to support themselves. Another subtle way to gain control is what researchers call *sandbagging*.[24] This takes place when people display weakness or low ability so that an opponent will reduce his or her effort. For example, during conflict, one relational partner may act hurt or defeated so that the other will lower his or her guard. Then, when the other is vulnerable, the sandbagger will spring back into action with a hurtful comment or a cutting remark.

Control strategies, in short, come in many different shapes and sizes. Those who wield the most control can appear on the surface to be relatively weak or submissive. Indeed, acting submissive in a relationship may give someone a lot of power if his or her partner comes to depend on that submission as a form of ego gratification.

Occasionally, each of us may gravitate toward a position of oversubmissiveness and helplessness and avoid almost any form of responsibility and control. We want to be told what to do. At such times, we usually speak less frequently and when verbal messages do occur, their duration will probably be short, accompanied by a lower voice volume. Agreement and acceptance of others' remarks are likely. Nonverbally, the head and eyes are frequently lowered, appeasing smiles increase, and a greater physical distance is maintained.

Affection: The feeling of liking or caring for someone or something.

Affection To like and be liked by others is important to our interpersonal health. Even though we may find it momentarily distasteful, the opposite of affection—hostility, coldness, anger—can also be important for us. Experiencing hostility (giving and receiving) provides a useful benchmark for understanding the kind and amount of affection we and others require. Those who have had pleasant experiences with affection will probably be comfortable with both close and distant relationships, recognizing that the absence of affection does not mean they are not lovable people. Individuals who have had positive experiences with affection also may be more likely to give affection to others. Their tendency to give affection, in turn, will probably put them in a position to receive more affection than they would otherwise. Indeed, research suggests that people who are highly affectionate are more likely to engage in regular social activity and less likely to experience social isolation than those who are low in affection. Highly affectionate people also tend to report greater happiness, higher self-esteem, less depression, less stress, and greater overall mental health than their less affectionate counterparts.[25]

Immediacy: The degree of liking between communicators; the verbal linkage of the speaker with the content of his or her communication.

Although the concept of *affection* is generally associated with intimate behavior, it may incorporate behavior that is known as rewarding, supportive, generous, cooperative, sympathetic, warm, or sensitive. This broadened definition would then encompass behavior such as helping someone with a task, taking an interest in another's problems, or having someone endorse your self-image. The concept of **immediacy**, or the degree of liking between communicators, gives us some additional behavioral indicators. Immediacy is the verbal linkage of the speaker with the content of his or her communication—"we" has more immediacy (or liking) than the separation of the elements into "you and I."[26] Nonverbally, greater liking may be displayed in more touching, increased mutual gazes, decreased distance, a direct body orientation with open arms and body, leaning forward, nodding, and a positive facial expression and vocal tone.

Sometimes we meet someone with an excessive need for affection: "I need a lot of loving." It almost seems as if the person is trying to devour us—to the extent that other friends are resented because they take time away from the relationship. There may be many reasons for such behavior. In one case, it may be a fear of rejection; in another, the person may have just terminated a relationship in which the satisfaction of affection needs was painful and he or she is trying to recoup past losses.

Low affection needs also may be triggered by unpleasant experiences (being "burned") with others. Not wanting to get "emotionally involved," feeling that you are "unlovable," or distrusting the affection displays of others may naturally result in distant, superficial relationships. It is interesting that sometimes people who are especially sensitive to rejection will exhibit antagonism or jealousy toward others as a device to avoid getting too personal.[27] This hostility or jealousy then causes others to avoid giving affection, which, in turn, fulfills the person's prophecy that he or she can't trust others to provide for his or her affection needs. Another manifestation of wishing to avoid a high level of affection is found in the person who tries to make friends with everyone so he or she doesn't have to be close to any given individual.

Even in intimate relationships, affection needs are sometimes difficult to satisfy. For example, in marriages in which both the husband and wife are pursuing careers outside the home, both partners are trying to satisfy achievement needs at work and affection needs in their relationship. Too much emphasis on the satisfaction of achievement needs is not always compatible with a similar emphasis on affection needs. One partner may desire a great deal of affection after a career setback, but the other person's need for achievement may be soaring and it may be difficult to satisfy the other's affection needs. In other types of relationships, the husband may spend years emphasizing achievement needs while the wife seeks the satisfaction of affection needs; then when the husband wants to spend more time with his family, the wife gets a job that she hopes will fulfill her long-neglected needs for achievement. In some cases, the partners do not agree on what satisfies achievement and affection needs. A husband may say he is showing affection for his wife by working long hours, but the wife may not agree; a wife may think the time spent in raising the children should provide satisfaction for the husband's affection needs, but the husband may not agree.

In summary, interpersonal needs do exist. They do influence and are influenced by communication at various stages of the relationship. While some verbal and nonverbal behaviors that may accompany inclusion, control, and affection have been suggested here, you will find there are many ways to express such needs. Individual differences may be learned only with continued contact over a period of time—"When his moustache twitched, I knew he was mad."

The Role of Interpersonal Needs

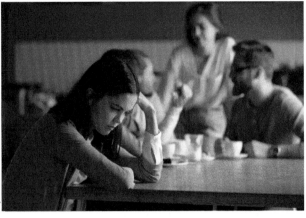

© fizkes/Shutterstock.com

For any given situation involving two people, we can plot and analyze the role of interpersonal needs. The example in **Figure 3.1** illustrates what one person (A) wants to give and what the other person (B) wants to receive. Similar plots can be developed for self-analysis (what A wants to give and receive) or perception of the other person (what A thinks B wants to give and receive).

One implication of Figure 3.1 is that interpersonal needs can be used to describe encounters or relationships in terms of compatibility: "Do you have (or want to express) what I don't have (or need)?" Obviously it becomes more complicated (but more accurate) when we add two more lines to the diagram: (1) what A wants to receive and (2) what B wants to give. Schutz's work suggests that a compatibility of inclusion needs is most critical for successful communication when becoming "part of the group" is dependent on mutual agreement—for example, joining a sorority. Interacting in close quarters for a short duration calls for compatibility of control needs—for example, a cross-country car trip. Affection compatibility is paramount when there is a close interdependency over a long period of time—as there is with roommates.

A number of researchers have examined these sorts of compatibility issues in terms of loneliness. People who are chronically lonely believe that their interpersonal needs are not being fulfilled—that they lack certain social

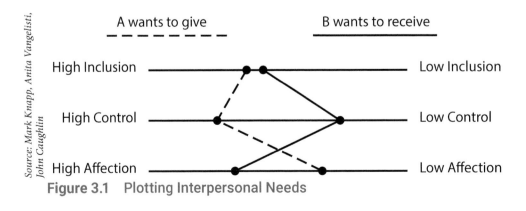

Source: Mark Knapp, Anita Vangelisti, John Caughlin

Figure 3.1 Plotting Interpersonal Needs

relationships.[28] They become lonely in part because they perceive that the discrepancy between the social relations they have and the social relations they desire is too large. They may, in reality, have a large number of friends, and they may even be involved in a romantic relationship. But if they believe they have too few friends[29] or that their romantic relationship lacks certain qualities,[30] they may feel extremely lonely. For some, inclusion may be the problem: they may feel that they aren't really accepted into the social (or task) groups they would like. Others may feel out of control of their interpersonal networks, relegating the cause of their loneliness to external or environmental forces.[31] Yet others may be lacking affection—whether it be from a parent, a friend, or a lover. What creates feelings of loneliness for one person may or may not create those feelings for another.[32]

Regardless of the type of need, Figure 3.1 illustrates that interpersonal needs occur in the context of a relationship. In some cases, our expectations about what a particular relationship ought to be like may intensify a need (e.g., coworkers should provide inclusion), whereas in others a need may intensify the relationship (e.g., a need for affection may "create" a love relationship). In both instances, however, the compatibility between one person's needs and the other's has substantial effects on the relationship. A number of researchers have discussed this concept in terms of symmetrical and complementary relationships.

Symmetrical Relationships Symmetrical encounters or relationships are characterized by each participant exchanging the same sort of behavior. Equality is the name of the game. If one person offers to give affection, the other also offers to give affection; if one wants to receive, the other wants to receive; if one has power, the other wants power; if one pleads helplessness, the other counters with an equivalent disability. This type of interpersonal meshing can be and is productive as long as the participants continue to see each other's individuality and respect each other's rights and needs. It does, however, have competitive overtones that may cause one or both persons to become overly concerned about their own rights and to classify satisfying the other's rights as a duty. Another potential problem concerns the methods used to maintain the "I'm the same as you are" girding necessary for symmetry. Lederer and Jackson outline the problem this way:

> The difficulty is that if A says, "You can't scare me, I've got a gun," and B retorts, "Well, you can't scare me either, I've got two guns," there is danger that this behavior will escalate until the only solution is for A and B to demonstrate their equality by shooting each other.[33]

Complementary Relationships Complementary encounters or relationships are based on differences. In this case, the partners are exchanging different and complementary sorts of behavior. One person controls, the other submits; one person leads, the other follows; one person gives affection, the other takes it. For example, a mother's need to feed and care for her baby is complemented by the

Symmetrical relationships: Relationships characterized by each participant exchanging the same sort of behavior; an equal relationship.

Complementary relationships: Relationships based on different and complementary behaviors; for instance, one person controls while the other submits, one person leads and the other follows.

baby's need to be fed and receive affection. Other contexts might include the roles played in doctor–patient or most student–teacher relationships. Since this pattern is completely dependent on the maintenance of the established roles, a potential problem arises when one person no longer wants to exchange behavior consistent with his or her role—there can be no lover without a beloved, no teacher without a student.[34]

Healthy relationships probably have both symmetrical and complementary patterns that vary over time and with topic areas. In situations where one person defines the relationship as symmetrical and the other defines it as complementary, we would expect the probabilities of strife to increase dramatically. For instance, many women are now seeking symmetry in areas where men have traditionally treated the situation as complementary. This same phenomenon can sometimes be seen in how parents and children communicate. The smooth-running, complementary pattern between parents and children may take a sharp turn when children reach adolescence. At this time, teenagers increasingly seek symmetrical interactions. Parents who insist on the maintenance of a complementary pattern for all interactions will find the relationship suffering and the communication gap widening.

Analyzing Our Own Needs and Those of Others

One of the obvious implications of our discussion of interpersonal needs is that we must spend time trying to understand our own needs so that we have a better idea of what we need from others and what we can offer them. This doesn't mean we should enter an encounter or a relationship with the expectation that we will always be able to satisfy all the needs of the other, or that the other person will always be able to satisfy all our needs. Sometimes only special people at special times can serve these functions. Sometimes we are made aware of our own needs only through the behavior of another person. You may find that you have a need to be very cautious in revealing personal information to others only when you ponder why others never tell you anything very personal. No matter how we obtain such knowledge of our needs, it is safe to say that an understanding of our interpersonal needs will raise the probabilities for successful social interaction.

Telling others to examine and understand their own interpersonal needs is an easy principle to preach, but it is not always easy to do. There are many reasons why it is difficult to analyze our own needs. These difficulties include the following: (1) We are not always aware of our needs, which may be changing from situation to situation, time to time. We are many different selves, *not* a single, *real* self. We can expect different patterns of interpersonal needs as we assess our self in relation to our parents, our self in relation to our lover, our self in relation to our teacher, or our self in relation to our employer. Sometimes our lack of awareness of interpersonal needs is due to our inattention to the cycles or rhythms of our life. Although we know little about the relationship of a person's biological cycles to his or her social behavior, it seems reasonable to postulate that such effects do occur—for example, "I don't know why I feel alienated and alone right now. I really have no reason to. People have invited me to parties; I have several really good friends." (2) For various reasons we may repress certain needs—for example, not wanting to face the fact that we are often submissive and usually enjoy it. (3) We may distort the strength of a particular need by producing a favorable perception of ourselves to fulfill our need for self-esteem. (4) We may also avoid talking to others about our interpersonal needs which, in turn, provides us with less understanding and awareness of these needs. Sometimes we can understand these needs only by comparing our feelings with those of others. There is, however, a paradox here. Our inclusion needs may be best understood by being included in conversations in which others discuss such needs. People who are able and willing to discuss their needs with others often understand their needs and are able to garner the social resources necessary to fulfill them.[35] In contrast, those who have difficulty making contact with others are, in all likelihood, the ones who need that contact the most.

Chronically lonely people are a case in point. Whether their needs lie primarily in the area of inclusion, control, or affection, people who are chronically lonely tend to see themselves and others as less competent communicators[36] and less interpersonally attractive and tend to act less involved in the conversations they have with others.[37] With these sorts of interpersonal issues, it is not surprising that lonely people often have difficulty connecting with others, understanding their own relational needs, and finding ways of getting their needs met.[38]

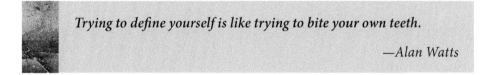

Trying to define yourself is like trying to bite your own teeth.

—*Alan Watts*

Closely intertwined with our self-analysis of interpersonal needs is our perception of the needs of others, an equally important task if we are to understand what they need and what they have to offer us. The bond between self-analysis and other-analysis is aptly illustrated in the following paraphrase of Hora's comment:

> To understand themselves, people need to be understood by another. To be understood by another, they need to understand the other.[39]

Sometimes our own predispositions, needs, and expectations color our perceptions of others. We might engage in selective perception—perceiving what we want to perceive. It is not uncommon, for instance, to see only good in those we like and only bad in those we dislike. Consciously or unconsciously, we sometimes behave in such a way that our perceptions of others must be confirmed. This process, known as a **self-fulfilling prophecy**, might begin with the assumption that another person is hostile. Assuming this is true, we begin to

Self-fulfilling prophecy: When an individual's expectations or predictions become true simply because the individual believes they are true and behaves as if they are true.

act defensive. Our defensiveness provokes some hostility in the other person, and we take great pride in the confirmation of our original assumption that the person was hostile.

Many things may act as barriers to accurate perceptions of others' needs: (1) The other person may wish to conceal his or her needs. (2) The same verbal and nonverbal behavior may be associated with two very different needs—an overbearing person can be reflecting high control and confidence or deep-seated anxiety and insecurity. (3) The process of selective interaction (interacting only with those like us) may prevent us from experiencing and being able to understand a broad spectrum of needs. (4) We sometimes place undue weight on momentary behavior patterns—we may observe people soon after they have been mistreated, when their self-presentation is focused on making the necessary corrections, and make judgments based on our observations. Despite these and other problems involved in accurate perceptions of others (and ourselves), the value of the process is undeniable, particularly to those who have constantly sought love from one who is incapable of returning it, or unwilling to do so.

Many communicator characteristics may influence messages exchanged during the course of a relationship. Interpersonal needs form the root system for the more visible manifestations of individual differences, interpersonal skills such as listening, role taking, role playing, perceived motivation, and various personality styles.

Interpersonal Needs Across the Lifespan

Throughout life we experience changes and fluctuations in our biological needs. Our interpersonal needs also are affected by the changing demands and experiences associated with different life stages. Thus, we can expect some differences in the communication behavior of people who form relationships at different life stages.

© fizkes/Shutterstock.com

Infancy and Childhood

Interpersonal needs are reflected in our behavior from the day we are born. In fact, some scholars believe our evolutionary heritage provides us with an inborn yearning for contact or inclusion with our world.[40] Infants whose biological needs have been provided for sometimes seem to cry for no reason, but inclusion (holding) and affection (cuddling, soothing sounds) often have a calming effect.

Even before language is understood or spoken, the child is gaining a rudimentary understanding of interpersonal needs. Patterns of being with others and being alone are established.[41] The child soon learns that not all time spent with others is the same. Sometimes good feelings are derived from extended mutual gaze, cuddling, and other displays of affection; sometimes hostile behavior elicits pain; and sometimes there seems to be an absence of affection *or* hostility. In an effort to provide experiences that will ultimately give the child more control over his or her environment, parents shift

© Rawpixel.com/Shutterstock.com

their children from breast-feeding to solid food, from a baby bed to a "big" bed, from home to school, and so on. For the child, the initial feelings of anxiety and having little control over these new environments are sharply contrasted with the security and control associated with behavioral patterns already mastered. So the infant is scanning his or her world, reacting to the actions of others, and trying to get a grasp on what is expected for getting along.

The developing child also is learning how to signal others that interpersonal needs have not been met. In infancy, these are unfocused expressions (crying, pulling, banging, smiling) of emotional states that may be associated with any number of needs. Gradually, the developing child is able to specify which particular needs are or are not being met. Even infants as young as one year old discriminate among persons with whom they interact—selectively teasing, begging, grabbing, playing, hugging, and aggravating.[42] The ability to *give* inclusion, control, and affection is similarly limited during this time but develops rapidly as early friendships are formed.

In preschool and early play relationships, the child's repertoire of communication skills associated with interpersonal needs continues to expand.[43] More sophisticated control strategies may characterize the parent-child relationship—for example, using one parent as leverage on the other or using primitive fear appeals ("I'm not coming home if you don't . . ."). Similarly, the child becomes more sophisticated in giving and withholding affection from his or her parents. Successful strategies are likely to be used again. Sometimes the play behavior of these preschool children reflects interpersonal needs. The actions of the child who continually bosses other children around may be linked to strong parental dominance. Bossing other children may be the only outlet for asserting dominance for that child. In more extreme cases, when a child consistently bullies his or her peers, the child may perceive that one or both parents are relatively uninvolved in his or her life.[44] When parents are uninvolved, some children try to exert control over peers as a way to cope with the fact that their needs for affection and inclusion are not being met by their parents. Childhood is a time for experimenting with various methods of self-presentation. Many of these behaviors stem from basic interpersonal needs, such as seeking attention, showing off, requesting things from others, looking for praise, and giving affection.

When the child enters school, he or she will observe a wide variety of social relationships and behaviors. School provides a glimpse at the popular and the unpopular, the liked and the disliked, the in-group and the out-group, and the aggressive and the docile. At about this time, first friendships take shape.[45] Up to this point, the child's perspective on friendship has been best described as "the people I'm with." Likes and dislikes are especially important. Often these early friendships are not long lasting. Rubin gives one explanation:

> Young children, who do not yet understand that one can regard someone both positively and negatively at the same time, are likely to deal with negative feelings by deciding—for the moment—that they aren't friends anymore.[46]

Another reason why some of these early relationships are fleeting concerns the rapidly changing needs of the participants. If a friend is selected because he or she meets your need for inclusion, it may not be long before you desire the company of a less extroverted, outgoing, and intense type of person. One child may like another because he or she is allowed to give as much control as is desired; but the shortcomings of this arrangement may become clear quickly, and a new friend who is able and willing to give some control in return (but not too much) is favored. Many of these likes and dislikes are based on sharing interests in certain activities rather than sharing values that transcend activities.[47] Children at this age also begin to develop ideas about who they should and should not play with.[48] This is a time of experimenting, a time of finding out about the nature of one's interpersonal needs in the context of a variety of relationships outside the home.

During the period of late childhood several important changes are taking place. First, there seems to be a greater recognition that our own interpersonal needs are closely intertwined with those of others. Gradually, we learn that friendship involves the satisfaction of the needs of others as well as our own. Second, our mastery of language and extensive experience with friendship making and breaking may prompt the gathering of information about the world in other ways. Sometimes we settle on a single "best friend"; sometimes books, magazines, videos, or television take precedence over activities involving other people.

Brenton noted that many children during this period start to feel like they need more privacy than they have had before. They begin to spend more time alone, and they do activities that allow them to be alone, such as reading, playing video games, or watching television. Some parents, often the mothers, are bothered by children's desires to be alone because they think a lack of friends means their child is not very attractive or has poor mental health.[49]

Late childhood is also a time for continued practice in giving inclusion, control, and affection in different ways to different people. We also develop an increased understanding of our own needs and abilities as we face new situations—for example, being "in charge" of babysitting or mowing the lawn.

Adolescence

Adolescence is a bridge between two very different life stages—childhood and adulthood. Teenagers and young adults often feel conflicts related to the life pattern they are leaving behind and the uncertainty of the one to come. Independence and the commitments and responsibilities that often accompany adolescence provide a major theme during this period. On the one hand, it is gratifying to be treated more like an "adult" and to be breaking away from dependence on parents; on the other hand, it would be nice not to have to contemplate the problems involved in going to college or getting a job or joining the Army or getting married; sometimes we would like our parents to take charge again.

Parent-child relationships during this time are moving from being predominantly complementary to predominantly symmetrical. This relational change, and the conflict sometimes associated with it, often means that both parents and adolescents express more negativity toward each other than they did in prior years.[50] Yet, even with an increase in expressed negativity, most adolescents feel they have relatively close, positive relationships with their parents.[51] The way adolescents feel about their relationships with their parents depends, in part, on the nature of the relationships they had with their parents when they were children. The growth and the changes that take place during adolescence, in other words, occur as part of an ongoing process that begins long before puberty.[52]

Some researchers have characterized this growth process as one involving a tension between individuality and connectedness. In terms of their verbal behavior, this means that adolescents may alternate between statements of (1) self-assertion (displaying awareness of one's own point of view and responsibility for communicating it clearly), (2) permeability (expressing responsiveness to the views of others), (3) mutuality (showing sensitivity and respect for others' views), and (4) separateness (expressing distinctiveness of self from others). Once individuation from the parent is achieved, conversations with parents will tend toward a balance among these four types of statements.[53]

Redefining the parent-adolescent relationship as a more symmetrical, individuated relationship often involves difficulties in understanding interpersonal needs. Parental concerns on matters of drugs and sex may cause a child to protest that the parent is exercising too much control over his or her life. But parental control in other areas may be more acceptable.[54] Parents may expect a continuation of the affection giving and receiving patterns practiced from early childhood. But the child is establishing other affection and inclusion patterns with peers. Inevitably, these friendships outside the home will alter interpersonal needs in family relationships. It is not unusual for parents to sense this change and criticize the child's new friends. This criticism may only serve to make the new friends seem more desirable and the parents less so.

Acceptance: Seeing another person as favorable; embracing or approving of another person.

Challenge: Calling another person to engage in a competition or test.

Adolescents' needs for inclusion, control, and affection—and the extent to which those needs are met—are influenced by their parents' communication skills. For instance, research shows that adolescents tend to feel better about themselves after a conversation with their parents if the parents show them **acceptance** (warmth, attentiveness, and affection) and if their parents **challenge** them (pushing the adolescents to strengthen their abilities).[55] Adolescents' perceptions of their parents' communication skills also can predict the adolescents' tendency to overreact to a stressful conversation. Those with parents who they think have better communication skills are less likely to overreact when talking about something stressful than those who do not think their parents are skillful communicators.[56]

It is also interesting to note that the degree to which parents understand adolescents' thoughts and feelings and the types of communication problems adolescents feel they experience with their parents do not necessarily determine how satisfied adolescents are with their parental relationship.[57] Both happy and unhappy adolescents report disagreements, misunderstandings, and other communication problems linked to control. The critical factor in distinguishing satisfied from dissatisfied adolescents seems to be the way they interpret these communication problems: Is my parent to blame? Did my parent have good intentions? Is my parent thinking about my well-being? Struggles between parents and their teenage children are so commonly reported in the popular press, it is understandable that we often ignore the fact that all relationships have periods of turmoil and that most relationships between parents and teenagers are not a constant parade of misunderstandings and fighting.

Friendships play an especially important role in reflecting interpersonal needs during adolescence. This is a time when peer-group comparisons in emotional, physical, and attitudinal areas are frequent: Do my friends feel as awkward as I do when they talk to a potential romantic partner?[58] Do other people my age have the same sexual urges that I have? How many people in my class also hate it when people "assume" something about you without asking first? Social groups are formed and provide a power base and a refuge from unwanted demands from the "outside" world. More than ever before, there is a recognition of the extent to which inclusion in a group can increase your personal leverage and power with other people and institutions. Individual friendships within the group often provide intense pleasure, and sometimes intense pain. Emotional responses are generally less inhibited at this time than they will be later in life. Thus, the emotional highs derived from idealized friends are subject to emotional lows when those friends behave in very normal, but not ideal ways by lying, not keeping a secret, or not accepting you as you are. This may trigger a disillusionment that others may label as "moody," and it may cause the person to go through a period of wanting to be alone. This is only one instance involving changing interpersonal needs relative to adolescent friendships with peers. The interpersonal needs involved in romantic relationships may change need patterns established with friendship groups and individual same-sexed friends. An adolescent's family situation also may affect friendship patterns and needs. An only child may need more friends than one who has several brothers and sisters in his or her own age category.

Brenton argued that most adolescents have very complex friendships.[59] They like to be part of a big group and not close off anyone, but they also want to be particularly close to someone special. They want friends who challenge them to grow, but they also sometimes drop friends if they focus too much on weaknesses or take advantage of vulnerabilities. Adolescents often want to trust others, but they are also learning that even so-called friends cannot always be trusted. In short, the best way to describe adolescent friendships might be: It's complicated.

Despite the inherent complexity and occasional strain in the parent-child relationships and peer friendships that occur during this period, adolescents gradually increase their ability to understand the perspective of the other person and communicate more in terms of their needs.[60]

Adulthood

Just because we are labeled an "adult" does not mean we behave similarly to all others who wear this label. Our behaviors and our values as adults are influenced by a multitude of factors, including the degree to which our needs were satisfied when we were children.[61] At the same time, the fact that every adult is different does not mean that all adults follow very different patterns of development. Some regularities in adult life are brought about because many adults in this society face similar decisions about similar tasks at similar times of their lives. This research reveals the existence of several distinguishable stages or periods during adulthood.[62] Therefore, let's examine interpersonal needs during early, middle, and late adulthood.

For many adults, early adulthood is a time of adventure, a time to try and "master the world." The feeling of having actually "mastered the world" is not uncommon for young adults who find a compatible partner to live with or who savor the opportunity to live alone, obtain a respectable job and interpret initial successes as the beginning of a brilliant career, or feel they have achieved optimal independence from their parents and other controlling figures of the past. Some couples share the excitement and feeling of accomplishment from having a child during this period. For those who experience this sense of controlling their environment and being firmly in charge of their relationships at home and at work, the desire for control from others will probably be minimal. The one exception may be a mentor at work whose controlling and guiding actions are perceived as having a long-range payoff in promotions and increased responsibilities. In time, however, the partners of these people who want to give a lot of control in their relationships at home and work may want to give more control and receive less. The process of redistributing control needs for a person who feels comfortable and successful giving much and receiving little can be a difficult one. If this issue cannot be satisfactorily resolved, new work environments, new living partners, and even new social groups may be sought. Problems in aligning control needs will surely affect inclusion and affection needs as well. The preceding is only one of the many possible sobering experiences that may arise during this time. Others include finding out that working hard doesn't always bring success, having to face the fact that people can be treacherous and cruel, confronting the knowledge that life situations are not always "fair," or being told that "trying" isn't good enough.

Normally, opportunities for giving and receiving inclusion are high during this period of exploring and reaching out. But an occupation that involves moving to a new community may require the effort to establish a new social group. And some people who remain unmarried may desire more inclusion than they are able to achieve. Singles may also desire opportunities to give and receive more affection as well. Cohabiting or married people may experience optimum levels of giving and receiving affection during the early relationship stages, but the introduction of children or increased demands at work may require new efforts to regain satisfactory levels of affection for both partners.[63]

Early adulthood is a time when the analysis of one's own and others' interpersonal needs is probably undertaken in a more superficial way than at other stages in adulthood. It is not uncommon to find a greater emphasis on having one's own needs satisfied than considering how to understand and achieve satisfaction of both partners' needs. It is also a time when the confidence derived from early successes may lead to commitments in the areas of inclusion, affection, and control that are beyond the individual's ability to fulfill.

In contrast, one of the primary themes of middle adulthood is a thorough review and reassessment of established relationships and life goals. What have I done with my life? What can I realistically expect to do? What do I really get and give to my spouse, my children, my friends, my work, my community, and myself? What are my central values and how are they reflected in my life? This is not to say that we don't reflect on such questions at earlier points in our lives. But it is likely that the analysis in middle adulthood is much deeper and the answers hold more significance than at earlier times. Answers to these and similar questions provide a basis for putting the past and the future in perspective. People often realize during this stage that decisions concerning possible changes in their life should be made before change becomes too difficult. As a result, some aspects of life are modified; some things are intensified; some are reworked; some are rejected; some new goals may be set; and some new behaviors may be tested. Thus, in some areas the person will be emphasizing his or her strengths from the past—carving out a niche, sinking deeper roots; in other areas, there may be feelings of uncertainty and awkwardness reminiscent of adolescence.

Primary relationships may undergo changes in the composition of interpersonal needs. For example, in traditional husband-wife relationships, the wife may now wish to enter or reenter the world of work outside the home. As a result, she may be able to give and be desirous of giving more control; coworkers may help satisfy inclusion needs; and affection displays may also change. Communicative exchanges during this time will surely reflect these changing or challenged needs of both husband and wife. People in middle adulthood also are likely to experience interaction changes with their parents and children.[64] Both aging parents and adolescent children are going through life transitions that also involve reevaluation and redirection. Thus, we can expect the parents of the person in middle adulthood to ask for increasing control and certainty not any less inclusion or affection while their teenagers are often looking for less control and inclusion and a different style of affection.

In later adulthood, one's aging parents may still be a concern, but children may have left the home. Two themes typically characterize this period: (1) The adult is experiencing clear signals of decreasing strength and other health-related changes, and (2) it is a time when active involvement in civic affairs may be high. While in early adulthood, future-oriented goals encourage people to expand their social network and seek out new relationships with acquaintances, in later adulthood, the situation can be quite different. As individuals age, they begin to see time as more limited and, as a consequence, tend to emphasize goals that are more oriented to the present. These present-oriented goals (e.g., meeting current needs for inclusion or affection) often encourage people to limit many of their social relationships to those that are emotionally satisfying.[65] Indeed, research suggests that as people near the end of their lives, they often discontinue relationships with people they do not feel close to and focus their efforts on family members and close social companions.[66]

Control needs may be low at this time because people may have achieved either the external credentials of power, the sense of internal control of self, or both. Indeed, some research suggests that in many cases, older couples show more personal support and submission than do younger couples in which one partner tries to exert control.[67] In other cases, control may be displayed in a more self-assured manner than it was at earlier life stages. There may be a sense of needing more inclusion in the near future that impels a person during this period to immerse himself or herself more than ever in community activities. The focus has shifted to the satisfaction of the needs of others. The family may be a high priority for giving affection, but if these needs have been neglected for many years, reestablishment may be difficult. It also is important to acknowledge that the needs of older adults often are stereotyped, even by friends and family. These stereotypes can be influenced—in both positive and negative ways—by the ways older adults communicate.[68]

The Older Adult

Interpersonal needs continue to change throughout the period of later life too. Older adults may experience several different need patterns. Certainly the interpersonal needs of a recently retired couple that is active and healthy will differ greatly from those persons who are socially isolated and physically dependent on others.

© Kzenon/Shutterstock.com

Generally, the interpersonal needs of these older adults are linked to changes in three areas: (1) health and mobility, (2) social contacts, and (3) financial condition. Naturally, these factors affect interpersonal needs at earlier life stages as well, but the impact during this period is often more dramatic. A fourth factor, which often plays a central role in changing needs during the early period of older adulthood, is retirement from work. Established patterns for giving and needing inclusion, affection, and control will be challenged when one or both partners no longer have the satisfactions, irritations, and time spent at work. Although many treat retirement as an opportunity to form new friendships[69] and pursue new interests, it is difficult to ignore the number and variety of social contacts one "leaves behind" in the work environment.[70] This theme of a gradually constricting social life is well known to the older adult.

It is said that we die in this order: socially, psychologically, and biologically. With decreasing health and mobility, older adults are gradually less able to give inclusion to others. Other factors that contribute to the social isolation of the older adult may cause inclusion needs to rise. Such factors include the deaths of friends and relatives, leaving friends and acquaintances because of a change of residence or retirement, dropping club memberships because of financial burdens.

Some of the communication behaviors associated with the increased inclusion needs of many older adults include the following:

1. To compensate for the decreasing amount of total communication with others, some older adults will "talk your arm off." Those who are bitter about what is happening may communicate very little. Still others, with limited social experiences, may have little to say.

2. When communication does take place, some will be hesitant to discuss controversial topics or to disagree too strongly for fear further alienation and social isolation may occur. Others may express their general resentment with their life situation by being especially disagreeable.

3. With less opportunity for comparing experiences and attitudes with others, some will communicate a lack of trust—fearing others will take advantage of them; others, motivated by the same fear, may communicate in a friendly, docile, and submissive manner.

4. With a constricted social world, it is not unusual for the topics of conversation to focus on oneself—health problems, impact of cold weather, hobbies, and so on. Those who spend much of their time alone may even

carry on covert dialogues with themselves. Those who realize that self-oriented communication may grow tiring for listeners will ask questions about the other's life experiences.

5. It is not uncommon for older adults to be more interested in making younger friends than friends their own age. Intergenerational ties between grandparents and grandchildren are sometimes very strong. Making new friends in older age categories may have limited rewards. They may have less to give to the friendship, and ill health or death may mean an earlier termination to the relationship than would occur with a younger friend.

6. As the acuity of an older adult's visual and auditory receptors declines, isolation from social processes may occur even in the presence of other people. Many times older adults prefer to talk to only one other person at a time. Memory also plays a part in maintaining a coherent conversation and, when memory fails, the older adult may risk a monologue unrelated to the previous conversation or let others talk until the direction of the conversation is once again pinpointed.

Older adults will also communicate messages that signal decreasing inclusion in the affairs of others. These signals may be similar in nature to those leave-taking cues used to signal the termination of a conversation or a relationship (see Chapter 2, pp. 32–34). Decreasing access may take the form of ordering and dividing up possessions. But indicators may be even more explicit: "Oh, I don't have to worry about that. . . . I won't be around much longer." The manifestations of supportiveness and salve for the future may be shown in many ways: "You've been a good daughter, Veronica . . . don't fret about me . . . just take care of your family." There may be additional supportive linkages in an older person's will, and if there is a desire to express some *non*supportive evaluations of others, a will is the perfect instrument because, unlike everyday leave-taking, there is no possibility of having to face the offended party. The summarizing function of leave-taking may take the form of a life review.[71] Although the life review has been subjected to little systematic study, its occurrence in late life is believed to be a response to a need for reconciling one's past and putting it into an acceptable (to oneself) framework as aligned with earlier goals and values. The extent to which this review manifests itself as dialogue and the depth of that dialogue are unknown. Thus, the processes enacted when one ends a conversation, a relationship, or a life have some distinct parallels. As detailed in an earlier work, the communicative processes that characterize the beginning and middle stages of conversations, relationships, and the life span may also have remarkable similarities.[72]

Some people respond to their shrinking social world by giving up. Others, however, accept the losses and begin to take steps reminiscent of behavior that characterized earlier growth stages. In an intensive study of male aging, Reichard and others found the following patterns of adjustment to be healthy: (1) mature—constructive rather than defensive or impulsive patterns, (2) rocking chair—taking it easy through dependence on others, and (3) armored—maintaining effective defenses against anxieties. The unhealthy adjustment patterns included (1) angry—becoming hostile and blaming others for one's life situation and (2) self-haters—blaming oneself for dissatisfactions with life.[73] Other research indicates that expressing optimism about aging, resisting antiaging messages, communicating wishes about care with family members, and encouraging the use of new technology are associated with successful aging.[74]

Even though most elderly people experience limitations in their social lives, researchers have found that older adults often are happier than younger adults[75] and that many older adults forge new personal ties in the form of dating relationships, friendships, and contacts with people from volunteer organizations.[76] Some of the elderly are even using the Internet to develop new relationships. In at least one study, those who were highly involved with the online community reported lower life stress and noted that they were relatively satisfied with the social support they received from their Internet companions.[77]

Of course, a number of older adults live with a spouse or romantic partner. Older people with live-in partners are often less dependent on friends and acquaintances for social support than are those who are divorced or widowed. For people who live alone, friends, children, and grandchildren play a much more important role in alleviating feelings of loneliness.[78] In fact, research suggests that older adults who participate in community service and social activities tend to be more satisfied with their lives than those who do not.[79] While access to interpersonal relationships may decrease over time, the need for human contact seems to be relatively constant. To illustrate, two sociologists quote a 64-year-old woman as saying:

> I suppose that hope does spring eternal in the human breast as far as love is concerned. People are always looking for the ultimate, perfect relationship. No matter how old they are, they are looking for this thing called love.[80]

Although the focus for most of the preceding discussion of older adults has been on inclusion needs, it should be clear that control and affection needs also are susceptible to the processes of aging. Older adults face gradually less ability to give control and greater needs for control by others. This society has typically invested little interest and credibility in our older population. As a result, control strategies for older adults are sometimes based on making others feel guilty or ashamed. Similarly, the ability to give affection in a variety of ways also decreases, but the need for affection from others remains. Because of their increased need for physical care, some older adults may appreciate acts of compassionate love focused on caring for their health and well-being more than they did in their younger years.[81]

Interpersonal Needs of Women and Men

As we try to understand our own interpersonal needs and those of others, it may be useful to examine some possible differences between men and women. Some of these differences are related to the way we express the giving and needing of inclusion, affection, and control. Men and women are sometimes taught to express the same feeling or attitude in different ways or to value certain behaviors more than others.

It is not uncommon, for instance, for men and women to communicate affection needs in different ways. Men are sometimes taught to repress emotions, to "stay cool" and express excitement only in certain places—for example, sports events. Directly talking about a need for affection from others or admitting the desire to give more affection to others is difficult for men who exhibit these characteristics.[82] Some women, on the other hand, are taught to be more demonstrative about their feelings. These women may feel freer to express emotions, although affection displays must be muted when there is danger of communicating too much intimacy. Men and women also may react differently to the expression of affection in relationships with members of the same sex. Some men fear that any affection displays between men may be associated with homosexuality; thus, male-male friendships among men raised with these values will express affection in very indirect ways.

Men who have stereotypical sex-role characteristics also rely on external signs of control—signs that show everybody "who is in charge." The competition to "get ahead" in sports, school, and work is often measured by one's "accomplishments" for these men. Women who were raised to accept and behave according to the sex-role stereotype for women typically express control indirectly—that is, a willingness to be "in charge" of situations even though it is not obvious to others. For these women, getting ahead and being in control are not so much associated with accomplishments for oneself as with the development of effective interpersonal relationships with others. **Figure 3.2** shows one person's view of what men and women who adopt stereotypical sex roles think about.

The traditional male sex role emphasizes inclusion in the activities of others in order to do things together. Traditional female sex roles emphasize inclusion in the activities of others for sharing emotions and reactions to experiences.[83] As a result, speed, muscles, coordination, and skills associated with winning various games are important to these men, while looks and communication skills are important for their female counterparts. Men with traditional sex-role orientations typically find it hard to admit they need other people—preferring to express stoically, "I can get along by myself."

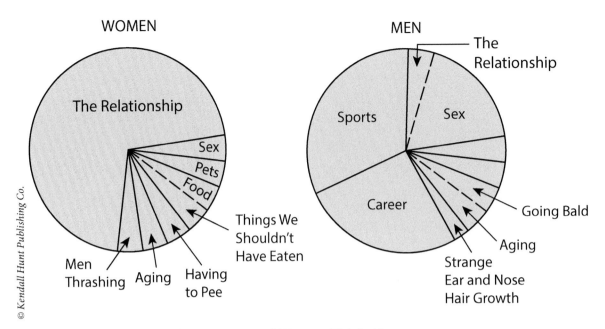

Figure 3.2   Stereotype of What Men and Women Think About

A number of scholars describe gender differences in communication by noting that men tend to value instrumental behavior, emphasize individual achievement, and focus on activities, whereas women tend to value affective behavior, emphasize relationships, and focus on communication.[84] Deborah Tannen, a well-known linguist, suggests that women and men define conversation in very different ways. She states that for men, "conversations are negotiations in which people try to achieve and maintain the upper hand if they can, and protect themselves from others' attempts to put them down and push them around." In contrast, for women, "conversations are negotiations for closeness in which people try to seek and give confirmation and support, and to reach consensus. They [women] try to protect themselves from others' attempts to push them away."[85] The complementary nature of these two perspectives allows both women and men to bring important strengths to their cross-gender relationships. However, the differences can also create misunderstandings. Women may wonder why men don't seem to be interested in discussing the details of what happened during the day while they were apart; men may wonder why women want to spend so much time talking about "trivial" issues. Women may feel that intimate talk precedes great sex; men may feel that great sex produces intimacy. Women may ask their male partners why they never say "I love you"; men may respond with frustration because they feel they do a great deal to show their female partners that they care.

So you want to know about communication and same-sex couples . . .

The similarities in patterns of relationship initiation, maintenance, and dissolution for gay, lesbian, and heterosexual couples far outnumber the differences.

What do same-sex couples want in a partner? Gay men, lesbians, and heterosexuals want similar characteristics in their partners—dependability, affection, similar interests, similar religious beliefs, and so on. Gender probably plays a greater role in some preferences than sexual orientation—for example, gay men emphasize physical attractiveness in partner selection and lesbians tend to emphasize personality and feelings. Gay men are drawn toward a stereotypical masculine appearance whereas lesbians do not show a common preference for partners who are stereotypically masculine or feminine in appearance.

How do same-sex couples initiate romantic relationships? The processes of initiation and what same-sex couples do on dates are similar to patterns followed by heterosexual couples. Lesbian romantic relationships often develop out of established friendships.

How do same-sex couples maintain close relationships? Some patterns differ, but the ways gay men and lesbians maintain their relationships are very similar to the ways heterosexual couples maintain relationships. Matters pertaining to equity and equality are often stressed in close gay and lesbian relationships. Sharing household tasks is not inevitable with same-sex couples, but it is far more common than among heterosexual couples. Gay men and lesbians do express a commitment to establishing enduring relationships, but it is also true that the breakup rate over a five-year period is higher for same-sex couples than for opposite-sex couples. Part of this finding is a function of the barriers that make it more difficult for heterosexual married couples to dissolve their relationships—barriers that may be less salient for same-sex couples. Gay men and lesbians also are more likely to maintain ties to their ex-partners than are heterosexual couples.

What about sexual behavior? Gay men are more likely than lesbians or heterosexuals to seek sexual intimacy on a first date, but sexual satisfaction for gays and lesbians, as for heterosexual couples, is linked to relationship satisfaction. Gay men report more nonmonogamous relationships than do lesbians and heterosexuals overall, but past research on civil unions suggests that they have fewer nonmonogamous relationships when they make a legal commitment, such as in marriage.

What about relationship quality? Research does not indicate any significant differences between lesbians, gay men, or heterosexuals on any measure of relationship quality and satisfaction initially or over time. This is especially true when equity is perceived as high. The nature of influence tactics between relationship partners in all types of relationships has more to do with power than gender or sexual orientation. Some same-sex couples fight less about money management than do heterosexual couples because they do not merge their funds, but fighting over other issues such as power, jealousy, self-esteem, and substance abuse are common to all couples. The incidence of physical and verbal abuse does not vary significantly between same-sex and opposite-sex couples.

* * * * * * * * * * * * * * * * * * * *

There is much more to be learned about the communication behavior among same-sex couples. The preceding points are only a brief beginning. In various places throughout the book, other aspects of same-sex interaction are addressed. For those interested in more in-depth coverage, see L. M. Diamond and K. L. Blair, "The Intimate Relationships of Sexual and Gender Minorities." In A. L. Vangelisti and D. Perlman, eds. *The Cambridge Handbook of Personal Relationships*, 2nd ed., pp. 186-198. New York: Cambridge University Press, 2006; L. M. Diamond, K. A. Rith, and M. R. Butterworth, "The Family Relationships of Sexual minorities." In A. L. Vanglisti, ed. *The Routledge Handbook of Family Communication*, 2nd ed., pp. 179-189. New York: Routledge, 2013; D. P. McWhirter, and A. M. Mattison, *The Male Couple: How Relationships Develop*. Englewood Cliffs, NJ: Prentice Hall, 1984; and L. A. Peplau, and L. R. Spalding, "The Close Relationships of Lesbians, Gay Men, and Bisexuals." In C. Hendrick and S. S. Hendrick, eds. *Close Relationships: A Sourcebook*, pp. 111–123. Thousand Oaks, CA: Sage, 2000.

In discussing gender differences such as these, it is important to underline two basic points. First, women and men are more similar to each other than they are different. Men and women both place a great deal of value on interpersonal relationships, both benefit from social support, and both fear isolation and loneliness.[86] Furthermore, when differences in motivation (e.g., to focus on relational issues)[87] or status (e.g., leadership position)[88] are controlled, many of the distinctions that we observe in men's and women's communication patterns disappear. The gender differences that have been found between the ways men and women communicate are actually quite small.[89] Of course, small differences can (and do) have important influences in our interpersonal relationships.

Second, it is virtually impossible to isolate any behavior that is exclusively performed by men and women. Most of us do not limit ourselves to rigid, unchanging stereotypical behaviors associated with males or females. We change our behavior based on who we are talking to, what we are talking about, and where we are.[90] On the other hand, some patterns of behavior can be linked with the expectations typically associated with male and female performance in this society. When we seek explanations for a person's communication behavior based on interpersonal needs, gender is an important consideration. It is sometimes inappropriate to judge a member of the opposite sex by your own experiences. Also, men and women sometimes perform similar tasks with similar needs at different stages in the life cycle. In today's society, many people are trying to break the bonds of stereotypical sex roles. Some men are taking charge of household tasks and child care and some women are becoming primary wage earners.[91] These role changes have altered the way men and women interact. Men are no longer expected to be invulnerable to life's stressors, but instead they are expected to be sensitive to their own and others' emotions. Women are expected to be competent communicators both in the home and in the workplace. Although these changes provide people with the opportunity to choose from a variety of behavioral styles, they also can be confusing because the behaviors of women and men are not as predictable as they once were.

Our interpersonal needs, the intensity with which they are felt, and the changes they undergo are heavily grounded in the rewards and costs we associate with our experiences in giving and needing inclusion, control, and affection. When the costs of giving affection to another seem to outweigh the benefits, our need to give affection may decrease and our need to receive affection from that person may increase. The need to give a lot of control may diminish if we feel rewarded by someone when we give little control. Unfortunately, interpersonal needs are not simply determined by our experiences with one other person. A husband's need to give and/or receive control in his relationship with his wife may be a result of his control experiences with his friends, relatives, coworkers, and children. Thus, the rewards and costs accumulated in one relationship for various interpersonal needs may tell only part of the story.

Control, inclusion, and affection can be manifested in a variety of ways. One person's "moderate" need for inclusion may be perceived as "excessive" by another; giving affection may mean performing the role of a sympathetic listener in one situation and giving money in another. Thus, it is important for those who want to become more effective communicators (1) to try to observe the various ways people communicate interpersonal needs and (2) to experiment with various ways of communicating the giving and receiving of inclusion, affection, and control. A person who has not experienced and experimented with giving control in different ways may find it difficult to manage a department of people who desire to be controlled in different ways; a person who limits himself or herself to giving affection in romantic relationships may find it difficult to recognize and give affection in other types of relationships.

Summary

The messages we make and our interpretation of others' messages are affected by many factors. This chapter showed how the nature of interpersonal messages may be affected by the nature of the communicators—particularly the interpersonal needs of those communicators. Each of us wants to give and receive varying amounts and types of affection, control, and inclusion. These interpersonal needs may be expressed in a variety of ways ranging from stereotypical manifestations such as exerting control by ordering people around to highly idiosyncratic messages that may be shared only by the relationship partners, such as putting a hand behind your back to say "I love you."

When both communicators want to give and receive the same sort of behavior, the relationship is labeled a symmetrical one; when one communicator wants to give what the other wants to receive, the relationship is called a complementary one. We noted that one difficulty parents and their teenage children sometimes experience concerns the shifting from a basically complementary relationship to one that is predominantly symmetrical. Many of our relationships have both symmetrical and complementary patterns that vary over time and with topic areas.

The last part of the chapter showed how age and gender affect our interpersonal needs. Throughout our life span we are faced with accomplishing certain tasks and adjusting to certain changes related to finances and health. As we move from infancy through old age, these life conditions will alter our interpersonal needs and our communication behavior with our primary partners, friends, acquaintances, and the multitude of store clerks and bureaucrats who pass briefly in and out of our lives. Men and women may show some similarities and some differences in the time and manner in which interpersonal needs are manifested. Those men and women who adhere to conventional sex-role expectations in this society are more likely to reveal the greatest differences in their overt behavior.

Many communicator characteristics can potentially influence the messages we exchange as we move in and out of various relationships. But interpersonal needs form a strong root system for many of the more visible manifestations. Understanding our own interpersonal needs and those of others is a worthy goal for improving communication in our relationships with others. It is, however, a difficult and never-ending task. Sometimes we aren't aware of our own needs; sometimes we repress or distort them in our messages to others; and sometimes the same style of behavior is associated with very different needs.

Selected Readings

Interpersonal Needs

Baumeister, R. F., and Leary, M. R. "The Need to Belong: Desire for Interpersonal Attachments as a Fundamental Human Motivation." *Psychological Bulletin* 117 (1995): 497–529.

Frandsen, K. D., and Rosenfeld, L. B. "Fundamental Interpersonal Relations Orientations in Dyads: An Empirical Analysis of Shutz' FIRO-B as an Index of Compatibility." *Speech Monographs* 40 (1973): 113–122.

Le, B., and Agnew, C. R. "Need Fulfillment and Emotional Experience in Interdependent Romantic Relationships." *Journal of Social and Personal Relationships* 18 (2001): 423–440.

McAdams, D. P. *Intimacy: The Need to Be Close.* New York: Doubleday, 1989.

———. "Personal Needs and Personal Relationships." In S. W. Duck, S. E. Holofoll, W. Ickes, and B. M. Montgomery, eds., *Handbook of Personal Relationships: Theory, Research and Interventions*, pp. 7–22. New York: Wiley, 1988.

Pickett, C. L., Gardner, W. L., and Knowles, M. "Getting a Cue: The Need to Belong and Enhanced Sensitivity to Social Cues." *Personality and Social Psychology Bulletin* 30 (2004): 1095–1107.

Prager, K. J., and Buhrmester, D. "Intimacy and Need Fulfillment in Couple Relationships." *Journal of Social and Personal Relationships* 15 (1998): 435–469.

Watzlawick, P., Beavin, J. H., and Jackson, D. D. *Pragmatics of Human Communication.* New York: W. W. Norton, 1967.

Communication Throughout the Life Span

Asher, S. R., and Weeks, M. S. "Friendships in Childhood." In A. L. Vangelisti and D. Perlman, eds., *The Cambridge Handbook of Personal Relationships*, 2nd ed., pp. 119–134. New York: Cambridge University Press, 2018.

Bigelow, B., Tesson, G., and Lewko, J. *Learning the Rules: The Anatomy of Children's Relationships.* New York: Guilford, 1996.

Blieszner, R. "A Lifetime of Caring: Dimensions and Dynamics in Late-Life Close Relationships." *Personal Relationships* 13 (2006): 1–18.

Blos, P. *On Adolescence: A Psychoanalytic Interpretation.* New York: Free Press, 1962.

Branje, S. Laursen, B., and Collins, W. A. "Parent-Child Communication During Adolescence." In A. L. Vangelisti, ed., *The Routledge Handbook of Family Communication.* 2nd ed., pp. 271–286. New York: Routledge, 2013.

Brenton, M. *Friendship.* Chapters 5–9. New York: Stein and Day, 1975.

Cappella, J. N. "The Biological Origins of Automated Patterns of Human Interaction." *Communication Theory* 1 (1991): 4–35.

Madsen, S. D., and Collins, W. A. "Personal Relationships in Adolescence and Early Adulthood." In A. L. Vangelisti and D. Perlman, eds., *The Cambridge Handbook of Personal Relationships.* 2nd ed., pp. 135–147. New York: Cambridge University Press, 2018.

Dailey, R. M. "Testing Components of Confirmation: How Acceptance and Challenge from Mothers, Fathers, and Siblings are Related to Adolescent Self-Concept." *Communication Monographs* 77 (2010): 592–617.

Denham, S. A. *Emotional Development in Young Children.* New York: Guilford, 1998.

Dunn, J. *Children's Friendships: The Beginnings of Intimacy.* Malden, MA: Wiley-Blackwell, 2004.

Elkind, D. *All Grown Up and No Place to Go.* Reading, MA: Addison-Wesley, 1984.

Erikson, E. H. *Identity: Youth and Crisis.* New York: W. W. Norton, 1968.

Fingerman, K. L., Birditt, K., Nussbaum, J., and Ebersole, D. S. "Generational Juggling: Family Communication at Midlife." In A. L. Vangelisti, ed., *The Routledge Handbook of Family Communication.* 2nd ed., pp. 97–111. New York: Routledge, 2013.

Gopnik, A., Meltzoff, A. N., and Kuhl, P. K. *The Scientist in the Crib: What Early Learning Tells Us About the Mind.* New York: Perennial, 2001.

Grotevant, H. D., and Cooper, C. R. "Individuation in Family Relationships: A Perspective on Individual Differences in the Development of Identity and Role-Taking Skill in Adolescence." *Human Development* 29 (1986): 82–100.

Gruenbaum, B., Depowski, N., Shaw, K. E., and Bortfeld, H. "Infant Communication." In A. L. Vangelisti, ed., *The Routledge Handbook of Family Communication.* 2nd ed., pp. 241–255. New York: Routledge, 2013.

Harwood, J., Rittenour, C. E., and Lin, M. "Family Communication in Later Life." In A. L. Vangelisti, ed., *The Routledge Handbook of Family Communication*, 2nd ed., pp. 112–126. New York: Routledge, 2013.

Hinde, R. A. *Towards Understanding Relationships.* Chapters 21 and 22. New York: Academic Press, 1979.

Lamb, M. E., Bornstein, M. H., and Teti, D. M. *Development in Infancy.* 4th ed. Mahwah, NJ: Erlbaum, 2002.

Larson, R., and Richards, M. H. *Divergent Realities: The Emotional Lives of Mothers, Fathers, and Adolescents.* New York: Basic Books, 1994.

Mehler, J., and Dupoux, E. *What Infants Know.* Cambridge: Blackwell, 1994.

Montemayor, R., Adams, G. R., and Gullota, T. P., eds. *Personal Relationships During Adolescence.* Thousand Oaks, CA: Sage, 1994.

Noller, P., and Callan, V. *The Adolescent in the Family.* New York: Routledge, 1991.

Nussbaum, J. F., and Coupland, J., eds. *Handbook of Communication and Aging Research.* 2nd ed. Mahwah, NJ: Erlbaum, 2004.

Nussbaum, J. F., Pecchioni, L. L., Robinson, J. D., and Thompson, T. L. *Communication and Aging.* 2nd ed. Mahwah, NJ: Erlbaum, 2000.

Pecchioni, L. L., Wright, K. B., and Nussbaum, J. F. *Lifespan Communication.* Mahwah, NJ: Erlbaum, 2005.

Rodnick R., and Wood, B. "The Communication Strategies of Children." *Speech Teacher* 22 (1973): 114–124.

Sheehy, G. *Passages: Predictable Crises of Adult Life.* New York: E. P. Dutton, 1976.

Sillars, A., Koerner, A., and Fitzpatrick, M. A. "Communication and Understanding in Parent-Adolescent Relationships." *Human Communication Research* 31 (2005): 102–128.

Wood, B. S. *Children and Communication.* Englewood Cliffs, NJ: Prentice Hall, 1976.

Communication and Gender

Aries, E. *Men and Women in Interaction: Reconsidering the Differences.* New York: Oxford University Press, 1996.

Ashmore, R. D., and Del Boca, F. K. *The Social Psychology of Female-Male Relations: A Critical Analysis of Central Concepts.* New York: Academic Press, 1986.

Canary, D. J., and Dindia, K. eds. *Sex Differences and Similarities in Communication.* Mahwah, NJ: Erlbaum, 1998.

Helgeson, V. S., and Mascatelli, K. "Gender and Relationships." In A. L. Vangelisti and D. Perlman, eds., *The Cambridge Handbook of Personal Relationships*, 2nd ed., pp. 186–198. New York: Cambridge University Press, 2018.

Kramarae, C. *Women and Men Speaking.* Rowley, MA: Newbury House, 1981.

Palomares, N. A. "Women are Sort of More Tentative than Men, Aren't They? How Men and Women Use Tentative Language Differently, Similarly, and Counterstereotypically as a Function of Gender Salience." *Communication Research* 36 (2009): 538–560.

Peplau, L. A., DeBro, S. C., Venigas, R. C., and Taylor, P. L. *Gender, Culture, and Ethnicity: Current Research About Women and Men.* Mountain View, CA: Mayfield, 1999.

Tannen, D. *You Just Don't Understand: Women and Men in Conversation.* New York: William Morrow, 1990.

Wood, J. T. *Gendered Lives: Communication, Gender, and Culture.* 2nd ed. Belmont, CA: Wadsworth, 1997.

Notes

[1] For example, Prager and Buhrmester found that the fulfillment of certain needs was associated with intimate communication (see K. J. Prager and D. Buhrmester, "Intimacy and Need Fulfillment in Couple Relationships," *Journal of Social and Personal Relationships* 15 [1998]: 435–469). Also, a study by Le and Agnew revealed that need fulfillment predicted positive emotional experience in romantic relationships (B. Le and C. R. Agnew, "Need Fulfillment and Emotional Experience in Interdependent Romantic Relationships," *Journal of Social and Personal Relationships* 18 [2001]: 423–440).

[2] W. C. Schutz, *FIRO: A Three-Dimension Theory of Interpersonal Behavior* (New York: Holt, Rinehart and Winston, 1958). Inclusion, control, and affection not only reflect Schutz's work, but consistently over the last six decades, have appeared in studies of interpersonal relations as major forces that affect human behavior. They seem to be basic responses to our environment and are reflected in the way we assign meaning to both verbal and nonverbal behavior. Osgood labeled the dimensions *Dynamism, Potency*, and *Evaluation*; Mehrabian called them *Responsiveness, Power*, and *Immediacy*. Cf. C. E. Osgood, G. J. Suci, and P. H. Tannenbaum, *The*

Measurement of Meaning (Urbana: University of Illinois Press, 1957); A. Mehrabian, *Nonverbal Communication* (Chicago: Aldine, 1972). More recently, Sheldon et al. found that autonomy, competence, and relatedness were consistently ranked among individuals' top four psychological needs (see K. M. Sheldon, A. J. Elliot, Y. Kim, and T. Kasser, "What Is Satisfying About Satisfying Events? Testing 10 'Candidate Psychological Needs.' " *Journal of Personality and Social Psychology* 80 [2001]: 325–339).

3   D. D. Von Dras and I. C. Siegler, "Stability in Extraversion and Aspects of Social Support at Midlife," *Journal of Personality and Social Psychology* 72 (1997): 233–241.

4   A. Thorne, "The Press of Personality: A Study of Conversations Between Introverts and Extroverts," *Journal of Personality and Social Psychology* 53 (1987): 718–726.

5   R. E. Lucas and F. Fujita, "Factors Influencing the Relation Between Extroversion and Pleasant Affect," *Journal of Personality and Social Psychology* 79 (2000): 1039–1056.

6   L. F. Barrett and P. R. Pietromonaco, "Accuracy of the Five-Factor Model in Predicting Perceptions of Daily Social Interactions," *Personality and Social Psychology Bulletin* 23 (1997): 1173–1187.

7   Thorne, "The Press of Personality."

8   J. J. Gross and R. W. Levenson, "Emotional Suppression: Physiology, Self-Report, and Expressive Behavior," *Journal of Personality and Social Psychology* 64 (1993): 970–986.

9   C. L. Picket, W. L. Gardner, and M. Knowles, "Getting a Cue: The Need to Belong and Enhanced Sensitivity to Social Cues," *Personality and Social Psychology Bulletin* 30 (2004): 1095–1107.

10   J. J. Lynch, *The Broken Heart: The Medical Consequences of Loneliness in America* (New York: Basic Books, 1977).

11   B. R. Burleson, T. L. Albrecht, and I. G. Sarason, eds., *Communication of Social Support: Messages, Interaction, Relationships, and Community* (Thousand Oaks, CA: Sage, 1994); B. C. Feeney and N. L. Collins, "Social Support in Close Relationships." In A. L. Vangelisti and D. Perlman, eds., *The Cambridge Handbook of Personal Relationships.* 2nd ed. (New York: Cambridge University Press, 2018), pp. 282–296; E. L. MacGeorge, B. Feng, and B. R. Burleson, "Supportive Communication." In M. L. Knapp and J. A. Daly, eds., *Handbook of Interpersonal Communication.* 4th ed. (Thousand Oaks, CA: Sage, 2011), pp. 317–354;

12   B. H. Gottlieb, "Social Support and the Study of Personal Relationships," *Journal of Social and Personal Relationships* 2 (1985): 351–375; H. W. Jones, "The Psychology of Loneliness: Some Personality Issues in the Study of Social Support." In I. G. Sarason and B. P. Sarason, eds., *Social Support Theory, Research and Applications* (The Hague, Holland: Martinus Nijhoff 1985).

13   P. N. Christensen and D. A. Kashy, "Perceptions of and by Lonely People in Initial Social Interaction," *Personality and Social Psychology Bulletin* 24 (1998): 322–329.

14   K. J. Rotenberg and J. Kmill, "Perception of Lonely and Non-Lonely Persons as a Function of Individual Differences in Loneliness," *Journal of Social and Personal Relationships* 9 (1992): 325–330; B. H. Spitzberg and D. J. Cupach, "Loneliness and Relationally Competent Communication," *Journal of Social and Personal Relationships* 2 (1985): 387–402.

15   B. P. Buunk and K. S. Prins, "Loneliness, Exchange Orientation, and Reciprocity in Friendships," *Personal Relationships* 5 (1998): 1–14.

16   J. R. Coyne, C. Wortman, and D. Lehman, "The Other Side of Support: Emotional Overinvolvement and Miscarried Helping." In B. H. Gottlieb, ed., *Marshaling Social Support* (Newbury Park, CA: Sage, 1988); J. J. Lynch, *The Language of the Heart* (New York: Basic Books, 1985).

17   H. L. Fritz and V. S. Helgeson, "Distinctions of Unmitigated Communion from Communion: Self-Neglect and Overinvolvement with Others," *Journal of Personality and Social Psychology* 75 (1998): 121–140.

18   T. C. Sabourin, D. A. Infante, and J. E. Rudd, "Verbal Aggression in Marriages: A Comparison of Violent, Distressed but Nonviolent, and Nondistressed Couples," *Human Communication Research* 20 (1993): 245–267.

19   A. L. Vangelisti, M. L. Knapp, and J. A. Daly, "Conversational Narcissism," *Communication Monographs* 57 (1990): 251–274.

20   M. S. Mast, "Dominance as Expressed and Inferred Through Speaking Time," *Human Communication Research* 28 (2002): 420–450; W. T. Rogers and S. E. Jones, "Effects of Dominance Tendencies on Floor Holding and Interruption Behavior in Dyadic Interaction," *Human Communication Research* 1 (1975): 113–122; K. J. Tusing and J. P. Dillard, "The Sounds of Dominance: Vocal Precursors of Perceived Dominance During Interpersonal Influence," *Human Communication Research* 26 (2000): 148–171.

21   A. Mehrabian, *Nonverbal Communication* (Chicago: Aldine, 1972).

22 R. B. Exline, S. L. Ellyson, and B. Long, "Visual Behavior as an Aspect of Power Role Relationships." In P. Pilner, L. Krames, and I. Holloway, eds., *Advances in the Study of Communication and Affect.* vol. 2. (New York: Plenum, 1975), pp. 21–51.

23 D. T. Gilbert and D. H. Silvera, "Overhelping," *Journal of Personality and Social Psychology* 70 (1996): 678–690.

24 J. A. Sheppard and R. E. Socherman, "On the Manipulative Behavior of Low Machiavellians: Feigning Incompetence to 'Sandbag' an Opponent," *Journal of Personality and Social Psychology* 72 (1997): 1448–1459.

25 K. Floyd, "Human Affection Exchange: V. Attributes of the Highly Affectionate," *Communication Quarterly* 50 (2002): 135–152; also see K. Floyd and S. Riforgiate, "Affectionate Communication Received from Spouses Predicts Stress Hormone Levels in Healthy Adults," *Communication Monographs* 75 (2008): 351–368.

26 M. Wiener and A. Mehrabian, *Language Within Language: Immediacy, A Channel in Verbal Communication* (New York: Appelton-Century-Crofts, 1968). For an example, see S. Gildersleeve, J. A. Singer, K. Skerrett & S. Wein, "Coding 'We-ness' in Couple's Relationship Stories: A Method for Assessing Mutuality in Couple Therapy," *Psychotherapy Research* 27 (2017): 313–325.

27 G. Downey and S. I. Feldman, "Implications of Rejection Sensitivity for Intimate Relationships," *Journal of Personality and Social Psychology* 70 (1996): 1327–1343. Also see S. L. Murray, P. Rose, G. M. Bellavia, J. G. Holmes, and A. G. Kusche, "When Rejection Stings: How Self-Esteem Constrains Relationship-Enhancement Processes," *Journal of Personality and Social Psychology* 83 (2002): 556–573.

28 For reviews see J. de Jong Gierveld, T. van Tilburg, and P. A. Dykstra, "New Ways of Theorizing and Conducting Research in the Field of Loneliness and Social Isolation." In A. L. Vangelisti and D. Perlman, eds., *The Cambridge Handbook of Personal Relationships* (New York: Cambridge University Press, 2018). 2nd ed., pp. 391–404; L. A. Peplau and D. Perlman, "Perspectives on Loneliness." In L. A. Peplau and D. Perlman, eds., *Loneliness: A Sourcebook of Current Theory. Research and Therapy* (New York: Wiley-Interscience, 1982), pp. 1–20.

29 One study demonstrated that the size of young people's social network was negatively associated with their loneliness. The same study suggested that for older people, the quality of their social ties was more important than the size of their network. (See L. R. Green, D. S. Richardson, T. Lago, and E. C. Schatten-Jones, "Network Correlates of Social and Emotional Loneliness in Young and Older Adults," *Personality and Social Psychology Bulletin* 27 [2001]: 281–288).

30 C. Segrin, H. L. Powell, M. Givertz, and A. Brackin, "Symptoms of Depression, Relational Quality, and Loneliness in Dating Relationships," *Personal Relationships* 10 [2003]: 25–26.

31 J. de Jong-Gierveld, "Personal Relationships, Social Support, and Loneliness," *Journal of Social and Personal Relationships* 6 (1989): 197–221; B. H. Spitzberg and D. J. Cupach, "Loneliness and Relationally Competent Communication," *Journal of Social and Personal Relationships* 2 (1985): 387–402.

32 See, for example, S. M. Moorman, "Dyadic perspectives on marital quality and loneliness in later life," *Journal of Social and Personal Relationships* 33 (2016): 600–618.

33 W. J. Lederer and D. D. Jackson, *The Mirages of Marriage* (New York: W. W. Norton, 1968), p. 162.

34 D. C. Dryer and L. M. Horowitz, "When Do Opposites Attract?: Interpersonal Complementarity Versus Similarity," *Journal of Personality and Social Psychology* 72 (1997): 592–603.

35 M. K. Conn and C. Peterson, "Social Support: Seek and Ye Shall Find," *Journal of Social and Personal Relationships* 6 (1989): 345–358.

36 Christensen and Kashy, "Perceptions of and by Lonely People."

37 R. A. Bell "Conversational Involvement and Loneliness," *Communication Monographs* 52 (1985): 218–235.

38 R. A. Bell and M. E. Roloff, "Making a Love Connection: Loneliness and Communication Competence in the Dating Marketplace," *Communication Quarterly* 39 (1991): 58–74; also see T. Nishimura, T. Murakami, and S. Sakurai, "Do Not Overlook Lonely Children: Additional Evidence from Two Longitudinal Studies," *Journal of Social and Personal Relationships* 35 (2018): 956–976.

39 T. Hora, "Tao, Zen, and Existential Psychotherapy," *Psychologia* 2 (1959): 236–242.

40 Baumeister, R.F. and Leary, M.R., "The Need to Belong: Desire for Interpersonal Attachments as a Fundamental Human Motivation," *Psychological Bulletin*, 117 (1995): 497–529.

41 J. N. Cappella, "The Biological Origins of Automated Patterns of Human Interaction," *Communication Theory* 1 (1991): 4–35. B. Gruenbaum, N. Depowski, K. E. Shaw, and H. Bortfeld, "Infant Communication." In A. L. Vangelisti, ed., *The Routledge Handbook of Family*

Communication. 2nd ed. (New York: Routledge, 2013), pp. 241–255.

42 A. Gopnik, A. N. Meltzoff, and P. K. Kuhl, *The Scientist in the Crib: What Early Learning Tells Us About the Mind* (New York: Perennial, 2001).

43 J. Dunn, *Children's Friendships: The Beginnings of Intimacy* (Malden, MA: Wiley-Blackwell, 2004).

44 R. Shetgiri, H. Lin, and G. Flores, "Trends in Risk and Protective Factors for Child Bullying Perpetration in the United States," *Child Psychiatry & Human Development* 44 (2013): 89-104; A. L. Spriggs, R. J. Iannotti, T. R. Nansel, and D. L. Haynie, "Adolescent Bullying Involvement and Perceived Family, Peer, and School Relations: Commonalities and Differences Across Race/Ethnicity," *Journal of Adolescent Health* 41 (2007): 283–293.

45 For a review see S. R. Asher and M. S. Weeks, "Friendships in Childhood." In A. L. Vangelisti and D. Perlman, eds., *The Cambridge Handbook of Personal Relationships.* 2nd ed. (New York: Routledge, 2018), pp. 119–134.

46 Z. Rubin, *Children's Friendships* (Cambridge, MA: Harvard University Press, 1980), p. 73.

47 W. K. Rawlins, *Friendship Matters: Communication, Dialectics, and the Life Course* (New York: Aldine de Gruyter, 1992).

48 C. L. Martin, R. A. Fabes, S. M. Evans, and H. Wyman, "Social Cognition on the Playground: Children's Beliefs About Playing with Girls Versus Boys and Their Relations to Sex Segregated Play," *Journal of Social and Personal Relationships* 16 (1999): 751–771.

49 M. Brenton, *Friendship* (New York: Stein and Day, 1975), p. 57. Reprinted with permission of Stein and Day Publishers.

50 D. J. Flannery, R. Montemayor, M. Eberly, and J. Torquati, "Unraveling the Ties That Bind: Affective Expression and Perceived Conflict in Parent-Adolescent Interactions," *Journal of Social and Personal Relationships* 10 (1993): 495–509.

51 W. A. Collins, "Relationships and Development During Adolescence: Interpersonal Adaptation to Individual Change," *Personal Relationships* 4 (1997): 1–14.

52 S. Branje, B. Laursen, and W. A. Collins, "Parent-Child Communication During Adolescence." In A. L. Vangelisti, ed., *The Routledge Handbook of Family Communication.* 2nd ed. (New York: Routledge, 2013), pp. 271–286.

53 H. D. Grotevant and C. R. Cooper, "Individuation in Family Relationships: A Perspective on Individual Differences in the Development of Identity and Role-Taking," *Human Development* 29 (1986): 82–100.

54 J. G. Smetana, "Adolescents' and Parents' Conceptions of Parental Authority," *Child Development* 59 (1988): 321–335.

55 R. M. Dailey, "Testing Components of Confirmation: How Acceptance and Challenge from Mothers, Fathers, and Siblings are Related to Adolescent Self-Concept," *Communication Monographs* 77 (2010): 592–617.

56 T. D. Afifi, D. A. Granger, A. Denes, A. Joseph and D. Aldeis, "Parents' Communication Skills and Adolescents' Salivary α—Amylase and Cortisol Response Patterns," *Communication Monographs* 78 (2011): 273–295.

57 A. Sillars, A. Koerner, and M. A. Fitzpatrick, "Communication and Understanding in Parent-Adolescent Relationships," *Human Communication Research* 31 (2005): 102–128; A. L. Vangelisti, "Older Adolescents' Perceptions of Communications Problems with Their Parents," *Journal of Adolescent Research* 7 (1992): 382–402.

58 F. S. Christopher, S. J. McKenney, and F. O. Poulsen, "Early Adolescents' 'Crushing': Pursuing Romantic Interest on Social Stage," *Journal of Social and Personal Relationships* 33 (2016): 515–533.

59 Brenton, M. *Friendship*, p. 74.

60 E. M. Ritter, "Social Perspective-Taking Ability, Cognitive Complexity and Listener Adapted Communication In Early and Late Adolescence," *Communication Monographs* 46 (1979): 40–51.

61 T. Kasser, R. Koestner, and N. Lekes, "Early Family Experiences and Adult Values: A 26-Year, Prospective Longitudinal Study," *Personality and Social Psychology Bulletin* 28 (2002): 826–835.

62 R. L. Gould, *Transformations: Growth and Change in Adult Life* (New York: Simon & Schuster, 1978); D. J. Levinson, *The Seasons of a Man's Life* (New York: Knopf, 1978); R. S. Sears and S. S. Feldman, eds., *The Seven Ages of Man* (Los Altos, CA: William Kaufmann, 1964); G. Sheehy, *Passages: Predictable Crises of Adult Life* (New York: Dutton, 1976); G. E. Valliant, *Adaptation to Life* (Boston: Little, Brown, 1977).

63 R. C. Barnett and C. Rivers, *She Works/He Works: How Two-Income Families Are Happier, Healthier, and Better Off* (New York: HarperCollins, 1996); R. L. Repetti, "Effects of Daily Workload on Subsequent Behavior During Marital Interaction: The Roles of Social Withdrawal and Spouse Support," *Journal of Personality and Social Psychology* 57 (1989): 651–659; D. N. Ruble, L. S.

Hackel, A. S. Fleming, and C. Stangor, "Changes in the Marital Relationship During the Transition to First-Time Motherhood: Effects of Violated Expectations Concerning Division of Household Labor," *Journal of Personality and Social Psychology* 55 (1988): 78–87; P. Schwartz, *Peer Marriage* (New York: The Free Press, 1994).

64 K. L. Fingerman, K. Birditt, J. Nussbaum, and D. S. Ebersole, "Generational Juggling: Family Communication at Midlife." In A. L. Vangelisti, ed., *The Routledge Handbook of Family Communication.* 2nd ed. (New York: Routledge, 2013), pp. 97–111.

65 L. L. Carstensen, "A Life-Span Approach to Social Motivation." In J. Heckhausen and C. S. Dweck, eds., *Motivation and Self-Regulation Across the Life Span* (New York: Cambridge University Press, 1998).

66 F. R. Lang, "Endings and Continuity of Social Relationships: Maximizing Intrinsic Benefits Within Personal Networks When Feeling Near to Death," *Journal of Social and Personal Relationships* 17 (2000): 155–182.

67 P. H. Zietlow and C. A. VanLear Jr., "Marriage Duration and Relational Control: A Study of Developmental Patterns," *Journal of Marriage and the Family* 53 (1991): 773–785. Also see R. W. Levenson, L. L. Carstensen, and J. M. Gottman, "Long Term Marriage: Age, Gender, and Satisfaction," *Psychology and Aging* 8 (1993): 301–313.

68 C. Y. Chen, N. Joyce, J. Harwood, and J. Xiang, "Stereotype Reduction through Humor and Accommodation during Imagined Communication with Older Adults" *Communication Monographs* 84 (2017): 94–109.

69 T. van Tilburg, "Support Networks Before and After Retirement," *Journal of Social and Personal Relationships* 9 (1992): 433–445.

70 C. M. Avery and F. M. Jablin, "Retirement Preparation Programs and Organizational Communication," *Communication Education* 37 (1988): 68–80.

71 J. E. Birren, *The Psychology of Aging* (Englewood Cliffs, NJ: Prentice Hall, 1964), pp. 273–279.

72 M. L. Knapp, *Social Intercourse: From Greeting to Goodbye* (Boston: Allyn & Bacon, 1978), Chapter 6.

73 S. Reichard, F. Livson, and P. G. Petersen, *Aging and Personality* (New York: Wiley, 1962).

74 C. Fowler, J. Gasiorek, and H. Giles, "The Role of Communication in Aging Well: Introducing the Communicative Ecology Model of Successful Aging," *Communication Monographs* 82 (2015): 431–457; J. Gasiorek, C. Fowler, and H, Giles, "What Does Successful Aging Sound Like? Profiling Communication About Aging," *Human Communication Research* (2015): 577–602.

75 Y. Yang, "Social Inequalities in Happiness in the United States, 1972–2004: An Age-Period-Cohort Analysis," *American Sociological Review* 73 (2008): 204–226.

76 W. A. Peterson and J. Quadagno, *Social Bonds in Later Life: Aging and Interdependence* (Newbury Park, CA: Sage, 1985).

77 K. Wright, "Computer-Mediated Social Support, Older Adults, and Coping," *Journal of Communication* 50 (2000): 100–118.

78 P. A. Dykstra, "The Differential Availability of Relationships and the Provision and Effectiveness of Support to Older Adults," *Journal of Social and Personal Relationships* 10 (1993): 255–370; for a review of research on older adults' communication in these relationships see J. Harwood, C. E. Rittenour, and M. Lin, "Family Communication in Later Life." In A. L. Vangelisti, ed., *The Routledge Handbook of Family Communication.* 2nd ed. (New York: Routledge, 2013), pp. 112–126.

79 R. E. Harlow and N. Cantor, "Still Participating After All These Years: A Study of Life Task Participation in Later Life," *Journal of Personality and Social Psychiatry* 71 (1996): 1235–1249.

80 K. Bulcroft and M. O'Conner-Roden, "Never Too Late," *Psychology Today* 20 (1986): 66–69.

81 See, for example A. K. Sabey, A. J. Rauer, and M. L. Haselschwerdt, "'It's Not Just Words Coming from the Mouth': The Nature of Compassionate Love among Older Couples," *Journal of Social and Personal Relationships* 33 (2016): 640–665.

82 For reviews, see V. S. Helgeson and K. Mascatelli, "Gender and Relationships." In A. L. Vangelisti and D. Perlman, eds., *The Cambridge Handbook of Personal Relationships.* 2nd ed. (New York: Cambridge University Press, 2018), pp. 186–198; L. A. Peplau, S. C. DeBro, R. C. Venigas, and P. L. Taylor, *Gender, Culture, and Ethnicity: Current Research About Women and Men* (Mountain View, CA: Mayfield, 1999); J. T. Wood, *Gendered Lives: Communication, Gender, and Culture.* 2nd ed. (Belmont, CA: Wadsworth, 1997).

83 R. Martin, "'Girls Don't Talk About Garages!': Perceptions of Conversation in Same- and Cross-Sex Friendships," *Personal Relationships* 4 (1997): 115–130; W. K. Rawlins, "Communication in Cross-Sex Friendships." In L. P. Arliss and D. J. Borisoff, eds., *Women and Men Communicating: Challenges and Change* (New York: Harcourt Brace Jovanovich, 1993), pp. 51–70; S. M. Rose

"Same- and Cross-Sex Friendships and the Psychology of Homosociality," *Sex Roles* 12 (1985): 63–74.

84 L. K. Acitelli, "Gender Differences in Relationship Awareness and Marital Satisfaction Among Young Married Couples," *Personality and Social Psychology Bulletin* 18 (1992): 102–110; C. Sedikides, M. B. Oliver, and W. K. Campbell, "Perceived Benefits and Costs of Romantic Relationships for Women and Men: Implications for Exchange Theory," *Personal Relationships* 1 (1994): 5–21; S. Sprecher and C. Sedikides, "Gender Differences in Perceptions of Emotionality: The Case of Close Heterosexual Relationships," *Sex Roles* (1993): 511–530; T. A. Wills, R. L. Weiss, and G. R. Patterson, "A Behavior Analysis of the Determinants of Marital Satisfaction," *Journal of Consulting and Clinical Psychology* 42 (1974): 802–811; J. T. Wood and C. C. Inman, "In a Different Mode: Masculine Styles of Communicating Closeness," *Journal of Applied Communication Research* 21 (1993): 279–295.

85 D. Tannen, *You Just Don't Understand: Women and Men in Conversation* (New York: William Morrow, 1990).

86 See, for example, B. R. Burleson, "The Experience and Effects of Emotional Support: What the Study of Cultural and Gender Differences Can Tell Us About Close Relationships, Emotion, and Interpersonal Communication," *Personal Relationships* 10 (2003): 1–23; A. W. Kunkel and B. R. Burleson, "Assessing Explanations for Sex Differences in Emotional Support: A Test of the Different Cultures and Skill Specialization Accounts," *Human Communication Research* 25 (1999): 307–340; A. L. Vangelisti and J. A. Daly, "Gender Differences in Standards for Romantic Relationships," *Personal Relationships* 4 (1997): 203–219.

87 See, for example, K. J. K. Klein and S. D. Hodges, "Gender Differences, Motivation, and Empathic Accuracy: When It Pays to Understand," *Personality and Social Psychology Bulletin* 27 (2001): 720–730. Also see B. R. Burleson, A. J. Holmstrom, and C. M. Gilstrap, "'Guys Can't Say *That* to Guys': Four Experiments Assessing the Normative Motivation Account for Deficiencies in the Emotional Support Provided by Men," *Communication Monographs* 72 (2005): 468–501.

88 See, for example, A. H. Eagly and B. T. Johnson, "Gender and Leadership Style: A Meta-Analysis," *Psychological Bulletin* 108 (1990): 233–256.

89 B. R. Burleson, A. W. Kunkel, W. Samter, and K. J. Werking, "Men's and Women's Evaluations of Communication Skills in Personal Relationships: When Sex Differences Make a Difference—And When They Don't," *Journal of Social and Personal Relationships* 13 (1996): 201–224; D. J. Canary, K. S. Hause, "Is There Any Reason to Research Sex Differences in Communication?" *Communication Quarterly* 41 (1993): 129–144; K. Dindia and M. Allen, "Sex Differences in Self-Disclosure: A Meta-Analysis," *Psychological Bulletin* 122 (1992): 106–124; D. J. Goldsmith and S. A. Dun, "Sex Differences and Similarities in the Communication of Social Support," *Journal of Social and Personal Relationships* 14 (1997): 317–337.

90 N. A. Palomares, "Explaining Gender-Based Language Use: Effects of Gedner Identity Salience on References to Emotion and Tentative Language in Intra- and Intergroup Contexts," *Human Communication Research* 134 (2008): 263–286; N. A. Palomares, "Women are Sort of More Tentative than Men, Aren't They? How Men and Women Use Tentative Language Differently, Similarly, and Counterstereotypically as a Function of Gender Salience," *Communication Research* 36 (2009): 538–560.

91 See J. Y. Lee and S. J. Lee, "Caring is Masculine: Stay-At-Home Fathers and Masculine Identity," *Psychology of Men and Masculinity* 19 (2018): 47–58.

CHAPTER 4

LEARNING OUTCOMES

Students will . . .

. . . recognize a number of the ways patterns of work affect personal relationships.

. . . describe how differences in, and changes in, relationship styles can influence communication.

. . . explain the effect of attitudes toward self-fulfillment on social interaction.

. . . describe how messages from the mass media both reflect and shape the way people see their relationships.

. . . identify the six different types of perceptions of the physical environment and know how they affect the messages communicators send and receive.

. . . explain how people are incorporating technology into their communication with relational partners.

. . . define the four different affordances of communication technologies.

KEY TERMS

asynchronicity	formality
communication interdependence theory	internet compulsion
	passive strategies
constraint	privacy
distance	surveillance
editability	triangulating
familiarity	warmth

The Communication Environment: Cultural and Physical

Dear Dr. Knapp,

I don't understand why I can't find a guy who is honest with me. It is so easy to say you believe in telling the truth and so hard (for some) to do it. When I grew up, I was encouraged to tell the truth and to treasure that in others. But the last two relationships I've been in have made me wonder if I expect too much. Then I see these politicians who lie to the public and I wonder if honesty is really valued or whether we just say it is.

In Search of Truthfulness

The society or culture within which a relationship develops reflects certain guidelines or "teachings" about how people are expected to behave in various types of relationships. The extent to which individuals are exposed to these guidelines and the extent to which they subscribe to them will affect the type of communication behavior they exhibit with their communication partners. The cultural values and trends associated with honesty may, for some, make this a pivotal issue in the success or failure of a relationship.

Different societies approach relationships and social interaction in different ways.[1] Some societies place more emphasis on the practical aspects of marriage than others;[2] some advocate more indirect communication than others;[3] some see close family ties as more important than others;[4] and some are more tolerant of negative marital communication than others.[5] There also are differences in beliefs and values within societies (e.g., regional differences) that may influence the way people approach their personal relationships.[6] Most of the time, the assumptions that guide social interaction in various cultural environments are unspoken. As a consequence, people often are unaware of the impact that their social background has on their interpersonal relationships. This chapter explores several important characteristics of U.S. society that may influence communication. It also examines the possible effects of specific communication environments within the larger U.S. culture and their influence on what people say.

> *The organism, then, is in a sense responsible for its environment. And since organism and environment determine each other and are mutually dependent for their existence, it follow that life-process, to be adequately understood, must be considered in terms of their interrelations.*
>
> —*George Herbert Mead*

Human communication does not take place in a vacuum. Every time we communicate, we are surrounded and influenced by a set of conditions that help determine why we did or did not interact in a particular way. In Chapter 3 we explored the potential influence of each communicator's interpersonal needs on communication behavior in developing and deteriorating relationships. In this chapter, our focus is on the influence emanating from communication environments. These environments range in size from the society at large to a classroom or an elevator. To illustrate, consider a jealous male who confronts a friend he suspects is his competition by saying, "You make me so mad I could *kill* you." Two observers comment on the conditions that prompted such a statement:

Analysis 1. It's the climate of the times. Today people generally are less patient with others and put less energy into building close relationships. They think they have a right to express their anger no matter how it makes other people feel. Anger and violence are glorified on TV and in videogames. He's just expressing himself the way other people do.

Analysis 2. I think it was entirely a function of the setting itself—the environment in which the confrontation took place. If his girlfriend and several of his other friends hadn't been around, it would have been different. Because it was a public setting, he felt he had to speak to all the audiences present. He was trying to be "macho" for his friends and tell his girlfriend how much he loves her. The fact that the confrontation took place right outside the athletic building may also have contributed to the strength of the statement.

You can probably think of several other explanations—including the possible role of interpersonal needs. But the preceding analyses adequately represent the scope of this chapter. Which analysis is correct? Like most situations involving complex human behavior, there is some truth in each analysis; each contributes a share of the total picture.

The Influence of the Cultural Environment

One of the analyses just presented explained the jealous boyfriend's behavior as a reflection of the climate of the times. What are the current trends in U.S. society that comprise the climate of the times? Trends in many areas go together to make up the climate of the times, but our concern is with four areas: (1) patterns of work, (2) relationship styles, (3) attitudes toward self-fulfillment, and (4) messages from the mass media. How will these societal conditions affect our interpersonal communication directed toward the development of relationships?

Patterns of Work

More than ever before in this nation's history, both husband and wife are employed outside the home. In 1940, less than 28 percent of women worked and only about one-third of those who worked were married. At the time of this writing, approximately 70 percent of women work outside the home, and most of those who do work are married. In addition, millions of unmarried couples live together and maintain separate full-time jobs and careers. The monetary gains and increased feelings of self-fulfillment may provide important benefits for a couple's relationship, but this pattern of work also may bring about relationship stress, particularly when two careers are involved.[7]

Work environments can be deceptively alluring. The variety of people and potential relationships may provide a stimulating contrast to a single individual whose habits you know well; the rewards you receive for showing your skill in accomplishing tasks may seem personally more gratifying than the rewards your spouse provides; the topics discussed may somehow seem more "important" than those discussed at home. As a result, the effort expended for maintaining a satisfying relationship may not be enough, and conflict may develop. Of course, there are times when the workplace is stressful. The stress people experience at work can influence the way they communicate later in the day. Research shows that one partner's work-related stress can affect the way both partners feel when they interact with each other at home.[8]

When both partners in a relationship are working outside the home, it may take special planning to find the time to resolve conflicts and to talk about work-related stress. It is not unusual for dual-career couples to have difficulty finding the time necessary to build friendships—although the quantity and variety of people available in the work setting should be high. When friendships with people at work are pursued without the participation of the other spouse, problems may develop. If the friendship is with a member of the opposite sex, jealousy may occur; if it is a friendship with a member of the same sex, a partner may feel slighted—wondering why that time cannot be spent together. And when dual-career couples decide to have children, many decisions regarding responsibilities and priorities must be agreed upon to head off potential areas of relationship strife.

Many of the problems faced by couples in which both partners work outside the home also face couples in which only one partner leaves the home to work. However, the intensity of the problems faced by dual-career couples and our general lack of preparation for dealing with these issues force us to look closely at this trend. Even couples who are able to free themselves of traditional expectations for appropriate marital behavior and who are able to manage their time and support each other's efforts and achievements may face special difficulties in maintaining a rewarding relationship. For example, families and careers develop and change over time, and the behavior most advantageous for the family may be counterproductive for enhancing a career or vice versa. To add to the complexity, each partner may be at a different stage in his or her respective career.

Although the preceding paragraphs seem to emphasize the possible problems in two wage-earner families, many couples are succeeding in such relationships. In fact, studies show that most people who work outside the home are relatively happy with their family life.[9] To succeed, however, couples must adapt their expectations and communication behavior to a set of conditions quite different from the working patterns of previous generations. [10] Flexibility and compromise are the bywords for couples today.

Often career advancement is dependent on moving to a new location. This presents dual-career couples with difficult choices. It also has the potential to affect how we view other relationships. During the 1970s and 1980s, this nation experienced a particularly high rate of mobility. As one author noted, the U.S. was a "society of torn roots."[11] Songwriter and singer Carole King may have put it most succinctly when she said that, "Doesn't anybody stay in one place anymore?"

Although Americans still move more frequently than people in many other countries, the trend to relocate has slowed. In the early 1970s, only about 10 percent of the employees who were asked by their corporation to change locations resisted. In the 1990s, roughly one-third of the employees asked to move resisted—even though they were sometimes promised fatter-than-usual salaries.[12] The U.S. Census Bureau has found that movement from one residence to another has decreased from about 20 percent in the mid-1980s, when one in five people moved every year, to about 10 percent.[13]

But while physical mobility has decreased, the rate of change that people encounter in the workplace has not. Today's employee must be prepared to deal with a fast-paced, constantly changing work environment. Phrases such as "high-speed management," "reinventing the workplace," and "rapid downsizing" reflect the continual state of flux that characterizes many organizations. Many employees in the United States now are working more hours, earning less, and under more pressure to adapt than they have been in several decades.[14] Job descriptions change quickly to accommodate fluctuations in the marketplace. People constantly have to learn new skills to keep up with advances in technology. For many, job security seems to be a thing of the past. It is not at all uncommon for employees to move from one job to another every three or four years.

How are interpersonal relationships affected by a high degree of change? First, rapid change may affect our expectation for how long relationships will last. Virtually everything we do is based on a culturally taught assumption regarding how long things last. As children, we learn how long Mommy or Daddy spends at the office; how long dinner lasts; how long a vacation is; how long a friend can play at our house. If the pace of life accelerates, we will come to expect things to last for a shorter time. In other words, we can become culturally conditioned toward building and dissolving relationships quickly.

Movement from one relationship to another in rapid succession may also affect the trust, support, and long-term commitment desired in many relationships. If we expect most of our relationships to change, we may feel it necessary to rely less on others and more on ourselves—thus avoiding the very relatedness we seek.

Another result of frequent change is the possibility of building a wide range of acquaintances and friends. One study, cited by Milgram, asked a number of people from different lifestyles to keep a diary of those with whom they came in contact over a 100-day period. On the average, each person listed some 500 names. Milgram's own research, based on the idea that "it's a small world," suggested that each American has a pool of 500 to 2,500 acquaintances.[15] Even more surprising was Milgram's finding that a message given to anyone in the United States and passed only to people known on a first-name basis can reach any other person in the United States with an average of about five intermediaries. For example, a wheat farmer in Kansas was trying to get a message to an unknown graduate student in Cambridge, Massachusetts. The farmer gave it to his Episcopal priest who gave it to another priest in Cambridge who happened to know the graduate student. All this seems to suggest that Americans have developed a fantastic repertoire of acquaintances from which to select close friends.

The rapid changes we have seen in technology over the past decade also have affected our relationships by increasing the number of channels we have for communication. Our interactions with others used to be limited to phone calls, letters, or face-to-face conversations; most of us now also use texts, e-mail, and social media sites to keep "in touch" with people we care about. Relational partners are able to contact each other more easily—if they can't reach each other on the phone, they can always try sending a text message or an e-mail. This increased number of channels not only gives us greater access to those we love, it also gives us access to a larger number of people. For example, we can "meet" and "talk" with individuals from all over the world on the Internet. Cyberspace has created a whole new environment for social interaction. Indeed, research has begun to show that a fairly large proportion of those who use the Internet as a social vehicle form ongoing personal relationships, including friendships or romantic relationships, with some of the people they "meet."[16] Of course, the increased number of channels for communication comes with costs. One potential cost involves the choices that people make about which channel is most appropriate for the messages they want to send.[17] Making the wrong choice (e.g., using e-mail when a phone call would have been more appropriate) can result in negative impressions, misunderstandings, and even conflict. Another potential difficulty emerges from the anonymity associated with some of these new technologies. The Internet is one channel that allows individuals to easily conceal their identity and their intentions from each other. Some research suggests that deception is not only common but is expected among frequent Internet users.[18] Yet another cost involves the increased access we get to each other with all of these different communication channels. Although the greater access is convenient, it can create a need for more privacy. Having a cell phone go off several times during the course of a romantic evening may spoil the mood of one or both partners. Knowing that almost anyone can plug the name of a dating partner into an Internet search engine may make people more cautious about where and when they reveal their personal information.[19] As our privacy needs increase, we will begin to turn off our cell phones, remove our names from web sites, use caller I.D. to screen our calls, and limit the time we devote to answering e-mail messages.[20]

Frequent changes in our social environment also provide an opportunity to "start over" or outlive an undesirable past. In a new social setting, new modes of behavior can be communicated without an audience that is contaminated by, and holding you to, past behavior. You can interact with people anonymously on the Internet without ever revealing anything about your personal history. Similarly, when you move from one city to another or even from one job to another, you can change some of your behaviors without having to explain why. Each of us needs to have some intimate relationships, but we also need to be "the stranger on the train" too—to have situations in which commitments are not demanded. In fact, some people are more comfortable if they have only a minimal number of relationships in which strong commitments are necessary. Frequent change serves this need.

In summary, the patterns of work that you and others practice in this society will affect the way your relationships develop. We've examined only two possible forces: employment of both relationship partners and changing work environments. Economists and business forecasters suggest that in the future more couples will be working in their homes. The implications of this prolonged proximity to family members will certainly affect the conduct and expectations for these relationships.

Relationship Styles

In today's society, we have a greater variety of relationship styles available to us (with social approval) than ever before. It is an "era of options." Many people still choose to develop and conduct relationships in the manner of previous generations, but the number of people choosing alternative lifestyles is significant. Some are choosing to be married, and some aren't; some choose to live alone while others prefer to live with one or more people; some live with a partner of the same sex, and others choose a partner of the opposite sex; some decide to have children, and some don't; some raise their children with a spouse, and some don't; some have a sexual relationship before marriage, and some don't.

The variety of available relationship styles is quite extensive. To illustrate these trends and to show how dramatic changes have occurred in this society's acceptance of such trends, consider the following findings reported in several national studies:[21]

- Today, households consisting of a married couple with at least one young child are in the minority.
- Approximately 50 percent of the adult population in the United States is married, down from 72 percent in 1960.
- In 1970, men married at about 23 years of age and women married at about 21. Today, the average groom is 30 years old and the average bride is 28.
- More than half of couples who marry for the first time live together before they are married, whereas 50 years ago almost none did.
- In 1970, a little over 28 percent of adults in the United States were divorced, widowed, or always single. Today, that number has increased by about 50 percent.
- More than 50 percent of children are likely to be born into or spend part of their childhood in a single-parent family.
- The number of children living in homes with their grandparents increased 64 percent since 1991, when 4.7 million children lived with a grandparent. Today that number is 7.8 million.
- Nearly one in six people who get married (17 percent) marry someone from a different race, up from only 3 percent of newlyweds who were intermarried in 1967.
- Roughly 83 percent of people believe it is acceptable to be married and not have children.
- Seventy-five percent of people in the United States say it is morally acceptable to be single and have children.
- Although the vast majority of Americans (about 90 percent) still believe that extramarital sex is morally wrong, over 70 percent believe that premarital sex is morally acceptable.
- About 62 percent of U.S. adults believe that same-sex marriage should be legal.
- In 2017, approximately 10 percent of LGBT couples were married. Today, a majority (61 percent) of same-sex couples who live together are married.

A number of scholars have argued that one of the preeminent questions for people entering relationships in today's society is how to preserve warmth and closeness while at the same time holding onto this newfound freedom to choose. Whatever forms of interpersonal communication develop in response to this era of options for relationship styles, certain relationship needs will have to be satisfied. And a diversity of relationship types will have to be maintained to meet them. These needs include the following:

1. Individuals must know people who share their concerns; otherwise, they may develop feelings of social isolation or boredom.

2. They must know people they can depend on in a pinch; otherwise, they may develop a sense of anxiety and vulnerability.

3. They must have one or more really close friends, with ready access to those friends; otherwise, they may experience emotional isolation or loneliness.

4. They must know people who respect their competence; otherwise, they may manifest a decreased self-esteem.[22]

Attitudes Toward Self-Fulfillment

Up until the late 1950s, most Americans adhered to what has been called a "giving/getting" compact with society; that is, you get out of the system only as much as you put in. Self-denial and sacrifice were commonly accepted practices. In the late 1960s and throughout the 1970s, however, a new set of values emerged. Some people called it the "Me Decade"; others referred to it as cultural narcissism.[23] People were disenchanted because they felt they weren't getting back as much as they gave; that there was no payoff for self-denial and sacrifice; that individuals had a right to seek self-fulfillment by seeking gratification of whatever needs they felt; that if they didn't satisfy their desires today, tomorrow would be too late. The preoccupation with one's own improvement and satisfaction seemed well on the road to new heights as our society entered the era of options. It seemed that everyone would be able to achieve self-fulfillment.

But focusing exclusively on oneself often does not lead to self-fulfillment. As psychologist Marion Solomon notes, "It is assumed that members of both sexes can 'have it all'—a successful career and a happy family life . . . everyone gets what he or she wants. But that is not what most men and women experience."[24] National pollster Daniel Yankelovich suggests that by the early 1980s, people began to realize that even though they could have many things in life, having "everything" was not necessarily what they wanted. Yet for some, it was not clear what they wanted to have or what they were willing to give up. In Yankelovich's words:

> Among the people I interviewed, many truly committed self-fulfillment seekers focus so sharply on their own needs that instead of achieving the more intimate relationships they desire, they grow farther apart from others. In dwelling on their own needs, they discover that the inner journey brings loneliness and depression. They are caught in a debilitating contradiction: their goal is to expand their lives by reaching beyond self, but the strategy they employ constricts them, drawing them inward toward an ever-narrowing, closed-off "I." People want to enlarge their choices, but seeking to "keep all options open," they diminish them.[25]

Many scholars concur that the me-first, satisfy-all-my-desires attitude often leads to superficial and unsatisfying relationships. Why then, do many of today's young people seek material gain with such great fervor? Some argue that the continued emphasis on materialism is not so much an effort to satisfy desires as it is an effort to find security—security that often eludes people in a world in which economic prospects, personal safety, and even interpersonal relationships seem unstable.[26] So, one of the results of a cultural environment that has emphasized social diversity—represented by many alternative (and acceptable) lifestyles—is that the promise of self-fulfillment has been high. But increased social diversity has also meant that some aspects of human contact have been more difficult—for example, we become choosier about social ties, we focus on our own needs to the exclusion of those of others, we find it harder to identify people with exactly matching interests, values, schedules, and tastes.

Although the greater diversity of relationships sometimes makes finding and maintaining relationships complex, there seems to be a trend away from self-centeredness and toward a greater commitment to all types of relationships. Today, more than ever, we hear people talking about developing healthy relationships, building bridges between different groups, and strengthening community ties. This is not to say that people will leave self-centeredness completely behind. As Amitai Etzioni, a professor and former White House advisor, notes,

> To suggest that most adults thrive on bonding is not to suggest that their individuality needs to be lost as they become immersed in a relationship. . . . To suggest a higher valuation of the we-ness of being a couple . . . does not entail giving up a personal identity.[27]

Focusing on oneself can play an important role in developing a strong identity and achieving personal ambitions. The current trend suggests not that we subvert ourselves, but rather that we emphasize a commitment to others—that we recognize the centrality of relationships to our lives. This increased focus on relationships may be encouraged by several factors. For instance, the proliferation of self-help books and websites emphasizing the importance of interpersonal relationships to individuals' health and happiness may encourage people to make a stronger commitment to their associations with others. Additionally, because many of the relationship types we see today (e.g., cohabiting couples, stepfamilies, gay/lesbian couples) are not fully supported by our social institutions, it is possible that the people involved in these relationships rely on an increased sense of commitment to maintain their ties to each other.[28] Some also argue that an increased commitment to interpersonal relationships and community is necessary if we are to deal with many of the economic and societal difficulties we face today.[29]

Messages from the Mass Media

Images of what relationships are like and how people should communicate in them are also featured in the daily messages we receive from television, magazines, music, books, and movies.[30] Some of these images reinforce stereotypes while others try to portray preferred or idealized behavior; some capture the reality we live in pretty well while others seem to be mostly fiction; some seem to have a sizable impact on us while others have minimal influence; some we consciously accept, reject, or discuss with friends while others may affect us in more subtle ways. Nevertheless, the images of communication and relationship development in the mass media are based on reciprocal influence: our behavior contributes to what appears in the mass media and the images portrayed in the mass media have an impact on our everyday expectations and behavior.

Popular Literature

In the 1970s, Kidd examined all popular magazines in the United States with a circulation of more than one million over a twenty-year period.[31] She was primarily interested in articles that gave advice about interpersonal relations and how they reflected and influenced the climate of the times. She identified what she called *two visions*.

Vision I, prominent from the 1950s to the early 1960s, presented life in this society as relatively unchanging and consistent. If you wanted to be an interpersonal success, all you had to do was learn the ten easy steps and apply them to almost any situation. Articles during this period often were based on the premise that effective interpersonal relations are manifest only when everyone is happy. Therefore, communicators were advised to make every effort to elicit happiness in others. This could be done by giving compliments when you didn't want to or listening attentively and supportively to dull and boring interchanges. In short, it was argued that one's personal enrichment would be strengthened by trying to make others happy. This, of course, meant constantly thinking of others before yourself and avoiding confrontation, disagreement, and conflict at all costs. People were encouraged to avoid dating those with whom they argued by telling them they were "busy." This strategy was supposed to be in the best interests of both parties because it avoided further immediate conflict arising out of telling the other person you simply didn't want to date them. Wives were advised to pretend to be satisfied during sex with their husbands even if they were not. This was described as "the worthiest duplicity on earth" in a 1957 article in *Reader's Digest*. Togetherness was another primary theme. Both men and women were supposed to enjoy their family so much they didn't even want a night out. If they did, there was a problem in their relationship. Thus, Kidd's analysis shows that the popular magazines of the 1950s and early 1960s advised American readers on how to create a good impression, put aside genuine personal feelings, and live up to a predetermined standard.

From the early 1960s to the early 1970s, a new set of guidelines for interpersonal behavior emerged (Vision II). These guidelines reflected a changing society. The idea of a single ever-effective standard for success was abandoned. Life and relationships were recognized as constantly changing entities. "Not all marriages are alike and cannot be measured by the same standard." Readers were encouraged to forsake the idea of self-sacrifice to make others happy and to substitute being their real selves. Only by being themselves were they ultimately going to be able to make others happy. Again, a corollary prescription followed. Rather than avoid conflict, people were encouraged to feel free to come together in an atmosphere of openness in which *any* feelings, no matter how argumentative, could be aired. The mere act of communication was the elixir for productive human relationships. No matter what the problem is, "we can talk it out."

To investigate whether the guidelines set out by Vision II have changed, a group of researchers conducted another study that followed up on Kidd's findings. Prusank, Duran, and DeLillo examined articles in popular women's magazines published from 1974 to 1993.[32] They found that the vision of interpersonal relationships portrayed during this time period differed from the views portrayed by Vision I and Vision II. Several interesting patterns make up what these researchers called Vision III. First, the content of Vision III articles represented a "softening" of the previous two visions. For instance, rather than present a strong orientation toward others (Vision I) or toward the self (Vision II), Vision III often took the middle ground, providing readers with relationship-oriented reasons for engaging in self-oriented behaviors (e.g., "it will make your romantic relationship more interesting"). Second, "equality" was an important component of Vision III. Relationship health and stability were obtained when there was a sense of balance between partners. Readers were not necessarily encouraged to distribute tasks equally, but instead to take advantage of their differences by distributing work on the basis of expertise. Third, to have a satisfying relationship with another person, people were told they must first have "knowledge"—both of themselves and of others. Such knowledge was said to provide relational partners with understanding and a realistic view of their own and others' expectations. Fourth, and finally, change in relationships was acknowledged, but it was described as predictable and cyclical (e.g., "all relationships go through difficult times").

Of course, it is important to remember that Vision III, as described here, emerged from popular women's magazines. Magazines typically read by men were not examined. It may be that the orientation toward relationships depicted in Vision III is one that was portrayed only in women's magazines. To examine this possibility, Duran and Prusank conducted another study comparing relational themes in women's and men's popular magazine articles.[33] Although they found that the types of relationships (e.g., romantic, dating) as well as the issues (e.g., sexual relations, understanding the opposite sex) raised in men's and women's magazines were similar, they also found some interesting differences. Articles in women's magazines were more likely to present relationships as complex phenomena and to take a cooperative, accommodating approach to relational issues. By contrast, articles in men's magazines tended to depict relationships as simple and often approached relational issues from a competitive, adversarial stance. The goal of many women's magazine articles was to help women understand men, whereas the goal of the men's articles often was to offer men a means to protect themselves from women. Findings such as these suggest that although the messages about relationships that are portrayed in popular magazines change over time, the way magazines and other popular media deal with relational issues likely depends on their audience.

Another important idea to consider is that none of the three visions discussed here gave much consideration to issues that talk could not resolve, to individuals who could not conform to disclosure norms, to couples who had difficulty understanding their relational expectations, or to situations in which separation would offer satisfactions unattainable by co-presence. Coping with these issues may be the substance of today's society and the content of what historians might call Vision IV.

Another type of popular literature that has been studied by researchers is the romance novel. In her study of romance novels, Hubbard examined the role relationships depicted between men and women across four decades.[34] Not unlike

Kidd's study, Hubbard found that during the 1950s the characters in romance novels played very traditional, complementary roles. Without exception, the hero was portrayed as "masterful, tall, handsome, passionate and powerful, educated, and engaged in a successful career." The heroine, on the other hand, was "young, small, isolated from family and friends, modestly educated, and low in self-esteem." She achieved personal fulfillment through romance, marriage, and family, whereas his needs were met through his own achievements.

In the 1960s and 1970s, these roles began to change. The typical heroine started to recognize the inequality of her relationship with the hero and made tentative efforts to change the situation. She sometimes insulted her partner as "despicable and arrogant," sought a traditionally male-dominated career, or declared that "nature intended her to be more than a docile showpiece." Her efforts, however, were usually destined for failure. In some cases, her own fragility, lack of support systems, or lack of education prevented her from making any independent moves. In others, the hero led her "gradually and forcefully" to see "the error of her ways."

Characters portrayed in the early 1980s were quite different from those of the three previous decades. Both the hero and the heroine became more realistic and lifelike. He was sometimes tall, handsome, and affluent but was not necessarily so. In many cases, he depended on the heroine to "help him reach his full potential." She was sometimes young, other times middle aged; sometimes small, other times nearly six feet tall. She was "most often highly skilled, artistic, or well-educated." The relationship between these two "new" characters also changed. They both became sensitive to interpersonal matters and caring about their relationship. They respected one another's ambitions and treated love, in part, as a pragmatic venture, focusing on "whether a permanent relationship will work, whether the parties are compatible, and whether the needs and desires of both participants can be satisfied."

In short, the characters of the early 1980s begin to portray what some scholars and trend forecasters have identified as the unifying theme of the early twenty-first century: the triumph of individual choice and responsibility. Individual respect, power, and sexual equality become the basis on which relationships are built. People do not seek relationships simply to fulfill needs for love or belonging, but also to fulfill self-actualization needs. They want to find meaning in their life and they believe that having a romantic relationship is part of that process. While, as Hubbard notes, it may be a number of years before we can accurately assess whether such ideals for romanticism have been accepted by the general public, many trend forecasters and sociologists argue that they have not only been accepted, but that they are thoroughly ingrained in our current understandings of interpersonal relationships.[35]

Television and Movies

Television and movies are important parts of our culture. In the average household, for example, the TV set is on about seven hours a day with actual viewing averaging about three hours a day. One of the prominent themes during both day and night programming concerns family and social relationships.

Television and movies today reflect different set of cultural norms and values than was seen in previous decades. The problems addressed in family situation comedies are more likely to be "Zak's anxiety over upcoming exams renders him temporarily impotent" rather than "Peter breaks Mom's favorite vase"; the inevitable "happy ending" of the past often is replaced with ambiguous or qualified happiness; the explicit "lesson" ("So always make sure you put a stamp on an important letter") is often more implicit or hidden among several possible "lessons" to avoid the charge of "preaching." Certainly many of the formal portrayals of days gone by have been replaced with images of a more casual society—fathers in family sitcoms of the past usually ate dinner in a tie and jacket. Sexual norms also have changed. Although the frequency of most types of sexual content on American prime-time network programming has actually decreased since 1975, the frequency of content related to gay male and lesbian sexuality has increased.[36] Similarly, analyses of both afternoon (soap operas) and evening programming show that references to or suggestions of sexual intercourse are more likely when the participants are unmarried than when they are married.[37]

As television programing moves away from happy endings, simple lessons, and conservative sexual norms, the effects of viewing television on our ideas about society and social relationships also are likely to change. Media influence the way we perceive certain social groups and social issues. For instance, one study demonstrated that exposure to different types of media content was associated with different beliefs about minority groups.[38] People who watched more TV entertainment programs thought that African Americans held higher socioeconomic positions, whereas those who watched more TV news believed that the same group held relatively lower socioeconomic positions. Most scholars agree that findings such as these reflect the fact that viewers often accept the portrayals that television presents. TV entertainment programs tend to feature models of financially successful African Americans, while TV news often depicts African Americans in lower socioeconomic contexts.[39]

Other studies similarly reveal that viewing certain types of programs can affect people's views about relationships and relational concerns. For example, research shows that people who watch soap operas are more likely than those who do not to overestimate the incidence of divorce, single parenthood, abortions, and sexually transmitted diseases in the real world.[40] Watching TV and movies also can influence what people think constitutes a good relationship. Systematic studies of TV shows and movies with romantic themes (such as romantic comedies) indicate that certain implicit beliefs about relationships are prevalent in the content.[41] For example, although storylines about "love at first sight" and living "happily ever after" may seem like stereotypes of a bygone era, those themes are still quite prominent in TV programs and movies.[42] Although such beliefs may seem harmless, they also may foster unrealistic notions about relationships, such as the idea that true love is so powerful that people who are in love do not need to expend effort maintaining their relationship.

Even though researchers have found links between the content of television and movies and people's attitudes about relationships, they are careful to note that people do not automatically accept what they see as reality. In some cases, the media influence people's perceptions and behaviors;[43] in others, they do not.[44] In yet other cases, the influence depends on viewers' motivation[45] or their perceptions of how realistic the programing is.[46] Furthermore, many scholars argue that television is not as much an *influence on* our perceptions as it is a *reflection of* our beliefs and stereotypes. If this is the case, television programming shows us what we expect (or what we want) to see and may reinforce our biases. For instance, researchers have found that the tendency to view romantic programming (e.g., romantic comedies, soap operas) is positively associated with idealistic expectations about marriage.[47] One explanation for these findings is that romantic programs cultivate unrealistic views of marriage, but it also is possible that people who idealize marriage have a tendency to watch programs that are romantic. Whether television is an influence on our perceptions, a reflection of our beliefs, or both, TV programming provides us with interesting information about the way society views interpersonal relationships.

Television programs also can serve as a vehicle for discussions about communication and relationships. The way we respond to what we see on TV can affect those around us. For instance, sometimes children's social skills are influenced by the way parents and children talk about TV characters.[48] Parents can provide guidance concerning characteristics that a child perceives he or she shares with a TV character. A child may identify with the constant victimization that Charlie Brown receives, but parents may point out how Charlie sticks with his relationships and how they all become friends at the end. Children (and adults) also may show identification with characters by imitating them. But again, input from family and friends (positive or negative) may be the critical factor determining the adoption of this behavioral style. Social skills also can be strengthened or weakened by the type of parental participation in a child's reenactment of TV episodes—for example, the hero saving the heroine or the monster terrorizing the helpless victim. In one study, children who were exposed to television programs portraying families whose members communicated in a concerned and supportive manner were more likely to perceive real-life family communication as similarly affiliative than were those who were not exposed to such programs. This was particularly true when the verbal and viewing behavior of their parents endorsed such perceptions.[49]

Finally, it should be noted that television and movies also may affect our understanding of and participation in various kinds of relationships by what they do *not* show. Studies continue to demonstrate that women, minorities, and nonconventional families are underrepresented characters on television.[50] Interaction patterns common to, for example, blue-collar families or certain ethnic minorities may be so rare (or stereotypical) that the implicit message is that such patterns are "nonstandard" and should gradually be abandoned if the group wants to advance in this society.

The Influence of the Immediate Physical Environment or Setting

Pictured in **Figure 4.1** are several settings where people meet and talk. There is also a list of statements. Try to match the statements with the environment you think is most and least likely to stimulate each statement.

You probably found some statements and environments that seemed to go together immediately and others that were more difficult to classify. Some statements may appear to fit several environments and others seem suited to only one.

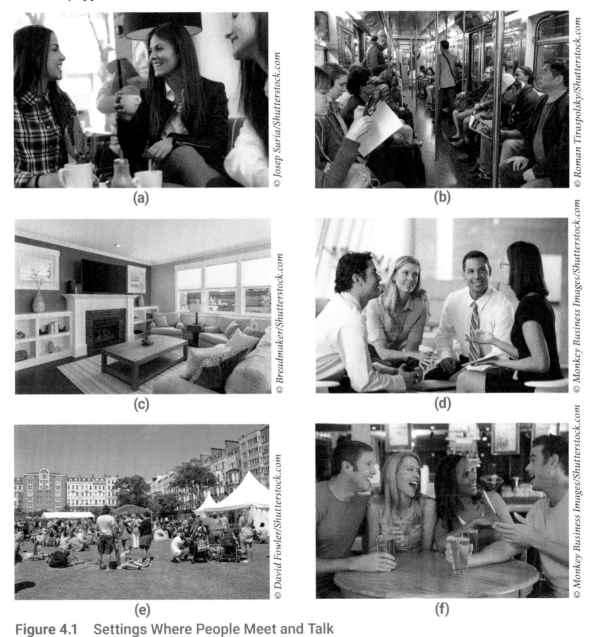

Figure 4.1   Settings Where People Meet and Talk

Statement	Most Likely to Appear in Setting:	Least Likely to Appear in Setting:
1. Good morning, Mr. Freedle. How are you today?	_____	_____
2. I just don't want to talk about it here. This just isn't the place to talk about such personal problems.	_____	_____
3. It was indeed a pleasure to make your acquaintance. I hope we meet again sometime.	_____	_____
4. Marge, I just don't know what I'm going to do. I feel so frustrated and confused about my relationship with Willie.	_____	_____
5. Now look, Grover, this is an important job we've been assigned and we have to do it right, so let's get to work.	_____	_____
6. Hey, dude . . . what's happenin'?	_____	_____
7. Oh wow! That's really weird!	_____	_____
8. Have you been here before?	_____	_____
9. So you're from Louisville. I remember one time I drove through there. Isn't there a . . .?	_____	_____
10. I feel so at ease and secure when I'm with you, Tyrone . . . if it isn't love it's so close it doesn't matter.	_____	_____
11. You're not going to believe what I just heard.	_____	_____
12. It really hurts me when you don't listen to me and you continually ask me to do things you know I don't want to do. You make me feel so small and insignificant when you do that.	_____	_____
13. You wanna go someplace this weekend?	_____	_____

The ease or difficulty in matching dialogue to setting is closely related to the ease or difficulty you had in answering such questions as: Who is likely to say this? To whom is the statement most likely directed? What environments do these people usually visit? What intimacy level does this statement suggest? What intimacy level does this setting suggest? Like any perceptual task, the job became increasingly difficult as the stimuli became more ambiguous. Environments and verbalizations representing extreme forms of intimacy, formality, and so on were obviously easier to code, but like most situations involving the attribution of meaning, the boundaries were not always so clear.

We do know, however, that each setting includes certain elements that may affect the communication-relationship interface.[51] People's perceptions and past experiences in a particular environment can evoke emotions that influence the way they interact with others. We also know that people enter settings with certain established relationships and communicative intents. The existing relationship (stranger, friend, enemy) and the purpose for communicating (small talk, marriage proposal, counseling) affect one's perception of the environment and may prompt the participants to restructure the environment to approximate more closely their relationship and purpose. Such restructuring can take the form of moving closer or farther away; arranging objects to create moods—the last-minute staging of one's home for that special, intimate evening by lighting candles, putting on soft music, preparing drinks, fluffing pillows on the couch, hiding dirty dishes, trash, and other nonintimate material associated with daily living; arranging the objects in the environment to establish or reflect certain role relationships, to demarcate boundaries, or to encourage greater affiliation. The typical "executive suite," for instance, may not be designed to encourage personal counseling, but chairs and other artifacts can be altered and arranged to make it more conducive to a helping relationship rather than a more formal, business relationship. Sometimes communicators will perceive seemingly inappropriate settings as appropriate. This is most often the case when the relationship bond is strong and the urgency to communicate is great. Lovers who will soon be parted sometimes seem oblivious to the rather cold and public features of an airport terminal, as evidenced by their intimate displays of verbal and nonverbal behavior. In short, the environment acts upon us, but we may also act upon the environment.

Any communication setting is composed of four major components: (1) the natural environment, (2) architectural structure and design features, (3) movable objects, and (4) the presence or absence of other people. Each of these components has the potential for facilitating or inhibiting certain kinds of communication.

To the extent that the natural environment influences our mood, stress-level, and sense of well-being,[52] it may have an effect on how we communicate with others. Most of us have felt unusually depressed on dark, overcast days or felt a surge of good feelings as we experienced the first signs of spring. Similarly, many of us have felt edgy or tense in a crowded urban area or calm and relaxed when on a long drive in the country. Although many factors in the natural environment, such as sun spots, moon positions, humidity, and noise, may affect our behavior, social scientists have been particularly interested in temperature and barometric pressure. Some believe extremely hot or cold weather will increase irritability and bring on a mild depression; others argue that temperature extremes affect our irritability only when they are prolonged; still others believe that our mood is more negative when barometric pressure drops. In one study, students showed less interpersonal attraction for other students as temperature and humidity increased.[53] Some studies associate aggressive acts with increases in temperature and humidity.[54] Others suggest that the positive association between aggression and temperature actually tapers off at a certain point when the temperature is too hot.[55] Most researchers agree that there are a lot of factors that interact with temperature and humidity to bring on aggressive acts—for example, prior provocation, the presence of aggressive models, or perceived ability to leave the environment.[56]

Extensive research in human ecology affirms the different psychological and social effects of environmental factors such as walls, room size, lighting, materials (wood, metal, tile, cloth), soundproofing, doors, hallways, chairs, desks, tables, fences, and many, many more.[57] The various features that make up our environment can affect our psychological and physiological well-being as well as the way we interact with others.[58] For instance, one investigation showed that children in classrooms without windows were more sociable (talkative) in class than were those exposed to some natural light.[59] A potential reason for these findings is that the children in windowless classrooms produced higher levels of a stress hormone (cortisol) than did the other children. The increased talkativeness of the children in the windowless classrooms may have been a reaction to their comparatively higher levels of cortisol. Another investigation demonstrated that people can use cues from the physical environment (e.g., cleanliness, level of decoration, neatness) to form impressions of others.[60] Participants in this study were asked to evaluate the personality of individuals after looking at their offices and bedrooms. In a considerable number of cases, participants' ratings of the individuals who occupied these spaces matched the actual personality of the occupants.

In addition to being affected by various aspects of the environment, communication settings also may be affected by the presence or absence of others. When other people are part of the setting, they may be seen as active or passive participants, depending on the degree to which they are perceived as involved (speaking or listening) in the conversation. In most instances, others are perceived as active, if for no other reason than that they are able to overhear what is being said. There are, however, situations in which other persons are granted the dubious title of "nonperson" and the main participants behave accordingly. This may occur in high-density situations, but it also is common with just one other person. Cab drivers, janitors, and children have been known to achieve nonperson status with some regularity. The presence of nonpersons, of course, allows the free, uninhibited flow of interaction because as far as the active participants are concerned, they themselves are the only human interactants present. Some parents have been known to talk to other people about highly personal aspects of their small children's lives in the children's presence as if they weren't there. Naturally, any perceptible response by the nonperson (verbal or nonverbal) to what is being said automatically reinstates "person" status.

When others are perceived as an active ingredient in the environment, it may facilitate or inhibit certain kinds of communication. The chief difference in communication with active others is that messages must be adapted to multiple audiences rather than to a single listener. Even telephone conversations, when the third party can hear only one of the interactants, are altered to account for the uninvited listener. Sometimes the existence of these additional audiences presents such a strain or threat that one or both communicators leave the scene. On the other hand, the appearance of a third party provides an opportunity to ease out of a conversation with an undesirable other by dumping the focus of interaction on the third party and making a polite exit. The presence of others may increase our motivation to look good in what we say and do, which can be detrimental (distorting information) or beneficial. The benefits of looking good in the presence of others are exemplified in the form of constructive approaches to conflict (see Chapter 8). In numerous cases, the presence of others prohibits overt fighting from arising at all. Certainly such benefits may be temporary in nature—for example, "catching it" later.

Generally, we would expect to find more breadth and depth of communication when the interdependence among those present is high; when interdependence is medium or low, communication will probably be less personal, more ritualistic, and more stereotyped—a form of communication designed for a broader, less specific audience.

Our Perceptions of Communication Environments

Any effort to provide a framework for looking at the interdependence of environmental stimuli and human communication necessitates a consideration of what these environments are. The range of interpersonal settings confronting us is staggering. We communicate in restaurants, public restrooms, classrooms, dormitories, churches, cars, all forms of public transportation, homes, elevators, offices, parks, theaters, bars, hotels, institutions, and on street corners. Despite this diversity, each environment has a particular configuration of features that causes us to perceive it in certain ways. These perceptions, in turn, help structure the messages we choose to make. Some perceptions foster communication typical of early stages of development in relationships; some foster communication typical of more intimate stages; some environments generate perceptions that provide an "ideal" setting for communication in deteriorating relationships. The following sections are about different types of perceptions and include hypotheses about the kind of communication that may flow from these perceptions.[61]

Perceptions of Formality Sometimes we perceive our environment along a formal-informal continuum. Perceived formality may be based on any number of stimuli within the setting. It may be based on the decor or on the normal functions associated with a particular room—most kitchens offer a more formal setting than do most bedrooms. Perceived formality may derive from the apparel worn by those present—black tie, come as you are, uniforms. As discussed earlier, the mere presence of others may designate greater formality; it follows that increasing the number of participants many times increases the formality of the setting. Using the dimensions of communication in developing relationships presented in Chapter 1, we would hypothesize that as formality

Formality: A relatively strict adherence to rules or conventions.

increases, we are more likely to find communication that has less breadth and depth. In addition, we are likely to see communication that is more stylized (the prescribed range of responses is narrower), less relaxed, more hesitant, and generally more difficult.

Perceptions of Warmth Warmth, as discussed here, is a broader concept than one's physiological reaction to temperature. When environments are perceived as warm, we are more inclined to linger, to feel relaxed and comfortable. Warmth may be associated with plants, woodwork, carpeting, soft chairs, drapes, lack of harsh lighting, or soundproofing. Although most research on human reactions to color has not attempted to alter systematically the color of an entire environment, it does tell us that colors may have a distinct impact on our perceptions of warmth or coldness of a setting. Wexner, for example, found the color blue to be the most frequently associated with the following mood tones: secure, comfortable, tender, soothing, calm, peaceful, and serene.[62] Several experiments have tested the effects of "beautiful" and "ugly" rooms. In many respects, warm and cold settings are analogous to beautiful and ugly ones. The ugly or cold room was described as producing monotony, fatigue, headaches, discontent, irritability, and hostility. Beautiful rooms elicited descriptive words such as: pleasure, comfort, enjoyment, importance, and energy. Participants in the beautiful rooms wanted to continue their activities while those in ugly rooms engaged in a wide range of avoidance or escape tactics. Beautiful rooms also seem to elicit more positive evaluations, better recall, and more effective problem solving.[63] Fast food chains often attempt to design environments that will remain inviting (some warmth) but encourage rapid turnover (some coldness).

The aforementioned research does not offer much specific data regarding actual communication behavior. We would, however, predict that the greater the perceived warmth, the more likely we would find personal, spontaneous, and efficient communication patterns.

Warmth: A sense of comfort, affability, or hospitality.

> *I don't like cold weather, and I found the schools cold, so I selected art. I liked that room because it was so warm. Of course, I loved my teacher too. But it was only years later that I accepted the fact that I generated heat because I was so happy in that room.*
>
> —Louise Nevelson

Privacy: Confidentiality; a freedom from being observed or disturbed by others.

Perceptions of Privacy Doors and walls (enclosed places) usually connote more private settings. When a person is seen entering an office and closing a door that is usually left open, curious viewers may ponder the need for privacy and the specific content of the private communication. Privacy also may be perceived in open places—without any doors or walls. The critical determinant is that the setting is not subject to other people freely entering or overhearing the active participants' conversation. However, even enclosed settings, without other people, can sometimes connote a certain publicness—a therapeutic interview in a large lecture hall.

A number of studies have demonstrated that people's ability to manage privacy within their environment is associated with a sense of well-being.[64] Privacy allows individuals the chance to engage in solitary activities (e.g., quiet contemplation), but it also creates an opportunity for intimate communication.[65] Having privacy enables us to share something special with others. For instance, personal objects of one or both communicators in the environment may contribute to perceptions of privacy—family pictures, a toothbrush, trinkets. Accessibility to these objects ("You can use my toothbrush") will increase as intimacy increases. Giving a loved one access to private objects shows that privacy involves more than just closing ourselves off from the outside world. It also gives us the opportunity to open ourselves up to those we trust.[66] Settings perceived as private usually encourage closer speaking distances, greater depth and breadth of topics discussed, and communication designed to fit a special relationship with one or two other people. In other words, our communication is likely to be flexible and spontaneous.

Perceptions of Familiarity Unfamiliar environments are much like unfamiliar people—typically calling for more cautious and hesitant communication. The slow, deliberate, and tentative nature of such communication is compounded only when we meet an unfamiliar person in a totally unfamiliar setting. We generally prefer familiar places.[67] Since we are uncertain of the norms or typical responses associated with unfamiliar environments, there is increased pressure to suspend overt judgments of the other person. Hence, initial communication in unfamiliar settings will probably be more awkward and difficult as we try to go slowly until we can associate this environment with one we know. For example, the spontaneity of children is sometimes severely curtailed on that first visit to Grandma's house. We would predict that familiar environments, even though they also are perceived as formal and public, will allow greater flexibility in communicating than unfamiliar environments, even though they also are perceived as informal and private. At least in the familiar environment, we know the range of acceptable responses. One explanation given for the stereotyped structures of fast-food restaurants is that they allow a mobile, constantly changing society to readily find a familiar predictable place that will guarantee minimum demands for active contact with strangers. When a relationship is in its early stages of development and the participants are in an unfamiliar setting, we would predict little or no rapid movement toward greater intimacy. This is provided, of course, that the people involved don't perceive a strong outside threat that would throw them together. In fact, in an unfamiliar setting, the most likely topic for small talk will be the environment itself. Even intimates, when confronted with unfamiliar settings, will initially linger longer at the experimenting stage.

> **Familiarity:** Being well-known, recognizable, or understood.

Perceptions of Constraint Part of our total reaction to a setting is based on our perception of whether (and how easily) we can leave it. There can be a definite difference in an individual's perception of confinement or constraint when his or her in-laws are visiting for an evening versus visiting for a month. The intensity with which we perceive an environment as constraining also is closely related to the space available to us and the privacy of that space. Many environments seem to be only temporarily constraining—a long car trip—but there are

> **Constraint:** A feeling of being limited or restricted.

those that most of us would consider rather extreme cases of environmental constraint—certain institutional settings (prisons, nursing homes), spacecraft, and the settings allowed a sequestered jury during a long trial.

A study by Taylor and others presents some information about how people communicate in *anticipation* of such conditions. Navy personnel were ostensibly being considered for a stint in an undersea capsule. They were told they would have to live and work with another sailor. Then they were allowed to talk over an intercom for three hours with a person they might be teamed with (actually a confederate). Some subjects were told the confinement would last three weeks; others were told they would live underwater for six months. When the conversations of the subjects were analyzed, there was generally less self-disclosure in the situations in which long-term commitment was expected, and especially when the confederate gave negative or unfavorable responses.[68] This study deals only with strangers and the expected environmental constraints, not interaction as it develops within a confined setting. It does suggest the possibility that there will be an initially slow revelation of personal information when physical and/or psychological constraint is perceived as high. In the same manner, we might expect such conditions to extend the duration of other communication behaviors typical of early stages in a relationship.

Perceptions of Distance Another important environmental perception concerns how close or far away the environment forces us to conduct our communication with another person. Very often identifiable facets of the environment create greater physical distance—tables, chairs, desks, offices on a different floor, houses in different parts of the city. Distance perceptions, however, are based on both physical and psychological proximity. An individual may be seated close to someone and still not perceive it as a close environment—for example, if both people are sitting in immovable chairs that are not facing each other. Romantic partners who live 500 miles away from each other may not perceive they have a long-distance relationship if both own private planes and have unlimited funds for visits and phone calls. Also, women and men tend to use space in different ways. Women usually interact with each other at closer distances than do men. But when a threat is perceived, women tend to increase their distance from the source of the threat and leave the scene more quickly than do men.[69]

> **Distance:** A reflection of detachment, remoteness, or a lack of intimacy.

As the intimacy of the relationship increases, there is a gradual shrinking of the distance barrier; in the same manner, shrinking the distance barriers can facilitate more intimate communication. Thus, we can intentionally reduce or extend distances we deem inappropriate. The closest proximity is usually associated with love, comfort, and protection. The corresponding communication behaviors include touching, a softer voice, and so on. When the setting forces us into close distances that are not desired—such as elevators, eight people in a compact car, or crowded buses—we will probably find people making efforts to increase distance psychologically and thereby reflect a less intimate feeling. This may include less eye contact, body tenseness and immobility, cold silence, nervous laughter, joking (often about the intimacy), and other strategies designed to keep the conversation public and directed to all present. If people must talk under such conditions, they usually avoid anything but small talk, trying to offset the unavoidable intimacy messages imposed by the environment.

A few qualifying remarks are in order. The preceding discussions focused on only some of the dimensions along which settings may be perceived. Little research and a lot of speculation are behind the hypothesis here that intimate communication is more often associated with settings perceived as informal, warm, private, familiar, unconstrained, and close. The discussion of these perceptions was generally limited to extreme examples—either formal *or* informal, public *or* private. In daily life, many of our perceptions are not so polarized and are more accurately represented as points on a continuum. For clarity of discussion, each dimension was discussed separately, but again typically we experience a mixture of these perceptions for any given setting. In an elevator, for instance, you may perceive it as close, familiar, and only temporarily confining, but it may also be public (assuming others are present), formal, and cold. It is this combination of intimate and nonintimate factors that acts on and interacts with the choice of what we ultimately say. In some cases, we may perceive one dimension so strongly that it will override other perceptions, provide the critical influence, and possibly even block any awareness that other perceptions were made.

Even though we know that environments add substance to our perceptions of communication situations, we are unsure exactly how these perceptions relate to the messages we produce. We know that people get used to and adapt to inappropriate settings, but we're not sure how that process works. We also know that careful selection of the environment may make a difference in the outcome of the encounter and the resulting relationship. In fact, sometimes we deliberately select incongruous settings—reprimanding someone in an intimate setting in order to soften the impact or to show personal concern.

The Influence of New Media and Communication Technologies

Just a few decades ago, mobile telephones did not exist. E-mail was something only a few people in the military and elite universities used. Nobody had heard of text messaging—unless you count telegrams. There was no such thing as browsing the web and certainly no online dating sites or social media sites. Millions of Americans can remember a time when the idea of video chat was literally something out of science fiction.[70]

Given the dramatic changes in communication technologies in the past few decades, it is not surprising that many scholars and pundits have asked what impact these technologies have on us and our relationships.[71] One common assumption is that the rapid increase in online connections has undermined the quality of our relationships. In fact, numerous writers have been concerned that online activity would come at the expense of maintaining the deeper relationships that people had prior to the internet becoming widely available.[72]

To be sure, there are times when the use of communication technologies can contribute to relational deterioration. For example, the internet can provide a means for a romantic partner to engage in infidelity and/or to form emotional attachments outside the relationship.[73] Moreover, some married people become compulsive internet users, which means that even though they have negative experiences while using the internet, and they would like to use it less, they find it difficult to control their online activities. Peter Kerkhof and his colleagues studied **internet compulsion** in marriage and found that when a spouse experiences extreme internet compulsion, it tends to foreshadow relational deterioration.[74]

Internet compulsion: An irresistible urge to have access to and use the Internet.

Phenomena like internet infidelity and internet compulsion make compelling media stories. Yet, it is important to recognize that internet infidelity and internet compulsion do not represent most people's experiences. For instance, the same Kerkhof study that showed that compulsive internet behavior was detrimental to marriages also showed that non-compulsive internet usage was actually associated with marital well-being. In other words, it appears that relationships suffer only if people use the internet in destructive ways, but most people who use the internet do not use it in such ways. In fact, in a systematic review of all the evidence, Boase and Wellman concluded that there was "little evidence of the internet harming social relationships or detracting from time spent socializing in person."[75]

In short, the effects of the internet and other communication technologies depend on how they are used. It is therefore important to think about how and why they are used in relational communication. A key concept in understanding the use of communication technologies is an affordance.

Affordances

Affordances refer to the communication acts or functions that are made possible by particular features of a communication channel. The internet and social media sites make it possible to announce major events in your life to hundreds of people immediately and all at once. This would be difficult to do without technological help. Being able to text makes it possible to tell your relational partner something without engaging in an entire conversation. Every mode of communication has certain affordances. Rather than trying to list every possible affordance for every possible communication technology, scholars have tried to identify affordances that are particularly noteworthy because they help define what is distinctive about certain communication modes.

Editability: A state of being correctable, changeable, or modifiable.

One commonly discussed affordance is **editability**.[76] Editability refers to the fact that, with certain kinds of new media, like an online dating site, you can experiment with different phrases and descriptions, changing it as many times as you want. This is obviously not something you can do if you meet somebody face to face—once you have said something, you can't unsay it. Also, notice that editability is a feature of some aspects of the internet but not others. If you are using the internet for a video chat, for example, you will not be able to edit your messages indefinitely.

Another important affordance that some new communication technologies have is **asynchronicity**, which means that whatever message you compose is not necessarily received by the target right away. If you decide to talk with your partner on the phone, that mode of communication would not afford you with asynchronicity. Whatever you say over the phone will be heard practically immediately by the other person. If you decide to say something to your partner by e-mail, however, your partner is unlikely to read it immediately, and might not even see it for hours or even longer.

Asynchronicity: A quality that occurs when objects or events exist or happen at two differnet times.

By definition, affordances allow us to do things with our communication. That might sound like an inherently good thing, but it is important to recognize that affordances also allow for communication acts that we might not like. For example, social media sites can afford users opportunities for **surveillance**. Researchers have repeatedly found that people use social media sites (e.g., Facebook or Instagram) to check up on relational partners or friends.[77] Social media sites can be used to figure out where others have been, who they were with, and so forth. Usually, this behaviour is innocuous, but it can be intrusive and even dangerous in extreme cases. Some people even use social media sites to gather information so that they can stalk somebody.

Surveillance: Close monitoring or observation. Being well-known.

As the examples of various affordances illustrate, advances in communication technologies are not inherently good or bad for relationships. The value of affordances is based on how they are actually used. Thinking about affordances is useful because it encourages us to think about what exactly is really new about emerging communication technologies—and what is not actually unique to these technologies. According to internet scholar Nancy Baym, research on the internet is "a domain too often plagued by the notion that everything is new," but this view often ignores ways of communicating that have been around for a long time.[78] Some authors, for example, suggest that new technologies allow people to engage in routine relational communication, even when the people are separated by long distances.[79] Yet people have been able to communicate via telephone and via mail for a very long time—so communicating across distances is not really new. Also, some new technologies allow people to "lurk" on social media sites and other interactive webpages. Lurking on the internet is clearly a new phenomenon, and some scholars have argued that it is important because it allows you to find out about people without interacting with them.[80] At first, it might seem like the ability to find out about people without interacting with them would be an affordance that is unique to certain kinds of internet sites. Upon further reflection, however, it is clear that people have been able to find out about others without interacting with them for a very long time. For example, the possibility of unobtrusively watching how somebody interacts with others is not exclusive to the internet. Rather than approaching somebody at a party, for instance, you might seek to learn about this person by watching how he or she interacts with other people at the party. This strategy can yield information that would be crucial in deciding whether to initiate interaction with that person. If you observe the person being nasty to someone else, for instance, you might decide to check out somebody else. Or, after watching this person hold hands with somebody else, you might reasonably conclude that this person already has some kind of relational partner at the moment. In 1979, Charles Berger called such observations of others **passive strategies**, which involves techniques for observing another to glean information without directly interacting.[81] Given that Berger described passive strategies in the 1970s, it is clear that the ability to unobtrusively learn about another person predates the internet by a long time. There are undoubtedly unique aspects of online lurking, but the possibility of unobtrusive observation is not one of them.

Passive strategies: Strategies that are indirect; for example, watching, listening, and observing.

As such examples illustrate, when thinking about the effects of new communication technologies, it is important to think not only about what has changed but also what has not changed. One cannot really understand the impact of these technologies on our relationships if one assumes that everything one does with them is an entirely new phenomenon. In most instances, the introduction of a new technology brings some tweaks to the way some relationships are negotiated, but the underlying principles of how relationships develop remain very similar to what they have been. Another example that illustrates how new communication media can change some features of relational communication without undermining the general principles of relational development is the phenomenon of online dating.

Online Dating

Online dating refers to initiating a relationship via the internet. This can occur though an online dating site, such as Match.com or eHarmony, or it can also happen via mobile app, such as Tinder or mobile versions of dating websites. Online dating in the U.S. has become very common; in fact, one nationally representative study of over 19,000 people who married between 2005 and 2012 found that more than a third of the relationships were first initiated online.[82]

© Jane Kelly/Shutterstock.com

The term "online dating" is a bit of a misnomer because, even though it is common for people to meet through such sites, if the relationship endures very long, the people usually end up meeting in person and continuing with a relationship that is both offline and online. Thus, it is probably more accurate to refer to the interaction that occurs on such sites as "online relationship initiation" (or maybe "online relationship experimentation").

Because online dating sites are primarily geared toward finding partners and initiating relationships, much of the research on these sites has examined what people put in their online profiles and how people react to others' profiles. The content of people's profiles is often precisely what you would expect from the social exchange theory that was discussed in Chapter 2. People are strategic about the information that they present, trying to focus on the things that would make them a rewarding relational partner and minimizing the things that would make it costly to date them.[83] For example, they carefully choose profile pictures that they think are flattering, and people often exaggerate, portraying themselves as a bit more attractive than they think they actually are. Interviews with people who have used online dating sites suggest that many people who use such sites tend to use the metaphor of a marketplace to describe dating.[84] Therefore, presenting themselves in the most positive light possible gives them the best possible market value.

Not surprisingly, people who view others' online dating information are somewhat suspicious of what they see, and they typically attempt to determine if the person who put up the profile is being deceptive.[85] One strategy some people use to account others' potential exaggerations is to make adjustments—for example, if a man says he is 6' tall, someone considering his profile might assume that means he's about 5'10". Another strategy people use is **triangulating** the information provided with other sources of available information. For example, people will look for clues to see if a profile picture is an old one (e.g., a dated hairstyle might imply that the person's looks have deteriorated). People sometimes augment their viewing of profiles with visits to an internet search engine to see if they can find any additional, and potentially less flattering, information or pictures.[86]

Triangulating: Verifying data or information with several different methods or sources of data.

One of the biggest questions about online dating is how these relationships compare to other relationships in terms of happiness and longevity. If we went by just the advertisements for the online dating sites, the answer would be clear. Various sites pair people based on different information and mathematical formulas, and some claim that this allows them to find better mates for online daters than they could possibly find themselves. Notwithstanding the claims made by these sites, the scientific evidence for these claims is mixed, at best. In the aforementioned study of over 19,000 people married between 2005 and 2012, those who met online were slightly less likely to divorce and were slightly happier than were people who met offline. The differences were very small, however, and they might not be attributable to meeting online. Some of the online dating sites screen out people for various reasons; for example, eHarmony has a propriety algorithm for screening—so we do not know exactly how they pick which people to refuse, but we know that they do screen out some prospective daters. Although eHarmony will not reveal their criteria, it has been reported that they often screen out people with a history of depression.[87] Given that depression is related to being unhappy in one's relationships, it is possible that the martial satisfaction ratings for eHarmony are boosted by excluding people with depression (or other characteristics) that would lead to less positive evaluations of their marriages. Without companies releasing full details about how they screen and match people, it will be impossible to say whether any differences between meeting online versus in person are effects of the service or simply the service picking clients more prone to be happy. Even if it were to turn out that online dating sites have a positive impact on finding a suitable mate, it is clear that the differences would be very small—so small that the average person probably would not notice the difference. In short, no company's mathematical formula seems to capture sure-fire love.

Given that some of the online dating companies have spent a great deal of time and money developing their matching techniques, it raises the question: "Why are online dating services not particularly effective at creating satisfying relationships?" One explanation that Eli Finkel and his colleagues proposed is that the sites base their matching models on flawed assumptions about what is important in relationships.[88] Such sites typically match people based on various similarities in personality, attitudes, and beliefs. As discussed in more detail in Chapter 5, similarity does play a role in initial attraction,[89] but there are a number of other factors that determine whether a relationship will be satisfying in the long run. Finkel and his co-authors argue that although we are generally attracted to people who we think are similar to us, actual similarity between partners is not a particularly powerful predictor of who ends up happy in the long run. Instead, thinking you are similar to your partner seems to matter more than whether you actually are similar. Moreover, people who have good, satisfying relationships often come to see themselves as more similar to each other than they actually are.[90] Online dating sites cannot easily account for such factors in relationships.

Communication Technologies in Romantic Relationships

Although online dating is a special case in that it begins with a period in which all relational communication happens electronically, it is important to recognize that communication technologies are integral to most modern relationships. For many college students, access to their mobile phone and texting has become so crucial for connecting with others that they may experience significant anxiety if their mobile phones are taken away.[91]

Despite their importance in modern relationships, communication technologies in personal relationships are not replacing face-to-face communication. Communicating with a relational partner is not a zero-sum activity in which using one mode of communication (e.g., text messaging or instant messaging) necessarily decreases the extent to which you use other modes (e.g., face-to-face conversations). For example, in a study of how people use instant messaging to maintain relationships, Ramirez and Bronbeck found that the more people used instant messaging with particular partners, the more they also e-mailed them, talked to them on the phone, and talked with them face-to-face.[92] In another study, Caughlin and Sharabi found that the closer people's romantic relationships were, the more likely they were to use various modes of communicating in their relationship.[93] In close relationships, people typically do not choose communicating with technology or talking face to face; they communicate both with technologies and in person. Typically, as people get closer, they simply communicate more, both in terms of frequency of communication and in terms of using more means of communicating. A couple who primarily texts or talks in person early in a relationship will continue to text and talk, even if as they get closer they also add phone calls, direct messages via social media, or even video chats (e.g., via Skype or Facetime).[94]

Recognizing that people use multiple modes of communication in their relationships implies that we cannot always look at the modes separately.[95] Because people use these various modes in conjunction with each other, to understand the meaning of what is communicated through one mode, we often have to think of it in relation to what was communicated through another mode. Let's say, for example, that a couple had a great morning talking together until the boyfriend had to go to lecture. During the lecture, the girlfriend sends him a text saying, "When will your class be OVER?" In isolation, the text message would probably be understood as a request for information, and maybe he would text back something like "in 30 minutes." But given that they had just had pleasant face-to-face interaction before the class and they probably expect more face-to-face interaction after the class, he understands that the message means something more like "I miss you and can't wait to see you again." So, instead of giving her a time estimate, he texts back, "LUMU!"[96]

As the texting in class example illustrates, communication technologies sometimes allow us to have one conversation during a different type of interaction. Part of the meaning of the interaction may derive from the connection between the two modes of communication; for example, one feature of text messaging is it is possible to send somebody a private message even when that person is with other people, and the fact that it is a private message that is received while others are co-present makes the words mean something different than if the person just said the same words without the others co-present. The content of the message might be the same, but using texting to send private messages despite other people being present can send a relational message about the specialness of the interaction.

The flipside of texting with one person with others present, of course, is that this also can send a tacit relational message of exclusion to the person not privy to the texts. Texting with third parties while one's relational partner is present can interfere with relational communication. This illustrates a point that is crucial for understanding technology in relationships: The *way* people use communication technologies in relationships matters. The meaning of phone usage is shaped by what the partners do with their phones. If they use their phones to connect with others (and avoid talking to each other) when they are together, it means something entirely different than if they use their phones to create a private connection just for themselves in a crowded room.

© jesadaphorn/Shutterstock.com

There are many different possible connections among modes of communication in relationships. **Table 4.1** lists some examples. When reading the table, keep in mind that although these examples are all phrased in terms of what communication technologies can do in relation to face-to-face communication, these connections can be reciprocal. Just as you can use a communication technology to coordinate a face-to-face encounter, you can also use a face-to-face conversation to arrange communication via another communication channel. Imagine, for example, that Billy is planning to study abroad next term without his girlfriend Sally. In their last face-to-face conversation before Billy leaves, he might discuss with Sally how, they will always make sure to be available for a

Table 4.1	
Connections between Communication Technologies and Face-to-Face Conversations	**Examples**
Using technology to *coordinate* face-to-face conversations	• Sending an e-mail to arrange a meeting. • Texting in a crowd to find your partner.
Using technology to *extend conversations* that began face-to-face	• Sending a text after a heated argument to get the last word. • Phoning to say "I love you" one more time after an affectionate encounter.
Using technology to *allow a private side conversation* within a larger group conversation.	• Using instant messaging with one person to make fun of the other people in a meeting. • Texting a comment about sex to your romantic partner while you are both having dinner with your family.
Using digital media to *provide a topic* for face-to-face conversation.	• Asking a partner to look at someone's Facebook post so you can talk about it together. • Talking about the kid yodelling in Walmart that you both saw on YouTube.
Using communication technology to *supplement* a conversation.	• Using your smart phone to look up the answer to a question that comes up in conversation. • When describing an ex-partner to a friend, pulling up the ex-partner's Facebook page to illustrate a comment.
Using communication technology to *regulate* face-to-face conversations	• Setting a meeting reminder on your phone. • Having a friend call during a date to provide a potential escape if the evening is unsatisfactory.

Source: Mark Knapp, Anita Vangelisti, John Caughlin

Skype session at 2 p.m. local time—no matter what else is going on. Or, when saying goodbye to your partner for the day, you might say, "IM me later, okay?" Any of the examples in Table 4.1 could be reversed.

In addition to having various functional connections like the ones described in Table 4.1, it is important to recognize that communication technologies and face-to-face communication can both be utilized as part of the same conversation. So, for example, a couple may start a conversation face-to-face, then comment on it while they are apart via text. Later, they might talk on the phone about the same topic, before getting together again and talking face-to-face. Even though it occurs across these various channels, the partners can recognize it as all being part of the same "conversation." Various communication technologies and face-to-face communication do not work in isolation; they are often interconnected with each other in complex ways.

Moreover, as relationships become close, it does not just increase the frequency that people use various modes, it also increases the interconnections among various modes of communication; for example, people who are close may discuss the same topic multiple times using different means of communicating, essentially keeping a topic of conversation going over multiple encounters both when physically copresent and when apart. According to **communication interdependence theory**, the extent connections between modes of communication—and the smoothness transitioning among them—is a sign of a close relationship. In general, people who are able to switch easily among various modes of communication are more satisfied with their relationships than are people who have more trouble switching among modes.[97] This suggests that communicative efficiency in contemporary relationships often entails the ability to use multiple modes of communication and being able to switch among them seamlessly. It is important to recognize, however, that interconnections among modes of communication are not always satisfying. If people are using multiple modes of communication to extend their opportunities to express jealousy or engage in repeated arguments, the interconnections among modes of communication can amplify the impact of such negative impact of such interactions.[98]

Communication interdependence theory: A theory that explains the associations between the rewards and costs of interpersonal communication and people's expectations for, and satisfaction with, their interactions.

Summary

The basic theme of this chapter is a simple one: when we examine the reasons why people communicate the way they do, we must consider the potential influence of the environment within which that communication takes place. Communication and relationships are influenced in different ways by different cultures. This chapter focused on some of the characteristics of U.S. society and how various aspects of the environment are used and interpreted in that society. We examined the environment from three perspectives: (1) the cultural environment, represented by behaviors, attitudes, and values shared by enough people to exert an influence on the messages we make; (2) the physical environment, represented by natural or human constructions that frame our conversations and relationships; and (3) the technological environment in which contemporary relational communication occurs.

To summarize, we discussed four areas within the cultural environment: (1) patterns of work, (2) relationship styles, (3) attitudes toward self-fulfillment, and (4) messages from the mass media. Couples who try to combine a marriage, family, and career may find some personal and financial benefits, but they must also work especially hard to develop the communication skills necessary to offset potential relationship difficulties in such pursuits. Although our society is not as mobile as it was a few years ago, the fast-paced changes that many of us currently encounter in the workplace still affect the way we maintain our relationships and establish new friendships. In today's society, many different relationship styles are acceptable, so it should be easier for this generation to satisfy what Weiss believes we all need—relationships with people who share our concerns, people on whom we can depend in a pinch, one or more really close friends who are easily accessible, and those who respect our competence. Some people will no doubt be more confused as the number of relationship options becomes greater, but greater choice is definitely the trend. We also noted that the number of people who are preoccupied with their own self-interests seems to be diminishing. Some scholars and trend forecasters even believe we have moved into an era in which interpersonal and group commitments will supersede individual commitments and self-actualization is defined, in part, by the relationships people form with others—at least to a greater extent than we've experienced in the past thirty years in this culture. We concluded our discussion on the influence of culture by reviewing the messages we receive from popular literature, television, and movies concerning relationship growth and decay.

The second part of the chapter discussed the physical environment and its interrelationship with the messages communicators send and receive. Several perceptions were proposed in which are seen the component parts (architecture, objects, people, and the natural environment) of communication settings—formality, warmth, privacy, familiarity, constraint, and distance.

The last section of the chapter examined the influence of new communication technologies on relationships. Although much has changed in recent years with communication technologies, the evidence suggests that rather than being entirely changed by new technologies, people in relationships use communication technologies strategically. New communication technologies are not supplanting face-to-face interaction; instead, people are incorporating technologies into their relational communication in ways that create interconnections between face-to-face interaction and the technologies.

The possible effect of interpersonal needs discussed in the preceding chapter and the possible effect of communication environments in this chapter represent some major forces that influence communication behavior in developing relationships. Obviously, in any given situation or relationship, other factors may have a major modifying influence on message making—for example, individual values, roles, expectations, self-images, motivations, past history, reference groups, prescribed or perceived time to communicate, and the repertoire of communication skills available. Thus, like the proverbial blind men examining different parts of an elephant, we may accurately describe some influential factors in a communication situation but omit others necessary for a full understanding of what happened. It is the nature of human communication to be incomplete; we can't say everything about anything. We can, however, strive to increase the precision, accuracy, and relevance of what we do say. It is hoped that these two chapters have made you aware of the tremendous complexity attending human interaction and the multitude of contingencies attached to each human action. Trying to understand human communication is a humbling experience—with one's certainty of explanation often inversely correlated with one's grasp of the possible influential factors. Each communicator is a party to something different from, yet a part of, both of them—their relationship. A person cannot denounce the insensitivity of a friend or acquaintance without simultaneously denouncing a part of himself or herself. Any individual change in attitudes or behavior is diffused out across every other facet of one's personality, which, in turn, affects the partner to the relationship and, eventually, the relationship itself.

Selected Readings

The Sociocultural Environment

Bellah, R. N., Madsen, R., Sullivan, W. M., Swidler, A., and Tipton, S. M. *Habits of the Heart: Individualism and Commitment in American Life.* New York: Harper & Row, 1985.

Lasch, C. *The Culture of Narcissism: American Life in an Age of Diminishing Expectations.* New York: W. W. Norton, 1979.

Naisbitt, J., Naisbitt, N., and Philips, D. *High Tech/High Touch: Technology and Our Accelerated Search for Meaning.* New York: Broadway Books, 1999.

Packard, V. A. *A Nation of Strangers.* New York: David McKay, 1972.

Rainer, T. S., and Rainer, J. *The Millennials: Connecting to America's Largest Generation.* Nashville, TN: LifeWay Research, 2011. Toffler, A. *Future Shock.* New York: Bantam Books, 1971.

———. *The Third Wave.* New York: William Morrow, 1980.

Yankelovich, D. *New Rules: Searching for Self-Fulfillment in a World Turned Upside Down.* New York: Random House, 1981.

The Physical Environment

Brown, B. B., Werner, C. M., and Altman, I. "Relationships in Home and Community Environments: A Transactional and Dialectical Analysis." In A. L. Vangelisti and D. Perlman, eds., *The Cambridge Handbook of Personal Relationships*, pp. 673–708. New York: Cambridge University Press, 2006.

Evans, G. W., and McCoy, J. M. "When Buildings Don't Work: The Role of Architecture in Human Health." *Journal of Environmental Psychology* 18 (1998): 85–94.

Gudykunst, W. B., Ting-Toomey, S., and Nishida, T., eds. *Communication in Personal Relationships Across Cultures.* Thousand Oaks, CA: Sage, 1996.

Knapp, M. L., and Hall, J. A. *Nonverbal Communication in Human Interaction.* 7th ed. Boston, MA: Wadsworth, 2010.

Mehrabian, A. *Public Places and Private Spaces.* New York: Basic Books, 1976.

Plaut, V. C., Markus, H. R., and Lachman, M. E. "Place Matters: Consensual Features and Regional Variation in American Well-Being and Self." *Journal of Personality and Social Psychology* 83 (2002): 160–184.

Steele, F. I. *Physical Settings and Organization Development.* Reading, MA: Addison-Wesley, 1973.

Stokols, D., and Altman, I., eds. *Handbook of Environmental Psychology.* vol. 1. New York: Wiley 1987.

Valentin, J., and Gamez, L., eds. *Environmental Psychology: New Developments.* Nova Science, 2010.

Dual Careers

Aldous, J., ed. "Dual-Earner Families." Special issue of *Journal of Family Issues* 2 (1981).

Barnett, R. C., and Rivers C. *She Works/He Works: How Two-Income Families Are Happier, Healthier, and Better Off.* New York: HarperCollins, 1996.

Bell, R. A., Roloff, M. E., Van Camp, K., and Karol, S. H. "Is It Lonely at the Top?: Career Success and Personal Relationships." *Journal of Communication* 40 (1990): 9–23.

Bryson, J. B., and Bryson, R., eds. "Dual-Career Couples." Special issue of *Psychology of Women Quarterly* 3 (1978): 5–120.

Crompton, R. *Employment and the Family: The Reconfiguration of Work and Family Life in Contemporary Societies.* New York: Cambridge University Press, 2006.

Gilbert, L. A. *Two Careers/One Family: The Promise of Gender Equality.* Newbury Park, CA: Sage, 1993.

Schwartz, P. *Peer Marriage.* New York: The Free Press, 1994.

Silberstein, L. R. *Dual-Career Marriage: A System in Transition.* Hillsdale, NJ: Erlbaum, 1992.

Interpersonal Relations and the Mass Media

Alberts, J. K. "The Role of Couples' Conversations in Relational Development: A Content Analysis of Courtship Talk in Harlequin Romance Novels." *Communication Quarterly* 34 (1986): 127–142.

Bryant, J., and Bryant, J. A. *Television and the American Family.* 2nd ed. Mahwah, NJ: Erlbaum, 2001.

Dixon, R. L., and Azocar, C. L. "Priming Crime and Activating Blackness: Understanding the Psychological Impact of the Overrepresentation of Blacks as Lawbreakers on Television News." *Journal of Communication* 57 (2007): 229–253.

Doyle, M. V. "The Rhetoric of Romance: A Fantasy Theme Analysis of Barbara Cartland Novels." *The Southern Speech Communication Journal* 51 (1985): 24–48.

Duran, R. L., and Prusank, D. T. "Relational Themes in Men's and Women's Popular Nonfiction Magazine Articles." *Journal of Social and Personal Relationships* 14 (1997): 165–189.

Galician, M. L., and Merskin, D. L., eds. *Critical Thinking about Sex, Love, and Romance in the Mass Media: Media Literacy Applications*. Mahwah, NJ: Erlbaum, 2007.

Gerbner, G., Gross, L., Morgan, M., and Signorielli, N. "The 'Mainstreaming' of America: Violence Profile No. 11." *Journal of Communication* 30 (1980): 10–29.

Hetsroni, A. "Three Decades of Sexual Content on Prime-Time Network Programming: A Longitudinal Meta-Analytic Review." *Journal of Communication* 57 (2007): 318–348.

Kidd, V. "Happily Ever After and Other Relationship Styles: Advice on Interpersonal Relations in Popular Magazines, 1951–1973." *Quarterly Journal of Speech* 61 (1975): 31–39.

Macnamara, J. R. *Media and Male Identity: The Making and Remaking of Men*. New York: Palgrave McMillan, 2006.

Prusank, D. T., Duran, R. L., and DeLillo, D. A. "Interpersonal Relationships in Women's Magazines: Dating and Relating in the 1970s and 1980s." *Journal of Social and Personal Relationships* 10 (1993): 307–320.

Segrin, C., and Nabi, R. L. "Does Television Viewing Cultivate Unrealistic Expectations about Marriage?" *Journal of Communication* 52 (2002): 247–263.

Zillman, D., Bryant, J., and Huston, A. C., eds. *Media, Children, and the Family*. Hillsdale, NJ: Erlbaum, 1994.

Interpersonal Relations and New Communication Technologies

Baym, N. K. *Personal Connections in the Digital Age*. Cambridge, UK: Polity Press, 2010.

Boase, J., and Wellman, B. "Personal Relationships: On and Off the Internet." In A. L. Vangelisti and D. Perlman, eds., *The Cambridge Handbook of Personal Relationships*, pp. 709–723. New York: Cambridge University Press, 2006.

Henline, B. H., Lamke, L. K., and Howard, M. D. "Exploring Perceptions of Online Infidelity." *Personal Relationships* 14 (2007): 113–128.

Punyanunt-Carter, N. and Wrench, J. S., eds., *The Impact of Social Media in Modern Romantic Relationships*. Lanham, MD: Lexington Books, 2017.

Vitak, J., and Ellison, N. B. "Personal Relationships and Technology in the Digital Age." In A. L. Vangelisti and D. Perlman, eds., *The Cambridge Handbook of Personal Relationships* 2nd ed., pp. 481–493. New York: Cambridge University Press, 2018.

Walther, J. B. "Theories of Computer-Mediated Communication and Relationships." In M. L. Knapp and J. A. Daly, eds., *The SAGE Handbook of Interpersonal Communication*. 4th ed., pp. 443–480. Thousand Oaks, CA: Sage, 2011.

Wright, K. B., and Webb, L. M. eds. *Computer-Mediated Communication in Personal Relationships*. New York: Lang, 2011.

Notes

1. J. G. Oetzel and S. Ting-Toomey, "Intercultural Perspectives on Interpersonal Communication." In M. L. Knapp and J. A. Daly, eds., *The Sage Handbook of Interpersonal Communication* 4th ed. (Thousand Oaks, CA: Sage, 2011) pp. 563–596.

2. R. Goodwin and C. Findlay, "'We Were Just Fated Together' . . . Chinese Love and the Concept of *yuan* in England and Hong Kong," *Personal Relationships* 4 (1997): 85–92.

3. T. Holtgraves, "Styles of Language Use: Individual and Cultural Variability in Conversational Indirectness," *Journal of Personality and Social Psychology* 73 (1997): 624–637.

4. S. G. Timmer, J. Veroff, and S. Hatchett, "Family Ties and Marital Happiness: The Different Marital Experiences of Black and White Newlywed Couples," *Journal of Social and Personal Relationships* 13 (1996): 335–359.

5. K. W. Halford, K. Hahlweg, and M. Dunne, "The Cross-Cultural Consistency of Marital Communication Associated with Marital Distress," *Journal of Marriage and the Family* 52 (1990): 487–500; J. G. Oetzel, S. Ting-Toomey, M. Chew-Sanchez, R. Harris, R. Wilcox, and S. Stumpf, "Face and Facework in Conflicts with Parents and Siblings: A Cross-cultural Comparison of Germans, Japanese, Mexicans, and U.S. Americans," *Journal of Family Communication* 3 (2003): 67–93.

6. V. C. Plaut, H. R. Markus, and M. E. Lachman, "Place Matters: Consensual Features and Regional Variation in American Well-Being and Self," *Journal of Personality and Social Psychology* 83 (2002): 160–184; J. A. Vandello and D. Cohen, "Patterns of Individualism and Collectivism Across the United States," *Journal of Personality and Social Psychology* 77 (1999): 279–292.

7. P. R. Amato, D. R. Johnson, A. Booth, and S. J. Rogers, "Continuity and Change in Marital Quality Between 1980 and 2000," *Journal of Marriage and Family* 65 (2003): 1–22.

8. See, for example, J. A. Lavner and M. A. Clark, "Workload and Marital Satisfaction Over Time: Testing Lagged Spillover and Crossover Effects during the Newlywed Years," *Journal of Vocational Behavior* 101 (2017): 67–76; N. A. Roberts and R. W. Levenson, "The Remains of the Workday: Impact of Job Stress and Exhaustion on Marital Interaction in Police Couples," *Journal of Marriage and Family* 63 (2001): 1052–1067.

9. K. J. Kiecolt, "Satisfaction with Work and Family Life: No Evidence of a Cultural Reversal," *Journal of Marriage and Family* 65 (2003): 23–35.

10. K. M. Shockley and T. D. Allen, "'It's Not What I Expected': The Association between Dual-Earner Couples' Met Expectations for the Division of Paid and Family Labor and Well-Being," *Journal of Vocational Behavior* 104 (2018): 240–260.

11. V. Packard, *A Nation of Strangers* (New York: David McKay, 1972), pp. 7–8.

12. R. C. Barnett and C. Rivers *She Works/He Works: How Two-Income Families Are Happier, Healthier, and Better Off.* (New York: HarperCollins, 1996); A. Toffler, *The Third Wave* (New York: William Morrow, 1980).

13. "2018 Geographic Mobility Data Released," *U.S. Census Bureau*, November 27, 2018, retrieved from https://www.census.gov/newsroom/press-releases/2018/geographic-mobility.html.

14. B. Covert, "Americans Work Too Much Already, *The Nation* (September 28, 2018); J. Liberty, "The Erosion of the Middle Class—Why Americans are Working Harder and Earning Less," *The Mind Unleashed* (December 30, 2018).

15. S. Milgram, "The Small World Problem," *Psychology Today,* 1 (1967): 60–67.

16. For a review see J. B. Walther "Theories of Computer-Mediated Communication and Relationships." In M. L. Knapp and J. A. Daly, eds., *The SAGE Handbook of Interpersonal Communication.* 4th ed. (Thousand Oaks, CA: Sage, 2011), pp. 443–480.

17. Parks examined some of the relational demands that influence the choices people make about which channel to use when they communicate (see M. R. Parks, "Embracing the Challenges and Opportunities of Mixed-Media Relationships," *Human Communication Research* 43 (2017): 505–517).

18. K. M. Wolff, "Impression Management, Anonymity, and Deceptive Communication in Computer Chat." Paper presented at the annual meeting of the Central States Communication Association, Chicago, 1998.

19. M. A. Ostrom and M. Marshall, "Have You Googled Your Date? Searches Get Personal," *Austin American Statesman* (May 19, 2003) D1, D5.

20. J. Naisbitt, N. Naisbitt, and D. Philips, *High Tech/High Touch: Technology and Our Accelerated Search for Meaning* (New York: Broadway Books, 1999).

21. J. Adler, "Tomorrow's Child," *Newsweek* (November 2, 1998), pp. 54–64; L. L. Bumpass and H. Lu, "Trends in cohabitation and implicatins for children's family contexts in the United States," *Population Studies* 54 (2000): 29–41; M. W. Chapman, "Gallup: 71% of Americans Say Premarital Sex is Fine; 89% Say Adultry is Wrong," CNS News.Com, retrieved from https://www.cnsnews.com/news/article/michael-w-chapman/gallup-89-americans-say-adultery-wrong-71-say-pre-marital-sex-fine; Executive Summary, "The Decline of Marriage and Rise of New Families," Pew Research Center, retrieved from https://www.pewsocialtrends.org/2010/11/18/the-decline-of-marriage-and-rise-of-new-families/; R. Frye, "The Share of Americans Living Without a Partner has Increased, Especially among Young Adults," Pew Research Center, retrieved from https://www.pewresearch.org/fact-tank/2017/10/11/the-share-of-americans-living-without-a-partner-has-increased-especially-among-young-adults/; Gallup, "Gay and Lesbian rights: In Depth Topics A to Z," retrieved from https://news.gallup.com/poll/1651/gay-lesbian-rights.aspx; A. W. Geiger and G Livingston, "8 Facts About Love and Marriage in America," Pew Research Center, retrieved from https://www.pewresearch.org/fact-tank/2019/02/13/8-facts-about-love-and-marriage/; K. Joyner and G. Kao, "Interracial Relationships and the Transition to Adulthood," *American Sociological Review* 70 (2005): 563–581; J. A. Sweet and L. L. Bumpass, "Young Adults' Views of Marriage, Cohabitation, and Family." In S. J. South and S. Tolnay, eds., *The Changing American Family: Sociological and Demographic Perspectives* (San Francisco, CA: Westview,

1992), pp. 143–170; A. Thornton and L. Young-DeMarco, "Four Decades of Trends in Attitudes Toward Family Issues in the United States: The 1960s Through the 1990s," *Journal of Marriage and Family* 63 (2001): 1009–1037; U.S. Census Bureau, "Census Bureau Reports 64 Percent Increase in in Number of Children Living with a Grandparent over the Last Two Decades," retrieved from http://www.census.gov/newsroom/releases/archives/children/cb11-117.html; E. Wildsmith, N. R. Steward-Streng, and J. Manlove, "Childbearing Outside of Marriage: Estimates and Trends in the United States," *Child Trends Research Brief* (2011), publication #2011-29.

22 R. S. Weiss, "The Fund of Sociability," *Trans-Action* (July–August 1969). Weiss also notes the need for adults to nurture children. In a society with an increasing number of childless couples, we might see this need fulfilled vicariously through social work (the Big Brothers Big Sisters program), professional work (nurturing students), the children of other couples, or, we suppose, through pets or plants.

23 C. Lasch, *The Culture of Narcissism: American Life in an Age of Diminishing Expectations* (New York: Norton, 1979); P. Marin, "The New Narcissism," *Harper's* (October 1975), pp. 45–50. A best-selling book in the late 1970s was R. J. Ringer, *Looking Out for Number 1* (New York: Fawcett, 1978).

24 M. Chen, "The Issue with Millenials Isn't Narcissism But Our Depressing Culture of Mass Consumption," *Think: Opinion, Analysis, Essays* (January 20, 2018).

25 D. Yankelovich, "New Rules in American Life," *Psychology Today* 15 (1981): 40.

26 N. Howe and B. Stauss, *13th Gen: Abort, Retry, Ignore, Fail?* (New York: Vintage Books, 1993). See also J. Giles, "Generalizations X," *Newsweek* (June 6, 1994): 62–70; D. M. Gross and S. Scott, "Proceeding with Caution," *Time* (July 16, 1990): 56–62.

27 A. Etzioni, *The Spirit of Community: Rights, Responsibilities, and Communitarian Agenda* (New York: Crown, 1993).

28 W. J. Doherty, "Private Lives, Public Values," *Psychology Today* 25 (1992): 35–37.

29 T. S. Rainer, and J. Rainer, *The Millennials: Connecting to America's Largest Generation.* (Nashville, TN: LifeWay Research, 2011).

30 C. M. Bachen and E. Illouz, "Imagining Romance: Young People's Cultural Models of Romance and Love," *Critical Studies in Mass Communication* 13 (1996): 279–308.

31 V. Kidd, "Happily Ever After and Other Relationship Styles: Advice on Interpersonal Relations in Popular Magazines, 1951-1973," *Quarterly Journal of Speech* 61 (1975): 31–39.

32 D. T. Prusank, R. L. Duran, and D. A. DeLillo, "Interpersonal Relationships in Women's Magazines: Dating and Relating in the 1970s and 1980s," *Journal of Social and Personal Relationships* 10 (1993): 307–320.

33 R. L. Duran and D. T. Prusank "Relational Themes in Men's and Women's Popular Nonfiction Magazine Articles," *Journal of Social and Personal Relationships* 14 (1997): 165–189.

34 R. C. Hubbard, "Relationship Styles in Popular Romance Novels, 1950 to 1983," *Communication Quarterly* 33 (1985): 113–125.

35 S. B. Kaufman, "Self-Actualizing People in the 21st Century: Integration with Contemporary Theory and Research on Personality and Well-Being," *Journal of Humanistic Psychology* (in press).

36 A, Hetsroni, "Three Decades of Sexual Content on Prime-Time Network Programming: A Longitudinal Meta-Analytic Review," *Journal of Communication* 57 (2007): 318–348.

37 B. S. Greenberg and R. Busselle, "What's Old, What's New: Sexuality on the Soaps," *Siecus Report* 24 (1996):14–16; B. S. Greenberg, D. Graef, C. Fernandez Collado, F. Korzenny, and C. K. Atkin, "Sexual Intimacy on Commercial Television During Prime Time," *Journalism Quarterly* 57 (1980): 30–37. Also see F. R. Dillman Carpentier, E. M., Stevens, L. Wu, and N. Seely, "Sex, Love, and Risk-N-Responsibility: A Content Analysis of Entertainment Television," *Mass Communication and Society* 20 (2017): 686–709.

38 G. B. Armstrong and K. A. Neuendorf with J. E. Brentar, "TV Entertainment, News, and Racial Perceptions of College Students," *Journal of Communication* 42 (1992): 153–176. See also T. L. Dixon and C. L. Azocar, "Priming Crime and Activating Blackness: Understanding the Psychological Impact of the Overrepresentation of Blacks as Lawbreakers on Television News," *Journal of Communication* 57 (2007): 229–253.

39 O. H. Gandy and P. W. Matabane, "Television and Social Perceptions Among African-Americans and Hispanics." In M. K. Asante and W. B. Gudykunst, eds., *Handbook of International and Intercultural Communication* (Newbury Park, CA: Sage, 1989).

40 J. D. Brown and J. R. Steele, "Sexuality and the Mass Media: An Overview," *Siecus Report* 24 (1996): 3–9.

41 V. Hefner and B. J. Wilson, "From Love at First Sight to Soul Mate: The Influence of Romantic Ideals in Popular Films on Young People's Beliefs about Relationships," *Communication Monographs* 80 (2013): 150–175; B. M. Holmes, "In search of my 'one and only': Romance-oriented media and beliefs in romantic relationship destiny." *Electronic Journal of Communication* 17 (2007). For an analysis of reality dating shows like *The Bachelor*, see A. L. Ferris, S. W. Smith, B. S. Greenberg, and S. L. Smith, "The Content of Reality Dating Shows and Viewer Perceptions of Dating," *Journal of Communication* 57 (2007): 490–510. A key finding of this study was that salient attitudes expressed on these shows include the notions that women are sex objects, dating is a game, and men are driven by sex. Similar attitudes, albeit probably in less extreme forms, are also prevalent in prime time television: see: J. L. Kim, C. L. Sorsoli, K. Collins, B. A. Zybergold, D. Schooler, and D. L. Tolman, "From Sex to Sexuality: Exposing the Heterosexual Script on Primetime Network Television," *Journal of Sex Research* 44 (2007): 145–157.

42 B. M. Holmes and K. R. Johnson, "Where Fantasy Meets Reality: Media Exposure, Relationships Beliefs and Standards, and the Moderating Effect of a Current Relationship." In E. P. Lamont, ed., *Social Psychology: New Research* (Hauppauge, NY: Nova Science, 2009), pp 117–134.

43 A. Mulac, L. L. Jansma, and D. G. Linz, "Men's Behavior Toward Women After Viewing Sexually Explicit Films: Degradation Makes a Difference," *Communication Monographs* 69 (2002): 311–328; B. J. Wilson, D. Linz, E. Donnerstein, and H. Stipp, "The Impact of Social Issue Television Programming on Attitudes Toward Rape," *Human Communication Research* 19 (1992): 179–208.

44 W. J. Brown and M. J. Cody, "Effects of a Prosocial Television Soap Opera on Promoting Women's Status," *Human Communication Research* 18 (1991): 114–142.

45 V. Hefner and B. J. Wilson, "From Love at First Sight to Soul Mate: The Influence of Romantic Ideals in Popular Films on Young People's Beliefs about Relationships," *Communication Monographs* 80 (2013): 150–17; P, X, Kuo and M. Ward, "Contributions of Television Use to Beliefs about Fathers and Gendered Family Roles among First-Time Expectant Parents," *Psychology of Men and Masculinity* 17 (2016): 352–362.

46 H. Gamble and L. R. Nelson, "Sex in College Relationships: The Role Television Plays in Emerging Adults' Sexual Expectations in Relationships," *Communication Monographs* (2016): 83: 145–161.

47 C. Segrin and R. L. Nabi, "Does Television Viewing Cultivate Unrealistic Expectations About Marriage?" *Journal of Communication* 52 (2002): 247–263.

48 P. Messaris and C. Sarett, "On the Consequences of Television-Related Parent-Child Interaction," *Human Communication Research* 7 (1981): 226–244. See also D. J. Atkin, B. S. Greenberg, and T. F. Baldwin, "The Home Ecology of Children's Television Viewing: Parental Mediation and the New Video Environment," *Journal of Communication* 41 (1991): 40–52.

49 N. L. Buerkel-Rothfuss, B. S. Greenberg, C. K. Atkin, and K. A. Neuendorf, "Learning About the Family from Television," *Journal of Communication* 32 (1982): 191–201.

50 Research conducted by G. Gerbner, reported in "TV Stereotypes Persist, Study Shows," *Austin American Statesman* (June 19, 1993), 3; G. Gerbner, L. Gross, M. Morgan, and N. Signorielli "Living with Television: The Dynamics of the Cultivation Process." In J. Bryant and D. Zillmann, eds., *Perspectives on Media Effects* (Hillsdale, NJ: Erlbaum, 1986), pp. 17–40; A Mulac, J. J. Bradac, and S. K. Mann, "Male/Female Language Differences and Attributional Consequences in Children's Television," *Human Communication Research* 11 (1985): 481–506; R. Riffe, H. Goldson, K. Saxton, and Y. C. Yu, "Females and Minorities in TV Ads in 1987 Saturday Children's Programs," *Journalism Quarterly* 6 (1989): 129–136; T. Skill, J. D. Robinson, and S. P. Wallace, "Portrayal of Families on Prime-Time TV: Structure, Type and Frequency," *Journalism Quarterly* 64 (1987): 360–398.

51 The influence of the physical environment on the way people feel and behave has been studied extensively by researchers who are interested in retail sales and marketing. See, for example, A. Dijksterhuis, P. K. Smith, R. B. van Baaren, and D. H. J. Wigboldus, "The Unconscious Consumer: Effects of the Environment on Consumer Behavior," *Journal of Consumer Psychology* 15 (2005): 193–202; M. Helmefaulk and B. Hulten, "Multi-Sensory Congruent Cues in Designing Retail Store Atmosphere: Effects on Shoppers' Emotions and Purchase Behavior," *Journal of Retailing and Consumer Services* 38 (2015): 1–11; A. V. Madzharov, L. G. Block, and M. Morrin, "The Cool Scent of Power: Effects of Ambient Scent on Consumer Preferences and Choice Behavior," *Journal of Marketing* 79 (2015): 83–96.

52 For information on the association between the physical environment and individuals' mood, stress, and well-being, see C. Bertram and K. Rehdanz, "The Role of Urban Green-Space for Human Well-Being," *Ecological Economics* 120 (2015): 139–152; C. Keltz, G. W. Evans, and

K. Roderer, "The Restorative Effects of Redesigning the Schoolyard: A Multi-Methodological, Quasi-Experimental Study in Rural Austrian Middle Schools," *Environment and Behavior* 47 (2015): 19–59; M. Triguero-Mas, P. Dadvand, M. Cirach, D. Martínez, A. Medina, A. Mompart, X.. Basagaña, R. Gražulevičienė, and M. J. Nieuwenhuijsen, "Natural Outdoor Environments and Mental and Physical Health: Relationships and Mechanisms," *Environment International* 77 (2015): 35–41.

53 W. Griffitt, "Environmental Effects of Interpersonal Affective Behavior: Ambient Effective Temperature and Attraction," *Journal of Personality and Social Psychology* 15 (1970): 240–244; W. Griffitt and R. Veitch, "Hot and Crowded: Influence of Population Density and Temperature on Interpersonal Affective Behavior," *Journal of Personality and Social Psychology* (1971): 92–98.

54 C. A. Anderson and K. B. Anderson, "Violent Crime Rate Studies in Philosophical Context: A Destructive Testing Approach to Heat and Southern Culture of Violence Effects," *Journal of Personality and Social Psychology* 70 (1996): 740–756; C. A. Anderson, B. J. Bushman, and R. W. Groom, "Hot Years and Serious and Deadly Assault: Empirical Tests of the Heat Hypothesis," *Journal of Personality and Social Psychology* 73 (1997): 1213–1223; National Advisory Commission on Civil Disorders, "Report of the National Advisory Commission on Civil Disorders" (Washington, DC, 1968), p. 71. For a discussion of the controversy surrounding the association between heat and aggression see B. J. Bushman, M. C. Wang, and C. A. Anderson, "Is the Curve Relating Temperature to Aggression Linear or Curvilinear? Assaults and Temperature in Minneapolis Reexamined," *Journal of Personality and Social Psychology* 89 (2005): 62–66; E. G. Cohn and J. Rotton, "The Curve Is Still Out There: A Reply to Bushman, Wang, and Anderson's (2005) 'Is the Curve Relating Temperature to Aggression Linear or Curvilinear?'" *Journal of Personality and Social Psychology* 89 (2005): 67–70; P. A. Bell, "Reanalysis and Perspective in the Heat-Aggression Debate," *Journal of Personality and Social Psychology* 89 (2005): 71–73; B. J. Bushman, M. C. Wang, and C. A. Anderson, "Is the Curve Relating Temperature to Aggression Linear or Curvilinear? A Response to Bell (2005) and to Cohn and Rotton (2005)," *Journal of Personality and Social Psychology* 89 (2005): 74–77.

55 J. Rotton and E. G. Cohn, "Violence Is a Curvilinear Function of Temperature in Dallas Replication," *Journal of Personality and Social Psychology* 78 (2000): 1074–1081.

56 R. A. Baron and P. A. Bell, "Aggression and Heat: The Influence of Ambient Temperature, Negative Affect, and a Cooling Drink on Physical Aggression," *Journal of Personality*

and *Social Psychology* 33 (1976): 245–255; R. A. Baron and P. A. Bell, "Aggression and Heat: Mediating Effects of Prior Provocation and Exposure to an Aggressive Model," *Journal of Personality and Social Psychology* 31 (1975): 825–832.

57 S. Augustin, *Place Advantage: Applied Psychology for Interior Architecture* (New York: John Wiley & Sons, 2009); R. Sommer, *Tight Spaces: Hard Architecture and How to Humanize It* (Englewood Cliffs, NJ: Prentice Hall, 1974); M. L. Knapp, J. A. Hall, T. G. Horgan. *Nonverbal Communication in Human Interaction*. 8th ed. (Boston, MA: Wadsworth, 2014).; A. Mehrabian, *Public Places and Private Spaces* (New York: Holt, Rinehart and Winston, 1973), pp. 162–165; O. Newman, *Creating Defensible Space* (U.S. Department of Housing and Urban Development, P.D. & R, 1996). R. Sommer, *Design Awareness* (San Francisco: Rinehart Press, 1972).

58 G. W. Evans and J. M. McCoy, "When Buildings Don't Work: The Role of Architecture in Human Health," *Journal of Environmental Psychology* 18 (1998): 85–94.

59 R. Kuller and C. Lindsten, "Health and Behavior of Children in Classrooms with and Without Windows," *Journal of Environmental Psychology* 12 (1992): 305–317.

60 S. D. Gosling, S. J. Ko, T. Mannarelli, and M. E. Morris, "A Room with a Cue: Personality Judgment Based on Offices and Bedrooms," *Journal of Personality and Social Psychology* 82 (2002): 379–398.

61 A related schema for analyzing *situations* (a broader concept than settings) was advanced by Altman and Taylor. Their framework includes situational formality, situational confinement, and situational interdependence. Cf. I. Altman and D. A. Taylor, *Social Penetration* (New York: Holt, Rinehart and Winston, 1973), pp. 162–165. Other reviews and conceptualizations of social situations include M. Argyle, A. Furnham, and J. A. Graham, *Social Situations* (Cambridge, MA: Cambridge University Press, 1981); L. C. Miller, M. J. Cody, and M. L. McLaughlin, "The Situations and Goals as Fundamental Constructs in Interpersonal Communication Research." In M. L. Knapp and G. R. Miller, eds., *Handbook of Interpersonal Communication*. 2nd ed. (Beverly Hills, CA: Sage, 1994), pp. 162–198.

62 L. B. Wexner, "The Degree to Which Colors (Hues) Are Associated with Mood-tones," *Journal of Applied Psychology* 38 (1954): 432–435. See also D. C. Murray and H. L. Deabler, "Colors and Mood-Tones," *Journal of Applied Psychology* 41 (1957): 279–283.

63 A. H. Maslow and N. L. Mintz, "Effects of Esthetic Surroundings: I. Initial Effects of Three Esthetic Conditions upon Perceiving 'Energy' and 'Well-Being' in Faces,"

Journal of Psychology 41 (1956): 247–254. See also N. L. Mintz, "Effects of Esthetic Surroundings: II. Prolonged and Repeated Experiences in a 'Beautiful' and 'Ugly' Room," *Journal of Psychology* 41 (1956): 459–466.

64 P. B. Harris, B. B. Brown, and C. M. Werner, "Privacy Regulation and Place Attachment: Predicting Attachments to a Student Family Housing Facility," *Journal of Environmental Psychology* 16 (1996): 287–301; C. M. Werner, I. Altman, and B. B. Brown, "A Transactional Approach to Interpersonal Relations: Physical Environment, Social Context and Temporal Qualities," *Journal of Social and Personal Relationships* 9 (1992): 297–323.

65 D. M. Pedersen, "Psychological Functions of Privacy," *Journal of Environmental Psychology* 17 (1997): 147–156.

66 I. Altman, *Environment and Social Behavior: Privacy, Personal Space, Territory and Crowding* (New York: Irvington Press, 1975); I. Altman, "A Personal Perspective on the Environment and Behavior Field." In R. M. Downs, L. S. Liben, and D. S. Palermo, eds., *Visions of Aesthetics, the Environment and Development: The Legacy of Joachim F. Wohlwill* (Hillsdale, NJ: Erlbaum, 1991), pp. 113–138; S. Petronio "Communication Boundary Management: A Theoretical Model of Managing Disclosure of Private Information between Marital Couples," *Communication Theory* 1 (1991): 311–335.

67 U. Ritterfeld and G. C. Cupchik, "Perceptions of Interior Spaces," *Journal of Environmental Psychology* 16 (1996): 349–360.

68 D. A. Taylor, I. Altman, and R. Sorrentino, "Interpersonal Exchange as a Function of Rewards and Costs and Situational Factors: Expectancy Confirmation-Disconfirmation," *Journal of Experimental Social Psychology* 5 (1969): 324–339.

69 J. R. Aiello, "Human Spatial Behavior." In D. Stokols and I. Altman, eds., *Handbook of Environmental Psychology* (New York: Wiley, 1987), pp. 389–504.

70 If you have a hard time believing this, go search for "Jetsons video phone" at youtube.com. *The Jetsons* was a cartoon popular in the 1960s and 1970s that depicted a futuristic family.

71 J. N. Bailenson, N. Yee, J. Blascovich, and R. E. Guadagno, "Transformed Social Interaction In Mediated Interpersonal Communication." In E. A. Konjin, S. Utz, M. Tanis, and S. B. Barnes, eds., *Mediated Interpersonal Communication* (New York: Routledge, 2008), pp. 77–99.

72 See, for example, J. M. Twenge, B. H. Spitzberg, and W. D. Campbell, "Less In-Person Social Interaction with Peers Among U.S. Adolescents in the 2st Century and Links to Loneliness," *Journal of Social and Personal Relationships* 36 (2019): 1892–1913.

73 H. A. K. Groothof, P. Dijkstra, and D. P. H. Barelds, "Sex Differences in Jealousy: The Case of Internet Infidelity," *Journal of Social and Personal Relationships* 26 (2009): 1119–1129.

74 P. Kerkhof, C. Finkenauer, and L. D. Muusses, "Relational Consequences of Compulsive Internet Use: A Longitudinal Study Among Newlyweds," *Human Communication Research* 37 (2011): 147 – 173.

75 J. Vitak and N. B. Ellison, "Personal Relationships and Technology in the Digital Age," In A. L. Vangelisti and D. Perlman, eds., *The Cambridge Handbook of Personal Relationships* 2nd ed. (New York: Cambridge University Press, 2018), pp. 481–493.

76 C. L. Toma, and J. T. Hancock, "Looks and Lies: The Role of Physical Attractiveness in Online Dating Self-Presentation and Deception," *Communication Research* 37 (2010): 335–351.

77 See, for example, J. Fox and R S. Tokunaga, "Romantic partner monitoring after breakups: Attachment, dependence, distress, and post-dissolution online surveillance via social networking sites," *Cyberpsychology, Behavior, and Social Networking* 18 (2015): 491–498; M. Phillips, and B. H. Spitzberg, "Speculating about Spying on MySpace and Beyond: Social Network Surveillance and Obsessive Relational Intrusion," In K. B. Wright and L. M. Webb, eds., *Computer-Mediated Communication in Personal Relationships* (New York: Lang, 2011), pp. 344–367.

78 N. K. Baym, "A Call for Grounding in the Face of Blurred Boundaries," *Journal of Computer-Mediated Communication* 14 (2009): 720–723.

79 J. Stephenson-Abetz and A. Holman, "Facebook and the Negotiation of "Old" and "New" During the Transition to College," *Western Journal of Communication* 76 (2012): 175–193.

80 A. Ramirez, Jr., "The Effect of Interactivity on Initial Interactions: The Influence of Information-Seeking Role on Computer-Mediated Interaction," *Western Journal of Communication*, 73 (2009): 300–325.

81 C. R. Berger, "Beyond Initial Interaction: Uncertainty, Understanding, and the Development of Interpersonal Relationships." In H. Giles and R. St. Clair, eds., *Language and Social Psychology* (Oxford, UK: Blackwell, 1979), pp. 122–144.

82 Cacioppo, J. T., Cacioppo, S., Gonzaga, G. C., Ogburn, E. L., and VanderWeele, T. J. "Marital Satisfaction and Break-ups Differ across On-line and Off-line Meeting Venues." *Proceedings of the National Academy of Sciences* 110 (2013): 10135–10140.

83 C. L. Toma and J. T. Hancock, "A New Twist on Love's Labor: Self-Presentation in Online Dating Profiles," In K. B. Wright and L. M. Webb, eds. *Computer-Mediated Communication in Personal Relationships* (New York: Lang, 2011), pp. 41–55.

84 R. D. Heino, N. B. Ellison, and J. L. Gibbs, "Relationshopping: Investigating the Market Metaphor in Online Dating," *Journal of Social and Personal Relationships* 27 (2010): 427–447.

85 C. L. Toma and J. T. Hancock, "What Lies Beneath: The Linguistic Traces of Deception in Online Dating Profiles," *Journal of Communication* 62 (2012): 78–97.

86 J. L. Gibbs, N. B. Ellison, and C. Lai, "First Comes Love, Then Comes Google: An Investigation of Uncertainty Reduction Strategies and Self-Disclosure in Online Dating," *Communication Research* 38 (2011): 70–100.

87 P. Farhi, "They Met Online, but Definitely Didn't Click" *Washington Post* (May 13, 2007): D01. Retrieve online: http://www.washingtonpost.com/wp-dyn/content/article/2007/05/12/AR2007051201350.html.

88 E. J. Finkel, P. W. Eastwick, B. R. Karney, H. T. Reis, and S. Sprecher, "Online Dating: A Critical Analysis From the Perspective of Psychological Science," *Psychological Science in the Public Interest* 13: (2012): 3–66.

89 M. Decuyper, M. De Bolle, and F. De Fruyt, "Personality Similarity, Perceptual Accuracy, and Relationship Satisfaction in Dating and Married Couples," *Personal Relationships* 19 (2012): 128–145.

90 M. M. Morry, "Relationship Satisfaction as a Predictor of Similarity Ratings: A Test of the Attraction Similarity Hypothesis," *Journal of Social and Personal Relationships* 22 (2005): 561–584; M. M. Morry, M. Kito, and L. Ortiz, "The Attraction–Similarity Model and Dating Couples: Projection, Perceived Similarity, and Psychological Benefits," *Personal Relationships* 18 (2011), 125–143.

91 D. Skierkowski and R. W. Wood, "To Text or Not to Text? The Importance of Text Messaging Among College-Aged Youth," *Computers in Human Behavior* 28 (2012): 744–756.

92 A. Ramirez, Jr. and K. Broneck, "'IM me': Instant Messaging as Relational Maintenance and Everyday Comunication," *Journal of Social and Personal Relationships* 26 (2009): 291–314.

93 J. P. Caughlin and L. Sharabi, L. "A Communicative Interdependence Perspective of Close Relationships: The Connections between Mediated and Unmediated Interactions Matter. *Journal of Communication* 63: 873–893.

94 C. Haythornthwaite, "Social Networks and Internet Connectivity Effects." Information, Communication & Society 8 (2005): 125–147; G. Sparks, *Media Effects Research: A Basic Overview.* 4th ed. (Boston, MA: Wadsworth, 2013); L. L. Sharabi, and J. P. Caughlin, J. P. "Usage Patterns of Social Media across Stages of Romantic Relationships." In N. Punyanunt-Carter & J. S. Wrench, eds., *The Impact of Social Media in Modern Romantic Relationships.* (Lanham, MD: Lexington Books, 2017), pp. 15–29; S. H. Taylor, and N. N. Bazarova. "Revisiting Media Multiplexity: A Longitudinal Analysis of Media Use in Romantic Relationships." *Journal of Communication* 68 (2018): 1104–1126.

95 The discussion of the connections among various communication modes is based partly on the Caughlin and Sharabi study but also on some general principles of interpersonal communication. One lesson scholars of interpersonal communication have learned is that it is easy to overestimate the extent that different channels of communication operate independently. For example, popular magazines, television shows, and webpages frequently claim to show how to read "body language." The idea that one can look at facial expressions, gestures, and body posture as a language that can be read implies that these nonverbal cues operate in a self-contained system that can be understood on its own. Yet careful study of nonverbal communication has shown that it is often the *connections* between what we say and the nonverbal cues that is most meaningful. A smile, for example, means something very different if both you and your partner are saying "I love you" versus if you are smiling when trying to convince your partner to forgive you for kissing somebody else. The meaning of the smile has to be understood in relation to what is being talked about. A smile, or any other nonverbal cue, does not constitute a self-contained "language" that can be understood apart from other channels of communication. For a much more thorough discussion of the connections between verbal and nonverbal communication, see M. L. Knapp, J. A. Hall, T. G. Horgan. *Nonverbal Communication in Human Interaction.* 8th ed. (Boston, MA: Wadsworth, 2014).

96 LUMU is an abbreviation for "Love you. Miss you." Obviously, he would want to keep his response brief because he knows that he should not be texting in class.

97 J. P. Caughlin and L. Sharabi, L. "A Communicative Interdependence Perspective of Close Relationships: The Connections between Mediated and Unmediated Interactions Matter. *Journal of Communication* 63: 873–893; N. Wang, D. J. Roaché, and K. B. Pusateri. "Interconnection of Multiple Communication Modes in Long-Distance Dating Relationships." *Western Journal of Communication* (2018): 1–24.

98 J. L. Bevan. "Romantic Jealousy in Face-to-Face and Technologically-Mediated Interactions: A Communicative Interdependence Perspective." *Western Journal of Communication* 81 (2017): 466–482; K. B. Pusateri, D. J. Roaché, and N. Wang. "The Role of Communication Technologies in Serial Arguments: A Communicative Interdependence Perspective." *Argumentation and Advocacy* 52 (2015): 44–60.

PART III

Interaction Patterns for Coming Together

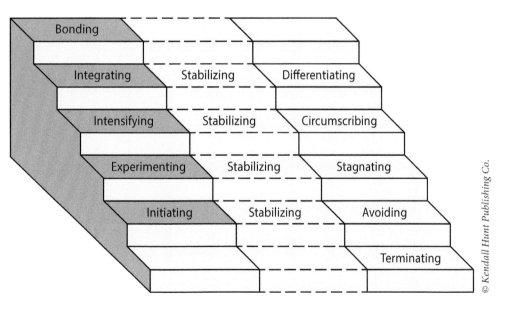

© Kendall Hunt Publishing Co.

CHAPTER 5

KEY TERMS

attribution theory

chain of reciprocal events

fundamental attribution error

implicit personality theory

matching hypothesis

negativity effect

perceptual anesthesia

phantom-other technique

Polyanna Principle

primacy

recency

selective perception

self-fulfilling prophecy

self-serving bias

spiral of reciprocal perceptions

stereotype deductively

stereotype inductively

stereotyping

The Genesis of Dialogue

Dear Dr. Knapp, . . .

I've been dating this guy and I really enjoy his company. The problem is that we are very different people with very different views on things. For example, he is a "bleeding heart liberal," and I'm a "closed-minded conservative"; he has a Ph.D. in math, and I took my one mandatory math class just hoping to get my B.A.; he is militant about cigarette smoking, and I don't really care. From big to little issues we seem to be different. At first we ignored the differences, but now that the relationship is getting more intense, we have started to discuss them. Neither of us particularly wants to change or have the other person change. So my question is, what is the chance of our being able to move ahead in our relationship? We're obviously attracted to each other for reasons other than similarities— why do we like each other so much? In the long run, will these differences overrule all the other compatible/good aspects of our relationship?

Wondering If It Will Work

This chapter does not list any human characteristics that will invariably predict relationship success or failure. It does discuss why people get together and how they go about sizing each other up. Perhaps an understanding of these processes may be helpful in setting realistic expectations for how predictable our perceptions of others can be.

> *Getting to know someone, entering that new world is an ultimate, irretrievable leap into the unknown. The prospect is terrifying. The stakes are high. The emotions are overwhelming.*
>
> —*Eldridge Cleaver*

To give birth to an encounter is to give life to a relationship. Like the birth of a child, the first moments in the life of a relationship are often critical in determining the length and quality of its life. Over four decades ago, Psychiatrist Leonard Zunin argued that the first four minutes of interaction with a stranger may be the most crucial time in determining whether an encounter or relationship will blossom or die. Furthermore, he suggested that the quality of a married couple's relationship can generally be predicted by assessing the interaction during the first four minutes after the couple is reunited following a working day.[1] Whether the critical time frame is four seconds, four minutes, or fourteen minutes is not clear, but research conducted since Zunin made these arguments indicates that the early moments of coming together may have a significant impact on the communication and relationship that follows.

Like the birth of a baby, some relationships are delivered easily—even routinely; others are wrought with complications. Perhaps it is an understanding of these potential complications and important consequences of initial interaction that often causes us to enter first encounters with feelings of apprehension, uncertainty, and cautious anticipation. Even the first few moments with a friend can be charged with some uncertainties: Were there events that may have profoundly affected either of your lives since you were last together and that may alter the original basis for the friendship? What is the friend's present mood? The stress often associated with new encounters causes some people to avoid them like the plague. However, avoidance of encounters with new and unfamiliar people is increasingly difficult in a mobile, high-tech society that requires more and more time to be spent at the early stages of developing relationships. And, as we pointed out in Chapter 2, most relationships do not advance beyond the experimenting stage.

Given the importance and the inescapable frequency of these early phases, we can now address the central question for this chapter: What interpersonal processes are enacted when we first come together with other people? The obvious point of departure is to consider the question of why people come together in the first place.

Getting Together

Sometimes people deliberately set out to find a relationship partner, but usually the initial period of relationship development does not involve much prior planning. Instead, relationships spring to life because people are in proximity to other people. What brings people into contact with other people?

Davis identified four human *impulses* that seem to push people together: (1) the impulse to receive stimulation, (2) the impulse to express experiences, (3) the impulse to assert oneself, and (4) the impulse to enhance enjoyment of certain activities.[2] Even though this may not be a comprehensive list, it goes a long way toward answering our question of why people come together.

© fizkes/Shutterstock.com

The Impulse to Receive Stimulation

Many times we seek encounters with others simply to get excitement, variety, or a change of pace from an existence that may be temporarily stale. Such conditions may arise when people have few social contacts or when they have many social contacts. In the latter case, one may feel conditions are overly familiar or repetitive: "All we seem to do is go to the same places, talk to the same people about the same old things." In the United States, certain time periods seem more likely to trigger this impulse for stimulation. Weekends are a particularly good example. Another example is late winter and early spring when people who live in relatively cold climates get "cabin fever." During this period, some travel to warmer regions, while others seek new forms of stimulation outdoors (e.g., snowboarding) because they are bored and tired of being "stuck" inside.

The Impulse to Express Experiences

A divorced friend of the senior author recently spent the better part of an hour telling him how great it was to be alone and how much he enjoyed the solitude. The author was struck by the fact that possibly a large part of this person's satisfaction with solitude was due to the fact that he had a friend to whom he could relate this experience. Each of us has a reservoir of private experiences that at some point must overflow onto others. Usually we'll try to find specific others who will provide protection, comfort, and security for unpleasant private experiences and who will increase our enjoyment of pleasant experiences. There is a great deal of wisdom in the oft-stated belief that the most intolerable form of punishment is total isolation from human contact. Part of the impulse to express experiences is motivated by a desire to discover how they compare with the experiences of others—the subject of the next section.

The Impulse to Assert Oneself

No matter how we choose to define it, our identity, or our self, is largely the result of testing its potential components against other people.[3] We know ourselves by knowing others, by what they think of us and say to us. Sure, we sometimes talk to ourselves and test out ideas and feelings in our own imagination, but without social comparison we quickly lose our perspective for efficient daily interaction. Each of us has to feel we have some influence or control over our psychosocial environment. Our ability to assert some control and to fulfill our goals affects the way we interpret our social world.[4] Researchers have found that those who do not believe they have such control also tend to feel that they have fewer social relationships than they would like—they are lonely in comparison to other people.[5] The only way for these and other people to develop a sense of control and to measure their social impact is to seek out the actions and ideas of others.

When we find ourselves in a situation in which our feelings or environment are confusing, ambiguous, or changeable, the need for social contact and comparison increases dramatically. We seek social contact in an effort to reduce the uncertainties surrounding us. We want to make sense out of our world. The anguish felt by one of our students whose father died subsided considerably after she discussed her feelings with other students who had also experienced the death of a parent. It wasn't long before she said to us, "I realize that I'm in much better shape than a lot of people I've talked to, so I've started counseling them." Without knowing it, many of the people this student had talked to provided her with an indirect form of social support. By asserting herself and comparing herself to others, she realized that her situation was not as bad as it could be. Our initial interaction with strangers also reflects how we try to reduce the uncertainty of who they are. We ask, "Where are you from?" "What do you do?" "Do you know somebody I know?" It is not as necessary to seek encounters with others when the object of our testing is some physical reality— "Is the sun shining?"—but attitudes, values, and beliefs demand testing in the social arena.

Schachter's classic experiment illustrates how induced anxiety or fear may cause individuals to come together in an attempt to reduce their uncertainties.[6] Some female undergraduates were brought to a laboratory for the alleged purpose of serving as subjects in an experiment dealing with the physiological effects of electric shock. Some subjects were told the shocks would be extremely painful but "would do no permanent tissue damage." Other subjects were told the shocks would be mild, resembling a tickle or a tingle. While the equipment was supposedly being prepared, the women were asked to wait in another room. When given the choice of waiting alone or with others, two-thirds of the women in the high-fear treatment group wanted to wait with others; two-thirds of the women in the low-fear group chose to wait alone or said they didn't care what room they waited in. A follow-up study indicated the high-fear subjects did not want to wait with just anybody; they wanted to wait with subjects in their own treatment group. As Schachter observed: "Misery doesn't love just any kind of company, just miserable company." This finding held true even when subjects were not allowed to speak to one another. Just the presence of others and the observation of nonverbal cues seemed to be enough to provide information on how others were reacting, and how others' reactions compared with one's own feelings. It should be noted that fear accompanied by the thought that you might be forced to reveal some threatening emotion will likely keep people apart rather than bring them together.

The Impulse to Enhance Enjoyment of Certain Activities

Sometimes the desire to encounter others is associated with an event or an activity that is more fun with others than alone. There may be times when Auto-Bridge or Auto-Monopoly or eating Thanksgiving dinner alone is enjoyable, but usually the participation of others enhances the pleasure.

When people want to share an event or an activity with someone, they may seek out new relationships. Evidence of this can be seen in the subscription patterns associated with online dating sites. Executives of some of these sites report that their business increases during the first quarter of the year right after New Year's until Valentine's Day. These executives suggest that people who were single during the holiday season often resolve to find a companion with whom they can share their activities in the new year. Executives of other dating sites note that they see a spike in business during the spring and summer months. The founder of one site noted that "the weather gets better and people want to find someone to share the nice weather with."[7]

Conditions That Facilitate or Impede Initial Interactions

Now that we have some idea of the general impulses that bring people together, we should note that there are certain conditions that facilitate and/or impede the initiation of communication with others. This is not to say that people are typically conscious of these conditions. Most times, we meet and talk with others without thinking about the surrounding circumstances. Our failure to carefully consider these circumstances, however, doesn't prevent them from affecting our relationships. For instance, one of the most important facilitators of social interaction is having something in common. Although researchers find that we base our selection of romantic partners more on infatuation than on a careful assessment of the commonalities we share with potential partners,[8] the similarities we share with potential partners affect our relationships. The list of things that people may discover in others and consider to be important commonalities is almost endless. A few examples will suffice.

Before you even meet the other person you may find out things about him or her that are also true of you—religion, birthplace, age, sex, group membership (a sociology student), race, attitudinal orientation (liberal), or interests (collecting rhinos). These things can be uncovered by a common acquaintance, a news story, social media sites, a dating service, or a host of other sources. Perhaps you have had previous interaction with this person and found him or her socially attractive. Whether you discover these commonalities beforehand or during the interaction, they will facilitate the initiation or duration of an encounter. Other commonalities may be derived from a common interest in an activity that facilitates the encounter—you both like to play handball. The very fact that you are in the same setting and exposed to the same stimuli—a party, an art class, or the site of a tornado disaster—with another person may suggest certain commonalities. Or the encounter may be facilitated by a common friend. Sometimes a third person or object provides the catalyst for an encounter—a stalled car or a petition that needs signatures. When this added stimulus has unusual features, it may literally beg for comment. A cast on your arm or leg or some unusual hair style may provide the focus for that often elusive opening line, and walking your pet vulture around the block on a leash would be hard for neighbors to ignore. Obviously, people can also meet by accident—literally. More than one relationship that led to marriage has started when "we just bumped into each other on the street."

It is interesting that the previously mentioned facilitators can also impede coming together. There are many instances where this happens. You and another person may both enjoy a common activity, but the activity itself may have certain sanctions against interacting—chess tournaments or attending the symphony. Two very career-oriented individuals may not take the time away from their work to participate in social gatherings. Similarly, two people who are shy may both avoid social interaction because of the anxiety it causes them. Even if they are not shy, people who are attracted to each other may both decide against "making the first move" because they are both worried about being rejected.[9] At a party, a woman may find a great deal in common with an attractive man only to discover later that he is holding hands with another man. Same group membership may also work against coming together; you may not even want to associate with a person in the same group. You may be living in a small university town and desperately want to find acquaintances who are not affiliated with the university. Unusual features also may act as barriers to encounters, such as having a physical disability, wearing a wedding ring to a speed dating event, or reading *Fifty Shades of Grey* in church.[10]

 At the moment of meeting, parting begins.

—*Patrick Hughes and George Brecht*

The process of determining whether a given stimulus is a facilitator or a barrier to an encounter involves establishing your individual criteria for coming together with others. In essence, you are asking yourself whether this person has the characteristics that will make it worthwhile to initiate an encounter. Do the location, appearance, and behavior of the other and your own mood and purposes suggest that an encounter is desirable at this time? Will you have to expend a great deal of energy on this encounter, never to see the person again? Will the other person define the encounter as legitimate under those circumstances? In order to understand more fully some of the things we consider when processing these questions, we need to look at the process of person perception.

Sizing Up the Other Person

The process of perceiving other people is rarely translated (to ourselves or others) into cold, objective terms: "She was five feet, eight inches, tall; had blonde hair; and wore a plaid skirt." More often, we try to get inside the other person's mind to pinpoint his or her attitudes, emotions, motivations, abilities, ideas, perceptions, and traits. Although research suggests that our methods for assessing others' feelings and behaviors are usually quite imprecise,[11] we sometimes behave as if we can accomplish this difficult maneuver almost instantaneously—perhaps with a two-second glance.[12]

© fizkes/Shutterstock.com

We try to obtain information about others in many ways. Berger suggests several methods for reducing uncertainties about others: (a) unobtrusively watching a person interacting with others, particularly with others who are known to you so you can compare the observed person's behavior with the known others' behavior; (b) observing a person when social behavior is relatively uninhibited or when a wide variety of behavioral responses are called for; (c) deliberately structuring the physical or social environment so as to observe the person's responses to specific stimuli; (d) asking people who have had or have frequent contact with the person about him or her; and (e) using various strategies in face-to-face interaction to uncover information about another person—questions, self-disclosures.[13] Of course, we also use technology to gather information about others. Social media sites, Google, and other data bases can provide information about people's current activities and about their history that is difficult to obtain in face-to-face settings.[14]

Berger and Kellermann note that the strategies people use to reduce their uncertainty about others may be viewed as plans for reaching social goals. When our social goals involve obtaining information about another person, we may also have a number of higher-level goals that influence our choice of strategies.[15] For instance, the higher-level goal of social appropriateness may prevent us from asking new acquaintances about their age, income, or sexual preferences—even if we would like to obtain that information. Getting to know someone is a never-ending task, largely because people are constantly changing and the methods we use to obtain information are often imprecise. You may have known someone for ten years and still know very little about him or her. If we accept the idea that we won't ever fully know another person, it enables us to deal more easily with those things that get in the way of accurate knowledge, such as secrets and deceptions. It also will keep us from being too surprised or shocked by seemingly inconsistent behavior. Ironically, those things that keep us from knowing another person too well may be just as important to the development of a satisfying relationship as those things that enable us to obtain accurate knowledge about a person (e.g., disclosures and truthful statements). Sometimes a degree of uncertainty about our partners can help us sustain our relationships.[16]

Why Perceptions Differ

When several different people look at the same person, it is not unusual for each of them to see different things; when you alone observe one behavior or one person at two different times, you may see different things. The following are but some of the factors that contribute to these varying perceptions:

1. Each person's perceptions of others are structured by his or her own cultural conditioning, education, and personal experiences. Adults teach children what they think are the critical dimensions to look for in other people.[17] In the United States, individuals are trained to develop their auditory and visual sensors and to pay less attention to information that could be obtained from touching or smelling. As an individual, a person may have had previous experiences with tall, powerful, red-headed males that cause him or her to recoil in fear. The experiences of another may cause him or her to see the same person as a good lover, a warm and gentle person, a dull person, a dogmatic person, an athlete, and so on.

2. Sometimes perceptions differ because of what we choose to observe and how we process what we've observed. It is not necessarily true that person perception is based on observations of a particular person. Your observations may be totally dominated by what others have told you about this person, or you may focus primarily on the situation or role relationship. Most people do not use the same yardstick to measure their parents, their friends, and strangers. It is often difficult to see our own children or spouses as others do. An aggressive child may be perceived very differently at home by his or her parents than by a stranger when the child displays the same behavior. We have a tendency to minimize the faults of those we love[18] and to see our own relationships in a more positive light than we see others' relationships.[19] Furthermore, we do not mentally process everything we observe. There are moments when we will look for, see, respond to, and interpret a particular set of cues and other times when the same cues will go unnoticed or will be disregarded. Even when two people attend to the same cluster of cues and receive the same impressions, the language used to express these impressions may be sufficiently different to suspect different perceptions.

3. Sometimes we see only what we want to see or don't see what may be obvious to others because of our own needs, desires, or temporary emotional states. This is a process known as **selective perception**. Selective perception is obviously more difficult when contradictory information is particularly vivid, but it can be done. We can ignore the stimulus—"He's basically a good boy, so what I saw was not shoplifting." We can reduce the importance of the contradictory information—"All

Selective perception: Sensing (e.g., seeing or hearing) only a portion of available information, often due to cognitive or emotional biases.

kids get into mischief. Taking a comic book from the drugstore isn't such a big deal." We can change the meaning of the contradictory information—"It wasn't shoplifting, because he was going to pay for it later." We can reinterpret previously observed traits to fit the contradictory information—"I can see now how he tried to manipulate and use me. He ran errands for me so I wouldn't report his shoplifting!" Or we can infer new traits—"I still think he's a kind and pleasant kid, but he doesn't seem to be very honest or dependable." In each attempt to deal with seemingly contradictory information, an effort was made to see the boy's behavior as making sense.

When we learn that an old childhood acquaintance has been charged with a mass murder, we may selectively recall a variety of behaviors and incidents that were relatively unimportant to our previous image of this person but will now help to explain the new image.[20] Factors such as how much time has passed and what our role was in the situation influence the sorts of memories we develop.[21] And there will always be some who, after reconstructing the past, must say, "I always *knew* something like this would happen." Encountering people who are consistently puzzling to us probably leads us to terminate association with them.

In view of these and other factors affecting our perception of others, it is difficult to isolate those characteristics that typify an accurate perceiver or a good judge of other people. Although no definitive conclusions from empirical research can be made at this time, the following characteristics have been explored and seem to be possessed by a good judge: breadth of personal experience; ability to process complex stimuli and complex relationships; intelligence; self-insight (seeing and accepting both positive and negative qualities in oneself); and the ability to assume a detached role, like a third-person observer. Certainly, it is not a single skill that makes a person a good judge of others. Scholars have long argued that some people are good at knowing themselves; others at understanding their friends; and still others are most accurate in judging strangers.[22] Each procedure seems to involve different perceptual and cognitive operations and few of us are good at all three.

What are these mental gyrations we perform when perceiving others? Several related theories will help us understand how we form impressions of others.

The Processes of Perceiving Others

Even though it may seem logical that our impressions of others are based on the sum of all we know about them, research and actual experience would suggest that our impressions are often more than this. In the 1940s, Soloman Asch advanced the idea that we organize individual traits to form a whole, and this gestalt impression affects the judgment we make about each individual trait.[23] In short, this theory suggests that if we assess the totality of another person as negative, this will negatively affect our perceptions of individual traits associated with this person.

Kelley's experiment illustrates this concept by showing how the identification of a person as either "warm" or "cold" can affect a wide range of perceptions.[24] Half of Kelley's class received this description of a new instructor who would teach their class:

> Mr. _____ is a graduate student in the Department of Economics and Social Science here at M.I.T. He has had three semesters of teaching experience in psychology at another college. This is his first semester teaching Economics 70. He is 26 years old, a veteran, and married. People who know him consider him to be a rather warm person, industrious, critical, practical, and determined.

The other half of the class received the exact same description with the exception of the word *warm,* which was changed to *cold.* A class discussion with the new instructor followed. After the instructor left, the class evaluated him. Those who were told he was warm rated him as significantly more considerate, informal, sociable, popular, good natured, humorous, and humane than those who were told he was cold. During the actual class discussion, only 32 percent of those who thought he was cold participated; 56 percent of those who saw him as warm interacted with him.

As an outgrowth of this work on *central traits,* it was proposed that all human beings operate with an **implicit personality theory.** This simply means that each of us has a mental catalog of traits in our heads. As soon as we obtain information on one trait or a cluster of traits, we seem to assume automatically that other traits will also be characteristic of the person being observed. Given this mental matrix, the knowledge that someone is warm or cold may or may not change our impression of the person, depending on how we weigh and interrelate the characteristics of warmth or coldness with other perceived characteristics.[25]

Implicit personality theory: A theory that suggests people believe that certain personality traits are likely to co-occur.

Suppose we told you we were going to fix you up with a blind date who was good looking, rich, intelligent, blunt, and independent. How would you assess this person on the following characteristics?

Cautious _____	or	_____ Rash
Reliable _____	or	_____ Unreliable
Generous _____	or	_____ Stingy
Considerate _____	or	_____ Inconsiderate
Short _____	or	_____ Tall
Successful _____	or	_____ Unsuccessful
Conventional _____	or	_____ Eccentric
Humble _____	or	_____ Proud
Self-Respecting _____	or	_____ Servile
Sincere _____	or	_____ Insincere
Kind _____	or	_____ Cruel
Quiet _____	or	_____ Talkative
Romantic _____	or	_____ Unromantic

How do your answers compare with those of others? When regularities are found in person perception, it might be due to an implicit personality theory derived from being a member of contemporary U.S. culture. However, evidence also suggests that individuals have rather stable implicit personality theories of their own that may not be grounded in a particular culture. For example, research shows that some people believe personality traits are relatively fixed (unlikely to change), whereas other people see traits as more malleable (likely to change). In at least two different cultures, those who saw personality traits as fixed tended to make stronger predictions about others' behavior (e.g., "She is shy, so she probably won't go to the party") than did those who saw the traits as malleable (e.g., "She is shy, but she still might like to go to the party").[26] People whose implicit theories suggest that personality traits are fixed tend to make more extreme judgments about individuals and groups than do those who believe personality traits are likely to change.[27]

As human beings, we each have a need for structuring our world and for finding invariant properties in people so that they can be organized and classified. It would be literally impossible to function socially if we tried to react to each individual stimulus as a separate and unique aspect of our world, in spite of the fact that it probably is. Instead, we choose to say it is often a "difference that doesn't make a difference" and engage in what we know as stereotyping. **Stereotyping** is a way of simplifying our environment so that we can handle it. Sometimes we **stereotype inductively**, which is inferring personality or group membership on the basis of specific features—height, skin color, vocal resonance, or baldness. Other times we **stereotype deductively**. We start with a more abstract category such as group membership or personality and infer specific features—"If he's Jewish, he must have a big nose." Of course, while stereotyping simplifies our social environment and makes our lives more manageable, it can also create more problems. Stereotyping shapes the inferences we make about other people.[28] It affects the type of questions we ask when seeking information about others.[29] Unless we are careful, our stereotypes can prevent us from meeting, interacting, and relating to people we might otherwise care a great deal about.

A slightly different, yet related, approach to identifying how we perceive other people is outlined in the following phases of the inference process.[30] Sarbin, Taft, and Bailey suggest that person perception begins with a system of postulates, or premises, within the perceiver: "Team sports require cooperation; cooperative people tend to have many friends." A syllogistic major premise is then derived from this system of postulates: "People who enjoy team sports tend to be cooperative." Then the perceiver searches for and observes occurrences relevant to the major premise: "Jack plays football." The occurrence must then be converted into a general class: "Football is a team sport." The inferential conclusion, then, is that "Jack is probably cooperative" and the perceiver's prediction is that "Jack probably has many friends."

Sometimes we attribute certain characteristics or qualities to others on the basis of their overt actions. **Attribution theory** is concerned with whether a specific behavior is due to a person's personality (typically recurring patterns

Stereotyping: Formulating an overgeneralized belief about a particular category or group of people.

Stereotype inductively: Inferring individuals' personality or group membership based on their specific features.

Stereotype deductively: Inferring individuals' specific features based on their personality or group membership.

Attribution theory: A theory that suggests people are motivated to explain others' behavior, particularly when the behavior is unexpected and/or negative.

of behavior) or whether it is due to the situation or circumstances impinging on the person. Jumping up in the air and giving a "V for victory" sign is certainly appropriate behavior for a cheerleader at a sporting event, but it would seem rather odd as the result of having pointed out a fallacy in your partner's reasoning during a dinner party. Sometimes when we perceive a person's behavior as a deviation from the norm, we consider it as a reflection of his or her personality—he or she did it out of choice rather than in response to constraints of the situation. Sometimes, of course, it is just the opposite; we see more conventional behavior as "typical" of that person while norm violations are seen as "called for by the circumstances." Generally, we seem more prone to attribute the actions of others to more enduring dispositions and to discount situational demands. This tendency to overestimate the influence of dispositional factors and underestimate the role of situational factors in others' behavior is called the **fundamental attribution error**. The reason we often make this error is obvious. If a behavior is part of a person's personality, it is carried from situation to situation and, hence, our predictions about this person are made considerably easier.

A number of researchers have found that we also tend to interpret our own behavior in more positive, generous ways than we do others' behavior. For instance, in performing a task, we sometimes take credit for successful task outcomes, but blame circumstances or other people for failures. This tendency to enhance outcomes associated with our own behavior is called the **self-serving bias**. Although a great deal of research supports the idea that we sometimes engage in the self-serving bias, studies also suggest that we are less likely to do so when it means blaming someone we care about for a failure.[31] Our knowledge of other people and our attitudes toward them affect the judgments we make. For instance, research shows that in the context of an ongoing romantic relationship, our attributions for our partner's behavior depend, in part, on how satisfied we are with the relationship. When we are happy with a relationship, we are more likely to attribute our partner's positive behaviors to his or her personality ("She's being polite because she's a wonderful person") and negative behaviors to situational factors ("She's acting irritable because she had a bad day at work"). On the other hand, when we are distressed or unhappy with a relationship, we will use situational factors to explain positive behaviors ("She's only being polite because we have guests over") and personality variables to explain negative behaviors ("She's acting irritable because she's an inconsiderate person").[32]

As for attributions about our own behavior, we seem to be even more likely to accept situational explanations with the passage of time. With time we also seem to see our own behavior as more similar to others—for example, "I guess I'm more like my Dad than I ever thought I'd be." Apparently, two things happen as time passes: (1) we tend to consider more of the potentially influential features of a situation on our behavior and (2) we may have less need to be seen as a person who had control over the situational influences that may have affected our behavior.[33]

Fundamental attribution error: The tendency to overestimate the influence of dispositional factors in other people's behavior and overestimate the role of situational factors in one's own behavior.

Self-serving bias: The tendency to interpret one's own behavior in more positive, generous ways than others' behavior.

Although numerous studies confirm our predisposition to engage in certain biases when we judge the causes of others' behavior, there are a number of situations in which these biases do not apply. For example, some have noted that conversational norms affect our attributional judgments.[34] Our assumptions about how we are supposed to respond to and interpret questions about others can influence the causal statements we make.[35] The mood we are in when we interpret others' behavior also can affect our attributions.[36] In addition, the artificial conditions and the strong constraints on participants to be "logical" in most of these studies may have influenced the findings.[37]

Seeing or Hearing Yourself in Others

We cannot divorce ourselves from the process of person perception. We are at the same time both the observer and the observed, inextricably a part of our own observations. What I think that you think of me reverberates back to what I think of myself. What I think of myself, in turn, affects the way I act toward you. The way I act toward you, in turn, influences how you feel toward yourself and the way you act toward me. Laing, Phillipson, and Lee called this the **spiral of reciprocal perspectives**.[38] The following case illustrates how this spiral can operate:

© XiXinXing/Shutterstock.com

Brittany thinks Gilbert is needy. Gilbert thinks Brittany is kind of nasty sometimes. Brittany believes that Gilbert always wants more and more from her—that he is always looking for more assurances and affection, even though she is just as affectionate with Gilbert as she has ever been with any other boyfriend. Gilbert really likes Brittany, but he finds it mean and hurtful when she talks about her past boyfriends. Brittany realizes that Gilbert sometimes gets upset when she talks about old boyfriends, so she tries not to, but she also feels like Gilbert makes unreasonable demands on her. She occasionally tries to help him understand that people need some space in any relationship. In fact she has always needed space. Gilbert understands that Brittany thinks he's too needy, so he tries to act cool and not ask for too many assurances. But, because he feels like Brittany has thrown her more extensive experience in his face, he sometimes wonders if she is being mean on purpose and whether she is really serious about their relationship. When he talks to her in an effort to get reassurance, Brittany is exasperated because she feels that if she didn't want to be with him, she wouldn't be. Brittany gets tired of the neediness sometimes, and rolls her eyes at Gilbert, acting with a mix of anger and annoyance. When she calms down, she tries to help Gilbert understand again that it's not normal to be constantly asking for reassurance, and she resents him not trusting her. Gilbert views such attempts as

Spiral of reciprocal perceptions:
A concept suggesting that individuals simultaneously observe others, are observed by others, and are influenced by both sets of observations.

condescending, and perhaps even hostile. The more Brittany tries to convince Gilbert that nothing is wrong with their relationship, the more Gilbert starts to think she is nasty and uncommitted to him. Staying with her in such circumstances makes him start to question whether he really is good enough to be with her. He sometimes thinks, "I must be a huge loser to stay with somebody who is so nasty to me. I think she might just be toying with me. I guess she's right that I'm needy and pathetic." They get trapped in a cycle in which the more each tries to understand and respond to the other's perspective, the more they make their relationship unpleasant for both of them, with the neediness and nastiness continuing to spiral to the point that neither one of them can control it. Their problems are no longer in either person's control—the negative spiral is something they created together, and the more each one tries to stop it, the more it spirals into more and more negative thoughts and feelings.

By the nature of human interaction, we are a part of what we are observing. Sometimes, however, we explicitly project our own qualities onto others; after all, if the trait is a part of us, it must be true of others—"Everyone is dishonest; it's only human." It is possible, of course, to reverse the process and see characteristics opposite from our own in others—"I may be tough, but most people are spineless." Thus, the needs, values, and desires of the perceiver help structure and become a part of the perception. Why?

Well, sometimes we are so tuned in to looking for certain aspects of another person, we focus only on those things that will fulfill our current needs. If you see a potential marriage partner only as a "good lay," it may be due to the fact that you are so focused on one dimension, you ignore other potentially important characteristics of the person. In the same manner, we sometimes allow our own needs or insecurities to influence our perceptions of the other person. For instance, studies suggest that individuals who are troubled by self-doubt have fewer positive perceptions of their partner and underestimate the strength of their partner's feelings for them. Feeling less loved by a less valuable partner, in turn, is associated with less satisfaction and less optimism about the future than the partner's feelings of love and commitment warrant.[39]

Perceptual anesthesia: A distortion in what individuals sense due to their inner drives.

Perceptual distortion caused by the perceiver's inner drives is particularly evident in the early stages of infatuation. H. L. Mencken called this condition **perceptual anesthesia.** Of course, it doesn't help matters that our partner might try to present what he or she wants us to see. Bach and Deutsch pointed out that people may create a connection that seems very deep and real to them without even talking about topics that ultimately would prove important if they were to establish a long-term bond. For instance, a couple can meet, hook up, and feel like they are in love without ever talking about topics that might be important to them, such as their core values or beliefs.[40] The hypothetical example below illustrates how this could happen when (1) people see what their needs demand them to see and (2) people present themselves to others how they want to be seen. In this scenario, Eric and Chantal are attending the year's first meeting of their campus astronomy club. This is Eric's second year in the club, and Chantal is a new member.

What They Said	**What They Thought**
ERIC: Welcome to the club.	*Man! I should have something better to say. I sound boring.*
CHANTAL: Thanks. What's your name?	*This guy seems geeky but cute...just my type.*
ERIC: I go by Eric.	*I hope she doesn't find out my real name is Sheldon. I still don't understand why my mother named me that, and now with everyone knowing Sheldon Cooper, people associate my name with a socially inept geek. It's just better if she doesn't know that.*
CHANTAL: My name is Chantal.	*I wonder why he said, "I go by Eric." What's his real name? This guy is a bit mysterious.*
ERIC: So how'd you get interested in astronomy?	*What a wonderful thing to live in a time when cute girls are interested in science like I am!*
CHANTAL: Gosh. I've just always found the stars beautiful, and as I've learned more, it's just become more and more interesting.	*He doesn't need to know that I never looked through a telescope before my last boyfriend showed me his. He'd probably think I'm an idiot.*
ERIC: Yeah. Me too.	*We have so much in common!*
CHANTAL: So when is this meeting going to start?	*I know there are other novices in here so if we can just start the meeting before he asks me too many questions, I won't look stupid.*
ERIC: That's a good question. I think they are deciding whether the sky is clear enough to bother walking up to the observatory tonight.	*If I get a vote, we are definitely taking that long walk to the most romantic spot around tonight.*
CHANTAL: That would be cool with me. My place is up that direction.	*I wonder if I can get Eric to take a detour to my place afterwards.*
ERIC: Oh, that's convenient for you.	*Wow—she lives in THAT neighborhood? She's hot, smart, AND rich. Why is she still talking to me? I wonder . . .*
CHANTAL: Yeah. It's not so convenient for getting to class, but I love it up there.	*I'd love it a bit more if he'd joined me up there tonight.*

After a few minutes, the meeting started. The group decided to just do an introductory talk because it was a bit too cloudy to bother with the observatory. But in the moments before the meeting, Eric and Chantal began a pattern of selectively revealing information and imagining just the right information. Their conversation gained quite a momentum. After the meeting, Eric expresses his disappointment that they didn't get to go to the observatory, and says, "I'm sure we could have seen SOMETHING up that way." Chantal replies, "I agree. Let's head up that direction anyway and see." On the way there, they selectively revealed more about themselves and filled in just the right things about each other in their minds, focusing on the ways they were compatible. They ended up having an amazing night that spilled over into the next day. They both felt an incredible bond and even expressed love for each other. Their experience together seemed magical. They parted feeling like their love was truly special and unique.

But in reality, they knew very little about each other. They carefully avoided certain topics like politics and instead paid attention to their illusions about each other. It may be that some couples who meet in such circumstances are fortunate enough that they end up remaining enamored with each other as they find out more. But alas, that was not the case for Eric and Chantal, as the magic in their bond turned out to be an illusion based on infatuation.

It was easy to see that "things aren't always what they seem to be" in the get-acquainted dialogue of Chantal and Eric. But it is worth noting that the "things aren't always what they seem to be" phenomenon continues throughout the life of a relationship. For instance, the anger in the yelling apparently directed at you by your partner may be motivated by your partner's anger with himself or herself; your partner may disclose something very personal to you, but the hidden intent may be to see if this information makes you "squirm" rather than to be helpful to the relationship; statements apparently designed to support your ego and compliment you may be insincere; feigned weakness may be an attempt to dominate you.

Thus far, we've emphasized how inserting ourselves into the process of person perception can distort our image of the other person. The disadvantages of such distortions are clear, but on occasion advantages may also accrue. For instance, if you need affection and you underestimate a person's liking for you, you may be extremely happy at the slightest show of interest or acceptance—and you might not be as disappointed if you are rejected. Similarly, overestimating a person's liking for you may cause you to exert a great deal of energy for that person. That exertion, in turn, may elicit increased liking from your partner.

We can change reality by changing our perceptions; it can work for us or against us. Once again we see the relationship between our initial perceptions, our behavior based on these perceptions, the impact of our behavior on the other person's perceptions and behavior, and our subsequent perceptions based on the responses of the other person. Research shows, for example, that individuals who feel less valued by their partners read more into stressful events, feel more hurt when their partners are ill-behaved or moody, and respond to being hurt by behaving badly toward their partners.[41] The bad behavior these individuals display toward their partners most likely sets the stage for their partners' behaving badly toward them, and so on. When this cycle, or **chain of reciprocal events**, is structured (usually unconsciously) in such a way that the other person's response possibilities are limited to actions that will only reaffirm initial perceptions, we have a phenomenon Merton called the **self-fulfilling prophecy**.[42] In short, we begin with a false definition of another person, behave toward this person as if our definition were true, and eventually elicit new behavior from the other person that makes the original perception seem true.[43] For instance, I may see you as a very threatening person. Since I cannot trust you and feel that you might cause me harm, I buy a gun to protect myself. You find out that I bought a gun,

Chain of reciprocal events: A series of behaviors that are elicited and returned mutually by partners.

Self-fulfilling prophecy: When an individual's expectations or predictions become true simply because the individual believes they are true and behaves as if they are true.

which causes your feelings of insecurity to skyrocket. As a result, you also buy a gun. As soon as I find out you have a gun, it is easy for me to proudly state that my first impression was indeed accurate—you can't be trusted, and you pose a definite threat to my welfare. My impression of you has been proven by a self-proving mechanism.

Finally, it should be noted that many of our perceptions of others may have an optimistic bias in them.[44] Apparently many of us are inclined to see the good, the pleasant, and the positive to a far greater extent than we see the less pleasant things. Consider the following findings which Matlin and Stang cite to support the existence of a **Pollyanna Principle**.[45]

- People tend to evaluate other people—students, instructors, strangers—positively.
- Most people describe themselves as optimists, claiming that their present mood is positive, and that their lives are happy at work and at home.
- The average person rates himself or herself as "better than average," even though this is mathematically impossible.
- People judge pleasant events to be more likely to occur than unpleasant events, even when the actual probabilities are equivalent.
- Even when people have seen pleasant and neutral stimuli equally often, they report that the pleasant stimuli were more frequent.
- People remember events as more pleasant with the passage of time.
- People overestimate the importance of pleasant events and underestimate the importance of unpleasant events.
- In a free-association task, people produce a greater number of responses to pleasant stimuli, and they produce them more quickly. Further they recall the responses to pleasant stimuli more accurately.

The reasons why these behaviors occur is not entirely clear, but if we are affected by our observations of others, we may simply be trying to create a positive social environment for ourselves. Looking forward to people and events with the expectation that they will be positive may bring about a self-fulfilling prophecy in some cases in which the outcome may have otherwise been less positive.[46] On the other hand, optimism that is grossly unwarranted and unrealistic may cause others to see you as socially inept and out of touch with reality.

Although we tend to perceive most of our life events in a positive light, a number of researchers have found that when forming initial impressions of others, we tend to weight negative events and characteristics more heavily than positive ones.[47] Initially, many researchers explained this **negativity effect** by noting that negative events and characteristics may be the most informative. Since we believe that most events are positive, negative events are seen as relatively rare. Therefore, when negative events occur, we assume that they will provide us with more information than we usually receive.[48] More recent research on initial interaction, however, has demonstrated that this may not be the case.

Negativity alone does not seem to predict how informative an event or characteristic is. Instead, *typicality* (i.e., how unusual an event or characteristic is) seems to be the more important factor. When we observe something that is atypical or unusual in an initial interaction, it stands out in our mind—we tend to remember it and use it in forming our first impressions of others.[49]

First and Last Impressions

Most of us realize how critical first impressions can be. We try to "get off to a good start" when we meet others by presenting ourselves in the best possible light. Unless we have a good supply of friends and really don't care what happens to our relationship with a new person, it is risky business to say, "I don't care what people think of me at first. Let them see my shortcomings right off the bat. Eventually, this strategy will lead to a better relationship." Because first impressions are often so important, this strategy may lead nowhere. Research and everyday observations confirm the fact that first impressions are often lasting ones.

© Antonio Guillem/Shutterstock.com

Asch's work shows how important initial information can be in forming an impression of someone.[50] He asked some people to describe a person who was characterized by the following adjectives: intelligent, industrious, impulsive, critical, stubborn, and envious. Other people were asked to describe a person who was envious, stubborn, critical, impulsive, industrious, and intelligent. The only difference in the two tasks was the order in which the adjectives appeared. Those who received the description beginning with the word *intelligent* described the person in much more positive terms than those who read the adjective list initiated by the word *envious*. The perceivers apparently created an image based on the early adjectives and proceeded to interpret the remaining adjectives so they would fit the first impression.

While first impressions are obviously important, they can be overdone. You can make yourself look so good that it sets unsustainable expectations. This may cause problems later. Bach and Deutsch, for example, provided an account of Doug and Helen, a couple who learned that the impression Helen made was just a little too good.[51] Doug found this out when he asked her why they never went backpacking anymore, and Helen said she didn't really like backpacking. This confused Doug because one of the reasons he fell for Helen was he thought they had a love of backpacking in common. Early in their relationship, she said that she had such a great time on a hike with friends. He confronted her about why she deceived him regarding her opinion about hiking, and she said didn't know what he was talking about. She DID have a good time on that hike, and she commented at the time on how much fun she had and how beautiful the scenery was. She also particularly enjoyed the time when they ditched their friends and made love in the gorgeous wilderness. But, Helen also noted that this did not mean she liked lugging around a heavy backpack and wondered if they could maybe just drive to see some nature and then go to a nice hotel instead. Doug took this very hard and wondered what happened to the Helen he thought he knew.

Helen clearly let Doug think she was more outdoorsy than she really was. She truly did enjoy their first experience backpacking, but mostly because she was into Doug—not really because she loved the trail or the hiking. It also is important to note that Doug probably was so excited about finding someone who shared his love of the outdoors, that he didn't pick up on cues that Helen was not as much in love with the hike as she was with him.

The issue of first and last impressions is particularly relevant to the early phases of relationship development because we are receiving so much previously unknown information about the person. But people in long-established relationships also grapple with these decisions when hitherto unknown or seemingly contradictory attitudes, behaviors, or habits are revealed. In some cases, people try to ignore or undermine the new information.[52] But even then, the information influences the way they relate to each other. Even though the topic of Doug and Helen's conversation dealt with perceptions about past behavior, Doug's impression of Helen's interest in camping out will now affect their current relationship.

There are at least two reasons why first impressions can be so dominant: (1) We have a tendency to want to size up another person quickly in order to reduce any uncertainties. (2) We have a tendency to avoid admitting we made a mistake. This is often done by clinging to our first impression rather than revising our opinion according to more recent contradictory information.

In spite of the seeming predominance of first impressions, we do judge others by what they did last. Notice how the following dialogue moves rapidly from potatoes to honesty and from today to "ever since we've known each other":

JOHN: These potatoes are kinda bland.

MARY: That's the way I've always fixed them. You've eaten them before and haven't said anything.

JOHN: I've eaten them, but I haven't always liked 'em.

MARY: For God's sake, John, why don't you tell me when you don't like something? You never seem to be honest with me . . . and it's not just the potatoes either . . . it's a lot of things . . . ever since I've known you, you have kept things from me.

Boxer Muhammad Ali was described as "washed up" when he lost a decision to Ken Norton; shortly thereafter Ali was voted Athlete of the Year when he defeated George Foreman. In turn, George Foreman was considered too old and out of shape after more than a decade of boxing inactivity. This changed as soon as he regained the heavyweight championship at age 45. It is not uncommon that the most recent actions are considered most important when they represent a dramatic reversal from a previous impression or there is a compelling reason to believe your first impression was inaccurate.

Obviously, the question of whether we will base our perceptions of another on **primacy** (first impressions) or **recency** (last impressions) cannot be fully answered unless we know which traits we see as susceptible to change and which traits we see as permanent. It's the difference between "once a cheat, always a cheat" and "sure he cheated in college, but look what he's done lately—he's a U.S. senator."

Primacy: The state of being first or primary.

Recency: The state of being most current or proximate.

The Many Faces of Attraction

© Dragon Images/Shutterstock.com

From the previous section's discussion of the process of perceiving others, it should be clear that one aspect of sizing up another person is deciding whether we are attracted to that person. Judgments concerning another person's attractiveness are made continually throughout each stage of coming together and coming apart. The criteria for such judgments will often change at various stages, but some feelings of attraction or repulsion emerge before (based on reputation) or very early in the encounter or relationship. We make judgments about our attraction to people in both intimate and nonintimate relationships. We even have stable relationships with people we aren't very attracted to. The extent to which you feel attracted to other people will surely affect how you communicate with them and, sometimes, whether you communicate with them at all.

In everyday conversation, we usually think first of physical attractiveness when someone says he or she is attracted to a person. Although this is perhaps the most obvious referent, interpersonal attraction is a more complex phenomenon. McCroskey and McCain identified three types of attraction: (1) social attraction—"He would fit into my circle of friends"; (2) physical attraction—"I think she's quite pretty"; and (3) task attraction—"My confidence in her ability to get the job done makes me want to work with her."[53]

Which factors are the most important in determining our attraction to another individual?

Reward or Punishment?

Some people believe they are attracted to particular others because they obtain personal rewards; they like those who like them, even those who they anticipate will like them. Rewards may also be associated with communication competence[54] or interaction styles—that is, somebody who listens attentively, who responds directly to your statements and questions. As noted in earlier chapters, perceived rewards are not always as obvious as simply observing that one person praised or complimented another. The perceiver may feel the flattery is not deserved or phony and question the sincerity of the communicator. Or the perceiver may be so certain that he or she isn't any good at something that he or she may respond favorably to someone who confirms it. What are rewards for some, then, may be costs for others. Some people may show attraction for others who physically and/or mentally abuse them. Some of these relationships are short lived; others have hidden and offsetting rewards; in still others, the abused person may feel that the relationship isn't particularly good, but it is the "best I can do." Indeed, researchers have found that people with poor self-concepts tend to be more committed to spouses who think poorly of them than they are to spouses who think well of them.[55]

The rewards or costs we perceive to be associated with our attraction for another person do not always emanate from that individual. For instance, one study demonstrated that women who were asked to rate men's physical attractiveness were influenced by ratings made by female peers—particularly when those peer ratings were negative.[56] Other studies have revealed that the quality of both men's and women's dating relationships is affected by family and friends.[57]

Perceptions of relational rewards and costs also sometimes differ for men and women. Some scholars argue that these differences exist because our society teaches females and males to value different aspects of relationships.[58] Others feel that the distinctions are the result of thousands of years of evolutionary forces.[59] Regardless of how they originally developed, it is important to note that these distinctions are often small. By and large, men and women tend to have more relational similarities than differences. For example, when one group of researchers asked people to rate the importance of various relational rewards and costs, they found both women and men felt that some of the most important rewards of romantic relationships were companionship, happiness, and feeling loved or loving another person.[60] The most significant costs reported by both genders were stress and worry about the relationship, sacrifices, and increased dependence on the other. The researchers also noted that although there were far more similarities than differences in men's and women's ratings, several interesting differences did emerge. Women rated intimacy, self-growth, self-understanding, and positive self-esteem more highly than did men, and women saw loss of identity and innocence about relationships as more serious costs. In contrast, men felt sexual gratification was a more important benefit and monetary loss was a more significant cost than did women. While the number of gender differences here may be small, it is easy to imagine how the differences might affect communication between male and female romantic partners.

For many years, conventional courtship wisdom has held that a woman who plays hard to get somehow offers sufficient reward to attract males. Apparently, it is not only a matter of how hard a woman is for a particular male to get, but also how hard she is for other men to get. The greatest attraction, according to Walster and her colleagues, occurs when the woman is easy for the subject to get but hard for others to get.[61] Other researchers have qualified these findings, noting that both men and women who are extremely selective (i.e., described as never having "met a guy [girl] she [he] liked enough to go 'steady' with") are less attractive than those who are moderately selective.[62]

Near or Far?

Proximity also may facilitate or curtail attraction. A great deal of research verifies the fact that we are more likely to develop friendships with people we are exposed to more often ("To know him is to love him"). It may be that you share the same office, attend the same classes, occupy the same dorm room, or come from the same neighborhood. Conversely, we may try to obtain closer proximity to people we are attracted to—for example, two students living in two separate dorms who agree to share an apartment. Although technology has made it easier for people to communicate with each other when they are apart,[63] those who are attracted to each other usually want some degree of proximity.

Obviously, increasing exposure by decreasing distance allows us to obtain more information more quickly about another person. And, for this reason, we can think of many examples of when we have been in close proximity to someone and have not been attracted to him or her. This is particularly true when it soon became clear that we differed on some basic and fundamental attitudes or beliefs ("Familiarity breeds contempt"). However, this fact does not limit the tremendous potential of proximity in fostering and influencing attraction. As one of our colleagues astutely noted, "It's tough to be close when you're far away."

Proximity was found to be a most influential factor in the development and maintenance of romantic relationships in commercial organizations. Sometimes the two people worked in the same area of the building and sometimes they just shared the same elevator every morning and evening; or they were assigned to work on a task together; or the proximity was on an irregular basis—one was a receptionist in another office. The proximity of the two participants' work group and supervisor also influenced the course of these relationships. When supervision was not close and when there was little pressure from a work group to terminate the relationship, it was more likely to continue.[64] While these relationships continue, proximity is an advantage; when there is no desire to prolong the relationship, proximity is a problem and efforts will no doubt be made to decrease the possibilities of copresence.

So you want to know about communication and long-distance romantic relationships . . .

Can they work? Yes. But the chances of success are better if (1) both parties see the need for the long-distance relationship (LDR) and are committed to making it work; (2) both parties know that the LDR will end and when; (3) for both parties, the degree of commitment to the relationship is strong and the relationship is firmly established prior to the separation; (4) both parties initiate voice-to-voice contact on a regular basis, preferably every day; (5) both parties are willing to talk about the "trivial" things that have been going on in their lives as well as the "big" things; (6) both parties talk about and have ways to deal with relationships with others that may negatively impact the LDR; and (7) both parties try to achieve copresence as much as possible.

What are some common problems? Problems include (1) not having the things that the other partner brings to the relationship leading to a desire to find someone else to meet those needs, (2) unfounded jealousy or a lack of understanding of the other person's situation (compared to yours), and (3) losing touch with how your partner is growing and changing resulting from not sharing enough information and feelings on a regular basis.

Are there any good things about long-distance relationships? Yes. (1) Both parties may learn skills related to self-reliance that can later enhance the relationship, (2) both parties have more free time to pursue personal projects, and (3) both parties can develop new interests and friends that will enhance the relationship when it is no longer a LDR.

What is it like when couples get together during the LDR? It is not uncommon for short visits together during a LDR to follow this pattern: (1) great elation is felt at first and the couple does as much as they can to show their intimacy; (2) this is followed by a period of relaxing, which sometimes reveals potential areas of threat to the relationship; and (3) before the couple has satisfactorily dealt with these potential problems, it is time for one partner to leave.

* *

There is much more to be learned about LDRs. The preceding points are only a brief beginning. In various places throughout this book, other aspects of romantic LDRs are addressed. For those interested in more in-depth coverage, see Belus, J. M., Pentel, K. Z., Cohen, M. J., Fischer, M. S., and Baucom, D. H. "Staying Connected: An Examination of Relationship Maintenance Behaviors in

Long-Distance Relationships." *Marriage & Family Review* 55 (2019): 78–98; Kelmer, B., Rhoades, G. K., Stanley, S., and Markman, H. J. "Relationship Quality, Stability, and Commitment in Long-Distance Relationships." *Family Process* 52 (2013): 257–270; Sahlstein, E. M. "Relating at a Distance: Negotiating Being Together and Being Apart in Long-Distance Relationships." *Journal of Social and Personal Relationships* 21 (2004): 689–710; Stafford, L., and A. J. Merolla "Idealization, Reunions, and Stability in Long-Distance Dating Relationships." *Journal of Social and Personal Relationships* 24 (2007): 37-54.

Similarity or Dissimilarity?

The phrase *birds of a feather flock together* reminds us of another important source of attraction—similarity. Many studies confirm the fact that we often desire and select friends, dates, and spouses who are similar to us in morals, background (social class, occupation), interests, goals, ways of expressing ideals (language choices, dynamism), attitudes (political leaning, etc.), or appearance (size, features).[65] There are at least three underlying reasons why we seem to gravitate to similar others: (1) We assume similar characteristics will reflect a common view of the world. (2) If we share a lot in common, our interaction will require less hard work. Dissimilar others may ask us to justify our beliefs and force us to keep track of referents for a host of expressions that we can assume with similar others. Similar others also seem to provide a promising information-per-time-unit investment. In a culture in which the pressures for getting things done rapidly is high, similarity seems to grease the path. Sometimes we even fake similarities in order to get more information about another. Dissimilarity, it is presumed, bogs us down. Dissimilar others may have to start their relationship by learning about each other at very basic levels—"Now how does that handshake go?"—which inevitably forecasts a long time before the individuals in the relationship can begin to deal with more personal matters. (3) Similar others also seem to give us a better chance of being liked.

Phantom-other technique: Technique in which the researcher asks subjects to evaluate people they think are real but are actually made up to vary in key ways (e.g., being very similar or very dissimilar to research participants).

Many of the experiments testifying to the relationship between similarity and attraction have used Byrne's **phantom-other technique**. According to this technique, subjects are asked to inspect a questionnaire supposedly filled out by another person. Actually, the experimenter has filled out the questionnaire, so it will be either similar or dissimilar to the subject's own attitudes and beliefs on a variety of issues. When subjects are asked to indicate how much they like the phantom-other, a greater liking is consistently expressed for those who agree with the subject's opinions.[66] Although it is at times true that "opposites attract," the overwhelming evidence seems to point in the other direction; we are drawn to people who are similar to us, and more specifically, to those who agree with us.

Several qualifications regarding this general principle of attitude similarity and attraction are in order.[67] For example, researchers have found that we tend to assume we are more similar to attractive others than we are to less attractive others.[68] If we are very attracted to someone, we may perceive a number of similarities between ourselves and that person that might otherwise go unnoticed. Indeed, research suggests that people in satisfying, stable relationships tend to perceive more similarities between themselves and their partners than actually are there.[69] It is also important to remember, however, that perceived similarities do not always lead to attraction. People may be trying to renounce a fate they hope to avoid—the hard of hearing may not want to meet the deaf. In one experiment, people were led to believe that they were similar in attitudes and beliefs to another person except that the other person had had "a nervous breakdown and was seeing a psychiatrist."[70] In such cases, subjects were more anxious to avoid their partner than if the partner had dissimilar attitudes and beliefs. Here, similarity was threatening. People could not dismiss the idea that "this could happen to me" (because the person is so like me) when they had to face it directly. You may also find that you don't perceive a similarity that others perceive[71] or that you are similar to someone in ways that seem to be of little relevance for a particular kind of relationship (e.g., bowling partners who are both Presbyterian). Attitude similarity may lead to attraction, but other offsetting costs may inhibit relationship development. For example, your similar other may live thousands of miles away; the similar other may express a dislike for someone you care about deeply; or the similar other is dissimilar on a single characteristic that overrides any attraction you might feel based on all the similarities.

Other qualifications concerning this general principle of attitude similarity and attraction concern changes in people over time. In the early stages of a relationship, similarity may be based on a wide range of background factors and relatively superficial opinions and interests. As the relationship intensifies, certain topics, beliefs, and values may emerge as the most critical areas of similarity—those areas that must be similar if the relationship is to continue. You may find some similarities are initially appealing, but disastrous to a long-term relationship—for example, similarities on things you don't like about yourself or on the need to dominate. You may initially value your partner's imagination and creativity but detest it when you find he or she is also a liar. Partners in a relationship do not always grow at the same speed or in the same direction, but changes in the relative importance of external factors, physical attributes, attitude similarity, need similarity, and the like do change with time:

> HUSBAND: I don't understand all your proposals for weird and deviant sexual adventures. When we got married, we agreed sex was beautiful, not something to be abused.
>
> WIFE: It is beautiful and I'm not proposing we abuse it. All I'm suggesting is some variety—something different from the "same ol' thing."

This dialogue also points up another qualification. Two people may assume similarity on the basis of a general statement ("Sex is beautiful") but end up disagreeing about the particular behaviors associated with the general statement ("*This* sex is not beautiful"). The degree of pleasantness or unpleasantness regarding attitude similarity or dissimilarity obviously depends on how deeply held the attitude in question is. We can like a person generally and still disagree with or dislike certain of his or her attitudes or features, providing the disliked attributes are not basic or core values.[72]

Dissimilarities are not always unattractive. Sometimes exposure to dissimilar attitudes may help strengthen our own beliefs—shoring up or modifying our position on an issue by examining a contrasting one. At times the dissimilarities are irrelevant for the particular relationship sought. The other person may not rigidly adhere to or argue a dissimilar belief or the dissimilarity may not challenge our most cherished beliefs. Sometimes when dissimilar others say they like us, this positive evaluation may override the perceived differences.[73] And we may be attracted to dissimilar others because they represent something we'd like to be like—an ideal.[74]

Like similarities, dissimilarities can change over time as people interact with each other. In one study, the attitude similarity of couples at the time of engagement and after eighteen years of marriage was analyzed.[75] Happily married couples showed more attitude differences at engagement but became more alike. Unhappily married couples became more unlike each other. Another study demonstrated that female roommates who spent more time talking to each other tended to be more similar than those who did not talk as much.[76] The researchers argued that conversation between friends may be an important way for them to develop and maintain similarity. Conversations also allow people to deal with their differences. Friends and marital partners develop norms to smooth out differences and iron out possible problem areas.

Of course, the time and effort that partners spend dealing with their differences is not the only way interaction affects perceptions of similarity. In fact, studies show that even the act of engaging in the pleasantries of initial interaction with another person enhances interpersonal attraction. People who know they have different attitudes on a topic and who have a chance to interact with each other are more attracted to each other than are those who don't have a chance to interact.[77] Some assume these findings are the result of individuals' desire to have a stable, predictable, and controllable communication environment—and that interacting with others helps them to attain this goal.[78] Others feel that similarity on some issues leads to increased interaction and that the interaction then leads to increased similarity.[79] Although it is apparent that quality communication plays an important role in attraction,[80] we clearly have a lot to learn about how interaction affects perceptions of similarity and dissimilarity. After all, it is the way we talk about ourselves—not the comparison of our answers on questionnaires—that causes others to perceive us as similar or dissimilar to them. Some people learn to like each other after a bad start (perceived dissimilarity or negative reactions). Furthermore, we may be more attracted to someone whose reaction toward us has changed from negative to positive than we might be toward someone we liked from the beginning.[81] Similarly, we might be very negative toward someone who originally liked us and then shifted to dislike, even more negative, perhaps, than toward a person we didn't think much of from the beginning.

Another important qualification to the similarity-attraction principle is that there are instances in which we seek out people who are known to be different. Seeking out people with vastly different backgrounds and attitudes is usually an infrequent activity determined by our own free choice as the seeker. We usually engage in this when we don't feel we'll be rejected by the dissimilar other(s), and when we are in need of putting our unique identity in sharp contrast with others—escaping from the another-face-in-the-crowd syndrome. Just as there are times when we wish to emphasize our similarities with others, there are also times when we seek to emphasize our uniqueness.[82]

People can be similar in a variety of ways. Research has tended to emphasize similarities in personal preferences (attitudes, beliefs, values, interests, goals) and personal characteristics (age, race, sex, status, looks, background). But people also perceive similarities and dissimilarities in communication style (ways of expressing ideas, language choices, topic selection); communicative norms (sharing an understanding and acceptance of cultural roles and rituals); personal needs (immediate and long-term individual and interpersonal needs); and situational factors (sharing perceptions of the pros and cons associated with a particular situation). For example, Burleson and his colleagues found that people with similar communication values were more likely to become friends than were those with dissimilar values[83] and that spouses tended to have relatively similar levels of communication skills.[84] These findings suggest that some degree of similarity with regard to communication issues is important for relationships. But while some of these similarities and dissimilarities may be central to any type of attraction—task, physical, or social—others probably are not. There are likely some similarities that are especially important in one type of attraction and not in others. The factors important for task attraction may take into consideration, for example, the fact that the task may not last long and may demand a type of expertise that a long-term romantic relationship would not profit from.

Beauty or Beast?

We now return to physical attractiveness. It is safe to say that the evidence from contemporary United States culture overwhelmingly supports the notion that *initially* we respond much more favorably to people perceived as physically attractive than to those seen as less attractive. In short, "what is beautiful is good." Summarizing numerous studies in this area, it is not at all unusual to find subjects evaluating physically attractive persons as more likely than unattractive persons to possess a wide range of socially desirable traits—success, personality, popularity, sociability, sexuality, persuasiveness, and often happiness.[85] In other cultures, the positive traits associated with physical attractiveness may differ, but the judgments in favor of "what is beautiful" are fairly consistent.[86] People tend to agree about others' attractiveness, and individuals who are attractive to others are aware that they are pretty or handsome.[87]

Judgments linked to a person's attractiveness begin early in life (preschool, kindergarten), apparently reflecting similar attitudes and evaluations made by teachers and parents. It is important to note that less attractive people usually are not discriminated against as long as their performance is impressive. As soon as performance declines, however, the less attractive individual may receive more sanctions than the attractive one. For the less attractive readers of this book, bear with us. The picture is not entirely bleak. For instance, attractive people are not consistently rated more intelligent or more trustworthy. And unattractive couples have been judged by others to be more happily married than physically attractive couples. Handsome men do not seem to score any better on tests measuring happiness, self-esteem, and psychological well-being. And although attractive women seem to score slightly better on such measures than unattractive ones, this doesn't seem to be a lasting result. For example, middle-aged women who had been identified as attractive or unattractive in college were tested later in life. By middle age, the attractive college women seemed to be less happy, less satisfied with their lives, and less well-adjusted than their plain counterparts.[88] Furthermore, in management positions, attractive women sometimes face charges that they are succeeding because they are attractive rather than because they are competent. And, in one of the few studies of physical attractiveness that linked attractiveness ratings with social interaction, women who received more variable ratings on physical attractiveness were more satisfied with their social encounters.[89]

Although it is not true of all studies on physical attractiveness, most use photographs that, prior to the study, are judged to fall into the beautiful or into the ugly category. Hence, in most cases, we are not reporting results from observations of live, moving, talking human beings in a particular environment and we are not generally dealing with subtle differences in physical attractiveness that lie between the extremes. Although there does seem to be a general consensus in this culture on who is and who isn't physically attractive, this methodological consideration should offer further consolation to those who fear their yearbook picture may have been placed in the wrong category. When we judge people's physical attractiveness, we usually consider a whole range of factors beyond what we might see in a single photograph—for example, we observe the way they talk, the way they move, the way they treat us. Furthermore, our assessment of an individual's attractiveness may change over time. Research indicates that most people have had an experience when someone they thought was only moderately attractive actually became much more attractive to them.[90] In some cases, people noted that their perceptions changed because they modified the criteria they used to judge physical attractiveness; in others, they said they came to appreciate certain physical traits in the other person that they did not previously find attractive.

Situations also change judgments of physical attractiveness. For example, Mickey Gilley's classic country song about how "all the girls get prettier at closing time" prompted some social psychologists to test the idea.[91] Information about the general attractiveness of patrons in several bars at different times leading up to closing time confirmed the idea that both men and women perceive a significant increase in attractiveness of others in the bar as closing time draws near. Although alcohol intake was not controlled in this study, there may still be some truth in the lyrics Gilley sings: "Ain't it funny, ain't it strange, the way a man's opinions change, when he starts to face that lonely night." Judgments of attractiveness in this context, then, change as the number of available partners diminishes. These judgments also may be affected by seeing someone considered to be extremely attractive just prior to meeting another person. College men, for instance, who viewed attractive women on television just prior to rating the attractiveness of some college women rated the college women lower on attractiveness than another group of men who did not see the women on television.[92]

In light of the general preference for a physically attractive partner, we might suspect dating patterns would reflect these preferences. Such a hypothesis would certainly be confirmed by a series of studies at the universities of Texas, Illinois, and Minnesota. In these investigations, physical attractiveness superseded a host of other variables in determining liking for one's partner and desire to date in the future. Although both men and women reported that the other's physical appearance was the most important contributor to their feelings of attraction, a number of studies show that men tend to place more value than do women on youth and physical attractiveness when selecting a partner. Women, in contrast, tend to value earning potential more than do men. In addition, research has demonstrated that the greater emphasis men place on physical attractiveness applies to both male-female and same-sex relationships.[93] Regardless of sexual orientation, men tend to rate partners' physical attractiveness as more important than do women.

The finding that men value physical attractiveness more than women (and that heterosexual women place more value on the earning potential of their partners) has been replicated in a number of studies across a variety of age groups and cultures.[94] Even so, it is important to qualify the results of these investigations. First, the fact that this pattern of findings is cross-cultural does not necessarily mean that it is "inborn" or that it is a result of evolutionary forces. Some scholars argue that the emphasis men place on physical attractiveness is socialized or taught by most cultures.[95] Second, men and women often rate other traits such as kindness and intelligence as highly as they rate physical attractiveness or earning potential.[96] Men and women both evaluate a number of traits when selecting a mate—physical attractiveness and earning potential are only part of the package. Third, research suggests that men's and women's preferences for short-term mates may differ from their preferences for long-term partners. These studies demonstrate, for example, that women are as likely as men to prioritize physical attractiveness in short-term relationships.[97] Fourth, some researchers have found that differences in the importance that men and women assign to physical attractiveness is larger when self-report data are examined than when behavioral data are tested. In other words, when men and women are asked to report their preferences in potential mates, men are more likely than are women to say that physical attractiveness affects their choice, but when participants' behaviors are examined, both men's and women's choice of a partner is most influenced by the partner's physical attractiveness.[98]

If both women and men always pursued the most attractive partners they could find, people who were highly attractive would probably end up with more dating opportunities than they desired. There are times, however, when attractive persons are almost untouched in the mainstream of dating behavior. Why? Elaine Walster and her colleagues proposed what they called the matching hypothesis.[99] Since this hypothesis was presented, other studies have confirmed its validity. Essentially, the **matching hypothesis** argues that each person may be attracted to only the best-looking partners, but reality sets in when actual dates are made. You may face an unwanted rejection if you select only the best-looking person available, so the tendency is to select a person similar to yourself with respect to physical attractiveness. Hence, the procedure seems to be to try to maximize the attractiveness of our choice while simultaneously minimizing the possibilities of rejection. If you have high self-esteem, you might seek out highly attractive partners in spite of a considerable gap between your looks and those of your partner. Self-esteem, in this case, will affect the perception of and possible reaction to rejection. Confirmation of the matching hypothesis has also been obtained by examining middle-aged, middle-class couples[100] as well as younger college-aged friends.[101] And in another research project, it was found that couples who were similar in physical attractiveness during early stages of relationship development tended to make more courtship progress (achieve more breadth and depth of intimacy) over a nine-month period. Partners in the early phases of relationship development who were dissimilar in attractiveness were more likely to break up.[102]

Sometimes we find couples who appear to be mismatched with regard to their physical attractiveness. One study suggests that evaluations of males may change dramatically if they are viewed as married to someone very different in general physical attractiveness.[103] Unattractive men who were married to attractive women were judged, among other things, as making more money, as more successful in their occupation, and as more intelligent than an attractive man with an attractive wife. Judges must have reasoned that for an unattractive man to marry an attractive woman, he must have offset this imbalance by succeeding in other areas, such as making money.

Matching hypothesis: The tendency of individuals to select a partner who is similar to them with regard to physical attractiveness.

Summary

What forces bring people together to communicate and begin the process of building a relationship? How do we form impressions of others when we encounter them? What factors influence our judgments of other people as attractive? In short, what is the nature of the genesis of dialogue, what are those cognitive and behavioral processes enacted during the initial stages of encounters and relationships? These were the questions posed and addressed in this chapter.

People are drawn to each other for many reasons. We noted a few: (1) the impulse to receive stimulation, (2) the impulse to express experiences, (3) the impulse to assert and learn more about oneself, and (4) the impulse to enhance the enjoyment of certain activities.

Once in the immediate presence of others (and sometimes prior to copresence), we begin to form impressions of the other person. What we see in others, and how we perceive them, may be influenced by a host of factors: (1) our own cultural, educational, and personal background; (2) what we choose to observe and how we process what we observe; and (3) our own needs, desires, and emotional states. Environmental stimuli (noted in Chapter 4) also will affect what we see in another person.

Once the factors that influence our perceptions have been identified, our analysis of the formation of impressions becomes more complex. A total picture evolves out of dynamic interaction between our own personality, the other's personality, the fragments of these personalities that each of us chooses to dribble out or magnify on a particular occasion, what others tell us, what modifications are imposed by the setting or time available, and so on. Although it is unrealistic to expect a precise mental roadmap of how person perception works, we have some general theories that are useful for description and explanation—attribution theory, implicit personality theory, gestalt impression formation, the concept of central traits, inference processes, and stereotyping.

Sometimes certain forces are set in motion that cause us to feel particularly attracted to another person. On the basis of the research reviewed in this chapter, the following conditions seem to be most likely to provide a basis for attraction across most situations: (1) personal rewards derived from the other person, (2) proximity, (3) similarity of attitudes and beliefs, and (4) physical attractiveness. In some cases, however, the effects of any one of these factors may be neutralized or overridden by one or more of the other factors. Situational constraints and pressures will also affect the attraction process. It should also be clear that many of the processes discussed in this chapter are not limited to first encounters, strangers, or the commencement of an encounter. They were presented in this chapter because they may be more evident or dramatic during initiating and experimenting stages. Although this book has overtones of a distinct chronology, it is obvious that human communication cannot be rigidly fixed in an unchanging order. General patterns can be observed, but impression formation and attraction forces are obviously important at all stages of development and deterioration in relationships.

Selected Readings

Personal Perception

Fletcher, G. J. O., N. C. Overall, M. D. Friesen, and C. L. Nicolls "Social Cognition in Romantic Relationships." In A. L. Vangelisti and D. Perlman, eds., *The Cambridge Handbook of Personal Relationships,* 2nd ed., pp. 230–242. New York: Cambridge University Press: Sage, 1993.

Goffman, E. *The Presentation of Self in Everyday Life.* Garden City, NY: Doubleday Anchor, 1959.

Hastorf, A. H., Schneider, D. J., and Polefka, J. *Person Perception.* Reading, MA: Addison-Wesley, 1970.

Jones, E. E., and Nisbett, R. E. "The Actor and the Observer: Divergent Perceptions of the Causes of Behavior." In E. E. Jones et al., eds., *Attribution: Perceiving the Causes of Behavior.* Morristown, NJ: General Learning Press, 1973.

Kelley, H. H. "The Processes of Causal Attribution." *American Psychologist* 28 (1973): 107–128.

Laing, R. D., Phillipson, H., and Lee, A. R. *Interpersonal Perception: A Theory and a Method of Research.* New York: Springer, 1966.

Murray, S. L., Bellavia, G. M., Rose, P., and Griffin, D. W. "Once Hurt, Twice Hurtful: How Perceived Regard Regulates Daily Marital Interactions," *Journal of Personality and Social Psychology* 84 (2003): 126–147.

Roloff, M. E., and Berger, C. R., eds. *Social Cognition and Communication.* Beverly Hills, CA: Sage, 1982.

Schneider, D. J. "Implicit Personality Theory: A Review." *Psychological Bulletin* 27 (1973): 294–309.

Srivastava, S., McGonigal, K. M., Richards, J. M., Butler, E. A., and Gross, J. J. "Optimism in Close Relationships: How Seeing Things in a Positive Light Makes Them So." *Journal of Personality and Social Psychology* 91 (2006): 143–153.

Swann, W. B., Jr., and Gill, M. J. "Confidence and Accuracy in Person Perception: Do We Know What We Think We Know About Our Relationship Partners?" *Journal of Personality and Social Psychology* 73 (1997): 747–757.

Taylor, S. E., *Positive Illusions: Creative Self-Deception and the Healthy Mind.* New York: Basic Books, 1989.

Interpersonal Attraction

Aron, A., Steele, J. L., Kashdan, T. B., and Perez, M. "When Similars Do Not Attract: Tests of a Prediction from the Self-Expansion Model." *Personal Relationships* 13 (2006): 387–396.

Albada, K. F., Knapp, M. L., and Theune, K. E. "Interaction Appearance Theory: Changing Perceptions of Physical Attractiveness Through Social Interaction," *Communication Theory* 12 (2002): 8–40.

Berscheid, E., and Walster, E. H. *Interpersonal Attraction.* Reading, MA: Addison-Wesley, 1969.

Burleson, B. R., and Denton, W. H. "A New Look at Similarity and Attraction in Marriage: Similarities in Social-Cognitive and Communication Skills as Predictors of Attraction and Satisfaction." *Communication Monographs* 59 (1992): 268–287.

Buss, D. M. *The Evolution of Desire: Strategies of Human Mating.* New York: Basic Books, 1994.

Byrne, D. *The Attraction Paradigm.* New York: Academic Press, 1971.

Hatfield, E., and Sprecher, S. *Mirror, Mirror: The Importance of Looks in Everyday Life.* Albany: State University of New York Press, 1986.

Huston, T. L., ed. *Foundations of Interpersonal Attraction.* New York: Academic Press, 1974.

Lykken, D. T., and Tellegen, A. "Is Human Mating Adventitious or the Result of Lawful Choice? A Twin Study of Mate Selection." *Journal of Personality and Social Psychology* 65 (1993): 56–68.

McCroskey, J. C., and McCain, T. A. "The Measurement of Interpersonal Attraction." *Speech Monographs* 41 (1974): 261–266.

Murstein, B. I. *Who Will Marry Whom? Theories and Research in Marital Choice.* New York: Springer, 1976.

Sprecher, S., "Effects of Actual (Manipulated) and Perceived Similarity on Liking in Get-acquainted Interactions: The Role of Communication," *Communication Monographs* 81 (2014): 4–27.

Notes

1. L. Zunin, *Contact: The First Four Minutes* (New York: Ballantine, 1979).

2. M. S. Davis, *Intimate Relations* (New York: Free Press, 1973), pp. 31–35.

3. B. R. Schleker and M. F. Weigold, "Interpersonal Processes Involving Impression Regulation and Management," *Annual Review of Psychology* 43 (1992): 133–168.

4. C. R. Berger, "Goals, Plans, and Mutual Understanding in Relationships." In S. Duck, ed., *Individuals in Relationships* (Newbury Park, CA: Sage, 1993), pp. 30–59; C. R. Berger, *Planning Strategic Interactions* (Mahwah, NJ: Erlbaum, 1997).

5. C. H. Solano, "Loneliness and Perceptions of Control: General Traits Versus Specific Attributions." In M. Hojat and R. Crandall, eds., *Loneliness: Theory, Research and Theory* (Newbury Park, CA: Sage, 1989), pp. 201–214.

6. S. Schachter, *The Psychology of Affiliation* (Stanford: Stanford University Press, 1959).

7. J. Saranow, "Is There a Season for Love? Dating Sites Trade Theories," *Wall Street Journal Online* (May 7, 2003).

8. D. T. Lykken and A. Tellegen, "Is Human Mating Adventitious or the Result of Lawful Choice? A Twin Study of Mate Selection," *Journal of Personality and Social Psychology* 65 (1993): 56–68.

9. J. D. Vorauer and R. K. Ratner, "Who's Going to Make the First Move? Pluralistic Ignorance as an Impediment to Relationship Formation," *Journal of Social and Personal Relationships* 13 (1996): 483–506.

10. Several of these and other barriers to relationship development are noted in S. B. Woll and P. C. Cozby, "Videodating and Other Alternatives to Traditional Methods of Relationship Initiation." In W. H. Jones and D. Perlman, eds., *Advances in Personal Relationships* (Greenwich, CT: JAI Press, 1987), vol. 1, pp. 69–108.

11. M. J. Levesque and D. A. Kenny, "Accuracy of Behavioral Predictions at Zero Acquaintance: A Social Relations Analysis," *Journal of Personality and Social Psychology* 65 (1993): 1178–1187; W. B. Swann Jr. and M. J. Gill, "Confidence and Accuracy in Person Perception: Do We Know What We Think We Know About Our Relationship Partners?" *Journal of Personality and Social Psychology* 73 (1979): 747–757.

12. The fact that we often make such rapid judgments needs little supporting evidence. Whether or not these judgments based on a glance are accurate is often questioned. Sudnow, on the other hand, argues that "for many activities, the single glance is a maximally appropriate unit of interpersonal observation." See D. Sudnow, "Temporal Parameters of Interpersonal Observation." In D. Sudnow, ed., *Studies in Social Interaction* (New York: Free Press, 1972), pp. 259–279.

13. C. R. Berger, "Beyond Initial Interaction: Uncertainty, Understanding, and the Development of Interpersonal Relationships." In H. Giles and R. N. St. Clair, eds., *Language and Social Psychology,* (Baltimore, MD: University Park Press, 1979), pp. 122–144.

14. J. Vitak and N. V. Ellison, "Personal Relationships and Technology in the Digital Age." In A. L. Vangelisti and D. Perlman, eds., *The Cambridge Handbook of Personal Relationships* 2nd ed. (New York: Cambridge University Press, 2018), pp. 481–493.

15. C. R. Berger and K. Kellermann, "Acquiring Social Information." In J. A. Daly and J. M. Wiemann, eds., *Communicating Strategically* (Hillsdale, NJ: Erlbaum, 1994), pp. 1–31.

16. D. E. Brashers, "Communication and Uncertainty Management," *Journal of Communication* 51 (2001): 477–497; L. K. Knobloch and D. H. Solomon, "Information Seeking Beyond Initial Interaction: Negotiating Relational Uncertainty Within Close Relationships," *Human Communication Research* 28 (2002): 243–257.

17. B. R. Burleson, J. G. Delia, and J. L. Applegate, "The Socialization of Person-Centered Communication: Parental Contributions to the Social-Cognitive and Communication Skills of their Children." In M. A. Fitzpatrick and A. L. Vangelisti, eds., *Perspectives on Family Interaction* (Newbury Park, CA: Sage, 1995), pp. 34–76.

18. S. L. Murray and J. G. Holmes, "The (Mental) Ties That Bind: Cognitive Structures That Predict Relationship Resilience," *Journal of Personality and Social Psychology* 77 (1999): 1228–1244.

19. P. A. M. Van Lange, C. E. Rusbult, A. Semin-Goossens, C. A. Gorts, and M. Stalpers, "Being Better Than Others But Otherwise Perfectly Normal: Perceptions of Uniqueness and Similarity in Close Relationships," *Personal Relationships* 6 (1999): 269–289.

20. M. Snyder and S. W. Uranowitz, "Reconstructing the Past: Some Cognitive Consequences of Person Perception," *Journal of Personality and Social Psychology* 36 (1978): 941–950.

21. M. G. Frank and T. Gilovich, "Effect of Memory Perspective on Retrospective Causal Attributions," *Journal of Personality and Social Psychology* 57 (1989): 399–403;

C. K. Scott, R. W. Fuhrman, and R. S. Wyer, "Information Processing in Close Relationships." In G. J. O. Fletcher and F. D. Fincham, eds., *Cognition in Close Relationships* (Hillsdale, NJ: Erlbaum, 1991), pp. 37–67; E. R. Smith, "Mental Representation and Memory." In D. T. Gilbert, S. T. Fiske, and G. Lindzey, eds., *The Handbook of Social Psychology,* 4th ed. (Boston: McGraw-Hill, 1998), pp. 391–445.

22 P. E. Vernon, "Some Characteristics of the Good Judge of Personality," *Journal of Social Psychology* 4 (1933): 42–58.

23 S. Asch, "Forming Impressions of Personality," *Journal of Abnormal and Social Psychology* 41 (1946): 258–290.

24 H. H. Kelley, "The Warm-Cold Variable in First Impressions of Persons," *Journal of Personality* 18 (1950): 431–439.

25 J. Wishner, "Reanalysis of 'Impressions of Personality,'" *Psychological Review* 67 (1960): 96–112.

26 C. Chiu, Y. Hong, and C. S. Dweck, "Lay Dispositionism and Implicit Theories of Personality," *Journal of Personality and Social Psychology* 73 (1997): 19–30.

27 S. R. Levy, S. J. Stoessner, and C. S. Dweck, "Stereotype Formation and Endorsement: The Role of Implicit Theories," *Journal of Personality and Social Psychology* 74 (1998): 1421–1436.

28 D. Dunning and D. A. Sherman, "Stereotypes and Tacit Inference," *Journal of Personality and Social Psychology* 73 (1997): 459–471.

29 Y. Trope and E. P. Thompson, "Looking for Truth in All the Wrong Places? Asymmetric Search of Individuating Information About Stereotyped Group Members," *Journal of Personality and Social Psychology* 73 (1997): 229–241.

30 T. R. Sarbin, P. Taft, and D. E. Bailey, *Clinical Inference and Cognitive Theory* (New York: Holt, Rinehart and Winston, 1960).

31 C. Sedikides, W. K. Campbell, G. D. Reeder, and A. J. Elliot, "The Self-Serving Bias in Relational Context," *Journal of Personality and Social Psychology* 74 (1998): 378–386.

32 F. D. Fincham, S. R. Beach, and D. H. Baucom, "Attribution Processes in Distressed and Nondistressed Couples: 4. Self-Partner Attribution Differences," *Journal of Personality and Social Psychology* 52 (1987): 739–748; F. Grigg, G. J. O. Fletcher, and J. Fitness, "Spontaneous Attributions in Happy and Unhappy Dating Relationships," *Journal of Social and Personal Relationships* 6 (1989): 61–68; B. R. Karney, T. N. Bradbury, F. D. Fincham, and K. T. Sullivan, "The Role of Negative Affectivity in the Association Between Attributions and Marital Satisfaction," *Journal of Personality and Social Psychology* 66 (1994): 413–424.

33 D. T. Miller and C. A. Porter, "Effects of Temporal Perspective on the Attribution Process," *Journal of Personality and Social Psychology* 39 (1980): 532–541.

34 K. Fiedler, G. R. Semin, and C. Koppentsch, "Language Use and Attributional Biases in Close Relationships," *Personality and Social Psychology Bulletin* 17 (1991): 147–155.

35 D. J. Hilton. "Conversational Processes and Causal Explanation," *Psychological Bulletin* 107 (1990): 65–81.

36 J. P. Forgas, "On Being Happy and Mistaken: Mood Effects on the Fundamental Attribution Error," *Journal of Personality and Social Psychology* 75 (1998): 318–331.

37 G. Fontaine, "Causal Attribution in Simulated Versus Real Situation: When Are People Logical, When Are They Not?" *Journal of Personality and Social Psychology* 32 (1975): 1021–1029.

38 R. D. Laing, H. Phillipson, and A. R. Lee, *Interpersonal Perception: A Theory and a Method of Research* (New York: Springer Publishing Co., Inc., 1966, and Tavistock Pubs.).

39 S. L. Murray, J. G. Holmes, D. W. Griffin, G. Bellavia, and P. Rose, "The Mismeasure of Love: How Self-Doubt Contaminates Relationship Beliefs," *Personality and Social Psychology Bulletin* 27 (2001): 423–436. Also see S. L. Murray, J. G. Holmes, and D. W. Griffin, "Self-Esteem and the Quest for Felt Security: How Perceived Regard Regulates Attachment Processes," *Journal of Personality and Social Psychology* 78 (2000): 478–498.

40 G. G. R. Bach and M. Deutsch, *Pairing* (New York: Avon Books, 1971).

41 S. L. Murray, G. M. Bellavia, P. Rose, and D. W. Griffin, "Once Hurt, Twice Hurtful: How Perceived Regard Regulates Daily Marital Interactions," *Journal of Personality and Social Psychology* 84 (2003): 126–147. Also see S. L. Murray, D. W. Griffin, P. Rose, and G. M. Bellavia, "Calibrating the Sociometer: The Relational Contingencies of Self-Esteem," *Journal of Personality and Social Psychology* 85 (2003): 63–84.

42 R. K. Merton. "The Self-Fulfilling Prophecy," *Antioch Review* 8 (1948): 193–210.

43 See, for example, G. Downey, A. L. Freitas, B. Michaelis, and H. Khouri, "The Self-Fulfilling Prophecy in Close Relationships: Rejection Sensitivity and Rejection by Romantic Partners," *Journal of Personality and Social Psychology* 75 (1998): 545–560.

44 S. E. Taylor, *Positive Illusions: Creative Self-Deception and the Healthy Mind* (New York: Basic Books, 1989).

45 M. W. Matlin and D. J. Stang, *The Pollyanna Principle: Selectivity in Language, Memory and Thought* (Cambridge, MA: Schenkman, 1979). Pollyanna was an irrepressibly cheerful child heroine who always seemed to find a bright side in even the most tragic circumstances. See E. H. Porter, *Pollyanna* (Boston: L. C. Page, 1913).

46 See S. Srivastava, K. M. McGonigal, J. M. Richards, E. A. Butler, and J. J. Gross, "Optimism in Close Relationships: How Seeing Things in a Positive Light Makes Them So," *Journal of Personality and Social Psychology* 91 (2006): 143–153.

47 For a review, see S. T. Fiske, "Attention and Weight in Person Perception: The Impact of Negative and Extreme Behavior," *Journal of Personality and Social Psychology* 38 (1980): 889–908.

48 Another explanation is that negative events have a greater impact on us than do positive events. If this is the case, the ability to focus on and recall negative events may help us protect ourselves from potential harm.

49 K. Kellermann, "The Negativity Effect in Interaction: It's All in Your Point of View," *Human Communication Research* 15 (1989): 147–183.

50 Asch, "Forming Impressions," pp. 258–290.

51 G. R. Bach and M. Deutsch, *Pairing* (New York: Avon Books, 1971).

52 C. De La Ronde and W. B. Swann, Jr., "Partner Verification: Restoring Shattered Images of Our Intimates," *Journal of Personality and Social Psychology* 75 (1998): 374–382.

53 J. C. McCroskey and T. A. McCain, "The Measurement of Interpersonal Attraction," *Speech Monographs* 41 (1974): 261–266.

54 R. L. Duran and L. Kelly, "The Influence of Communicative Competence on Perceived Task, Social, and Physical Attraction," *Communication Quarterly* 36 (1988): 41–49.

55 W. B. Swann Jr., J. G. Hixon, and C. De La Ronde, "Embracing the Bitter 'Truth': Negative Self-Concepts and Marital Commitment," *Psychological Science* 3 (1992): 118–121.

56 W. G. Graziano, L. A. Jensen-Campbell, L. L. Shebilske, and S. R. Lundgren, "Social Influence, Sex Differences, and Judgments of Beauty: Putting the *Interpersonal* Back in Interpersonal Attraction," *Journal of Personality and Social Psychology* 65 (1993): 522–531.

57 C. R. Agnew, T. J. Loving, and S. M. Drigotas, "Substituting the Forest for the Trees: Social Networks and the Prediction of Romantic Relationship State and Fate," *Journal of Personality and Social Psychology* 81 (2001): 1042–1057; C. M. Bryant and R. D. Conger, "The Influence of In-Laws on Change in Marital Success," *Journal of Marriage and Family* 63 (2001): 614–626; C. M. Bryant and R. D. Conger, "Marital Success and Domains of Social Support in Long-Term Relationships: Does the Influence of Network Members Ever End?" *Journal of Marriage and the Family* 61 (1999): 437–450; J. J. Lehmiller and C. R. Agnew, "Marginalized Relationships: The Impact of Social Disapproval on Romantic Relationship Commitment," *Personality and Social Psychology Bulletin* 32 (2006): 40–51; M. R. Parks and M. Adelman, "Communication Networks and the Development of Romantic Relationships: An Expansion of Uncertainty Reduction Theory," *Human Communication Research* 10 (1983): 55–79; M. R. Parks, C. M. Stan, and L. L. Eggert, "Romantic Involvement and Social Network Involvement," *Social Psychology Quarterly* 46 (1983): 116–131; S. Sprecher and D. Felmlee, "The Influence of Parents and Friends on the Quality and Stability of Romantic Relationships: A Three-Wave Longitudinal Investigation," *Journal of Marriage and the Family* 54 (1992): 888–900.

58 D. Tannen, *You Just Don't Understand* (New York: William Morrow, 1990).

59 D. M. Buss, *The Evolution of Desire: Strategies of Human Mating* (New York: Basic Books, 1994); J. A. Simpson and D. T. Kenrick, eds., *Evolutionary Social Psychology* (Mahwah, NJ: Erlbaum, 1996).

60 C. Sedikides, M. B. Oliver, and W. K. Campbell, "Perceived Benefits and Costs of Romantic Relationships for Women and Men: Implications for Exchange Theory," *Personal Relationships* 1 (1994): 5–21.

61 E. Walster et al., "'Playing Hard To Get': Understanding an Elusive Phenomenon," *Journal of Personality and Social Psychology* 26 (1973): 113–121.

62 R. A. Wright and R. J. Contrada, "Dating Selectivity and Interpersonal Attraction: Toward a Better Understanding of the 'Elusive Phenomenon'," *Journal of Social and Personal Relationships* 3 (1986): 131–148.

63 C. J. Billedo, P. Kerkhof, and C. Finkenauer, "Just a Facebook Away: The Use of Social Network Sites for Relational Maintenance in Long-Distance and Geographically-Close Romantic Relationships," *Cyberpsychology, Behavior and Social Networking* 18 (2015): 152–157.

64 R. E. Quinn. "Coping with Cupid: The Formation, Impact and Management of Romantic Relationships in Organizations," *Administrative Science Quarterly* 22 (1977): 30–45. Also see J. P. Dillard and K. Miller, "Intimate Relationships in Task Environments." In S. W. Duck,

D. F. Hay, S. E. Hobfoll, W. Ickes, and B. M. Montgomery, eds., *Handbook of Personal Relationships* (Chichester: Wiley, 1988), pp. 449–465.

65 See, for example, L. K. Acitelli, D. A. Kenny, and D. Weiner, "The Importance of Similarity and Understanding of Partners' Marital Ideals to Relationship Satisfaction," *Personal Relationships* 8 (2001): 167–185; D. Gibbons and P. M. Olk, "Individual and Structural Origins of Friendships and Social Position Among Professionals," *Journal of Personality and Social Psychology* 84 (2003): 340–351; R. M. Houts, E. Robins, and T. L. Huston, "Compatibility and the Development of Premarital Relationships," *Journal of Marriage and the Family* 58 (1996): 7–20; E. C. Klohnen and G. A. Mendelsohn, "Partner Selection for Personality Characteristics: A Couple-Centered Approach," *Personality and Social Psychology Bulletin* 24 (1998): 268–278; J. C. McCroskey, V. P. Richmond, and J. A. Daly, "The Development of a Measure of Perceived Homophily in Interpersonal Communication," *Human Communication Research* 1 (1975): 323–332.

66 D. Byrne, *The Attraction Paradigm* (New York: Academic Press, 1971); D. Byrne, "An Overview (and Underview) of Research and Theory Within the Attraction Paradigm," *Journal of Social and Personal Relationships* 14 (1997): 417–431.

67 For a review of some of these issues, see "Chautauqua: The Role of Communication in the Similarity-Attraction Relationship," *Communication Monographs* 59 (1992): 164–212.

68 G. Marks, N. Miller, and G. Maruyama, "Effect of Targets' Physical Attractiveness on Assumptions of Similarity," *Journal of Personality and Social Psychology* 41 (1981): 198–206.

69 S. L. Murray, J. G. Holmes, G. Bellavia, D. W. Griffin, and D. Dolderman, "Kindred Spirits?: The Benefits of Egocentrism in Close Relationships," *Journal of Personality and Social Psychology* 82 (2002): 563–581.

70 D. W. Novak and M. J. Lerner, "Rejection as a Consequence of Perceived Similarity," *Journal of Personality and Social Psychology* 9 (1968): 147–152. For an extension of Novak and Lerner's findings, see also M. J. Lerner and E. Agar, "The Consequences of Perceived Similarity: Attraction and Rejection, Approach and Avoidance," *Journal of Experimental Research in Personality* 6 (1972): 69–75.

71 B. Park and C. Flink, "A Social Relations Analysis of Agreement in Liking Judgments," *Journal of Personality and Social Psychology* 56 (1989): 506–518.

72 C. J. Lutz-Zois, A. C. Bradley, J. L. Mihalik, and E. R. Moorman-Eavers, "Perceived Similarity and Relationship Success Among Dating Couples: An Idiographic Approach," *Journal of Social and Personal Relationships* 23 (2006): 865–880.

73 A. Aron, J. L. Steele, T. B. Kashdan, and M. Perez, "When Similars Do Not Attract: Tests of a Predction from the Self-Expansion Model," *Personal Relationships* 13 (2006): 387–396.

74 It is interesting to note that similarity to the "ideal self" is a two-edged sword—it seems to generate both attraction and repulsion. Herbst, Gaertner, and Insko found that attraction to a partner increased and then decreased as the partner became more similar to and then surpassed individuals' ideal self (see K. C. Herbst, L. Gaertner, and C. A. Insko, "My Head Says Yes but My Heart Says No: Cognitive and Affective Attraction as a Function of Similarity to the Ideal Self," *Journal of Personality and Social Psychology* 84 (2003): 1206–1219).

75 L. M. Uhr, "Personality Changes During Marriage" (Ph.D. diss. University of Michigan, 1957).

76 F. M. Deutsch. L. Sullivan, C. Sage, and N. Basile, "The Relations Among Talking, Liking, and Similarity Between Friends," *Personality and Social Psychology Bulletin* 17 (1991): 406–411. Also see J. L. Davis and C. E. Rusbult, "Attitude Alignment in Close Relationships," *Journal of Personality and Social Psychology* 81 (2001): 65–84.

77 S. Sprecher, "Effects of Actual (Manipulated) and Perceived Similarity on Liking in Get-acquainted Interactions: The Role of Communication," *Communication Monographs* 81 (2014): 4–27.

78 M. Sunnafrank, "Communicative Influences on Perceived Similarity and Attraction: An Expansion of the Interpersonal Goals Perspective," *Western Journal of Speech Communication* 50 (1986): 158–170.

79 V. Blankenship, S. M. Hnat, T. G. Hess, and D. R. Brown, "Reciprocal Interaction and Similarity of Personality Attributes," *Journal of Social and Personal Relationships* 1 (1984): 415–432.

80 S. Sprecher and S. Duck, "Sweet Talk: The Importance of Perceived Communication for Romantic and Friendship Attraction Experienced During a Get-Acquainted Date," *Personality and Social Psychology Bulletin* 20 (1994): 391–400.

81 E. Aronson and D. Linder, "Gain and Loss of Esteem as Determinants of Interpersonal Attractiveness," *Journal of Experimental Social Psychology* 1 (1965): 156–171. See also G. L. Clore, N. H. Wiggins, and S. Itkin, "Gain and Loss in Attraction: Attributions from Nonverbal

Behavior," *Journal of Personality and Social Psychology* 31 (1975): 706–712; G. L. Clore, N. H. Wiggins, and S. Itkin, "Judging Attraction from Nonverbal Behavior The Gain Phenomenon," *Journal of Consulting and Clinical Psychology* 43 (1975): 491–497.

82 C. R. Snyder and H. L. Fromkin, *Uniqueness: The Human Pursuit of Difference* (New York: Plenum, 1980).

83 B. R. Burleson, W. Samter, and A. E. Lucchetti, "Similarity in Communication Values as a Predictor of Friendship Choices: Studies of Friends and Best Friends," *The Southern Communication Journal* 57 (1992): 260–276.

84 B. R. Burleson and W. H. Denton, "A New Look at Similarity and Attraction in Marriage: Similarities in Social-Cognitive and Communication Skills as Predictors of Attraction and Satisfaction," *Communication Monographs* 59 (1992): 268–287.

85 E. Berscheid and E. H. Walster, "Physical Attractiveness." In L. Berkowitz, ed., *Advances in Experimental Social Psychology,* vol. 7 (New York: Academic Press, 1974), 158–215.

86 L. Wheeler and Y. Kim, "What Is Beautiful Is Culturally Good: The Physical Attractiveness Stereotype Has Different Content in Collectivistic Cultures," *Personality and Social Psychology Bulletin* 23 (1997): 795–800.

87 D. K. Marcus and R. S. Miller, "Sex Differences in Judgments of Physical Attractiveness: A Social Relations Analysis," *Personality and Social Psychology Bulletin* 29 (2003): 325–335.

88 Bersheid and Walster, "Physical Attractiveness," Cf. pp. 200–201 for reference to an unpublished manuscript by the authors and R. Campbell, "Grow Old Along with Me," 1972.

89 H. T. Reis, J. Nezlek, and L. Wheeler, "Physical Attractiveness in Social Interaction," *Journal of Personality and Social Psychology* 38 (1980): 604–617.

90 K. F. Albada, M. L. Knapp, and K. E. Theune, "Interaction Appearance Theory: Changing Perceptions of Physical Attractiveness Through Social Interaction," *Communication Theory* 12 (2002): 8–40.

91 J. W. Pennebaker, M. A. Dyer, R. S. Caulkins, D. L. Litowitz, P. L. Ackreman, D. G. Anderrson, and K. M. McGraw, "Don't the Girls Get Prettier at Closing Time: A Country and Western Application to Psychology," *Personality and Social Psychology Bulletin* 5 (1979): 122–125. "Don't All the Girls Get Prettier At Closing Time" written by Baker Knight, Singleton Music Co: BMI and sung by Mickey Gilley, *The Best of Mickey Gilley,* vol. 2, 1975, Columbia. Used with permission from Sixteen Stars Music, administered by HoriPro Entertainment Group, Inc.

92 D. T. Kenrick and S. E. Gutierres, "Contrast Effects and Judgments of Physical Attractiveness: When Beauty Becomes a Social Problem," *Journal of Personality and Social Psychology* 38 (1980): 131–140.

93 J. M. Bailey, S. Gaulin, Y. Agyei, and B. A. Gladue, "Effects of Gender and Sexual Orientation on Evolutionarily Relevant Aspects of Human Mating Psychology," *Journal of Personality and Social Psychology* 66 (1994): 1081–1093.

94 D. M. Buss, "Sex Differences in Human Mate Preferences: Evolutionary Hypotheses Tested in 37 Cultures," *Behavioral and Brain Sciences* 12 (1989): 1–49; S. Sprecher, Q. Sullivan, and E. Hatfield, "Mate Selection Preferences: Gender Differences Examined in a National Sample," *Journal of Personality and Social Psychology* 66 (1994): 1074–1080.

95 A. H. Eagly, *Sex Differences in Social Behavior: A Social-Role Interpretation* (Hillsdale, NJ: Erlbaum, 1987).

96 N. P. Li, J. M. Bailey, D. T. Kenrick, and J. A. W. Linsenmeier, "The Necessities and Luxuries of Mate Preferences: Testing the Tradeoffs," *Journal of Personality and Social Psychology* 82 (2002): 947–955.

97 M. F. Braun and A. Bryan "Female Waist-to-Hip and Male Waist-to-Shoulder Ratios as Determinants of Romantic Partner Desirability," *Journal of Social and Personal Relationships* 23 (2006) 805–819; N. P. Li and D. T. Kenrick "Sex Similarities and Differences in Preferences for Short-Term Mates: What, Whether, and Why," *Journal of Personality and Social Psychology* 90 (2006) 468–489.

98 S. Sprecher "The Importance to Males and Females of Physical Attractiveness, Earning Potential and Expressiveness in Initial Attraction," *Sex Roles* 21 (1989) 591–607.

99 E. Walster et al., "Importance of Physical Attractiveness in Dating Behavior," *Journal of Personality and Social Psychology* 4 (1966): 508–516.

100 B. I. Murstein and P. Christy, "Physical Attractiveness and Marriage Adjustment in Middle-Aged Couples," *Journal of Personality and Social Psychology* 34 (1976): 537–542.

101 L. L. Carli, R. Ganley, and A. Pierce-Otay, "Similarity and Satisfaction in Roommate Relationships," *Personality and Social Psychology Bulletin* 17 (1991): 419–426.

102 G. L. White, "Physical Attractiveness and Courtship Progress," *Journal of Personality and Social Psychology* 39 (1980): 660–668.

103 D. Bar-Tal and L. Saxe, "Perceptions of Similarly and Dissimilarly Physically Attractive Couples and Individuals," *Journal of Personality and Social Psychology* 33 (1976): 772–781.

CHAPTER 6

LEARNING OUTCOMES

After reading this chapter, students will . . .

. . . define the term "communication rule" and identify the six rules that have been found to apply to most types of relationships.

. . . describe the ways people learn, maintain, and violate communication rules.

. . . recognize the five different types of disclaimers.

. . . explain why violating communication rules sometimes is not negatively unsanctioned.

. . . identify the four steps in the greeting sequence and recognize the thirteen different types of greetings.

. . . describe the four points on the continuum of formality for forms of address.

. . . know the factors that affect how people respond to different opening lines.

. . . recognize the seven affinity-seeking strategies.

. . . define the six functions of small talk and explain why small talk focuses on some topics more than others.

KEY TERMS

affinity-seeking strategies

attenuation rule

communication norm

communication rule

disclaimer

ego depletion

eyebrow flash

script

small talk

Interaction Rituals

Dear Dr. Caughlin,

I have a question. I'd like to ask about "breaking the ice" when meeting a woman for the first time. I don't want her to think I'm too straightforward, but on the other hand shyness is just as bad if not worse. What I usually do is talk openly and tell her a lot about myself. I also try to get her to tell me about herself. My problem is that although everything seems normal at first, my relationships tend to drop off after only about a week. This drives me crazy, and I spend most of my time wondering what I do to offend these women. Can you give me any ideas about what I might be doing wrong?

Eager to Please

The first few seconds of talk with another person can be extremely important in setting the tone for further conversation and contact. This chapter discusses some of the factors that may facilitate or inhibit communication during this time. The extent to which we violate or adhere to certain interaction rules and how we choose to formulate our greetings, address terms, relational openings, and small talk should provide a basis for explaining why some contacts appear to be "winners" and some seem to be "losers."

> *Relational life wavers between order and disorder, certainty and uncertainty, permanence and change. Rituals help to balance these competing forces by providing order and formality in regions of relational life that may be easily threatened by disorder and informality.*
>
> —Arthur P. Bochner

Sometimes we simply don't know what to say, when to say it, or how to say it. At other times, the social situation seems almost to demand a certain kind of communication. It's as if both communicators are following a script written by someone else—a script each of them has performed before. And, although it often seems that we could make better use of our time than performing these rituals, we continue to "go through the motions." Interaction rituals may be short or long, performed by many or few, elaborate or plain, but they are an important part of the process of establishing, sustaining, and terminating relationships.[1]

Communication Rules

Communication rule: A followable prescription that indicates what communication behaviour (or range of communication behaviour) is obligatory, preferred, or prohibited in certain social situations.

Interaction rituals are created and sustained by the existence of communication rules. A **communication rule** is a followable prescription that indicates what communication behavior (or range of communication behavior) is obligatory, preferred, or prohibited in certain social situations.[2] It is a probability statement about the expectations for the situation—what is the likelihood that X must be said or that Y must not be said? Some of these rules are limited to a single person—"When Harry starts to yell at me, I will stop talking to him." Other rules apply to the behavior of both partners in a relationship—"If we have a fight, we won't go to bed while we're still angry at each other." There are also rules that pertain to specific groups of people—"When fathers want to show affection for their sons, they shouldn't kiss them on the lips." Then there are those rules that apply to most people in the society—"When someone greets you, you should return the greeting." From these examples, we can see that the influence of communication rules is not limited to initial interactions. On the contrary, as we will see in Chapter 8, people involved in long-term relationships develop and negotiate rules that are unique to those relationships.

Argyle and Henderson further argue that there are some rules that cut across different types of relationships. These researchers found that in Britain, Italy, Hong Kong, and Japan, people said that the following rules applied to most of their relationships: (1) partners should respect each other's privacy; (2) partners should look one another in the eye during conversation; (3) partners should not discuss with others what is said in confidence; (4) partners should not criticize one another in public; (5) partners should seek to repay debts, favors, and compliments—no matter how small; and (6) partners should (or should not) engage in sexual activity with each other.[3] Regardless of how specific or general a rule is, when an individual, couple, group, or society follows a rule most of the time, it is considered a **communication norm**—the most typical behavior relative to the rule.[4] People may acknowledge the existence of a rule but fail to follow it, so it doesn't become a norm. And sometimes people seem to be engaging in similar or normative behavior, but it is not rule-governed behavior—for example, they may depart from the norm without any positive or negative sanctions. Rules also may develop about who can make the rules. A husband may

Communication norm: An accepted way of communicating that most people agree with.

agree that he spends too much money but disagree that his wife should tell him to stop spending so much.

We begin learning about communication rules as children. Some of these rules give direction concerning what we say—for example, we learn "Mama" is not a form of address appropriate for all human beings, or we learn what is acceptable to say and what is not ("Don't say that ... it's not nice"). Other rules pertain to the structuring of conversations—we're taught not to talk when another person is talking[5] or not to start a conversation cold without some rapport building. We learn the implicit and explicit rules for getting the floor so we can talk, giving up the floor so the other will know it is his or her turn, maintaining our turn so another can't get in, and helping someone else maintain his or her turn as we inject occasional comments without interrupting the conversational flow. We also learn rules that help us manage certain conversational episodes. We know to be discrete when someone reveals private information to us,[6] to act concerned when someone is hurting,[7] and to try stay relatively calm and rational when having an argument in public.[8] Researchers remind us that the application of any rule to a situation or a relationship varies[9]—most of us know romantic partners who have no qualms about fighting in public—and that these variations serve to define the nature of our relationships.

Rules develop and are maintained in a variety of ways.[10] Sometimes we talk openly about the rule-related issue and negotiate a rule acceptable to both parties. Other times, we learn about an existing rule when people give us advice about how to handle a situation or when they sanction us for not following the rule. More often, though, rules are established in much more subtle ways. Metacommunication (see Chapter 1) may be the process that tells others how to behave relative to particular communicative responses. As a result of these "unspoken" processes used to establish agreed-upon rules of interaction, it is not uncommon for two people not to be able to state the specific rules that guide their behaviors.

Common sense tells us that learning and obeying these rules is crucially linked to the way others evaluate us. Allgeier, for instance, found that an individual's ratings of interpersonal attraction and adjustment increased as that person more closely approached an equal share of the talk time in a conversation.[11] Berger and his colleagues documented the fact that when people violate the norms of small talk (not reciprocating appropriate information, not giving the right number of compliments, or not following an impersonal-to-personal sequence of information giving), communicators were judged to be less attractive and too unpredictable.[12]

Test yourself. Examine the following situations and jot down two answers for each one. One answer should be based on what communication behavior would be generally expected or appropriate; the other based on generally *unexpected* or *in*appropriate communicative responses (rule violations).

1. You are in an intimate relationship with another person. He or she has just spent four hours preparing an elaborate gourmet meal for you. What do you say?

2. You are introduced to a stranger. The stranger smiles and extends his or her hand to greet you. What do you do?

3. You are on the brink of becoming engaged to person A. However, circumstances forced you to take a long trip with person B. You were sexually intimate with person B, but both of you agree it was "a one-time thing." You still plan the engagement with person A. On your return, person A asks you what happened on your trip. What do you say?

4. You enter an elevator. The only other person in the elevator is a stranger you find attractive. What do you say or do?

Now ask some of your friends to respond to these episodes. Are there communication rules for these situations? Is there enough agreement on the appropriate behavior so we can assume there is a communication norm operating?

In an effort to predict the permissible communication in the episodes, you had to consider a number of factors: How well did the communicators know each other? What topic were they discussing? What messages preceded the one you were asked to predict? What was the setting in which the message was delivered and received? Questions like these were the bases for a number of hypotheses developed by Roderick P. Hart and the senior author concerning the following interrelationships among speakers, listeners, situations, and expected messages.[13]

- When communicators are physically close, listeners expect more personal messages; less personal, or public, messages are expected when physical distance is greater.

- When the relationship between communicators is intimate, there is a greater demand for messages of affection; strangers are expected to supply messages that reflect less affection.

- When the speaker perceives the listener as higher in status, there is a greater demand for humility in message sending; when the listener is perceived as lower in status, dignity in message sending is expected—for example, a senator's constituents do not expect him or her to cry when addressing them.

- When the speaker perceives the listener as highly ego-involved in the topic, there is a greater demand for respectful message sending—the speaker would not criticize his mother-in-law in front of his wife; if listener ego-involvement is perceived as low, nonpretentious messages are required—students in required courses would not appreciate messages implying they should be happy to be there.

- When the listener's self-image is highly involved in the message, there is a greater demand for complimentary messages—"I'd like to go out with you . . . I really would . . . but . . ."; when the listener's self-image is not at stake, undramatic messages are called for—the speaker would not expect the listener to get "heated" during idle chatter about the World Series.

- When the listener's basic attitudes are salient due to the situation or the topic of discussion, there is a greater demand for seriousness in message sending; if the listener's basic attitudes are irrelevant to the situation or discussion, more flippant messages may be required—a football superfan would not expect to discuss the next college football season at Comic-Con.

- When the speaker's role in a situation is clearly defined, there is a greater demand for his or her messages to be consistent with that role; a lack of clarity regarding the speaker's role will call for nonpresumptuous message sending. The self-appointed "coordinator" at an informal party is a good example of a violation of the latter.

- When there is a great deal of formality between the communicators, there is a greater demand for messages that could be described as "nongauche"— "Hi, Queenie!" would not be an appropriate way to address the Queen of England; informality requires informal messages.

Naturally, the preceding list represents only some of the many interpersonal conditions that help structure the development of communication norms. You will no doubt think of others. At this point, you may be troubled by what seems to be a communicator's book of etiquette. When you see that "you *can't* do this," "you *must* do this," or "you *aren't supposed* to do this," it is an understandable reaction to question these edicts—to think of the exceptions. After all, people do violate the rules we've discussed, sometimes with little or no punishment from those around them. Why?

Violating Communicative Rules

Norms are brought vividly to our attention when they are violated. Telling a stranger you just met about your favorite way to have sex or refusing to give the same information to an intimate romantic partner are likely to be considered by most people as violations of communicative rules. The preceding violations were rooted in expectations that accompany certain kinds of relationships. But if an adult male turns to an unknown adult female standing next to him in a crowded elevator and says, "Elevators scare

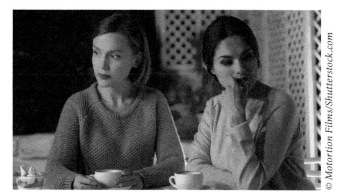
© Motortion Films/Shutterstock.com

me. Will you hold my hand until we get to the first floor?" everyone who hears it (and especially the female target) are likely to move as far away as possible from the speaker because he not only sought intimacy with a stranger, he did it in a place where everyone, even intimates, are expected to communicate in non-intimate ways. [14]

There are many ways to violate conversational rules. Ethnomethodologist Harold Garfinkel gave his undergraduate students the following assignment. Students were instructed to engage an acquaintance or a friend in ordinary conversation and, without indicating that anything was out of the ordinary, insist that the other person clarify the sense of his or her commonplace remarks. The following dialogues represent typical student experiences.[15]

Case One

"Hi, Evan. How is your girlfriend feeling?"

"What do you mean, how is she feeling? Do you mean physical or mental?"

"I mean how is she feeling? What's the matter with you?" (He looked peeved.)

"Nothing. Just explain a little clearer what do you mean."

"Skip it. How are your Med School applications coming?"

"What do you mean, how are they?"

"You know what I mean."

"I really don't."

"What's the matter with you? Are you sick?"

Case Two

On Friday night my husband and I were watching television. My husband remarked that he was tired. I asked, "How are you tired? Physically, mentally, or just bored?"

"I don't know. I guess physically, mainly."

"You mean that your muscles ache, or your bones?"

"I guess so. Don't be too technical."

(After more watching)

"All these old movies have the same kind of old iron bedstead in them."

"What do you mean? Do you mean all old movies, or some of them, or just the ones you have seen?"

"What's the matter with you? You know what I mean."

"I wish you would be more specific."

"You know what I mean! Just shut up!"

These conversations highlight how much we take for granted as we converse with others—how much we "let pass."[16] We assume that any important ambiguities in a person's discourse will be cleared up later. If we violate that rule too often (as illustrated in the cases presented), the other communicator will no doubt observe our violation and sanction us accordingly.

Like any rules, communicative rules require adherence. When the rule is broken, some type of sanctioning usually takes place—rejection, frustration, puzzled or disapproving looks, avoidance, reprimands, or simply a facial expression that visually says, "You're weird!" While this is usual, it is not always the case. For instance, in many of our interactions there is a norm for politeness that discourages us from letting others know that their behavior is strange or inappropriate. Even if someone is talking too much or disclosing information that is too personal, we will sometimes listen attentively to avoid being rude.[17] In other cases, we may not sanction a rule violation because we see the violation as positive. Under the right circumstances, what seems to be excessive displays of affection, involvement, or support from a loved one may be very much appreciated.[18] Also, there are times when we choose not to react negatively to rule violations because of a characteristic or behavior demonstrated by the rule violator.

One way to break communicative rules successfully, incurring little punishment, is to be perceived as a person who was not aware of the expectations for the situation,[19] or one who was aware but was incapable of doing anything about them. A person may be seen as irresponsible or naive ("He didn't know any better"). For example:

GRANDMA: How does my favorite boy like the nice warm sweater Grandma knitted for him?

CHILD: It's yucky.

Or he or she may be perceived as disabled ("She couldn't help it") or as boxed in ("He had no alternative"). A person may also get away with rule violations if seen as "just having fun" ("She didn't mean it").

Sometimes one rule can be violated, but other contiguous rules are not violated, so that one's total behavior is considered balanced. A high school teacher may talk about religion in the classroom but do so in an educational manner. Similarly, rules may be violated when people believe that accomplishing some other task (e.g., answering a phone call, comforting a crying baby) is more important than adhering to the rules.[20] As long as the violation does not violate the relationship, there should be less concern on the part of the message receiver(s).

Rule violations can also be offset by apologies,[21] but a more strategic method of defusing negative reactions is to acknowledge that the rule is about to be broken—a 25-year-old male says to a 45-year-old female stranger: "I know I probably shouldn't ask—and you don't have to answer if you don't want to—but how old are you?" **Disclaimers** of this type were the subject of study by Hewitt and Stokes.[22] They categorized the following types of disclaimers:

1. **Hedging.** This conveys that what follows is tentative and I'm willing to accept other views: "I'm no expert, of course, but . . ."; "I haven't thought this through very well, but . . ."; or "Let me play the devil's advocate here."

2. **Credentialing.** This conveys that I know you'll react unfavorably to what I'm about to say, but I'll try to establish special credentials that will soften that reaction: "Don't get me wrong, I like your work, but . . ." or, "I'm not prejudiced, some of my best friends are . . ."

3. **Sin Licenses.** This conveys that I know you'll react negatively, but that's the way it has to be: "What I'm going to do is contrary to the letter of the law but not its spirit".

4. **Cognitive.** This conveys that I realize you may think I'm losing touch with facts or reality, so I'll acknowledge the fact, thereby showing I am in control: "I know this sounds crazy, but . . ."

5. **Appeal for Suspended Judgment.** This conveys that I know you're going to be tempted to react unfavorably, but wait until you hear the whole story: "I don't want to make you angry by saying this, but I hope you will wait . . ." or "Hear me out before you explode."

If the rule violation is perceived as an isolated instance, it has a greater chance of being accepted, particularly if the significant others (interaction partners and others involved in the situation) can find some unusual, but plausible, explanation for the actions. For example, a person may break down and cry in front of a casual acquaintance who knows that that individual's brother just died of cancer.

A rule can be violated, and unpleasant reactions circumvented, by choosing the rule carefully. If the violated rule is not deeply internalized or ego-related to the relevant, or significant, other(s) or it is not bound by severe sanctions (violations are expected), punishment will be minimal. Asking a total stranger on the street if you can borrow their phone or forgetting the name of someone you were just introduced to would probably fall into this category. Notice how many times the slightest pause in regreeting a person you've been introduced to will cause them to help you by quickly restating their name. In some situations, people realize the rules are not widely known so that violators are given a greater range of behavior before the rule is considered violated. For example, there seem to be few widely accepted rules for interactions involving one's former spouse. And people who are overtly solicitous with a person who is disabled may, at first, be gently encouraged to interact in more conventional ways rather than be reprimanded. Argyle found that people reacted very negatively to violations that prohibited conversation from even taking place. These people considered the following to be totally disruptive: speaking an unknown language, being overly aggressive or disinterested, or responding to an idea by changing the topic. The same people reacted less negatively to violations of rules that would be considered nonessential for conversation to take place.[23] The following were considered only mildly disruptive to conversations: lying on the floor; sitting too close; sitting too far away.

We also know that some people get away with rule violations because they are done with class or style—the violations are not perceived as too gross or too crude. Those who proffer sexual invitations in the initiating or early experimenting stages of a relationship are no doubt acutely aware of this need for sophistication. We would suspect that as the intensity of the conversation and the use of loaded language increases, there is a corresponding increase in the possibility that one or both participants will feel that a rule has been violated.

Shimanoff notes three other reasons why rule violations may not be negatively sanctioned: (1) the violator may be of a higher status and it may, therefore, be in the best interests of the other person to overlook the violation; (2) the violation may be viewed as a violation for the purpose of emphasis or humor; and (3) the act of giving a negative evaluation to someone may, itself, violate a rule of politeness so it is not proffered.[24]

In some situations, people do not care about negative reactions to rule violations. The violation may be used to disorient, frustrate, or elicit defensiveness in others as a means to gain power over them. On other occasions, rule violations are used to get an early reading of the other person.[25] At such times, the person may feel he or she has an adequate number of friends and thus choose to channel the energy into developing relationships with only those who react well in a difficult situation—for example, a rule violation. Also, the person may be extremely fearful of investing time and energy in a close relationship that may end up being hurtful. At such times, rigidity, rejection, and/or responses in line with the norm for the given situation by the recipient may not provide the necessary motivation to develop a closer relationship. Attempts by the recipient to counter the original rule violation with an even stronger violation may also work against attraction in situations of this type. These outcomes pertain to rules or conventions developed by a pair to fulfill their specific needs and desires. These rules can be easily changed (if both participants so desire) and sanctions are normally applied only by the other party, although in some cases "outside executioners" are shipped in.[26]

Most communicative rules are considered informal, nothing like *Robert's Rules of Order*. This informal nature may cause wide variations in adherence. Some people feel almost an obligation to break a rule once it is brought to their attention; others will adhere tenaciously for fear of not being correct. Most of us lie between such extremes. We recognize and can appreciate the fact that communicative rules add predictability, order, and structure to our world. We also recognize that they can be changed—that violations are not necessarily tantamount to social incompetence. We recognize that rules often make life easier—keeping us from having to make an interminable number of interpersonal decisions during each encounter; yet we know that rules are limited—that changes in factors such as the physical environment or in someone's mood[27] may leave us without any clear code of conduct. We understand how helpful a knowledge of communication rules can be when facing new social situations—giving us guidelines for achieving certain communication goals such as acceptance, influence, understanding, and acknowledgment; and we realize the role communication rules play in the satisfaction of interpersonal needs—affection, ego support (or the lack of damage to it), inclusion, control, avoiding conflict, maintaining order, ensuring interaction (or the absence of it), and so on.

With this understanding of the backbone of interaction rituals, communicative rules, the rest of the chapter will explore four common, but important rituals—greetings, forms of address, relationship openings, and small talk.

The Rhetoric of Hello

On the surface, interpersonal greetings seem to be a rather quick, simple, and routinized way of initiating communication.[28] Generally we don't give much thought to what happens during those first few seconds of interaction unless something unusual happens—receiving a warm smile and a "hi" from an unknown passerby or receiving a fully documented medical report when we query, "How are you?" For some time, scholars have regarded greetings and other similarly routinized social sequences (e.g., ordering food at a restaurant) as conversational **scripts** or sequences of actions that we carry out automatically, with very little thought.[29] Although one of the defining features of conversational scripts is that they are predictable, it is important to note that scripts also are flexible and adaptive.[30] In the case of greetings, this means that we adjust what we say to the person we are greeting—depending on our relationship with the person, the mood he or she is in, and how the person responds to us.

Scripts: Sequences of actions that we carry out automatically, with very little thought.

It also is important to remember that just because we normally don't pay much attention to greetings doesn't mean that they are simple or unimportant. In a very real sense, when we say hello (verbally and/or nonverbally), we have implicitly agreed to interfere with another's life. It could be argued, then, that this seemingly insignificant intrusion into another's life brings with it an added responsibility for the other's welfare. Perhaps this is one reason why city dwellers are sometimes described as cold when they do not respond to the well-meaning salutations of strangers; the city dwellers are expressing a need not to get involved. Consider how you feel when a person you know passes you and fails to acknowledge your existence. Conversely, consider how difficult it is for you to intentionally ignore a greeting from an acquaintance. The act of initiating communication is the first step in becoming a part of another person's life. Even passing greetings between strangers provide a form of social recognition, affirmation of a fellow human being's existence, and mutual access to one another.

For our purposes, the most important feature of the greeting ritual is what it tells us about the relationship between the interacting parties.

Greetings and Relationships

Since the manner in which a greeting is performed will help structure the dialogue to follow, it is not surprising that greetings convey information about the relationship.[31] This information may appear in a variety of verbal and nonverbal behaviors. Strangers, for instance, might be more apt to engage in handshaking, formal forms of address (Mr.), and formal expressions such as "Good morning"; "Nice to meet you"; or "Pardon me, but . . ." Intimates may greet each other with an embrace or a kiss, avoid handshaking, use shortened verbalizations such as "Hey!" or some specialized nonverbal gesture unique to themselves. One form of these specialized greetings has been labeled the "friendly insult greeting"—"Hey, dummy!" or "You son-of-a-bitch, how ya doin?"[32] The "insult" is not intended to be taken literally at all, but the metamessage is that "we have such a close relationship, I am confident that you will understand that I mean the opposite of what I'm saying." Of course, there are times when it is not clear to the person being greeted that this is the case, so such greetings may be risky with all but the best of friends.

Status relationships may be noted in the ritual that requires a subordinate in the army to maintain a salute until it is returned by the greeted officer. Greetings by subordinates in executive suites may be proffered from a greater distance. Without belaboring the point, it should be clear that one of the things we say, when we say hello, is what the nature of our relationship is, so the forthcoming dialogue can follow suit. Although our choice of words and behaviors in these situations depends, in part, on our efforts to be socially appropriate (polite) and conversationally efficient,[33] the nature of our relationship with the person we are greeting can override the usual norms for both politeness and efficiency. For instance, researchers have noted that intimates disregard some of the steps that people usually go through when they greet each other on the telephone.[34] Even though politeness norms suggest that people should identify themselves at the beginning of a phone conversation, friends, family members, and lovers often skip over this step. Because they tend to recognize each other's voices and speak to each other frequently, intimates don't always need to identify themselves or the purpose of their call.

When people have been parted for a period of time, it is often necessary to dramatize relationship features. An overly enthusiastic greeting may communicate that the absence has not changed what was previously a good relationship. Hence, the amount of time separating our greetings with a particular person may affect the expansiveness of the greeting. Goffman has proposed an **attenuation rule** that argues that the expansiveness of the greeting will gradually subside with each subsequent greeting, especially when an individual is forced to greet a person numerous times during the day—which is the case in

Attenuation rule: A conversational rule suggesting that the expansiveness of a greeting will gradually subside with each subsequent greeting.

many offices.[35] One of our colleagues, Robert E. Smith, felt it was also the case at the professional conventions of communication scholars that he attends—as his composition testifies:

Convention Book of Days

I

Heeeeyyyy! Jim!

Good to see you!

Looking fantastic

When did you get in?

Flight down went OK

How are things at the university?

Congratulations

That's great about Carolyn

Jimmy, first string, Wow

Olivia, first clarinet, Great

Research going well?

Maybe dinner tomorrow

Heeeeyyyy! Matt . . .

II

Hi, Jim

Enjoying the convention?

Good paper last meeting

Cup of coffee, all right?

III

Hi, Jim

IV

(Buzz off, Jim)

This attenuation rule may also be applicable to the various stages of a relationship. For example, we would expect greetings in the early stages of a relationship to be more inflated or exaggerated than greetings between intimates. Relationships that are coming apart also may reflect a return to the more visibly formalized and stereotyped greetings. The very nature of the relationship between close friends, relatives, or married couples speaks so powerfully that the expansiveness of greeting behavior is allowed to subside and is instead expressed in many subtle and spontaneous ways. Kendon and Ferber have observed the following greeting sequence:[36]

1. **Sighting, Orientation, and Initiation of the Approach.**

2. **Distant Salutation.** This is the "official ratification" that a greeting sequence has been initiated and who the participants are. A wave, smile, or call may be used for recognition. Several types of head movements were noted. One, the "head dip," has also been observed in other situations as a marker to transitions between activities or shifts in psychological orientation. This movement was not observed if the greeter did not continue the approach.

3. **Approach.** As the greeters continued to move toward each other, gazing probably helped signal that channels were cleared for talking. An aversion of this gaze, however, was seen just prior to the close salutation stage. Grooming behavior and one or both arms positioned in front of the body also were observed at this point. When the participants were within ten feet of each other, mutual gazing, smiling, and a positioning of the head not seen in the sequence thus far were seen. The palms of the hands were sometimes turned toward the other person.

4. **Close Salutation.** As the participants negotiated a standing position, ritualistic comments such as "Hi, Will! How ya doin'?" were heard. And, if the situation called for body contact (handshakes, embraces), it would occur at this time.

Although it would be literally impossible to catalogue each specific verbal and nonverbal greeting behavior for each type of person in every situation and every kind of relationship, a general taxonomy has been developed.[37]

Nonverbally, greetings are frequently initiated by a vertical or sideways motion of the head accompanied by eye contact. Kendon notes that a head toss probably invites further interaction—as does a tilting of the head back and/or raising of the eyebrows. But nods or a lowering of the head while making some other greeting gesture (e.g., wave) is likely to be just a greeting-in-passing. One of the functions of eye contact is signaling that the channels of communication are open. Should you not wish to pursue a conversation with a person, the avoidance of eye contact is imperative since a prolonged mutual glance almost obligates you to extend the encounter. Other eye-related greeting behaviors include winks or what is known as an **eyebrow flash**, a distinct up-and-down movement of the eyebrows which is barely detectable. Some observations from other cultures suggest that the eyebrow flash may be a universal behavior attendant to greetings.[38] The hands also may be very active in the greeting process. Salutes, waves, handshakes, handslaps, and various emblematic gestures such as the peace sign, raised fist, or thumbs up may be seen. The hands also may be engaged in grooming attendant to the greeting—running fingers through one's hair. Touching, in the form of embraces, kisses, or hitting on the arm is also common. The mouth may take the form of a smile or an oval shape, which suggests a possible readiness for subsequent talk.

Eyebrow flash: A distinct up-and-down movement of the eyebrows which is barely detectable.

Sometimes we find ourselves in close contact with strangers and wish to signal that we do not want to greet them. Observations of people in such circumstances in a bar, shopping center, and on a college campus found the following nonverbal behaviors occurring in most of the situations: lip compression; lip bite; tongue-show; tongue-in-cheek; downward, lateral, and maximal lateral gaze avoidance; hand-to-face, hand-to-hand, hand-to-body, and hand-behind-head automanipulations; and postures involving flexion and adduction of upper limbs. These behaviors, which signaled "stay away" or "greeting will not be well received," abruptly ceased after the strangers left the scene.[39]

Verbally, greetings may be classified along the following lines:

1. Verbal salutes—"Good morning."
2. Direct references to the other person by name, nickname, or personal pronoun—"Hi, babe!" or "Jeremiah!"
3. Questions of personal inquiry—"What's new with you?" or "How ya doin'?"
4. Verbalizations expressing a desire to continue a past relationship—"Long time no see" or "Nice seeing you *again.*"
5. Compliments—"You're looking great."
6. References to here-and-now surroundings—"May I get you another drink?" or "Can you tell me who did that painting?"
7. References to people or things, outside the immediate interaction setting—"How do you like this weather we're having?"
8. References to the other's behavior—"I noticed you were sitting all alone over here."
9. References to oneself—"Boy, have I had a rough day!" or "Hi, I'm Mark Knapp."
10. Apologies—"Excuse me, but . . . "
11. Unexpected, humorous, or whimsical phrases designed to break the ice—"How's your love life?" or "This is the best drink I've had since breakfast."
12. Immediate topic initiation that usually excludes any preliminary comments—"The reason I wanted to talk to you . . . "
13. Single words or vocalizations that are essentially content free—"Well!" or muted grunting sound.

The preceding list of behaviors is representative, but not necessarily exhaustive. Any given greeting may fall into several of the categories discussed. A legitimate question at this point might be: So what? So what if we go to all the trouble to dissect greeting behavior? In answer, the major advantage of this classification system is that it may eventually help us understand more precisely what particular form greetings take at various stages of development and deterioration in human relationships. Once we are able to identify typical and regular patterns associated with specific stages and in specific situations, we have taken a giant step toward explaining the success or failure experienced later in the encounter.

For instance, if you greet a close friend with behaviors typically found in interactions with strangers, a greater quantity of subsequent messages about the relationship itself may be required to make up for this unexpected behavior.

Forms of Address

Like greetings, the way we address another person may be brief, but it can say volumes about the relationship we have with that person. We are able to communicate our relative status to the other person, how well we are acquainted with him or her, whether we are angry or affectionate toward him or her, and whether the situation is a formal or informal one— all by the way we choose to address that person.[40] Fortunately, most of us have a variety of names and titles that provide several options as forms of address—Colonel Maxwell Q. Black, Colonel Black, Sir, Max, Maxie, "Ol' Stonedface." If a person offers a limited number of mutations of his or her name, others will often invent their own variations. This does not mean, of course, that we don't have trouble deciding how to address people. When we have difficulty determining our relative status or degree of intimacy to another, choices are frustrating—the familiar student dilemma: Dr., Professor, Mr., Mrs., Ms., Miss, Herbert, or Mary Ellen? And what are the in-laws to be known as: Mr. and Mrs., Mom and Dad, Jim and Mavis, or should it wait until they can be Grandma and Grandpa?[41] As a rule, the more intimate we feel toward someone, the more we will be inclined to use less formal forms of address. The manifestations of this rule, and the exceptions to it, will be discussed in conjunction with the following continuum of formality for forms of address: (1) formal-impersonal, (2) ambiguous formality, (3) informal, and (4) intimate-affectionate.

© mirzavisoko/Shutterstock.com

Formal-Impersonal

The formal forms of address are generally used with strangers, new acquaintances, and those we perceive to have greater status than we do. In each case, the social distance between the communicators is high. Brown has identified what he believes is a universal norm underlying forms of address: Higher-status persons address subordinates with a form that people of equal status use when they are well acquainted or intimate (Will or Charlie); subordinates, on the other hand, must address the higher-status person with a form that people of equal status use when they are strangers or new acquaintances (Mr. Jennings).[42] This norm, which incorporates indices of status and affection, seems to have parallels in other behavior as well. For instance, Henley argues that people are most likely to initiate touching behavior with those of a status lower than their own—just as they do with people toward whom they feel affectionate.[43] Similarly, we've observed Ph.D.s calling the janitor they may see once or twice a week for thirty seconds by his nickname—"Hi, Mac." Researchers have argued that shorter names (like Mac) tend to be associated with approachability, whereas longer names (like Katherine or Alexander) tend to be linked to success and/or morality. Although this is clearly not always the case,[44] it may be part of the reason why people of a lower status are often addressed by their nicknames. Also, as we will note later, the use of nicknames generally is associated with people who feel more intimate with each other. Some observers of the current social scene have noted that women are more often called by their affectionate nickname (Abby, Izzie, or Lilly). Men are more often known by an informal nickname (Will or Tom, but not Willy or Tommy). In view of the parallels between affection and superiority presented thus far, such a finding (if it were true) would certainly have value for analyzing traditional perceptions of women in contemporary U.S. society.

Because formal names and titles often carry a sense of power or superiority, some researchers have investigated the extent to which we perceive certain names or titles as more masculine or feminine than others. For example, McConnell and Fazio found that people associated gender-marked, "man-suffixed" titles (e.g., chairman) with more masculine personality characteristics and "person-suffix" titles (e.g., chairperson) with relatively feminine characteristics.[45] They also found that individuals who had traditional beliefs about gender roles were more influenced by gender-marked titles than were those with liberal beliefs. Given that formal titles provide information about our status, it is important to consider that the choices we make with regard to the use of these titles also may send messages about our personality characteristics.

Formal forms of address are most often used when we perceive the other person's age, title, authority, eminence, or seniority as greatly above our own and when we feel this discrepancy needs to be manifested in the way we address the person. Formal forms of address also will manifest themselves when we fear the other person or when we want to build the addressee's ego through ingratiation strategies.

Ambiguous Formality

In the process of our life growth, our growth in school, or in our careers, we will periodically reach points at which the perception of ourselves, relative to another in a particular situation, is vague. In short, we just don't know how to address someone. It might be a situation in which we feel a particular person doesn't warrant deference any longer because status differences have grown fuzzy—calling parents by their first names rather than "Mom" or "Dad," or calling a dissertation advisor by his or her first name. Imagine the dilemma for the Nixon cadre during and after the Watergate coverup—Mr. President? Mr. Nixon? Dick? Sir? Ahhh...? It also might be a situation in which a person asks us to call him or her by his or her first name and we are reluctant to do so. There are any number of reasons why we will feel uncertainty or ambiguity about what to call someone. As a result, we may end up using any of the following strategies: (1) The most formal of the ambiguous forms of address includes Sir, Miss, Ma'am, Ms., and so on. (2) The playful in-between is exemplified by "Doc" for a Ph.D. (3) The least formal response to the ambiguous situation is what Little and Gelles call the *Hey you form of address*.[46] A good example is the extended and amplified "Ahhhhh . . . " (with upraised finger) in place of a name or title.

Informal

The informal forms of address are usually derived from a person's first name—Sam is an informal form of Samuel. In status-differentiated encounters, the higher-status individual will usually ask the subordinate to call him or her by a less formal name. Many times, people try to speed up a relationship by deliberately using another person's first name when the situation calls for a more formal appellation. When you encounter a car salesperson and become offended by the salesperson's casual and frequent use of your first name, it may be because you perceive a needed formality for your relationship (strangers) and for the situation (business deals), not to mention the feeling that his or her usage immediately limits you to either subordinate or peer status at best.

Intimate-Affectionate

The intimate-affectionate form represents the least formal of the forms used to address others. Ordinarily, this form is reserved for close friends or intimates. Even within this category, however, there seem to be subcategories of formality: (1) A further alteration of one's given name seems to be the most formal—Charlie or Trish. Sometimes names do not have natural intimate forms, so others will invent them—Marko for Mark. The usual manner of inventing these alterations is to add an *ie* or *y* to make an "ee" sound. Although most adult males regard this as too symbolic of childhood names, many exceptions do exist—Bobby Kennedy, Teddy Roosevelt, Jimmy Carter. A variation on given-name alteration is to use a person's middle name when it is not known to others and knowledge of it is symbolic of interpersonal closeness. (2) Nicknames that have been given because they are somehow associated with one's appearance, role, or activities represent the next lower level of formality—"Stretch," "Cupcake," "Boss," "Goose," or "Hands." Sometimes a name that starts out as a nickname becomes so commonly used in so many different relationships that it no longer has the uniqueness necessary to qualify as an intimate form of address—"Shaq" for basketball player Shaquille O'Neal. (3) Even more personal are those names that are considered traditional terms of endearment. These generally encompass terms designating the person as either sacred ("Angel"), an innocent small animal ("Chickadee"), or child ("Babe," "Honey Child") or a pleasant taste experience ("Sugar," "Honey"). (4) The most intimate forms of address seem to be those that have no apparent explanation, are often nonsensical, and are likely to be embarrassing if used in the presence of others—"Poopsie," "Booper," or "Snookums."

Although we would predict more personal forms of address between intimates, variations will appear, depending on how long intimacy has been established and what conditions exist in the environment for communicating. For instance, we are likely to find that longtime intimates may cease to use any mode of address. In addition, they may occasionally use the more formal forms, perhaps to emphasize closeness or just to be playful—"Thelma Z. Peters, I love you very much." The use of technology also may affect the way intimates address each other. Romantic partners may be more subtle about their expressions of affection on Facebook than they would be in a more private context.[47] Similarly, the presence of others may cause an individual to address a close friend in a very formal manner—in a graduate student's oral examination, you might hear close friends addressing each other as Dr. and Professor. Obviously, the audience is not the friend, and the friend understands. Formality may also change as the situation and roles change—Professor Ruggirello in the classroom becomes "Frank" in the touch football game.

As we mentioned earlier, the same form of address can be used to express anger or affection. Depending on the vocal inflection, the phrase "Look here, Baby Doll" could be demeaning and hateful or tender and loving. Naturally, the use of the intimate form greatly assists a demeaning vocal inflection in eliciting a defensive response. At other times anger or serious intent can be shown by simply increasing the degree of formality (and vocal volume). The following, familiar message construction seen in parent-child episodes illustrates this:

Most Intimate	Herbie, no.
	Herb, don't.
	Herbert, don't do that . . . please.
	Herbert Wilson—I've told you a hundred
	times not to do that!
Most Formal	Herbert Wilson Knapp—I want you to stop
	that this instant!

Relationship "Openers"

How do you begin a relationship? Earlier in this chapter, we noted that there are rules that help guide our communication choices. In most communication situations, we can recognize behaviors that are socially appropriate and others that are socially inappropriate. For instance, when greeting a superior, we tend to use more formal address terms than we would when greeting a peer. Even though rules such as these seem as if they should provide us with a prescription for how to begin relationships, they rarely do. In fact, often when we would like to initiate a relationship with someone, it is much easier for us to think of *in*appropriate behaviors than it is to think of appropriate ones. As a result, some people spend a great deal of time planning and rehearsing how to begin their first conversation with someone they are attracted to. The classic example of this involves what many refer to as the "opening line."

Many prescriptions for good and bad opening lines are offered by the media and friends and acquaintances. However, many do not identify important contingencies such as the relationship between the communicators and the setting, the nonverbal cues used by communicators,[48] and the ability of each communicator to elicit disclosure from the other.[49] Those prescriptions that fail to recognize the importance of such factors tend to take on the characteristics of interpersonal burlesque. One book, which says it will help women convince a man they want that the "have something that's worth looking closely into" is advertised by the following paragraph:

> In an easy to understand and personal way, this book teaches **EVERY-THING** a woman needs to know to catch her elusive **Mr. Right**. This book gives tips on how women can get the attention of a man she likes, how to get asked for a date, how to behave on a date, what to talk about, and how to win a man's love. How can women know if they have found **Mr. Right**, if they can't get men interested enough to ask for a second date? After reading this book, not only will there be a second date, there'll be a third and a fourth . . . Men will seek your company and they'll be the ones wondering if **YOU** may be the girl of their dreams.[50]

Another book, which sports "a proven system for effortlessly starting conversations, flirting & connecting with women, and leading conversations to sex" is advertised this way:

> Do you freeze up when you see an attractive girl? Do you run out of things to say? Do you struggle to attract women through conversation? It doesn't have to be this way . . . What if you could effortlessly strike up a conversation with any women, at any time, in any environment? What if you knew exactly how to keep the conversation going (so you never ran out of things to say)? What if you could command women's attention and instantly connect with them? What if you could turn any conversation from boring to "sexual"? That would all make your life a lot more fun, right? Well, it's not out of your reach. All of this is very possible. And you'll discover exactly how to do it in *Conversation Casanova*.[51]

Another author who believed it necessary to justify his classification of "Hello" as a good opening line comments: "This is a fantastic opening line. I wish I could take credit for it. Probably millions of relationships between men and women have begun on this basis. If you feel more comfortable with 'Hi,' the results will be equally good."[52] This same author identified the following as bad opening gambits between men and women:

1. Haven't I met you someplace before?
2. You are a beautiful person.
3. Let's go to bed.
4. I love you. Do you believe in love at first sight?
5. Do you think it will rain?
6. You look like a movie star.
7. Are you alone?
8. You look lonely.
9. Why are you here?
10. Where have I seen you before?

None but the most foolhardy would "guarantee success" with any message without some knowledge of who said it; to whom it was said; how it was said (vocal tone); whether, or how often, it had been said before; where it was said; or what messages preceded it or would follow it. The assumptions underlying these prescriptions from the popular press are, however, important. Recipes for cookbook communication designed to initiate encounters are based on the belief that (1) enough people have experienced difficulty in initiating communication to seek simple, guaranteed prescriptions and (2) a number of people in this culture attach a great deal of importance to these initial behaviors, recognizing their role in facilitating or inhibiting the communication that follows.

Only acceptable pickup line: "Hi, my name is [insert your name]. What's yours?"

—*Anonymous*

In an attempt to survey people who might actually use these opening lines and to categorize them according to different locations, psychologists Kleinke, Meeker, and Staneski asked several hundred college students in California and Massachusetts to write down all the opening lines they could think of that men might use with women at beaches, supermarkets, and bars.[53] After selecting the 100 most frequently cited openers, Kleinke and his colleagues asked 600 more students from the same two states to rate each line from "terrible" to "excellent." Both men and women respondents seemed to prefer the "direct" and "innocuous" lines over the "cute/flip" ones. But most men underestimated how much women were put off by the cute/flip approach. Some of the top-rated lines included the following:

In General Situations:

"I feel a little embarrassed, but I'd like to meet you." (direct)

At the Beach:

"The water is beautiful today, isn't it?" (innocuous)

At the Supermarket:

"Can you help me decide here? I'm a terrible shopper." (direct)

At the Bar:

"What do you think of the band?" (innocuous)

The bottom-rated lines included:

In General Situations:

"Is that really your hair?"

"Your place or mine?"

"You remind me of a woman I used to date."

At the Beach:

"Let me see your strap marks."

At the Supermarket:

"Do you really eat that junk?"

At the Bar:

"Bet I can outdrink you."

In another study, Murray found that the almost 3,000 opening lines he observed fell into three categories: questions (e.g., "How are you?"), advertisements/declarations (e.g., "My name is Heather"), and compliments (e.g., "I like your suit"). He also found that the use of sexual propositions and all three types of opening lines increased drastically from 10:00 p.m. to 11:00 p.m. and continued to increase at a slower rate until 1:00 a.m. Since his study was conducted in singles bars, this pattern is not surprising. As Murray himself notes, patterns of alcohol consumption, increased desperation (as closing time neared), and increases in perceived attraction (as desperation increased) probably account for this phenomenon.[54]

Although Murray's study focused on opening lines and sexual propositions in singles bars, the influence of alcohol on people's behavior during the early stages of relational development is apparent in other contexts as well. For instance, Mongeau and Johnson found that on first dates, binge drinkers were more likely to become sexually involved than were non–binge drinkers and that non–binge drinkers, in turn, engaged in more sexual involvement that nondrinkers.[55] They also found that men reported more intimate sexual expectations and involvement than did women. Of course, alcohol is not the only factor that can affect how receptive people are to opening lines and propositions. Research suggests that individuals who have experienced **ego depletion**—who have just engaged in a task that requires mental self-control—are less receptive to cute/flip opening lines and slightly more receptive to innocuous opening lines.[56]

Ego depletion: The idea that self-control draws on limited mental resources that can be used up.

A consistent theme that runs throughout all of these studies is that "good" opening lines rarely reveal the candid thoughts of the speaker. Granted, some people present themselves in a more direct, genuine way than do others.[57] But even the most direct lines (e.g., "I'd sure like to meet you") typically don't focus on relational or sexual issues. Douglas explains this by noting that although we might like to be more direct and efficient (e.g., "Do you find me physically attractive?"), we must balance our conversational efficiency with social appropriateness.[58] Certainly, it would be easier to reduce our uncertainty about potential relational partners by being more direct. However, since relational development is based on the wants and needs of *both* people, we must consider how the other person is going to respond to our direct inquiries. When we are first attracted to someone and we are uncertain about that person feels about us, this is a difficult task. In fact, even after people have been dating someone for a while, their uncertainty about the relationship can affect the requests they make of their partner. Research suggests, for example, that when individuals who are uncertain about their relationship ask their partner out for a date, their requests are less fluent, less affiliative, less focused on the relationship, less explicit, and perceived as less effective than requests made by people who are relatively certain about their relationship.[59]

In many cases, the response to an opening line or a request for a date is observable because the line is delivered and received in a face-to-face context. However, a number of different channels are available to those seeking a romantic relationship, including dating apps, internet chat rooms, video dating services, match makers, and personal ads. These alternative channels restrict some forms of communication (e.g., the ability to observe potential partners' nonverbal behavior, engage in deep self-disclosure) and allow for more freedom with regard to others (e.g., direct questions, impression management).[60] Researchers have found that people use more direct and intimate uncertainty reduction behaviors (e.g., they ask more intimate questions) when they engage in initial interactions online than they do when they meet face-to-face.[61] Individuals who use computer dating services report that these more direct communication strategies—combined with the ability to screen potential partners based on body type, education level, age, income, or hobbies—speed up the process of dating because they provide a way for potential partners to gather information about each other before they decide to initiate an interaction[62]

Although the communication that occurs between people who use these mediated channels may differ from face-to-face interaction, it does provide an indication of what some people think they want in a relational partner as well as what they believe others want. For instance, in studies of personal ads placed, several trends emerged: (1) heterosexual men wanted what heterosexual women offered—physical attractiveness, (2) heterosexual women sought what heterosexual men offered—financial security, (3) gay men emphasized physical attractiveness in their ads even more than did heterosexual men, and (4) lesbian women tended to deemphasize physical attractiveness as something to be sought or offered.[63] Personal ads placed by people over the age of 50 tend to put less emphasis on physical appearance than those placed by younger people and tend to focus on relational goals that are more restrained and less sexual.[64]

The increased use of alternative channels for meeting and communicating with potential dating partners has prompted the development of some new rules for initial interactions. In many cases, these rules compensate for the lack of nonverbal information that people are able to obtain from internet chat rooms, personal ads, or video dating services. Most people who are familiar with the current dating scene recommend that those who use mediated forms of communication to meet potential partners adhere to the following five guidelines:[65]

1. Remember that individuals who use dating apps or who place personal ads can lie. People who say they are tall may be short, those who act as if they are young may be old, and those who claim they are men may be women.

2. Ask people for specific information before you meet face-to-face (e.g., their age, occupation, and where they live). Be cautious of someone who gives you vague or inconsistent answers.

3. If you decide to meet someone face-to-face, agree to meet in a well-lighted, public place.

4. Tell a good friend or family member where and when your meeting will be.

5. Keep your first meeting simple (e.g., a meal or a drink). Spending an entire weekend together may sound romantic, but it does not offer you much flexibility if your meeting does not go as you planned.

Whether you initially interact with someone online, over the phone, or at a party, a "good" opening line doesn't ensure relationship development. Bell and Daly have found that people believe they use a number of other communication strategies to get people to like and appreciate them. These **affinity-seeking** strategies include behaviors that (1) demonstrate one's *control and visibility* (e.g., being dynamic and interesting), (2) encourage *mutual trust* (e.g., consistently fulfilling commitments), (3) display *politeness* (e.g., adhering to conversational rules), (4) demonstrate *concern and caring* (e.g., listening to and supporting the other), (5) *involve the other* (e.g., including the other in activities), (6) show *self-involvement* (e.g., participating in the other's activities), and (7) focus on *commonalities* (e.g., pointing out similarities). People who were reported as using many of these affinity-seeking strategies also were rated as being more likable, socially successful, and satisfied with their lives. The use of other-oriented

Affinity-seeking strategies: Communication strategies that individuals use to get others to like and feel positively toward them.

strategies (e.g., caring, listening, and including the other) seemed to best predict affinity. In addition, individuals' choice of affinity-seeking strategies depended on contextual and relational factors. People believed they used different strategies in task-oriented situations than in social situations, and they noted that status differences influenced their strategy choice.[66] These findings underline both the complexity and the mutuality of our initial interactions. When two people converse, both of them determine whether the conversation is successful and satisfying, and both determine whether to continue the relationship. It is impossible to plan a conversation in its entirety (choosing the appropriate greeting, form of address, opening line, and affinity-seeking strategy) because we don't know how the other person will respond to us.[67] Characteristics of that individual, the initial impression we establish, and the context will influence our interaction. Communication rules provide us with a guideline, but it is a very general and necessarily flexible guideline.

After achieving contact and making our initial approach to conversation, the most common type of communication typically follows.

Small(?) Talk

What we commonly know as **small talk** has been discussed by other authors using terms such as *grooming talk*, *phatic communion*, *superficial talk*, *social cosmetics,* and *cliché conversation*. For some, this activity seems to be unimportant, even repugnant. Powell[68] correctly identified small talk as superficial, conventional, and perhaps the lowest level of communication about oneself. Indeed, small talk is characterized by breadth, not depth. We might expect to find a fair range of topics discussed but little motivation to reveal seldom-seen parts of one's inner self.

While small talk often is seen as trivial, research suggests this view is a gross miscalculation of the role it plays in our relationships. Even though engaging in meaningful, substantive conversations is associated with our well-being,[69] the human condition is dependent on our ability to draw from a vast repertoire of topics, strategies, and feelings. We need intimate conversation, but we also need to be able to communicate at various levels of intimacy. Small talk represents a form of communication that is critical to developing and maintaining relationships. In some contexts, such as the workplace, small talk is associated with trust.[70] In other situations, such as cocktail parties, family gatherings, and first encounters, small talk is almost the demanded form of communication. Without the ability to engage another in small talk in these situations, our ability to connect with others would surely suffer.

© Robert Kneschke/Shutterstock.com

Those people who castigate small talk are probably expressing displeasure with the way in which it was conducted, not with the act of small talk per se. Like greetings, the act of engaging in small talk may be as important as the content of the exchange. Notice how engaging in small talk in the following example serves an important function in relationship building, even though the participants do not speak the same language:

> A U.S. businessman who, while traveling to Europe for the first time, finds himself seated across from a Frenchman at lunch. Neither speaks the other's language, but each smiles a greeting. As the wine is served, the Frenchman raises his glass and gesturing to the American says, "Bon appetit!" The American does not understand and replies, "Ginzberg." No other words are exchanged at lunch. That evening at dinner, the two again sit at the same table and again the Frenchman greets the American with the wine, saying, "Bon appetit!" to which the American replies, "Ginzberg." The waiter notices this peculiar exchange and, after dinner, calls the American aside to explain that "the Frenchman is not giving his name—he is wishing you good appetite; he is saying that he hopes you enjoy your meal." The following day the American seeks out the Frenchman at lunch, wishing to correct his error. At the first opportunity the American raises his glass and says, "Bon appetit!" to which the Frenchman proudly replies, "Ginzberg."[71]

Even when communicators speak the same language, listening may not be the intent and the exchange of noises assumes precedence over substance.

The prevention of silence is, itself, an important conversational goal fulfilled by small talk. For some, it is difficult to accept the fact that there are communicative exchanges that shouldn't be taken too literally: trivial conversation at parties doesn't mean everybody there (except us) was somehow devoid of intelligent things to say; and people who can't remember the topic of the sermon immediately upon leaving church may still have had a deeply religious experience. In many instances, the literal translation of the words spoken is less important than the fact that words have been spoken. When a new student walks into a professor's office and sees him or her surrounded by papers, furiously pounding at the computer, and asks, "Are you busy?" the professor doesn't usually turn around and say, "No, I'm relaxing." The student's words were intended to be translated, "Hello! There's somebody here to see you. I want to talk to you. I realize I'm interrupting you. You may not want to talk to me or you may not have time, so I'll ask a question that will give you the opportunity to ease out of this encounter by saying you're busy. I hope you appreciate the way I handled this interruption—so much so that you won't use the excuse I've given you." So, like this example of an opening line, small talk is often an end in itself. But small talk is also a means to an end—that is, it serves several important interpersonal functions.

Functions of Small Talk

Small talk is a way of maintaining a sense of community or fellowship with other human beings. It helps us cement our bond of humanness. Desmond Morris calls it a "friendly mutual aid system" akin to the grooming and licking rituals of nonhuman primates that provide feelings of comfort, security, and acceptance.[72] Hayakawa calls it "the language of social cohesion."[73] Keeping the lines of communication open with members of your own species and enjoying the togetherness of talking often take precedence over subject matter. In fact, small talk serves a number of functions. For example, in the jargon of Schutz's interpersonal needs, we could say small talk is particularly effective in satisfying inclusion needs,[74] since it is designed so that each party can (or must) contribute. Perhaps this is one reason that we find so little disagreement or conflict in small talk; supportiveness and affirmation are indispensable for maintaining effectively a sense of community with our fellow humans.

In addition to providing us with feelings of inclusion, small talk is an important mechanism for socialization. By observing and engaging in small talk, we learn how to function as a member of a group—whether that group is a family, an organization, or a society.[75] Small talk teaches us rules about how to structure our interactions. It tells us which group members are dominant and which are more submissive. Small talk shows children how to take turns and how to avoid interrupting others (e.g., "Just a minute dear; it's Daddy's turn to talk now"). It offers people who are new to organizations information about how the organization functions (e.g., "Remember the time when the copier machine was broken for two weeks?"). It teaches members of a society or a culture about what is acceptable and unacceptable at any given point in history (e.g., "Can you believe that just 25 years ago people used to . . . ?").

Small talk also serves as a proving ground or test for both new and established relationships. Small talk in this sense, then, becomes an "audition for friendship." We noted earlier how potential friends and acquaintances are visually filtered; during small talk, we apply a verbal filter. Small talk allows us to gather information about others so that we can decide if we are able and willing to begin to trust them.[76] Only after we are satisfied with the communication at the superficial level of small talk do we venture into "big talk"—communication characterized by greater focus and depth of personal disclosures. Sometimes we mistakenly associate seriousness exclusively with big talk. However, it is easy to think of many serious conversations (task-oriented business discussions or courtship games) that still offer only surface information about the participants.

People often assume that big talk is more important than small talk for maintaining relationships, but relational maintenance is an important function of small talk. Goldsmith and Baxter found that nearly half of all the conversations people reported having with acquaintances, friends, romantic partners, family members, and others consisted of relatively informal, superficial talk.[77] Likewise, Duck and his colleagues found that intimates really spend a relatively small portion of their everyday conversation engaged in self-disclosive discussions.[78] Even though intimacy is usually a precursor to self-disclosure, self-disclosure doesn't always characterize intimate relationships. For instance, one trick for the person seeking instant intimacy is to give the illusion of serious self-revelation that can be shrugged off as superficial small talk if the request for instant intimacy is denied; the other person has not truly become a confidant.

In established relationships, small talk may be dispensed with more quickly and easily, but it is a necessary prelude to more intimate dialogue. When romantic partners reunite after being separated for a period of time, they often feel the need to engage in some small talk. Talking about what happened while they were apart can assure them that their relationship has not changed and allow them to escalate to their past-relationship-level talk once again.

Small talk also provides a safe procedure for indicating who we are and how another can come to know us better. We're playing for time, trying to display our best features. If one of our many selves doesn't seem to work, we can always shift gears and bring out another self. Although most small talk centers on topics that are safe (and relatively bland), there are cases when it involves topics that are more risky—sometimes people tell rude jokes or gross stories when they engage in small talk.[79] This more colorful form of small talk can create a sense of intimacy when both speakers and listeners agree to participate (e.g., by laughing at a joke or elaborating on a story). Whether it focuses on safe or risky topics, small talk allows us to further reduce uncertainties about the other without revealing too much about ourselves too soon. The fewer the uncertainties, the greater the chances of accurate predictions about the person—and the greater the chances of moving from small talk to big talk.

Another function of small talk is to serve as an interpersonal pacifier. It is a nonthreatening, time-killing activity devoid of the pressures involved in more analytical or introspective processes. Some researchers have found that couples use small talk to avoid discussion of conflict.[80] Small talk, in short, can be a release, an escape valve, or a diversion from other kinds of talk that require more conscious thought.[81]

And finally, small talk provides a means for uncovering integrating topics, or, more simply, openings for more penetrating conversations and relationships. We now turn our attention to the nature of these topics, which is the information derived and exchanged during small talk.

Name, Rank, and Serial Number

When strangers meet for the first time, the first few minutes will usually be devoted to an exchange of demographic or biographical information—name, occupation, marital status, hometown.[82] Both people are attempting to obtain a sociological profile of the other in the hope that certain similarities will be uncovered and form a common ground for conversational pursuit. Of course, this depends on the number of environmental cues that are available. The exchange of biographical information is more involved when environmental cues do not provide much information about who a partner might be. In other situations, the environment allows participants to make more inferences with more certainty. Under such circumstances, the acquisition of information is likely to be less directed and less strategic.[83] For example, if you meet a person in a university building carrying books, you might not feel the need to ask if the person is a student, where the person goes to school, what general age range the person represents, and so forth. In some cases, the environmental forces will be so compelling that strangers will begin exchanging attitudes and opinions before seeking demographic data—for example, two delegates who meet at a political gathering. During the early information exchange—a period Berger calls the *entry phase*—a norm often seems to be operating that says: If I provide you with some information about myself, you will reciprocate by giving me an equal amount of information about yourself. Or, in simpler terms, "I'll tell you my hometown if you tell me yours."

The reason biographical information is so predominant in a new relationship is that it is something each party is sure to know about himself or herself, and it is generally nonthreatening because it is nonarguable. Sure, we could start an argument over somebody's hometown, but we generally reserve that for later.

Other topics commonly encountered in initial small talk may be derived from the situation or surroundings: "I'm building a house and I was wondering what kind of insulation you selected for this room." The weather seems to be a topic everyone knows, is a part of every situation, and is generally nonthreatening. The topic of weather will probably occur more often in certain areas of the country and at certain times during the year. Some sections of the country seem to have local guidelines for small talk topics. In Lafayette, Indiana, for instance, it is not unusual to talk about the dearth of good restaurants in the area or the fact that it's a "good place to raise kids." Another currently popular ploy is to talk about how much you hate small talk and how people really aren't open with each other. Of course, talking *about* openness meets all the necessary criteria for small talk and is very different from actually *being* open by disclosing more intimate aspects of your personality. Finally, Beinstein's research shows how the topics for small talk often will reflect the environment, the time allowed for interaction, the distance between the participants, and the ostensible purpose for the meeting.[84] She obtained data on topics discussed in twenty-eight barber shops, thirty beauty shops, and thirty pharmacies in Philadelphia during the summer. It is no surprise that vacations were a frequent topic in all the shops, nor that beauticians talked with their customers mainly about fashions, nor that pharmacists talked with their customers mainly about health problems. The only surprise may have been that barbers talked about vacations more than sports.[85]

Once we have sufficiently stocked our biographical warehouse, we can begin to focus on those aspects that seem to be productive avenues for further conversation (increase the depth) or pursue additional areas that seem logically related (increase the breadth). Upon learning that a couple is not married and just living together, you may choose to slowly tap the conditions and value system that led to that decision or you may seek another different, but related area—"Yeah, couples have a lot of different choices to make now. My sister got married with the understanding that she would not have any kids." More often than not, breadth is our choice with strangers and acquaintances; when depth is pursued, however, it is usually a brief foray unless the communicators already have a close relationship or unless special circumstances indicate that the other person needs and wants to uncover a particular inner area.

His own small talk, at any rate, was bigger than most people's large. "I believe it was Hegel who defined love as the ideality of the relatively of the reality of an infinitesimal portion of the absolute totality of the Infinite Being" he would chat at dinner.

—*Peter De Vries*

Thus, through small talk we eventually obtain knowledge about the other person—hobbies, interests, likes, dislikes, tastes, future plans, other acquaintances and friends. Gradually, small talk will move past the highly superficial, biographical level, and information will be gained about attitudes, opinions, goals, and specific ways of behaving—how the person handles mistakes, conflict, play, and support for others. It is only when we begin to tap those things that a person does not reveal to just anybody—topics that are held in the middle layers of Altman and Taylor's Social Penetration Model (see Chapter 2)—that we have moved from small talk to big talk.

Berger points out the usefulness of this harvesting of biographical information in predicting possible attitudes a person might hold—similar backgrounds may suggest similar attitudes.[86] It seems we work backward too, predicting possible biographical information from perceived attitudes. If we disagree or agree with someone, we sometimes try to relate that back to some previously uncovered aspect of background similarity or dissimilarity. It is likely, however, that when we're surprised (background dissimilarities turn into attitude agreements or background similarities turn into attitude

© Rocketclips, Inc./Shutterstock.com

disagreements), we will be less inclined to recall our earlier store of information and attribute the situation, instead, to the current phase of the relationship.

Small talk also aids friends and family who have been separated to pick up their relationship again. When people are separated, uncertainty increases and once again they have to start the feeling-out process. Since biographical data are the least apt to change, relational partners often start their small talk by asking what's been happening, what they've been doing since they last saw each other, and so on. By telling friends and family what happened during a separation, we help them to "catch up" with our past and provide them with knowledge that may facilitate their interaction with us in the future.[87] Most of us engage in this type of small talk on a more limited basis with roommates, family, and lovers when we talk with them about what happened in our day. "Debriefing" a relational partner about the events of our day seems to have an important function in our relationships. Researchers have found that spouses who spent more time talking together about the events of their day tended to be more relationally satisfied.[88]

In an attempt to summarize some of the material discussed thus far, let's look at a study conducted by Berger and his colleagues.[89] More than 200 adult residents of a Chicago suburb were asked to imagine they were observing a two-hour conversation between people meeting for the first time. These "observers" sorted 150 preselected statements into eight 15-minute segments. They were also asked to place those statements that they felt would not occur in a two-hour conversation of this type into a separate category. Generally, the results confirm what we've been saying thus far: demographic and superficial information about oneself tends to be disclosed to new acquaintances first; personal, sexual, and family problems are consistently placed in later time slots. Some noteworthy exceptions do exist—one's salary and age, although seemingly superficial information, are not disclosed early. In such cases, we might assume that speakers may not want listeners to infer deeper personality aspects from this biographical information. Table 6.1 presents a sampling of these results.

Table 6.1	Perceptions of When Information Might Be Revealed Between Strangers in a Two-Hour Conversation[90]

Zero to Fifteen Minutes:

1. I'm a volunteer at a local hospital.
2. I'm from New York.
3. My son is a freshman at Penn State.
4. I have a dog, three cats, and a parakeet.

Fifteen to Thirty Minutes:

1. My wife is a good cook.
2. I've been skiing only once.
3. I like hunting for antiques.
4. I really enjoy playing tennis.
5. The Chicago Bears are a lousy football team.

Thirty to Forty-Five Minutes:

1. I've never really had a vacation.
2. I wish I knew more about politics.
3. Most of my clothes are blue or green.
4. One of my favorite authors is Norman Mailer.
5. I wear contact lenses.

Forty-Five to Sixty Minutes:

1. I am thirty-five years old.
2. It bothers me to see young women cursing and swearing.
3. My parents were much more politically conservative than I am.
4. I make it a point to see the doctor, dentist, and optometrist once a year.
5. I want to give my children all of the things I never had as a child.

Sixty to Seventy-Five Minutes:	
1.	I don't like people who smile all the time.
2.	People who don't finish what they start always annoy me.
3.	I don't believe in evolution.
4.	I dislike my job so much I would like to quit tomorrow and move to a farm.
5.	Any American who is a Communist should be deported from the country.

Seventy-Five to Ninety Minutes:	
1.	I don't believe that there is an afterlife, but I'm really not sure.
2.	I hate lying in bed at night, listening to the clock tick.
3.	I wish my church was more relevant to my life.
4.	I believe in mercy-killing when there is absolutely no hope of survival.
5.	My mother-in-law really dislikes me.

Ninety to One Hundred Five Minutes:	
1.	I have a violent temper.
2.	I find it difficult to respond rationally when I am criticized.
3.	I suspect people's motives when they compliment me.
4.	I think we got married much too young.
5.	There are times when I feel I have wasted my life.

One Hundred Five to One Hundred Twenty Minutes:	
1.	Sometimes I'm afraid I won't be able to control myself.
2.	I wish my husband would feel free to cry as an emotional release.
3.	I don't really like myself very much.
4.	I often wonder why people don't like me.
5.	My husband and I stay together for the sake of the children.

Statements Perceived as Not Occurring in a Two-Hour Conversation Between Previously Unacquainted Persons:	
1.	I had my first sexual experience when I was twenty-one.
2.	I make $13,000 a year.
3.	I'm suspicious of my husband's constant need to work late.
4.	I have considered committing suicide on more than one occasion.
5.	We got married earlier than we'd planned because I was pregnant.

Adapted from C.R. Berger, R.R. Gardner, G.W. Clatterbuck, and L.S. Schulman (1976) Human Communication Research (2), *34-39.*

Whether you agree or disagree with the particular order of the preceding statements is irrelevant as long as you recognize that we all organize our revelations to others in some way. Some people may not mind mentioning their salary early in the conversation and even the people in this study—given additional information about the other person, (e.g., an investment counselor for people in lower income brackets) may have revealed the salary information. The point is that *whatever* information you perceive to be more personal about yourself will most likely be revealed to another person only after the exchange of more superficial information. Also, the more the two parties to a relationship expect and agree on such sequencing (and tolerate deviations from it) the greater the likelihood that they will experience satisfaction.[91] Naturally, there are exceptions. Bartenders, strangers on public transportation, and people who deliberately express a desire to listen to another person's troubles will experience a great deal more "unloading" of personal information during the early phases of the encounter. In many of these cases, there is no intent to build a relationship that would last beyond the needed catharsis. Relationships can and do develop under such circumstances, but they must, at some point, go back and exchange more superficial information.

Earlier, you will recall we suggested that even though small talk disgruntles many people, it is not the small talk per se that bothers them, it is the way in which small talk is usually conducted. The following are a few of the many possible sources of this irritation: (1) You might engage in a great deal of demographic information exchange with no opportunity or motivation to pursue any of the possible commonalities. Sometimes fraternity or sorority rush parties impose these conditions. Just as you finish providing a biographical overview, it is time to switch partners and go through the same routine again. (2) You may encounter a person who is locked into one specific subject—and he or she doesn't even want to talk about that subject in much depth. Hence, breadth is cut off and the chances of finding integrating topics are decreased. If a person's lone topic happens to be themselves, small talk may seem especially boring. However, dissatisfaction may not accrue if that person's lone subject is also one you enjoy talking to death. (3) You may feel that there is an inequality of information exchange. You end up giving all the information and the other person does not reciprocate. Unless you are performing a counseling function, extremely high or low amounts of talking may not be perceived favorably during initial interaction. People who talked 80 percent of the time were judged to be domineering, outgoing, selfish, inconsiderate, inattentive, impolite, cold, and disliked by their interaction partner. People who talked 50 percent of the time were evaluated as likable, warm, attentive, and polite. Those who talked only 20 percent of the time were viewed as submissive, introverted, unselfish, and unintelligent.[92] Rightly or wrongly, our perception of how much help the other person is giving us in continuing the dialogue is closely related to our perception of whether the other wants to continue the conversation and the relationship. With new acquaintances and strangers, small talk allows us to avoid the anxiety caused by long silences. Although this is confusing and/or irritating to the information giver, it may be that the receiver just doesn't understand the important role of questions in small talk. (4) You may also meet a person who violates the pleasantness norm in small talk and brings the conversation dangerously close to conflict before the relationship can withstand the strain.

In summary, we have a form of public dialogue that serves a number of crucial personal and social functions, is omnipresent, is quantitatively superior to almost any other form of talk, and according to Malinowski, is pan-cultural[93]— and we choose to call it *small talk!* The covert question underlying all small talk is, "Do you want our encounter and our relationship to continue?" Should both parties agree to sustain their association, they will make some rather specific plans regarding when and where. Should either or both participants feel less enthusiastic about pursuing the relationship, the where and when of the next meeting will probably be left vague—"I'll probably run into you sometime." This vagueness serves the purpose of leaving the door open but does not commit either party to inviting the other in immediately. Obviously, additional encounters are used to help verify knowledge previously obtained or inferred and provide a mechanism to learn new things. Additional encounters are necessary in order to look for consistency or disparity across situations, between what was said and what was observed, between what the person says and what others say. One of the important mechanisms for initiating additional encounters is a previously identified topic of common ground—"Professor Knapp! How's the rhino expert? You know, I saw a TV program on the rhino the other night. Did you see it?"

Summary

This chapter examined some of the ritualistic exchanges that affect our relationships with others. On the surface, these behaviors don't seem too important to the development of our relationships, but they can be critical. Much of social interaction is influenced by rules—personal, relationship, group, and society rules for communicating. When communication is not satisfying, it may be that a rule has been violated. Ordinarily people receive negative reactions for not following the established rules of interaction, but we mentioned several ways in which rules could be (and are) violated without incurring unwanted sanctions. Sometimes these rules are so well learned that we don't pay much conscious attention to them, yet we carry out entire sequences of behavior that are, to a great extent, rule governed. We examined four of these patterned behaviors: greetings, forms of address, relational openings, and small talk.

Perhaps the most obvious and seemingly incidental act of initiating encounters is the greeting. Greetings, however, are anything but incidental, since they carry important relationship information concerning formality, status, and intimacy. Forms of address and opening lines, like greetings, also help set the stage for the dialogue and relationship that will follow. While these three conversational rituals are relatively routine, it is important to remember that all three are also flexible. The beginning of any conversation is always mutually constructed by the participants.

In the same sense, we argued that the next phase of interaction that normally follows the opening line—small talk—is sometimes unfairly maligned. Several reasons were suggested why people might be nonplused by the way in which small talk is conducted, but it was also pointed out that effective small talk is critical to developing relationships and subsequent dialogue. Small talk helps us maintain a sense of community with our fellow human beings, offers an important mechanism for socialization, provides a nonthreatening and revealing proving ground for new and/or established relationships, offers a way to maintain our relationships, provides a safe procedure for indicating who we are and how others may come to know us, offers a diversion from uncomfortable "big" talk, and helps us uncover integrating topics. The discovery of these integrating topics is a facilitative thread for bringing two strangers together, but it is also an important ingredient of small talk in existing relationships. The content of greetings and small talk will change as relationships ebb and flow, but the structure will be similar and the functional significance to the relationship will persist.

Selected Readings

Communication Rules and Rituals

Bowers, J. W., Elliott, N. D., and Desmond, R. J. "Exploiting Pragmatic Rules: Devious Messages." *Human Communication Research* 3 (1977): 235–242.

Bruess, C. J. S., and Pearson, J. C. "The Function of Mundane Ritualizing in Adult Friendship and Marriage." *Communication Research Reports* 19 (2002): 314–326.

Campbell, K., Silva, L. C., & Wright. D. E. "Rituals in Unmarried Couple Relationships: An Exploratory Study." *Family & Consumer Sciences Research Journal* 40 (2011): 45–57.

Dindia, K., Timmerman, L., Langan, E., Sahlstein, E. M., and Quandt, J. "The Function of Holiday Greetings in Maintaining Relationships." *Journal of Social and Personal Relationships* 21 (2004): 577–593.

Goffman, E. *Interaction Ritual.* Garden City, NY: Doubleday, 1967.

_____. *Relations in Public.* New York: Harper & Row, 1971.

Gouldner, A. W. "The Norm of Reciprocity: A Preliminary Statement." *American Sociological Review* 25 (1960): 161–178. b

Hewitt, J., and Stokes, R. "Disclaimers." *American Sociological Review* 40 (1975): 1–11.

Hopper, R. "The Taken-for-Granted." *Human Communication Research* 7 (1981): 195–211.

Jones, E., and Gallois, C. "Spouses' Impressions of Rules for Communication in Public and Private Marital Conflicts." *Journal of Marriage and the Family* 51 (1989): 957–967.

Labov, W. "Rules for Ritual Insults." In D. Sudnow, ed., *Studies in Social Interaction,* pp. 120–169. New York: Free Press, 1972.

Pearce, W. B. "The Coordinated Management of Meaning: A Rules Based Theory of Interpersonal Communication." In G. R. Miller, ed., *Explorations in Interpersonal Communication.* pp. 17–36. Beverly Hills, CA: Sage, 1976.

Rothenbuhler, E. W. *Ritual Communication: From Everyday Conversation to Mediated Ceremony.* Thousand Oaks, CA: Sage, 1998.

Shimanoff, S. B. *Communication Rules.* Beverly Hills, CA: Sage, 1980.

Wiemann, J. M., and Knapp, M. L. "Turn-Taking in Conversations." *Journal of Communication* 25 (1975): 75–92.

Greeting Behavior

Baxter, L. A., and Philpott, J. "Attribution-Based Strategies for Initiating and Terminating Friendships." *Communication Quarterly* 30 (1982): 217–224.

Firth, R. "Verbal and Bodily Rituals of Greeting and Parting." In J. S. LaFountaine, ed., *The Interpretation of Ritual* pp. 1–38. London: Tavi-stock Publications, 1972.

Givens, D. "Greeting a Stranger: Some Commonly Used Nonverbal Signals of Aversiveness." *Semiotica* 22 (1978): 351–367.

Goffman, E. *Relations in Public.* New York: Basic Books, 1971.

LeFebvre, L. E. "Swiping Me Off My Feet: Explicating Relationship Initiation on Tinder." *Journal of Social and Personal Relationships* 35 (2018): 1205–1229.

Kendon, A., and Ferber, A. "A Description of Some Human Greetings." In R. P. Michael and J. H. Crook, eds., *Comparative Behavior and Ecology of Primates* pp. 591–668. London: Academic Press, 1973.

Knuf, J. "Greeting and Leave-Taking: A Bibliography of Resources for the Study of Ritualized Communication." *Research on Language and Social Interaction* 24 (1990/1991): 405–448.

Krivonos, P. D., and Knapp, M. L. "Initiating Communication: What Do You Say When You Say Hello?" *Central States Speech Journal* 26 (1975): 115–125.

Pillet-Shore, D. "Doing Introductions: The Work Involved in Meeting Someone New." *Communication Monographs* 78 (2011): 73–95.

Schiffrin, D. "Opening Encounters." *American Sociological Review* 42 (1977): 679–691.

Sprecher, S. "Relationship Initiation and Formation on the Internet." *Marriage & Family Review* 45 (2009): 761–782.

Forms of Address

Brown, R., and Ford, M. "Address in American English." *Journal of Abnormal Social Psychology* 62 (1961): 375–385.

Butler, C. W., Danby, S., and Emmison, M. "Address Terms in Turn Beginnings: Managing Disalignment and Disaffiliation in Telephone Counseling." *Research on Language and Social Interaction* 44 (2011): 338–358

Harré, R., Morgan, J., and O'Neill, C. *Nicknames: Their Origins and Social Consequences.* London: Routledge and Kegan Paul, 1979.

Kroger, R. O., Chang, K., and Leong, I. "Are the Rules of Address Universal?: A Test of Chinese Usage." *Journal of Cross Cultural Psychology* 10 (1979): 395–414.

Little, C. B., and Gelles, R. J. "The Social Psychological Implications of Forms of Address." *Sociometry* 38 (1975): 573–586.

Rausch, H. L., Marshall, K. A., and Featherman, J. M. "Relations at Three Early Stages of Marriage as Reflected by the Use of Personal Pronouns." *Family Process* 9 (1970): 69–82.

Small Talk

Alberts, J. K., Yoshimura, C. G., Rabby, M., and Loschiavo, R. "Mapping the Topography of Couples' Daily Conversations." *Journal of Social and Personal Relationships* 22 (2005): 299–322.

Beinstein, J. "Small Talk as Social Gesture." *Journal of Communication* 25 (1975): 147–154.

Berger, C. R., and Calabrese, R. J. "Some Exploration in Initial Interaction and Beyond: Toward a Developmental Theory of Interpersonal Communication." *Human Communication Research* 1 (1975): 99–112.

Berger, C. R., Gardner, R. R., Clatterbuck, G. W., and Schulman, L. S. "Perceptions of Information Sequencing in Relationship Development." *Human Communication Research* 3 (1976): 29–46.

Coupland, J. "Small Talk: Social Functions." *Research on Language and Social Interaction* 36 (2003): 1–6.

Goldsmith, D. J., and Baxter, L. A. "Constituting Relationships in Talk: A Taxonomy of Speech Events in Social and Personal Relationships." *Human Communication Research* 23 (1996): 87–114.

Levin, J., and Arluke, A. *Gossip: The Inside Scoop.* New York: Plenum, 1987.

Milek, A., Butler, E. A., Tackman, A. M., Kaplan, D. M., Raison, C. L., Sbarra, D. A., Vazire, S., and Mehl, M. R. "Eavesdropping on Happiness Revisited: A Pooled, Multisample, Replication of the Association Between Life Satisfaction and Observed Daily Conversation Quantity and Quality." *Psychological Science* 29 (2018): 1451–1462.

Zunin, L. *Contact: The First Four Minutes.* Los Angeles: Nash Publishing, 1972.

Notes

[1] For an extensive discussion of communication rituals, see E. W. Rothenbuhler, *Ritual Communication: From Everyday Conversation to Mediated Ceremony* (Thousand Oaks, CA: Sage, 1998).

[2] This definition is a modified version of one found in S. B. Shimanoff, *Communication Rules* (Beverly Hills. CA: Sage, 1980), p. 57.

[3] M. Argyle and M. Henderson, *The Anatomy of Relationships* (London: Heinemann, 1985).

[4] M. K. Lapinski and R. N. Rimal, "An Explication of Social Norms," *Communication Theory* 15 (2005): 127–147.

[5] It is worth noting that the rules governing the structure of a conversation may be as important to the overall relationship as the content. See J. M. Wiemann and M. L. Knapp, "Turn-Taking in Conversations," *Journal of Communication* 25 (1975): 75–92, which proposes that "Turn-taking in conversations not only helps us apportion the floor, but also serves a symbolic function of helping the interactants define their relationship."

[6] M. K. Venetis, K. Greene, K. Magsamen-Conrad, S. C. Banerjee, M. G. Checton, and Z. Bagdasarov, "'You Can't Tell Anyone But . . .': Exploring the Use of Privacy Rules and Revealing Behaviors," *Communication Monographs* 79 (2012): 344–365.

[7] B. R. Burleson, "Emotional Support Skills." In J. O. Greene & B. R. Burleson, eds., *Handbook of Communication and Socail Interaction Skills* (Mahwah, NJ: Lawrence Erlbaum, 2003), pp, 551–594.

[8] E. Jones and C. Gallois, "Spouses' Impressions of Rules for Communication in Public and Private Marital Conflicts," *Journal of Marriage and the Family* 51 (1989): 957–967.

[9] See, for example, K. E. Roggensack and A. L. Sillars, "Agreement and understanding about honesty and

deception rules in romantic relationships," *Journal of Social and Personal Relationships* 31 (2014): 178–199.

10 See, for example, L. A. Baxter, T. Dun, and E. Sahlstein, "Rules for Relating Communicated among Social Network Members," *Journal of Social and Personal Relationships* 18 (2001): 173–199.

11 A. R. Allgeier, "The Effects of Differential Amounts of Talkativeness on Interpersonal Judgments" (Ph.D. diss., Purdue University, 1975).

12 C. R. Berger, R. R. Gardner, M. R. Parks, L. Schulman, and G. R. Miller, "Interpersonal Epistemology and Interpersonal Communication." In G. R. Miller, ed., *Explorations in Interpersonal Communication* (Beverly Hills, CA: Sage, 1976), pp. 163–170.

13 These hypotheses were developed during a pro-seminar at Purdue University that was taught by R. P. Hart and the senior author.

14 For more examples, see M. S. Davis, *Intimate Relations.* (New York: The Free Press, 1973).

15 H Garfinkel, "Studies of the Routine Grounds of Everyday Activities," *Social Problems* 11 (1964): 225–250.

16 R. Hopper, "The Taken-for-Granted," *Human Communication Research* 7 (1981): 195–211.

17 J. A. Daly, D. J. Weber, A. L. Vangelisti, M. Maxwell, and H. L. Neel, "Concurrent Cognitions During Conversations: Protocol Analysis as a Means of Exploring Conversations," *Discourse Processes* 12 (1989): 227–244.

18 W. A. Afifi and S. Metts, "Characteristics and Consequences of Expectation Violations in Close Relationships," *Journal of Social and Personal Relationships* 15 (1998): 365–392; also see W. A. Afifi and J. K. Burgoon, "The Impact of Violations on Uncertainty and the Consequences for Attractiveness," *Human Communication Research* 26 (2000): 203–233.

19 M. L. McLaughlin, *Conversation: How Talk Is Organized* (Beverly Hills, CA: Sage, 1984).

20 C. A. Braithwaite, "Blood Money: The Routine Violation of Conversational Rules," *Communication Reports* 10 (1997): 63–73.

21 See N. Tavuchis, *Mea Culpa: A Sociology of Apology and Reconciliation* (Stanford, CA: Stanford University Press, 1991). But when offended parties see a rule violation as intentional, apologies often are not well-received. See C. W. Struthers, J. Eaton, A. G. Santelli, M. Uchiyama, and N. Shirvani, "The Effects of Attributions of Intent and Apology on Forgiveness: When Saying Sorry May Not Help the Story," *Journal of Experimental Social Psychology* 44 (2008): 983–992.

22 J. Hewitt and R. Stokes, "Disclaimers," *American Sociological Review* 40 (1975): 1–11.

23 M. Argyle, *Bodily Communication* (New York: International Universities Press, 1975), p. 65.

24 Shimanoff, *Communication Rules,* pp. 98–99.

25 See L. A. Baxter and W. Wilmot. "Secret Tests: Social Strategies for Acquiring Information About the State of the Relationship," *Human Communication Research* 11 (1984): 171–201, for a discussion of such "secret tests" in the context of romantic relationships.

26 To show how communicative rules change, one writer observed, "according to the rules of etiquette, as codified by Emily Post, divorced persons were supposed to meet socially as non-speaking strangers, the underlying theory being . . . that the divorce would not have been sought in the first place if the grievance of one of the parties had not been irreparable and unforgivable. But as divorces became more common, particularly with the advent and spread of 'friendly divorces,' this rule became difficult to enforce. In some social circles it would have meant that an awkwardly large number of people, including the friends of divorced persons, would find themselves in embarrassing situations. The old rule was therefore changed by consensus and later [re]formulated by Mrs. Post. Now it is quite proper for divorced persons to meet as friends." J. Bernard, *American Family Behavior* (New York: Harper & Row, 1942), pp. 210–211.

27 J. P. Forgas, "Asking Nicely? The Effects of Mood on Responding to More or Less Polite Requests," *Personality and Social Psychology Bulletin* 24 (1998): 173–185.

28 But a close examination of the conversational "work" that people do during introductions shows that they are quite complex (see D. Pillet-Shore "Doing Introductions: The Work Involved in Meeting Someone New," *Communication Monographs* 78 (2011): 73–95).

29 R. C. Schank and R. P. Abelson, *Scripts, Plans, Goals and Understanding* (Hillsdale, NJ: Erlbaum, 1977).

30 See R. C. Schank, *Dynamic Memory* (New York: Cambridge University Press, 1982) for the foundational ideas; K. Kellermann, "The Conversational MOP II. Progression Through Scenes in Discourse," *Human Communication Research* 17 (1991): 385–414; K. Kellermann, "Communication: Inherently Strategic and Primarily Automatic," *Communication Monographs* 59 (1992): 244–300; and K. Kellermann, S.

Broetzmann, T. Lim, and K. Kitao, "The Conversational MOP: Scenes in the Stream of Discourse," *Discourse Processes* 12 (1989): 27–62, for the application to initial interaction.

31 Research also suggests that greetings convey information about individuals' personality. For instance, Chaplin and his colleagues found that people's tendency to greet a confederate with a firm handshake was positively associated with extraversion and emotional expression and negatively associated with shyness and neuroticism. See W. F. Chaplin, J. B. Phillips, J. D. Brown, N. R. Clanton, and J. L. Stein, "Handshaking, Gender, Personality, and First Impressions," *Journal of Personality and Social Psychology* 79 (2000): 110–117.

32 W. G. Powers and R. B. Glenn, "Perceptions of Friendly Inside Greetings in Interpersonal Relationships," *Southern Speech Communication Journal* 44 (1979): 264–274; also see M. E. Ballard, S. Green, and C. Granger, "Affiliation, Flirting, and Fun: Mock Aggressive Behavior in College Students," *The Psychological Report* 53 (2003): Iss. 1, Article 3.

33 J. Laver, "Linguistic Routines and Politeness in Greeting and Parting." In F. Coulmas, ed., *Conversational Routine: Explorations in Standardized Communication Situations and Prepatterned Speech* (New York: Mouton, 1981), pp. 289–306; W. Douglas, "Affinity-Testing in Initial Interactions," *Journal of Social and Personal Relationships* 4 (1987): 3–15.

34 R. Hopper, *Telephone Conversation* (Bloomington: Indiana University Press, 1992); R. Hopper and K. Drummond, "Accomplishing Interpersonal Relationship: The Telephone Openings of Strangers and Intimates," *Western Journal of Communication* 56 (1992): 185–199.

35 E. Goffman, *Relations in Public* (New York: Basic Books, 1971), pp. 84–85.

36 A. Kendon and A. Ferber, "A Description of Some Human Greetings." In R. P. Michael and J. H. Cook, eds., *Comparative Behavior and Ecology of Primates* (London: Academic Press, 1973) pp. 591–668.

37 P. D. Krivonos and M. L. Knapp, "Initiating Communication: What Do You Say When You Say Hello?" *Central States Speech Journal* 26 (1975): 115–125.

38 I. Eibl-Eibesfeldt, "Similarities and Differences Between Cultures in Expressive Movement." In R. A. Hinde, ed., *Non-Verbal Communication* (Cambridge: Royal Society and Cambridge University Press, 1972) pp. 297–312.

39 D. Givens, "Greeting a Stranger: Some Commonly Used Nonverbal Signals of Aversiveness," *Semiotica* 22 (1978): 351–367.

40 See, for example, C. W. Butler, S. Danby, and M. Emmison, "Address Terms in Turn Beginnings: Managing Disalignment and Disaffiliation in Telephone Counseling," *Research on Language and Social Interaction* 44 (2011): 338–358; K. L. Fitch, "The Interplay of Linguistic Universals and Cultural Knowledge in Personal Address: Colombian *Madre* Terms," *Communication Monographs* 58 (1991): 254–272.

41 J. Jorgenson, "Situated Address and the Social Construction of 'In-Law' Relationships," *The Southern Communication Journal* 59 (1994): 196–204.

42 R. Brown, *Social Psychology* (New York: Free Press, 1965), chapter 2. Also see C. L. Kleinke, P. A. Staneski, and P. Weaver, "Evaluation of a Person Who Uses Another's Name in Ingratiating and Noningratiating Situations," *Journal of Experimental Social Psychology* 8 (1972): 457–466. Kleinke et al. propose that when we are dependent on a stranger (e.g., applicant to interviewer in job interview), and we use his or her first name, we run the risk of being perceived as insincere, phony, and less likable. Liking, however, may accrue when dependency is not an issue (e.g., noningratiation situation).

43 N. M. Henley, "The Politics of Touch." In P. Brown, ed., *Radical Psychology* (New York: Harper & Row, 1973), pp. 421–433. See also N. M. Henley, *Body Politics* (Englewood Cliffs, NJ: Prentice Hall, 1977).

44 Some researchers suggest that this generalization may be more accurate for men than for women because women's names often take a diminutive or feminine form (e.g., "ette" or "ie") at the end, even when they are relatively long. See A. Merhrabian and M. Piercy, "Affective and Personality Characteristics Inferred from Length of First Names," *Personality and Social Psychology Bulletin* 19 (1993): 755–758.

45 A. R. McConnell and R. H. Fazio, "Women as Men and People: Effects of Gender-Marked Language," *Personality and Social Psychology Bulletin* 22 (1996): 1004–1013.

46 C. B. Little and R. J. Gelles, "The Social Psychological Implications of Forms of Address," *Sociometry* 38 (1975): 573–586.

47 G. B. B. A. Mod, "Reading Romance: The Impact of Facebook Rituals Can Have on a Romantic Relationship," *Journal of Comparative Research in Anthropology and Sociology* 1 (2010): 61–77.

48 M. M. Moore. "Nonverbal Courtship Patterns in Women: Context and Consequences," *Ethology and Sociobiology* 6 (1985): 237–247.

49 D. R. Shaffer, C. Ruammake, and L. J. Pegalis, "The 'Opener': Highly Skilled as Interviewer or Interviewee," *Personality and Social Psychology Bulletin* 16 (1990): 511–520.

50 P. Clooney, *How to Talk to Men: Getting Men to Open Up and Start a Conversation* (Independently published, 2018). There is an abundance of books similar to this one including L. Braswell, *How to Be the Type of Girl Who Gets the Guy: How Confident, Self-Assured Women Handle Dating with Class and Sass* (CreateSpace, 2017) and V. Grace, *Get Him, Have Him & Keep Him Successfully: Ultimate Guide to Find Your Man, Keep His Interest and Continue Ahead for a Long Lasting Relationship* (Independently Published, 2018).

51 D. Perrotta, *Conversation Casanova* (Independently published, 2017). Books on this topic are regularly published. A couple of recent examples are: J. Beckettt, *The Woman Whisperer: How to Naturally Strike Up Conversations, Flirt Like a Boss, and Charm any Woman off Her Feet* (Independently published, 2016) and A. Ferebee, *The Dating Playbook For Men: A Proven 7 Step System To Go From Single To The Woman Of Your Dreams* (Knowledge for Men, 2019).

52 A. J. DuBrin, "The Meeting/Mating Game: How and Where To Play," *Single* 2 (1974): 48–51, 72–75.

53 C. L. Kleinke, F. B. Meeker, and R. A. Staneski, "Preference for Opening Lines: Preferences by Men and Women," *Sex Roles* 15 (1986): 585–600.

54 T. E. Murray, "The Language of Singles Bars." *American Speech* 60 (1985): 17–30.

55 P. A. Mongeau and K. L. Johnson, "Predicting Cross-Sex First-Date Sexual Expectations and Involvement: Contextual and Individual Difference Factors," *Personal Relationships* 2 (1995): 301–312.

56 G. W. Lewandowski, N. J. Ciarocco, M. Pettenato, and J. Stephan, "Pick Me Up: Ego Depletion and Receptivity to Relationship Initiation," *Journal of Social and Personal Relationships* 29 (2012): 1071-1084.

57 W. C. Rowatt, M. R. Cunningham, and P. B. Druen, "Deception to Get a Date," *Personality and Social Psychology Bulletin* 24 (1998): 1228–1242.

58 L. K. Knobloch, "Relational Uncertainty and Message Production Within Courtship: Features of Date Request Messages," *Human Communication Research* 32 (2006): 244–273.

59 W. Douglas, "Affinity-Testing in Initial Interaction," *Journal of Social and Personal Relation-ships* 4 (1987): 3–16.

60 See, for example, E. K. Ruppel, "Use of Communication Technologies in Romantic Relationships: Self-disclosure and the Role of Relationship Development," *Journal of Social and Personal Relationships* 32 (2015): 667–686; S. Sprecher, "Relationship Initiation and Formation on the Internet," *Marriage and Family Review* 45(2009): 761–782.

61 L. C. Tidwell and J. B. Walther, "Computer-Mediated Communication Effects on Disclosure, Impressions, and Interpersonal Evaluations: Getting to Know One Another a Bit at a Time," *Human Communication Research* 28 (2002): 317–348.

62 L. E. LeFebvre, "Swiping Me Off My Feet: Explicating Relationship Initiation on Tinder," *Journal of Social and Personal Relationships* 35 (2018); 1205–1229.

63 A. Feingold, "Gender Differences in Effects of Physical Attractiveness on Romantic Attraction: A Comparison Across Five Research Paradigms," *Journal of Personality and Social Psychology* 59 (1990): 981–993; R. Koester and L. Wheeler, "Self-Presentation in Personal Advertisements: The Influences of Implicit Notions of Attraction and Role Expectations," *Journal of Social and Personal Relationships* 5 (1988): 149–160; M. H. Gonzales and S. A. Meyers, "'Your Mother Would Like Me': Self-Presentation in the Personals Ads of Heterosexual and Homosexual Men and Women," *Personality and Social Psychology Bulletin* 19 (1993): 131–142.

64 J. Coupland, "Past the 'Perfect Kind of Age'? Styling Selves and Relationships in Over-50 Dating Advertisements," *Journal of Communication* 50 (2000): 9–30.

65 See, for example, L. Koss-Feder, "Getting Back into It," *Time* (Bonus Section, July 2002): G1–G3.

66 R. A. Bell and J. A. Daly, "The Affinity-Seeking Function of Communication," *Communication Monographs* 51 (1984): 91–115; R. A. Bell, S. W. Trablay, and N. L. Buerkel-Rothfuss, "Interpersonal Attraction as a Communication Accomplishment: Development of a Measure of Affinity-Seeking Competence," *Western Journal of Speech Communication* 51 (1987): 1–18; J. A. Daly and P. O. Kreiser, "Affinity Seeking." In J. A. Daly and J. M. Wiemann, eds., *Strategic Interpersonal Communication* (Hillsdale, NJ: Erlbaum, 1994), pp. 109–134; J. M. Honeycutt and J. Patterson, "Affinity Strategies in Relationships: The Role of Gender and Imagined Interactions in

Maintaining Liking Among College Roommates," *Personal Relationships* 4 (1997): 35–46.

67 In fact, Berger, Karol, and Jordan found that plan complexity was inversely related to verbal fluency. See C. R. Berger, S. H. Karol, and J. M. Jordan, "When a Lot of Knowledge Is a Dangerous Thing: The Debilitating Effects of Plan Complexity on Verbal Fluency," *Human Communication Research* 16 (1989): 91–119.

68 J. S. Powell, *Why Am I Afraid To Tell You Who I Am?* (Chicago: Argus Communications, 1969).

69 A. Milek, E. A. Butler, A. M. Tackman, D. M. Kaplan, C. L. Raison, D. A Sbarra, S. Vazire, and M. R. Mehl, "'Eavesdropping on Happiness' Revisited: A Pooled, Multisample Replication of the Association Between Life Satisfaction and Observed Daily Conversation Quantity and Quality." *Psychological Science* 29 (2018): 1451–1462.

70 D. D. Levine. "Small Talk: A Big Communicative Function in the Organization?" Paper presented to the Eastern Communication Association Convention, 1987.

71 J. C. Condon Jr., *Semantics and Communication* (New York: Macmillan, 1966), pp. 88–89.

72 D. Morris, *The Naked Ape* (New York: Dell, 1969).

73 S. I. Hayakawa, *Language in Thought and Action*, 4th ed. (New York: Harcourt Brace Jovanovich, 1978), ch. 6.

74 G. M. Sandstrom and E. W. Dunn, "Is Efficacy Overrated?: Minimal Social Interactions Lead to Belonging and Positive Affect," *Social Psychological and Personality Science* 5 (2014): 437–442.

75 See, for example, S. Blum-Kulka, *Dinner Talk: Cultural Patterns of Sociability and Socialization in Family Discourse* (Mahwah, NJ: Erlbaum, 1997); J. Coupland, "Small Talk: Social Functions," *Research on Language and Social Interaction* 36 (2003): 1–6.

76 Some research even suggests that people are more likely to trust robots when the robots engage in small talk with them. See, e.g., R. B. Paradeda, M. Hashemian, R. A. Rodrigues, and A. Paiva, "How Facial Expressions and Small Talk May Influence Trust in a Robot." In: A. Agah, J. J. Cabibihan, A. Howard, M. Salichs, and H. He, eds., *Social Robotics. ICSR 2016. Lecture Notes in Computer Science*, vol. 9979 (Springer Cham, 2016), pp. 169–178.

77 D. J. Goldsmith and L. A. Baxter, "Constituting Relationships in Talk: A Taxonomy of Speech Events in Social and Personal Relationships," *Human Communication Research* 23 (1996): 87–114.

78 S. Duck, D. J. Rutt, M. H. Hurst, and H. Strejc, "Some Evident Truths About Conversations in Everyday Relationships: All Communications Are Not Created Equal," *Human Communication Research* 18 (1991): 228–267.

79 J. Coupland and A. Jaworski, "Transgression and Intimacy in Recreational Talk Narratives," *Research on Language and Social Interaction* 36 (2003): 85–106.

80 J. M. Honeycutt and J. M. Wiemann, "Analysis of Functions of Talk and Reports of Imagined Interactions (IIs) During Engagement and Marriage," *Human Communication Research* 25 (1999): 399–419.

81 J. Levin and A. Arluke, *Gossip: The Inside Scoop* (New York: Plenum, 1987), pp. 28–29.

82 C. R. Berger and R. J. Calabrese, "Some Explorations in Initial Interaction and Beyond: Toward a Developmental Theory of Interpersonal Communication," *Human Communication Research* 1 (1975): 99–112.

83 For an in-depth commentary on the strategic and nonstrategic acquisition of information, see C. R. Berger, "Strategic and Nonstrategic Information Acquisition," *Human Communication Research* 28 (2002): 287–297.

84 J. Beinstein, "Conversations in Public Places," *Journal of Communication* 25 (1975): 85–95.

85 Other investigations on the types of topics people discuss have yielded similarly predictable results. Sherman and Haas, for example, have found that when women talk together, they tend to discuss relationship problems, family, health, reproductive concerns, weight, food, and clothing more frequently than men do. Men, on the other hand, focused more often on music, current events, and sports. See M. A. Sherman and A. Haas, "Man to Man, Woman to Woman," *Psychology Today* (1984): 72–73.

86 C. R. Berger, "Proactive and Retroactive Attribution Processes in Interpersonal Communications," *Human Communication Research* 2 (1975): 33–50.

87 S. R. Rodriguez, "'We'll Only See Parts of Each Other's Lives:' The Role of Mundane Talk in Maintaining Nonresidential Parent-Child Relationships," *Journal of Social and Personal Relationships* 31 (2014): 1134–1152. Also see J. A. Gilbertson, K. Dindia, and M. Allen, "Relational Continuity Constructional Units and the Maintenance of Relationships," *Journal of Social and Personal*

Relationships 15 (1998): 774–790 and S. J. Sigman, "Handling the Discontinuous Aspects of Continuous Social Relationships: Toward Research on the Persistence of Social Forms," *Communication Theory* 1 (1991): 106–127.

88 A. L. Vangelisti and M. A. Banski, "Couples' Debriefing Conversations: The Impact of Gender, Occupation, and Demographic Characteristics," *Family Relations* 42 (1993): 149–157.

89 C. R. Berger, R. R. Gardner, G. W. Clatterbuck and L. S. Schulman, "Perceptions of Information Sequencing in Relationship Development," *Human Communication Research* 3 (1976): 34–39.

90 C. R. Berger, R. R. Gardner, G. W. Clatterbuck, and L. S. Schulman, op. cit. Reprinted with permission from *Human Communication Research,* 2, 34–39.

91 See, for example, S. Blum-Kulka, *Dinner Talk: Cultural Patterns of Sociability and Socialization in Family Discourse* (Mahwah, NJ: Erlbaum, 1997); J. Coupland, "Small Talk: Social Functions," *Research on Language and Social Interaction* 36 (2003): 1–6.

92 C. L. Kleinke, M. L. Kahn, and T. B. Tully, "First Impressions of Talking Rates in Opposite-Sex and Same-Sex Interactions," *Social Behavior and Personality* 7 (1979): 81–91. Also see C. L. Kleinke and T. B. Tully, "Influence of Talking Level on Perceptions of Counselors," *Journal of Counseling Psychology* 26 (1979): 23–29.

93 B. Malinowski, "The Problem of Meaning in Primitive Languages." In C. K. Ogden and I. A. Richards, eds., *The Meaning of Meaning,* 10th ed., Supplement I (London: Routledge & Kegan Paul, 1949), pp. 296–336.

CHAPTER 7

LEARNING OUTCOMES

After reading this chapter, students will . . .

. . . be able to distinguish Lee's six styles of love.

. . . be able to explain Sternberg's three-part or triangular theory of love.

. . . know how love is distinct from liking and friendship.

. . . be able to explain how the seven foundations of intimacy explain how relationships differ.

KEY TERMS

altruistic love	love of beauty
anxious/ambivalent lovers	nonlove
	obsessive love
avoidant lovers	playful love
companionate love	realistic love
consummate love	responsiveness
cross-sex friendships	romantic love
empty love	self-fulfillment
fatuous love	secure lovers
infatuation	self-surrender
joint identity	
liking	

The Foundations of Intimate Dialogue

Dear Dr. Knapp,

My best friend just broke up with his girlfriend. My problem is that ever since this happened, our friendship has gotten a little too close. Before, while he was still dating his girlfriend, we'd play basketball once a week and maybe go out partying on Friday or Saturday night. Now that she's gone, he wants to do everything together. Don't get me wrong—the guy is still my best friend—but I don't want to spend every minute of my life with him. He's even starting to annoy the women I date. It's embarrassing. I don't want to hurt his feelings, but this is really beginning to bug me. How do I tell him this without hurting his feelings and our friendship?

Bugged to Death

When relationships become more intimate, the expectations for the relationship change. Establishing a close proximity to a person you care about may be crucial in reaching greater intimacy, but maintaining opportunities for separate activities may be just as crucial for the continuance of those feelings of intimacy. This chapter discusses different types of intimacy and several key factors associated with the development of intimacy. An understanding of these factors should provide additional insights into the how and why communication behavior changes as people develop closer relationships.

The subject was pornography. Many claimed expertise, but they couldn't agree on a definition. Resolution of the problem was deemed critical enough to warrant consideration by the U.S. Supreme Court. Reporters grilled the lawyers and decision makers relentlessly: "What is the specific nature of pornography? How can we define it?" Finally, one Supreme Court Justice verbalized what so many others felt but were afraid to say: "I can't tell you what it is, but I know it when I see it."

This chapter concerns advanced stages of human intimacy, stages that appear to have many definitions with little consensus. Many people feel they know or can identify it when they experience it; many others are much less certain. As with the pornography issue, there is certainly no shortage of public commentary on liking and loving. At one extreme are those who claim to know the answers, oftentimes giving conflicting advice. The internet and our popular literature are saturated with case histories, testimonials, diagnostic tests, and advice on almost every conceivable aspect of intimate relationships. Readers learn from so-called experts how to "rekindle your dying marriage," how to "find out if your boss really likes you," or how "one out of every five women is looking for you as her no-strings-attached lover" as this outlandish book advertisement in a popular men's magazine claimed:

> A distinguished American scientist shows you how three simple psychological insights can bring as many lovely young women to your bed as you could possibly wish for the rest of your life! . . . Not a single detail that you'll need (or want) to know is left out of this book . . .
>
> Never again will you have to lose out because you might not be the type of guy certain women go for . . . To put it all in a nut-shell: Once you learn to apply the principles of "SECRET FEMALE HYPNOTISM," you'll have the power to make women do *exactly as you wish.*

At the other extreme, are those who would rather remain uninformed. Former Senator William Proxmire, scorning what he called the "love racket," was reported as saying that people don't want to know the answers to what comprises romantic love; they want it to remain a mystery. Not even Dear Abby is willing to wrestle with love's complexity: "When you're in love, you'll know it. You won't have to ask."

So much for the extremes. The following material should go a long way toward demystifying some forms of human intimacy. It will give you a way to understand and explain your feelings associated with intimacy. But there is plenty of mystery left; we still have a lot to learn.

Types of Love

Many of the questions facing those who wish to study intimate relationships revolve around the oftentimes ambiguous terminology we use to label our experiences and feelings as they intensify toward another. Take the word *love,* for instance. We would probably be astonished if we told someone we loved them and they replied by asking, "What exactly do you mean by that?" When we are participants in the process of intimacy development, emotional distance is often difficult to achieve, and many of us seem to behave as if love had a single concrete referent that others will understand. On the other hand, we can look at the way others express love in a more detached manner and conclude that there are probably many ways of loving. Sociologist John Lee, like others before him, believed that the word *love* had many behavioral referents and that the assumption of a common referent was the biggest communication barrier between two people using the term. Both people say they are in love, but they may have different ways of showing it because they are working with different referents for the term. To test his idea, Lee sought answers from more than 100 people representing various walks of life. He asked them how they had met their beloved; what expectations they had for love; how they handled arguments, jealousy, breakups, reunions, sex, and absence; what their orientation toward life in general was; what their childhood was like; and many other questions. Listed next are six styles of loving that Lee identified. The first three he called *primary styles of love*; the last three are the result of mixing and combining elements of the primary styles.[1] Other combinations are obviously possible, but this list is sufficient to show that love may have many referents:

© Ekaterina Pokrovsky/Shutterstock.com

1. Love of Beauty These lovers are passionate and intense. They seem to have an immediate and powerful attraction to physical beauty. They have a clear concept of ideal beauty and get a noticeably heightened physiological reaction when they are confronted with persons approaching this ideal. They are eager for rapid self-disclosure and sexual intimacy. Sensations associated with touching the beloved are greatly enjoyed. The intensity this lover initially gives to a relationship must inevitably diminish, but successful long-term relationships can be achieved if satisfaction can be derived from relationship "highs" that occur less often and are, perhaps, less intense. Problems are normally associated with this lover's strong desire to find the ideal, which results in seeing things that aren't there. These lovers often experience strong emotional peaks and valleys.

Love of beauty: Style of love that is passionate, intense, and rooted in a powerful attraction to physical beauty.

Playful love: Style of love in which individuals consider love a game.

2. Playful Love These lovers seem to derive the most pleasure from playing the game. They often consider love to be less important than, say, work and believe in themselves so strongly that they feel they don't need much from others. As a result, they will not be very concerned about getting or giving involvement or dependency. Playing the game is often as rewarding as winning the prize. These lovers are interested in variety and good times and often have more than one romantic interest at a time. For people who are undemanding and self-sufficient, this style of love will be satisfying; but if one partner desires a deeper commitment, problems may arise. This advertisement for a book would be most likely to appeal to those who practice playful love: "Love is a game. Some play it poorly. And some play it well. If you want to play it brilliantly—so brilliantly you win almost every time—then its time you read *Connecting*."

Companionate love: Style of love based on friendship and companionship.

3. Companionate Love These lovers are patient; they let love grow naturally into a peaceful, enchanting affection. This love is based in friendship and companionship. They are generally not distressed by absences from their lover. The turbulence often generated by intense feelings or frivolity is not appealing to these lovers. In many ways, they are less preoccupied with their partners than lovers with other styles. They can offer considerable stability and predictability, which may work well until such behavior is perceived as a dull routine by someone desirous of more variety and excitement.

Obsessive love: Style of love that is possessive, consuming, and somewhat like an addiction.

4. Obsessive Love This style combines the passion of the love of beauty with the desire to hold back feelings and manipulate the relationship found in playful love. These lovers are consumed by and possessive of their relationship. Their style is similar to what Peele and Brodsky call *addictive love*[2] and is dangerously similar to drug addiction except that the lover is the object of dependency—a sort of interpersonal heroin. In this type of relationship, the slightest lack of enthusiasm by one partner will cause anxiety, pain, and/or jealousy in the other. These lovers need to be loved so much that they can't let the relationship take its course; they begrudge their partner's personal growth because they need the lover to fill their own self-emptiness. Their need for attention and affection is so strong and persistent that it is virtually impossible to satisfy. They alternate between peaks of ecstasy and depths of despair. Breakups are akin to a withdrawal from drug dependency and even the possibility of a breakup may lead to a variety of undesirable behaviors—for example, watching and following a person around, giving the person unwanted gifts and messages of affection, or stealing or damaging personal possessions.[3]

Realistic love: Style of love based on practicality and logic.

5. Realistic Love These lovers combine the control and manipulation of playful love with companionate love. Compatibility is examined and sought on the basis of practicality. Lee uses the phrase *computer dating type* to describe this style. Logical thought and attempts to minimize the role of feelings in important decisions are valued. Careful planning based on the pros and cons not only characterizes courtship, but even separation may be carefully designed to occur at an "appropriate" time. Changes in life goals and the need for a less predictable relationship may pose challenges to the viability of this style.

6. *Altruistic Love* These lovers view love as most major religions espouse—unselfish, patient, kind, generous, never jealous, never demanding reciprocity. A similar type of love is called "compassionate" and may be directed at a close relationship partner, strangers, or humanity in general. It involves caring, concern, tenderness, and an orientation toward supporting, helping, and understanding the target, particularly when he or she is suffering or in need. Compassionate love involves reaching out to strangers in despair, thinking deeply about the well-being of humankind, and choosing self-suffering if it would alleviate the suffering of others.[4] Lee reports that although some of his interviewees had episodes in their lives that approached this style, he did not find any saints. Few interviewees seemed to exhibit this style consistently throughout their lives. And although it may seem appealing to have a partner who constantly places your needs (and the needs of all people) ahead of his or her own, this also may create a problem. For instance, someone who is always "above" the pull of self-satisfaction may appear to be more of a spectator in life's activities than a full-fledged participant.

> **Altruistic love:** Style of love that is unselfish, patient, caring, and kind.

The preceding, styles of loving identified by Lee do a good job of making two important points: (1) love can manifest itself in many different ways and (2) different people may have different orientations or styles of loving.

We would expect love styles to manifest themselves differently depending on the degree of intimacy the couple feels and the length of time they have been together. The amount of experience you have with love in general or a particular style also will influence the likelihood a person will manifest it. Age may even influence the manifestation of some love styles. Do people prefer a partner with a love style similar to their own? There does seem to be a tendency for this preference among dating partners. And with the exception of obsessive and playful love, people with similar styles tend to find each other. Are certain styles preferred over others? Not surprisingly, altruistic love and companionate love have widespread appeal.[5] Love of beauty is also often associated with satisfying relationships, whereas playful love can undermine a couple's ability to cope together when they face stressors, contributing to an unhappy pairing.[6]

There is some evidence that certain communication styles may accompany each of these love styles.[7] People with obsessive and altruistic love styles reported a heightened concern for relationship intensification strategies; those with a playful love style identified with cute pickup lines, secret tests, and sex, but they were less interested in spending more time with their partners and talking about their relationship. In contrast, those with a love of beauty style wanted to spend more time with their partners and give them tokens of affection. Companionate lovers were less interested in the physical aspects of relationships and more interested in a partner with good communication skills, intelligence, compassion, and a sense of humor. Realistic lovers preferred directness in their communication choices and essentially wanted it all—good looks, sex, companionship, money, success, and so on.

Some research shows that women and men have different patterns of falling in love and tend to emphasize different styles. Women seem to fall in love earlier and more often than men as teenagers, but after about age twenty men fall in love more easily. Men seem to be more interested in the passionate, game-playing styles of love, whereas women emphasize friendship and practicality with some degree of possessiveness. Obviously, these general trends may not adequately represent the preferences of any given man, woman, or couple, and at least one study concludes that men and women are more similar in their conceptions of love than has previously been assumed.[8]

No matter which style of loving predominates for a person, there will be aspects of other styles that will be shown as well. To what extent do you think you show each of the styles identified by Lee? Select a person you love romantically and answer all the questions in **Table 7.1** with that person in mind.

Table 7.1 What is Your Love Styles Profile?					
Circle the number that best represents your attitude: 1 = Strongly Agree; 2 = Agree; 3 = Neutral; 4 = Disagree; 5 = Strongly Disagree.					
1. My lover and I have the right physical "chemistry" between us.	1	2	3	4	5
2. I feel that my lover and I were meant for each other.	1	2	3	4	5
3. My lover and I really understand each other.	1	2	3	4	5
4. My lover fits my ideal standards of physical beauty/handsomeness.	1	2	3	4	5
5. I believe that what my lover doesn't know about me won't hurt him/her.	1	2	3	4	5
6. I have sometimes had to keep my lover from finding out about other lovers.	1	2	3	4	5
7. My lover would get upset if he/she knew of some of the things I've done with other people.	1	2	3	4	5
8. I enjoy playing the "game of love" with my lover and a number of other partners.	1	2	3	4	5
9. Our love is the best kind because it grew out of a long friendship.	1	2	3	4	5
10. Our friendship merged gradually into love over time.	1	2	3	4	5
11. Our love is really a deep friendship, not a mysterious, mystical emotion.	1	2	3	4	5
12. Our love relationship is the most satisfying because it developed from a good friendship.	1	2	3	4	5
13. A main consideration in choosing my lover was how he/she would reflect on my family.	1	2	3	4	5

14. An important factor in choosing my lover was whether or not he/she would be a good parent.	1	2	3	4	5
15. One consideration in choosing my lover was how he/she would reflect on my career.	1	2	3	4	5
16. Before getting very involved with my lover, I tried to figure out how compatible his/her hereditary background would be with mine in case we ever had children.	1	2	3	4	5
17. When my lover doesn't pay attention to me, I feel sick all over.	1	2	3	4	5
18. Since I've been in love with my lover, I've had trouble concentrating on anything else.	1	2	3	4	5
19. I cannot relax if I suspect that my lover is with someone else.	1	2	3	4	5
20. If my lover ignores me for a while, I sometimes do stupid things to try to get his/her attention back.	1	2	3	4	5
21. I would rather suffer myself than let my lover suffer.	1	2	3	4	5
22. I cannot be happy unless I place my lover's happiness before my own.	1	2	3	4	5
23. I am usually willing to sacrifice my own wishes to let my lover achieve his/hers.	1	2	3	4	5
24. I would endure all things for the sake of my lover.	1	2	3	4	5

SCORING: Add your ratings for statements 1–4. This is your score for love of beauty or passionate love. Your total for statements 5–8 is your score for playful or game-playing love. Your total score for statements 9–12 is your score for compassionate or friendship love. Your total for statements 13–16 is your score for realistic love. Your total for statements 17–20 is your score for obsessive love. Your total for statements 21–24 is your score for altruistic love. Lower scores indicate greater agreement with the scale (e.g., a score of 4 would reflect very strong and positive attitude toward this type of love; a score of 20 would reflect a strong negative attitude toward this type of love).

Source: C. Hendrick, S. S. Hendrick, and A. Dicke (1998). The Love Attitudes Scale: Short Form. Journal of Social and Personal Relationships 15 (1988); 147–159. See also C. Hendrick and S. S. Hendrick. A Theory and Method of Love. Journal of Personality and Social Psychology 50 (1986); 392–402. Reprinted by permission of Sage Publications. Ltd.

Like Lee, Sternberg listened to people tell about their love relationships. His conclusion was that intimate relationships could be analyzed by examining three components: (1) *intimacy,* which includes feelings of closeness, sharing, communication, and support; (2) *passion,* which involves physiological arousal and an intense desire to be united with the loved one; and (3) *commitment,* which involves both the short-term decision to love another and the longer-term commitment to maintain it.[9]

These three dimensions of love have been useful in other studies that also have tried to identify the central dimension of love.[10] This three-part, or triangular, theory provided Sternberg with a way of identifying the eight different types of love relationships that follow (**Figure 7.1**).

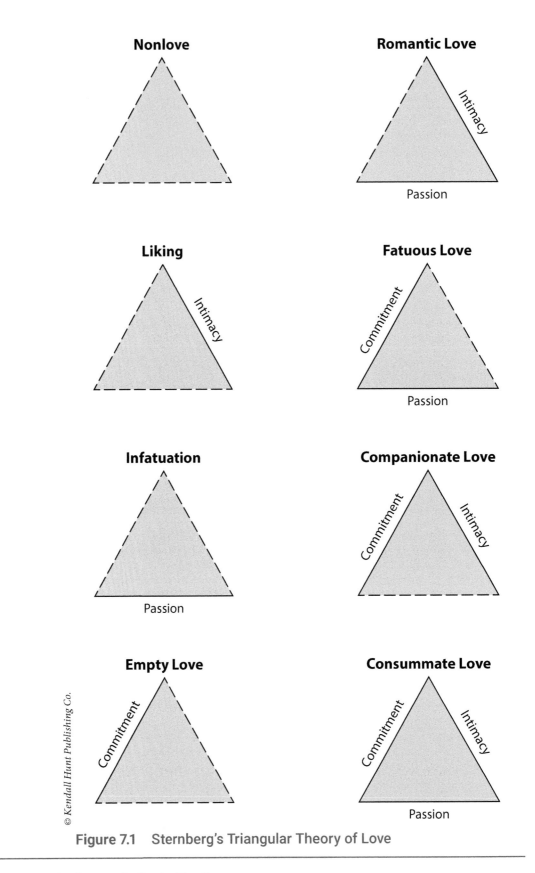

Figure 7.1   Sternberg's Triangular Theory of Love

Many of our relationships are not likely to emphasize any of the three dimensions of Sternberg's theory—resulting in a state called **nonlove**. When intimacy is the only component, there is the kind of closeness associated with *liking*. When passion is the only component, there is a high degree of arousal but no intimacy or commitment. This type of relationship love is **infatuation**. When commitment is the sole dimension (no passion or intimacy), it is what Sternberg calls **empty love**. A couple may be committed to staying in a relationship but feel no passion or intimacy toward each other. This may occur at the end of a long-term relationship or at the beginning of one. Romantic love is a combination of intimacy and passion. It is liking plus physical attraction, but commitment is absent. Physical attraction is what some have called sexual desire and found it to be an important aspect of romantic love.[11] A short-term affair may have these features. Sternberg points out that the intimacy dimension of **romantic love** is itself a complex phenomenon. It is composed of both general and specific feelings—for instance, feeling loved but also feeling loved by a person who is particularly good for you and a person who makes your relationship special. **Fatuous love** combines commitment and passion but excludes intimacy. This scenario might find a couple meeting and marrying within a week. But because they don't have the emotional support for long-term commitment provided by intimacy, the relationship may not last long. **Companionate love** has intimacy and commitment, but no passion. A long-term friendship or a marriage that has lost the physical attraction exemplifies this type of love. **Consummate love** contains all three dimensions. This kind of relationship, according to Sternberg, is difficult, but not impossible, to achieve. It also is difficult to maintain, but it is the kind of love that embodies the ideal for many seeking a love relationship.

To explain the foregoing eight types of relationships that result from combinations of Sternberg's three dimensions, it is necessary to talk as if a dimension did or did not exist. In reality, behaviors representing each dimension most likely occur in various degrees. Thus, passion may not be completely absent in companionate love, but may be of little influence in defining the nature of the relationship. In addition, these dimensions are changeable. Sometimes the magnitude of a given relationship dimension may change quickly; sometimes it is a gradual process that occurs over many years. Passion ammitment, for example, may gradually reverse the amount of influence each plays in defining a marital relationship the longer it lasts. In one test of Sternberg's theory, passion did decline as the length of a relationship increased—but primarily for females. Although the researchers thought intimacy levels also would decrease over time, this was not the case. Commitment was the best predictor of relationship satisfaction in long-term relationships.[12]

Liking Versus Loving

Efforts such as the preceding to sort out the varieties of love inevitably bring us to the task of differentiating liking and loving. Some believe that love is just the end result of intensifying one's liking for another; others believe you can love someone and not like them. At this point, let's examine several attempts to unravel liking and loving.

Nonlove: Relational state that lacks intimacy, passion, and commitment.

Infatuation: Type of love with high passion but no intimacy or commitment.

Empty love: Type of love that is high in commitment but low in passion and intimacy.

Romantic love: Type of love that combines passion and intimacy but lacks commitment.

Fatuous love: Type of love that combines commitment and passion but lacks intimacy.

Consummate love: Type of love that combines all three of Sternberg's dimensions: passion, intimacy, and commitment.

He had forbidden me to call love the lotus that turns into lettuce.

—*Peter De Vries*

Berscheid and Walster have contrasted liking with what they call passionate love (romantic and sexual attraction).[13] One distinguishing factor, they argue, may be the role of fantasy. Whereas liking may be based on a rather direct exchange of rewards between the participants, passionate love often is aroused by one's imagined fantasies—rewards are expected rather than actual. Should passionate love be heavily based on fantasy, a large letdown could be expected when reality-based information starts coming in during later stages of the relationship and the lesser rewards that can be obtained from this very real human being are realized. Other things being equal, liking will tend to increase as the time of interaction is extended. Passionate love, however, may erode over time, and as Berscheid and Walster put it, the best you can hope for after an extended period of time is an "afterglow." In this conceptual framework, *love may be necessary to propose marriage, but liking will be necessary to sustain it.*

Passionate love is intense, unstable, and sexual in nature. It is often characterized by emotional highs ("This perfect creature is always on my mind") and emotional lows ("I hate to think what will happen to me if I don't hear from my partner soon"). Liking, on the other hand, is far less intense, a great deal more stable, and generally devoid of sexual attraction.[14]

Liking: An attraction that is a result of positive reinforcement received from another person.

Liking is generally thought of as an attraction resulting from positive reinforcement received from another. *Loving,* however, is sometimes more complex. It is possible to fall in love with someone we know will cause us agony or suffering. According to Berscheid and Walster, it seems to be a process of experiencing some form of emotional arousal (either positive or negative) and having some rationale for labeling that arousal *love* that explains the many and seemingly conflicting emotions that may characterize love rather than liking. It also may help to clarify incidents when a person kills another he or she claims to love. A series of experiments in which subjects' physiological arousal was heightened by conditions representing fear, rejection, or frustration and who were given some situational rationale to conclude that this arousal was related to a positive attraction to others helped confirm the viability of this theory.

In a related set of studies, men experienced neutral (exercise), positive (comedy), or negative (anxiety) arousal. After arousal, these men viewed a videotape of either an attractive or unattractive woman whom they believed they would soon meet. Men with high arousal levels were more attracted to the attractive woman and more repulsed by the unattractive woman than similar men who did not experience high arousal. The aroused men had labeled their aroused state as sexual-romantic attraction or repulsion.[15] This type of research is based on the earlier work of Schachter, who proposed that any emotional experience depends on physiological arousal plus the individual's belief that he or she is experiencing a particular emotion—increased heart and respiration rates may be interpreted as either anger or joy, depending on what you see others in your immediate environment doing.[16] In summary, then, Berscheid and Walster's theory holds that individuals will experience passionate love if they are emotionally agitated and attribute their state to passionate love. When the arousal ceases, or the individuals cease to attribute their internal emotional state to passionate love, love will fade. Taking this a step further, individuals can experience something that makes them feel elated (perhaps an A in chemistry) and the unnamed emotional joy can later be labeled affection when they meet a friend. Thus, the emotional high from rewarding events can be transferred or generalized to other situations just as emotional lows can be projected onto people who were in no way responsible for them.

"*When I fell in love with you, suddenly your eyes didn't seem close together. Now they seem close together again.*"

Source: Esquire (December 1988)

Whereas many argue that the differences between liking and loving are quantitative (loving is simply a more intense form of positive attraction), Rubin believes that there are qualitative differences.[17] *Liking,* according to Rubin, has two major components: affection and respect. *Affection* is liking based on mutual interacting characterized by warmth, closeness, and fondness: "You really make me feel good. You always seem to say the right thing and you're fun to be around. I really like you." *Respect* is liking based on another's admirable characteristics outside the interpersonal domain. It is a cooler, more distant sort of liking: "I've always liked my boss. Even though he is dour and hard sometimes, he is bright and responsible" or "I still like and respect you, but I don't love you anymore." Affection and respect are coexisting dimensions of liking; a liked person may not receive both attributions, although most of us would prefer some of both. The components of *love,* based on Rubin's conceptualization and research are attachment, caring, and intimacy. *Attachment* consists of "powerful desires to be in the other's presence, to make physical contact, to be approved of, and to be cared for"—to be fulfilled by the other. *Caring* is the component in opposition to attachment, the view of love as giving rather than needing. When we care about another, their satisfaction and security become as important as our own. *Intimacy* is a postulate derived from the combination of attachment (self-fulfillment) and caring (self-surrender). Whereas these latter components are individual based, intimacy is the bond or link between the two people. It transcends the characteristics of each individual; it's the mixture.

Love Versus Friendship

© fizkes/Shutterstock.com

Related to scholarship on loving versus liking, researchers have also considered the differences between friendship and love. Davis and Todd started their research with the assumption that love and friendship share many characteristics but also differ on some crucial ones.[18] Their theory, shown in **Figure 7.2**, identifies eight characteristics of friendships. According to the theory, love relationships also contain these eight characteristics of friendship plus two other features: passion and caring. The research based on this theory provides much support. Studies comparing best friendships and close friendships (same- and opposite-sexed) with lovers have largely resulted in what one would expect from the theory.

Some exceptions have occurred, however. Being a "champion/advocate" does not seem to be a behavior particularly characteristic of lovers only; similarly, "enjoyment" appears to be more a factor in love relationships than in friendships. This research indicates that "typical" love relationships differ from

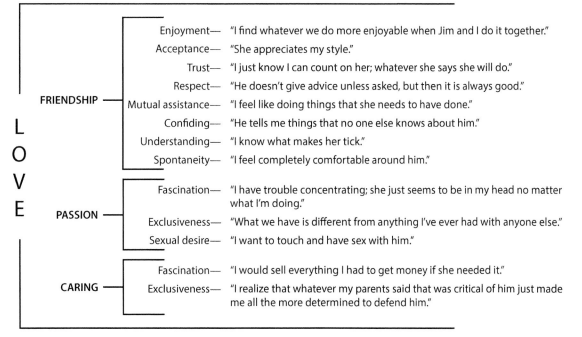

Figure 7.2 Love and Friendship

even very close friendships by having higher levels of fascination, exclusiveness, and sexual desire; a greater depth of caring (willing to give one's utmost when it is needed); and a greater potential for experiencing enjoyment.

Recent research on **cross-sex friendships** among heterosexual individuals indicates that the boundaries between love and friendship are sometimes blurred. People are not always sure if they have passion for each other. Sometimes one person has romantic intent while the other does not, making it difficult to determine whether the relationship is "just" a friendship or something else too.[19]

Cross-sex friendships: Ostensibly non-romantic friendships between a heterosexual man and heterosexual woman.

Negotiating cross-sex friendships can be challenging, and they sometime require special efforts to define or maintain them. Many cross-sex friends end up talking about their relationship in an attempt to clarify exactly what kind of connection they have or want. In some cases, cross-sex friends talk explicitly about how they do not want to introduce sexual or romantic elements into their relationship because they worry about damaging the friendship. Other times, cross-sex friends signal their intentions less directly; for example, cross-sex friends who wish to move toward a romantic relationship may be act supportive, exhibit affection, and flirt; whereas those who do not wish to make their cross-sex friendship romantic often talk about other romantic interests they have. If you talk enough about how you are really hot for somebody else, most cross-sex friends will get the idea that you are not particularly interested in them romantically, even if you don't say that explicitly. Of course, even such seemingly clear signals do not define the relationship forever. Sometimes people who fully intend to remain "just friends" change their mind or end up surprised to find that they develop a level of passion and caring that they didn't expect.

So you want to know about communication between friends . . .

Can a dog be man's best friend? Yes, and a woman's too. In a series of studies involving nearly 1,000 college students, Lawrence Kurdek found that some college students feel as close and attached to their pet dogs as they do to their siblings. Given that dogs (and other pets) can provide a person with a sense of companionship and a productive exchange of needs, they can be considered "friends." This only serves to remind us that we use the term *friend* to describe a variety of intimate and nonintimate relationships. A friend can be someone you hardly know or somebody you know best, somebody you like or somebody who is simply not disliked. Friends are often thought of as "low maintenance," but we sometimes have "high-maintenance" friends if the needs of each person are not being met. Friends, close friends, and best friends differ in the degree to which the other is known, the degree of commitment to maintaining the relationship, and the degree of interdependence experienced by the pair.

Ideally, how do friends behave? Not all friendships are alike and not all manifest the characteristics of an ideal friendship. But the closer the friendship, the more likely each person will perceive the other as trustworthy, dependable in times of need, accepting of the other's attitudes and behavior, caring and supportive, and fun and enjoyable to be around. The best of friends are able to keep your secrets, protect your vulnerabilities, stand up for you in your absence, enjoy your other friends, spend time with you, provide comfort during bad times and joy during good times, and disclose personal feelings or problems. The ease with which friends communicate during small talk is an important marker of their closeness.

Is the communication in male and female friendships different? Often it is. Women friends are more apt to talk about personal issues and share emotions; friendships between men typically revolve around shared activities and their talk is less personal. Male friends can exhibit signs of greater intimacy, but in the United States, social norms, gender roles, and homophobia often work against it.

Can a man and a woman be close friends without being romantically involved? This type of friendship is not as unusual as some think, but its frequency sharply decreases after college—especially when the participants develop other romantic relationships. Sexual desire, feelings of exclusivity, and perceptions of others are often barriers to such relationships. In some cases, college students report that they have had sex with a friend of the opposite sex but are not romantically involved with them.

How do friendships end? The reasons friendships fade away are not all that different from the reasons that romantic relationships fade away—for example, the relationship no longer meets your needs, dislike of something about the friend's behavior, or lifestyle changes that don't involve or aren't suitable to the friend. But most friendships are not characterized by a formal breakup. Instead, most are simply allowed to fade away through passive avoidance. This process doesn't help solve immediate problems with the friendship, but it leaves the door open for resuscitating it at a later date. Some friendships that have been in limbo for years can be easily reestablished.

* * * * * * * * * * * * * * * * * * *

There is much more to be learned about communication between friends. The preceding points are only a brief beginning. In various places throughout this book, particularly in this chapter, other aspects of this topic are treated. For those interested in more in-depth coverage, see Fehr, B. "The life cycle of friendship." In C. Hendrick and S. S. Hendrick, eds., *Close Relationships: A Sourcebook* (pp. 71–82). Thousand Oaks, CA: Sage, 2000; Hays, R. B. "Friendship." In S. W. Duck ed., *Handbook of Personal Relationships* (pp. 391–408). New York: Wiley 1988; Hojjat, M. and Moyer, A., eds., *The Psychology of Friendships*. New York, NY: Oxford University Press, 2017; Kurdek, L. A., "Pet Dogs as Attachment Figures," *Journal of Social and Personal Relationships* 25 (2008): 247-266; and Rawlins, W. K. *Friendship Matters: Communication, Dialectics, and the Life Course.* New York: Aldine de Gruyter, 1992.

Intimacy and Close Relationships

Some researchers have studied what it means to describe a relationship as "close" or "intimate." People can develop close bonds in different types of relationships, including friendships, romantic relationships, and family relationships.[20] Regardless of what type of relationships it is, a number of scholars have suggested that the defining characteristic of a close or intimate relationship involves the notion of **responsiveness**.[21] Responsiveness has been defined in different ways, but one useful way to think about responsiveness is when somebody does things out of consideration for the other person that he or she would not otherwise do. For example, if it so happens that two people both love to eat lunch outside under a tree, the fact that they do that at the same time does not necessarily mean that they are responding to each other in any way. In contrast, if one of those people would probably eat in the office if the other person wasn't

Responsiveness:
A core characteristic of intimate relationships marked by individuals doing things out of consideration for the other person that they would not otherwise do.

around but chooses to eat outside under the tree because the other person prefers that, that would be an indication of responsiveness. In close relationships, both people tend to be responsive to each other, and as a relationship becomes more intimate, the partners tend to become even more responsive to each other. Moreover, people in close relationships begin to notice if the other person is responsive to them. The extent that people believe their relational partner is supportive, understanding, and concerned with their needs is called *perceived responsiveness*. Perceived responsiveness is a crucial part of what makes people feel close in relationships; it predicts all kinds of positive outcomes in relationships, such willingness to put mutual needs over one's own needs, willingness to work on maintaining the relationship, and willingness to forgive transgressions in the relationship.

Although we know that a general sense of mutual responsiveness is an important part of what it means to have a close or intimate relationship, there are also more specific qualities associated with close relationships. Some that have been found repeatedly in studies of close and intimate relationships include: (1) Partners like to *spend time together*. They seek each other out and want to interact frequently. (2) They feel like they *mutually influence each other*—giving and receiving help and advice. (3) They say they *get positive feelings from the relationship*. This may involve any or all of the following: respect, trust, caring, warmth, sex, acceptance. (4) They feel like they *know and understand each other*—a feeling derived from disclosing to and confiding in their partner and having their partner do the same. (5) They *want their relationship to continue* and would be distressed if it did not. Keep in mind that even though these features may characterize many or even most close relationships, there are bound to be relationships that people describe as "close" that do not include one or more of the preceding features.

Even though we are increasing our understanding of the features that characterize and distinguish various types of relationships, we still have a lot to learn about how these features are communicated.[22] Not surprisingly, some of the ways people say they increase the intimacy of a romantic relationship include increasing contact; discussing the future of the relationship; giving social support, assistance, favors, and gifts; disclosing more personal information; using nicknames; increasing touching and flirting; enhancing one's appearance; having sex; and integrating one partner into the other partner's social network and family.[23] However, intimacy can be achieved and communicated in a variety of ways. Even when people are experiencing the same type of love, for example, they may have different ways to communicate it. Sometimes expressions of friendliness and caring can be misinterpreted as romantic behavior. Sometimes the reverse occurs.

But, of course, there are times when the ambiguity and confusion associated with communicating intimacy, closeness, love, and liking serve a useful purpose. At such times, we aren't interested in being "clear." However, when clarity is important, communicators must be especially vigilant about signals that will be misread and provide the contextual information necessary to clarify one's intent.

The preceding theory and research have probably provided an overdose of terms and lists of characteristics. OK, omit the word *probably*. What does it all boil down to? The following conclusions seem warranted at this time:

1. There are many levels and types of liking and loving. Liking and loving are phenomena that seem to vary in both degree and kind—even though some components of "closeness" may be similar across several types of relationships.

2. Emotional intensity seems to be more characteristic of love relationships than of friendships—particularly when first forming or when threats to the relationship are perceived.

3. The extent to which any characteristic or set of characteristics contributes to a relationship's definition is likely to change as the length of the relationship increases; some aspects will grow in importance, and some will become less important.

4. Relationships described with the word *love* may be further understood by examining the degree of intimacy, commitment, and passion that characterizes the relationship.

5. Love relationships that last a long time are more likely to have a strong friendship component to them even though this may not have characterized the relationship when it began.

6. Liking and loving have many overlapping features.

The love we give away is the only love we keep.

—*Elbert Hubbard*

There are still a lot of unanswered questions about the nature of intimacy and how it is manifested. Even though we are not now in a position to solve these long-standing puzzles by putting all the right pieces in all the right places, we do have some pretty good guesses about the nature of the pieces. Let's call these the *foundations of intimacy*: (1) personality and early experiences, (2) situational and developmental factors, (3) cultural guidelines, (4) emotional arousal and labeling, (5) self-fulfillment, (6) self-surrender, and (7) commitment to a joint identity. Although we may not know precisely how it is accomplished, these foundations combine in complex ways to produce the variety of intimate relationships possible. Some combinations may even produce similar feelings in two individuals but different behaviors. Part of the difficulty in understanding intimate relationships is that each foundation block is, at any time, subject to change by exerting influence on other foundation categories or by being influenced by forces from those other categories.

Foundations of Intimacy

Personality and Early Experiences

The participants in an intimate relationship bring to it their own unique experiences and behavioral orientations—commonly known as their personalities. Even though much of our temperament and behavior patterns are molded and influenced by our environment, there is some reason to believe that we enter the world with certain genetically based predispositions.[24] Whether innate or learned, these individual characteristics provide one source of explanation for how each of us approaches, avoids, sustains, and/or communicates intimacy.

If there are instincts or genetic predispositions, we need to examine the nature of early human experiences with attachment. Our early ancestors no doubt found value in close relationships because they provided protection and an opportunity for reproduction.[25] Using this knowledge as a backdrop for identifying acts of love among human beings today, Buss proposed the following: (1) Females are interested in males who can protect their young, so acts of love by men will be displays of resources that have the potential to be invested in the young: (2) Males, on the other hand, are interested in women's reproductive capabilities, so acts of love by women will involve appearance-enhancing acts designed to show reproductive viability.[26] Obviously, males and females communicate a variety of acts that show love, but these two tendencies, according to Buss, are deeply rooted in our development as a species.

Another source of our adult behavior can be traced to our experiences as children. Researchers often will examine the rewards and punishments parents administer and how these affect characteristics such as social dependency or achievement needs. It is clear that early experiences with affection will certainly have an impact on later attempts to build intimate relationships; it is not clear, however, what that impact will be. For instance, let's assume a child has had some type of early emotional deprivation, perhaps a lack of parental closeness. From this background, that adult may consider the process of intensifying a relationship as negative. He or she may fear the dependency and vulnerability of a commitment to intimacy: "I've been burned before and I'm not going to let it happen again." That same background, however, could cause that adult to desperately seek out many friends and cling to intimates in an effort to offset early unpleasant experiences. It is not uncommon to find a person seeking a primary relationship with someone who symbolizes characteristics of that person's mother or father. In some cases, it may be because of pleasant experiences with the parent, but it also may be an effort to find someone to exercise one's neuroses on. One study found that the extent to which a person was optimistic about his or her own future marital relationship depended on whether he or she perceived his or her parents as having a good marriage. Optimism about future love relationships in general, though, was most accurately predicted by actual dating experiences.[27] Being optimistic and hopeful about the future of a relationship often results in satisfying relationships because behavior is more likely to be perceived within a constructive and supportive frame. These perceptions may, in turn, elicit more supportive and constructive behavior.[28]

In an effort to identify specifically how our early childhood experiences with intimacy may influence our adult behavior, Hazan and Shaver studied patterns of attachment. Their research resulted in the identification of three adult attachment styles in romantic relationships: secure, avoidant, and anxious/ambivalent.[29] **Secure lovers** describe themselves as happy, friendly, trusting, and accepting of their partner despite known faults. They acknowledge that love rises and falls in many relationships but also believe that in some relationships love never fades. Their interpersonal behavior is believed to be constructive, warm, supportive, and optimistic. They are not interested in alternatives to their current relationship and regularly express their commitment.[30] **Avoidant lovers** say they fear intimacy and experience emotional extremes and jealousy. They believe romantic love is possibly an illusion, and if it does exist, it doesn't last long. They perceive that few potential partners exist for a satisfying love relationship, and they worry that partners may ask them to be more intimate than they perceive they can be. Their communication behavior is often characterized as detached, negative, and unsupportive. Bartholomew, however, points out that people who avoid relationships also can be independent, and self-reliant and genuinely prefer autonomy and freedom to the development of close relationships.[31] **Anxious/ambivalent lovers** seem to be a combination of what Lee called obsessive love and love of beauty. They report emotional extremes, obsession with the lover, jealousy, and extreme sexual attraction. They find it easy to fall in love, but they also believe it is rare to find a truly satisfying long-term love relationship. They worry that their partner doesn't want them or won't stay with them. Their communication style frequently leads to an escalation of conflict. They may seek a great deal of reassurance from their partner even though their own expressions of commitment are weak.

At first glance, one might think that everyone would prefer someone with a secure attachment style, but this does not seem to be the case. In fact, it is not unusual for dating partners to prefer those who have a similar style—a person with an anxious/ambivalent style preferring to date a person who is also

Secure lovers: Attachment pattern associated with being happy, friendly, trusting, and accepting of one's partner despite known faults.

Avoidant lovers: Attachment pattern in which people fear intimacy and experience emotional extremes and jealousy.

Anxious/ambivalent lovers: Attachment pattern in which people experience emotional extremes, obsession, jealousy, and extreme sexual attraction.

anxious/ ambivalent. Even though adults may manifest a dominant or preferred attachment style, the situation and the behavior of one's partner often will influence and alter these tendencies emanating from early attachment experiences.[32]

Beginning early in childhood, some people believe men and women experience friendship differently. The widely held belief, and it is supported by some research, is that women friends talk more than men friends—especially about feelings and relationships. Male friends, on the other hand, are believed to base their friendships more on doing things together and when they do talk they mainly talk about sports and work. If disclosing feelings and talking about one's friendship are used as the standard for close, satisfying friendships, then one might conclude that male friendships are pretty empty. The puzzling part is that many men seem very satisfied with their male friendships and feel that they have a real sense of closeness in some of them. Supporting this view is some research that challenges the traditional portrayal of male friendships. This research argues that affect is not missing from or a minor part of men's friendships and that women not uncommonly rely on doing things together as an important part of some of their friendships as well. Perhaps more important than any differences in communication between men's and women's friendships is the lesson that there are many ways friends can communicate that provide the energy necessary to develop and sustain close friendships.[33]

Another way of examining personality is to look at how it affects our perceptions of others. For instance, many believe that how well we are able to accept others is intimately linked to how well we accept ourselves. Hence, you may have more difficulty making close friends if you do not like yourself. Similarly, if you perceive yourself as unromantic or unlovable, you will probably find falling in love an infrequent experience. Low self-esteem seems to be a personality trait that will limit the frequency of intimate relationships. The chances of success are perceived as small by the individual with low self-esteem and, more often than not, these perceptions are confirmed. However, one research project concluded that those with low self-esteem were more likely than those with high self-esteem to show "greater love, greater liking and more trust for their romantic partners and evaluate their love mates more favorably."[34] This makes sense. If an individual has difficulty obtaining something, he or she would probably go to great lengths to hold onto it once it was obtained. The general lack of confidence stemming from low self-esteem will probably make it more difficult to build an intimate relationship with someone who closely approximates one's romantic ideal. It is not unusual, however, for many types of people, with many different personality configurations, to seek intimacy with those who have characteristics that are not only revered, but seemingly missing in their own lives—a mental midget marries a mental giant; the person with verbal diarrhea marries one with verbal constipation. There is a belief that somehow these characteristics will magically rub off on the person who lacks them. If the expectations for this personality osmosis are too great, it could lead (and has led) to bitter disappointment. On the other hand, idealizing one's partner, maintaining positive illusions about him or her, can be very beneficial to a relationship. It not only helps to maintain a relationship during times of stress, but one's partner may come to believe in and act out some of the aspects of your idealization. In this way, idealizing one's partner acts as a self-fulfilling prophecy—bringing about the relationship you desired.[35]

Finally, we can look at how our perception of another's personality may help structure our own behavior. It is quite possible, for instance, that the personality you adopt in a relationship is heavily dependent on personality characteristics you perceive in the other person. What you see in the other person, however, is contingent on the type of relationship (as it realistically exists and as you would like it to be), the situation, and the other person's perceptions. For instance, some will see male aggressiveness as menacing; others will see it as masculine. In like manner, an aggressive woman may inspire dread or desire. Or you may delight in a self-confident, aggressive, verbose, independent, shrewd, and witty person as your closest friend and bridge partner, but you may be repelled at the thought of having such a personality with you on a daily basis as a roommate or spouse. Further, you may desire a given set of personality characteristics in a person with whom you want to form an intimate relationship, but such characteristics are attractive only isolated from your own personality. Oil and water are independently attractive and useful; merger, however, is costly for both.

Some people will enter relationships with high self-esteem, patience, tolerance, and adaptability; others may possess distinctly dissimilar personality profiles. Some will have a configuration of predispositions that will prepare them for a wide range of relationships with a wide range of people; others' predispositions will prepare them for a more limited range of people and types of relationships. Of course, this does not suggest that certain personality characteristics are better than others or that behavior patterns are unchangeable. It does suggest that when we examine the communicative patterns in advancing stages of a relationship (intimacy), we cannot ignore the contribution of the early experiences and personalities of the participants.

Situational and Developmental Factors

Circumstances can sometimes play a sizable role in the facilitation or inhibition of intimate relationships. For example, some people who have lived abroad report becoming friends with other people from their home county, to whom they normally would not have been drawn. Some cultures do not accept outsiders readily; thus, foreigners need to socialize with one another if they want to socialize at all. Brenton noted that sometimes foreigner communities even start to feel like a "big family," and the people in those communities overlook negative things about each other that they otherwise wouldn't. Indeed, often when friends like these return to their home country, they find each other's negative qualities are more noticeable, and they no longer feel compelled to maintain their friendships—even though when they were abroad they thought of each other as almost like family.[36]

In a similar way, people who work together sometimes develop relationships that are strongly influenced by factors associated with the work situation. When people spend much of their day in close proximity with others, work on tasks together, eat lunch or socialize during breaks together, it is not surprising that friendships develop. In time, coworkers may increase the intimacy of their talk (problems at work or in their lives away from work) and expand the venues for talking (socializing after work).[37] Of course situational factors inherent in the work environment may act as inhibitors to relationship development as well. Working closely and talking with someone five days a week do provide a lot of information about that person in a relatively short period of time. It may or may not be information that prompts you to pursue a closer relationship.

Parents sometimes maneuver and pressure their children into circumstances that will restrict their intimacy choices. Sometimes such conditions will bring about premature or careless relationship choices; occasionally a child may marry a person who is not loved in order to spite the parents—to watch them squirm as the relationship begins its inevitable public demise. Regardless of how the situation materializes, some people simply find themselves thrown together; others find an almost conspiratorial set of external conditions that set up intimacy barriers. The term *spring fever* attributes one's feelings of intimacy to environmental changes associated with a new season of the year. Even though these situational forces no doubt contribute to one's feelings and perceptions, there are surely other contributing factors—the act of labeling one's emotional state with an intimacy term or biorhythmic cycles. Once an intimate relationship has been formed, its continuance may be heavily dependent on surrounding environmental circumstances. Many familiar statements of marital frustration reflect a maintenance of co-presence more than a sustenance of intimacy—"We had to stay together because of what separation might do to the kids" or "I know she treats me like scum, but I just couldn't handle things if she left."

Chronological age, by itself, is a relatively meaningless developmental barometer, but it is a fact that some situations, circumstances, or events are more likely to occur at certain times in one's life. For this reason, we cannot ignore the interaction between one's stage in life and the extant circumstances. This interaction often will reveal differences in one's knowledge and understanding of, experience with, and predispositions for intimacy. Consider, for instance, the possible variants in meaning of the word *love* for a suburban child of six, a twenty-one-year-old bride, a middle-aged divorcee, and an older widow recently admitted to a nursing home. We all have some expectations for what a good friend or a lover should be like, and this is partly derived from how we perceive and react to events at various times in our life cycle. Children are generally told that they must love, who to love, and what expressions would constitute a satisfactory demonstration of love; adults are expected to *experience* love. Applying the standards we learn as children (loving Grandpa and Nana, or "I'll be your friend if you give me a cookie") to an adult experience may make the recognition of love difficult at first. At certain times in our lives, a state of *intimacy readiness* may occur. Examples might be a lonely bachelor or an unhappily married woman, a college senior who expected to find a life partner in school but hasn't yet, or a person who might be described as "in love with love." Obviously, there are other times when we are more lethargic or indifferent toward building intimate relationships—we already have a satisfactory number of concurrent relationships. Finally, it should be noted that as a relationship develops a history of its own, it may be possible to look back and see that at certain junctures behavioral manifestations of love were most important while at other times liking behavior was paramount for sustaining the intimate relationship.

An analysis of the environmental forces, the surrounding events, and each of our own developmental stages in life will certainly provide some of the necessary information for understanding and analyzing the nature of intimate relationships and intimate communication patterns.

Cultural Guidelines

Throughout our daily lives, we are bombarded with messages about what constitutes the normative boundaries for assorted types of intimate relationships. Magazines, TV shows, internet sites, advertisements, comic books, songs, novels, and movies serve to influence expectations, attitudes, and behaviors associated with human intimacy. These messages may reiterate the romantic ideal, espousing that love will conquer all adversity. As a result, some people seek utopian relationships, which do not exist. Other messages may communicate this contemporary U.S. culture's encouragement of love and marriage—everyone is expected to fall in love; marriage is generally considered a good thing. It may be of interest to learn that marrying for love didn't really catch on until the late eighteenth century. Before then, marriage was thought of as a way to acquire wealth and property, forge political ties, and produce legitimate children. Marrying for practical reasons made sense to people who were looking for ways to ensure their survival and improve their standard of living.[38]

Our cultural guidelines also address the characteristics of people who are commonly thought to be most suited for the development of intimate relationships—pairs who are physically attractive, single, opposite-sexed, similar in age and social background, who have known each other for an appropriate length of time, and who sexually desire each other. Although many intimate couples do not fit these characteristics, the cultural guidelines are persistent. Our culture's standards are changing, but there are still many people who feel, for example, that unmarried, middle-aged women must be unattractive, and generally failures; unmarried middle-aged men still are frequently categorized as either gay or as individuals with mother complexes. Test yourself. Identify as many sources as you can that help communicate the U.S. norm that in mixed-gender, romantic love the woman should be younger than the man. This norm, and the previously noted examples, have been widely communicated and have received cultural reinforcement in the past. This does not suggest that people in the United States don't receive countercultural messages or that many people aren't adopting alternative (nontraditional) styles of intimacy. In time, some of these counter-normative messages may become the norm. One example of a transition from counter-normative behavior to more normative behavior concerns the familiar double standard regarding sexual behavior of men and women. Men, the previous norm told us, could experience sexual excitement and have intercourse without being in love; women, on the other hand, could not (without negative sanctioning) have sexual intercourse without being in love. Behavioral standards are now more similar for both sexes and receive greater acceptance, but this is a good example of how cultural guidelines encourage us to accept and label differently the same behavior in men and women. In fact, many cultural guidelines for the behavior of men and women in intimate relationships are in the process of changing. In the past, men were generally taught to shy away from overt emotional expressions; to express tenderness and affection in indirect, understated ways; to take responsibility for all important relationship decisions; and to be the initiator of intimate behavior. All of these relationship teachings are being questioned in current mass media portrayals of male and female behavior.

There is an entire cultural litany for U.S. intimacy with numerous subcultural variations, but the foregoing examples should be enough to remind us of how our culture provides guidelines around which we are expected to structure our perceptions and behavior in intimate relationships.

Emotional Arousal and Labeling

Throughout most of this book, we rely heavily on social and psychological factors to help us explain and understand interpersonal behavior. It would be a mistake, however, to ignore the role of body chemistry as a part of the process of experiencing intimate relationships.[39] For example, *oxytocin* is a hormone secreted by the pituitary gland that neuroscientists believe promotes close, intimate bonds. It has been shown to stimulate species contact, bonding and nurturing between parents and children, and affectionate and sexual behavior. PEA (*phenylethylamine*) or *dopamine* is an amphetamine-related compound that triggers euphoria and energizes romantic lovers. Dopamine also is critical to mate seeking and nesting for the prairie vole. But once mating is achieved, the male's brain starts producing an abundance of D1 receptors that attach themselves to dopamine and create stress and anxiety instead of pleasure when in the presence of other females. This explains why the male prairie voles remain true to their mates and why human males, in the absence of D1 receptors to block the dopamine, sometimes don't.[40]

© *Monkey Business Images/Shutterstock.com*

Body chemistry works in tandem with social factors in many ways, but none is more important than physiological arousal. Heightened emotions demand explanation or identifying labels. As soon as we've identified an emotional state as intense attraction for another person or as an extremely positive evaluation of another person, it will profoundly influence (1) our expectations for the type of relationship we are entering—if we label what we're feeling as love, we will then expect a different set of behaviors (performed and received) than if we labeled the same feelings as liking; (2) our perceptions of and consequent behavior toward the other person—what were faults before we labeled our feelings as love, now become mere idiosyncrasies; likewise, when we determine love is no longer an appropriate label for our feelings, idiosyncrasies may become faults again; and (3) our motivation to expend energy for the relationship, the fervor and excitement with which we carry out the role prescribed by our label.

Patterson believes this process also operates in conjunction with various nonverbal behaviors shown in intimate and nonintimate situations.[41] Briefly, he suggests that sufficient amounts of eye contact, touching, and proximity will create an arousal state in the other person. If these behaviors are labeled positive (liking, love, relief), they will be returned or reciprocated; if they are labeled negative (dislike, embarrassment, anxiety), we will enact offsetting, opposite, or compensatory behavior. In this theory, the emotional arousal precedes the act of labeling it. The process also may be reversed. We may have a preexisting label (Elmo loves me) that may or may not fit Elmo's behavior toward us. According to this theory, a big discrepancy between what we expect and what we get is highly arousing and will bring forth compensatory behavior; if the discrepancy is only moderate, this is moderately arousing and pleasurable and will elicit reciprocal behavior. Little or no discrepancy between the expected and observed behavior is not very arousing.[42]

> *When you're in love, you put up with things that, when you're out of love, you cite.*
>
> —*Miss Manners (Judith Martin)*

Emotional responses are an important part of intimate relationships, but sometimes these relationships develop through an orderly, dispassionate, and sober process. Intimacy develops gradually as a result of the interpersonal reward schedules adopted by the participants. Various forms of liking and loving may develop in this fashion. Empathic ability may be very strong, and personal feelings for the other individual may be intensely felt. It is not, however, the same type of emotional drunkenness that so often characterizes romantic intimacy. The allusion to alcoholic intoxication was not a stylistic accident. The same brand of ecstasy and irrationality have often been noted in both love and inebriation. Just one of many examples can be found in the song "Drunk on Love," in which Rihanna sings that being intoxicated with love is all she needs.

Like alcoholic intoxication, romantic passion often has a sobering, reality-based morning after. The intensity level of the physiological arousal simply cannot be maintained indefinitely. Lederer and Jackson would probably add an emphatic "Thank God!" to that last statement since they believe that during these periods of unbridled passion, rationality is temporarily shelved, and blinders are donned to ward off any unpleasant realities. They point out that the word *ecstasy,* a common label for one's emotions during a time of romantic love, is derived from a Greek word meaning *deranged* (in a state of being beyond all reason and self-control). Commenting further on potential distortions by a couple caught in this emotional tornado, Lederer and Jackson say: "Bad marriages, like death, are for others only . . . they are in such a passion (some call it romance), and are being driven so hard by the applause of society, that they cannot help themselves."[43] Permit us just one more analogy between those who treat themselves to alcohol and those who attribute their arousal to love. The drinker will often deny knowledge of any, and all, charges of abnormal behavior. We doubt the lover can be any better at transcending the situation when immersed in his or her emotions.

Exactly how we learn to label a particular, agitated emotional state as intimacy related is not entirely clear. When, as children, we learn a word such as *chair,* we can examine the referent by looking, touching, feeling, smelling, or even tasting. The referents for the term *intimate relationships* (lovers, close friends, intimates) and terms of intimacy (strong liking, loving, deep affection) are not available for sensory examination in the same way as a chair. We can observe others as lovers, close friends, or intimates and we can see how others exhibit strong liking, loving, and deep affection, but we cannot experience the emotions behind our observations. Hence, we have to rely on what others tell us. Novelist Graham Greene echoed this idea when he said:

> Hatred seems to operate the same glands as love; it even produces the same actions. If we had not been taught how to interpret the story of the Passion, would we have been able to say from their actions alone whether it was the jealous Judas or the cowardly Peter who loved Christ?[44]

We also know that our parents give us some early guidance in labeling by providing the meaning for various physiological conditions—"You're just afraid of the dark" or "You're disappointed because your good friend can't go too." As noted previously, there is a wealth of parental guidance concerning love, but most often this guidance does not cover the emotions associated with passionate or romantic love. Parents probably assume their children can't experience such feelings until they grow up.

During late adolescence, we have attained a fair grasp on the parameters of our own arousal tendencies, and we begin to look for plausible labels to explain various states of arousal. The surrounding environmental and social conditions help a great deal. Sometimes parents may try to assist in this labeling process by identifying a relationship with an early romantic partner as "infatuation" or "just a crush" rather than "love." *Infatuation* generally refers to strong affective feelings that have been terminated—or soon will be terminated. As we mentioned before, if people accept the label, behaviors congruent with the label will most likely follow. The temporary nature of the term *infatuation* may, in turn, serve to shorten the duration of the relationship if one or both parties begin to act in concert with the label. Sometimes we opt for the socially approved label because the costs may be too high for selecting another label. For instance, a person who did not want to be burdened with the responsibilities associated with the label *love* might label arousal as sexual excitement at one point in life, and the same feelings as love at another point. No doubt there have been many instances in which the label *romantic love* has been carefully avoided as an explanation of one's arousal in the presence of a same-sexed friend.

It should be clear that the process of learning to identify the feelings of intimacy and to label them accurately is a process subject to considerable variation. This is because it is a process primarily learned by social comparisons. Besides variation, Brenton also observed the relativity in the labeling process in his extensive study of American friendship patterns.[45] One striking aspect of Brenton's observations was the use of the word "close" to describe friendships. Some people who described their friendships as really close had relationships that would appear to others to be practically acquaintances. Some people may not want to have overly involved friendships, and their closest friends might not seem like very close friends to other people, but to them, they are "close." What counts as close is not objective; each person gets to decide for him or herself what they need from friendships and how they define them. Brenton's observation reminds us of a communication truism—that meanings are not in the words we use, but in us.

One final note. Labeling our state of emotional arousal is an ongoing process. The discussion here has focused mainly on the period of entry into intimacy. As we linger longer in an intimate relationship, we continue to evaluate and label our emotions. As an intimate relationship progresses, there may be periodic peaks that resemble the early ecstasy. In fact, the concept of the anniversary is probably an attempt to remind us of such feelings. Mostly, however, enduring intimate relationships reveal more stable and less intense physiological arousal than that experienced during earlier phases of intimacy. As we give more (or less) to the relationship, as we have (or don't have) our needs satisfied, and as we commit more of ourselves to a joint (or individual) identity, we will reevaluate the relationship and relabel our feeling states. We may continue to use the word *love* to describe the relationship, but the type of love and the intensity may change dramatically over the years. Relationships that are coming apart, may do so—not because of arousal labeled hatred or dislike—but because there is a perceived absence of *any* arousal, or, at least, the absence of any arousal that might receive a positive label concerning our relationship to our partner.

The Eskimos had fifty-two names for snow because it was important to them; there ought to be as many for love.

—*Margaret Atwood*

Self-Fulfillment

Self-Fulfillment: The extent to which our needs are fulfilled by the relationship.

Self-fulfillment, as a foundation for interpreting intimate relationships, is based on the assumption that the more our needs are fulfilled by the relationship, the greater will be our feelings of intimacy. We are, in essence, talking about the perceived rewards we receive—how effectively we perceive our partner as complementing our strengths and weaknesses or whether we find the needed similarity (or difference) in attitudes, values, physical attractiveness, sense of humor, and so forth. The following probably represent the most commonly discussed areas of need satisfaction in the pursuit of intimacy:

1. Affection Needs The satisfaction of one's need for affection is a minimal and basic requirement for intimacy. This overlaps with what some call a sense of belonging. Various verbal and touching behaviors might be an important manifestation in some relationships; in others, satisfaction of affection needs also may encompass sexual gratification. It should be obvious that the sex act, itself, does not necessarily mean the satisfaction of affection needs; and furthermore, sexual satisfaction doesn't always mean that affection needs are satisfied.

2. Self-Esteem Needs The parties to an intimate relationship must recognize and deal with ways in which self-respect, recognition, appreciation, and status can be communicated, and how often messages of this type are required. It is hard to contribute effectively to the joint identity of the relationship if one or both partners are uncertain about or don't think much of their own identities.

3. Security Needs In this context, security has a broad definition. It not only includes the rather primitive forms of security such as food, shelter, and friends, but it also includes a psychological security that is derived from the absence of threat, the presence of ego-supportive communication, and a healthy amount of predictability in the relationship and the environment.

4. Freedom Needs As people grow more intimate, it is almost inevitable that they will find it necessary to wrestle with questions concerning satisfaction of freedom needs. In some areas of activity, a person may want self-reliance and independence of action; in other areas, the same person may desire dependency and reliance on his or her partner. Many times these issues are reflective of individual perceptions of how much exclusivity the developing relationship demands. Have you ever had what you considered to be a "dear friend" who was great except for one thing—the friend was like a parasite and you were the host? Your friend, by not satisfying your freedom needs, was engaging in behavior that might eventually cause you to weigh your need for the friendship against your need for freedom. Whatever one's needs in this area, self-fulfillment can occur only when each partner does not feel too limited or restrained by the relationship. Of course, if you feel no restraining forces from the relationship, you might well examine whether you have the kind of intimacy you thought you did. You can ensure your disappointment in a relationship by demanding total freedom and total intimacy at the same time.

5. Equality Needs Although it is easy to write about the satisfaction of equality needs, it is considerably more difficult to specify what this means. Equality needs are linked to many of the other need areas previously mentioned. You may feel you need to be superior to your partner in some things; subordinate in others; and equal in others. Then, to make it even more confusing, on any given occasion you might want to be equal or subordinate in an area you had traditionally been superior in. Equality in a relationship also can be affected by involvement with the relationship. An imbalance of involvement with the relationship may cause an imbalance of power in the relationship. And, it is interesting to note, the person who is least interested in the relationship may, *for a time,* dictate the conditions of the relationship because the person who cares the most will defer most often to the wishes of the other. No matter what the intricate permutations of equality in a relationship might be, self-fulfillment will be enhanced if a person feels his or her needs for equality and/or inequality are generally met.

The rewards that lead to the satisfaction of the foregoing needs can be communicated in many ways. Such rewards may appear in utilitarian forms—doing favors, doing chores, or giving gifts. There may be direct expressions of feelings—interest or encouragement, or there may be indirect expressions—moral support. Some rewards may come through physical expressions. Sometimes psychological stimulation is found in the other person, "I can learn from you," or self-fulfillment may derive from being associated with someone talented in areas others respect—intelligence or interpersonal skills. It is important to remember that needs do change, and the ways of satisfying these needs also must change at various times in the relationship.

Some people just don't seem to have much self-fulfillment on the dimensions previously listed. Why do they maintain their friendships or marriages? First, let's recall that we are dealing with individual perceptions and priorities. What we perceive as a reward, or a satisfier, for a particular need may not be what others perceive; furthermore, some individuals attach so much importance to certain needs that other needs do not require much fulfillment. In other words, freedom needs may be very important to one individual but not so important to another; what may seem to be a strong reward to one person in the freedom area may seem to be tokenism to another. So, in some situations, outsiders may feel there is little self-fulfillment or need satisfaction while the participants feel that there is plenty.

In some situations, people do stay together when they are obtaining little self-fulfillment. Strong external forces may cause the relationship to continue, and adaptations are made. Among these adaptations might be (1) telling yourself that satisfactions will be forthcoming, and this is just a phase of the relationship that can be explained; (2) seeking satisfactions from other relationships—complaining about your "terrible relationship" to others or seeking more satisfaction and rewards from children or other lovers; (3) waiting for the external forces to dissolve so exit from the relationship will be easier; or (4) taking your dissatisfaction out on your partner and feeding neurotically on the mutual misery.

In summary, participants in an intimate relationship have a desire for self-fulfillment from the other—a need to be cared for. The degree of intimacy one perceives will certainly be affected by the extent to which this self-fulfillment has been met. It would, however, be inappropriate to conclude from this discussion that if all needs aren't satisfied, a relationship is in trouble or the partners in a relationship are wrong for each other. Inevitably, we will always have some needs unfulfilled, maybe not always the same ones, but the point is not to expect all needs to be completely fulfilled at the same time. The nature of human relationships is that they are constantly in process. Sometimes an attempt to satisfy all one's needs may boomerang. For example, a couple has, by their own standards, a good relationship with many satisfactions. One of the partners feels a deficiency in self-esteem–building messages from the other partner. Rather than dealing with this problem within the relationship, the dissatisfied partner finds such messages flowing freely from others in exchange for a casual sexual encounter. When the spouse becomes aware of the sexual encounters, he or she perceives it as the breaking of a sacred covenant of the relationship and seeks to terminate the relationship.

Self-Surrender

The process of evaluation is perhaps our most common cognitive activity. Most of these evaluations are oriented toward a concern for our own feelings—"What does it mean to me?" **Self-surrender** is a process of evaluation in which the response is more likely to be, "What does this mean to the other person's feelings?" Self-fulfillment dealt with needing; self-surrender deals with giving. The assumption undergirding this foundation of intimacy is that the extent to which one is willing to give to another person is reflective of the degree of intimacy he or she feels. Psychiatrist Harry Stack Sullivan believed that a full extension of this concept brought one to a state of love:

> When the satisfaction or the security of another person becomes as significant to one as is one's own satisfaction or security, then the state of love exists.[46]

Realistically few, if any, of us will reach a point at which our communication shows a genuine concern for the other person that is *consistently* as great as our concern for our own satisfaction. It is clear, however, that some people are able to achieve a greater degree of this than others are. When people are willing and able to make the other person's needs a priority, then acts they do on behalf of the other may benefit both themselves and the relationship. Indeed, showing concern for the other's needs, and sometimes even putting them ahead of one's own needs, can foster an even closer and more satisfying relationship. In fact, working to show attention to the other person's needs is not only associated with the partner becoming more satisfied, it also predicts that the person doing the

Self-surrender: Process in which people put the needs and feelings of the other person ahead of their own.

work will become more satisfied with the relationship.[47] Perhaps this happens because when a person has truly engaged in self-surrender, giving to one's partner may become satisfying in its own right.

Commitment to a Joint Identity

Thus far, the foundations we've discussed have focused on the individual parties to the relationship—their personality, their emotional arousal, their need for caring and giving. The idea of a **joint identity** concerns something much more abstract—the bond or link between the two people. It is something different from a simple algebraic summation of both person's attributes, attitudes, and behaviors. The blending of two individuals, like the blending of two chemicals, produces a new mixture. Indeed, properties of the two original chemicals are still in the new mixture, but there is also a substance with characteristics unlike anything the original chemicals had. It is the amount of commitment to this new mixture, or new identity, that characterizes this foundation for assessing intimacy in a relationship.

Joint identity: The blending of two individuals to create a new shared identity as a dyad or couple.

© Rawpixel.com/Shutterstock.com

For those engaged in cultivating this joint identity, it is possible to see a number of outward manifestations of their efforts. Sometimes these efforts will be very conscious and planned. For instance, the participants might discuss how the superstructure of the relationship far exceeds or transcends most of their individual needs and desires. This attempt to balance individuality and mutuality is a continuing concern for intimate partners. Often the very thing that enhances the joint identity will detract from the autonomy of one or both partners, and vice versa. Nevertheless, each partner must in some way demonstrate an ongoing commitment to the relationship as well as to himself or herself. Relationship commitment, like commitment to other things, requires an effort to become knowledgeable about it, devote time to it, make future plans based on it, speak favorably about it, and defend it against destructive forces. You can probably think of additional behaviors that show one's commitment to sustaining a relationship. Other manifestations of this joint identity may develop without a great deal of conscious programming. The partners find themselves using the same phrases, similar vocal inflection patterns, or even dressing similarly.

Mixed-sex pairs in our culture have traditionally used the marriage ritual to announce their movement toward a joint identity. A related issue concerns the accepted custom for the woman to adopt the man's last name and shed her own surname. If the name change was consistent with the joint identity concept, the two participants would adopt a totally new last name that might be preceded by their own family names—Mark L. Knapp-Landis and Anita L. Vangelisti-Landis.

I am good, you love me; therefore you are good. I am bad, you love me; therefore you are bad.

—*R. D. Laing*

Same-sexed pairs often announce their movement toward a joint identity by consistently engaging in common activities. Two professors in the field of communication, Larry Barker and Robert Kibler, wrote so many articles and books together that their names were almost inextricably linked. When others in the field were referring to a work authored by either Kibler or Barker alone, there often would be some confusion as to whether it was jointly done. This points out the fact that when people engage in behavior that seems to affirm a joint identity, it is not always without complications. Roommates may live together but not want to be seen as a common package in some settings; spouses may want to be invited some places as a couple but would prefer separate invitations to other functions. It is a common experience for the friends of a divorced couple to worry about whom to invite over first for fear the order of the invitations would communicate favoritism. Sometimes this dilemma is resolved by not inviting either person and results in both divorced individuals wondering whether the friends were really friends in the first place.

An example of the difficulties incurred by moving too quickly to establish a joint identity can be seen in the efforts made by businesses or organizations to fuse the corporate identity with the new employee's individual identity. New employees might feel a certain strain when it appears that they are being asked to commit themselves to this new identity before they even know the corporation. This situation usually occurs when the long-time employees try to pull the newly hireds into the "we" relationship too quickly—"We here at Purdue (IBM, or whatever) have always done it this way." It is not surprising to see many newly hireds respond with an "I-you" distancing move—"Well, I can understand why *you* have done it this way, but . . ."

Each of the seven foundations of intimacy, which have just been discussed, exerts its own influence on the *type* of intimacy you feel you have achieved and on the *intensity* with which you feel it. Whatever label you select to describe your intimate relationship with another person—deep affection, strong liking, romantic love, friendship—you should be able to account for your use of the label by examining your perception of the intimacy foundations in that particular relationship.[48] Obviously, there may be differences in your love for your grandfather, a lifelong friend, or your spouse; there also may be more similarities than you might imagine. Your own personal explanation for the qualitative and quantitative differences and similarities in your intimate relationships may be revealed as you ponder the influence of each intimacy foundation.

Summary

This chapter focused on the intricacies of intimacy—the more advanced stages of a relationship, which include intensifying, integrating, and bonding. First, we examined the terminology typically used to describe these more advanced growth stages of relationships. Although we didn't arrive at any neat, compact, and conclusive definitions, we uncovered some intriguing distinctions. One line of research, for instance, found at least six different *styles of loving*; another identified eight types of love relationships. These works suggest that the term *love* may have many referents and many overt manifestations. Although this last statement reverberates with triteness, we should recall how many times in this emotionally detached world of book reading, people act as if there were only one type of love and act accordingly. Furthermore, when people seeking a divorce say that they aren't in love, they may mean simply that they want a different type of love. A new intimate relationship may be the only way a person can shed old, displeasing habits and start over.

Next, distinctions between the terms *liking* and *loving* were sought. Love often involves a greater intensity of feelings and behaviors than liking, a quantitative difference, but there also seems to be a strong likelihood that qualitative differences between the two feeling states exist. Companionate features often accompany both liking and loving. We then compared love relationships to friendships, noting that the distinctions may be blurred in some cross-sex friendships. We concluded our effort to identify features or characteristics of relationships with our summary of the findings from studies that have examined *intimacy* and *closeness* as terms that refer to a variety of relationships.

The last part of the chapter focused on the seven *foundations of intimacy* that are necessary to understand and explain a variety of concepts related to close relationships—deep affection, romantic love, friendship, strong liking, and related terms. These foundations included personality and early experiences, situational and developmental factors, cultural guidelines, emotional arousal and labeling, self-fulfillment, self-surrender, and commitment to a joint identity. These broad categories provide the parameters for explaining different relationships and different individual labels. Obviously, they fall far short of the specificity we might like to have—for example, X type of love will most likely occur when the participants have A, B, and C personality characteristics, have D and E early experiences, and have F and G needs fulfilled, and so on, but they do provide a useful basis for greater understanding.

Intimacy/Liking/Loving

Acevedo, B. P., Aron, A., Fisher, H. E., and Brown. L. L. "Neural Correlates of Long-term Intense Romantic Love." *Social cognitive and affective neuroscience* 7 (2012): 145–159.

Aron, A., Fisher, H. E., Strong, G., Acevedo, B., Riela, S., and Tsapelas, I. "Falling in Love." In S. Sprecher, A. Wenzel, and J. Harvey, eds., *Handbook of Relationship Initiation*, pp. 315–336. New York: Psychology Press, 2008.

Berscheid, E., and Reis, H. T. "Attraction and Close Relationships." In D. T. Gilbert, S. T. Fiske, and G. Lindzey, eds., *The Handbook of Social Psychology,* vol. 2, pp. 193–281, 4th ed. New York: McGraw-Hill, 1998.

Caughlin, J. P., and Huston, T. L. "The Flourishing Literature on Flourishing Relationships." *Journal of Family Theory & Review* 2 (2010): 25–35.

Daly, J. A., and Kreiser, P. O. "Affinity Seeking." In J. A. Daly and J. M. Wiemann, eds., *Strategic Interpersonal Communication,* pp. 109–134. Hillsdale, NJ: Erlbaum, 1994.

Dunlop, W. L. "Love as Story, Love as Storytelling." *Personal Relationships* 26 (2019): 114–136.

Fehr, B. *Friendship Processes.* Thousand Oaks, CA: Sage, 1996.

Fisher, H. E. *Why We Love: The Nature and Chemistry of Romantic Love.* New York: Holt, 2004.

Fletcher, G. J. O., Simpson, J. A., Campbell, L., and Overall, N. C. "Pair-Bonding, Romantic Love, and Evolution: The Curious Case of Homo Sapiens." *Perspectives on Psychological Science* 10 (2015): 20–36.

Gottman, J. M., and Silver, N. *What Makes Love Last? How to Build Trust and Avoid Betrayal.* New York: Simon & Schuster, 2012.

Hatfield, E., and Rapson, R. L. "Passionate Love and Sexual Desire." In A. Vangelisti, H. T. Reis, and M. A. Fitzpatrick, eds., *Stability and Change in Relationships,* pp. 306–324, New York: Cambridge University Press, 2002.

Hendrick, S. S., and Hendrick, C. "Love." In C. R. Snyder and S. J. Lopez, eds., *Handbook of Positive Psychology,* pp. 472–484. New York: Oxford University Press, 2005.

Illouz, E. "Reason within Passion: Love in Women's Magazines." *Critical Studies in Mass Communication* 8 (1991): 231–248.

Laurenceau, J-P and Kleinman, B. M. "Intimacy in Personal Relationships." In A. L. Vangelisti and D. Perlman, eds., *The Cambridge Handbook of Personal Relationships,* pp. 637–653. New York: Cambridge University Press, 2006.

Lee, J. A. *The Colors of Love.* Englewood Cliffs, NJ: Prentice Hall, 1976.

Mashek, D. J., and Aron, A., eds. *Handbook of Closeness and Intimacy.* Mahwah, NJ: Erlbaum, 2004.

Mikulincer, M., and Shaver, P. R. "Attachment Theory as a Framework for Studying Relationship Dynamics and Functioning." In A. L. Vangelisti and D. Perlman, eds., *The Cambridge Handbook of Personal Relationships* 2nd ed., pp. 175–185. New York: Cambridge University Press, 2018.

Prager, K. J. "Intimacy in Personal Relationships." In C. Hendrick and S. S. Hendrick, eds., *Close Relationships: A Soucebook,* pp. 229–242. Thousand Oaks, CA: Sage, 2000.

Regan, P. *The Mating Game.* Thousand Oaks, CA: Sage, 2003.

Reis, H. T., and Aron, A. "Love: What is It, Why Does It Matter, and How Does it Operate?" *Perspectives on Psychological Science* 3 (2008): 80–86.

Seidman, S. *Romantic Longings: Love in America, 1830–1980.* Routledge, SUNY Albany Press, 1991.

Shaver, P. R., and Hazan, C. "A Biased Overview of the Study of Love." *Journal of Social and Personal Relationships* 5 (1988): 473–501.

Sheets, V. L. "Passion for Life: Self-Expansion and Passionate Love across the Life Span." *Journal of Social and Personal Relationships* 31 (2014): 958–974.

Sprecher, S. and Fehr, B. "Compassionate Love for Close Others and Humanity." *Journal of Social and Personal Relationships* 22 (2005): 629–651.

Sternberg, R. J., and Weis, K. *The New Psychology of Love.* Binghampton, NY: Vail-Ballou Press, 2006.

Tomlinson, J. M., Aron, A., and Hatfield, E. "Romantic Love." In A. L. Vangelisti and D. Perlman, eds., *The Cambridge Handbook of Personal Relationships* 2nd ed., pp. 407–421. New York: Cambridge University Press, 2018.

Notes

1. J. A. Lee, "Love-styles." In R. Sternberg and M. Barnes, eds., *The Psychology of Love* (New Haven: Yale University Press, 1988), pp. 38–67; also J. A. Lee, *The Colors of Love* (Englewood Cliffs, NJ: Prentice Hall, 1976).

2. S. Peele and A. Brodsky, "Love Can Be an Addiction," *Psychology Today* 8 (1974): 23–26.

3. W. R. Cupach and B. H. Spitzberg, *The Dark Side of Relationship Pursuit: From Attraction to Obsession and Stalking.* Mahway, NJ: Erlbaum, 2004.

4. S. Sprecher and B. Fehr, "Compassionate Love for Close Others and Humanity," *Journal of Social and Personal Relationships* 22 (2005): 629–651.

5. G. D. Morrow, E. M. Clark, and K. F. Brock, "Individual and Partner Love Styles: Implications for the Quality of Romantic Involvements," *Journal of Social and Personal Relationships* 12 (1995): 363–387. J. Hahn and T. Blass, "Dating Partner Preferences: A Function of Similarity of Love Styles," *Journal of Social Behavior and Personality* 12 (1997): 595–610.

6. A. Vedes, P. Hilpert, F. W. Nussbeck, A. K. Randall, G. Bodenmann, and W. R. Lind, "Love Styles, Coping, and Relationship Satisfaction: A Dyadic Approach," *Personal Relationships* 23 (2016): 84–97.

7. T. R. Levine, K. S. Aune, and H. S. Park, "Love Styles and Communication in Relationships: Partner Preferences, Initiation, and Intensification," *Communication Quarterly*, 54 (2006): 465–486.

8. S. S. Hendrick and C. Hendrick, "Gender Differences and Similarities in Sex and Love," *Personal Relationships* 2 (1995): 55–65; B. Fehr and R. Broughton, "Gender and Personality Differences in Conceptions of Love: An Interpersonal Theory Analysis," *Personal Relationships* 8 (2001): 115–136.

9. R. J. Sternberg, *The Triangle of Love.* (New York: Basic Books, 1988).

10. A. Aron and L. Westbay, "Dimensions of the Prototype of Love," *Journal of Personality and Social Psychology* 70 (1996): 535–555.

11. P. C. Regan, "Of Lust and Love: Beliefs About the Role of Sexual Desire in Romantic Relationships," *Personal Relationships* 5 (1998): 139–157.

12. M. Acker and M. H. Davis, "Intimacy, Passion and Commitment in Adult Romantic Relationships: A Test of the Triangular Theory of Love," *Journal of Social and Personal Relationships* 9 (1992): 21–50.

13. E. Berscheid and E. Walster, "A Little Bit About Love." In T. L. Huston, ed., *Foundations of Interpersonal Attraction* (New York: Academic Press, 1974), pp. 355–381.

14. S. Sprecher and P. C. Regan, "Passionate and Companionate Love in Courting and Young Married Couples." *Sociological Inquiry* 68 (1998): 163–185; E. Hatfield and S. Sprecher "Measuring Passionate Love in Intimate Relationships," *Journal of Adolescence* 9 (1986): 383–410.

15. G. L. White, S. Fishbein, and J. Rutstein, "Passionate Love and the Misattribution of Arousal," *Journal of Personality and Social Psychology* 41 (1981): 56–62. Also see D. Dutton and A. Aron, "Some Evidence for Heightened Sexual Attraction Under Conditions of High Anxiety," *Journal of Personality and Social Psychology* 30 (1974): 510–517.

16. S. Schachter, "The Interaction of Cognitive and Physiological Determinants of Emotional State." In L. Berkowitz, ed., *Advances in Experimental Social Psychology,* vol. 1 (New York: Academic Press, 1964), pp. 49–80. Not all arousal-labeling experiments support Schachter's theory. Maslach found aroused people reporting negative emotions in both happy and angry situations. See C. Maslach, "Negative Emotional Biasing of Unexplained Arousal," *Journal of Personality and Social Psychology* 37 (1979): 953–969; C. D. Marshall and P. G. Zimbardo, "Affective Consequences of Inadequately Explained Physiological Arousal," *Journal of Personality and Social Psychology* 37 (1979): 970–988.

17. Z. Rubin, *Liking and Loving* (New York: Holt, Rinehart and Winston, 1973).

18. K. E. Davis and M. J. Todd, "Friendship and Love Relationships." In K. E. Davis and T. O. Mitchell, eds., *Advances in Descriptive Psychology,* vol. 2 (Greenwich, CT: J. A. I. Press, 1982); K. E. Davis, "Near and Dear: Friendship and Love Compared," *Psychology Today* (February 1985) 22–30. Also see S. S. Hendrick and C. Hendrick, "Lovers as Friends," *Journal of Social and Personal Relationships* 10 (1993): 459–466.

19. L. K. Guerrero and A. M. Chavez, "Relational Maintenance in Cross-Sex Friendships Characterized by Different Types of Romantic Intent: An Exploratory Study." *Western Journal of Communication* 69 (2005): 339–358; H. Weger, Jr. and M. C. Emmett, "Romantic Intent, Relationship Uncertainty, and Relationship Maintenance in Young Adults' Cross-Sex Friendships." *Journal of Social and Personal Relationships* 26 (2009): 964–988.

20 B. Fehr, "How Do I Love Thee? Let Me Consult My Proto- type." In S. Duck, ed., *Individuals in Relationships* (New- bury Park, CA: Sage, 1993), pp. 87–120; G. M. Maxwell, "Behavior of Lovers: Measuring the Closeness of Rela- tionships," *Journal of Social and Personal Relationships* 2 (1985): 215–238; M. R. Parks and K. Floyd, "Mean- ings for Closeness and Intimacy in Friendship," *Journal of Social and Personal Relationships* 13 (1996): 85–107; E. Bersheid, M. Snyder, and A. M. Omoto, "The Relation- ship Closeness Inventory: Assessing the Closeness of Interpersonal Relationships," *Journal of Personality and Social Psychology* 57 (1989): 792–807; A. Aron, E. A. Aron, and D. Smollan, "Inclusion of the Other in the Self Scale and the Structure of Interpersonal Closeness," *Journal of Personality and Social Psychology* 63 (1992): 596–612; K. J. Prager and D. Buhrmester, "Intimacy and Need Fulfillment in Couple Relationships," *Journal of Social and Personal Relationships* 15 (1998): 435–469; T. Lippert and K. J. Prager, "Daily Experiences of Intimacy," *Personal Relationships* 8 (2001): 283–298; J. R. Frei and P. R. Shaver, "Respect in Close Relationships: Prototype Definition, Self-Report Assessment, and Initial Corre- lates, " *Personal Relationships* 9 (2002): 121–139.

21 A. Canevello and J. Crocker, "Creating Good Rela- tionships: Responsiveness, Relationship Quality, and Interpersonal Goals," *Journal of Personality and Social Psychology* 99 (2010): 78–106; H. H. Kelley, *Personal Rela- tionships: Their Structures and Processes.* Hillsdale, NJ: Erlbaum. 1979; E. P. Lemay, Jr., and M. S. Clark, "How the Head Liberates the Heart: Projection of Communal Responsiveness Guides Relationship Promotion." *Jour- nal of Personality and Social Psychology* 94 (2008): 647– 671; H. T. Reis, M. S. Clark, and J. G. Holmes, "Perceived Partner Responsiveness as an Organizing Construct in the Study of Intimacy and Closeness." In D. J. Mashek and A. Aron, eds., *Handbook of Closeness and Intimacy* (Mahwah, NJ: Erlbaum, 2004), pp. 201–225.

22 P. J. Marston, M. L. Hecht, M. L. Manke, S. McDaniel, and H. Reeder, "The Subjective Experience of Intimacy, Passion, and Commitment in Heterosexual Loving Relationships," *Personal Relationships* 5 (1998): 15–30; L. K. Guerrero, "Nonverbal Involvement Across Interac- tions with Same-Sex Friends, Opposite-Sex Friends and Romantic Partners: Consistency or Change?" *Journal of Social and Personal Relationships* 14 (1997): 31–58; J-P Larenceau and B. M. Kleinman, "Intimacy in Per- sonal Relationships." In A. L. Vangelisti and D. Perlman, eds., *The Cambridge Handbook of Personal Relation- ships.* (New York: Cambridge University Press, 2006), pp. 637–653.

23 J. H. Tolhuizen, "Communication Strategies for Inten- sifying Dating Relationships: Identification, Use and Structure," *Journal of Social and Personal Relationships,* 6 (1989): 413–434.

24 A. Thomas, S. Chess, and H. G. Birch, "Origins of Per- sonality," *Scientific American* (August 1970): 102–109.

25 J. K. Maner and S. L. Miller, "The Evolution of Romantic Relationships: Adaptive Challenges and Relationship Cognition in Emerging Adulthood." In F. D. Fincham and M. Cui, eds., *Romantic Relations in Emerging Adulthood,* (New York: Cambridge University Press, 2011), pp. 169–189; G. Wilson, *The Coolidge Effect: An Evolutionary Account of Human Sexuality* (New York: Morrow, 1981).

26 D. M. Buss, *The Evolution of Desire: Strategies of Human Mating* (New York: Basic Books, 1994).

27 K. B. Carnelley and R. Janoff-Bulman, "Optimism About Love Relationships: General vs. Specific Lessons from One's Personal Experiences," *Journal of Social and Per- sonal Relationships* 9 (1992): 5–20.

28 S. Srivastava, K. M. McGonigal, J. M. Richards, E. A. Butler, and J. J. Gross, "Optimism in Close Relationships: How Seeing Things in a Positive Light Makes Them So," *Journal of Personality and Social Psychology,* 91 (2006): 143–153. For more on the specific role of hopefulness in relationships, see A. J. Merolla, "Further Testing Hope's Role in Constructive Conflict Communication," *Com- munication Quarterly* 65 (2017): 481–501.

29 C. Hazan and P. Shaver, "Romantic Love Conceptual- ized as an Attachment Process," *Journal of Personal- ity and Social Psychology,* 42 (1987): 511–524; P. Shaver, C. Hazan, and D. Bradshaw, "Love as Attachment: The Integration of Three Behavioral Systems." In R. J. Sternberg and M. Barnes, eds., *The Psychology of Love.* (New Haven: Yale University Press, 1988).

30 M. Mikulincer, P. R. and Shaver, "Attachment Theory as a Framework for Studying Relationship Dynamics and Functioning." In A. L. Vangelisti and D. Perlman, eds., *The Cambridge Handbook of Personal Relationships,* 2nd ed., (New York, NY: Cambridge University Press, 2018), pp. 175–185; P. R. Shaver and M. Mikulincer, "Attach- ment Theory, Individual Psychodynamics, and Relation- ship Functioning." In A. L. Vangelisti and D. Perlman, eds., *The Cambridge Handbook of Personal Relation- ships.* (New York: Cambridge University Press, 2006), pp. 251–271.

31 K. Bartholomew, "Avoidance of Intimacy: An Attachment Perspective," *Journal of Social and Personal Relationships* 7 (1990): 147–178.

32 M. W. Baldwin and B. Fehr, "On the Instability of Attachment Style Ratings," *Personal Relationships* 2 (1995): 247–261. Also P. A. Frazier, A. L. Byer, A. R. Fischer, D. M. Wright, and K. A. DeBord, "Adult Attachment Style and Partner Choice: Correlational and Experimental Findings," *Personal Relationships* 3 (1996): 117–136.

33 B. Fehr, *Friendship Processes* (Thousand Oaks, CA: Sage, 1996)

34 "Seesaw Love," *Human Behavior* (August 1975): 35–36.

35 S. L. Murray, J. G. Holmes, and D. W. Griffin, "The Self-Fulfilling Nature of Positive Illusions in Romantic Relationships: Love Is Not Blind, but Prescient," *Journal of Personality and Social Psychology* 71 (1996): 1155–1180.

36 M. Brenton, *Friendship*. (New York, NY: Stein and Day, 1974).

37 P. M. Sias and D. J. Cahill, "From Coworkers to Friends: The Development of Peer Friendships in the Workplace," *Western Journal of Communication* 62 (1998): 273–299.

38 S. Coontz, *Marriage, A History: How Love Conquered Marriage*. (New York: Penguin Books, 2005).

39 E. Hatfield and R. L. Rapson, *Love, Sex, and Intimacy: Their Psychology, Biology, and History* (New York: HarperCollins, 1993); H. Fisher, *Anatomy of Love: The Natural History of Monogamy, Adultery and Divorce* (New York: Norton, 1992); and D. Ackerman, *A Natural History of Love* (New York: Random House, 1994).

40 B. J. Aragona, Y. Liu, J. T. Curtis, F. K. Stephan, and Z. Wang, "A Critical Role for Nucleus Accumbens Dopamine in Partner-Preference Formation in Male Prairie Voles," *Journal of Neuroscience, 23* (2003): 3483.

41 M. L. Patterson, "An Arousal Model of Interpersonal Intimacy," *Psychological Review* 83 (1976): 235–245. This theory is similar to one discussed earlier in this chapter. See S. Schachter and J. Singer, "Cognitive, Social, and Physiological Determinants of Emotional State," *Psychological Review* 69 (1962): 379–399.

42 D. N. Stern, "Mother and Infant at Play: The Dyadic Interaction Involving Facial, Vocal and Gaze Behavior." In M. Lewis and L. A. Rosenblum, eds., *The Effect of the Infant on Its Caregiver* (New York: Wiley, 1974). Also see J. N. Cappella and J. O. Greene, "A Discrepancy-Arousal Explanation of Mutual Influence in Expressive Behavior for Adult and Infant-Adult Interaction," *Communication Monographs* 49 (1982): 89–114.

43 W. J. Lederer and D. D. Jackson. *The Mirages of Marriage* (New York: W. W. Norton, 1968), pp. 42–43.

44 G. Greene, *The End of the Affair* (New York: Penguin Books, 1977). (Originally published, 1951, by Wm. Heinemann, London.)

45 M. Brenton, *Friendship*. (New York: Stein and Day, 1974).

46 H. S. Sullivan, *Conceptions of Modern Psychiatry* (New York: W. W. Norton, 1953), pp. 42–43.

47 R. M. Horne, and M. D. Johnson. "A Labor of Love? Emotion Work in Intimate Relationships," *Journal of Social and Personal Relationships* 36 (2019): 1190–1209. See also A. Kogan, E. A. Impett, C. Oveis, B. Hui, A. M. Gordon, and D. Keltner. "When Giving Feels Good: The Intrinsic Benefits of Sacrifice in Romantic Relationships for the Communally Motivated." *Psychological Science* 21 (2010): 1918–1924.

48 A full understanding of love, like other types of intimate relationships, is highly contextual and requires an analysis of the specific feelings, thoughts, and actions of the people involved. See A. E. Beall and R. J. Sternberg, "The Social Construction of Love," *Journal of Social and Personal Relationships* 12 (1995): 417–438.

PART IV

Interaction Patterns and the Maintenance of Relationships

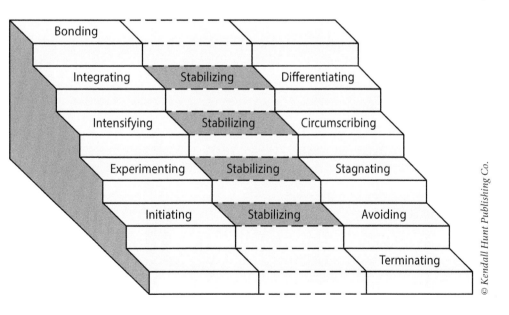

© Kendall Hunt Publishing Co.

CHAPTER 8

Maintaining Relationships Through Dialogue: Disclosures, Lies, and Fights

Dear Dr. Vangelisti,

I have been going out with a certain guy for a little less than a month now. At the beginning of the relationship, we both were attracted to each other, felt we had a lot in common, and had a great time together. One night, though, we had a long talk and I told him a lot of very personal things about myself. He just listened. From that night on, the relationship has been declining for me. I can only see our differences now and when we go out I don't have such a great time anymore. We still spend a lot of time together, but this doesn't help the situation. I have shut myself off except for purely social conversation. Can anything be done to save this relationship?

Too Much Too Soon

There are many ways to be open with others. Perhaps this writer's problem stems from a tendency to be open with nonintimates in ways that are normally reserved for our more intimate relationships. Openness, or self-disclosure, is only one communication pattern that gradually changes as relationships become closer. This chapter discusses several of these communication patterns as they occur in close relationships, including disclosing some personal information and withholding some, lying, and fighting fair.

Married life requires shared mystery even when all the facts are known.

—Richard Ford

Relationship Maintenance

Relationship maintenance: The various things people do to try to keep their relationship functioning at the desired level, countering other forces that may contribute to undesirable changes in the relationship.

The various ways human beings try to maintain close relationships through verbal and nonverbal behavior can be complex. In contrast, the "mate-retention" or "mate-guarding" processes of some insects and birds, although odd to us, seem relatively simple. The penis of male damselflies, for example, not only inseminates his mate but also brushes and scrapes out any sperm from other suitors. In addition, he remains physically attached to his mate until she has laid her eggs. Human interaction designed to maintain a close relationship also is concerned with the reproductive process, but it encompasses much more. This chapter and the next focus on the interaction patterns that are critical to maintaining a close relationship. Maintenance involves all those things people do to try to keep their relationship functioning at the desired level and countering other forces that may contribute to undesirable changes in the relationship. Although the focus may be on pleasant transactions, we believe effective relationship maintenance does not exclude the existence of unpleasant interactions as well.

It is our belief that maintenance behavior is not something new to the ongoing dialogue that helped shape the relationship. Maintenance, from this perspective, is the way the partners deal with the critical and repeated acts of discourse that constitute their relationship. It is the way they deal with conflict, their ability to use small talk for relational purposes, the judicious use of disclosures as well as secrets, their ability to make their partner feel their commitment and affection, their ability to engineer the proper mixture of teamwork and team play, the ability to provide for one another's privacy as well as togetherness, and the ability to develop the proper balance of predictable and novel communication patterns.

Relationship assurances: Relationship maintenance strategy involving showing or telling partners how much they mean to the person trying to maintain the relationship.

Sharing tasks: Relationship maintenance strategy of taking a fair amount of responsibility for tasks, offering to help.

Some researchers have identified what they believe to be seven primary areas involved in maintaining heterosexual romantic relationships.[1] These behaviors may be carefully planned and strategically implemented to achieve a maintenance goal, or they may be routine behaviors that are frequently enacted at a relatively low level of awareness. They include (1) *giving advice* (making recommendations for your partner's behavior), (2) **relationship assurances** (showing and telling your partner how much he or she means to you and stressing your commitment), (3) *effective conflict management* (proper and timely use of apologies, listening, cooperation, and forgiveness), (4) *appropriate openness* (sharing feelings and talking about the relationship), (5) *positive demeanor* (enacting an upbeat, cheerful style), (6) **sharing tasks** (taking a fair amount of responsibility for tasks, offering to help), and (7) *blending social networks* (spending time with common friends). Enacting all these behaviors would be ideal, but most close relationships are maintained with a mixture of positive and negative behaviors. It also should be noted that effectively maintaining a close relationship may require a heavy dose of one or two of the preceding seven maintenance behaviors at one point in time and little attention at other times.

The seven aforementioned maintenance strategies were first identified in reference to face-to-face relational communication, but they also apply to technologically mediated forms of communication; for example, one can offer a partner reassurances via text or social media.[2] Communication technologies also afford additional relational maintenance opportunities beyond those available in person. Interacting electronically can provide a sense that a relational partner has consistent **presence** in one's life, even when not physically present. Additionally, people can use social media to display electronic **tie signs**, which publicly demonstrate the existence and importance of one's relationship (e.g., relationship status statements, posting pictures of the dyad as a couple engaged in shared activities).[3]

Presence: The sense that relational partners are still together in a relationship, even when they are not physically co-present.

Tie signs: Public displays that demonstrate the existence and importance of one's relationship.

Moreover, it is important to recognize that people's perceptions of maintenance behaviors can be as important as (if not more so than) the behaviors themselves. Sometimes a behavior that is usually a positive maintenance behavior is perceived as negative if it is enacted at the wrong time—for example, a major demonstration of affection immediately after being accused of not giving enough affection. Sometimes a positive behavior such as "giving support" can be seen as negative if the sincerity of the performance is questioned. Maintenance also is about learning to let some irritating partner behavior go, learning the relationship doesn't always satisfy your every need, and learning which issues need attention and which ones don't. It is also helpful when people recognize and are grateful for their partner's efforts at maintenance; when people appreciate their relational partner, it tends to motivate them to be more responsive and engage in more relational maintenance efforts.[4] Each partner's commitment to the relationship and his or her perception of equity in the relationship will have a lot to do with how he or she enacts and views various maintenance behaviors.[5]

In this chapter and the next, we elaborate on various communication behaviors embedded in these maintenance strategies and routines. How do married couples say they maintain their relationships? Mostly, they report using *assurances,* but *sharing tasks* also is an important and often underappreciated maintenance behavior.[6]

Not all relationships require the same kind of maintenance. Some friendships, for example, require only infrequent contact to sustain them, while others would be lost without regular care and feeding. In the same way, relationships that may need a great deal of maintenance at one point in time may need far less at another. *Maintenance* itself means different things to different people. For example, it may require a far different set of skills to simply keep a relationship from disappearing than it does to keep a relationship at a point of which it is satisfying to both parties. As noted earlier, maintenance behavior involves virtually any type of interaction characterizing the relationship. Maintenance can be performed, though, by using only a small subset of these behaviors at any given time. The ability to identify which subset of behaviors acts in a relationship-maintaining way is, of course, part of the skill relationship caretakers must develop. Failure to maintain (appropriately care for) certain key communicative aspects of a relationship (e.g., conflict and affection) on a regular schedule may mean that eventually there will be need for repair or rejuvenation. When relationship-maintaining behavior is performed regularly for an extended period of time, it is difficult to appreciate its important effects. On the other hand, we are painfully aware of our relationship when it has not been properly maintained.

Self-Disclosure, Confidentiality, and Trust

Intimacy: Feelings of closeness, sharing, communication, and support.

The word **intimacy** is derived from Latin words meaning "to make known" and "innermost." For this reason, some people equate self-disclosure and intimacy. It is true that, as people increase their affection for another, they seem to reveal previously hidden aspects about themselves; however, we also find people disclosing very private information to complete strangers. With the rise of the internet and social media, it is more common than ever for people to divulge private information about themselves to a wide audience, even strangers, all at once.[7] Yet even in this environment in which much information is available online, people still are more apt to make intimate disclosures in person than via technological means.[8] Moreover, people make a distinction between the general broadcasting of information and private messages directed at a particular individual: Information is more relationally meaningful if it is told to a specific person rather than broadcast to a social network or the world.[9] Thus, self-disclosure between specific people seems to be a necessary condition for achieving intimacy, but it also may be possible to know a lot about someone and still not like them.

The Nature of Self-Disclosing Messages

Let's look at the composition of self-disclosing messages. By definition, self-disclosing messages reveal something about oneself. It might be relatively public information (twenty-nine years old and born in Muskogee, Oklahoma), but intimate disclosures usually refer to more personal matters, things people probably wouldn't find out unless you told them, and things you don't tell many people. For college students in one study, information related to their self-concept/image was cited most often as the most personal type of disclosure (e.g., fear of failure, perceptions of body image, prejudices, and self-esteem). Feelings about a romantic relationship were also rated as a highly personal disclosure (e.g., emotional ambivalence, plans for the future). But the disclosure of details associated with other types of information also was reported as likely to be limited to close and/or intimate relationship partners (e.g., masturbation, pornography, losing one's virginity, addictions, phobias, depression, eating disorders, physical abuse, death of a friend or family member, divorce, illegal activities, or unplanned pregnancy).[10]

Thus, your self-disclosures may reflect any breadth and depth combination, but intimate dialogue is primarily concerned with depth. Self-disclosures can focus on information, perceptions, or feelings; messages may be positive or negative, frequent or infrequent, long or short, accurate or inaccurate reflections of yourself, intentional or under less conscious control. They may be well timed or ill timed. Disclosure may be extensive on a topic at one time and minimal on the same topic at another time.

Based on the studies of self-disclosure conducted over the past forty years, we would suggest the dimensions in **Table 8.1** be used in order to determine the nature and strength of the message for each partner to the relationship.

Self-disclosures of "greater magnitude" would be known by fewer people, be personally owned ("*I feel*" rather than the more general "*People feel*"), and be specific. Specificity may be related to the other person or to the other person's behavior. It is more open and self-disclosive to say, "I feel _____ toward you, Merle" than it is to say, "I feel _____ toward people." Similarly, it is more revealing about yourself if you say, "You were late for our appointment" than to say, "You and I just operate by different rules." Self-disclosures of greater magnitude also involve more risk and make the discloser more vulnerable. Because of the discloser's perceived risk and vulnerability, he or she expects a comparable amount of understanding, acceptance, and assurance that the information will be kept confidential. If the recipient of the self-disclosure reciprocates with his or her own disclosure and it is of a similar magnitude, this in itself is likely to be a sign of mutual trust. Both interactants may go through the same motions but not engage in reciprocated disclosures of the same magnitude. If this inequitable reciprocation is known, the trust and comfort level for the person engaging in the more

Table 8.1	Dimensions of Self-Disclosure
Information	
Many Know	Few Know
Impersonal/Not Owned	Personal/Owned
Abstract	Specific
Expectations for Self	
Low Risk/Vulnerability	High Risk/Vulnerability
Expectations for Other	
Lack of Understanding/Acceptance	High Understanding/Acceptance
Not Reciprocated	Reciprocated
May Tell Others	May Not Tell Others

© Mark Knapp-Anita Vangelisti-John Caughlin

vulnerable disclosure is likely to be less. As with any message, there are many ways to present a self-disclosing message. Some stylistic choices may make your disclosure seem more open. For instance, disclosure *of* perceptions and/or feelings would probably be considered much more open and personal than disclosures *about* perceptions and/or feelings. Co-occurring nonverbal behavior will surely affect the perceived "depth" of the disclosure as well. It also should be noted that messages of self-disclosure are part of an ongoing process of interaction. From this perspective, the nature of self-disclosive messages at any given time will be affected by co-occurring behavior of each interactant.

People also make choices about when and how to self-disclose. Although it works differently with strangers, people in romantic relationships often reserve their deepest disclosures for when they can have a conversation in person rather than making such disclosures using a communication technology (e.g., texting, phone, e-mail).[11] This is not to suggest that romantic partners never make important disclosures via communication technologies, but the tendency to do so more often in person suggests that there is something about that mode of communication that romantic partners value when making important disclosures. Perhaps face-to-face conversations best afford them the ability to shape the meaning of their disclosures with cooccurring nonverbal behaviors.

Even though self-disclosure can be important in forming and maintaining an intimate relationship,[12] it may not always be the best communication strategy. To determine whether a communication strategy is "best," we need to have some measure of correspondence between responses sought and responses obtained.

Self-Disclosure as Catharsis

Catharsis:
Communicative release or unburdening that can occur with self-disclosure.

One motivation for engaging in self-disclosing communication is to achieve **catharsis**, or communicative release. We may have some need to free ourselves of information that is eating away at us, a desire to get something "off our chest." Even though disclosing our deepest secrets and releasing our inhibitions can sometimes have some positive effects on our health, the primary motivation for such revelations is personal, not communicative.[13]

Moreover, there is growing evidence that disclosing just to try unburdening oneself of negative emotions is usually not by itself particularly helpful to people—and can even be harmful. People who report gaining catharsis about a secret or venting their emotions about a secret can actually feel worse about the topic than do people who do not seek catharsis. Instead of catharsis, what people often need is to gain new insights about whatever troubles them, which may happen by talking with somebody, but it can also happen in other ways. In general, gaining understanding and insights about one's experiences appears to be more important for people's health than is dumping their negative emotions on another person.[14] Given that one can gain such insights by journaling or by talking with other people (e.g., other friends, counselors), one should always consider the impact on a relational partner before disclosing just for catharsis. Trying to achieve catharsis by talking about negative information can come at a cost to one's relational partner—knowing certain things can be a burden.[15]

Self-Disclosure as "The Need to Be Open"

Another motivation for disclosing personal information about yourself centers on the belief that it is best to "tell it like it is," "lay it on the line," and "reveal ourselves as we really are." Hiding and concealing information, according to this expressive orientation, is a reflection of being "hung up," "phony," or "a manipulator." To hold things in is dirty; letting them out is cleansing. From this perspective, "letting it all hang out" will lead to greater psychological adjustment as well as to closer relationships with fellow human beings. Here it is assumed that we can't communicate clearly if we have a lot to hide, that in true intimacy we need not weigh and measure our words because our partner will separate the wheat and chaff, keeping the grain and blowing the chaff away. Proponents of this orientation toward disclosure believe that when we keep things from others it is not for their sake but more for our own sake—our fear of retaliation, guilt, and so on.

Admittedly, we have all seen and probably experienced instances in business, government, education, or family life when people have deliberately withheld information. The reasons could be for personal gain; to avoid a potentially negative reaction; or to keep oneself, another person, or the relationship from getting hurt. In fact, some couples manage to make the avoidance of certain topics a positive thing for their relationship. Obviously, too little disclosure can be harmful, but too much disclosure also can be problematic.

Indiscriminate or overzealous disclosure can cause difficulties for both the receiver and the communicator. The person who feels compelled to engage in a great deal of intimate self-disclosure in almost any setting is no more adjusted than the person who hides almost everything from everyone regardless of setting. These indiscriminately high disclosers are not adapting their messages to their audience. For these persons, intimate self-disclosures are so common, they are nearly reduced to the level of cocktail party chatter. Such indiscriminate self-disclosure drains the force out of and cheapens people's feelings.

Because self-disclosure is important in close relationships but avoiding such disclosures can also be helpful, it is natural to ask when it is best to disclose and when it is best to avoid disclosures. This turns out to be a very complicated question because it depends on many factors. For example, avoiding self-disclosures in close relationships seems to work best when (1) the relationship partners see their avoidance of some issues as within the "normal" range, (2) each partner tends to emphasize other commonalities and positive aspects of their relationship, and (3) the avoidance of a particular topic or topics is not perceived as the way they commonly deal with relationship issues.[16] A variety of studies also suggest that couples who are able to avoid topics without drawing attention to the fact that they are avoiding topics tend to be more successful than couples who explicitly state that they are going to avoid a topic.[17] Let's say, for example, that you are not particularly fond of your

© Viktor Gladkov/Shutterstock.com

relationship partner's favorite band, but you don't really care what your partner listens to. If you simply don't disclose your opinion, that is likely to be much less of a big deal than if you sit down with your partner and explain: "Look, I do not think we can talk about music because your favorite band sucks, and I am worried that if we talk about music, I will be constantly reminded that your favorite band is crappy, and you will be constantly reminded that you have bad taste. So let's not talk about music." If you are going to not talk about a topic, it is usually better to just not talk about it rather than talking about not talking about it.

Even when people do have topics that they do not talk about, in close relationships is it important to feel like they *could* talk about those topics if they needed to. When people choose not to talk about something because they just don't want to talk, it tends to be less problematic than if they don't talk because they believe their partner wouldn't understand or would be judgmental. Having one person in a relationship who does want to talk about something while the other does not also can create problems. In sum, even people in really close and satisfying relationships often withhold disclosures and avoid talking about certain topics, but this is not necessarily problematic as long as they feel like they are generally open and that they can talk when they want or need to.[18]

Self-Disclosure as a Communication Strategy

An important task facing couples who seek to establish a close relationship is the negotiation of privacy boundaries.[19] These negotiations involve what can/should be shared and what is/should be off limits. The process of sharing more and more of yourself with another person inevitably highlights the offsetting need for a refuge from unwanted intrusions. It sounds simple enough, but these boundaries are not always clear—even to the person seeking privacy. Consider, for example, a man and a woman who have been sexually intimate for nearly two years even though they do not live together. One day, while the woman is in the shower shaving her legs, her boyfriend suddenly pulls aside the shower curtain and starts watching her. He says, "I just like to see you naked." Visibly upset, the woman tells her boyfriend to leave her alone. Later she tells him she felt "violated."

Self-disclosure, like any communication pattern, loses its capacity for accomplishing a variety of communicative goals if it is used indiscriminately.

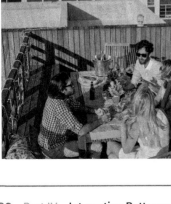

The critical question we should be asking ourselves is not, "What can I do to be totally open?" but "What do I want to accomplish and how can I do it best?" The latter question assumes that there is more than one alternative for what we want to say. Further, sometimes we don't want to be as direct or personal as a total openness perspective might suggest. To be effective communicators, we will want to consider the timing of our disclosure, the other person's capacity to respond, the kind of relationship we have with the target person, long-term versus short-term effects, the motives for the disclosure, how much detail is called for, and whether the disclosure is relevant to the current situation and feelings. We must remember that we can't say everything there is to say about anything anyway. Thus, we will be faced with selecting the information to be conveyed and the way to say it, whether we try to "tell it like it is" or not.

Because we have to be selective about what we say and how we say it, accuracy and reality become elusive goals in presenting ourselves to others and in perceiving what others are like:

> Owing to the very peculiar nature of knowledge about persons, relationships necessarily turn on somewhat misguided and misleading premises about other parties. Social order rests partly upon error, lies, deception and secrets, as well as upon accurate knowledge.[20]

One of the most intense reveal-hide quandaries for romantic couples concerns what one does after having had an extramarital affair. Two important decisions are associated with this issue—whether to tell and, if the answer is yes, how to do it. If the motivation for telling this secret is to work at improving the marriage, there is a much better chance of a productive outcome than if the motivation is to punish or hurt the other person or simply to relieve guilt feelings. Many couples survive the disclosure of an affair and use it to form a better relationship. This doesn't mean that there won't be anger, pain, and conflict. But these are not uncommon elements in the quest for intimacy even if there is no extramarital affair. Some people (and therapists) maintain a more secretive position (e.g., "what you don't know won't hurt you"). With certain circumstances and certain types of negotiated relationship rules, this may be an appropriate behavior. In other instances, the perpetrator's behavior change may negatively affect his or her spouse. And even though one person may not be hurt by what isn't known, the other person does know and that can affect the relationship too. Most people who report their experiences with an affair say the pain is not in the knowledge that one's partner had sex with another person, but in the private life that developed, the deceptions associated with that life, and the exchange of symbols associated with their intimacy—thereby reducing the intimacy value of such symbols for their own relationship.

The second question has to do with how one talks about an affair if it is revealed. The repair process may take a long time—perhaps even years. But the central theme for the person having the affair should be that his or her primary interest is in putting the affair and all that it represented aside and taking steps to improve the current relationship. The partner will want to hear negative things about the affair and at the same time positive signs of commitment (Chapter 9) about their own relationship. A partner may indicate he or she wants to hear all the details, but the extent to which details are provided should be cast in the framework of whether such details are necessary to dispense with the affair and get on with building the current relationship—that is, what purpose will knowledge of such details serve? Sometimes people say they want to hear things they really don't want to know. On the other hand, the person who had the affair usually overemphasizes the need to keep certain aspects secret. It is not so much that the person who finds out about an affair really wants to know all the gory details. They may be trying only to get confirmation that this is really an effort to expunge any ugly secrets from the marriage—for example, is the revealer sincere in his or her intentions?

Self-Disclosure as Manipulation

The irony of those who accuse secretive people of being manipulative is that self-disclosure also can be used as a manipulative device. We can deliberately disclose certain information to hurt, shock, or embarrass another person; we can take advantage of the reciprocity norm in order to try to elicit certain personal information or services from others. This latter strategy commonly occurs in attempts at *instant intimacy*. One version involves an effort to move quickly a new romantic relationship to what *seems* to be the intensifying stage. This can be done by one or both participants displaying the illusion that they have some special "vibes" that allow them to advance more quickly than most people. It is further illustrated by the way the two communicate with each other—using terms of endearment such as "you sweet thing" and exchanging intimate disclosures, usually about sex or other past and ongoing relationships. This communicative behavior can then be the rationale for why they feel the way they do—they find it easy to talk to each other. This behavior is usually initiated by one person with what seems to be a personal disclosure (and maybe most people would think of it in that category), but the discloser does not consider it private, and he or she is not subject to much risk. Like so many instances of disclosure in relationships, *perceived* disclosure and *perceived* reciprocity of disclosure are often more critical than what actually takes place. In the case of instant intimacy, the entire procedure is, of course, designed to get the other person to reciprocate with disclosures dealing with sexual and relationship matters. Once both parties have begun to verbally communicate *as if* they were at the intensifying stage, the intimate physical behavior that also is characteristic of the intensifying stage is legitimized. This strategy of talking to a person you don't know very well as if you did, in order to obtain the behavior characteristic of a friend or intimate, is not limited to romantic relationships. For instance, one woman we know uses this manipulative technique of rapid pseudo-disclosure when first going to a new hairdresser. In this case, the client is trying to establish a conversational climate characteristic of friends, assuming that a friend would give a better haircut than an acquaintance or stranger.

© Jacob Lund/Shutterstock.com

Self-Disclosure and Relationship Development

Certainly, self-disclosure contributes to the growth of a relationship that develops naturally and non-manipulatively. As was noted in earlier chapters, less intimate information will be exchanged in the experimenting stage. As people begin forays into the intensifying stage, we will see a flurry of more personal self-disclosures. These disclosures, then, will increase as the relationship moves into the integrating stage. Since most of the research on self-disclosure has been conducted on stranger-stranger dyads, much of our knowledge about self-disclosure at more intimate stages must remain speculative. **Figure 8.1** shows how the breadth and depth of self-disclosure changes as relationships vary in intimacy.

As noted earlier, one of the characteristics of self-disclosure is that it is often reciprocated—for example, my self-disclosure has a good chance of eliciting a self-disclosure from you. In fact, our expectations are so firmly set for this reciprocity in the initial stages of a developing relationship that we often perceive reciprocal disclosures when they aren't there. It seems reasonable to argue that if we don't feel a mutuality of disclosure in the intensifying stage, we probably won't get to the integrating stage—unless, of course, some external force propels us there. As the relationship advances into intimacy, one disclosure may not be followed immediately by a reciprocal one, but if the mutual reciprocity doesn't balance out over a period of time, adaptations in disclosure patterns will be made.

As a relationship reaches for more intimacy, disclosures will probably be more frequent than in relationships that have established themselves and stabilized at an intimate stage. For instance, the feelings of intensifying intimacy may cause certain restraints to be released—frankness may often override tact; as intimacy is sustained, attempts to reinstate the constraints may be made in order to preserve the relationship and let it stabilize. Thus, as an intimate relationship grows from initiating to intimacy, disclosure frequency and depth will eventually reach a point of stabilization and probably taper off. *Intimate relationships need to suppress some things or they may lose their intimacy.* This does not mean, however, that the relationship has reached the circumscribing stage. It is an *act* of circumscribing, but this act does not typify or represent the common communication patterns of the intimate couple, nor does it signal deterioration in the generally intimate character of the relationship.

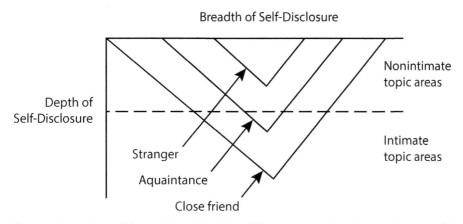

Figure 8.1   Breadth and Depth of Self-Disclosure for Three Types of Relationships

Source: Adapted from Irwin Altman and W. W. Haythorn, "Interpersonal Exchange in Isolation," Sociometry 28 (1965): 422.

Chilling effect:
Avoiding revealing
certain information
due to fears that its
revelation will result in
ridicule, rejection, or
conflict.

Not disclosing certain information or keeping secrets is not uncommon among couples and families. Sometimes secrets will harm a relationship, but it is not uncommon for those who perceive their relationship to be close to have secrets as well. Secrets may occur for strategic reasons or because of a "**chilling effect**" in which a person fears the revelation of certain information will result in ridicule, rejection, or conflict.[21] Baxter and Wilmot found that "taboo" topics may occur at virtually any relationship stage.[22] Some of these avoided topics include extra-relationship activities, talking about rules and expected behavior, previous relationships, negative self-disclosures, and topics from the past that can be expected to cause problems. But the most frequently reported subject to avoid, according to the students interviewed, is the relationship itself. People in platonic relationships, relationships with romantic potential, and those in established romantic relationships all felt the relationship would suffer by being discussed. For people who want to maintain a relationship, this belief is quite natural. But it doesn't mean that the relationship is a topic that is ignored. It may be discussed in indirect ways or inferred from the nature of conversations on other topics. Baxter, herself, found quite a variety of techniques used by students to acquire information about their relationships.[23] Some of these methods included (1) asking third parties; (2) trial intimacy moves—for example, through self-disclosures or touch; (3) putting yourself down to see how the other will respond; (4) using hypothetical situations to see how the other will respond; (5) asking the partner to do something for you that shows sacrifice of time and energy; (6) separating for a while to see how the other responds; and (7) deliberately putting the partner in a situation in which the nature of the relationship will be tested—for example, encouraging one's partner to be with another person.

In long-established intimate relationships, it is probably more difficult to identify what is personal and what is superficial, since the lines have been blurred (even to the participants) as the couple moves freely in and out of the two areas. Most of the research conducted on married couples shows more disclosure in couples who are more satisfied with their relationship.[24] However, it is significant that this disclosure doesn't seem to be just any kind of disclosure. The satisfied couples did not have as many *negative* disclosures of feelings. Often they resorted to more oblique ways of revealing negative perceptions—for example a husband who dislikes his wife interrupting him when he speaks may comment on the behavior of another couple observed at a party, "Wow, did you see how Caroline wouldn't let Larry get a word in edgewise?" Couples who trust each other somewhat less than the satisfied couples are more likely to focus directly on negative events and explanations. But when trust is at a low level, partners tend to communicate in less extreme ways in an effort to minimize the potential for conflict.[25]

Trust and Self-Disclosure

Trust: The degree of confidence people feel when they think about their relationship.

Self-disclosure of intimate information is based on trust. According to Rempel et al., **trust** is the degree of confidence you feel when you think about the relationship.[26] Trust is composed of three primary perceptions: predictability, dependability, and faith. *Predictability* is the expectation that your partner will act consistently in positive ways toward you; *dependability* means you can rely on your partner when it counts; and *faith* refers to the belief that your partner will continue to be responsive and caring in the future. High levels of trust are needed for intimate disclosures, but it is no guarantee of it. One of the reasons we see people disclosing highly personal information to strangers is that they realize there is minimal risk—i.e., the unknown and transient recipient usually cannot use the information against them. Ordinarily, disclosing highly personal information can make us vulnerable; it can give others power over us. This is why trust is so important. This also is why we try to get people to talk about themselves from the moment we meet them; we are trying to get to know where they stand, what they think and feel, so that we can have some control and find some predictability in the relationship. Recipients of self-disclosures should recognize the discloser's concerns—that the listener won't keep it confidential, that he or she won't reciprocate, that he or she won't understand or accept the disclosure. If we want a person to disclose more to us, we must make the person feel our appreciation for his or her trust in us and our acceptance and support for that person, not necessarily for the behavior or feeling that is the focus of the disclosure. This last issue is obviously easier said than done. It sometimes takes painstakingly long to get another person to understand that criticism of his or her behavior is not also a criticism of him or her as a person. It can be done, however.

© gpointstudio/Shutterstock.com

Lying

At first glance, it may seem strange that we include lying as a behavior involved in maintaining a close relationship. After all, honesty and close relationships go hand in hand. And some people report that honesty and trustworthiness are more desirable traits in a partner (for long- and short-term relationships) than almost any other—including an exciting personality, a good sense of humor, adaptability, dependability, and kindness/understanding.[27] And, as expected, people in close relationships report telling fewer lies to each other.[28] But most people realize that satisfying relationships somehow learn to appreciate and accommodate behavior that falls short of "the whole truth and nothing but the truth."[29] Decisions about truth telling and lying are at the very heart of what constitutes a close relationship. For many, the familiar promise "We won't lie to each other" is viewed as a covenant that will lead to and sustain greater intimacy. It is, however, worth noting that each partner may have different referents for what "agreeing not to lie" means. For instance, does it mean I have to tell you things that I know would hurt you and you probably wouldn't find out anyway? Does it mean I have to tell you I hate your outfit (if that's the way I feel) when you ask for my opinion? If I tell you I went to bed with another person, is it lying not to tell you the details? If acts of omission, exaggeration, vagueness, evasiveness, and substitution are all a part of the act of lying, then everybody lies. If we can't avoid lying, then what is the kind of behavior we are trying to avoid with the "we won't lie to each other" promise?

For most couples, the real issue is whether a lie will have a damaging effect on the relationship and whether the motivation for lying was well intended. Thus, when contemplating a lie, the following questions seem to be key: (1) Will this lie help both of us? If the lie is solely for the benefit of one partner, it is more likely to be viewed negatively and incur more relationship damage. Liar motivation is at issue here. The couple's short- and long-range mutual goals are the focus. From this perspective, we would expect most of the lies of people in close relationships to be motivated by a desire to help their partners. And that seems to be the case.[30] Lies designed to protect their partner from hurt, to help them build or maintain their self-esteem, to assist them in accomplishing their goals, and to show concern for their physical and mental states are the most common lies told by the most committed partners. This doesn't mean that self-oriented lies don't occur in close relationships. In fact, sometimes "closeness" itself facilitates or prompts self-oriented lying when the fear of losing it is high and when one's partner makes it clear that there is a high probability that such lies will be forgiven.[31] (2) Is the lie consistent with the rules of fairness in the relationship? That is, does one's partner operate by the same rules you do? Liar intentions are the concern now. If both partners agree that certain classes of lies are OK but others are not (e.g., lying about one's sexual prowess may be okay, but lying about having lunch with an ex-lover may not), then lies in the forbidden categories will incur more relationship damage. Sometimes, of course, a couple either assumes the other knows which categories are OK and which are not or they have not discussed the issue specifically. Thus, when an intentional lie in a category one partner believes is not acceptable occurs, the liar may argue that he or she was not aware of the rule and that it won't happen again. This is one way that fairness rules about lying are negotiated. (3) Does your partner (the one lied to) believe you have his or her best interests at heart—both generally and in this specific situation? If the answer is yes, the lie is likely to have less damage to the relationship. Even in situations in which the liar clearly violates the couple's agreed-upon norms for lying (e.g., lying about an affair), the damage to the relationship will be offset if the offender can convince his or her partner that the lie was consistent with other instances that indicated a concern for the partner's welfare.

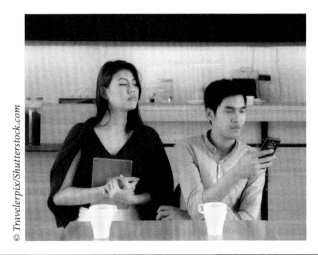

The best predictor of relationship termination as a result of a discovered lie is the perceived importance of the information lied about. This explains why those people who are more involved/committed to their relationship are going to have a greater emotional reaction to lies that impinge directly on the relationship.[32]

© Travelerpix/Shutterstock.com

The way that a liar and a lie detector behave in a close relationship is strongly influenced by certain conditions that are unlike those conditions that characterize less intimate relationships.[33] The first characteristic has to do with the kind of **mutual influence** exerted by the partners to a close relationship. Even in lies to nonintimates, we may be more involved in the lie than we care to admit. It is easy to condemn lies that we feel we had no part in. But we can influence a person's decision to lie, and we can give tacit approval to it once it occurs. A familiar behavior of this type is the hostess who knows a guest is lying about "what a nice party this has been" but recognizes the intent is to avoid unpleasantness, so she cooperates in the deception. In other instances, a person may make it so clear that he or she is intolerant and inflexible regarding a certain behavior that this person's partner feels the necessity to lie when experiences with that behavior occur. Thus, we may be well advised to reflect on our own role in another's decision to lie before we determine how much punishment is deserved. Additionally, the role of the deceived in the deceiver's behavior is likely to affect the deceived person's motivation and accuracy in detecting the deception as well as the way the liar performs the lie. Liars usually view their own lies as more altruistic, justified, and provoked by the target than they view the lies of others.[34] In close relationships, partners constantly negotiate interaction norms with the knowledge that each will play a role in the outcome. Lying should be no different. When the outcome is an undesirable one, however, responsibility is frequently attributed to one's partner.

> **Mutual influence:** Describes how people's behaviors in a relationship (e.g., lying and lie detection) are influenced by both themselves and their partner.

The second important characteristic of lies in close relationships concerns the increased possibility of **multiple exposure** to the lie. Lies to people we don't see that often do not require the same kind of development and/or repetition. This will surely affect the extent to which the liar will want to engage in a falsehood that requires long-term memory of details or whether it would be easier to engage in lies of omission.

> **Multiple exposure:** Characteristic of close relationships recognizing that interacting with the same person repeatedly can influence communicative outcomes (e.g., the ability to detect lies).

The third characteristic of intimates is that they are quite *familiar* with one another's behavior. This raises the question of detection accuracy. Most of the research on detection of liars has been done with people who don't know each other well. This research indicates that an untrained observer, looking at and listening to a stranger without the aid of any mechanical equipment, will be able to identify liars about half or slightly better than half the time. The percentage of accurate identification in everyday life is, in reality, probably lower due to the fact that most people tend to assume others are telling them the truth most of the time.[35] Thus, it is easier to deceive a person who has no reason to suspect that he or she is being lied to, and much of the research conducted asks subjects to "identify this person as a deceiver or nondeceiver"—an instruction that immediately forewarns subjects of possible deception.

Lie Detection

Although research on detecting lying among friends and intimates is sparse, Comadena found that intimates are generally more accurate than acquaintances. Friends, however, may exhibit more accuracy than spouses.[36] Spouses are committed to a relationship that may last a long time and involves daily contact. As a result, they may be more likely than good friends to develop a desensitization to behavior associated with lying. People in close relationships don't expect their partner to lie, and there also may be a strong desire not to be an accurate detector, as this wife attests:

> Little by little things were happening that didn't make sense, but I can remember making excuses for them myself . . . I didn't want to believe there was anything to find out . . . so I was being deceived from two angles. . . . I was deceiving myself . . . I didn't sit there when it was happening saying, "I am just fooling myself." You know, I, I, as I said, I made up a lot of excuses, and really believed them. . . . I didn't confide in anyone, too, because I was afraid of what they would tell me. I wanted to believe everything was going to be fine and I wasn't being deceived. If I told someone else they might tell me I was being deceived and I didn't want to hear that. . . . But as much as I wanted to be a detective and find him out, I didn't want to either. Because the truth, I was afraid more of the truth than living in the lie kind of.[37]

If intimates do want to detect the lies of their partners, they have several advantages. For example, in more intimate relationships, the partners have a mental record or backlog for verbal checking and verification. When people are able to compare statements to other potentially conflicting information, it increases the chances of correctly identifying a lie.[38] Furthermore, intimate partners have a history of having observed the other in many different emotional situations. Hence, intimates should have a better idea of what behavior exceeds the boundaries of normality for their partners. Changes in behavior or activity patterns often trigger partner alertness if not suspicion. In addition, intimates have considerably more motivation than acquaintances or mere observers to look closely for clues. Although greater intimacy may give one an advantage in being able to perceive a partner's lies, greater intimacy also may make partners less attentive to the possibilities of lies.[39] Thus, unless intimates have a reason for expecting a lie, they may be less apt to notice it. The first lies to intimate partners are likely to be the easiest to get away with. After all, the relationship was built on trust, so there is no reason to be suspicious. Even if lie goes undetected, it still may have a significant impact on the relationship.[40] For example, a person who has engaged in an important deception in a close relationship may get mad at him- or herself and take out his or her anger on a partner. Perceptions of his or her partner as being easily duped or as no more honest him—or herself may begin to take hold and alter feelings and discourse.

The Lies That Bind?

The other day, Jeremy woke up, and the first thing he saw was his fiancée, Gabriela, smiling at him. She said, "You're grinning. You must have been having a sweet dream. What was it about?"

Instinctively, he replied, "Oh, I was? I don't really remember. I guess I'm just happy to be here with you." Gabriela smiled, and they began a pleasant morning.

Later that day, the incident was bothering Jeremy because the truth was that he did remember his dream. He was outside on a beautiful day, on a beach by his favorite lake, acting goofy. He was running, laughing, and generally having a great time. But he wasn't with Gabriela in the dream; he was with his ex-girlfriend. And they were not just having a good time, they were flirting with each other and really happy about it. It was obvious that they would soon be hooking up, and in the dream, Jeremy was really excited about this prospect.

Now, Jeremy knows that the content of dreams doesn't always mean anything, and having this dream did not make him doubt his love or commitment to Gabriela one bit. But he still felt kind of bad that he lied to her about it. This was on his mind later when he had lunch with his sister, Shelby, and her boyfriend, Corbin. Because this was bothering him, he decided to tell them what happened and ask what they thought.

Shelby immediately said, "Don't even give it another thought, brother. Some silly old dream is not important. But if you told her, she might *think* it is important. Why make her feel bad or give her doubts when there is no reason she has to feel that way? Now, if it were something important—like if this made you doubt your feelings—of course you'd talk to her about that. But this is different. We have all kinds of thoughts every day, and we certainly have dreams that we can't control. It's just not reasonable to think you are going to tell her every thought you ever have, and it wouldn't do any good if you did. If it's important, sure, you talk about it. But otherwise, you have to think about whether there is a point, and if all it's going to do is make her feel bad or worried, there is no point. In fact, right now I'm noticing that the guy waiting on those tables over there has a really nice rear end, but normally I would keep that to myself because I am quite fond of this rear end right here." As she grabbed Corbin's backside, Shelby added in her best babytalk voice, "I don't need my little schmoopie to be worried about stupid stuff that doesn't really matter."

Looking a bit confused, Corbin chimed in, "Look, while I appreciate the public display of affection, I think you are wrong. He should have told her exactly what was on his mind, and he should still tell her. Good relationships are built on open and honest communication no matter what. Any time you tell a lie, it builds a barrier in that relationship, and good relationships are about building bridges—not barriers. So Jeremy, if you really love her, you have to be honest with her all the time. You can't build your relationship on lies."

As Jeremy thought about what both of them had said, Shelby laughed about the entire situation, and decided to get the last word: "Well, if that's the way you feel about things, Corbin, remember how you asked me if that shirt made you look cool, and I said that you didn't need the shirt to look cool because you *are* cool? Well, that was kind of deceptive because that shirt makes you look like a doofus."

****

Who do you agree with about lying—Corbin or Shelby? Are they both right or wrong? Are there times in relationships when lying can be "good"?

Although lie detection is no doubt an important skill on some occasions, there is always the danger of engaging in such acts too often. Those who go on a search-and-destroy mission for their partners' lies may find they have created more harm than good for the relationship. Suspicion can create suspicion to the point at which neither person trusts the other and the lie detector has created the very thing he or she set out to destroy. In addition, it is likely that such a campaign against lies may only drive the worst offenders underground so they can refine their strategies. Besides, relationships often rely on certain kinds of deceptions for sustenance. To wipe out any ability to deceive another may wipe out some important structural foundations for the relationship. This doesn't mean we shouldn't probe, question, and investigate situations in which a lie seems to harm the relationship; it simply means we should try to preserve the assumption of truthfulness rather than replace it with an assumption of deceit. If you're like us, there are some things you'd rather not know the "truth" about.

Socrates: What Plato is about to say is false.

Plato: Socrates has just spoken truly.

Are there any behaviors that are always associated with lying behavior and nothing else? No. There are behaviors that liars in nonintimate relationships regularly exhibit, such as speech errors, higher pitch, more hesitations, and fidgeting, but intimates may attend to more idiosyncratic cues.[41] We know one person whose wife listens for a barely audible gulp after a statement that is already suspected of being an untruth (e.g., "I dropped by the office to do some work," whereas "I stopped by the jeweler to check on your ring" would be the true statement). It is usually wise to look for clusters of behavior rather than a single cue. To say, "I knew he was lying because he didn't look at me," is just as risky as saying, "I knew he didn't have a large vocabulary because he used the word *liar* instead of *deceiver*." In order to increase the probability that we are accurate in detecting deception, we should look for clusters of cues—does his or her lack of eye contact fit with other things you've observed such as nervous movement and speech errors?

There does seem to be some stereotyped categories for lying behavior. Liars, for instance, will sometimes be observed exhibiting a cluster of **anxiety responses** resulting from guilt or psychological distress. These may include behaviors such as blushing, shaking, gulping, perspiring, voice tremors, speech errors, using fewer different words, and sending shorter messages. Sometimes observers key their observations on what they consider to be **excessive responses**. As noted earlier, excessive responses go beyond the boundaries of normal behavior for the individual being observed. It may be that the person is too inactive or too active; it might be that he or she talks excessively or engages in pronounced pauses and silences; it might be that he or she makes excessive eye contact (staring) or no eye contact at all; or it may be that he or she answers seemingly nonthreatening questions with extremely defensive remarks—"You're a little late this evening, dear. Where have you been?" "CAN'T I HAVE ONE PEACEFUL MOMENT BEFORE I GET THE THIRD DEGREE! IF YOU WANT TO KNOW MY WHERE-ABOUTS EVERY MOMENT OF THE DAY, HIRE A PRIVATE DETECTIVE!" Another category of behaviors people sometimes observe in liars is **incongruous responses**. Liars sometimes have a hard time keeping their stories straight. Verbally, a person may contradict some known fact of which the receiver is aware, or contradict his or her own earlier statement. Sometimes incongruity is shown when a person is being very careful and trying to maintain control in a situation that doesn't call for such behavior. Nonverbally, we might see some of the same inconsistency discussed earlier in this chapter—saying "I've always liked you" but exhibiting a host of nonverbal cues that attest otherwise. Finally, sometimes observers detect what might be called **indirect responses**. Verbal indirectness will take on the characteristics of some of the evasive tactics mentioned in Chapter 11—answering a question with a question or changing the subject. A person also could show verbal indirectness through vagueness—fewer verifiable factual assertions; fewer references to a verifiable past; fewer self-oriented statements for which a person could be held responsible; and more broad, sweeping generalizations. Nonverbally, indirectness may be seen, among other things, by not maintaining a direct body orientation when talking to another person or simply by increasing the distance between oneself and the listener. It should be clear from the preceding that many of the behaviors typically associated with liars also are manifested by people telling the truth. Thus, it is advisable to gather as much information about the situation as possible before charging the other with lying.

Of course, lie detection in close relationships is not always wholly dependent on observing the behavior of one's partner. Some of the most common methods involve obtaining information from third parties and finding evidence that contradicts the liar's story. In ongoing relationships, determining a partner has lied can take place over a considerable amount of time as one learns or recalls new information or one engages in more discussions, which may even include follow-up questions designed to probe for inconsistencies or elicit confessions.[42]

Anxiety responses: Cluster of behaviors resulting from guilt or psychological distress, such as blushing, shaking, or perspiring.

Excessive responses: Potential indicator of lying in which a response goes beyond the boundaries of normal behavior for the individual being observed.

Incongruous responses: Potential indicator of lying involving inconsistencies in one's statements or between the verbal and nonverbal messages.

Indirect responses: Potential indicator of lying involving evasiveness, vague responses, or few verifiable factual assertions.

Constructive Conflict

In Chapter 1, we proposed that communication at increased stages of intimacy would be characterized by more overt, evaluative judgments of the other person. Further, intimate relationships are characterized by increased breadth and depth. The paradox, then, is that the possibilities for conflict actually may increase as the relationship grows more intimate.[43] Obviously, the frequency and intensity of conflict will vary from couple to couple. Marital couples described as "traditionals" have fairly clear rules and roles and seem to have less overt conflict.[44] Assuming a relationship remains intimate, the frequency of conflict in most relationships will probably level off as the participants deal with numerous issues or the same issues numerous times. The problem, of course, is that the ineffective conduct of conflict can decrease intimacy.

Conflict is neither good nor bad. The way people choose to engage each other in conflict, however, can be judged as positive or negative depending on how it affects the participants and the relationship. There is also some indication that the nature of premarital conflict will be a good predictor of marital happiness after the first two-and-one-half years of married life.[45]

During the early years of marriage, the perceived negativity associated with conflict is strongly related to the likelihood of relationship dissolution—more so than the sheer number of fights. But an interesting reversal seems to occur after about eight years of marriage. At this point, the frequency of conflict becomes the best predictor of divorce. A high frequency of fighting between couples who have had eight years to negotiate a variety of issues associated with their relationship is a sign that they may not have been successful negotiators.[46]

For many couples, their "first big fight" can be a watershed event for the relationship. In a study that contrasted couples who broke up after their first big fight with those who stayed together, the first big fight provided a closer reading of the relationship:

> For survivors, the FBF [first big fight] typically renders explicit for the first time mutual feelings of commitment. Couples openly discuss previously unspoken concerns and gain a greater understanding of "where we stand" as a result. In contrast, those who broke up because of their FBF reported the onset of confusion about their relationship, the revelation of previously unknown aspects of their partner's personality, and the transformation of nonproblematic interaction into conversation that becomes at best, tense and sporadic. . . . The big difference between non-survivors and survivors was the way they perceived and handled conflict in their relationships. The survivors generally believed that a successful relationship required a joint effort in problem-solving, some sacrifice from both parties, and the ability and/or willingness to adjust one's own ways of doing things in order to mesh with the partner's way of doing things.[47]

The interpersonal costs of conflict can be high, but sometimes these apparent costs can be turned into profit. Profitable constructive conflict may (1) provide a greater understanding of the other, oneself, and the relationship; (2) clarify similarities and dissimilarities; (3) assist people in learning methods for coping with future conflict; and (4) reveal areas in which communicative effort and adaptation need to be strengthened. When conflict, or any force, threatens the continuance of a relationship, the participants learn a great deal about how solid the ties binding them are.

Although our major focus is on conflict between the parties in a close relationship, sources outside the relationship can influence the combatants in a variety of ways. For example, a person with a strong network of friends may show more confidence or even aggressiveness when fighting than one whose social world is constricted and who is overly dependent on the relationship within which the conflict occurs. The people who comprise a couple's social network also may be the source of arguments ("I just wish your friend, Julie, would keep her mouth shut"). Conflict coaches or consultants also may be found in one's social network, and they may either encourage or discourage a person to "confront" his or her partner.

Before the Fight

Before we get carried away with what may seem to be a "how to" manual for effective confrontation, let's face the fact that when our emotions are piqued, the probability that we will consciously try to plan our strategy for the ensuing conflict is severely lessened. For this reason, we could argue that those who are most effective in interpersonal conflict are those who foresee conflict and analytically weigh the nature of their partner and the nature of the conflict *prior to its appearance.* For instance, effective disputants surely consider the other's ability or inclination to deal with the problem (initiate, postpone, or delay indefinitely); the long- and short-range goals they want to accomplish with the confrontation (catharsis or behavior change); the surrounding environment's contribution to the intensity of the confrontation (public locale or private); and the mode of communication (written or oral).

Once we decide to enter the conflict situation, the *attitudes* we approach it with may be more important in determining the outcome or outcomes than any behavioral prescriptions. It seems that the most productive conflict will arise when both participants enter the encounter with the following orientations: (1) They recognize that not all conflicts can be resolved, that most will require more than a single encounter for a resolution satisfactory to both parties, and that they have the potential to solve this problem as a team. (2) They accept the fact that conflict is a natural part of all human relationships—that differences of opinion can, indeed, be helpful. (3) They have a desire to solve the problem

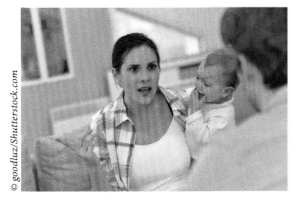
© goodluz/Shutterstock.com

arising out of a vested interest in the outcome (preserving the relationship) rather than just wanting to become a "winner." If one participant becomes the sole winner, the other becomes a loser, and when one party loses, the relationship loses. We knew a person, for instance, who had such a large vocabulary, breadth and depth of knowledge, and skill at formal debating techniques that he would always come away from a verbal duel seemingly unscathed—"victorious." However, nobody liked him. Who won? Conflict resides in the relationship, not in either individual. (4) They have an active concern for the feelings of the other person. (5) They maintain a flexibility that will allow them to see many possible outcomes other than personal victory— e.g., acquiescence, postponement, compromise.

Relationship partners who stay together long enough to expect periodic fights also tend to develop a sort of "code of conduct" for these fights. In one sense, these rules are formulated to reduce potentially harmful fight behavior, but ironically, the rules themselves often become the source of disagreement, which causes the participants to end up arguing about how they are arguing. Common examples of such rules include "We will not fight in front of the kids (or friends)"; "We will not 'hit below the belt'"; "We will not leave the scene in the middle of an argument"; or "We will not interrupt each other."

During the Fight

Now we arrive at the point at which people are communicating during the conflict itself. Which kind of strategies for conflict resolution are employed? Which of these strategies are best suited for constructive rather than destructive outcomes? To answer these questions, we are going to identify specific types of talk that typically characterize productive and unproductive fights. Before we do that, however, it is important to remember that in the absence of strategic thinking about conflict interaction, it is easy for us to be overtaken by excessive behavior associated with instinctive reactions to conflict. When we feel threatened, our "fight or flight" response is a natural first response. Unfortunately, many couples find themselves stuck in a distressingly extreme fight and/or flight pattern.[48] No doubt you will see the following patterns as too inaccurate and extreme to identify with. **Withdrawal** is a conflict pattern that arises when both parties want to flee the conflict. Both want relational peace and harmony so much that they almost never express negative feelings to each other. They see virtually all problems as "small" and are quick to find ways to keep from facing them. In such relationships, we would expect to find a relatively low level of intimacy coupled with an unspoken reservoir of tensions. It is not uncommon for those couples who withdraw from conflict to see themselves as martyrs who suffer in silence because they are "right" and their partner is "wrong." **Escalation** is the conflict pattern that develops when both parties want to fight rather than

Withdrawal: Conflict pattern that arises when both parties want to flee the conflict.

Escalation: Conflict pattern that develops when both parties want to fight rather than flee the conflict.

flee. In contrast to those who want to avoid conflict, these people want to pursue it. They have an urgency to express their anger and deal with problems immediately. When both parties respond to problems by exhibiting a desire to "get into the ring and settle it," we can expect the conflict to escalate. We also can expect both will be good at saying what's on their minds, but not so good at listening to their partners. It is not unusual that the fight-fight pattern produces repeated arguments about the same issues and leaves a residue of increased anger.

In some cases, these "volatile" couples can establish a satisfying relationship because they offset their anger with an equal or greater amount of affection and positive behavior. But tragically, in some cases, couples sense the futility of their fight-fight pattern for solving problems and seek to remedy the situation by going to the other extreme and becoming withdrawers. The pattern in which one person pursues the fight while the other withdraws is no more productive than is the pattern in which both persons manifest the same style of behavior. The *pursuit-withdraw* or withdraw-pursuit pattern feeds on itself, because in each case the responses are so predictable. The withdrawer can't understand why the pursuer is so upset by "little" things, and the pursuer can't understand why the withdrawer refuses to deal with problems. Frequently, though, pursuers feel less powerful in the relationship and are dissatisfied. Their pursuit is an effort to change that situation. But their partners perceive certain benefits from the status quo and are therefore uninterested in confronting issues that may threaten it. The result is withdrawal. The demand/withdraw pattern is illustrated in the following case study:

> Sally, a nurse in her 40s is married to Scott, a police officer, also in his 40s. Sally asks Scott about landscaping their yard while he was reading a newspaper. She asked him how much money he thought they could spend on landscaping and whether he was leaning toward rose bushes or rhododendrons in the front. He replied that it was up to her. In a somewhat agitated voice, Sally said, "Well, I need your input because we have to talk about how much we can spend." Scott continued reading the newspaper because he "didn't want to make things worse" by responding. He thought his silence would give her time to "calm herself down." But Sally became angrier. "Why don't you ever listen to me?" she said, raising her voice. Scott then got up and said he was going for a walk because their conversation was "going nowhere." Sally pursued him and demanded they discuss the landscaping. Scott felt that anything negative he might say about the landscaping project would generate Sally's anger, but it was Scott's silence that angered Sally the most about her relationship.[49]

Keep in mind that acts of withdrawal and pursuit are not, in and of themselves, "bad" for constructive conflict. People who engage each other in productive conflict will manifest withdrawal as well as a desire to fervently pursue a problematic issue. Withdrawal from a particular argument in order to rethink a problem may be the best course of action, but repeated withdrawal from issues central to the relationship is likely to be problematic.[50] With constructive problem solvers,

Can the way you communicate with people really affect your health? Yes. Research is increasingly establishing links between a person's physical well-being and his or her relationship communication. The way you communicate can affect your physiology (blood pressure, heart, glands, immune system, etc.); your physiology can affect the way you communicate (e.g., high levels of testosterone can lead to more aggressiveness); and your communication can significantly impact your partner's physiological health. Most of this research has been done with heterosexual couples, but we know that early family relationships also can affect one's vulnerability to various stress-related relationship disorders.

Which kind of relationship communication is not good for your health? Anything that creates undue stress is likely to affect body physiology negatively. Persistent and strong feelings of loneliness or anxiety associated with forming and/or maintaining a relationship can negatively affect the immune system. Hostility, signs of not caring, persistent domination, and avoiding issues are examples of some communication patterns that can create stress during conflict in heterosexual marriages. When stressful interactions occur repeatedly, it is even more likely to lead to physiological problems and even shorten one's life span. Those who mentally "can't let go" of an argument and vividly recall negative interactions also subject themselves to the negative effects of stress.

Which kind of relationship communication is better for your health? Those who experience instrumental and emotional support in their relationships are more likely to experience greater physical well-being. The greater number of such relationships (e.g., family, friends, romantic partner) the better it is for one's health. But it is not only the number of relationships that matters; having good communication in your relationships can be helpful, even if you do not have many friends and family members to call upon. For example, there is growing evidence that affectionate communication in relationships is related to the release of protective hormones (e.g., oxytocin) that reduce the impact of stressful situations. In other words, when partners are affectionate with each other, it seems to make the other stressful things that happen in their lives less damaging to their emotional and physical well-being.

Are married people healthier than single people? There is a widespread belief that being married somehow makes you live longer and enjoy a healthier life. It is true that marriage can be beneficial, but not all marriages are. People in troubled marriages tend to experience more health problems. And surveys show that the health and longevity of people who get married and stay married isn't all that different from people who stay single. One reason for this is many single people have other enduring relationships that are supportive and fulfilling, and these relationships confer many of the same benefits on people as do happy marriages. In short, people who are happy with their relationships (married or single) are likely to have a health advantage over people who are not satisfied with their relationships.

* * * * * * * * * * * * * * * * * * * *

There is much more to be learned about how relationships affect your health. The preceding points are only a brief beginning. In various places throughout this book, other aspects of this topic are treated. For those interested in more in-depth coverage, see Floyd, K. *Communicating Affection: Interpersonal Behavior and Social Context*. New York: Cambridge University Press, 2006; Holt-Lunstad, J. "Relationships and Physical Health." In A. L. Vangelisti and D. Perlman, eds., *The Cambridge Handbook of Personal Relationships* (2nd ed., pp. 449–463). New York, Cambridge University Press, 2018; Loving, T. J., Heffner, K. L., and Kiecolt-Glaser, J. K. "Physiology and Interpersonal Relationships." In A. L. Vangelisti and D. Perlman, eds., *The Cambridge Handbook of Personal Relationships* (pp. 385–405). New York: Cambridge University Press, 2006; and the entire issue of the April 2006 *Journal of Social and Personal Relationships, 23*.

withdrawal and pursuit behaviors are used strategically and as situationally adapted behavior—not as instinctively repeated and predictable behavior. Any pattern that consistently adheres to predictable extremes of behavior will not help couples effectively deal with disagreements. Fighting can be stressful and repeated fights with unsatisfactory conclusions can adversely affect the health of the combatants.

Obviously, people engage in a variety of conflict behaviors: withdrawing, demanding, losing control, compromising, negotiating, giving in, and so on.[51] What do couples who are satisfied with their relationship do? Exchanges during conflict between couples who are dissatisfied with their relationship are far more predictable than those of satisfied couples—for example, criticism inevitably gets criticism in response or telling the other person what they are thinking inevitably gets disagreement in response. Satisfied couples are more likely to provide novel responses. Gottman's work comparing the responses of satisfied and dissatisfied couples engaged in conflict provides us with concrete illustrations.[52]

Cross-complaining: Conflict pattern in which complaints are reciprocated between partners.

The dissatisfied couples tended to engage in more **cross-complaining**—that is, one person's complaint would be countered with the partner's complaint:

> H: I'm getting tired of eating hamburger every night.
>
> W: Well, I'm getting tired of cooking every night . . . every morning and every afternoon!

Satisfied couples were more likely to acknowledge the validity of each other's complaints. Dissatisfied marital couples were more likely to get bogged down in *arguments about how they were arguing*—for example:

> H: You don't have to get so emotional about it.
>
> W: I have to do something to make you pay attention when I'm talking. Otherwise, it's like talking to a brick wall.
>
> H: I do pay attention, but I'm not going to pay attention when you get hysterical.
>
> W: The only time you ever act like you're paying attention is when you are telling me not to do something.

Negative affect: Expressions of hostility or other negative emotions.

Satisfied couples were able to break out of such sequences earlier (e.g., "You're right, I was getting carried away") and get back to the original issue of disagreement. Dissatisfied couples generally communicated with more **negative affect**. The hostile vocal tone and facial expression accompanying a comment such as "You seem to be pretty calm considering what has happened" is likely to be taken as a criticism and responded to in a defensive manner. The same statement, without the accompanying negativity, is more likely to be perceived as a neutral or even concerned observation. Finally, dissatisfied couples tended to treat proposed solutions as they did the initial complaints—by *countering the partner's proposal with another proposal that was incompatible with it*. Satisfied couples were more likely to compromise, "give in," and look for mutually satisfying solutions.

Getting angry in a stressful situation is like trying to clean something with dirt

—Urbanky Aurel Petru

In addition to differences between satisfied and dissatisfied married couples, there also seem to be differences in the conflict behavior of husbands and wives. Unproductive conflict behavior is not the province of either the husband or wife. Husbands, as a group, reportedly have less ability than their wives to read nonverbal signals, less ability to deal with the communication of feelings, and less ability to remain involved in the conflict. If a husband is normally unwilling to be influenced by his wife's suggestions and emotional expressions, the marriage is not likely to last. Wives, on the other hand, also may contribute unproductive responses. They show less skill as a group at knowing when to keep a problem off the interaction table and less ability in achieving emotional detachment during conflict.

One set of tactics for constructive conflict resolution hinges on identifying and specifically stating the source of the conflict rather than presenting it generally. Assuming that conflict is situation-bound and temporary, rather than personality-bound and lasting, improves greatly the chances for resolving the conflict. For instance, an individual's approach to a situation-bound problem will be influenced by the fact that the change desired is well within reach, not deeply hidden in the habits of the other. Sometimes, however, the real grievance is hidden because the trigger for the conflict is only a distant and minute manifestation of a deeper issue. An example of a hidden grievance was the dialogue about TV watching outlined in Chapter 1. When people fight about one person spending too much money, the "real" issue may be rooted in that person's need to buy love, to build self-esteem, to show who is in control, an expression of a value system that focuses on the here-and-now rather than the future—or a host of other feelings and attitudes. Novelist Diane Johnson gives a most detailed and vivid description of how much often lies beneath the surface in conflict situations:[53]

> The fights were all conducted in the same phrases but each phrase was just a formula, stood for pages and pages, a very long list, of hate and pain. I didn't understand this at the time, I admit. I didn't understand for example that every time Gavin said, "And then you bought that fucking chair," which he did say obsessively in the course of every fight, he really meant, "You defied me and went and did what you wanted just as you always do, causing me to feel unimportant and wretched and unattended, unlike my mother, who does what I want, which makes me feel manly, and, because it is an ugly chair which I hate, you are also assailing my comfort and my position in the household, making me feel unwanted and uncomfortable here: and by buying that hideous old secondhand chair when I had said not to, you were reproaching me financially, you were complaining that we couldn't afford a new one, another way of saying, as you constantly seem to, that now that we have all these loathsome brats I ought to disregard my personal development and think about earning money for them, something a man is not obliged to do, as I infer from my own family, where my father's career was sacrosanct and my mother's whole concern was my father, and instead you stick me with all these brats whom you don't even take care of properly, witness their dirty faces and wet pants, and have the nerve to complain to me about needing help and freedom when I did not ask you to bring these brats into the world and when I did, good naturedly, help you bring the chair home and help you upholster it, that's when I stuck the upholstery needle in my eye you were not sorry although I could have been blinded which is another way of saying castration which is really your game isn't it, isn't it?
>
> There were a number of other formulas: why don't you ever play with the children (me to G.); why don't you ever clean up around here (G. to me); you are rude to our friends (me to G.); you neglect our children and home (G. to me). We would trot these and others out at each quarrel like dominoes and line them up on the board. I was really dumb, I never did

understand the game; I would dump over the board, screeching, "Why are you always bringing up that chair? Can't you forget it? Why do you want to ruin our family about some old chair, what a crazy obsession, sometimes I think you are crazy," and that's when he hit me.

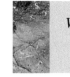

We are going to have peace even if we have to fight for it.

—*Dwight D. Eisenhower*

Conflicts also arise when a person is feeling frustrated, irritable, or depressed because of some event totally unrelated to the person with whom he or she eventually argues. This emotional state simply spills over onto the person at hand and topics of friction are manufactured, even though these topics would be relatively unimportant on another occasion. Conflict may arise out of almost any topic area, but the three most common in marital disputes are *financial matters, communication,* and *sex.* Other frequent sources of dispute include child raising; personal habits—e.g., sleeping and waking patterns, neatness, what and when to eat; responsibilities at home; how to spend leisure time; in-laws and friends; religion; alcohol and drugs; and jealousy. Any of these topics may be a source of superficial or serious disagreement, depending upon whether it is linked to basic values of the participants.

Couples often fight about seemingly "little things," but when such fights persist, it is often a sign that these "little things" are linked to important values. Power and intimacy are examples of topics that represent core values associated with the relationship, and conflict in these areas has been found to be frequent and damaging.[54] It is also important to recognize that there is no objective way to classify certain topics as "little things"; if somebody thinks some topic is really important, then it is to them and probably to the relationship as well. What could be a nearly unnoticed issue in other circumstances can become a major irritant and source of conflict. In general, if people are uncertain about their relationship or they believe that their partner interferes with (rather than facilitates) their daily activities and goals, they are more likely to think of seemingly little topics as more major conflict issues.[55] Regardless of why they think so, if partners believe their conflicts are severe, the quality of the relationship may depend on them addressing the issues directly, even if the discussions are uncomfortable.[56]

The various sources of conflict are usually the result of behavior in the immediate present, but the past may enter in—"Remember when you did. . . . Well, I never forgave you for that and . . ." Stockpiling sources of conflict from the past provides an almost limitless warehouse of problems that could be introduced; when this happens, the stockpiler's partner will worry more about defensive maneuvers than the problems themselves. Besides identifying the specific cause of the conflict, participants to a constructive outcome generally present the issues or problems one at a time. Admittedly, many issues may be intertwined, but if either participant in the argument feels an information overload, the problem becomes much more difficult to understand and resolve. An example of a subtle escalation to information overload occurs when one participant's complaint is met with a counter complaint or a counter demand over and over until the original complaint is forgotten.

Another set of tactics associated with constructive conflict deals primarily with methods of information exchange and methods of encoding messages. Using this set of tactics, the participants will generally provide each other with enough feedback so that each person's viewpoint is understood by the other person. Obviously, disagreement still may exist when people understand each other, but many conflicts are grounded in misunderstanding. Sometimes when the emotional level of the argument is high, the participants will agree to guidelines for structuring the interaction; these are much like the formal rules used in bargaining. Although this is not a common practice in interpersonal encounters, for which the rules are generally more implicit, sometimes the interactants must stop themselves from stepping on each other's words. In heated conflict situations, any word has the potential to be explosive. The word *precious* does not seem particularly "loaded" out of context, but said in a sarcastic tone in the context of a controversial issue, it can be highly provocative—"Well, I hope you and your *precious* magazine are happy with each other!" In the same way, both partners may use profanity, but it may become problematic only when its perceived use is to disparage or belittle the other.[57] In order to redirect or depress unproductive emotional intensity, some have suggested the use of a ground rule. Using this ground rule, you have to repeat what the other person said (to his or her satisfaction) before stating your own opinion. This drains a good deal of the emotion out of a heated debate and contributes to an understanding of the other's ideas. Generally, responses in constructive conflict are characterized by a spirit of inquiry rather than certainty—knowing what your partner thinks and feels, not knowing what your partner *should* think and feel. Chronic complaining and sarcasm are generally absent because the goal is solving a problem, not gaining superiority over the other person. Although there is less derogatory labeling of the other person ("jerk," "chicken," "numbnut"), we find more statement labeling in constructive conflict. **Statement labeling** is simply the identification of a statement as a fact, feeling, or inference. Notice the differences in this example:

Statement labeling: The identification of a statement as a fact, feeling, or inference.

Inference Not Labeled	Inference Labeled
CLYDE: I saw your car parked in front of his house.	CLYDE: I saw a car that looked an awful lot like yours parked in front of his house and I just assumed it was yours.
EMMA: Oh you did, did you? Ol' Eagle-eye, huh? I suppose you got in the car to check the registration in the glove compartment? Or perhaps you checked the serial number?	EMMA: Well, you assumed wrong. It wasn't mine.

A study by Sillars suggests that Emma and Clyde might have profited from a lesson in qualifying and labeling their statements about what's going on in a conflict interaction.[58] When Sillars asked couples to view a videotape of an argument they had with their partner and report their thoughts and feelings, the interactants tended to avoid using qualifiers like "from my perspective, it looks like . . ." or "I'm not sure, but he seems to be. . . ." Inference labeling also was infrequent. Instead, these couples tended to be quite assertive and confident about their analysis of what transpired on the videotape, saying things such as "She's lying" and "He wants to change the topic because he knows I'm right."

More pausing and reflection, rather than a constant rapid-fire exchange of opinions, are usually a part of constructive conflict. These time-outs serve both the speaker and the listener. The person who pauses may communicate that he or she is indeed giving serious thought to the ideas presented by the other. The pausing time can be useful for getting a grip on one's feelings or for deciding how to phrase an idea. It also can be useful for just cooling off or for considering the many ramifications of the other's messages. It can be valuable time to reflect on the pattern of resolution that previous arguments with this person have taken and how this conflict is likely to come out.

Negative problem talk: Expressing problems in a way that the negative tone overshadows the problem itself.

Negative solution talk: Presenting unreasonable, unrealistic, or impractical solutions.

Mindreading: Assuming complete knowledge of the other person's thoughts and motives.

Critical talk: Focusing on your and your partner's flaws.

Listening talk: Showing that you have heard and understood your partner's message.

Positive problem talk: Attempting to provide information about the problem in a focused, specific, and relatively neutral manner.

As a result of studying couples in conflict for many years, Notarius and Markman concluded that certain types of talk make constructive conflict more likely and certain types of talk make it less likely. For constructive conflict,[59] they suggest *decreasing* the following: (1) **Negative problem talk**—that is, the problem is presented in such a way that the speaker's position on the problem overshadows the problem itself. This can be done by a nasty tone of voice, sarcasm, pessimism, yelling, and so on. (2) **Negative solution talk**—that is, presenting unreasonable, unrealistic, impractical solutions. Usually, it will be clear from the proposed solution that one's partner is somehow responsible for any perceived inadequacies in the proposed plans. (3) **Mindreading**—that is, the assumption of complete knowledge of the other person's thoughts and motives. (4) **Critical talk**—that is, evaluating oneself or one's partner by focusing on the flaws. Critical talk can be especially harmful because, as Notarius and Markman say: "One zinger will erase twenty acts of kindness."

At the same time we are trying to decrease the frequency of the preceding, Notarius and Markman suggest we try to *increase* (1) **Listening talk**—that is, talk that shows you have at least heard and perhaps understood your partner's message. Making your partner feel understood does not mean you must agree with him or her. It may mean only that you communicate your involvement through nods, eye gaze, posture, and a verbalization that acknowledges what your partner has said (without a tone of voice or other comments that evaluate the worth of the message). (2) **Positive problem talk**—that is, attempts to provide information about the problem in a focused, specific, and relatively neutral manner.

When trying to solve a problem, it is important to determine whether the problem demands action or demands listening, comforting, and stroking. Some people who, upon hearing the basic outline of a problem, start trying to devise action plans for the two parties involved. No matter how many solutions people have in their bags of tricks, or how pragmatic those solutions, it still is a restricted communicative response pattern if action is the only type of response. Sometimes people just need to lay out a problem to another person who cares about them—the child who complains that another child has been mean to him or her may want only to be held and soothed. Compromise is the hallmark of constructive conflict and, more often than not, the ability to compromise arises out of the ability to understand that our partner's view of reality is just as real and just and as "right" as ours.

After the Fight

Participants in constructive conflict are aware that issues are in process—that the end of any given argument or confrontation does not neatly wrap up the issue forever. Following an argument on a certain issue are several common behaviors: (1) The *confrontation is periodically reviewed* after both participants have cooled off and gained distance—"Boy, you really had me worried the other night when you were yelling and your hand started curling around the butcher knife." (2) The *participants apprise each other with progress reports on the agreed solutions*—"Wait a minute, I thought we agreed to tell each other when we'd be late getting home." (3) **Reassurance rituals** *follow the argument*—a bouquet of flowers with a card that reads "together again" or the familiar kiss (or shake) and make up. These reassurance rituals also may take the form of supportive statements for new behavior that reflects congruence with the agreed-on solution. They are an effort to reestablish the unity of the pair since the confrontation had numerous overtones of differentiating. The absence of such rituals may, of course, be the source of another conflict—"If you really cared about me, you would have . . . " (4) *Forecasts and tests are presented to each other* that offer hypothetical situations to provide information on areas of potential conflict in a generally detached rather than involved climate—"What would you do if you were away from me and an attractive man wanted to sleep with you?" If a firm stand is taken in these hypothetical discussions, it may serve to strengthen the commitment of both parties to the behavior or attitude in question. It also follows, however, that if future behavior does not seem to be congruent with the earlier stated position, one party may be doubly angry.

Reassurance rituals: Attempts to reestablish the unity of the pair after a conflict has suggested differentiation.

One of the most important lessons to be learned about conflict resolution is the ability to let the other people **save face**.[60] People often say things they don't mean, but this propensity is particularly evident during conflicts. If one participant holds the other to everything he or she says and obliges that person to defend it, he or she will. The defense may be judged logically feeble, but it won't lack for emotional vigor—a pattern not representative of constructive conflict. Even if it seems clear to one person that the other is totally wrong, it is helpful in future dialogues if the fault is shared—"I guess I wasn't making myself very clear, and. . . . " Kicking a person while he or she is down is the antithesis of efforts at face saving. Nor is the self-serving line "See! I told you . . . ," which emphasizes who "won" or who was "right" but may also create greater distance between the relationship partners. Apologies, if done well, can go a long way toward healing wounds caused by arguments and in establishing a constructive basis for future interactions (see insert below).

Save face: Attempts to minimize the importance of the conflict to each other's identity.

Making an Apology

Apologies, like any communication behavior, are effective to the extent that they get the response that the communicator wants. Thus, an apology can be effective and not follow these recommendations. Still, the following advice provides some useful general guidelines for making your apologies more effective.

- If your goal is to make an effective apology, begin by avoiding *pseudo-apologies*. Pseudo-apologies start out like an apology but end up putting the blame on the other person. For example, "I'm sorry you can't take a joke." Instead of saying, "I'm sorry you're so upset," you might consider, "I'm sorry I did X, which upset you" Using conditional terms such as, "I'm sorry *if* I upset you" can create doubt about whether you perceived the other person as upset and/or suggest that you might not be sorry if the target of your behavior wasn't visibly upset.

- Effective apologies acknowledge the specific offense and explain what happened but do not emphasize excuses for the behavior. Lengthy and repeated efforts directed at "the reason I did X was . . ." may give the impression you are trying to legitimize the behavior or blame it on somebody else rather than apologize for it.

- Effective apologies are given earnestly and sincerely. Expressions of regret and remorse are not taken or given lightly. The person giving the apology should look directly at the other person and communicate how important that other's reactions and feelings are to him or her. Don't appear to be grudgingly saying it: "Ok, I guess . . . well . . . maybe I was wrong . . . and . . . well . . . um . . . ok, so I'm sorry."

- Effective apologies are unhurried. The apology may serve only as a prelude to a longer discussion. A hurried apology signals that it is being performed as a duty and there are other priorities that the apologizer wants to get to.

- Effective apologies offer to make amends and/or make promises for change in the future. Obviously, any concrete actions illustrating such intentions will serve as powerful testimony to any verbal statements.

- Apologies, like any other communication behavior, can be overdone. Apologizing too often will eventually reduce its impact and effectiveness; not apologizing enough may deprive a relationship of an important form of healing.

* *

For more on apologies, see S. J. Scher and J. M. Darley, "How Effective Are the Things People Say to Apologize? Effects of the Realization of the Apology Speech Act," *Journal of Psycholinguistic Research*

26 (1997): 127–140; S. Heitler, *The Power of Two: Secrets of a Strong and Loving Marriage.* Oakland, CA.: New Harbinger, 1997; A. Freeman and R. DeWolf, *Woulda, Coulda, Shoulda: Overcoming Regrets, Mistakes, and Missed Opportunities.* New York: HarperCollins Perrenial, 1992.

The act of face saving often attempts to negate or minimize the importance, relevance, or even existence of the other person's potentially embarrassing or destructive behavior. **Forgiveness,** on the other hand, requires the acknowledgement of a behavior perceived by at least one person to be damaging to him- or herself or to the relationship. Forgiveness may be given in order to recognize the transgressor's remorse, to preserve the relationship, or both. Forgiveness is not likely to occur when the transgression is too severe, has occurred too often, or is believed to be ongoing. When the transgressor has not apologized or the sincerity of the apology is questioned, forgiveness also is less likely.[61] By offering forgiveness, the forgiver is not saying the behavior was acceptable. Instead, forgiveness is intended to communicate the desire to avoid retaliation, put the hurtful act away, and move on to more constructive acts for the relationship. Forgiveness can be given verbally or nonverbally, unconditionally or conditionally. Conditional forgiveness may mean that "you are forgiven if it doesn't happen again."[62]

> Forgiveness: Expressing the desire to avoid retaliation, put the hurtful act away, and move on to more constructive acts for the relationship.

Most of us want others to forgive us our mistakes, but many people find it difficult to forgive others. Forgiveness incorporates sympathy, compassion, and tenderness, and this is not easy when another's behavior has hurt them. Saying you forgive someone and then acting in ways that show you have not is all too common and can make matters even worse. When the person supposed to be receiving forgiveness realizes he or she is still being punished for the transgression, that person may think he or she has nothing to lose by committing another destructive act—usually initiated by an argument about whether he or she has truly been forgiven. Research shows that the people who are best able to forgive are those who are best able to empathize with the emotional and behavioral perspective of the transgressor. In addition, those who have difficulty thinking of a time when they offended someone seem far less likely to have forgiven someone when they were offended.[63]

To avoid giving the wrong impression caused by our emphasis on conflict, we reiterate several important points: First, conflict is inevitably a part of intimate relationships. No matter how intimate our relationship is, it will have both constructive and destructive conflict. Since intimates are more committed to the relationship, they will try to minimize the destructive conflict; so we would predict less destructive conflict among intimates. Second, the behaviors that we detailed as representative of constructive conflict are simultaneously extraordinarily important and useful and extremely hard to put into practice. Such behaviors are especially difficult to incorporate into your own style of conflict management, once conflict has begun. And since few of us have the motivation to practice conflict strategies in the absence of conflict, the best advice may be to practice observing, analyzing, and reflecting on the conflicts of others in an effort to gain a greater understanding of and control over your own behavior.[64]

Summary

This chapter addressed three areas of communication that are crucial in the maintenance of relationships. In the area of self-disclosure, the primary question for relationship partners is what to reveal and what to keep secret. Relationships maintain themselves with the proper dosage of both. Disclosing personal information about oneself is typical of partners who desire increased intimacy. These acts of revelation about self are frequently reciprocated when each person wants to increase intimacy. And, although disclosures may be fewer in number as a relationship ages, self-disclosures still can be a potent force in gaining intimacy and trust. Each couple develops their own norms for the content, timing, style, and impact of self-revelations. Since disclosures from or about oneself also can be manipulative or hurtful, we proposed a model for assessing the nature of a disclosure for each partner. This model depicts self-disclosures varying on the following dimensions: how many people know the information and how many can be told, how personal or "owned" the information is, how specific it is, how much risk/vulnerability there is for the discloser, how much understanding/acceptance is expected from the target, and whether reciprocity is expected.

In the area of lying, the primary questions for relationship partners involve the establishment of rules concerning lies and identifying which behavior would constitute a violation of the rules. We don't like to talk about it in this manner, but lies can both help as well as destroy a relationship. In close relationships, we identified three characteristics that affect the nature of lies and lie detection. Mutual influence was the phrase we used to indicate how each partner to a close relationship plays a part in the way lying develops and the impact it has on the relationship. Sometimes we do not want to face the possibility that our behavior precipitated lying on the part of our partner or that by "looking the other way" we give tacit approval to it. Close relationships also have the potential for multiple exposure to a lie. This is bound to affect both the liar's and the detector's strategies. Because trust is a characteristic of close relationships, a liar's first lies will not be suspected. But once suspicion is raised and there is a desire to uncover the lie, a person who knows the liar and his or her behavior best will probably be the best detector. Some stereotypical categories of lying behaviors were presented under the headings of anxiety responses, excessive responses, incongruous responses, and indirect responses.

In the area of fighting, the primary question for the relationship partners is how to engage in constructive conflict so the relationship will profit. Conflict in close relationships is a fact of life that, like lying, has the capacity to completely destroy a relationship or to strengthen it. Withdrawal from the interaction and a lack of sensitivity to feelings were two common problems associated with conflict resolution by couples in unsatisfactory marriages. Our discussion of constructive conflict identified many suggestions for positive behavior, but one of the most important is the overall attitude each partner brings to the conflict. If each partner believes he or she can solve the problem only as part of a team and that it is worth working on for the good of the relationship, many of the specific techniques we mentioned will come naturally.

Relationship Maintenance

Canary, D. J., and Dainton, M., "Maintaining Relationships." In A. L. Vangelisti and D. Perlman, eds., *The Cambridge Handbook of Personal Relationships*, pp. 727–743. New York: Cambridge University Press, 2006.

Dainton, M., and Aylor, B. "Routine and Strategic Maintenance Efforts: Behavioral Patterns, Variations Associated with Relational Length, and the Prediction of Relational Characteristics." *Communication Monographs* 69 (2002): 52–66.

Gordon, A. M., Impett, E. A., Kogan, A., Oveis, C., and Keltner, D. "To Have and to Hold: Gratitude Promotes Relationship Maintenance in Intimate Bonds." *Journal of Personality and Social Psychology* 103 (2012): 257–274.

Johnson, A. J. "College Students' Use of Relational Management Strategies in Email in Long-Distance and Geographically Close Relationships." *Journal of Computer-Mediated Communication* 13 (2008): 381–404.

Merolla, A. J. "Relational Maintenance and Noncopresence Reconsidered: Conceptualization Geographic Separation in Close Relationships." *Communication Theory* 20 (2010): 169–193.

Ogolsky, B., and Monk, J. "Maintaining Relationships." In A. L. Vangelisti & D. Perlman, eds., pp. 523–537. *Cambridge Handbook of Personal Relationships*. New York: Cambridge University Press, 2018.

Stafford, L., Dainton, M., and Haas, S. "Measuring Routine and Strategic Relational Maintenance: Scale Revision, Sex Versus Gender Roles, and the Prediction of Relational Characteristics." *Communication Monographs* 67 (2000): 306–323.

Tong, S. T., and Walther, J. B. "Relational Maintenance and CMC." In K.B. Wright and L.M. Webb, eds., pp. 98–118. *Computer-Mediated Communication in Personal Relationships*. New York: Lang, 2011.

Self-Disclosure, Confidentiality, and Trust

Baxter, L. A., and Wilmot, W. W. "'Secret Tests': Social Strategies for Acquiring Information About the State of the Relationship." *Human Communication Research* 11 (1984): 171–201.

Bazarova, N. N. "Online Disclosure." In C. R. Berger and M. E. Roloff, eds., *The International Encyclopedia of Interpersonal Communication*. Hoboken, NJ: Wiley-Blackwell, 2015.

Caughlin, J. P., Petronio, S., and Middleton, A. V. "When Families Manage Private Information." In A. L. Vangelisti ed., *Routledge Handbook of Family Communication*, 2nd ed., pp. 321–337. New York: Routledge, 2013.

Caughlin, J. P., Scott, A. M., Miller, L. E., & Hefner, V. "Putative Secrets: When Information is Supposedly a Secret." *Journal of Social and Personal Relationships* 26 (2009): 713–743.

Derlega, V. J., and Chaikin, A. L. *Sharing Intimacy: What We Reveal to Others and Why.* Englewood Cliffs, NJ: Prentice Hall, 1975.

Dindia, K. "Self-Disclosure, Self-Identity, and Relationship Development: A Transactional/Dialectical Perspective." In S. Duck, ed., *Handbook of Personal Relationships.* 2nd ed., pp. 411–426. New York: Wiley, 1997.

Finkenauer, C., Kerkhof, P., and Pronk, T. "Self-Disclosure in Relationships: Revealing and Concealing Information about Oneself to Others." In A. L. Vangelisti and D. Perlman, eds., *The Cambridge Handbook of Personal Relationships* 2nd ed., pp. 271–281. New York: Cambridge University Press, 2018.

Holmes, J. G. "Trust and the Appraisal Process in Close Relationships." In W. H. Jones and D. Perlman, eds., *Advances in Personal Relationships,* pp. 57–104. London: Jessica Kingsley, 1991.

Jourard, S. *Self-Disclosure: The Experimental Investigation of the Transparent Self.* New York: Wiley, 1971.

Kim, J., and Dindia, K. "Online Self-Disclosure: A Review of Research." In K. B. Wright and L. M. Webb, eds., *Computer-Mediated Communication in Personal Relationships,* pp. 156–180. New York: Lang, 2011.

Parks, M. R. "Ideology in Interpersonal Communication: Off the Couch and Into the World." In M. Burgoon, ed., *Communication Yearbook 5,* pp. 79–107. New Brunswick, NJ: Transaction, 1982.

Petronio, S. "Communication Privacy Management Theory: Understanding Families." In D. O. Braithwaite, E. A. Suter, and K. Floyd, eds., *Engaging Theories in Family Communication: Multiple Perspectives,* 2nd. ed., pp. 87–97. New York: Routledge, 2018.

Rosenfeld, L. B. "Self-Disclosure Avoidance: Why Am I Afraid To Tell You Who I Am." *Communication Monographs* 46 (1979): 63–74.

Ruppel, E., Gross, C., Stoll, A., Peck, B. S., Allen, M., and Kim, S. "Reflecting on Connecting: Meta-Analysis of Differences Between Computer-Mediated and Face-to-Face Self-Disclosure." *Journal of Computer-Mediated Communication* 22 (2017): 18–34.

Vangelisti, A. "Family Secrets: Forms, Functions and Correlates." *Journal of Social and Personal Relationships* 11 (1994): 113–135.

Lying

Cole, T. "Lying to the One You Love: The Use of Deception in Romantic Relationships." *Journal of Social and Personal Relationships* 18 (2001): 107–129.

DePaulo, B. M., Lindsay, J. J., Malone, B. E., Muhelbruck, L., Charlton, K., and Cooper, H. "Cues to Deception." *Psychological Bulletin* 129 (2003): 74–118.

Ekman, P. *Telling Lies: Clues to Deceit in the Marketplace, Politics, and Marriage.* 4th. ed., New York: Norton, 2009.

Knapp, M. L., McGlone, M. S., Griffen, D. J., and Earnest, W. *Lying and Deception in Human Interaction* 2nd. ed. Dubuque, IA: Kendall Hunt, 2016.

Knapp, M. L., and Comadena, M. E. "Telling It Like It Isn't: A Review of Theory and Research on Deceptive Communications." *Human Communication Research* 5 (1979): 270–285.

Knapp, M. L., Hart, R. P., and Dennis, H. S. "An Exploration of Deception as a Communication Construct." *Human Communication Research* 1 (1974): 15–29.

Levine, T. R., and Knapp, M. L. "Lying and Deception in Close Relationships." In A. L. Vangelisti and D. Perlman, eds., *The Cambridge Handbook of Personal Relationships* 2nd ed., pp. 329–340. New York: Cambridge University Press, 2018.

Levine, T. R. "Truth-Default Theory (TDT): A Theory of Human Deception and Deception Detection." *Journal of Language and Social Psychology* 33 (2014): 378–392.

Levine, T. R. "New and Improved Accuracy Findings in Deception Detection Research." *Current Opinion in Psychology* 6 (2015): 1–5.

McCornack, S. A., and Parks, M. R. "Deception, Detection and Relationship Development: The Other Side of Trust." In M. L. McLaughlin, ed., *Communication Yearbook 9,* pp. 377–389. Beverly Hills, CA: Sage, 1986.

McGlone, M. S., and Knapp, M. L., eds., *The Interplay of Truth and Deception: New Agendas in Theory and Research.* NY: Routledge, 2009.

Rowatt, W. C., Cunningham, M. R., and Druen, P. B. "Deception to Get a Date." *Personality and Social Psychology Bulletin* 24 (1998): 1228–1242.

Vrij, A. "Detecting Lies and Deceit: Pitfalls and Opportunities in Nonverbal and Verbal Lie Detection." In C. R. Berger, ed., *Interpersonal Communication: Handbooks of Communication Science*, vol 6, pp. 321–346. Berlin, Germany: De Gruyter Mouton, 2014.

Conflict

Alberts, J. K. "An Analysis of Couples' Conversational Complaints." *Communication Monographs* 55 (1988): 182–197.

Birditt, K. S., Brown, E., Orbuch, T. L., and McIlvane, J. M. "Marital Conflict Behaviors and Implications for Divorce over 16 Years." *Journal of Marriage and Family* 72 (2010): 1188–1204.

Booth, A., Crouter, A. C., and Clements, M., eds., *Couples in Conflict.* Mahwah, NJ: Erlbaum, 2001.

Canary, D. J., and Canary, H. E. "Conflict in Close Relationships." In C. R. Berger, ed., *Interpersonal Communication: Handbooks of Communication Science: Vol 6*, pp. 177–199. Berlin, Germany: De Gruyter Mouton, 2014.

Caughlin, J. P., Basinger, E. D., and Sharabi, L. L. (2017). "The Connections between Communication Technologies and Relational Conflict: A Multiple Goals and Communication Interdependence Perspective. In J. A. Samp, ed., *Communicating Interpersonal Conflict in Close Relationships: Contexts, Challenges and Opportunities*, pp. 57–72. New York: Routledge, 2017.

Caughlin, J. P., Vangelisti, A. L., and Mikucki-Enyart, S. "Conflict in Dating and Marital Relationships." In J. G. Oetzel and S. Ting-Toomey, eds., *Sage Handbook of Conflict Communication: Integrating Theory, Research, and Practice*, 2nd ed., pp 161–186. Thousand Oaks, CA: Sage, 2013.

Gottman, J. M., and Silver, N. *What Makes Love Last? How to Build Trust and Avoid Betrayal.* New York Simon & Schuster, 2012.

Markman, H. J., Stanley, S. M., and Blumberg, S. L. *Fighting for Your Marriage: Positive Steps for Preventing Divorce and Preserving a Lasting Love.* San Francisco, CA: Jossey-Bass, 2001.

McNulty, J. K, and Russell, M. "When 'Negative' Behaviors are Positive: A Contextual Analysis of the Long-Term Effects of Problem-Solving Behaviors on Changes in Relationship Satisfaction." *Journal of Personality and Social Psychology* 98 (2010): 587–604.

Noller, P., Feeney, J. A., Bonnell, D., and Callan, V. J. "A Study of Conflict in Early Marriage," *Journal of Social and Personal Relationships* 11 (1994): 233–252.

Olson, D. H., and Ryder, R. G. "Inventory of Marital Conflicts (IMC): An Experimental Interaction Procedure." *Journal of Marriage and the Family* 32 (1970): 443–448.

Olson, L. N., and Dohahey, A. "Four Horsemen of the Apocalypse: A Framework for Understanding Family Conflict." In D. O. Braithwaite, E. A. Suter, and K. Floyd, eds., *Engaging Theories in Family Communication: Multiple Perspectives*, 2nd. ed., pp. 154–163. New York: Routledge, 2018.

Overall, N. C., and McNulty, J. K., "What Type of Communication during Conflict is Beneficial for Intimate Relationships?" *Current Opinion in Psychology* 13 (2017): 1–5.

Peterson, D. R. "Conflict." In, H. H. Kelley et al., eds. *Close Relationships,* pp. 360–396. New York: Freeman, 1983.

Roloff, M. E., and Chiles, B. W. "Interpersonal Conflict: Recent Trends." In M. L. Knapp and J. A. Daly, eds., *Handbook of Interpersonal Communication,* 4th ed., pp. 423–442. Thousand Oaks, CA: Sage, 2011.

Siegert, J. R., and Stamp, G. H. "'Our First Big Fight' as a Milestone in the Development of Close Relationships." *Communication Monographs* 61 (1994): 345–360.

Sillars, A. L. "Interpersonal Conflict." In C. R. Berger, M. E. Roloff, and D. R. Roskos-Ewoldsen, eds., pp. 273–290. *Handbook of Communication Science,* 2nd ed., Los Angeles, CA: Sage, 2010.

Sillars, A. L., and Canary, D. J. "Family Conflict Communication and Linkages to Relational Quality." In A. L. Vangelisti, ed., *The Routledge Handbook of Family Communication*, 2nd ed., pp. 338–357. New York: Routledge, 2013.

Whitton, S. W., James-Kangal, N., Rhoades, G. K., and Markman, H. J. "Understanding Couple Conflict." In A. L. Vangelisti and D. Perlman, eds., *The Cambridge Handbook of Personal Relationships* 2nd ed., pp. 297–310. New York: Cambridge University Press, 2018.

Wile, D. B. *After the Fight: A Night in the Life of a Couple.* New York: Guilford Press, 1993.

Notes

1. L. Stafford, M. Dainton, and S. Haas, "Measuring Routine and Strategic Relational Maintenance: Scale Revision, Sex versus Gender Roles, and the Prediction of Relational Characteristics," *Communication Monographs* 67 (2000): 306–323; M. Dainton and B. Aylor, "Routine and Strategic Maintenance Efforts: Behavioral Patterns, Variations Associated with Relational Length, and the Prediction of Relational Characteristics," *Communication Monographs* 69 (2002): 52–66; D. J. Canary and L. Stafford, *Communication and Relational Maintenance* (New York: Academic Press, 1994); also see K. Dindia, "Relational Maintenance." In C. Hendrick and S. S. Hendrick, eds., *Close Relationships: A Sourcebook* (Thousand Oaks, CA: Sage, 2000), pp. 287–299; B. G. Ogolsky and J. R. Bowers, "A Meta-Analytic Review of Relationship Maintenance and Its Correlates," *Journal of Social and Personal Relationships* 30 (2012): 343–367.

2. M. K. Laliker and P. J. Lannutti. "Remapping the Topography of Couples' Daily Interactions: Electronic Messages." *Communication Research Reports* 31 (2014): 262–271.

3. S.T. Tong and J.B. Walther. "Relational Maintenance and Computer-Mediated Communication." In K.B. Wright and L.M. Webb, eds., *Computer-Mediated Communication in Personal Relationships*, pp. 98–118. (New York: Lang 2011).

4. A. M. Gordon, E. A. Impett, A. Kogan, C. Oveis, and D. Keltner. "To Have and to Hold: Gratitude Promotes Relationship Maintenance in Intimate Bonds." *Journal of Personality and Social Psychology* 103 (2012): 257–274.

5. D. J. Canary and M. Dainton, "Maintaining Relationships." In A. L. Vangelisti and D. Perlman, eds., *The Cambridge Handbook of Personal Relationships,* pp. 727–743 (New York: Cambridge University Press, 2006). C. E. Rusbult, S. M. Drigotas, and J. Verette, "The Investment Model: An Interdependence Analysis of Commitment Processes and Relationship Maintenance Phenomena. In D. J. Canary and L. Stafford, eds., *Communication and Relational Maintenance*, pp. 115–140 (New York, Academic Press, 1994).

6. D. Canary and L. Stafford, "Relational Maintenance Strategies and Equity in Marriage." *Communication Monographs* 59 (1992): 243–267.

7. N. N. Bazarova, "Online Disclosure." In C. R. Berger and M. E. Roloff, eds., The International Encyclopedia of Interpersonal Communication. (Hoboken, NJ: Wiley-Blackwell, 2015).

8. L. Emanuel, G. J. Neil, C. Bevan, D. S. Fraser, S. V. Stevenage, M. T. Whitty, and S. Jamison-Powell. "Who am I? Representing the Self Offline and in Different Online

Contexts. *Computers in Human Behavior* 41 (2014): 146–152; E. Ruppel, C. Gross, A. Stoll, B. S. Peck, M. Allen, and S. Kim, "Reflecting on Connecting: Meta-Analysis of Differences Between Computer-Mediated and Face-to-Face Self-Disclosure." *Journal of Computer-Mediated Communication* 22 (2017): 18–34.

9   J. Hall, "When is Social Media Use Social Interaction? Defining Mediated Social Interaction." *New Media & Society* 20 (2018): 162–179; J. Lee, O. Gillath, and A. Miller "Effects of Self and Partner's Online Disclosure on Relationship Intimacy and Satisfaction." *PLOS ONE* 14: (2019) e0212186.

10   A. Mathews, V. J. Derlega, and J. Morrow, "What Is Highly Personal information and How Is It Related to Self-Disclosure Decision-Making? The Perspective of College Students," *Communication Research Reports* 23 (2006): 85–92.

11   E. K. Ruppel, "Use of Communication Technologies in Romantic Relationships: Self-disclosure and the Role of Relationship Development," *Journal of Social and Personal Relationships* 32 (2015): 667–686; E. K. Ruppel, C. Gross, A. Stoll, B. S. Peck, M. Allen, and S. Kim. "Reflecting on Connecting: Meta-Analysis of Differences between Computer-Mediated and Face-to-Face Self-Disclosure," *Journal of Computer-Mediated Communication* 22 (2016): 18–34.

12   S. Sprecher, "The Effects of Self-Disclosure Given and Received on Affection for an Intimate Partner and Stability of the Relationship," *Journal of Social and Personal Relationships* 4 (1987): 115–127; J. S. Gore, S. E. Cross, and M. L. Morris, "Let's be Friends: Relational Self-Construal and the Development of Intimacy," *Personal Relationships,* 13 (2006): 83–102.

13   J. W. Pennebaker, *Opening Up: The Healing Power of Expressing Emotions*, rev. ed. (New York: Guilford Press, 1997).

14   A. E. Kelly, J. A. Klusas, R. T. von Weiss, and C. Kenny, "What is it about Revealing Secrets That is Beneficial?" *Personality and Social Psychology Bulletin* 27, (2001): 651–665; M. Shim, J. N. Cappella, and J. Y. Han, "How Does Insightful and Emotional Disclosure Bring Potential Health Benefits? Study Based on Online Support Groups for Women with Breast Cancer," *Journal of Communication* 61 (2011): 432–454.

15   S. Petronio, "The Ramifications of a Reluctant Confidant." In A. C. Richards and T. Schumrum, eds., *Invitations to Dialogue: The Legacy of Sidney Jourard* (Dubuque, IA: Kendall/Hunt Publishers, 2000), pp. 113–132.

16   M. E. Roloff and D. E. Ifert, "Conflict Management Through Avoidance: Withholding Complaints, Suppressing Arguments, and Declaring Topics Taboo." In S. Petronio, ed., *Balancing the Secrets of Private Disclosures* (Mahwah, NJ: Erlbaum, 2000), pp. 151–163; also see M. E. Roloff, and C. N. Wright, "Conflict Avoidance: A Functional Analysis." In T. D. Afifi and W. A. Afifi, eds., *Uncertainty, Information Management, and Disclosure Decisions* (New York: Routledge, 2009), pp. 320–340; W. A. Afifi and L. K. Guerrero, "Motivations Underlying Topic Avoidance in Close Relationships." *Balancing the Secrets of Private Disclosures* (Mahwah, NJ: Erlbaum, 2000), pp. 165–179.

17   J. P. Caughlin and A. M. Scott, "Toward a Communication Theory of the Demand/Withdraw Pattern of Interaction in Interpersonal Relationships." In S. Smith and S. R. Wilson, eds., *New Directions in Interpersonal Communication* (Thousand Oaks, CA: Sage, 2010), pp. 180–200; M. E. Roloff and D. Ifert, "Antecedents and Consequences of Explicit Agreements to Declare a Topic Taboo in Dating Relationships," *Personal Relationships* 5 (1998): 191–205.

18   J. P. Caughlin, S. Mikucki-Enyart, A. V. Middleton, A. Stone, and L. Brown, "Being Open without Talking about It: A Rhetorical/Normative Approach to Understanding Topic Avoidance in Families after a Lung Cancer Diagnosis. *Communication Monographs* 78 (2011): 409–436; E. Donovan-Kicken, and J. P. Caughlin, "A Multiple Goals Perspective on Topic Avoidance and Relationship Satisfaction in the Context of Breast Cancer," *Communication Monographs* 77 (2010): 231–256.

19   S. Petronio, ed., *Balancing the Secrets of Private Disclosures* (Mahwah, NJ: Erlbaum, 2000); S. Petronio, "Communication Privacy Management of Families: What Do We Know?" *Journal of Family Theory and Review* 2 (2010): 175–196; J. Burgoon, "Privacy and Communication." In M. Burgoon, ed., *Communication Yearbook* 6 (Beverly Hills, CA: Sage, 1982), pp. 206–249; T. J. Cottle, "Is Privacy Possible? Exposing Ourselves in Public," *New Republic*, March 8, 1975, pp. 19, 21; P. J. Priest, *Public Intimacies: Talk Show Participants and Tell-All TV* (Cresskill, NJ: Hampton Press, 1995).

20   G. J. McCall and J. L. Simmons, *Identities and Interaction* (New York: Free Press, 1966), pp. 195-196.

21   T. D. Afifi and L. Olson, "The Chilling Effect in Families and the Presure to Conceal Secrets," *Communication Monographs* 72 (2005): 192–216; T. D. Afifi, L. Olson, and C. Armstrong, "The Chilling Effect and Family Secrets: Examining the Role of Self-Protection, Other Protection,

and Communication Efficacy," *Human Communication Research* 31 (2005): 192–216; J. P. Caughlin, W. A. Afifi, K. E. Carpenter-Theune, and L. E. Miller, "Reasons for, and Consequences of, Revealing Personal Secrets in Close Relationships: A Longitudinal Study," *Personal Relationships* 12 (2005): 43–59.

22 L. A. Baxter and W. W. Wilmot, "Taboo Topics in Close Relationships," *Journal of Social and Personal Relationships* 2 (1985): 253–269. Also see A. Vangelisti, "Family Secrets: Forms, Functions and Correlates," *Journal of Social and Personal Relationships* 11 (1994): 113–135; and M. E. Roloff and D. Ifert, "Antecedents and Consequences of Explicit Agreements to Declare a Topic Taboo in Dating Relationships." *Personal Relationships* 5 (1998): 191–205.

23 L. A. Baxter, "Secret Tests: Social Strategies for Acquiring Information About the State of the Relationship," *Human Communication Research* 11 (1984): 171–201. For a discussion of reasons for revealing or hiding information about one's relationship from one's friends, see L. A. Baxter and S. Widenmann, "Revealing and Not Revealing the Status of Romantic Relationships to Social Networks," *Journal of Social and Personal Relationships* 10 (1993): 321–337.

24 Self-disclosures can help each partner reduce uncertainties. See L. K. Knobloch, L. E. Miller, B. J. Bond, and S. E. Mannone, "Relational Uncertainty and Message Processing in Marriage," *Communication Monographs* 74 (2007): 154–180. A related study, not using married couples, found that positive disclosures resulted in more interpersonal attraction, regardless of the depth of disclosure. See S. J. Gilbert and D. Horenstein, "The Communication of Self-Disclosure: Level versus Valence," *Human Communication Research* 1 (1975): 316–322.

25 J. K. Rempel, M. Ross, and J. G. Holmes, "Trust and Communicated Attributions in Close Relationships," *Journal of Personality and Social Psychology* 81 (2001): 57–84.

26 J. K. Rempel, J. G. Holmes, and M. P. Zanna, "Trust in Close Relationships," *Journal of Personality and Social Psychology* 49 (1985): 95–112; J. G. Holmes and J. K. Rempel, "Trust in Close Relationships." In C. Hendrick, ed., *Reviews of Personality and Social Psychology: Close Relationships,* vol. 10 (Newbury Park, CA: Sage, 1989), pp. 187–219.

27 S. Stewart, H. Stinnett, L. B. Rosenfeld, "Sex Differences in Desired Characteristics of Short-Term and Long-Term Relationship Partners." *Journal of Social and Personal Relationships* 17 (2000): 843–853; H. LaFollette and G. Graham, "Honesty and Intimacy," *Journal of Social and Personal Relationships* 3 (1986): 3–18.

28 B. M. DePaulo and D. A. Kashy, "Everyday Lies in Close and Casual Relationships," *Journal of Personality and Social Psychology* 74 (1998): 63–79.

29 S. D. Boon and B. A. McLeod, "Deception in Romantic Relationships: Subjective Estimates of Success at Deceiving and Attitudes Toward Deception," *Journal of Social and Personal Relationships* 18 (2001): 463–476.

30 DePaulo and Kashy, "Everyday Lies,"; B. M. DePaulo and K. L. Bell, "Truth and Investment: Lies Are Told to Those Who Care," *Journal of Personality and Social Psychology* 71 (1996): 703–716; S. Metts, "An Exploratory Investigation of Deception in Close Relationships," *Journal of Social and Personal Relationships* 6 (1989): 159–179; S. Zhang and L. Stafford, "Relational Ramifications of Honest but Hurtful Evaluative Messages in Close Relationships," *Western Journal of Communication* 73 (2009): 481–501.

31 T. Cole, "Lying to the One You Love: The Use of Deception in Romantic Relationships," *Journal of Social and Personal Relationships* 18 (2001): 107–129.

32 S. A. McCornack and T. R. Levine, "When Lies Are Uncovered: Emotional and Relational Outcomes of Discovered Deception," *Communication Monographs* 57 (1990): 119–138.

33 D. E. Anderson, M. E. Ansfield, and B. M. DePaulo, "Love's Best Habit: Deception in the Context of Relationships." In P. Philippot and R. S. Feldman, eds., *The Social Context of Nonverbal Behavior* (New York: Cambridge University Press, 1999), pp. 372–409.

34 M. E. Kaplar and A. K. Gordon, "The Enigma of Altruistic Lying: Perspective Differences in What Motivates and Justifies Lie Telling Within Romantic Relationships," *Personal Relationships* 11 (2004): 489–507.

35 T. R. Levine, "Truth-Default Theory (TDT): A Theory of Human Deception and Deception Detection," *Journal of Language and Social Psychology* 33 (2014): 378–392.

36 M. E. Comadena, "Accuracy in Detecting Deception: Intimate and Friendship Relationships." In M. Burgoon, ed. *Communication Yearbook* 6 (Beverly Hills, CA: Sage, 1982), pp. 446–471. Also see S. A. McCornack and M. R. Parks, "Deception Detection and Relationship Development: The Other Side of Trust." In M. L. McLaughlin, ed., *Communication Yearbook* 9 (Beverly Hills, CA: Sage, 1986), pp. 377–389.

37 L. F. Werth and J. Flaherty, "A Phenomenological Approach to Human Deception." In R. W. Mitchell and N. S. Thompson, eds., *Deception: Perspectives on Human and Nonhuman Deceit* (Albany: SUNY Press, 1986), p. 296.

38 T. R. Levine, "New and Improved Accuracy Findings in Deception Detection Research," *Current Opinion in Psychology* 6 (2015): 1–5.

39 T. R. Levine and S. A. McCornack, "Linking Love and Lies: A Formal Test of the McCornack and Parks Model of Deception Detection," *Journal of Social and Personal Relationships* 9 (1992): 143–154.

40 B. J. Sagarin, K. v. L. Rhoads, and R. B. Cialdini, "Deceiver's Distrust: Denigration as a Consequence of Undiscovered Deception," *Personality and Social Psychology Bulletin* 24 (1998): 1167–1176.

41 B. M. DePaulo, J. J. Lindsay, B. E. Malone, L. Muhelbruck, K. Charlton, and H. Cooper, "Cues to Deception," *Psychological Bulletin* 129 (2003): 74–118.

42 H. S. Park, T. R. Levine, S. A. McCornack, K. Morrison, and M. Ferrara, "How People Really Detect Lies," *Communication Monographs* 69 (2002): 144–157.

43 M. E. Roloff and K. P. Soule, "Interpersonal Conflict: A Review." In M. L. Knapp and J. A. Daly, eds., *Handbook of Interpersonal Communication,* 3rd ed. (Thousand Oaks, CA: Sage, 2002), pp. 475–528. Conflict also is called confrontation; difference of opinion; friendly debate; knock-down, drag-out; discussion; little misunderstanding; spat; disagreement; argument. The choice of labels is often related to (1) one's perception of the magnitude or intensity of the conflict or (2) one's need to reduce or increase the *actual* magnitude or intensity of the conflict—to make the conflict *seem* more trivial or more critical to the relationship than it actually is. Probably the most volatile conflicts take place (1) when the issue is clearly linked to basic and deeply held values and (2) when the relationship has few accumulated rewards.

44 M. A. Fitzpatrick, "Negotiation, Problem Solving and Conflict in Various Types of Marriages." In P. Noller and M. A. Fitzpatrick, eds., *Perspectives on Marital Interaction* (Philadelphia: Multilingual Matters, 1988), pp. 245–270.

45 C. Kelly, T. L. Huston, and R. M. Cate, "Premarital Relationship Correlates of the Erosion of Satisfaction in Marriage," *Journal of Social and Personal Relationships* 2 (1985): 167–178.

46 K. A. McGonagle, R. C. Kessler, and I. H. Gotlib, "The Effects of Marital Disagreement Style, Frequency, and Outcome of Marital Disruption," *Journal of Social and Personal Relationships* 10 (1993): 385–404; R. S. Malis and M. E. Roloff, "Demand/Withdraw Patterns in Serial Arguments: Implications for Well-Being," *Human Communication Research* 32 (2006): 198–216.

47 J. R. Siegert and G. H. Stamp, "'Our First Big Fight' as a Milestone in the Development of Close Relationships," *Communication Monographs* 61 (1994): 345–360.

48 C. Notarius and H. Markman, *We Can Work It Out: Making Sense of Marital Conflict* (New York: Putnam, 1993); N. A. Klinetob and D. Smith, "Demand-Withdraw Communication in Marital Interaction: Tests of Interspousal Contingency and Gender Role Hypotheses," *Journal of Marriage and the Family* 58 (1996): 945–957; G. Bodenmann, A. Kaiser, K. Hahlweg, and G. Fehm-Wolsdorf, "Communication Patterns During Marital Conflict: A Cross-Cultural Replication," *Personal Relationships* 5 (1998): 343–356.

49 This is a somewhat modified version of an actual therapy case reported in G. H. Kline, N. D. Pleasant, S. W. Whitton, and H. J. Markman, "Understanding Couple Conflict." In A. L. Vangelisti and D. Perlman, eds., *The Cambridge Handbook of Personal Relationships.* (New York: Cambridge University Press, 2006.), pp. 445–462.

50 J. P. Caughlin and T. D. Afifi, "When Is Topic Avoidance Unsatisfying? Examining Moderators of the Association Between Avoidance and Dissatisfaction," *Human Communication Research* 30 (2004): 479–513; R. M. Dailey and N. A. Palomares, "Strategic Topic Avoidance: An Investigation of Topic Avoidance Frequency, Strategies Used, and Relational Correlates," *Communication Monographs* 71 (2004): 471–496.

51 A. L. Sillars and D. J. Canary, "Family Conflict Communication and Linkages to Relational Quality." In A. L. Vangelisti, ed., *The Routledge Handbook of Family Communication.* (New York: Routledge, 2013), 2nd ed., pp. 338–357; M. A. Rahim, "A Measure of Styles of Handling Interpersonal Conflict," *Academy of Management Journal* 26 (1983): 368–376.

52 J. M. Gottman, "Emotional Responsiveness in Marital Conversations," *Journal of Communication* 32 (1982): 108–120; J. M. Gottman, *Marital Interaction* (New York: Academic Press, 1979).

53 D. Johnson, *The Shadow Knows* (New York: Knopf, 1974), pp. 62–63. Copyright © 1974 by Diane Johnson. Reprinted by permission of Sll/Sterling Lord Literistic, Inc.

54 L. A. Kurdek, "Areas of Conflict for Gay, Lesbian, and Heterosexual Couples: What Couples Argue About Influences Relationship Satisfaction," *Journal of Marriage and the Family* 56 (1994): 923–934.

55 J. A. Theiss and L. K. Knobloch, "An Actor-Partner Interdependence Model of Irritations in Romantic Relationships," *Communication Research* 36 (2009): 510–537.

56 J. K. McNulty and V. M. Russell, "When "Negative" Behaviors are Positive: A Contextual Analysis of the Long-term Effects of Interpersonal Communication." *Journal of Personality and Social Psychology* 98: (2010): 587–604.

57 S. L. Young, "What the _____ Is Your Problem?: Attribution Theory and Perceived Reasons for Profanity Usage During Conflict," *Communication Research Reports* 21 (2004): 338–347.

58 A. Sillars, L. J. Roberts, T. Dun, and K. E. Leonard, "Stepping into the Stream of Thought: Cognition During Marital Conflict." In V. Manusov and J. H. Harvey, eds., *Attribution, Communication Behavior, and Close Relationships* (New York: Cambridge University Press, 2001), pp. 193–210; A. Sillars, L. J., Roberts, K. E. Leonard, and T. Dun, "Cognition During Marital Conflict: The Relationship of Thought and Talk," *Journal of Social and Personal Relationships* 17 (2000): 479–502.

59 Notarius and Markman, *We Can Work It Out.*

60 S. Metts, "Face and Facework: Implications for the Study of Personal Relationships." In S. Duck, ed., *Handbook of Personal Relationships,* 2nd ed. (New York: Wiley, 1997), pp. 373–390.

61 J. W. Younger, R. L. Piferi, R. L. Jobe, and K. A. Lawler, "Dimensions of Forgiveness: The Views of Laypersons," *Journal of Social and Personal Relationships* 21 (2004): 837–855; J. R. Meyer and K. Rothenberg, "Repairing Regretted Messages: Effects of Emotional State, Relationship Type, and Seriousness of Offense," *Communication Research Reports* 21 (2004): 348–356.

62 V. R. Waldron and D. L. Kelley, "Forgiving Communication as a Response to Relational Transgressions," *Journal of Social and Personal Relationships* 22 (2005): 723–742.

63 M. E. McCullough, E. L. Worthington Jr., and K. C. Rachal, "Interpersonal Forgiving in Close Relationships," *Journal of Personality and Social Psychology* 73 (1997): 321–336; J. W. Younger, R. L. Piferi, R. L. Jobe, and K. A. Lawler, "Dimensions of Forgiveness: The Views of Laypersons," *Journal of Social and Personal Relationships* 21 (2004): 837–855.

64 S. L. Braver and V. Rohrer, "Superiority of Vicarious over Direct Experience in Interpersonal Conflict Resolution," *Journal of Conflict Resolution* 22 (1978): 143–155.

CHAPTER 9

Maintaining Relationships Through Dialogue: Commitment and Intimacy

Dear Dr. Caughlin,

My girlfriend is really nice except she keeps bugging me to say and do stuff to convince her I love her. I tell her I love her every time we are together. But that isn't enough for her. Then I get mad and that doesn't help. What's wrong with her? Is she insecure or something? What can I do? I do love her.

Stumped

There are many ways to communicate the degree of intimacy and commitment one feels for his or her partner. The phrase "I love you" is one way of communicating how you feel about your partner, and sometimes it will be enough. But intimates reveal the kind of relationship they have and want through the language and behavior evidenced in a variety of communicative situations. Some types of talk that are especially revealing about the nature of the relationship are explored in this chapter. The extent to which partners are able to construct dialogue that defines a mutually satisfactory relationship is the extent to which they are able to adequately maintain their relationship.

> *It is the nature of the ongoing verbal and nonverbal behavior that defines intimacy and distinguishes intimate relationships from their less intimate counterparts.*
>
> —*Mark L. Knapp*

The process of maintaining relationships, like the process of establishing relationships, is critically dependent on an understanding of the messages partners exchange. Messages that directly or indirectly communicate information about the closeness or intimacy of the relationship are especially important in determining why relationships are maintained and how satisfying they are to the participants. We begin our understanding of these messages with an examination of commitment and how it can be effectively communicated during the maintenance of close relationships.

Commitment and Commitment Talk

Commitment takes many forms. The form that comes most readily to mind is a kind of commitment based on each partner's degree of attraction for the relationship and each other—a **want to** type of commitment. But we know that people stay in relationships for other reasons as well. Sometimes commitment is based on what one or both partners feel they **have to** do—not what they want to do. This perspective may be associated with the perception that there aren't any good alternatives; that the relationship would be more difficult to end than to keep together; that too much has been invested in the relationship to terminate it; or that coping with the reactions of others would be too difficult. The decision to continue a relationship also can be based on feelings of obligation—an **ought to** orientation. This may be related to the kind of relationship ("Once you get married, you ought to stay married") or to the other person in the relationship ("I was the one who got him into this relationship, so I ought to stay with him").[1] While the obligatory nature of *ought to* commitment motives at first may seem less desirable than *want to* motives, it can be important in sustaining relationships through difficult periods when *want to* motives are challenged. On the other hand, if a couple stays together solely because they think they *ought to*, they may not derive much satisfaction.[2] The important thing to remember about these three different types of commitments is that they will reflect and be reflected in different types of relationship talk.[3] This can be seen in the following six dimensions associated with the strength of one's *want to* commitment.[4]

Perceiving a Rewarding Future

We use information gleaned from interactions with our partner to forecast the future. The extent to which we see a *rewarding future* with our partner increases the strength of our commitment to the relationship. Once the partners have sustained a relationship long enough for the nature of future talk to achieve some reality, the nature of subsequent future talk (and its effects) will change. Talk about the future takes many forms. It may be specifically directed at the future of the relationship, or it may be more general; it may focus on the immediate future or on long-range plans and goals; and it may emphasize the couple or only one partner. Each of these foci has the potential to signal a rewarding future. As with other patterns of communication, we would predict that attempts at constructing rewarding future talk would become more frequent when strain on

Commitment talk: Communication that implicity or explicitly reflects and demonstrates relational commitment.

Want to commitment: Type of commitment based on attraction to the relationship.

Have to commitment: Type of commitment based on obstacles to leaving the relationship.

Ought to commitment: Type of commitment based on a sense of moral obligation to stay in the relationship.

the relationship is felt and there is a desire to "fix" it—for example, "Let's move out of this place to somewhere we can start over. I'll get a job that allows me to be home more and we can have a baby."

© fizkes/Shutterstock.com

Identifying with the Relationship

Our commitment is also gauged by the extent to which we *identify with the relationship.* Just as members of a corporation vary in the extent to which they believe in and accept the company's goals and values, members of a relationship vary in the degree to which they identify with it. In Chapter 2, we said that progress toward more intimacy brought the participants from an "I" orientation to a "We" orientation. More spontaneous plural pronoun use, greater perceptions of unity between the partners, and more relationship centrality are part of what happens when romantic couples become strongly committed to each other.[5] These same couples may, of course, perceive several gradations between "I" and "We" that reflect their growing identification with the relationship, even though these points may be next to impossible to describe.

Perceiving Fewer Attractive Alternatives

The development of any relationship will require the elimination of some alternatives. And higher levels of commitment can be communicated by indicating that there are *fewer attractive alternatives.* In fact, one researcher found the best predictor of relationship failure was high attentiveness to alternatives. As one author put it, "Even if the grass is greener on the other side of the fence, happy gardeners will be less likely to notice."[6] Alternatives may be other potential relationships, but they can also be one's work, a hobby, and so on. When these alternatives are attractive enough to replace some or all of the relationship, it can detract from the perceived commitment to that relationship.

A Willingness to Exert Effort for the Relationship

Most of us have many demands on our time. Those things we single out to devote time, energy, and resources to are perceived as the things we are most committed to. A *willingness to exert effort* on behalf of the relationship may be as varied as helping your partner study for a test or spending time listening to his or her problems. Effort on behalf of the relationship also may involve *sacrifice*—that is, giving up some immediate personal desire in the interest of benefitting the relationship or one's partner. Of course, by benefitting the relationship or one's partner, a person may, in the long term, benefit him- or herself. With committed partners, sacrifice seems to be a natural and appropriate way to express their feelings. It is not the kind of sacrifice that is done with the intent to make the other person feel guilty or indebted. Nor is it something that is done disproportionately by only one partner. Effort in the form of sacrifice may involve major life changes (one person quits a job in order to move to the distant city where his or her partner got a job) or it may simply involve saying something constructive rather than retaliating when one's partner says something demeaning or negative during a fight.[7]

Investing More in the Relationship

As a result of our efforts on behalf of the relationship, we accrue *greater investments* in the relationship. This, in itself, influences commitment. As investments increase, commitment to the relationship also is likely to increase.

Accepting Responsibility for Your Commitment

The last dimension deals with one's *responsibility for relationship commitment.* Commitment strength is related to perceptions that a person's behavior is freely chosen and that he or she is accountable for it. Even though it may be clear that external forces played an important role in the relationship, partners may still attribute their commitment to their free choice—which will have the effect of increasing perceived commitment.

Principle of Least Interest: The person with less interest in a relationship tends to have more control over it and typically determines the outcomes of the relationship, including whether it endures.

When two people are widely discrepant about the preceding dimensions, the **Principle of Least Interest** is relevant. This principle states that the person with less interest in the relationship tends to have more control over it. That is, the person who is less committed to the relationship typically determines the outcomes of the relationship, including whether it endures.

When relationships persist despite different levels of commitment, there will probably be a lot of talk directed at the subject of commitment, and if the partners do not reduce the discrepancy, it can lead to conflict and hostility.[8] When relationship transgressions occur, they often are perceived as indicative of a lowered level of commitment to the relationship. If one partner was highly committed to the relationship, the transgression presents a quandary—for example, should he or she give up something that he or she was strongly committed to or work with his or her partner in order to preserve the relationship?

Since these dimensions do not account for the possibility of strong *ought to* or *have to* motives, the relationship may continue with each partner having very different levels of commitment—for example, one partner who is maintaining the relationship "for the sake of the kids." And even if both partners are extremely committed to the relationship, they are not likely to find themselves closely bunched on the far right of **Figure 9.1** for very long. The far right is a point that represents strong commitment, but it is not necessary to remain at this point once you have demonstrated your ability to get there. For example, once you have thoroughly identified with this relationship through a commitment to "We," you are then allowed to step back and enjoy a bit more of an "I" orientation. But if commitment is ever in question, this will again require movement toward the far-right position. These dimensions are useful for assessing the development of a relationship, but it is not uncommon for people to report a

Figure 9.1	Cognitive/Affective Commitment to the Relationship					
	Prediction of Future Rewards from This Relationship					
Low	1	2	3	4	5	High
	Identification with the Relationship/Sharing Values					
Low	1	2	3	4	5	High
	Unattractive Alternatives to the Relationship					
Low	1	2	3	4	5	High
	Willingness to Exert Effort on Behalf of the Relationship					
Low	1	2	3	4	5	High
	Amount Invested in the Relationship					
Low	1	2	3	4	5	High
	Personal Responsibility for Commitment to the Relationship					
Low	1	2	3	4	5	High

Source: Mark Knapp-Anita Vangelisti-John Caughlin

less systematic development: "Commitment wasn't an issue. We just kept doing things and seeing each other and then one day . . . there we were." In situations such as this, the dimensions in Figure 9.1 can be useful for retrospective analyses.

One final complicating factor about using these dimensions as a guide to commitment concerns the dynamics of interaction. Remember we are dealing with the behavior of two people. Imagine a situation in which both parties are strongly committed to the relationship. Each wants to expend a lot of effort on behalf of the relationship, but one person seems to be doing so much of this that the other person backs off. Since the partner engaging in frequent displays of effort for the relationship perceives little effort on the part of his or her partner, efforts may be intensified with no desired increase forthcoming from the other. Of course, talk about commitment will ensue, and since both partners feel a strong commitment, the type of behavior expected by each in the future can be negotiated. This example points out the importance of *initiation and reciprocity* to the communication of commitment. Initiating acts of commitment have an intensity to them that overshadows the reciprocity of the same act. If you are the first person to say, "I love you," and your partner says, "I love you too," you may perceive a less intense commitment from your partner if he or she doesn't initiate the sentiment on occasion.

Since the phrase "I love you" is such a crucial one in the talk of commitment, let's look at how it manifests itself in dialogue.[9] When dating couples tape-recorded private conversations about their relationship and about the first time "I love you" occurred in their relationship, three types of dialogue were revealed.

The first is called *declaration of love–reciprocation of love.* As the following conversations illustrate, both partners want to express their love, but the actual dialogue allows the pair to gradually work up to explicit declarations.

Example 1

MALE: We've been spending a lot of time together, and I've really begun to feel close.

FEMALE: Yeah, I've felt us growing together into something special. It feels good!

MALE: Maybe we're failing in love! (laughs)

FEMALE: I know, I love you.

MALE: I love you too. (pause) But, I don't know what we'll do now.

FEMALE: Let's just enjoy it. I don't know when I've been so happy!

MALE: Me, too!

In the following conversation, we have an example of *declaration of love–pseudo-reciprocation of love*. These are instances when the other partner's readiness to reciprocate "I love you" is incorrectly assessed.

Example 2

MALE: I've wondered how you feel about me.

FEMALE: Well, I know people see us together all the time.

MALE: I'm beginning to—well—want you around all the time.

FEMALE: You're very special to me.

MALE: I love you.

FEMALE: I do, too. (pause) Now I'm really confused though. I mean, I feel close to you, but I've always considered you a friend. I guess more than a friend now. I don't know.

MALE: Yeah, well, I thought there was something wrong.

The third type is a *declaration of love–refutation of love*. Here the declarer again misconstrues the partner's readiness to reciprocate, but instead of simply being "confused" as in Example 2, the partner is clearly unready to reciprocate.

Example 3

FEMALE: You know, I've really enjoyed our summer. You know, dating and stuff.

MALE: Yeah, well, me too.

FEMALE: I love you, Jack.

MALE: Well, (pause) there's no way you could "love" me after only knowing me only a couple of months.

FEMALE: I love you, anyway.

MALE: I'm sorry, I'm not sure, and I feel pressured.

FEMALE: Well, you're playing with my emotions! I'm gonna treat you so you'll eventually fall in love with me!

MALE:	But I'm not ready for that! I think we should just cool off for a while and not see each other.
FEMALE:	(sobbing) Oh, I give up!

Once a relationship has achieved intimacy and become stabilized, how is the phrase "I love you" manifested? The following discussions by married couples reveal situations when "I love you" is suspect as a forecast for a request or to take the edge off bad news, to recapture feelings of commitment, and to gain assurance that commitment is still there.

Example 4

FEMALE:	Let's see, oh, I know how we say it. It was like this: You called me from work and said: "Joan? I love you" and I said: "I know, me too, what's wrong!?"
MALE:	What!? Why'd you say that!?
FEMALE:	Well, when you start off by telling me you love me you usually did something wrong. Oh, I know, it was 'cause we couldn't go out to eat dinner to celebrate our anniversary.
MALE:	Well, I love you, too.
FEMALE:	I know. (laughs)

Example 5

MALE:	You know, I think we got in the habit of saying "I love you" as—as, well, as a way to assure each other we still care, and in the madness in the midst of both of our careers, the relationship is still the most important thing. Sure, on the phone, we'd both say: "I love you, see you later," and as a way to call each other like: "Hi, love."
FEMALE:	Yeah.
MALE:	But remember when you got that great job and I saw you walking toward me on campus?
FEMALE:	Yeah, I was excited.
MALE:	We hugged and both said: "I love you." That was different.
FEMALE:	I guess we both knew we had jobs we always wanted, but yeah, that meant a lot. It meant *we* were still the most important thing.

Example 6

FEMALE:	I don't know. This is interesting. Do you still love me?
MALE:	Why do you ask?
FEMALE:	Well, I guess I haven't heard you say it in a while.
MALE:	Of course I love you.
FEMALE:	I love you, too. I guess it just feels good to hear it once in a while.
MALE:	Yeah. Now that you mention it, it *does* feel good!

In troubled relationships, the "I love you" phrase may not be enough to convince one's partner he or she is loved. It has become an empty phrase because there have not been enough follow-up behaviors that specifically testify to the declaration of love. Specific behaviors that complement more abstract statements of commitment are always important, but especially so in relationships that are questioning the extent of one's commitment. When 248 people of various ages and from various types of relationships were asked what they did or said to show their commitment to their partner, their responses fell into the following categories:[10]

- Provide Affection—state love, give gifts, show feelings, be intimate.
- Provide Support—build partner up, support decisions, give assistance.
- Maintain Integrity—be faithful, and honest, keep promises.
- Share Companionship—do things together, have fun together, include partner.
- Make Effort to Communicate—listen, stay in contact.
- Show Respect—accept differences, allow individual time, trust partner.
- Create Relational Future—celebrate relational milestones, plan future.
- Create Positive Relationship Atmosphere—be courteous, stay positive, defend partner.
- Work Together on Relationship Problems—talk about problems, manage relationship conflict effectively.
- Express Commitment—explicitly tell partner of intention to remain in the relationship.

Of course, it is not always what you do to show your commitment, but *how you do it* that counts. In fact, the way we enact our commitment talk is at least as important as the content itself. As we noted with the initiation process, *intensity* has a lot to do with the perceived strength of the commitment talk. This may involve rapt attention and focus achieved through long mutual gazes and close proximity; voice volume ("He just kept yelling 'I love Linda' as we walked down the street. It was embarrassing, but it meant a lot to me"); or absolute statements ("I'll *always* love you" or "I'll *never* leave you"). It is important to note that the intensity of commitment talk may be different for establishing a relationship and maintaining it. The absolute statements may taper off as the length of a relationship increases and there is a more rational endorsement of the tentative nature of life and love in general. The use of absolute statements often appears in the early phases of intensifying as an abundance of superlatives—"You have the *greatest* mind of any woman I've ever met." Although this behavior seems to taper off as the relationship stabilizes at a high level of intimacy, it can recur quickly if it appears there is trouble in the relationship and at least one person wants to save it. This pattern is consistent with the idea put forth earlier that as we move toward intimacy we move on a continuum from rigid to flexible in our communication. This idea, however, also suggests that there are certain critical points within advanced stages of intimacy at which rigidity rears its ugly head. It is interesting that the absolutism of the courtship pattern can be beneficial in cementing the commitment of the two parties. It becomes a problem only if the superlatives and "all-ness" terms are interpreted rigidly and used against the other later—"You said you'd do *anything* I wanted . . . well, I want. . . . "

Repetition is another way of performing commitment talk that has the potential for increasing its impact on the relationship. During the early attempts to reach for more intimacy, couples often repeat their commitment over and over—using virtually the same words each time. The first time a person tells you that he or she loves you, it has strong dramatic import. Commitment continues to take the form of "I love you" until, like any word or phrase, it begins to lose its effectiveness. When a person begins to say the words *I love you* like a programmed robot, there will probably be a move to show love in new ways by actions or dialogue that say *I love you* in different ways. In short, the constant repetition of this one phrase has diminished reward value, and new forms of proof often are called for. This is why we may be deceived by analyzing conventional statements about closeness in a relationship when we look at people who have been stabilized at a high level of intimacy for a long time. These couples will have many different ways of stating their commitment, and the frequency will no doubt taper off with intimacy sustained by "reminders" of commitment. When the relationship is threatened or when a partner's commitment is questioned and there is a desire to rejuvenate the relationship, frequent repetition of commitment (often in stereotypical forms used earlier to build the relationship) will recur.

Messages of commitment also vary in the extent to which they reflect *effort* by the communicator. Willingness to expend effort for the relationship was discussed earlier in the context of what is said; here we are dealing with *how* it is said (or done). When others feel we are "working" hard at showing our commitment, the strength of the message more likely will be seen as greater. This doesn't mean you will necessarily respond positively to it. It may be from an ardent lover you don't love.

Commitment talk also may gain strength from *explicitness*. It is harder to back down from messages for which there can be little misinterpretation. Vagueness and equivocation signal less commitment. Obviously, in long-term relationships, commitment talk may seem less explicit to an outsider, but the participants can read into such statements an explicitness of an earlier time. Sometimes this process even allows some rewriting of history—allowing two people who have decided to live out their remaining years together to mentally recall a past that wasn't there—for example, "Bill and I have always given each other 110 percent." Explicitness of commitment talk in the presence of others may sometimes be embarrassing, but it also serves as testimony that a person is willing to stand behind you socially as well as personally.

When commitment is **codified**, it has the effect of making it more permanent—it is a lasting relationship symbol. Writing down one's commitment is commonly done in letters and poems. Some couples also attempt to formalize the conventional marriage contract. These efforts take the form of agreements specifying the division of household responsibilities; rules for sharing income and expenses; expectations for relationships with others outside the marriage;

Codified: (Codification of commitment)—a lasting symbol of partners' intentions for relationship over the long-term.

clauses for changing, renewing, and terminating the contract; as well as others. These efforts are attempts to minimize potentially vast differences in expectations between marriage partners and/or to protect one's resources if the relationship should fail. In addition, such specifics make interpretation of the marriage contract easier than with the traditional contract, which was couched in such lofty, ambiguous terminology that it was subject to almost any interpretation. Some believe that almost any kind of formalized contract is an admission of one's inability to deal with issues as they arise. For these people, contracts suggest a lack of faith and trust in the relationship itself and the parties to the relationship. They may simply want to live together without any type of contract or legally binding document. Over time, however, an informal, unwritten contract or set of rules may develop even for these people. There are obviously many reasons for these formal prenuptial agreements, but there may be downsides.

Any time we make a rule, we begin to limit our alternatives for dealing with unexpected or unforeseen circumstances. When we write that rule down, we make it more permanent. When we ask that our rule be made a legally binding document, we have made it even more difficult to adapt to new and changing circumstances. On one hand, this rigidity serves as testimony to the strength of commitment. Simultaneously, however, it adds a permanence—a hardening that may increase the probabilities of maladaptive communication strategies emerging. For instance, sometimes couples feel that the contract signifies ownership. Either explicitly or implicitly, messages may be based upon the fact that the other person "belongs to me"—"You're my wife and you'll do as I tell you." Some feel the contract tends to increase one's laxity in communicating. That is, the energy expended during courtship can now be forgotten, the hunt is over, the quarry has been captured, and relaxation is the order of the day. Still others believe that the contract legitimizes intrusion into the other's behavior, thoughts, and feelings to the extent that the other person feels no personal identity or freedom—"Now that we've married I can open all your mail, demand to know where you are every minute," and so on. In short, some believe that the existence of a formal relationship contract brings about communication patterns that would never be used in a similar but contract-free relationship. The fact is, however, that nobody knows if this belief is true. No research specifically indicates the prevalence of certain communication patterns in contract relationships that do not exist in contract-free relationships. Still, the existence of a contract probably does influence the way the participants talk to each other, but exactly how much influence and what form that influence takes are yet to be determined. If a person's level of relationship commitment is clear to (i.e., he or she doesn't have to think about it very long), the more likely he or she will enact various behaviors that will signal that level of commitment.[11] But if a person wanted to know which behaviors would help him or her effectively communicate commitment, we would suggest the following. The absence of or opposite of these also may mean commitment is not being effectively communicated:

1. Repeat your commitment over and over in different ways. (Follow "I love you" talk with specific acts that prove it.)
2. Use unqualified, absolute statements.
3. Talk about future relationship rewards.

4. Make public statements of your commitment to the relationship.

5. Make your statements of commitment to the relationship more permanent—for example, in writing.

6. Do things that show effort—that you've gone to a lot of trouble.

7. Initiate at least as much as you respond—showing you don't always wait for the other person to express his or her commitment first.

Personal Idioms

Intimates have some unique speech patterns that distinguish them from nonintimates. Intimates normally have a greater sociological, psychological, and communicative history to their talk. Sometimes, then, they can present a great deal of information in a very few words. The following quote expresses the issue of simplification quite well:

> [T]he speech of intimates is played out against the backdrop of assumptions common to the speakers, against a set of closely shared interests and identifications, against a system of shared expectations; in short, it presupposes a "local cultural identity" which reduces the need for the speakers to elaborate their intent verbally and to make it explicit.[12]

As a result of their relationship history, intimates often develop an interpersonal jargon with private symbols and private meanings, known only to the intimate pair. In addition, they develop words and phrases commonly used by others that have special meanings for them. In such cases, intimates can refer to things in a public gathering that most people interpret one way but that the intimates interpret another—perhaps exchanging a knowing glance or wink to confirm the "special" interpretation. Galvin and Brommel provide this exemplary testimony from one of their informants.

> My sister and I have a long history of intimacy. Since early childhood, we have shared unique communication behavior. Our intimate name-calling is truly unique. Gail refers to me as "Sis," "K. C.," or "Coops." I, in return, call her "Kitten," "G. K.," or "Li'l Coops." As a result of doing many activities together, we acquired the duplex nickname of "The Coop Sisters." Occasionally, my mother refers to me by the name Loree. This is my middle name and the name of her grandmother whom she loved deeply. She is the only one who calls me this. "G. K." and I have always shared some type of personal jargon. This ritual began with our secret language of "witchtalk." "Witchtalk" meant saying the exact opposite of what one really meant. Now, in our current jargon, a romantic relationship is "official" only if one has been kissed by the male and "the bone" refers to a male who is sexually exciting. We also share a peculiar

© Mirelle/Shutterstock.com

handshake which can be interpreted as meaning "I agree with you 100 percent" or "I can identify with you."[13]

These "personal idioms" serve at least two useful functions for the intimates. First, they serve to make the pair a more cohesive unit—to reinforce the identity of the couple as something special or unique. This special language sets them off from those who "don't know the language." The private jargon developed by less intimate groups such as fraternal organizations, prisoners, and soldiers also supports group cohesiveness. Second, personal idioms help a couple define relationship norms. Intimates need to address many issues—such as, how shall we refer to sex, sexual organs, things we don't like about each other, and affectionate feelings? Sometimes personal idioms are an effective substitute for more direct, explicit terminology.

Our interest in these personal idioms prompted us to conduct two studies.[14] We collected 545 idioms from couples ranging in age from 20 to 76. The personal idioms reported to us were classified into the following categories:

1. *Expressions of Affection.* These phrases expressed love and reassured or complimented one's partner. "So Much" and "Hunch Nickle" as well as pulling on the right ear lobe were all idioms reported to mean, "I love you."

2. *Teasing Insults.* This category combines playfulness and derogation— usually through the tactic of "kidding." "Futtbutt," which referred to a woman's buttocks, and "Animal," which was used to refer to unduly aggressive behavior, are examples. Perhaps the act of making a partner's idiosyncrasy the subject of everyday teasing comments or gestures is a way to tell the partner the behavior is bothersome without threatening the equilibrium of the relationship.

3. *Partner Nicknames.* These terms of address included names such as "Boo," "Honski," "Bake," "Tooty," and "Mopsy."

4. *Names for Others.* These were names used for people outside the relationship. For example, "Pizza King" was the label given to a next-door neighbor's lover; "Mr. Finch" designated a person trying to compensate for small size; and "Motz" was a slow, disorganized person.

5. *Requests and Routines.* Sometimes it was necessary for the couple to communicate something in front of others without actually saying it. Thus, "What's new?" was interpreted by one couple as "I'm bored and ready to leave"; for another couple, "Let's go for a bike ride" meant "Let's go outside and smoke some dope." Sometimes these routines were within the confines of the relationship. "Week Thursday," for instance, meant "I'll attend to it at my convenience."

6. *Confrontations.* These idioms, like the teasing insults, showed displeasure or criticism of the partner's behavior, but the teasing or playful element of the former category was absent. "Jelly Beans" was a brief way to say, "You're talking over my head and I don't understand you"; "Pulling a Mrs. Oswald" indicated "You've made lukewarm soup again." Twisting one's wedding ring was a nonverbal command to the partner, "Don't you dare do (or say) that."

7. *Sexual Invitations.* Ways of proposing sexual intercourse included phrases such as "Let's go home and watch some TV" and "Aren't you getting awfully hot?"

8. *Sexual References and Euphemisms.* These idioms referred to male genitals ("Bozo," "Bodacious"), female genitals ("Wuzzer"), or sexual intercourse ("Boogie-Woogie").

Does the use of personal idioms contribute to a couple's satisfaction or closeness? Two studies indicate this may occur, but certain types of idioms are probably less related than others to satisfying relationships.[15] Requests, teasing insults, and confrontations, for example, seem to be less related to intimacy.

Sometimes friends and romantic partners will use the speech register we more frequently associate with parents talking to their infants—that is, parentese or babytalk. Personal idioms commonly occur as a part of this speech pattern as in these examples. You'll have to supply the vocal intonation:

"Hewo, I wuv you, Jellybean." "Oh, Punkin, are you okay?" "I'm sorryyy. Please forgive meee. I looove you." "Awww, is my lil' Jer-Bear not feeling well?"

Babytalk among friends and romantic partners is more likely used to express affection or to signal playfulness. Even though babytalk can be used sarcastically or to create distance, it's primary function seems to be the establishment and maintenance of emotional closeness.[16]

The use of personal idioms is likely to decline as the length of the relationship increases. Their frequency and impact on the relationship seem most powerful at the early stages of a developing relationship. They can, of course, have a powerfully negative impact when used with a partner who is trying to reduce or eliminate any signals that would suggest closeness and intimacy. Idioms tend to develop and receive use during the period when people want to emphasize commitment to the relationship the most—from serious dating through about the first three years of cohabitation or marriage. When personal idioms are no longer used, it may be due to one or more of these reasons: (1) situational changes (e.g., an idiom that mimicked one partner's mother was dropped when the mother died), (2) stated displeasure with the idiom by a partner, (3) relationship changes (e.g., feeling the relationship is "cemented" or feeling that matters previously represented by an idiom can be addressed more directly), (4) need changes (e.g., the couple no longer feels the need to communicate the information represented by the idiom), or (5) the need for variety (e.g., the idiom simply became tiresome or was replaced by another one).

The idioms develop in a variety of ways. Sometimes they are derived from slurred words or baby talk. One respondent said, "In college we used to say 'peatheart' which later became 'peep' and is now 'peepee.'" Personal characteristics can be a source for idioms, such as the woman who complained too often about how fat her butt was and gained the name "Futtbutt." Idioms also come from pleasantly memorable events, songs, or books. For instance, one person said, "I saw one character in a Peanuts comic strip call another his 'sweet little Baboo' and I liked it." Another source includes people previously known by one or both partner prior to the couple's relationship. As one person reported, "Motz is an old neighborhood character out of my childhood who hung out at the local candy store. He was a funny guy who was very slow and kind of dumb." Many personal idioms arise out of the need to remedy a situation or solve a problem—whether it is deciding what to call sexual organs or how to ask the other person if he or she is ready to leave a party without being rude to the host.

The expression of ideas in a "different way"—whether it is through the use of personal idioms or some other way—is perhaps the most evident difference in speech patterns between intimates and nonintimates. In fact, close friends or intimates sometimes look upon these highly personalized verbal exchange patterns as private possessions. Hence, it can be disturbing to hear (or hear about) a close friend or intimate talking in a similar manner with another of his or her friends. Goffman says this is particularly true if the intimate does not know the other friend.[17]

Giving Compliments and Gifts

One person told us that her husband gives her at least one compliment a day. They have been married more than thirty-five years. Even if we assume this couple's experience is unusual, it raises the question of whether complimenting is a speech act that has the ability to serve important maintenance functions in close relationships. After all, compliments

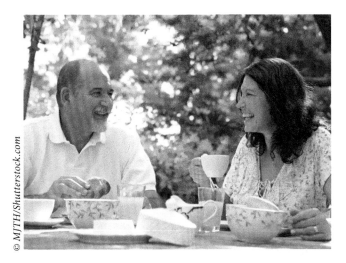

© MJTH/Shutterstock.com

tell others what we value, and that, in turn, provides a guide for what might make us happy. But compliments, like criticism, can be threatening. They are an evaluation of another person. You may say you like how I do the dishes. This may not be something I want to be complimented on or wish to become the family expert on, lest I be the person stuck with the job forever. And we know people sometimes use compliments manipulatively, so we sometimes maintain a healthy distrust of compliments—especially with those whom we suspect have something to gain from us.

We conducted several studies of the compliments people give and found that more than half of the nearly 1,000 compliments we examined were directed at friends, relatives, and lovers.[18] We not only give more to those we feel close to, but more than 75 percent of the givers and receivers reported positive feelings from the act. In fact, the perceived frequency of compliments has been linked to relationship satisfaction in one study.[19] Although complimenters acknowledged that compliments can be used manipulatively and as part of "meaningless" politeness routines, more than two-thirds of the compliments we collected were said to be deserved or earned. Which things seem to get complimented most? Appearance, attire, and performance (which may include work, play, verbal, or activities related to domestic skills). The most meaningful compliments, however, focused on positive feelings expressed about the relationship and/or the complimenter's partner, especially if the compliment focused on the whole person or the person's personality—for example, "Your courage was what first attracted me to you."[20]

As long as the compliment is perceived as sincere and addresses something valued by the receiver, it may go a long way toward maintaining intimacy. In fact, some couples spend a lot of time complimenting themselves on maintaining a good relationship—"We sure are a good team." In this way, both partners are rewarded for their efforts directed toward maintaining the relationship.

Like compliments, the giving of gifts is a way of periodically making a statement about the relationship. The gift statement, like other statements designed to maintain the relationship at a desired level of intimacy, may be effectively or ineffectively performed.

When gifts are given can be a crucial determinant of their impact on the relationship. There are times when gifts are normally expected, such as Christmas and birthdays. *Not* giving a gift on these occasions is potentially a strong negative statement about the relationship. Still, some couples may establish their own norms, which do not sanction the absence of gift giving on traditional gift giving occasions. Giving a gift to a person you feel close to when it is not expected is like getting an unexpected compliment. It has the potential to communicate a special concern for the relationship, because there was no obligatory day of perceived celebration that precipitated it. Yet sometimes the obligatory occasion is generated by the relationship and gifts are used to "make up" after an unpleasant fight or to lift the spirits of a partner who feels "down." In such cases, the gift carries the message that the giver wants to restore the feelings of closeness between them. Earlier in this chapter, we noted that the overuse of the phrase "I love you" could drain it of its value as a statement of intimacy. The person who gives gifts so often that they no longer seem "special" runs a similar risk. Needless to say, showering too many gifts on a loved one is not in the top 1,000 concerns for most couples.

The gift giver is faced with a number of decisions about the nature of the gift and the process of giving it, which affect the way it is received. What makes a good gift? The general answer is that it should be tailored to the needs and desires of the recipient while, at the same time, serving as a relationship statement. This could mean that a husband could give his wife, the ardent gardener, a shovel for her birthday and have it well received. For this to happen, however, the wife must be desirous of the shovel and perceive such a gift as thoughtful and caring commentary on their relationship. The danger, of course, is that the gift is received as "impersonal" and symbolic of the husband's desire to encourage more work on the part of his wife. Besides, buying things in another person's area of expertise runs the risk of presuming you know what they, the experts, need. When partners are choosy about gifts in the area in which they feel particularly skilled, it is wise to set clear expectations for the giver's behavior or to accept what is given graciously.

Gift givers sometimes act as if they are tailoring the gift to the interests of the other person, but on closer examination, the gift also is given to the giver as well—for example, a husband who gives his wife sexy lingerie for her birthday. As long as the wife sees this as a statement of relational closeness, the shared nature of the gift will not be a concern. Anniversaries are occasions when gifts are often expected to have a shared nature to them—for example, a trip to a place where something important to the relationship happened or a gift that symbolizes special times in the history of the relationship. Like any statement about the relationship, the best gifts reflect effort and involvement on the part of the giver and are devoid of any perceived obligations attached to them.

During the process of giving and receiving gifts, couples will negotiate their own norms. When one person responds unenthusiatically to a gift and thus hurts the feelings of the giver enough to withdraw from future gift giving, the demand for discussing personal norms is strong. Subsequent to forgetting a gift-giving occasion, a couple may agree that it is appropriate for forecasts to be given (e.g., "My birthday is next Friday"), while another couple may find this detracts from the positive impact of gift giving (e.g., "You give me gifts only because I tell you to"). One couple may treat Valentine's Day as an occasion for intense celebration; another may agree to "skip" Valentine's Day because it is not unique to their relationship. When gifts are exchanged, there will inevitably be differences in cost, effort, number, and so on. Over time, couples may agree on the acceptable ratio—for example, "We always spend about the same on each other" or "You'll always spend three times more on me than I will on you." The process of negotiating these norms, and the relative pleasure or displeasure associated with the giving and receiving of the gifts, is a good example of the concept of relationship maintenance.

Giving Comfort and Advice

Life does not always go smoothly. Each partner in a close relationship experiences his or her share of emotional distress. Sources of hurt may be external to the relationship or centered within it. Generally, this not-uncommon pain is caused by failing at something integral to one's self-concept or being rejected by someone who is valued. Those who share a close relationship expect their partners to help them through these periods of stress with the adroit use of comforting messages.[21] In fact, we can reasonably expect that a couple's skill with comforting messages is a crucial barometer of intimacy, and each partner's ability to manage this style of communication will have a lot to do with how the relationship is maintained. Comforting is a two-way street. If the comforter is an emotional wreck, the intended recipient of the comforting also may feel emotionally unstable. But when comforting one's relationship partner makes the partner feel better, the one giving the comfort and affection also may feel better.[22]

When the need for comfort has been determined and the helper is committed to providing comfort, it is important to find an environment conducive to comforting, to initiate the comforting when the recipient is ready, and to adapt the messages to the history and capabilities of the person as well as the nature of the hurt. At a minimum, the comforter's behavior should be focused on lessening or alleviating the other's unpleasant feelings. If, in the process, the comforter also is able to get the person to understand better what happened and pursue ways of feeling better, optimum results will be achieved.

Because people in close relationships have developed expectations for the way their partners communicate and because these people may be willing to accept communication behavior from their partners that they wouldn't accept from most people, it is hard to pinpoint the "ideal" comforting strategy for intimates. We can, however, identify those patterns that have been useful for a wide range of people with varying levels of intimacy. These involve (1) talk about feelings, (2) talk about the value of the person being helped, and (3) signals that underscore the authenticity of the helper's responses.[23]

The success or failure of comforting behavior often hinges on whether and how the helper talks about feelings. Some men, for example, may have a harder time than women talking about feelings.[24] But men or women who ignore, dismiss as somehow uncalled for, or even condemn the feelings of the injured person are not likely to succeed at comforting. There may be situations in which the comforter may want to minimize the significance of the problem causing the pain or even encourage the person to emotionally "lighten up," but if these strategies are not accompanied by other nonverbal and/or verbal messages of comfort and support, the person being comforted may not feel very comforted. Nevertheless, it is not uncommon to hear a potential comforter dismiss another person's feelings. Consider the following examples:

"You shouldn't be so upset about what he said to you."

or

"Hey, don't take it so hard. These things happen. It's no big deal."

At a minimum, people like to have their feelings recognized and accepted. Sometimes that is sufficient in itself. For example:

> "I'm sorry you don't feel well. I'd feel the same way. It's OK." (Hug) "Go ahead and cry."

Sometimes the recognition and acceptance of the other's feelings serve as a prelude to a more extended interaction, which is designed to accomplish other goals—namely, reinforcing the value of the other and the sincere involvement of the helper:

> I know it must hurt . . . and you have a right to be angry. He had no business talking to you that way. You've always been a class act—never saying anything bad about him and this is the gratitude he shows! I love you very much and I'm in this thing with you. If you want to look for another job, I'll help you. You need to work in a place that appreciates you.

In this example, the comforter indicates acknowledgment and acceptance of the person's feelings but goes on to explore the reasons for the hurt and the inherent goodness of the person. Exploring the reasons for the hurt may lead to an interaction that will help the distressed person gain insight and understanding about what happened. Effective comforting is often characterized by the comforter's ability to establish conditions favorable to effective coping and problem solving by the person who feels the hurt. The need to emphasize the value of the distressed person stems from the fact that he or she may be questioning his or her own worth, and that is why he or she feels distressed. Another important feature of the last example is its attempt to show that the helper is thoroughly involved and that his or her responses are genuine—not just "going through the motions" of helping. The helper expresses commitment to the relationship by proposing a shared course of action and by condemning the person who made the injurious remarks. The condemnation of the person making the injurious remarks serves a useful purpose, but it may be perceived as somewhat presumptuous by the injured person. After all, the comforter was not the person who was mistreated. As a result, it is not uncommon for the distressed person to argue with the comforter about how evil the source of pain is and even go so far as to defend it. What is important for the comforter in a close relationship, though, is to make sure he or she is clearly aligned with their partner—communicating the message that anyone who hurts the partner is, in essence, hurting both. Once that is established, there is no need to further berate the person who caused the hurt unless the partner encourages it.

Advice is often an integral part of comforting. On the basis of her research, Goldsmith offers the following advice about advice-giving:

> First, do not make advice the first or only response to a close relational partner's distress and recognize that sometimes people talk about problems for reasons other than seeking advice. Second, recognize that there is more to advice than just solving the problem. Effective advice givers appear to consider how the advice makes them look, how it makes the other person look, and what it says about the relationship. Third, recognize the negotiated character of these sequences: Is the other person seeking advice? Is the other person at a point, emotionally, to receive it?[25]

Persuasion

We don't always like to think of ourselves as a person who tries to "change" our partner, but, like it or not, people in close relationships are constantly trying to influence the thoughts, feelings, and actions of their partners. It is the stuff and substance of negotiating a relationship. Whenever we ask for something, give advice, criticize, or complain, we have entered a persuasive environment. What are the typical areas of intended influence in close relationships? In one study, people in close relationships identified six primary persuasive goals:

© Monkey Business Images/Shutterstock.com

1. Giving advice about your partner's lifestyle ("Tell your father we don't want his money.")

2. Giving advice about your partner's health ("You've got to stop smoking.")

3. Recommending a change in the relationship ("Let's spend some time apart.")

4. Requesting a change in your partner's political stance ("If you vote for him, you're voting to give away more of the money we make.")

5. Asking your partner to share an activity ("I wish you'd jog with me.")

6. Asking your partner for help ("I wish you'd help me clean this place on Saturdays.").[26]

With these goals in mind, how do people in close relationships actually go about trying to influence their partners? What strategies do they use? There is no shortage of information about persuasive strategies and processes.[27] **Table 9.1**, for example, highlights a variety of approaches available to men and women trying to maintain relationships through persuasion.[28]

In close relationships, both men and women use a variety of persuasive strategies, but there can be dramatic differences in the behavior of men and women in abusive relationships. Battered and abused women, for example, try to cope with a relationship in which they have little power and control by using persuasive techniques designed to seek more power and control. Although women in nonabusive relationships try, at times, to seek power too, it is done within a relationship in which power and control do not seem permanently imbalanced—and that makes a difference. Battered women will sometimes use more indirect tactics such as ingratiation, promises, alluring and deceptive behavior, and sometimes they seek power by using aggressive strategies such as threats and warnings. Women whose husbands do not

Table 9.1	Persuasive Strategies Used to Get Cooperation
Strategy	**Description**
Ask	Without giving any particular reasons, simply ask your partner for cooperation
Present Information	Present facts or evidence in support of your appeal
Mention Personal Benefits	Show how one or both of you would benefit
Mention Benefits to Others	Show your partner how his or her cooperation will benefit others
Butter Up	Make your partner feel important/wonderful
Mention Relationship	Use the relationship as a reason for cooperating—"As my best friend, I hope you'll do this for me."
Bargain with Favor	Offer to do a favor in exchange for cooperation
Bargain with Object	Offer your partner a highly desired physical object or money
Mention Similar Behavior	Tell you partner about others who have done or would do the same thing
Make Moral Appeal	Appeal to a moral value—"It's the right thing to do."
Emotional Appeal	Cry, beg, throw a tantrum, sulk, or use some other emotional display
Criticize	Attack your partner on a personal level, trying to make him or her feel personally inadequate
Deceive	Mislead your partner
Threaten	Inform your partner of the negative things that will result from not cooperating
Force	Physically assault your partner or use some other means of force

Source: Mark Knapp–Anita Vangelisti–John Caughlin

batter them are more likely to hint, disagree, and discuss issues—strategies that rely on assumptions of shared power and shared perspectives in the relationship.[29]

Even though we have much to learn about persuasion in close relationships, it is reasonable to expect that the degree of intimacy or closeness itself will play a role in the enactment of persuasive strategies. For example, persuasion theory tells us it is crucial to establish trust in order to increase the possibilities of accomplishing persuasive goals. Trust, as it happens, also accompanies increased feelings of intimacy. With this in mind, the strategy designated as "Ask" in Table 9.1 would seem well suited to those who feel greater closeness in their relationship. Elaborate and lengthy justifications, explanations, and inducements do not seem to capture the essence of persuasion between intimates. We also might expect that greater intimacy would carry with it the expectation that partners would perceive more obligations to *grant* resources and wishes to their partners. Similarly, there may be a greater felt obligation among intimates to *offer* resources to their partners without any request being made.[30] If this is true, increasing intimacy means an increasing expectation that your partner will attend to at least some of your needs without enactment of overt persuasion. All these assumptions about what intimates expect and will do also suggest that if expected behavior is not forthcoming, it will trigger an influence attempt in the form of a complaint or criticism.[31] Different degrees of intimacy or closeness also accentuate the role of mutual goals as a part of the persuasive goals of a single partner. The greater the intimacy and interdependency, the greater the difficulty in distinguishing between the persuasive efforts and outcomes of an individual and a couple. For intimates, the specter of the relationship is never far from any effort on the part of one partner to influence the other.

© Galina Tcivina/Shutterstock.com

The process of building a close relationship also means a growing familiarity with the expected responses of one's partner. This knowledge provides a foundation for the design of persuasive messages. Sometimes the unique characteristics and responses of one's partner in an intimate relationship may prompt the use of strategies that are not well understood by outsiders. Familiarity with one's partner also will give valuable information about what language to use and avoid, what is the best and worst timing for persuasive attempts, which topics are more subject to change and which topics aren't, which responses signal that it is best to "back off" and which responses signal receptivity, and so on. This is not to suggest that familiarity provides a foolproof basis for predicting which strategies are going to work. It does suggest that the familiarity gained in long-term, intimate relationships is an important factor in determining the selection of persuasive strategies.

> *More than anything else, women want you to make them laugh.*
>
> —*Anonymous*

Because relationship partners typically spend more time with each other in closer proximity as intimacy increases, this also will affect the manner in which persuasion unfolds in those relationships. As proximity increases, relationship partners will have opportunities to use multiple strategies, change strategies that don't work, return to an issue at another time, bring up the subject in a different context (e.g., when friends or relatives are present), revisit an issue that was not initially resisted but upon reflection needs to be, repeat a persuasive message over and over to a captive audience, and so on. In short, proximity will exert its own influence on how people in developing relationships influence each other.

The effectiveness of persuasive strategies used during the maintenance of close relationships will depend on a variety of factors. As we have noted, persuaders in this context have several potential advantages, (1) audience familiarity, (2) repeated opportunities to accomplish their goals, (3) the trust implicit in close relationships, and (4) the obligations to cooperate associated with building intimacy. Of course, all these factors can backfire as well. This can occur when the persuader uses strategies that are perceived by his or her partner as a lack of audience familiarity—for example, "You know I can't stand it when you use that word!"; when the repeated opportunities for persuasion are abused—for example, "You keep hammering on the same thing and I'm sick of it!"; and when the persuader is perceived as taking advantage of the trust and/or obligations inherent in the relationship.

No matter what you are trying to accomplish through persuasion, it is important for your partner to feel that you have an overriding concern for the relationship; that your individual goals are, in some way, linked to your mutual relationship goals; that you have specific ideas about how your goals can be accomplished and what each of you can contribute in order for them to come about; and that you are not interested in short-term goals at the expense of long-term relationship damage (e.g., using threats, emotional blackmail, or excessive negativity). If the recipient of persuasion attempts believes that the goals are relationally oriented rather than selfish, it can increase the persuasiveness of messages. In married couples, for example, when one person develops a chronic illness (e.g., diabetes) sometimes the partner of the ill person is able to foster the sense that they are both in this situation together, meaning that it is expected for spouses to be involved in each other's health behaviors. In such situations, spouses are often appreciative of influence attempts (e.g., a reminder that baked salmon is a better choice than donuts for dinner). But the exact same reminder can be seen as nagging or controlling if they haven't created the sense that each spouse's health is an issue that they, as a couple, works on together.[32]

Sex talk: Discussions about sex, including the ways that people negotiate the initiation, acceptance, and refusal of sexual activity.

Sex Talk

We talk *about* sex with acquaintances, friends, and romantic partners. In addition, romantic partners negotiate ways of *initiating, accepting,* and *refusing* sexual intercourse. They also must negotiate the appropriate type of talk (if any) *during* sexual intercourse. All these types of sex talk can have profound effects on the relationship. Similarly, ineffective relationship talk can profoundly affect a couple's sexual behavior.[33]

© *Pressmaster/Shutterstock.com*

Like other areas requiring relationship maintenance, problems can arise from too much or too little talk. When a person is described as "preoccupied with sex" because his or her conversations are so often filled with sex-related information or when a person won't talk about sexual matters when the topic is appropriate, these communicative orientations are likely to require modification for effective relationship maintenance.

Sexual topics include: discussing one's body parts, sexual preferences, sexual experiences, sexual fantasies, safe sex, sexual responsiveness, and sexual receptiveness. During sex, talk may focus on what feels good and not so good; what you want your partner to do or not do; and what verbal and/or nonverbal behavior will increase or decrease arousal.

Most research seems to suggest that during the early stages of relationships, men more frequently initiate sexual intercourse and women often play the role of accepting or refusing. As the length of a romantic heterosexual relationship increases, the couples will develop a more complex initiation pattern suited to the particular culture they develop. This may or may not involve more initiation efforts on the part of the woman.[34] We also know that the frequency of sexual intercourse as a marker of intimacy decreases as the relationship establishes itself as an intimate one. Like other types of communication we have discussed, quantity gradually gives way to quality in long-term relationships. When relationship partners experience strains on their relationship or other stressors, however, one or both partners may want to increase the frequency of sexual behavior in order to reestablish closeness and help maintain each other's emotional well-being. One study that examined the link between daily stress and sexual activity in established relationships found that sex can be useful for both men and women in relieving stress and maintaining emotional well-being, but the link between sex and psychological health was evident only in couples who were otherwise satisfied with their relationships. There was no evidence that people in unhappy relationships benefitted psychologically from having sex with each other.[35]

The question of how people go about initiating and responding to sex has received some attention.[36] We know it is a mistake to assume it will "happen naturally" all the time, because so many people report problems in accomplishing this act. Some of these problems are related to making difficult distinctions between affectionate behavior and sexual behavior. They may be separate activities or one and the same. Overall, men are more likely to misperceive behavior that was intended to be affectionate as sexual than are women, which can lead to embarrassment or even anger that could result in sexual aggression.[37]

Sometimes the misinterpretation of signals is not related to misperceiving affection and sex but to the misperception of sexual signals. There are many reasons why we communicate ambiguously and indirectly when we initiate and respond to requests for sex. Although it serves some important purposes, this behavior also increases the possibilities for misinterpretation. For example, sexual invitations may begin with various kinds of nonverbal posturing or sexual innuendo. This approach makes one's interest in sex a possible topic for discussion but does not formally make a proposal for sex.[38] If the target of these "interest" signals responds with similar signals of interest, this provides a context for increasing the clarity of the sexual invitation, if, indeed, that is the intended goal. If interest signals are not reciprocated, this keeps both parties from having to face the possible difficulties involved in a direct and unambiguous rejection. Temporary or "incomplete" rejections also are subject to misinterpretation—for example, "I don't want to ruin our relationship right now by having sex. I want it to be the right person and the right time and I've got to figure all this out." This response also can be an effective "test" in that a person who wants a long-term relationship and might qualify as the "right" person would not persist in requesting sex at this time. Dating and married couples also gravitate toward ambiguous messages because they don't want to "ruin the mood" or "hurt feelings." "Having a headache" became so familiar as a way of politely saying "no" to sex that it is now a cultural stereotype.

Sometimes a person is not sure whether he or she wants to engage in sex, and these mixed messages confuse the partner.[39] In a study that asked women if they had ever offered "token resistance" to sex (e.g., "I'm tired") even when they intended to engage in it, 39 percent of 610 college women said they had.[40] Most said they had only responded in this way a few times. These women reported offering token resistance because they didn't want to be labeled loose or promiscuous; because they were afraid of a sexually transmitted disease; because it was against their beliefs; and because they were angry with their partner— "I wanted him to beg because I was angry with him." Women also reported agreeing to have sex when they didn't really want to.

Contrary to those who believe men want to have sex at any time under any circumstances, men also sometimes engage in token resistance.[41] Regardless of gender, token resistance and other "mixed signals" can create problems in understanding one another's intentions.[42] Additional talk or less ambiguous talk should be helpful in clarifying these responses. Sometimes a definitive "no" may be necessary, and a direct no should be taken as such. Overwhelmingly, when either a man or woman actually says "no," that is exactly what they mean.

Still, in heterosexual negotiations about sexual activity, it is not uncommon for both males and females to contribute to the resulting misinterpretations. In trying to resist an invitation for sex, individuals may not always be direct. For example:

DIRECT:	"Please don't do that."
	"I don't want to do this."
LESS DIRECT:	"I don't think I know you well enough for this."
	"I can't do this unless you are committed to me."
INDIRECT:	"It's getting late."
	"I'm seeing someone else."

The less direct a person's resistance message is, the greater the likelihood the initiator will not understand it as communicating resistance. For example, 38 percent of the men who judged the resistance statement, "I don't think I know you well enough for this" said it meant "She wants to go further but wants me to know that she usually only does this with people she has known longer." Thirty-five percent of the men responding to the statement, "I'm seeing someone else" thought it meant, "She might want to go further, but wants me to be discreet, so that the other guy doesn't find out." Women say they use less direct and indirect strategies for communicating resistance because they are worried about offending, hurting, or angering the man. While such concerns are worth considering, they should not override making one's intentions clear.[43]

Most of the research targeted at identifying specific signals or strategies associated with the initiation of sex and the response to these initiations has not examined the sequential development of the process.[44] Instead, various verbal and nonverbal signals are listed. For example, various kinds of intimate touching, pressing bodies together so they touch at as many places as possible, kissing "deeply" or on many body parts, and looking at the other person in a sexy manner are all mentioned as common nonverbal signals. Verbal signals may vary in directness and include comments such as "I'd like to be alone with you," "You sure look sexy in that outfit," and "Let's make love." As noted in the section on personal idioms, intimate couples often have unique phrases for verbally signaling a desire for sex. So many factors help define the situation as sexual for long-term intimates that the repertoire of initiating behaviors may not be as large as they exhibited at earlier relationship stages. Mutuality of action in close relationships may even make the idea of initiation and response inappropriate. For example, who is the initiator when one person in a close relationship indicates a "readiness" for sex which, in turn, prompts the other partner to initiate it? Also, consider the couple who gets into the habit of having sex Saturday and Sunday mornings after they wake up. In this context, initiation and acceptance/rejection behaviors look very different. In addition, couples who share a bedroom and bathroom area also have a situation that offers opportunities for seeing the other person in a very private way, which may also increase the chances of sexual behavior at times when both partners are in this area. Sexual communication involves signals emanating from the partners (e.g., grooming/dress, touching, talking), signals emanating from the environment (e.g., privacy, bad weather outside, quiet, dark), timing (e.g., choosing the right moment/time since last sexual intercourse), and individual factors (e.g., how relaxed and spontaneous each feels and the role of one's olfactory, visual, and tactile senses). When one's partner also is ready for sexual behavior, a good indicator is the extent to which the initiation behavior is reciprocated or at least countered with an act of equal intimacy. Research suggests that it is common for lack of resistance to sexual advances to be used to communicate readiness for sex, but more explicit discussions about sex tend to be associated with more positive outcomes, including the chances that a first sexual encounter becomes a positive turning point in a relationship.[45] The lack of reciprocation, acting interested in something else, being "too tired," and verbally indicating "no" are common ways to decline sex.

Like other messages that can be associated with intimacy, sex has many meanings. It may be a way to communicate love, pleasure, duty, dominance, relief of frustration, stress, loneliness, or revenge. It may be enacted as a way to gain resources, social status, experience or to keep one's partner from an interest in alternative relationships.[46] It also may have different meanings at different stages of a relationship. Saying you "enjoy sex" during the early years of a long-term relationship may indeed mean you enjoy the sex itself; after thirty years of sex with the same partner, saying you "enjoy sex" may simply mean you enjoy being close to your partner. If sex is going to be an act that effectively maintains an intimate relationship, each partner needs to be committed to negotiating an effective way of initiation, acceptance, and rejection of signals related to sex. Each also must make an effort to infuse these overtures, the sexual act itself, and the after-play with the meaning that most closely fits the desired relationship definition.

Because sex can mean so many different things, how couples talk about sex is probably at least as important to the relationship as the sex itself. One study found that the way a partner attempts to initiate sex is more important than the frequency of sex: initiation attempts involving pressure or coercion were associated with greater relational conflict and dissatisfaction, but more constructive requests for sex were associated with less conflict and more satisfaction—even when the couples did not actually engage in sex.[47] Additionally, revealing positive feelings after sex seems to foster relational satisfaction and closeness.[48] Couples also would be well advised to spend more time talking about each other's particular sexual thoughts, emotions, and behavior rather than relying on the many stereotypes of men and women in general, which may or may not be accurate for any individual.[49] The importance of talk about sex, however, does not suggest that the sex itself is unimportant. Indeed, enjoyment of sex can elicit positive communication among relational partners.[50] Relationship satisfaction and expressing your sexual desires, fantasies, and preferences to your partner often go hand in hand.

Intimate Play

Play is a form of behavior that can be extremely important to the maintenance of a relationship as a whole. In one study, playfulness was found to be a strong correlate of relationship closeness in same-sexed friendships and in opposite-sexed romantic relationships.[51] Some of the personal idioms discussed earlier were specifically designed for play. Play is a type of behavior that can provide a source of mutual pleasure and can help maintain the equilibrium of a relationship. Tensions inevitably build up, and play behavior can redirect these energies toward activity that is for the mutual enjoyment of the partners without conscious planning by the partners. It is not uncommon for couples to report play behavior with their partner prior to sex. Even the tensions created during safe-sex and condom-use talk are sometimes alleviated through various forms of play, such as children's games, parody, and sexual teasing.[52] "Trying to have fun" together does not qualify as intimate play because the ambiguity of whether this is play or something more serious has been removed—and the benefits of play with it. Play also is a way to express thoughts that would normally be suppressed.[53] As such, it becomes an effective problem-solving activity. It also can serve as a source of arousal when the relationship is in need of such stimulation. Play is not likely to occur if more basic relationship needs are not met.

As important as play can be, it is infrequently flagged as "play" behavior. Instead, invitations to play involve abrupt topic changes, exaggerating or expanding normal behavior, outrageous or put-on behavior, invitations to engage in some playful activity, and nonverbal cues that indirectly suggest that the current activity is being dropped in favor of something less serious. Sometimes one partner will play *for* his or her partner (the other is a willing audience member); sometimes one partner will play *with* the partner (both are willing participants in play); and sometimes only one partner is willing to play—a situation that involves playing *at* one's partner.[54] The latter case is not likely to reap the same benefits of play derived from the first two for the relationship.

Intimacy Without Words

The language of intimacy does not hinge entirely on the spoken word. A relatively brief, but familiar, movie scene goes like this: two people are alone in an environment where intimacy can occur; they simultaneously make eye contact and hold it; any verbal behavior at this point is soft or unintelligible; after a brief period of silence with eye contact maintained, they move closer until they are in each other's arms; they close their eyes and kiss; then they kiss again with greater intensity and in some cases, complete the scene by descending together onto a bed or other suitably flat surface. All this nonverbal behavior has set the stage for them to act like intimates in the next scene.[55]

The potential impact of **nonverbal messages** in relationships with a long history is probably stronger than in short-term relationships because the participants know the language better. Couples who are low in marital satisfaction typically misunderstand each other's nonverbal signals more (although the husband is by far the least accurate); look at each other more than do satisfied couples—particularly when negative messages are involved; look more while speaking than do partners in satisfied marriages; and see negative nonverbal signals as more intentional, controllable, and stable than do satisfied couples. In any close relationship, the negative nonverbal signals are more likely to draw attention and demand explanation.[56]

Nonverbal messages: Messages that use means other than words to convey meanings.

Sometimes our reliance on multiple sensory input for our interpersonal messages can be a barrier when we are forced to reduce the input channels—the long-distance telephone call (where vocal cues are the sole nonverbal input) may prompt one intimate to query, "Are you OK? Is anything wrong?" As we suggested earlier in this book, strangers and acquaintances will rely much more on widely understood, stereotyped, and precisely coded messages—words, commonly used (often iconic) gestures, and the most conventional facial expressions. Men and women who don't know each other that well are quite able, for example, to identify nonverbal behaviors associated with flirting. Among men, flirting may involve more flirtatious glances, more smiling, and more slanting of the head to one side while looking, and women recognize this as flirting behavior.[57] Intimacy, however, is brought about by, and brings about, the use of a broader spectrum of nonverbal messages.

Since the nonverbal messages in intimate relationships become less stereotyped, it becomes more difficult to generalize about what nonverbal behavior in such relationships might be like. We can, however, assume that two people who feel they have an intimate relationship will exhibit indices of affection more often. Thus, we can outline some common nonverbal behaviors associated with greater liking, warmth, or affection, and predict that they will occur more frequently in intimate relationships. With each of the nonverbal behaviors discussed in the following paragraphs, it is evident that the behaviors themselves fit the terminology commonly used to describe intimate situations—private, personal, proximate, permeable. This is logical, for if intimacy is the "closest" type of relationship, its nonverbal manifestations should psychologically or physically reflect closeness and efforts to reduce separating distances. One qualification is in order. In Chapter 7, Rubin's conceptualization of the term *liking* was reported. You will recall that he designated two dimensions: affection and respect. Certainly if one likes another only on the respect dimension, some of the behaviors we are about to mention would be modified, absent, or totally reversed—we expect less touching directed at a person we respect but do not feel any affection for.

Touching is an act that reduces physical distance of the parts touched to zero; naturally, we would expect more touching, longer touches, and touching in a greater number of places among intimates. The type of touch employed in intimate relationships also is different from that used in more superficial relationships; it generally includes more stroking and caressing than patting. Obviously, touching one another plays an integral role in the behaviors characteristic of intimate relationships—giving encouragement, expressing tenderness, showing emotional support, aiding in grooming (combing hair, adjusting clothes), replacing a long verbalization. Intimates show more permeability on the verbal level, which is manifested by self-disclosures; they also manifest permeability on the nonverbal level by allowing their partners access to body parts unavailable to nonintimates. One common exception to this norm involves the kiss on the lips. Ordinarily, such a kiss would be limited to intimates or those with whom we would like greater intimacy, but social, polite kisses also can be observed between new acquaintances—a TV talk show host giving a "peck" to contestants. Some feel that sexual touching is the highest form of human intimacy; however, others find it easier to give access to their body than to give access to their feelings—"Sure I went to bed with her, but I didn't tell her I loved her. We hardly said anything."

Morris believes that heterosexual couples in Western cultures normally go through a sequence of steps—like courtship patterns of other animals—on the road to sexual intimacy.[58] Notice that each step, aside from the first three, involves some kind of touching: (1) eye to body; (2) eye to eye; (3) voice to voice; (4) hand to hand; (5) arm to shoulder; (6) arm to waist; (7) mouth to mouth; (8) hand to head; (9) hand to body; (10) mouth to breast; (11) hand to genitals; (12)

genitals to genitals and/or mouth to genitals. Morris believes that these steps generally follow the same order, although he admits there are variations. One form of skipping steps, or moving to a level of intimacy beyond what would be expected, is found in socially formalized types of bodily contact—the good-night kiss or the hand-to-hand introduction.

Mrs. Arpeggio darted her husband a look not to be missed, by which he must have sensed without seeing her, as if by marital radar.

—Peter De Vries

The specific pattern referred to in the following post-World War II example is not descriptive of today's courtship patterns in Britain and the United States, but it does make the point that people with different cultural experiences may have different expectations for the sequence of steps involved in courtship.[59]

> During the last years of World War II and the early postwar years, hundreds of thousands of U.S. soldiers were stationed in or passed through Great Britain. . . . Both American soldiers and British girls accused one another of being sexually brash. Investigation of this curious double charge brought light on an interesting punctuation problem. In both cultures, courtship behavior from the first eye contact to the ultimate consummation went through approximately thirty steps, but the sequence of these steps was different. Kissing, for instance comes relatively early in the North American pattern (occupying, let us say, step 5) and relatively late in the English pattern (at step 25 let us assume), where it is considered highly erotic behavior. So when the U.S. soldier somehow felt that the time was right for a harmless kiss, not only did the girl feel cheated out of twenty steps of what for her would have been proper behavior on his part, she also felt she had to make a quick decision: break off the relationship and run; or get ready for intercourse. If she chose the latter, the soldier was confronted with behavior that according to his cultural rules could only be called shameless at this early stage of the relationship.

Since pupil dilation seems to occur under conditions of emotional arousal, sexual arousal, interest, and attentiveness, we would certainly look for a greater frequency of this behavior among intimates. Further, mutual eye glances, eye contact, or the colloquial "making eyes" should occur more often and for longer periods of time. If we look at the functions served by mutual eye contact, it is easy to see why such a predication makes sense: mutual eye gazing can signal that communication channels are open rather than closed. It can psychologically reduce the physical distance between the communicators—pulling them closer to each other. It is a useful method for getting visual feedback. Research suggests that we look at those things that are rewarding to us or toward which (whom) we have a positive attitude. Keep in mind, however, that there may be exceptions here, too. Long-term intimates may have many other ways to communicate messages formerly communicated through eye gaze. They also may show less eye gaze because they have agreed (perhaps implicitly) to communicate deference through reduced eye gaze. Like the verbal patterns mentioned earlier, we would expect eye gaze to peak during early formation of an intimate relationship, stabilize at a lower level, and peak again during relationship crises.

Mehrabian's research on nonverbal immediacy (see Chapter 3) isolated a number of other behaviors one might expect to see among some intimates.[60] Again, such behaviors are most likely to be seen during times when relationship commitment is perceived to be in greatest demand. These behaviors include nodding, leaning forward, maintaining open arms and body positions, direct body orientation to the other person, and postural congruence. Positive facial expressions (happiness, interest, joy, amusement) also might reflect greater intimacy than do negative expressions. It should be noted, however, that frequency of behavior may not always be a very telling indicator. You may smile only on rare occasions, but those occasions may contribute heavily toward the perceptions of intimacy in your relationship. In addition, it is unlikely that such immediacy cues will increase indefinitely with greater intimacy, and there are reasons to think they might even diminish at certain levels of intimacy. In the United States, there are certain emotion "display rules" that people tend to follow, which lead them to frequently mask any negative emotions that they feel and express positive ones, even when they are not feeling overly positive.[61] Much of the time with acquaintances and friends, you might try to "be on your best behavior." Yet if a relationship becomes quite intimate, the tendency to mask negative and emphasize positive emotions may diminish; for example, after two people begin cohabiting and they are around each other all the time, they may be surprised to find out that neither of them is *really* happy and interested ALL the time.

The stereotyped intimate vocalizations may include a lower pitch, softer voice, slower rate, and a somewhat slurred enunciation.[62] But romantic partners also may perceive vocal behavior that shows interest and involvement in them as intimate too.[63] Long-term intimates are likely to communicate intimacy on the vocal level through a wide variety of behaviors. The absence of vocal sounds (silence) also is a potentially important part of intimate communications. Words, in fact, sometimes serve to create a greater distance than silence in some intimate contacts—such as sexual intercourse. As relationships grow, participants continue to exchange information until they become more and more comfortable being silent in one another's presence. Silences often are very uncomfortable at early stages of a relationship. They cause people to desperately scan their minds for some appropriate small talk to fill them. These silences may be perceived by participants as suggesting too strongly a communication pattern characteristic of intimacy. Hence, the extent to which we feel comfortable with another in silence can be vivid testimony to how well we know him or her. Of course, it also can be vivid testimony to how much we dislike a person or how little interest we have in getting to know a person. But these are hardly "comfortable" silences. Thus, silence may reflect distance as well as closeness.[64] Silences are usually charged with the words and deeds preceding them, so a silence can generate a tremendous range of meanings, some of which are listed in Table 9.2.

Table 9.2 Some Meanings of Silence	
Agreement	Disagreement ("Silent Treatment")
Thoughtfulness	Ignorance
Revelation (We often say much about the people we are describing by what we choose to omit.)	Secrecy ("If he didn't have something to hide, he'd speak up.")
Warmth (Binding the participants)	Coldness (Separating the participants)
Submission	Attack (Not answering a letter—or worse, not answering a comment directed at you)
Gaining attention	Boredom
Consideration	Inconsideration

Source: Mark Knapp-Anita Vangelisti-John Caughlin

Just as there are norms governing public silences (in churches, courtrooms, libraries, hospitals, at funerals), intimates also may have their own norms for when and where silences should occur. It may be during the playing of "You and I" by Lady Gaga rather than the "Star-Spangled Banner," the place may be the bedroom instead of the courtroom, but interpersonal norms for silences seem to be a common corollary of intimacy.

Up to this point, we've focused entirely on nonverbal behavior that is directly tied to the human body itself. Clothing and other apparel also may show the merging of intimates' identities.

Although we would predict that communication between intimates would be more accurate, the sending of nonverbal, emotional messages (like verbal ones) is not a perfected art. We sometimes send confusing messages. Some people, in fact, have particularly severe problems that either keep them from communicating intimate messages or propel them toward intimate messages when they don't want to send them.

Beier reported a study of newlyweds who were asked to portray different moods to see how well others could identify those moods.[65] This research found that some people are not very good at conveying different types of moods or emotions. Instead, for whatever reason, some people seem stuck presenting a consistent mood, regardless of the instructions or the situation. One newlywed woman, for instance, was viewed by neutral observers as consistently hostile and angry, even when she was trying to appear fearful, seductive, indifferent, happy, and sad. In another case, observers thought a woman was always extremely seductive, even when she was trying to seem angry, fearful, or sad. Obviously, there is great potential for relationship challenges if a person's sad, angry, or fearful mood is routinely interpreted as being seductive instead.

Summary

This chapter has focused on those communicative behaviors involved in the maintenance of relationship commitment and intimacy. In addition to commitment, we discussed personal idioms, compliments, gifts, comforting, persuasion, sex talk, intimate play, and intimacy without words.

Each of the verbal and nonverbal behaviors noted may be more prominent during periods when commitment to intimacy is in greater demand—for example, during early attempts to establish intimacy and during relationship crises when intimacy needs to be reasserted. In addition, we noted that intimates can (and do) negotiate different behavioral patterns from those shown by most people. With these qualifications in mind, this chapter suggested the following:

1. Commitment is communicated by addressing the future rewards in the relationship, by identifying with the relationship, by rejecting competing alternatives to the relationship, by showing a willingness to exert effort on behalf of the relationship, by investing a lot in the relationship, and by accepting personal responsibility for commitment to the relationship.

2. The communication of commitment involves repeating your commitment; using unqualified ways of expressing your commitment; talking about future rewards; making public statements of your commitment; taking action to make your declarations of commitment more permanent, as in writing them down; showing effort in your commitment talk; and initiating commitment talk as much as providing responses to your partner's initiations.

3. The communication of intimacy can be done through the use of personal idioms and private meanings unique to the intimate couple.

4. Compliments and gifts tell the other person what you value. A good gift, like a good compliment, is tailored to the needs and desires of the recipient. When you believe gifts and compliments are deserved and given without some ulterior motive, they more effectively serve relationship maintenance.

5. Comforting messages help relationship partners when they are feeling "down" or hurt. The most important goal in comforting is to sincerely involve yourself in the recognition and acceptance of your partner's feelings in an effort to lessen the hurt. Subsequently, comforting messages also should help your partner understand and cope with what happened and to feel better about him- or herself.

6. Persuasive messages focus on efforts to change your partner's thoughts, feelings or behavior or the relationship itself. This involves giving advice, asking for help, challenging attitudes and beliefs, complaining,

criticizing, and so on. Relationship maintenance through persuasion depends on each partner's ability to tap into a reservoir of knowledge about the other; their ability to use the close proximity of the target to their advantage; and their ability to integrate the trust and felt obligations inherent in the relationship into their strategies.

7. Sex talk is often a major problem in close romantic relationships because the methods used to initiate and respond are so often subject to misinterpretation. Effective maintenance requires being sensitive to distinctions between communicating affection and communicating sex. When the ambiguity of nonverbal messages creates problems, verbal clarity is in order.

8. Play is a valuable behavior for building and maintaining close relationships. It enables couples to enact "time-outs" when necessary. Play also is instrumental in couples dealing with tensions, expressing difficult messages, providing mutual pleasure, and solving problems.

9. Nonverbal messages are important at all stages of intimacy, but being able to read these signals effectively is critical to long-term satisfaction.

Throughout this chapter, we have not tried to separate or distinguish same-sexed pairs from different-sexed pairs in terms of the behavior discussed. This may be unsettling to some, confusing to others. The goal of signaling intimacy is one shared by same-sexed and different-sexed pairs. Differences in the way some of these signals are manifested may occur, but in some cases the messages will be similar. Traditionally, our society has not referred to same-sexed pairs as intimates because it might connote a sexual relationship. As a result, some of the differences in expressing intimacy to members of the same sex may be a result of social sanctions. Instead of saying, "I love you" repeatedly, then, same-sexed relationships may substitute another phrase that is designed to express intimacy and repeat it.

Obviously, some communication patterns common to intimate relationships have not been discussed. We noted earlier in the book, for instance, that we would expect to see an increasing number of pair-references over self-references. And, although the topic of feedback was implicit in much of the material covered, it should be clear that feedback is important as a way of giving help to another. After all, if we want to learn how our behavior matches up with our intentions, who is more suited to provide believable testimony than the one we feel closest to?

As a relationship begins to escalate toward intimacy, an increasing number of behaviors (outlined in this chapter) are manifested as intimate dialogue. At first there will probably be a cautious testing to see if the other person wants to move the relationship to a more intimate level. If one person injudiciously and wrongly assumes that the relationship is more intimate than it really is and begins behaving as if it were, we may see the other person helping the imprudent partner save face. Rather than bluntly telling the person that he or she has inaccurately perceived the situation, the partner may communicate this idea by saying: "It's not you. . . . I just don't want to get involved with any-one right now," or "Yeah, we really do have fun . . . but I've got so much work to do right now; I don't know how long it's going to be before I can get out again." It also should be evident that intimates occasionally exhibit behaviors that are more characteristic of acquaintances or even strangers. Less intimate, nonverbal behavior and extreme forms of politeness may appear as a function of playfulness, but it also will vividly remind the participants from whence and how far they've come.

Commitment

Ackerman, J. M., Griskevicius, V., & Li, N. P., "Let's Get Serious: Communicating Commitment in Romantic Relationships." *Journal of Personality and Social Psychology* 100 (2011): 1079–1094.

Agnew, C. R., and VanderDrift, L. E. "Commitment Processes in Personal Relationships." In A. L. Vangelisti and D. Perlman, eds., *The Cambridge Handbook of Personal Relationships* 2nd ed., pp. 437–448. New York: Cambridge University Press, 2018.

Arriaga, X. B., and Agnew, C. R. "Being Committed: Affective, Cognitive, and Conative Components of Relationship Commitment." *Personality and Social Psychology Bulletin* 9 (2001): 1190–1203.

Bui, K-V. T., Peplau, L. A., and Hill, C. T. "Testing the Rusbult Model of Relationship Commitment and Stability in a 15-Year Study of Heterosexual Couples." *Personality and Social Psychology Bulletin* 22 (1996): 1244–1257.

Etcheverry, P. E., Le, B., Wu, T., and Wei, M. "Attachment and the Investment Model: Predictors of Relationship Commitment, Maintenance, and Persistence." *Personal Relationships* 20 (2013): 546–567.

Fehr, B. "Laypeople's Conceptions of Commitment." *Journal of Personality and Social Psychology* 76 (1999): 90–103.

Johnson, M. P. "Personal, Moral and Structural Commitment to Relationships: Experiences of Choice and Constraint." In Warren H. Jones and Jeffrey M. Adams, eds., *Handbook of Interpersonal Commitment and Relationship Stability* pp. 73–88. New York: Plenum, 1999.

Knapp, M. L., and Taylor, E. H. "Commitment and Its Communication in Romantic Relationships." In A. L. Weber and J. H. Harvey, eds., *Perspectives on Close Relationships*, pp. 153–175. Needham Heights, MA: Allyn & Bacon, 1994.

Konstam, V., Curran, T., Celen-Demirtas, S., Karwin, S., Bryant, K., Andrews, B., and Duffy, R. "Commitment among Unmarried Emerging Adults: Meaning, Expectations, and Formation of Relationships." *Journal of Social and Personal Relationships* 36 (2019): 1317–1342.

Kurdek, L. A. "Attractions and Constraints as Determinants of Relationship Commitment: Longitudinal Evidence from Gay, Lesbian, and Heterosexual Couples." *Personal Relationships* 7 (2000): 245–262.

Ramirez, Jr., A. "An Examination of the Tripartite Approach to Commitment: An Actor-Partner Interdependence Model Analysis of the Effect of Relational Maintenance Behavior." *Journal of Social and Personal Relationships* 25 (2009): 943–965.

Rhoades, G. K., Stanley, S. M., and Markman, H. J. "Should I Stay or Should I Go? Predicting Dating Relationships Stability from Four Aspects of Commitment." *Journal of Family Psychology* 24 (2010): 543–550.

Rusbult, C. E., and Buunk, B. P. "Commitment Processes in Close Relationships: An Interdependence Analysis." *Journal of Social and Personal Relationships* 10 (1993): 175–204.

Segal, N., and Fraley, R.C. "Broadening the Investment Model: An Intensive Longitudinal Study on Attachment and Perceived Partner Responsiveness in Commitment Dynamics. *Journal of Social and Personal Relationships* 33 (2016): 581–599.

Schoebi, D., Karney, B. R., and Bradbury, T. N. "Stability and Change in the First 10 Years of Marriage: Does Commitment Confer Benefits beyond the Effects of Satisfaction?" *Journal of Personality and Social Psychology* 102 (2012): 729–742.

Surra, C. A., and Boelter J. M. "Dating and Mate Selection." In: G. Peterson and K. Bush, eds. *Handbook of Marriage and the Family*, 211–232. Boston, MA: Springer, 2013

Tran, P., Judge, M., and Kashima, Y. "Commitment in Relationships: An Updated Meta-analysis of the Investment Model." *Personal Relationships* 26 (2019): 158–180.

Weigel, D. J., and Ballard-Reisch, D. S. "Constructing Commitment in Intimate Relationships: Mapping Interdependence in the Everyday Expressions of Commitment." *Communication Research* 41(2014): 311–332.

Whitton, S., Stanley, S., and Markman, H. "Sacrifice in Romantic Relationships." In A. L. Vangelisti, H. T. Reis, and M. A. Fitzpatrick, eds., *Stability and Change in Relationships,* pp. 156–181. New York: Cambridge University Press, 2002.

Personal Idioms

Bell, R. A., and Healey, J. G. "Idiomatic Communication and Interpersonal Solidarity in Friends' Relational Cultures." *Human Communication Research* 18 (1992): 307–335.

Bell, R. A., Buerkel-Rothfuss, N. L., and Gore, K. E. "'Did You Bring the Yarmulke for the Cabbage Patch Kid?' The Idiomatic Communication of Young Lovers." *Human Communication Research* 14 (1987): 47–67.

Bombar, M. L., and Littig, L. W. "Babytalk as a Communication of Intimate Attachment: An Initial Study in Adult Romances and Friendships." *Personal Relationships* 3 (1996): 137–158.

Bruess, C. J. S., and Pearson, J. C. "'Sweet Pea' and 'Pussy Cat': An Examination of Idiom Use and Marital Satisfaction Over the Life Cycle." *Journal of Social and Personal Relationships* 10 (1993): 609–615.

Keltner, D., Capps, L., Kring, A. M., Young, R. C., and Heerey, E. A. "Just Teasing: A Conceptual Analysis and Empirical review." *Psychological Bulletin* 127 (2001): 229–248.

Hopper, R., Knapp, M. L., and Scott, L. "Couples' Personal Idioms: Exploring Intimate Talk." *Journal of Communication* 31 (1981): 23–33.

Van Fleet, M., and Feeney, B. C. "Play Behavior and Playfulness in Adulthood." *Social and Personality Psychology Compass* 9 (2015): 630–643.

Compliments and Gifts

Cheal, D. J. "The Social Dimensions of Gift Behavior." *Journal of Social and Personal Relationships* 3 (1986): 423–439.

Doohan, E. M., and Manusov, V., "The Communication of Compliments in Romantic Relationships: An Investigation of Relational Satisfaction and Sex Differences and Similarities in Compliment Behavior," *Western Journal of Communication,* 68 (2004): 170–194.

Deutsch, M. "The Interpretation of Praise and Criticism as a Function of Their Social Context." In D. Barnlund, ed., *Interpersonal Communication.* New York: Houghton Mifflin, 1968.

Kille, D. R., Eibach, R. P., Wood, J. V., and Holmes, J. G. "Who Can't Take a Compliment? The Role of Construal Level and Self-Esteem in Accepting Positive Feedback from Close Others." *Journal of Experimental Social Psychology* 68 (2017): 40–49.

Knapp, M. L., Hopper, R., and Bell, R. A. "Compliments: A Descriptive Taxonomy." *Journal of Communication* 34 (1984): 12–31.

Comforting and Social Support

Blair, K. L., Holmberg, D., and Pukall, C. F. "Support Processes in Same-and Mixed-Sex Relationships: Type and Source Matters." *Personal Relationships* 25 (2018): 374–393.

Bippus, A. M. "Recipient's Criteria for Evaluating the Skillfulness of Comforting Communication and the Outcomes of Comforting Interactions." *Communication Monographs* 68 (2001): 301–313.

Burleson, B. R. "Understanding the Outcomes of Supportive Communication: A Dual-Process Approach." *Journal of Social and Personal Relationships* 26 (2009): 21–38.

Clark, C. *Misery and Company: Sympathy in Everyday Life.* Chicago: University of Chicago Press, 1997.

Feeney, B. C., and Collins, N. L. "Social Support in Close Relationships." In A. L. Vangelisti and D. Perlman, eds., *The Cambridge Handbook of Personal Relationships* 2nd ed., pp. 282–296. New York: Cambridge University Press, 2018.

Goldsmith, D. J. *Communicating Social Support.* New York: Cambridge University Press, 2004.

Jones, S. M., and Bodie, G. D. "Supportive Communication." In C. R. Berger, ed., *Interpersonal Communication: Handbooks of Communication Science:* Vol 6, pp. 371–394. Berlin, Germany: De Gruyter Mouton, 2014.

Maguire, K. C. *Stress and Coping in Families.* Cambridge, UK: Polity Press, 2012.

Sarason, B. R., and Sarason, I. G., "Close Relationships and Social Support: Implications for the Measurement of Social Support." In A. L. Vangelisti and D. Perlman, eds., *The Cambridge Handbook of Personal Relationships*, pp. 429–443. New York: Cambridge University Press, 2006.

Persuasion

Craddock, E., vanDellen, M. R., Novak, S. A. and Ranby, K. W. "Influence in Relationships: A Meta-Analysis on Health-Related Social Control." *Basic and Applied Social Psychology* 37 (2015): 118–130.

Cody, M. J., Canary, D. J., and Smith, S. W. "Compliance-Gaining Goals: An Inductive Analysis of Actors' Goal Types, Strategies, and Successes." In J. A. Daly and J. M. Wiemann, eds., *Strategic Interpersonal Communication*, pp. 135–161. Hillsdale, NJ: Erlbaum, 1994.

Dillard, J. P., "Interpersonal Influence." In C. R. Berger, ed., *Interpersonal Communication: Handbooks of Communication Science: Vol 6*, pp. 155–176. Berlin, Germany: De Gruyter Mouton, 2014.

Falbo, T., and Peplau, L. A. "Power Strategies in Intimate Relationships." *Journal of Personality and Social Psychology* 38 (1980): 618–628.

Knobloch, L. K., and Schmelzer, B. "Using the Emotion-in-Relationships Model to Predict Features of Interpersonal Influence Attempts." *Communication Monographs* 75 (2008): 219–247.

Roloff, M. E., Janiszewski, C. A., McGrath, M. A., Burns, C. S., and Manrai, L. A. "Acquiring Resources from Intimates: When Obligation Substitutes for Persuasion." *Human Communication Research* 14 (1988): 364–396.

Sanders, R. E., and Fitch, K. L. "The Actual Practice of Compliance Seeking." *Communication Theory* 11 (2001): 263–289.

Wilson, S. R. *Seeking and Resisting Compliance*. Thousand Oaks, CA: Sage, 2002.

Wilson, S. R., Dorrance Hall, E., Gettings, P. E., and Pastor, R. G. "A Multiple Goals Analysis of Families Attempting to Encourage U.S. Service Members to Seek Behavioral Healthcare: Linking the GPA Model and Confirmation Theory. *Communication Research*. Advance Online Publication: https://doi.org/10.1177/0093650215617507

Sexual Communication

Afifi, T. D., Joseph, A., and Aldeis, D. "Why Can't We Just Talk about It?: An Observational Study of Parents' and Adolescents' Conversations about Sex." *Journal of Adolescent Research*, 23 (2008): 689–721.

Afifi, W. A., and Lee, J. W. "Balancing Instrumental and Identity Goals in Relationships: The Role of Request Directness and Request Persistence in the Selection of Sexual Resistance Strategies," *Communication Monographs* 67 (2000): 284–305.

Afifi, W. A., and Weiner, J. "Seeking Information about Sexual Health: Applying the Theory of Motivated Information Management." *Human Communication Research* 32 (2006): 35–57.

Christopher, F. S., and Frandsen, M. M. "Strategies of Influence in Sex and Dating." *Journal of Social and Personal Relationships* 7 (1990): 89–105.

Denes, A. "Toward a Post-sex Disclosures Model: Exploring the Associations among Orgasm, Self-disclosure, and Relationship Satisfaction." *Communication Research* 45 (2018): 297–318.

Denes, A. "Pillow Talk: Exploring Disclosures after Sexual Activity." *Western Journal of Communication* 76 (2012): 91–108.

Faulkner, S. L, and Lannutti, P. J. "Examining the Content and Outcomes of Young Adults' Satisfying and Unsatisfying Conversations about Sex." *Qualitative Health Research* 20 (2010): 375–385.

Harvey, J. H., Wenzel, A. and Sprecher, S., eds., *The Handbook of Sexuality in Close Relationships*. Mahwah, N.J.: Erlbaum, 2004.

Kisler, T. S., and Christopher, F. S. "Sexual Exchanges and Relationship Satisfaction: Testing the Role of Sexual Satisfaction as a Mediator and Gender as a Moderator." *Journal of Social and Personal Relationships* 25 (2008): 587–602.

Lefkowitz, E. S., Gillen, M. M., and Vasilenko, S. A. "Putting the Romance Back into Sex: Sexuality in Romantic Relationships." In F. Fincham and M. Cui, eds., *Romantic Relationships in Emerging Adulthood 213–233*. New York: Cambridge University Press, 2011.

Shotland, R. L., and Craig, J. M. "Can Men and Women Differentiate Between Friendly and Sexually Interested Behavior?" *Social Psychology Quarterly* 51 (1988): 66–73.

Sprecher, S., Christopher, F. S., Regan, P., Orbuch, T., and Cate, R. "Sexuality in Personal Relationships." In A. L. Vangelisti and D. Perlman, eds., *The Cambridge Handbook of Personal Relationships* 2nd ed., pp. 311–326. New York, NY: Cambridge University Press, 2018.

Play

Adelman, M. B. "Play and Incongruity: Framing Safe-Sex Talk." *Health Communication* 3 (1991): 139–155.

Aune, K. S., and Wong, N. C. H. "Antecedents and Consequences of Adult Play in Romantic Relationships," *Personal Relationships* 9 (2002): 279–286.

Burghardt, G. M. *The Genesis of Animal Play: Testing the Limits.* Cambridge, MA: MIT Press, 2006.

Baxter, L. A. "Forms and Functions of Intimate Play in Personal Relationships." *Human Communication Research* 18 (1992): 336–363.

Betcher, R. W. "Intimate Play and Marital Adaptation." *Psychiatry* 44 (1981): 13–33.

Glenn, P. J., and Knapp, M. L. "The Interactive Framing of Play in Adult Conversations." *Communication Quarterly* 35 (1987): 48–66.

Pellegrini, A. D., and Smith, P. K., eds., *The Nature of Play: Great Apes and Humans.* New York: Guilford Press, 2005.

Pellis, S. M., and Pellis, V. C. "Play Fighting." In H. T. Reis and S. Sprecher, eds., *Encyclopedia of Human Relationships.* Thousand Oaks, CA: Sage, 2009.

Nonverbal Behavior

Andersen, P. A., Guerrero, L. K., and Jones, S. M. "Nonverbal Behavior in Intimate Interactions and Intimate Relationships." In V. Manusov and M. L. Patterson, eds., *The Sage Handbook of Nonverbal Communication*, 259–277. Thousand Oaks, CA: Sage, 2006.

Guerrero, L. K. and Floyd, K. *Nonverbal Communication in Close Relationships.* Mahwah, NJ: Erlbaum, 2006.

Knapp M. L., Hall J. A., and Horgan, T. G. *Nonverbal Communication in Human Interaction,* 8th ed. Boston, MA: Wadsworth, 2014.

Matsumoto, D., Hwang, H. C., and Frank, M G., eds. *APA Handbook of Nonverbal Communication.* Washington, DC: American Psychological Association, 2016.

McCormick, N. B., and Jones A. I. "Gender Differences in Nonverbal Flirtation." *Journal of Sex Education and Therapy* 15 (1989): 271–282.

Noller, P. *Nonverbal Communication and Marital Interaction.* New York: Pergamon Press, 1984.

Patterson, M. L. *More than Words: The Power of Nonverbal Communication.* Barcelona, Spain: Editorial Aresta, 2011.

Notes

[1] M. P. Johnson, "Commitment A Conceptual Structure and Empirical Application," *The Sociological Quarterly* 14 (1973): 395–406. Also see M. P. Johnson, "Commitment to Personal Relationships." In W. H. Jones and D. Perlman, eds., *Advances in Personal Relationships* (London: Jessica Kingsley, 1991), 117–143; J. M. Adams and W. H. Jones, "The Conceptualization of Marital Commitment: An Integrative Analysis," *Journal of Personality and Social Psychology* 72 (1997): 1177–1196; M. P. Johnson, J. P. Caughlin, and T. L. Huston, "The Tripartite Nature of Marital Commitment: Personal, Moral, and Structural Reasons to Stay Married," *Journal of Marriage and the Family* 61 (1999): 160–177.

[2] For a particularly poignant example, see N. D. Kristof, "Who Needs Love? In Japan, Many Couples Don't." *New York Times,* February 11, 1996, A1, A6.

[3] A. R. Ramirez, Jr., "An Examination of the Tripartite Approach to Commitment: An Actor-Partner Interdependence Model Analysis of the Effect of Relational Maintenance Behavior." *Journal of Social and Personal Relationships* 25 (2008): 943–965; C. K. O'Riordan, "Examining the Communication of Personal Commitment: An Actor-Partner Interdependence Model Analysis," *Southern Communication Journal, 72* (2007): 229–245.

4   M. L. Knapp and E. H. Taylor, "Commitment and Its Communication in Romantic Relationships." In A. L. Weber and J. H. Harvey, eds., *Perspectives on Close Relationships* (Needham Heights, MA: Allyn & Bacon, 1994), 153–175. Other studies of commitment characteristics include X. B. Arriaga and C. R. Agnew, "Being Committed: Affective, Cognitive, and Conative Components of Relationship Commitment," *Personality and Social Psychology Bulletin* 9 (2001): 1190–1203. B. Le and C. R. Agnew, "Commitment and Its Theorized Determinants: A Meta-Analysis of the Investment Model," *Personal Relationships* 10 (2002): 37–57.

5   C. R. Agnew, P. A. M. Van Lange, C. E. Rusbult, and C. A. Langston, "Cognitive Interdependence: Commitment and the Mental Representation of Close Relationships," *Journal of Personality and Social Psychology* 4 (1998): 939–954. One qualitative study of people's lay conceptualizations of commitment found that many people consider "working as a team" to be an indication of commitment; see V. Konstam, T. Curran, S. Celen-Demirtas, S. Karwin, K Bryant, B. Andrews, and R. Duffy, "Commitment among Unmarried Emerging Adults: Meaning, Expectations, and Formation of Relationships." *Journal of Social and Personal Relationships* 36 (2019): 1317–42.

6   R. S. Miller, "Inattentive and Contented: Relationship Commitment and Attention to Alternatives," *Journal of Personality and Social Psychology* 73 (1997): 758–766.

7   S. Whitton, S. Stanley, and H. Markman, "Sacrifice in Romantic Relationships." In A. L. Vangelisti, H. T. Reis, and M. A. Fitzpatrick, eds., *Stability and Change in Relationships* (New York: Cambridge University Press, 2002), 156–181.

8   S. M. Stanley, G. K. Rhoades, S. B. Scott, G. Kelmer, H. J. Markman, and Frank D. Fincham. "Asymmetrically Committed Relationships." *Journal of Social and Personal Relationships* 34 (2017): 1241–1259; S. M. Stanley, G. K. Rhoades, G. Kelmer, S. B. Scott, H. J. Markman, and F. D. Fincham, "Unequally into 'Us': Characteristics of Individuals in Asymmetrically Committed Relationships." *Family Process* 58 (2019): 214–231; W. Waller, *The Family: A Dynamic Interpretation.* (New York: Gordon, 1938).

9   W. F. Owen, "Mutual Interaction of Discourse Structures and Relational Pragmatics in Conversational Influence Attempts," *Southern Speech Communication Journal* 52 (1987): 103–127.

10 D. J. Weigel and D. S. Ballard-Reisch, "Investigating the Behavioral Indicators of Relational Commitment." *Journal of Social and Personal Relationships* 19 (2002): 403–423.

11 P. E. Etcheverry and B. Le, "Thinking About Commitment: Accessibility of Commitment and Prediction of Relationship Persistence, Accommodation, and Willingness to Sacrifice," *Personal Relationships,* 12 (2005): 103–123.

12 B. Bernstein, "Elaborated and Restricted Codes: Their Social Origins and Some Consequences," *American Anthropologist* 66 (1964): 60–61.

13 K. M. Galvin and B. J. Brommel, *Family Communication: Cohesion and Change* (Glenview, IL: Scott, Foresman, 1982), p. 5.

14 R. Hopper, M. L. Knapp, and L. Scott, "Couples' Personal Idioms: Exploring Intimate Talk," *Journal of Communication* 31 (1981): 23–33.

15 R. A. Bell, N. L. Buerkel-Rothfuss, and K. E. Gore, "'Did You Bring the Yarmulke for the Cabbage Patch Kid?' The Idiomatic Communication of Young Lovers," *Human Communication Research* 14 (1987): 47–67; C. J. S. Bruess and J. C. Pearson, "'Sweet Pea' and 'Pussy Cat': An Examination of Idiom Use and Marital Satisfaction Over the Life Cycle," *Journal of Social and Personal Relationships* 10 (1993): 609–615.

16 M. L. Bombar and L. W. Littig Jr., "Babytalk as a Communication of Intimate Attachment: An Initial Study in Adult Romances and Friendships," *Personal Relationships* 3 (1996): 137–158.

17 E. Goffman, *Presentation of Self in Everyday Life* (Garden City, NY: Doubleday Anchor, 1959), p. 50.

18 M. L. Knapp, R. Hopper, and P. A. Bell, "Compliments: A Descriptive Taxonomy," *Journal of Communication* 34 (1984): 12–31; M. L. Knapp, R. Hopper, and R. A. Bell, "I Really Loved Your Article, But You Missed Your Deadline," *Psychology Today* 19 (1985): 24–28.

19 E. M. Doohan and V. Manusov, "The Communication of Compliments in Romantic Relationships: An Investigation of Relational Satisfaction and Sex Differences and Similarities in Compliment Behavior," *Western Journal of Communication,* 68 (2004): 170–194. Even romantic partners who typically discount praise (low self-esteem) feel better about themselves if they are able to reframe the compliment by describing what it means to them and how significant it is to their relationship. See also D. C. Marigold, J. G. Holmes, and M. Ross, "More Than

Words: Reframing Compliments from Romantic Partners Fosters Security in Low Self-Esteem Individuals," *Journal of Personality and Social Psychology,* 92 (2007): 232–248.

20 Doohan and Manusov, "The Communication Compliments"; Knapp, Hopper, and Bell, *"Compliments."*

21 B. R. Burleson, "Comforting Messages: Features, Functions, and Outcomes." In J. A. Daly and J. M. Wiemann, eds., *Strategic Interpersonal Communication* (Hillsdale, NJ: Erlbaum, 1994), 135–161.

22 K. Floyd, J. A. Hess, L. A. Miczo, K. K. Halone, A. C. Mikkelson, and K. J. Tusing, "Human Affection Exchange: VIII. Further Evidence of the Benefits of Expressed Affection," *Communication Quarterly,* 53 (2005) 285–303; K. Floyd, C. Hesse, M. T. Haynes, "Human Affection Exchange: XV. Metabolic and Cardiovascular Correlates of Trait Expressed Affection," *Communication Quarterly,* 55 (2007): 79–94.

23 A. P. Barbee, T. L. Rowatt, and M. R. Cunningham, "When a Friend Is in Need: Feelings About Seeking, Giving, and Receiving Support." In P. A. Andersen and L. K. Guerrero, eds., *Handbook of Communication and Emotion* (New York: Academic Press, 1998), 281–301; A. M. Bippus, "Recipient's Criteria for Evaluating the Skillfulness of Comforting Communication and the Outcomes of Comforting Interactions," *Communication Monographs* 68 (2001): 301–313; B. R. Burleson and W. Samter, "Consistencies in Theoretical and Naïve Evaluations of Comforting Messages," *Communication Monographs,* 52 (1985): 102–123.

24 B. R. Burleson, A. J. Holmstrom, and C. M. Gilstrap, "'Guys Can't Say That to Guys': Four Experiments Assessing the Normative Motivation Account for Deficiencies in the Emotional Support Provided by Men," *Communication Monographs,* 72 (2005): 468–501.

25 D. J. Goldsmith, *Communicating Social Support.* (New York: Cambridge University Press, 2004), p. 78.

26 J. P. Dillard, "Types of Influence Goals in Personal Relationships," *Journal of Social and Personal Relationships* 6 (1989): 293–308.

27 J. P. Dillard, J. W. Anderson, and L. K. Knobloch, "Interpersonal Influence." In M. L. Knapp and J. A. Daly, eds., *Handbook of Interpersonal Communication,* 3rd ed. (Thousand Oaks, CA: Sage, 2002) 425–474.

28 This table is adapted with permission of Taylor and Francis Group LLC—Books, from B. G. Rule and G. L. Bisanz, "Goals and Strategies of Persuasion: A Cognitive Schema for Understanding Social Events." In M. P. Zanna, J.

M. Olson, and C. P. Herman, eds., *Social Influence: The Ontario Symposium, vol. 5* (Hillsdale, NJ: Erlbaum, 1987), 185–206; permission conveyed through Copyright Clearance center, Inc.

29 J. E. Rudd and P. A. Burant, "A Study of Women's Compliance-Gaining Behaviors in Violent and Non-Violent Relationships," *Communication Research Reports* 12 (1995): 134–144.

30 M. E. Roloff, C. A. Janiszewski, M. A. McGrath, C. S. Burns, and L. A. Manrai, "Acquiring Resources from Intimates: When Obligation Substitutes for Persuasion," *Human Communication Research* 14 (1988): 364–396.

31 See J. K. Alberts, "An Analysis of Couples' Conversational Complaints," *Communication Monographs* 55 (1988): 182–197; J. K. Alberts, "A Descriptive Taxonomy of Couples' Complaint Interactions," *Southern Communication Journal* 54 (1989): 125–143; K. Tracy, D. Van Dusen, and S. Robinson, "'Good' and 'Bad' Criticism: A Descriptive Analysis," *Journal of Communication* 37 (1987): 46–59.

32 K. S. Rook, K. J. August, M. A. Parris Stephens, and M. M. Franks, "When Does Spousal Social Control Provoke Negative Reactions in the Context of Chronic Illness? The Pivotal Role of Patients' Expectations." *Journal of Social and Personal Relationships* 28 (2011): 772–789.

33 W. R. Cupach and J. Comstock, "Satisfaction with Sexual Communication in Marriage: Links to Sexual Satisfaction and Dyadic Adjustment," *Journal of Social and Personal Relationships* 7 (1990): 179–186.

34 N. B. McCormick, "Come-Ons and Put-Offs: Unmarried Students' Strategies for Having and Avoiding Sexual Intercourse," *Psychology of Women Quarterly* 4 (1979): 194–211; E. Grauerholz and R. T. Serpe, "Initiation and Response: The Dynamics of Sexual Interaction," *Sex Roles* 12 (1985): 1041–1059; M. Brown and A. Auerback, "Communication Patterns in Initiation of Marital Sex," *Medical Aspects of Human Sexuality* 15 (1981): 105–117; E. S. Byers and L. Heinlein, "Predicting Initiations and Refusals of Sexual Activities in Married and Cohabiting Heterosexual Couples," *Journal of Sex Research* 26 (1989): 210–231.

35 T. Ein-Dor and G. Hirschberger, "Sexual Healing: Daily Diary Evidence that Sex Relieves Stress for Men and Women in Satisfying Relationships," *Journal of Social and Personal Relationships* 29 (2012): 126–139.

36 McCormick, "Come-ons"; C. J. Jesser, "Male Responses to Direct Verbal Initiatives of Females," *Journal of Sex Research* 14 (1978): 118–128; T. Edgar and M. A.

Fitzpatrick, "Communicating Sexual Desire: Message Tactics for Having and Avoiding Intercourse." In J. P. Dillard, ed., *Seeking Compliance: The Production of Interpersonal Influence Messages* (Scottsdale, AZ: Gorsuch Scarisbrick, 1990), 107–112; S. Metts and W. R. Cupach, "The Role of Communication in Human Sexuality." In K. McKinney and S. Sprecher, eds., *Human Sexuality: The Societal and Interpersonal Context* (Norwood, NJ: Ablex, 1989).

37 W. A. Afifi and A. A. Lucas, "Information Seeking in the Initial Stages of Relational Development." In S. Sprecher, A. Wenzel, and J. Harvey, eds., *Handbook of Relationship Initiation* (New York: Psychology Press, 2008): 135–151; B. H. La France, D. D. Henningsen, A. Oates, and C. M. Shaw, "Social-Sexual Interactions? Meta-Analyses of Sex Differences in Perceptions of Flirtatiousness, Seductiveness, and Promiscuousness," *Communication Monographs* 76 (2009): 263–285.

38 It should be noted that the ambiguity of some sexual messages is at the core of many disputes about sexual harassment and rape. This underscores the importance of understanding the multi-interpretation potential of messages about or related to sex.

39 L. F. O'Sullivan and M. E. Gaines, "Decision-Making in College Students' Heterosexual Dating Relationships: Ambivalence About Engaging in Sexual Activity," *Journal of Social and Personal Relationships* 15 (1998): 347–363.

40 C. L. Muehlenhard and L. C. Hollabaugh, "Do Women Sometimes Say No When They Mean Yes? The Prevalence and Correlates of Women's Token Resistance to Sex," *Journal of Personality and Social Psychology* 54 (1988): 872–879; R. L. Shotland and B. A. Hunter, "Women's 'Token Resistance' and Compliant Sexual Behaviors Are Related to Uncertain Sexual Intentions and Rape." *Personality and Social Psychology Bulletin* 21 (1995): 226–236.

41 C. L. Muehlenhard and C. S. Rodgers. "Token Resistance to Sex: New Perspectives on an Old Stereotype." *Psychology of Women Quarterly* 22 (1998): 443–463.

42 R. L. Shotland and J. M. Craig, "Can Men and Women Differentiate Between Friendly and Sexually Interested Behavior?" *Social Psychology Quarterly* 51 (1988): 66–73; L. B. Koeppel, Y. Montagne-Miller, D. O'Hair, and M. J. Cody, "Friendly? Flirting? Wrong?" In P. J. Kalbfleisch, ed., *Interpersonal Communication: Evolving Interpersonal Relationships* (Hillsdale, NJ: Erlbaum, 1993), 13–32.

43 M. T. Motley and H. M. Reeder, "Unwanted Escalation of Sexual Intimacy: Male and Female Perceptions of Connotations and Relational Consequences of Resistance Messages," *Communication Monographs* 62 (1995): 355–382. Also see G. Y. Lim and M. E. Roloff, "Attributing Sexual Consent," *Journal of Applied Communication Research* 27 (1999): 1–23.

44 A few studies have viewed sexual interaction as a process. See Grauerholz and Serpe, 1985; T. Perper, and D. L. Weis, "Proceptive and Rejective Strategies of U.S. and Canadian Women," *The Journal of Sex Research* 23 (1987): 455–480.

45 J. A. Theiss and D. H. Solomon, "Communication and the Emotional, Cognitive, and Relational Consequences of First Sexual Encounters Between Partners," *Communication Quarterly,* 55 (2007): 179–206; S. E. Hickman and C. L. Muehlenhard, "'By the Semi-Mystical Appearance of a Condom': How Young Women and Men Communicate Sexual Consent in Heterosexual Situations," *Journal of Sex Research*, 36 (1999): 258–272.

46 C. M. Meston and D. M. Buss, "Why Humans Have Sex," *Archives of Sexual Behavior* 36 (2007): 477–507.

47 C. E. Leavitt and B. J. Willoughby. "Associations between Attempts at Physical Intimacy and Relational Outcomes among Cohabiting and Married Couples." *Journal of Social and Personal Relationships* 32 (2015): 241–262.

48 A. Denes, "Pillow Talk: Exploring Disclosures after Sexual Activity." *Western Journal of Communication* 76 (2012): 91–108; A. Denes, "Toward a Post-Sex Disclosures Model: Exploring the Associations Among Orgasm, Self-Disclosure, and Relationship Satisfaction." *Communication Research* 45 (2018): 297–318.

49 J. L. Montesi, R. L. Fauber, E. A. Gordon, and R. G. Heimberg, "The Specific Importance of Communicating about Sex to Couples' Sexual and Overall Relationship Satisfaction." *Journal of Social and Personal Relationships* 28(2010): 591–609; S. Sprecher, F. S. Christopher and R. Cate, "Sexuality in Close Relationships." In A. L. Vangelisti and D. Perlman, eds., *The Cambridge Handbook of Personal Relationships.* (New York: Cambridge University Press, 2006), 463–482.

50 A. Denes, "Pillow Talk: Exploring Disclosures after Sexual Activity." *Western Journal of Communication* 76 (2012): 91–108.

51 L. A. Baxter, "Forms and Functions of Intimate Play in Personal Relationships," *Human Communication Research* 18 (1992): 336–363.

52 M. B. Adelman, "Play and Incongruity: Framing Safe-Sex Talk," *Health Communication* 3 (1991): 139–155.

53 R. W. Betcher, "Intimate Play and Marital Adaptation," *Psychiatry* 44 (1981): 13–33.

54 For an analysis of the structure of play, see P. J. Glenn and M. L. Knapp, "The Interactive Framing of Play in Adult Conversations," *Communication Quarterly* 35 (1987): 48–66.

55 Davis recounts a similar example in his book. (See M. S. Davis, *Intimate Relations.* (New York: The Free Press, 1973.)

56 P. Noller, *Nonverbal Communication and Marital Interaction* (New York: Pergamon Press, 1984); V. Manusov, "An Application of Attribution Principles to Nonverbal Behavior In Romantic Dyads," *Communication Monographs* 57 (1990): 104–118.

57 J. A. Simpson, S. W. Gangestad, and C. Nations, "Sociosexuality and Relationship Initiation: An Ethological Perspective of Nonverbal Behavior." In G. J. O. Fletcher and J. Fitness, eds., *Knowledge Structures in Close Relationships* (Mahwah, NJ: Erlbaum, 1996), 121–146.

58 D. Morris, *Intimate Behavior* (New York: Random House, 1971), 71–101.

59 P. Watzlawick, *How Real Is Real?* (New York: Random House, 1976), 63–64.

60 A. Mehrabian, *Nonverbal Communication* (Chicago: Aldine Publishing Co., 1972).

61 J. G. Hayes and S. Metts, "Managing the Expression of Emotion," *Western Journal of Communication* 72 (2008): 374–396.

62 J. R. Davitz, *The Communication of Emotional Meaning* (New York: McGraw-Hill, 1964), p. 63.

63 B. LePoire, C. Shepard, A. Duggan, and J. Burgoon, "Relational Messages Associated with Nonverbal Involvement, Pleasantness, and Expressiveness in Romantic Couples," *Communication Research Reports* 19 (2002): 195–206.

64 There have been many words written about silence. If you wish to pursue the topic, the following should provide a diverse introduction: J. V. Jensen, "Communicative Functions of Silence," *ETC: A Review of General Semantics* 30 (1973): 249–257; T. J. Bruneau, "Communicative Silences: Forms and Functions," *Journal of Communication* 23 (1973): 17–46; R. L. Johannesen, "The Functions of Silence: A Plea for Communication Research," *Western Speech* 38 (1974): 25–35; A. Jaworski, *The Power of Silence: Social and Pragmatic Perspectives* (Newbury Park, CA: Sage, 1993).

65 E. G. Beier, "Nonverbal Communication: How We Send Emotional Messages," *Psychology Today* 8 (1974): 53–56.

PART V

Interaction Patterns for Coming Apart

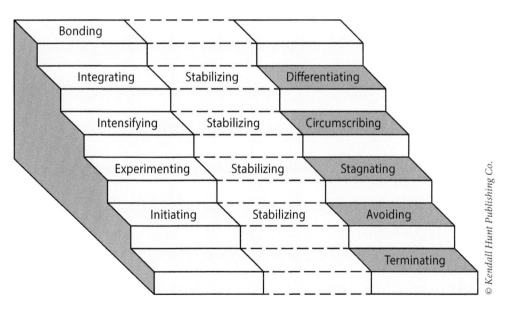

© Kendall Hunt Publishing Co.

CHAPTER 10

Communication and the Process of Relationship Disengagement

Dear Dr. Knapp,

How do you know when a relationship is over? This seems like a very simple question, but I think I may be staying in a relationship that has already ended. I've been involved in this relationship for almost six years. It was great for the first five years. Sure, we had a few rough times, but we always seemed to work things out. The last six months have been terrible. I went to Europe to study for a semester, and now that I've returned, everything has changed. We seem unaware of each other's needs and feelings. It is like we are bored with each other. We have not had any big fights or anything. We just seem to be drifting apart. What happened?

Confused

There are many reasons why relationships come apart. In this case, it may have been a combination of the two people spending so much time away from each other, each pursuing different interests, and growing in different directions during that time. In previous chapters, we've discussed how people get together. This chapter and the next focus on how relationships come apart and how people communicate the feelings and ideas associated with relationship disengagement.

> *It takes a couple seconds to say Hello but takes forever to say Good-bye.*
>
> —Anonymous

The bonds that hold people in relationships can dissolve with abrupt suddenness; they can degenerate over a period of years as if small but regular doses of poison were at work, or they can loosen as the people in the relationship drift apart. The end of a relationship may be intensely volatile and threatening; it may resemble long-simmering coals that never seem to get around to bursting into flames. Or as life-giving energies are increasingly withheld from the relationship, the participants may just grow weary of a dull and unrewarding copresence.

Terminating Relationships

Obviously, messages that communicate distancing, disengagement, and de-escalation are not limited to the termination stage of a relationship. They can and do occur in all the other interaction stages as well.

There are instances when a relationship begins to deteriorate before it starts; that is, one person does not return the normal approaching features of the greeting ritual. A common example is found in the numerous distancing moves performed by urban shoppers when they are approached by a homeless person; the shoppers avoid eye contact and verbalizations, stiffen up, and try to physically move away from the greeter. The avoidance of a greeting from an acquaintance or friend is an especially severe step toward relationship de-escalation, providing the snub cannot be effectively explained as accidental—"Oh, Jeez, I didn't see you," or "Wow, I didn't even realize you were talking to me. My mind was a million miles away." The reason that the absence of a greeting to an acquaintance or friend can be so devastating is that, among other things, the greeting ritual acknowledges the other's humanity and existence, a courtesy expected by all but one's most detested enemies.

People may move directly to the avoiding or terminating stages following a greeting ritual. Since neither party has much time and energy invested in the relationship at this point, one person will not notice if the other unilaterally arranges things so that future contact is avoided. In large gatherings when an individual is meeting many new people, it is not uncommon for both parties to agree effervescently to "try to get together sometime" without the least commitment to such a course of action. Often both parties will accurately send and receive the metamessage: "Nice to meet and be with you at this time, but we probably won't be together again. If we are, that's fine." Sometimes, of course, one party either misses the metamessage or sincerely wishes to extend the duration of the association.

Obviously, many things may occur during the initiating stage that make the development of the relationship slower or decay-prone—greeting a person with the wrong name, exhibiting inappropriate greeting behavior for the type of relationship established, or observing some stigmatizing feature that runs against expectations for a desirable person with whom to build a relationship (height, weight, disability, race).

There may be similar complications for two individuals who find themselves at the experimenting stage. When small talk is in order and one or both persons clam up, argue, jabber meaninglessly, or in some other way avoid fulfilling the interpersonal contract, relationship development is naturally put in greater jeopardy. Sometimes the two participants simply cannot find an integrating topic; or when integrating topics have been established, a simple phrase may serve to shatter and disintegrate—"Yes, my husband always says. . . . " uttered in a context in which at least one party expected the other to be unmarried. At other times, de-escalation from experimenting may not be intentional, but because of other commitments, other friends, living arrangements, or differing lifestyles, it may be difficult to arrange meetings and the couple may drift into the avoiding stage.

For most of us, the most vivid referent for a terminated relationship centers on a relationship that grew beyond the experimenting stage into intensifying, integrating, or bonding. Our involvement in these relationships is stronger and the withdrawal process is likely to be more dramatic. But even relationships that have been intimate manifest termination signals before the termination stage. Just as we are made aware of our eventual biological death prior to old age and as some conversational partners nervously look at their watch soon after a conversation begins, established intimate relationships also may provide some early signs of possible termination.

Reasons for Breaking Up

Virtually anything that creates relationship stress could be considered a source of relationship dissolution. Marriage therapists and clinical psychologists seem to agree, however, that a breakdown in communication is one of the major forces that pulls relationships apart. The focus on ineffective or problematic communication as a cause of relationship dissolution is not new. Indeed, a 1979 survey of marriage counselors identified

© Vera Agency/Shutterstock.com

the following ten as the most common trouble areas for couples.[1] In order of frequency, these included (1) a breakdown in communication, (2) the loss of shared goals or interests, (3) sexual incompatibility, (4) infidelity, (5) the excitement or fun has gone out of the marriage, (6) money, (7) conflicts about children, (8) alcohol or drug abuse, (9) women's equality issues, and (10) in-laws. More recent studies have confirmed the perceived centrality of communication to healthy marital functioning.[2] For example, a national survey of adults in the United States indicated that people felt the most common cause of marital dissolution was a lack of effective communication.[3] In fact, individuals noted that ineffective communication was more likely to lead to relational demise than money problems, interference from relatives/in-laws, sexual problems, previous relationships, or children. Another investigation that followed couples over the first three years of marriage revealed that satisfaction with communication was more often associated with overall marital satisfaction than were several other indices (e.g., satisfaction with finances, with ability to visit with friends and family, or sexual satisfaction).[4] Participants in other studies noted that "communication" and "not able to talk together" were among the most frequently cited reasons for their divorce.[5] In most of these studies, communication "problems" or "breakdowns" generally referred to the fact that couples didn't seem to talk to each other about matters that were central to the continuance of a close relationship—they didn't indicate what they felt or what they wanted from the relationship.

Research conducted by Gottman,[6] Markman,[7] Belsky,[8] and other scholars[9] suggests another communication pattern that is symptomatic of eventual relationship termination. Distressed couples tend to exchange and perceive a lot of negativity in their interactions. When compared with nondistressed couples, their communication includes more sarcasm, more negative feelings reciprocated, and more interpretations of the other's behavior as showing negativity. Distressed couples also engage in more "problem escalation," in which partners alternate between one presenting a problem and the other responding negatively to it.[10] Longitudinal studies show that couples become less happy and more likely to divorce when partners are more hostile toward each other,[11] when they invalidate each other's communication,[12] when they withdraw from each other,[13] when husbands reject their wives' influence, and when wives initiate problem solving with negative behavior.[14]

Of course, it would be a mistake to assume that communication is the only "cause" of relationship decay. Relationships usually come apart for a variety of reasons, including (1) dissatisfaction with one's *partner*—not receiving the expected rewards from the partner; (2) disillusionment with the *relationship*—the purposes for forming the relationship have been accomplished; (3) difficulties with *individual characteristics*--psychological or behavioral tendencies that interfere with the maintenance of rewarding relationships;[15] (4) problems with *others* who form the relationship network—in-laws, friends, former or current lovers;[16] (5) strains created by background variables—race, education;[17] and (6) inability to deal with stresses imposed by *circumstances*—relocation, unemployment.[18]

Two studies provide some particularly interesting information about why people end their relationships. One of these investigations focused on former spouses' reasons for divorcing.[19] The other examined former dating partners' reasons for breaking off the relationships.[20] **Table 10.1** presents the reasons generated by both studies and the percentage of men and women who agreed that the termination of their relationship could be attributed to one or more of these reasons.

Table 10.1 Reasons for Divorce

Reason	Women's Reports	Men's Reports
Infidelity	25.2%	15.6%
Incompatible	19.1	19.5
Drinking or drug use	13.7	5.2
Grew apart	9.9	9.1
Personality problems	8.4	10.4
Lack of communication	6.1	13.0
Physical or mental abuse	9.2	0.0
Loss of love	3.1	6.5
Not meeting family obligations	4.6	1.3
Employment problems	3.8	2.6
Don't know	0.0	9.1
Unhappy in marriage	3.1	2.6
Financial problems	3.1	1.3
Physical or mental illness	1.5	3.8
Personal growth	2.3	2.6
Interference from family	1.5	2.6
Immature	1.5	2.6
Other	2.3	6.5

Source: Adapted from "People's Reasons for Divorcing: Gender, Social Class, the Life Course, and Adjustment," by Paul R. Amato and Denise Previti, Journal of Family Issues 24 (2003): 602–626.

Reasons for the Termination of Dating Relationships

Reason	Women's Reports	Men's Reports
Becoming bored with the relationship	76.7%	76.7%
Differences in interests	72.8	61.1
Woman's desire to be independent	73.7	50.0
Man's desire to be independent	46.8	61.1
Differences in backgrounds	44.2	46.8
Conflicting sexual attitudes	48.1	42.9
Conflicting marriage ideas	43.4	28.9

Woman's interest in someone else	40.3	31.2
Living too far apart	28.2	41.0
Man's interest in someone else	18.2	28.6
Pressure from woman's parents	18.2	13.0
Differences in intelligence	19.5	10.4
Pressure from man's parents	10.4	9.1

Source: Reprinted by permission of BASIC BOOKS, a member of Perseus Books Group.

© Daniel Jedzura/Shutterstock.com

A degree of caution should be exercised in comparing the two studies because they were conducted by different researchers, at different times, using different methods. With this said, we can make a few careful observations. First, there are a number of similarities between the reasons former spouses gave for their divorces and the reasons dating partners gave for their breakups. For instance, both groups frequently noted that incompatibility ("Incompatible" and "Differences in interests") was a reason for ending their relationships. In addition to similarities such as this one, there also are notable differences. Some of the reasons given for ending a marriage (e.g., "Drinking or drug use," "Not meeting family obligations") were not noted by former dating partners and some of the reasons given for ending a dating relationship (e.g., "Living too far apart") were not provided by former spouses. Differences such as these may reflect distinctions in the criteria that people use to evaluate marital and dating relationships.

Second, the percentage differences in Table 10.1 between men and women also remind us that there are two, sometimes very different, sides to every breakup. In both of these studies, women were more likely to initiate the end of the relationship. The finding that women were credited with initiating more breakups than men does not necessarily mean that they are less tolerant of relationship problems. It may indicate that women are more cognizant of problems in their relationships. In fact, some research suggests that "men appear to be less aware of and/or less willing to accept responsibility in the dissolution process."[21] It also is possible that women are simply more direct in their expression of a need to end a relationship. Some men who say their partner initiated the breakup may be dissatisfied with the relationship, but instead of overtly initiating a breakup, they engage in behavior that eventually drives the woman to do the job. Thus, it isn't always the least involved partner who officially seeks the termination. The more involved partner can be influenced by the less involved partner's frustrating and unrewarding behavior.[22] In such cases, the broken-up-with can take the position, "I wanted to stay together, but she [he] wanted to end it." The "blame," then, falls on the partner—not the self.

Breakups also affect people's post-relationship feelings in different ways. Sometimes the behavior of one person will reflect the opposite of the other—the extent that one person feels relief in the breakup, the other feels regret. Some individuals cope with the loss by relating to others more, whereas others become more reserved.[23] In the dating couples previously discussed, men seemed to have had a more difficult time reconciling themselves to the fact that the relationship was over and that they were no longer loved by their partner than did women. When men initiated the breakup, though, the couple was more likely to maintain a relationship at a lower level of intimacy—that of friends.

Many of the differences we see in post-relationship feelings are attributable to people's perceptions of their relationship and their ability to deal with loss. Researchers have found that people who were more satisfied with their relationship were more likely to remain friends after they broke up than those who were less satisfied.[24] At the same time, individuals who were more committed to their relationship (e.g., those who perceived their relationships to be closer, who had more lengthy relationships, and who perceived they had fewer relationship alternatives) tended to be more distressed following a breakup.[25] Studies also have demonstrated that people who were insecure and anxious about close relationships experienced more physical and emotional distress after their romantic relationship ended.[26] In contrast, those who were extroverted, open, and resilient were able to adapt to their breakups.[27] Individuals who had more resources to cope with the dissolution of their relationship (e.g., those who felt they had more social support, who perceived the breakup was controllable, and who had higher self-esteem) also were likely to be less distressed and to feel that they recovered from the breakup.[28] Regardless of how each person initially responds to the dissolution of a relationship, it is important to remember that these initial responses, feelings, needs, and attributions tend to change over time.[29]

A study of gay and lesbian couples further reveals that the reasons partners give for disengagement do not seem to be affected by couples' sexual orientation.[30] In this study, gays and lesbians who had recently experienced a separation from their partners were asked to provide the major reason why their relationship ended and to rate the distress they felt about the separation. The data provided by these couples then were compared to similar data collected from heterosexual couples. The study's findings show that those in gay or lesbian relationships did not differ from heterosexual couples in reasons for their separation or in the level of distress they experienced. Although gay and lesbian couples face some different social and relational challenges than heterosexual couples do, the reasons people in these relationships give for breaking up and the distress they feel about losing their relationship appear to be quite similar.

Although there seems to be a fairly consistent set of reasons for breakups, there are many differences in the way relationships come apart.[31] Some relationships take years to end. For a number of reasons, the partners may be ambivalent about whether they want to leave one another and may attempt several reconciliations. Other relationships die quickly. Dissolution is wrought in a deliberate, unambiguous manner. Davis distinguishes between those relationships that simply "pass away" and those that seem to manifest a "sudden death."[32]

Passing Away

Relationships, says Davis, may slowly lose their vitality for innumerable reasons, but the following three seem to be especially crucial—and typical. For people bent on maintaining a relationship, these three reasons represent especially difficult forces for the relationship to withstand. The presence of any of the following situations, however, should not connote a feeling of inevitable termination. It may be that a knowledge of these potential problems and motivation to develop skills for dealing with them is the best insurance against these factors leading to a breakup.

1. A new intimate may enter the relationship scene. If the standing relationship is made up of a same-sexed pair, and the new friend is of that same sex, one person may face the problem of integrating a threesome in which two are compatible with him or her but neither of these two is compatible with each other. If a new intimate of the opposite sex enters an established heterosexual relationship, he or she may pose dilemmas for the original pair such as deciding with whom to spend how much time and energy; trying to communicate with the old intimate in the same way, yet still developing a set of activities

with the new intimate that cannot be freely communicated to the old intimate; making decisions regarding the type and frequency of favors for each intimate; and realizing that the process of integrating with the new intimate will eventually cause oneself to become a new person. Keep in mind that we are talking about a situation in which people feel the same sense of commitment to the new relationship as they did to the old. In situations in which commitment to the new relationship is low or commitment to the old relationship is waning, social psychologists note that individuals' responses to dilemmas such as these will depend on (a) how satisfied they were with the old relationship before the new person emerged, (b) the amount of resources they have invested in the old relationship, and (c) the quality of the best available alternative(s) to the old relationship.[33]

The entrance of a new intimate or "rival" into the life of an established relationship may cause jealousy. Jealousy is a reaction to a perceived loss or threat to a relationship. The cause of this threat or loss may be actual or imagined—jealous feelings do not depend on whether the threat or loss actually exists but whether a partner *perceives* a loss or a threat to the relationship.

What does research tell us about what makes men and women most jealous in heterosexual relationships? The answer to this question still is open to debate. Studies repeatedly have found that men report being more jealous of a partner's sexual infidelity, whereas women report being more jealous of a partner's emotional infidelity. There are several explanations for this pattern of findings. One of these has been offered by psychologists who use evolutionary theories to account for human behavior. This explanation suggests that men are more likely to be jealous of a partner's sexual infidelity because they are concerned with establishing the paternity of their offspring and that women are more likely to be jealous of a partner's emotional infidelity because they are concerned with losing their mate's resources.[34] A second explanation involves what researchers have called the **double-shot hypothesis**.[35] The double-shot hypothesis suggests that men will be more distressed by their female partner's sexual infidelity because they believe that women who are sexually unfaithful probably will also be emotionally unfaithful. By contrast, women will be more distressed by their male partner's emotional infidelity because they believe that when men are emotionally unfaithful, they probably also will be sexually unfaithful. Yet a third explanation for this pattern of gender differences in jealousy is that the amount of jealousy people feel depends, in part, on the extent to which they perceive the new intimate has characteristics that are important to the way they define themselves as a relational partner. Women may define themselves more in terms of their ability to provide emotional support, whereas men may define themselves more in terms of their sexual prowess.

In addition to studies supporting these three explanations, some research suggests that, in fact, this pattern of gender differences in jealousy may not exist. Scholars adopting this stance argue that the methods many researchers have used to collect their data have biased their findings. To support their argument, these scholars have conducted studies demonstrating that when men and women are asked to choose whether sexual or emotional infidelity will make them more jealous, men choose sexual infidelity and women choose emotional infidelity. But if you allow men and women to rate their feelings of jealousy in both situations (e.g., on a seven-point scale) or if you observe people's physiological reactions, both women and men are more distressed by sexual infidelity than emotional infidelity.[36] These researchers also have found that men's and women's ratings of how jealous they would feel about sexual and emotional

Double-shot hypothesis: Suggests that (a) men will be more distressed by their female partner's sexual infidelity because they believe that women who are sexually unfaithful probably will also be emotionally unfaithful, and that (b) women will be more distressed by their male partner's emotional infidelity because they believe that when men are emotionally unfaithful, they probably also will be sexually unfaithful.

infidelity vary depending on the age of respondents, the characteristics of the rival, the contextual information given to respondents, and whether the infidelity was face-to-face or online.[37]

Of course, people get jealous about issues other than the perceived sexual and emotional alliances of their partners. The jealousy brought about by the perception of a new intimate may encompass several types:

- **Time Jealousy**—The feeling that one does not have enough time with the partner.
- **Person Jealousy**—One partner may be threatened (or irritated) by a specific person the other has chosen to relate to but not be threatened by others.
- **Opportunity/Situation Jealousy**—One person may have unique opportunities/experiences that exclude the partner, who then feels cheated, or one person may be invited to participate in experiences with people at times or in places that exclude the partner. [38]

Some degree of jealousy may benefit a relationship by showing care and concern, but jealousy and the other emotions that come with it also may lead to unhealthy responses—for example, wallowing in self-pity, planning revenge, or even threatening violence.[39] Equating jealousy to love, therefore, is a dangerous thing to do.[40] Jealousy, like love, involves a physiological reaction, which, when labeled, calls forth a learned script for appropriate behavior. It is important to note, however, the way people define "appropriate behavior" depends on a number of factors including their immediate goals and how secure they feel about their relationship.[41] The degree to which individuals *experience* jealousy is not always clearly reflected by the way they *express* jealousy.[42] For instance, people who feel jealous during the initial stages of relationship development may pretend not to be jealous because they are worried about how their partner will react to their feelings. In contrast, those who have progressed beyond the initial stages may feel more confident about openly expressing jealousy to their partner.

Ordinarily those who are most dependent and insecure and subscribe strongly to a value system supporting possessiveness of private property and total togetherness in relationships are most likely to experience jealousy.[43] But researchers also have found that the sort of relationships people are in affects the degree to which they feel jealous. For example, one survey of nearly 25,000 people revealed that those who had been divorced or separated felt more jealous in their relationships than those who were married or widowed. In addition, individuals who were cohabiting with their partners tended to be more jealous than those who were married. One explanation for these findings is that the people who felt more jealousy also felt less commitment in their relationships than they would like.[44] Another explanation is that those who were more jealous believed they had less control and predictability in their relationships.[45] As a result of feeling more uncertain, these individuals may have begun to perceive their relationships in different (i.e., more threatening, more negative, even more fearful) ways.

How do people cope with jealous feelings? Men are more likely to work on repairing their damaged self-esteem, whereas women seem to concentrate on repairing the damaged relationship. Jealousy, though, is rarely an individual's problem—it typically involves a *relationship*—and the most effective method of coping is an exchange of expectations, assumptions, and feelings relating to the behavior in question. This allows both partners to work on adjustments if both are committed to preserving the relationship.

2. Interaction distance (availability for interaction) may expand. Over time, increased distance often causes a relationship to fade. For many relationships, in which at least one party would like to maintain the intimacy level, the following pattern is understandable and predictable: (a) An intense siege of messages about the relationship precedes the act of increasing distance between the participants (anticipating, no doubt, the possible effects of the separation on the relationship). (b) An initial spurt of communication activity (daily letter writing and telephoning), which is designed to maintain the previous intimacy level, follows the separation. (c) Gradually, over time, the intimacy level previously known attenuates. Some of the strong debilitating forces brought about by expanded interaction distance include decreased physical and psychological stimulation, awkward and infrequent receiving and giving of favors, curtailed or indirect information exchange on all topics (especially the relationship), and experiences and activities performed without the intimate, that can eventually cause misalignment of previously synchronized attitudes and behaviors. Research suggests that the restricted communication experienced by long-distance dating partners is often accompanied by a tendency to idealize the relationship.[46] It is possible that this idealization is part of what helps some people to maintain long-distance relationships for a time. But viewing the relationship in an idealized, unrealistic way also may make for a difficult transition period if and when the partners decrease the distance between them. Obviously, all this does not suggest that the relationship cannot be maintained at a different stage; it simply points to the difficulty of maintaining (for a length of time) a fairly intimate relationship without proximity.[47]

3. The normal processes of individual psychological and physical development over the course of the relationship **may sap strength from the relationship**. The more narrowly focused and rigidly defined a relationship is, the more vulnerable change makes it. People may grow at different rates and in different directions. What may have attracted them to each other at one point in their lives may become a point of difference should, say, one person's values change in a certain area. Over time, a quality that initially seemed "exciting and different" may become "unpredictable and weird."[48] Things happen. Physical beauty changes. One person learns and constantly observes the most irritating and unpleasant aspects of the other person along with the desirable behaviors. Events such as the entrance of a child into the relationship, a sickness or an accident, a promotion or a demotion, a new job, or a new location occur and may profoundly alter the congruence of attitudes, interests, and habits. It seems that as a relationship deteriorates, the balance of attractions and level of involvement for the two parties become unequal, whereas during the process of becoming more intimate the attractions and involvement seem to be more balanced.

It has been observed that intimate communications will sometimes decrease (and acquaintance messages increase) in an aging intimate relationship because one or both partners do not expend the energy necessary to maintain the intimacy level: "He doesn't show affection for me like he used to." If the absence of messages consonant with an intimate relationship violates expectations for the relationship, difficulties are surely on the horizon. For various reasons, however, some people who have previously held an intimate relationship are satisfied with a relationship maintained at the acquaintance level. Love, as the preceding chapters said, takes many forms, and companionship is, for some, a viable form.

More often than not, the changes just discussed are slow and subtle, with many ups and downs. Each person will be gathering data—"If you really loved me, you'd . . . "; but the magnitude of the changes may not be recognized or admitted for some time. Once the differences are highlighted, it may be even longer before one or both persons arrive at a satisfactory answer to the question of whether the changes can be "lived with" or whether there are grounds for moving the relationship to another stage or to termination. After people answer this question, their dependence on their partner, commitment to the relationship, desire to avoid conflict, concern for their partner, or fear of being alone may extend the process of coming apart even further.[49]

Sudden Death

If the preceding factors are analogous to a relationship slowly bleeding to death, the following is like an unexpected decapitation. Certainly the *actual* death of one partner would be an example of a relationship suddenly dissolving, but Davis provides several other instances in which relationships experience sudden death.

1. In some instances, the partners in a relationship have lost feelings of intimacy but continue to act out their roles because it is difficult to sever the relationship. **Once certain ties are loosened through the efforts of both persons, the relationship is quickly over**, sometimes to the shock of people who knew them. Perhaps the constraining bond may be the fact that both persons work in the same office and must cooperate in order to accomplish business goals; perhaps it is the feeling that "we need to stay together for the sake of the children." Interpersonal unpleasantries are repressed and sometimes cause such inner turmoil that the hostility leaks out for others to see anyway. In any case, once the work environment can be changed or the children have become self-sufficient, the relationship may terminate suddenly.

When the researchers who conducted the previously discussed study of dating couples asked their 103 students to identify the time at which the breakup occurred, the data revealed that the school calendar may act as a relationship tie that delays or facilitates breakups. Most of the 400 breakups reported occurred at the end of the school year (May/June), the beginning of the school year (September), and during the winter break in December/January. When breakups were initiated by the less involved partner, they usually occurred at the end of the school year, over the summer, or at the beginning of the school year; when the more involved partner initiated the breakup, it usually occurred during the school year. The authors comment on their findings by saying:

© fizkes/Shutterstock.com

> This pattern of breakups suggests that factors external to a relationship (leaving for vacations, arriving at school, graduation, etc.) may interact with internal factors (such as conflicting values or goals) to cause relationships to end at particular times. For example, changes in living arrangements and schedules at the beginning or end of a semester may make it easier to meet new dating partners (e.g., in a new class) or make it more difficult to maintain previous ties (e.g., when schedules conflict or one moves away). Such changes may raise issues concerning the future of a relationship: Should we get an apartment together? Should we spend our vacation apart? Should I accept a job out of state? Should we get together after vacation? If one has already been considering terminating a relationship, such changes may make it easier to call the relationship off. For example, it is probably easier to say, "While we're apart we ought to date others" than to say, "I've grown tired of you and would rather not date you any more." If one is to attribute the impending breakup to external circumstances, one may be able to avoid some of the ambivalence, embarrassment, and guilt that may be associated with calling a relationship off.[50]

2. Sometimes **one person wants to terminate the relationship and the other does not**. If the unwilling partner is skillful enough, he or she can keep the relationship in a state of limbo almost indefinitely—by promising "I'll change" at critical junctures or instituting various rejuvenation techniques such as a weekend at a resort. As a result of the unevenness inherent to such a relationship and the knowledge that it is not working for oneself, the dissatisfied partner often decides to act unilaterally and swiftly, trying to avoid any prolongation attempts by the other. Such

action is not taken without the possibility of real stress for the terminator. For instance, the terminator must often try to accomplish this maneuver while at the same time avoiding extreme hostility from the other and pangs of guilt for oneself. Hence, rather than take the initiative, the terminator sometimes will try to increase the costs for the unwilling partner sufficiently so that termination will soon become a bilateral decision.

> *Almost anything is easier to get into then out of.*
>
> Mrs. Frederick Lewis Allen

3. A variation on the preceding situation concerns relationships in which **expectations for the rate of relationship development differ**, which again prompts one person to lay the relationship to rest. If one person feels the development is too fast, he or she may request a slowdown, trying to keep the relationship at its current level while waiting to "see how things develop." If the other person does not provide the necessary slowdown mechanisms, a rapid, injudicious decision, often rejection, may be forced. Equally injudicious, of course, is a reluctant acceptance to advance the relationship when one's motivation is feeling guilty rather than feeling intimacy. Relationship escalation based primarily on the need gratification of one person (as in this case) may not have much staying power. The whole episode described here is dangerously similar to the coping strategy of some children—"If you don't play my way, I'll take my bat and go home." When the pace of a relationship's development is too slow, the antithesis of sudden death may appear—the agonizingly slow process in which one or both parties moves toward termination out of boredom or disgust.

Since it isn't always crystal clear for people in a relationship when one of them is ready to advance the relationship, and since pushing advancement at the wrong time can be destructive, escalation efforts often have escape valves. That is, after having suggested an escalation, one can, if necessary, indicate "I didn't think you really meant it *that* way" or "You didn't think I was serious, did you?" or upon rejection, "Who cares? I wasn't really into him/her anyway."

4. Another instance of sudden death may occur when **neither party wants to end the relationship, but due to some unforeseen event, a quick termination is precipitated**. It may be an argument that gets out of hand when things are said that cut deeply and cannot be forgotten easily. Or it may be that a smooth-running relationship acquires a deadly amount of friction when two people begin competing in the same job environment or for the same award.

5. As was mentioned in previous chapters, intimates develop formal and informal covenants or rules of conduct between themselves; some of these are trivial and easily changeable; some are considered more sacred and inviolable.[51] The latter are usually closely linked to one's core beliefs or

expectations and form the foundation and linkages for other dimensions of the relationship. If **one of these sacred covenants is broken**, it dramatically increases the chances of a sudden termination of the relationship.[52] One reason for this is that there are generally few, if any, adequate excuses ("I was drunk") or methods of correction ("I'll never do it again") that can satisfactorily offset the damage brought about by the violation.

Although we have given examples of how communication changes during the process of relationship disengagement, it is important to acknowledge that there are situations when communication changes very little, if at all. In some cases, partners may care about each other a great deal or they may be very good at disguising their dissatisfaction. In either of these two situations, couples may maintain positive patterns of communication right up to the point at which their relationship ends and even through the dissolution process. In other cases, partners may have entered their relationship with relatively negative communication patterns. When this happens, the negative patterns that partners brought to the relationship may be enough to erode any positive feelings that initially brought them together. If partners' communication patterns are relatively unchanging, the dissolution of their relationship may come as a surprise to one or both of them (e.g., "But things are the same as they always have been").

Duck has suggested four phases leading to the dissolution of relationships.[53] While these phases may be more appropriate for some relationships than others, they do point out important issues that relationship partners often have to deal with. In the **intra-psychic phase**, the major activity is the assessment of the other person's behavior and evaluating the extent to which that behavior provides a justification for terminating the relationship. In the **dyadic phase**, the partners discuss the perceived problems associated with the relationship. The major question underlying this interaction is, "Should the relationship be repaired, redefined or dissolved?" In the **social phase**, the participants concern themselves with the public acknowledgement to the social networks associated with the relationship that the relationship is being dissolved. In the **grave-dressing phase**, the major activities are focused on physically, psychologically, and socially ending the relationship. One common concern during this phase is to reconceptualize the relationship so that what happened "makes sense" to each participant. Duck and his colleague, Rollie, later added a **resurrection** phase to the model, which involves the possible lessons partners learn from the previous relationship as they get ready for future relationships.[54] Again, it is important to acknowledge that the phases do not describe all relationships. Rather, they provide a framework for examining the various behaviors partners engage in as their relationship comes apart. For instance, research that looked the way people use social media sites to adjust to relationship dissolution suggests that many of the behaviors people engage in on these sites after a breakup reflect the social, grave-dressing, and resurrection phases.[55]

Making sense of the prior relationship and learning lessons from the dissolution process is important for both partners. Much of this sense making occurs when participants develop an account or story about what caused the breakup.[56]

Intra-psychic phase: A phase or stage or relationship dissolution during which individuals assess their partner's behavior and evaluate the extent to which that behavior provides a justification for terminating the relationship.

Dyadic phase: A phase or stage of relationship dissolution during which partners discuss the perceived problems associated with the relationship.

Social phase: A phase or stage of relationship dissolution during which partners concern themselves with the public acknowledgment to the social networks associated with the relationship that the relationship is being dissolved.

Grave-dressing phase: A phase or stage of relationship dissolution during which partners focus on physically, psychologically, and socially ending the relationship.

Resurrection: A phase or stage of relationship dissolution during which partners consider lessons they have learned from the previous relationship as they get ready for future relationships.

Explaining why the breakup happened helps partners "work through" the changes brought on by relational dissolution and deal with any threats they may feel to their identity. Research suggests that the accounts partners develop often differ depending on whether the person formulating the account was the "dumper" (the one who ended the relationship) or the "dumpee" (the one who was left by his or her partner).[57] Dumpers tend to dismiss the notion that the breakup involved conflict, externalize responsibility for the breakup, and depict themselves as empathetic. Dumpees also tend to externalize responsibility for the breakup, but they emphasize their agency or active role, point out positive changes in themselves, and deny being injured.

Harvey, Orbuch, and Weber argued that those who fail to create an account of their breakup tend to have more difficulty coping with the losses they experience.[58] During the social and grave-dressing phases, when participants disclose their breakup account to others, they begin to bridge the gap that often exists between their private thoughts about the relationship and their social world. By explaining what went wrong, they are able to hear themselves think aloud, confide their feelings in others, deal with new information, and maintain relationships with their social network.[59]

The fact that a relationship has passed away slowly or has experienced a sudden demise does not necessarily finalize one's association with it. Sometimes postparting problems can linger long after the relationship has formally disengaged. Partners may get mental or emotional flashes of the past relationship when they encounter shared places or activities. A word or phrase spoken by another person may resemble something the departed one used to say. Perhaps old memories return when one partner is confronted with a task he or she had previously cooperated on or the other person used to perform alone. In addition to this **pentimento**,[60] partners may find post-relationship blues in the process of trying to disengage the social circles and relatives without experiencing more interpersonal trauma. Then, there are the dilemmas of building new relationships by trying to unlearn the subtleties of the private language (and modes of thinking) developed and used with one's previous partner. These relationship remnants are bound to characterize relationship termination. It is important to review and reflect on one's own needs and communication patterns for application to future relationships. There is a point, however, where work on new relationships will heavily blot out the old; if not, the reruns may become pathological.

Pentimento: An underlying image that reappears in a painting over time after it has been painted over.

Communication During Relationship Decay: Return of the Stranger

In an effort to find out what specific types of strategies people use when they want to break off a relationship, Cody asked students to recall a heterosexual relationship in which they had taken the initiative in breaking off.[61] Students were asked to write down what they said and/or did to accomplish that task. The students used relationships that had been going on for as long as two years, but the average length was about six months. Although this study was conducted with students, the range of strategies reported would appear to apply to other populations. The statements listed in **Table 10.2** provide a sense of the kinds of things respondents said. The statements formed five groupings: (1) positive tone, (2) negative identity management, (3) justification, (4) behavioral de-escalation, and (5) de-escalation.

The strategies for terminating a relationship listed in Table 10.2 were then used by Cody to further investigate relationship decay. He found, for instance, that people in more intimate relationships were more likely to justify their intentions and employ de-escalation and positive-tone strategies than those disengaging from less intimate relationships. In these less intimate relationships, behavioral de-escalation was more likely to be employed. Cody also believed that the causes for the breakups would affect the strategies used, so he asked students to identify the causes of their breakup and correlated the causes selected with the strategies selected.

Some of these findings include the following: (1) Students who perceived the relationship problems as the fault of their

© Alicia G. Monedero/Shutterstock.com

Table 10.2 Disengagement Strategies

Positive tone:

1. I said I was very sorry.
2. I said I still cared for him very much.
3. I tried to avoid us leaving on bad terms.
4. I assured her that really didn't want to hurt his/her feelings.
5. I tried to end things on a positive note.

Negative identity management:

6. I suggested that he would probably want to date others and be happy.
7. I told her that a better person for her was out there ready to be found.
8. I told him that we should both probably play the field a bit before deciding on a forever person.
9. I said that when the time was right, we'd both find the right person.
10. I told her that this would be an opportunity to check out other people.

Justification:

11. I said that the relationship was just not making me happy anymore.
12. I explained that I wasn't getting what I needed from the relationship anymore.
13. I said that I was changing and the relationship no longer fit with what I wanted.
14. I told him that if relational partners are not happy, then it's best not to keep dating.
15. I said that I just thought it was time for us to go in different directions.

Behavioral de-escalation:

16. I never really told her. I just started avoiding her until she got the idea.
17. I just kind of stopped agreeing to meet up with him so I never really had to officially break it off.
18. We never discussed breaking up. I just stopped calling her back.

De-escalation:

19. I said that I just felt more distance than I should, so we should take a break and see what happens.
20. I told him that we needed to slow things down for a while, that we've always been honest with each other and we needed to take some time before seeing if we wanted to go further with the relationship.
21. I said that we should take a break from each other for a while and if we stayed honest and respectful with each other we might end up together in the end.
22. I told her that maintaining the relationship had gotten too stressful for now and that maybe someday the timing will be better for us to make a go of it.
23. I told him that I thought the relationship had become kind of bad for us, and we needed to take some time apart to figure out if we could become strong enough on our own to be good for each other.

Adapted from: From M. J. Cody, "A Typology of Disengagement Strategies and an Examination of the Role Intimacy Reactions to Inequity and Relational Problems Play in Strategy Selection," Communication Monographs 49 (1982): 163.

partner chose justification strategies and avoided positive tone and de-escalation. In such instances, the disengager would be expected not to employ strategies that would increase the likelihood of future contacts. (2) When the relationship problem was perceived as a partner's inability or lack of interest in compromising (taking the other for granted; didn't contribute enough to the relationship), the disengager was more likely to use justification and de-escalation strategies and less likely to use positive-tone strategies. (3) It was only when the breakup was initiated by feelings of constraint or lack of freedom that the negative-identity strategy was used along with de-escalation, positive tone, and justification.

Two studies conducted after Cody's investigation extended his findings. One, by Banks, Altendorf, Greene, and Cody, found that the quality of relational partners' networks influenced strategy choice. Partners who reported high levels of overlap in their social networks were more likely to employ positive tone, de-escalation, and justification strategies.[62] Like intimacy, being involved in one another's social network seems to encourage consideration for the other's feelings and accountability for one's own behavior during a breakup. The other study, conducted by Sprecher, Zimmerman, and Abrahams, found that individuals who felt more compassion, caring, and empathy for their partner were more likely to select compassionate strategies (like positive tone) than were those who did not feel as much of those emotions. Sprecher and her colleagues also found that the reason for the breakup affected the strategies people thought they would use. Individuals who were told to imagine the reason they were breaking up with a partner involved a **partner-locus problem** (cheating) were less likely to use compassionate strategies than were those who were told to imagine the reason they were breaking up involved an **external problem** (moving) or a **dyad-locus problem** (different values).[63]

Partner-locus problem:
A problem stemming from a quality or characteristic of the partner.

External problem:
A problem caused by the situation or context.

Dyad-locus problem:
A problem linked to qualities or characteristics of the couple.

Although the preceding studies validate the notion that disengagement strategies are recalled by individuals who experience a breakup, the actual process of disengagement is probably much less conscious and much more complex than the strategies suggest. Recalled strategies probably do not accurately reflect all of the subtleties of the breakup process.[64]

In Chapter 1, eight general characteristics of communication were outlined. These characteristics would most likely be found in the early stages of communicating with an unknown quantity—a stranger. As relationships decay, partners to the relationship seem to design messages in such a way that interaction patterns gradually take on the same "stranger" characteristics—messages that are narrow, stylized, difficult, rigid, awkward, public and hesitant and that suspend judgments. Some of these message qualities may evidence signs of distance before others. For example, some couples may quit talking about their goals for the future or their sexual desires before they begin to suspend judgments. Others may continue to discuss their sexual desires but may withhold their judgments and opinions on a variety of issues to gain a sense of power or superiority over each other.[65] Boiling this down, it seems that people communicate de-escalation of a relationship by producing messages that communicate (1) an increasing physical and psychological distance, and (2) an increasing disassociation with the other person. These messages can be direct and unambiguous, or they can be indirect and subtle. When emotional confrontations about relationship termination are not desired, the initiator may try to avoid the partner (e.g., stop frequenting familiar places, stop asking about the partner)[66] or may use strategies that take some of the blame for the dissolution (e.g., apologizing, expressing regret).[67] Confrontations also can be avoided by using distance and disassociation signals to "hint" at the need for relationship disengagement. These more indirect approaches may represent a perceived need to protect oneself, a desire to protect one's partner, or a feeling of doubt that the termination is really desired. And, while indirect approaches typically extend the time it takes to accomplish a breakup, indirectness was a common strategy reported by students in terminating friendships— although the students felt it would be less likely with very close friendships.[68] In most cases, the process probably shows fluctuations between indirect and direct strategies.

Distance

Distance may be communicated by various withdrawal strategies or by the erection of barriers to symbolize withdrawal. We would expect, for instance, to see actual physical distance between the interacting communicators increase. We also would predict an increase in the time between interactions as well as a shorter duration for each encounter (less total communication). Perhaps early stages of decay may manifest lengthy interactions, but if they remain unrewarding, less time will be devoted to such discussions. In this same regard, the participants may make it harder to contact one another by sending nonspecific messages about where and when contact can be made—"Where can I reach you?" "Don't bother, I'll call you" or "When will you be coming over to pick up your stuff?" "Whenever I feel like it."

Nonimmediacy: Distance as communicated by the communication content; not liking.

Distance also may be communicated by the communication content, or, in Mehrabian's terms, **nonimmediacy** (not liking). We would expect less variety in the topics discussed and probably less information volunteered about one's personal activities and self. For the participants in a disintegrating relationship, a rationale will be increasingly perceived for *not* exchanging the same amount of information as when the relationship's future looked bright and secure. After all, how much are you willing to invest in a stock that seems on the verge of bankruptcy? As a reflection of this communicative closure, a lot more statements like "Don't worry about that. It doesn't concern you" or "I can't talk to you about anything anymore without you getting ugly" will be transmitted. If the relationship was well advanced, the amount of talk about the relationship might be fairly high initially, but again, if such talk continues to produce sour results, its frequency will taper off quickly. Our guess is that the same general usage level of superlatives and absolute statements that the pair exhibited in the growth process will be found at this stage—but now the statements are heavily laden with negativity. For instance, instead of, "You're the *most amazing* person I've ever met in my entire life—the very *best*" we might hear, "You *never* think of my needs—*never* have—you're the *most* self-centered person I've *ever* known." Speaking of needs, it should be a natural part of this process to see fewer favors exchanged. Not only is the motivation for favor giving decreasing, but many times unsolicited favors by the other are discouraged. They may simply activate the psychological forces behind the norm of reciprocity, which can produce a feeling of indebtedness at a time when one is trying to clear the books.

Finally, distance can be communicated through nonverbal behaviors. Some of the more obvious nonverbal manifestations might include (1) less direct body orientation; (2) less total eye contact; (3) eye contact for shorter durations, except in those instances where it is used to intimidate or threaten during verbal communication or preceding physical combat; (4) less touching; (5) a colder vocal tone; and (6) silences filled with discomfort, embarrassment, and disaffection rather than warmth.

As noted in Chapter 2, Hess suggests that most of the distancing behaviors we describe here fall into three general categories.[69] The first category is *avoidance*. Avoidant behaviors include those that prevent an interaction or reduce interaction time. The second is *disengagement*. Behaviors that fall into this category include hiding information about oneself, using nonimmediacy, or treating the other person as a stranger. The third and final category is *cognitive dissociation*. Disregarding the other's message, derogating the other person, and emotionally detaching oneself from the other are behaviors that reflect people's efforts to cognitively dissociate themselves from a relationship partner.

The following reports illustrate a wife's need to achieve nonverbal distance during a time when she was contemplating divorce. They also show how the husband's account of the same behavior was very different. He either failed to recognize the wife's marital dissatisfaction, recognized it and didn't want to face it, or didn't see the connection between cuddling and the decreasing intimacy in the marriage. The wife said,

> Steve always put his arm around me to cuddle before we went to sleep. I wasn't in the mood for it and for the first time I told him so. I can't stand being on the verge of divorce and still cuddling every night. He just turned over and went to sleep.

Her husband described the same event as follows:

> Joanne and I have always held each other before going to sleep, so I put my arm around her as usual. She said, "I'm not in the mood," so I thought, "OK" and went to sleep.[70]

Disassociation

Disassociation is usually reflected in an increasing concern for oneself, and a resulting decrease in concern for the relationship. This focus on self results in communicative behaviors that flow naturally from such an orientation. For

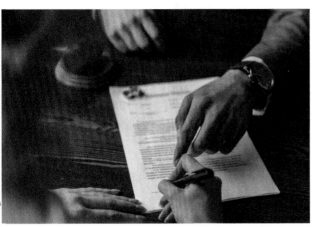

instance, if your main concern was preserving the self (to the exclusion or minimization of the process of preserving the relationship), you would be inclined toward less compromise in disagreements, adopting the illusory, "I win, you lose" stance, with its corollary that there is only one view of reality which is "right." The reason we use the word *illusory* is that so many times the strategies used to "win" only produce tremendous costs to the self-proclaimed "victor." As these costs for communicating orally mount, movement toward the stagnating stage can be expected.

Disassociation also is reflected in an increase in individual experiences and fewer activities jointly performed by the partners to the relationship. In the same manner, language that ties the pair into a single unit will be increasingly abandoned—more "I," "me," "my," and "mine" expressions replace the "we," "our," and "us." When the pair terms are used, it is likely to be in the context of pointing out how "we are different in the following ways" leading to the oft-spoken and ironic conclusion that "I guess I never really knew you." Since the prognosis for the relationship's future is tenuous at best, the past tense is used most often in communicating in an attempt to rewrite the relationship's history so that current actions make sense. The only necessary future-tense discussions concern what kind, if any, of relationship the future holds.

The attempt to emphasize differences and accentuate individuality may take many forms—buying clothes that illustrate differences, showing preferences for food or art work that obviously deviate from known preferences of the other, pursuing contrary interests; or widespread verbalization of certain inharmonious attitudinal positions. Individuality also can be reflected in speech patterns. Word choice, accent, rate of speaking, or even the amount of talk may show increasing divergence when at least one partner attempts to disassociate himself or herself from the other person.[71] As noted earlier in this chapter, communication during relationship decay tends to move increasingly toward the type of communication used with strangers. As one person disassociates himself or herself from a particular other, communication takes on more interpersonal etiquette, more formal names and titles, and the avoidance of endearment terms. (See **Figure 10.1**).

A note on the complexity of the foregoing behaviors seems to be in order. Identifying a relationship on the decline through observation of its communication patterns is difficult. This is because the observers need, but often don't have, a baseline measure of typical communication against which current patterns can be compared. Suppose observers see, for instance, that a couple exhibits several distancing and disassociation features in their communication behavior. Perhaps this simply reflects a form of adaptation made by this particular couple and not a signal of relationship decay. Or, observers might see a certain amount of distancing and disassociation maneuvers when the observed people are trying to move a relationship back (perhaps from intensifying to experimenting) but are not trying to terminate it. In order to communicate this desired change in the relationship ("Can't we just be friends instead of lovers?"), the couple finds it necessary to turn down their proximity and integration sensors—just as it is necessary in the termination process. It's a matter of degree. In another instance, observers may see distancing or disassociation behavior, but the relational partners themselves may not even be aware that they are sending distancing or disassociation messages. Ironically, one partner may accuse the other of such behavior only to increase the chances of such behavior appearing, whether it was extant in the first place or not.

> *Every exit is an entry somewhere else.*
>
> —*Tom Stoppard*

Similarly, it is sometimes nearly impossible to sort out cause-effect relationships. When a wife began going skiing alone, was this in itself an act of disassociation, or was an enjoyable activity for the wife the start of many new activities, which eventually turned a simple hobby into a divisive force in the relationship?

© 2008 C. Herscovici, London/Artists Rights Society (ARS), New York.

Figure 10.1 Rene Magritte's "The Lovers" aptly illustrates the feeling of distance and disassociation.

A final qualification concerns the fact that in every relationship, even the most intimate ones, there will be some messages that communicate distance and disassociation. The critical question is, "When are these de-escalation messages of sufficient strength or quantity to indicate that a relationship has taken a downward spiral?" Until research supplies more specific answers, the answer will probably continue to emanate from the feelings of each individual. Our guess is that if we listen to our feelings (rather than what we or others *think* we should feel), those feelings will signal warnings, maybe not to the degree of danger or to the cause of the danger but to the need for some scrutiny of the relationship.

The Farewell Address

Unlike other speeches called farewell addresses, the relationship farewell address is not restricted to a certain time frame. It may extend over a period of hours, days, or months. It does, however, have some features that are common to other farewell speeches and to the goodbye ritual we perform so many times every day. Probably the most important commonality is the belief by the participants and others that the act of leave-taking is not a separate, isolated unit of discourse. The farewell address will reflect facets of the total relationship history, although those facets are often magnified to the point at which the participants may very well see their exhibited behavior as a distortion or misrepresentation of their "normal" style. For example, leave-taking may be characterized by a lot of yelling and nastiness, which the pair feels are atypical of their relationship, but which was more typical than they wish to admit.

In a study of everyday leave-taking in human transactions, three functions of leave-taking behaviors were identified: (1) summarizing the substance of the discourse, (2) signaling the impending decreased access between the communicators, and (3) signaling supportiveness.[72] Although this study focused on specific conversations, the three functions form a useful paradigm for analysis even when the situation observed changes from a conversation to an ongoing relationship. For instance, as suggested by the first function of leave-taking, the termination of some conversations calls for the recapitulation or summarizing of salient points—as in the case of a professor counseling a student on how to study more effectively for his or her exams. Similarly, some relationship farewells require a historical summary, usually emphasizing the unpleasant aspects of the relationship to provide a rationale for the imminent action.

The final moments of a conversation also show the second function of conversational leave-taking—verbal and nonverbal efforts to communicate the impending decrease in communicative access. Put another way, we let people know we are going to be absent from them for awhile. The latter phases of a relationship also communicate this decreased access. As we've noted, there are many ways of showing decreased access by increasing psychological and physical distance. A farewell address may, however, be more explicit—"After July 1, we will have to see each other only once a month. Oh, maybe we'll run into each other accidentally someplace, but I'm not going out with you again." Perhaps the strongest act that communicates the certainty of decreased access for disengaging married couples is that of deciding how to divide household objects and/or time spent with children.

The third function of conversational leave-taking is to signal a form of supportiveness for what has transpired ("Thanks for your time; I think you really helped me"). It also offsets inaccessibility signals by suggesting future contact ("OK, let's do this again sometime") and communicates the idea that the conversation is terminated, but not the relationship. Have you ever noticed how many future plans people make that never come about—but it doesn't matter? All that really matters between friends is that they continue to talk about a future. When the farewell address is designed to communicate the fact that there will be no future relationship, this function obviously cannot be achieved. However, many farewell addresses leave open the possibility for some kind of future relationship—even if it is something slightly more than stranger status.[73] As a result, signs of supportiveness may be evident in the farewell rhetoric of decaying relationships. The parties may agree to be friendly and helpful to each other when occasional future contact is made; they may reflect on the decaying process supportively—"It could have been a lot worse if you hadn't . . . and I want you to know I appreciate it." The parties may express welfare concern—"Yeah, well . . . take care of yourself." Once separation has formally occurred, it is not at all unusual to hear reminiscences such as: "Sure we had some bad times, but . . . " In fact, supportiveness may be just as critical for relationship termination as it is for conversation termination—which may help to explain why nonsupportive terminations so often take a high psychological toll.

A comparison between conversational and relational leave-taking is worthy of note. In conversations there are two very common methods of verbally explaining why one is leaving. One of these is called an **internal legitimizer**, because the leaver takes sole responsibility for the act of leaving—"Well, I think that is all I have to say." The other pattern is called an **external legitimizer**, because the justification for leaving is derived from forces external to the leaver—"I can see other people are waiting to see you, so I'll be going." Leaving a relationship also can be expressed or justified from internal or external perspectives. Some people will reflect on personal behaviors and attitudes that may have contributed to the deterioration of the relationship; others are more inclined to focus their reflection on people and events external to themselves. Although research suggests that dissatisfied couples tend to give internal, stable explanations for the negative events in their relationship (e.g., "because she is insensitive to my needs"),[74] it is very possible that once partners terminate the relationship, their explanations will change (e.g., "because we were both hurting"). The notion that people often focus on internal or external causes for relational dissolution does not suggest that combination of the two perspectives is unheard of; in reality, most relationships are abandoned because of a combination of internal and external forces. The perspective emphasized will probably depend on relational factors such as the duration of the association, the relationship stage, and the

Internal legitimizer: A communication strategy that focuses on individuals' responsibility for a particular behavior.

External legitimizer: A communication strategy that focuses on external forces such as the situation or the environment.

degree to which the partner feels invested in the relationship. Individual factors such as the partner's personality, mood (e.g., sad or guilty),[75] and mental state (e.g., depressed or lonely)[76] also should affect the explanation he or she formulates.

Finally, let's examine the familiar farewell, or goodbye, itself. Although the term *goodbye* is possibly our most common referent for leave-taking expressions, it is not really common in daily exchanges. It probably has a greater frequency in children's leave-taking than in adults; and some form of it is probably used more to terminate telephone conversations than face-to-face encounters. The feature most relevant to our current analysis, however, is the hypothesized finality communicated by the term *goodbye* in face-to-face transactions. Goffman believes we now use *goodbye* primarily in situations in which the interactants will be apart for an extended period of time.[77] Further, we would expect *goodbye* to be found in more formal situations than informal situations. Thus, it seems reasonable to hypothesize that the farewell address is more likely to contain *goodbyes* that simultaneously communicate formality, finality, and extended absence.

A hypothetical goodbye rant created by Davis includes formality ("You'll be hearing from my lawyer."); finality ("We're through."); extended absence ("I never want to see you again."); rules for future engagement ("Don't call me. Don't ask me for anything."); and the division of co-owned aspects of the relationship ("You can have the house, but I'm taking the baby.").[78]

Summary

Our goal in this chapter has been to elaborate on those processes enacted when relationships come apart. We briefly outlined how relationship termination may occur in less intimate associations, but the major emphases in the chapter dealt with terminations of more intimate relationships. These relationships may pass away or, because of special circumstances, experience a sudden death. After the relationships have been officially terminated, the participants may continue to experience relationship flashbacks, which should gradually attenuate over time.

The second part of this chapter identified the general nature of communication during relationship decay as an increasing psychological and physical distance and continued disassociation from the other person. In short, communication behavior in decaying relationships will increasingly reflect patterns associated with strangers rather than those associated with intimates. Specifically, as a relationship moves toward termination, we would expect to find, among other characteristics,

- Increasing physical distance between the interactants
- Increasing time between interactions
- Shorter encounters
- Less personal information exchanged
- Less relationship talk
- Fewer favors given and/or asked for
- Less verbal immediacy
- Superlatives and absolutistic statements couched in negative rather than positive evaluations
- Less nonverbal immediacy—less touching, colder vocal tone, less eye contact
- An increasing concern for self rather than for the relationship or the other person
- Less compromising because of an increasing win-lose orientation
- More individual rather than mutual activities
- Decreasing use of endearment terms and private language—a return to a less particularized set of etiquette norms
- Differences accentuated in clothes, food, and other preferences.

Although we might agree that the preceding list of behaviors seems to occur in disintegrating relationships, this does not suggest we won't find some evidence of the same behaviors in relationships that are growing or moving back to earlier stages. These behaviors, however, will not be common in intimate relationships. The question of whether these behaviors are associated with a dying relationship or with one that has a temporary virus can be answered by looking at the frequency with which a given behavior occurs and seeing whether other behaviors seem to be communicating the same distancing and disassociation messages. We might find, for instance, relational partners who have infrequent verbal interactions but send many nonverbal messages of affection. Hence, for this couple, one behavior that might communicate distance is offset by others that communicate closeness.

To further illustrate the similarities between communication in encounters and relationships, we looked at relationship farewells through the lens of research data on saying goodbye in conversations. Parallels were suggested along functional lines—in both conversations and relationships evidence of the need to summarize, to clarify the impending decreased access, and to show supportiveness during the goodbye ritual was found.

Relationship Termination

Baxter, L. A. "Strategies for Ending Relationships: Two Studies." *Western Journal of Speech Communication* 46 (1982): 223–241.

Cody, M. J. "A Typology of Disengagement Strategies and an Examination of the Role Intimacy Reactions to Inequity and Relational Problems Play in Strategy Selection." *Communication Monographs* 49 (1982): 148–170.

Cupach, W. R., and Metts, S. "Accounts of Relational Dissolution: A Comparison of Marital and Nonmarital Relationships." *Communication Monographs* 53 (1986): 311–334.

Doering, J. "Face, Accounts, and Schemes in the Context of Relationship Breakups." *Symbolic Interaction,* 33 (2010): 71–95.

Duck, S. "A Topography of Relationship Disengagement and Dissolution." In S. Duck, ed., *Personal Relationships 4: Dissolving Personal Relationships,* pp. 1–30. New York: Academic Press, 1982.

Hill, C. T., Rubin, Z., and Peplau, L. A. "Breakups Before Marriage: The End of 103 Affairs." *Journal of Social Issues* 32 (1976): 147–168.

Kurdek, L. A. "The Nature and Correlates of Deterrents to Leaving a Relationship." *Personal Relationships* 13 (2006): 521–535.

Lannutti, P. J., and Cameron, K. A. "Beyond the Breakup: Heterosexual and Homosexual Post-Dissolutional Relationships." *Communication Quarterly* 50 (2002): 153–170.

Levinger, G. "A Social Exchange View on the Dissolution of Pair Relationships." In R. L. Burgess and T. L. Huston, eds., *Social Exchange in Developing Relationships,* pp. 169–193. New York: Academic Press, 1979.

Orbuch, T. L., ed. *Close Relationship Loss: Theoretical Approaches.* New York: Springer-Verlag, 1993.

Sprecher, S., Zimmerman, C. and Abrahams, E. M. "Choosing Compassionate Strategies to End a Relationship: Effects of Compassionate Love for Partner and the Reason For Breakup." *Social Psychology* 51 (2010): 66–75.

Weber, A. L., Harvey, J. H., and Orbuch, T. L. "What Went Wrong: Communicating Accounts of Relationships Conflict." In M. L. McLaughlin, M. J. Cody, and S. J. Read, eds., *Explaining One's Self to Others: Reason-Giving in a Social Context,* pp. 261–280. Hillsdale, NJ: Erlbaum, 1992.

Leave-Taking

Adato, A. "Leave-Taking: A Study of Commonsense Knowledge of Social Structure." *Anthropological Quarterly* 48 (1975): 255–271.

Albert, S., and Kessler, S. "Ending Social Encounters." *Journal of Experimental Social Psychology* 14 (1978): 541–553.

Goffman, E. *Relations in Public.* New York: Basic Books, 1971, pp. 79–91.

Knapp, M. L., Hart, R. P., Friedrich, G. W., and Shulman, G. M. "The Rhetoric of Good-bye: Verbal and Nonverbal Correlates of Human Leave-Taking." *Speech Monographs* 40 (1973): 182–198.

LeBaron, C. D., and Jones, S. E. "Closing Up Closings: Showing the Relevance of the Social and Material Surround to the Completion of Interaction." *Journal of Communication* 52 (2002): 542–565.

Schegloff, E. A., and Sacks, H. "Opening Up Closings." *Semiotica* 4 (1973): 289–327.

Sigman, S. J. "Handling the Discontinuous Aspects of Continuous Social Relationships: Toward Research on the Persistence of Social Forms." *Communication Theory* 1 (1991): 106–127.

Divorce

Amato, P. R., and Irving, S. "A Historical Perspective on Divorce in the United States." In M. Fine and J. Harvey, eds., *Handbook of Divorce and Relationship Dissolution,* pp. 41–58. Mahwah, NJ: Erlbaum, 2005.

Amato, P. R., and Previti, D. "People's Reasons for Divorcing: Gender, Social Class, the Life Course, and Adjustment." *Journal of Family Issues* 24 (2003): 602–626.

Coleman, M., Ganong, L., and Mitchell, S. N. "Divorce and Postdivorce Relationships." In A. L. Vangelisti and D. Perlman, eds., *The Cambridge Handbook of Personal Relationships,* 2nd ed., pp. 106–116. New York: Cambridge University Press, 2018.

Emery, R. E. *Renegotiating Family Relationships: Divorce, Child Custody, and Mediation,* 2nd ed. New York: Guilford Press, 2012.

Gottman, J. M. *What Predicts Divorce?: The Relationship between Marital Processes and Marital Outcomes.* Hillsdale, NJ: Erlbaum, 1994.

Kurdek, L. A. "Predicting Marital Dissolution: A 5-Year Prospective Longitudinal Study of Newlywed Couples." *Journal of Personality and Social Psychology* 64 (1993): 221–242.

Levinger, G. "A Social Psychological Perspective on Marital Dissolution." *Journal of Social Issues* 32 (1976): 21–47.

Levinger, G., and Moles, O. C., eds. *Divorce and Separation.* New York: Basic Books, 1979.

Markman, H. J., Rhoades, G. K., Stanley, S. M., Ragan, E. P., and Whitton, S. W. "The Premarital Communication Roots of Marital Distress and Divorce: The First Five Years of Marriage." *Journal of Family Psychology* 24 (2010): 289–298.

Ponzetti, J. J., and Cate, R. M. "The Divorce Process: Toward a Typology of Marital Dissolution." *Journal of Divorce* 11 (1988): 1–20.

Weiss, P. *Marital Separation.* New York: Basic Books, 1975.

Jealousy

Buunk, A. P., Dijkstra, P., and Massar, K. "The Universal Threat and Temptation of Extradyadic Affairs." In A. L. Vangelisti and D. Perlman, eds., *The Cambridge Handbook of Personal Relationships,* 2nd ed., pp. 353–364. New York: Cambridge University Press, 2006.

Clanton, G., and Smith, L. G., eds. *Jealousy.* Englewood Cliffs, NJ: Prentice Hall, 1977.

DeSteno, D., Bartlett, M. Y., Salovey, P., and Braverman, J. "Sex Differences in Jealousy: Evolutionary Mechanism or Artifact of Measurement?" *Journal of Personality and Social Psychology* 83 (2002): 1103–1116.

Dijkstra, P., Groothof, H. A. K., Poel, G. A., Laverman, T. T. G., Schrier, M., and Buunk, B. P. "Sex Differences in the Events That Elicit Jealousy Among Homosexuals." *Personal Relationships* 8 (2001): 41–54.

Guerrero, L. K., and Andersen, P. A. "Jealousy Experience and Expression in Romantic Relationships." In P. A. Andersen and L. K. Guerrero, eds., *Handbook of Communication and Emotion: Research, Theory, Applications, and Contexts,* pp. 155–188. San Diego, Ca: Academic Press, 1998.

Hart, S. L., and Legerstee, M., eds., *Handbook of Jealousy: Theory, Research, and Multidisciplinary Approaches,* Malden, MA: Blackwell, 2010.

Salovey, P. *The Psychology of Jealousy and Envy.* New York: Guilford, 1991.

Wurmser, L., and Jarass, H., eds., *Jealousy and Envy: New Views About Two Powerful Feelings,* New York: Taylor and Francis, 2008.

Notes

1 C. Safran, "Troubles That Pull Couples Apart: A Redbook Report," *Redbook* (January 1979): 83, 138–141.

2 For a review, see A. L. Vangelisti, "Interpersonal Processes in Romantic Relationships." In M. L. Knapp and J. A. Daly, eds., *Handbook of Interpersonal Communication,* 4th ed. (Thousand Oaks, CA: Sage, 2011), pp. 597–631.

3 "How Americans Communicate: A National Survey." Prepared by Roper Starch for the National Communication Association, 1998.

4 A. L. Vangelisti and T. L. Huston, "Maintaining Marital Satisfaction and Love." In D. J. Canary and L. Stafford, eds., *Communication and Relational Maintenance* (San Diego, CA: Academic, 1994), pp. 165–186.

5 A. J. Hawkins, B. J. Willoughby, and W. J. Doherty, "Reasons for Divorce and Openness to Reconciliation," *Journal of Divorce and Remarriage* 53 (2012): 453–463; H. C. Williamson, T. P. Nguyen, T. N. Bradbury, and B. R. Karney, "Are Problems that Contribute to Divorce

Present at the Start of Marriage, or Do They Emerge Over Time?" *Journal of Social and Personal Relationships,* 33 (2016):1120–1134.

6 J. M. Gottman, *Marital Interaction: Experimental Investigations* (New York: Academic Press, 1979); J. M. Gottman, *What Predicts Divorce? The Relationship Between Marital Processes and Marital Outcomes* (Hillsdale, NJ: Erlbaum, 1994).

7 H. Markman, "The Longitudinal Study of Couples' Interactions: Implications for Understanding and Predicting the Development of Marital Distress." In K. Halweg and N. Jacobson, eds., *Marital Interaction: Analysis and Modification* (New York: Guilford, 1984), pp. 253–281; H. J. Markman, G. K. Rhoades, S. M. Stanley, E. P. Ragan, and S. W. Whitton, "The Premarital communication Roots of Marital Distress and Divorce: The First Five Years of Marriage," *Journal of Family Psychology* 24 (2010): 289–298.

8 J. Belsky and K. H. Hsieh, "Patterns of Marital Change During the Early Childhood Years: Parent Personality, Coparenting, and Division-of-Labor Correlates," *Journal of Family Psychology* 12 (1998): 511–528.

9 B. R. Karney and T. N. Bradbury, "Neuroticism, Marital Interaction, and the Trajectory of Marital Satisfaction," *Journal of Personality and Social Psychology* 72 (1997): 1075–1092; K. A. McGonagle, R. C. Kessler, and I. H. Gotlib, "The Effects of Marital Disagreement Style, Frequency, and Outcome on Marital Disruption," *Journal of Social and Personal Relationships* 10 (1993): 385–404; P. Noller, "Negative Communications in Marriage," *Journal of Social and Personal Relationships* 2 (1985): 289–301.

10 D. Revenstorf, K. Hahlweg, L. Schindler, and B. Vogel, "Interaction Analysis of Marital Conflict." In K. Hahlweg and N. S. Jacobson, eds., *Marital Interaction: Analysis and Modification* (New York: Guilford, 1984), pp. 159–181.

11 T. L. Huston, J. P. Caughlin, R. M. Houts, S. E. Smith, and L. J. George, "The Connubial Crucible: Newlywed Years as Predictors of Marital Delight, Distress, and Divorce," *Journal of Personality and Social Psychology* 80 (2001): 237–252; L. Matthews, K. Wickrama, and R. Conger, "Predicting Marital Instability from Spouse and Observer Reports of Marital Interaction," *Journal of Marriage and the Family* 58 (1996): 641–655.

12 H. Markman and K. Hahlweg, "The Prediction and Prevention of Marital Distress," *Clinical Psychology Review* 13 (1993): 29–43.

13 C. L. Heavey, A. Christensen, and N. M. Malamuth, "The Longitudinal Impact of Demand and Withdrawal During Marital Conflict," *Journal of Consulting and Clinical Psychology* 63 (1995): 797–801; L. J. Roberts, "Fire and Ice in Marital Communication: Hostile and Distancing Behaviors as Predictors of Marital Distress," *Journal of Marriage and the Family* 62 (2000): 693–707.

14 J. Gottman, J. Coan, S. Carrere, and C. Swanson, "Predicting Marital Happiness and Stability from Newlywed Interactions," *Journal of Marriage and the Family* 60 (1998): 5–22.

15 J. E. Salvatore, S. L. Lonn, J. Sundquist, and K. S. Kendler, "Genetics, The Rearing Environment, and the Intergenerational Transmission of Divorce: A Swedish National Adoption Study," *Psychological Science* 29 (2018): 370–378; V. Jockin, M. McGue, and D. T. Lykken, "Personality and Divorce: A Genetic Analysis," *Journal of Personality and Social Psychology* 71 (1996): 288–299; D. T. Lykken, "How Relationships Begin and End." In A. L. Vangelisti, H. T. Reis, and M. A. Fitzpatrick, eds., *Stability and Change in Relationships* (New York: Cambridge University Press, 2002), pp. 85–105.

16 C. M. Bryant and R. D. Conger, "Marital Success and Domains of Social Support in Long-Term Relationships: Does the Influence of Network Members Ever End? *Journal of Marriage and the Family* 61 (1999): 437–450; M. Cleek and T. A. Person, "Perceived Causes of Divorce: An Analysis of Interrelationships," *Journal of Marriage and the Family* 47 (1985): 179–191.

17 T. L. Orbuch, J. Veroff, H. Hassan, and J. Horrocks, "Who Will Divorce: A 14-Year Longitudinal Study of Black Couples and White Couples," *Journal of Social and Personal Relationships* 19 (2002): 179–202.

18 For instance, researchers have found that economic stress is linked to marital distress; see R. Conger, M. Rueter, and G. Elder Jr., "Couple Resilience to Economic Pressure," *Journal of Personality and Social Psychology* 76 (1999): 54–71.

19 P. R. Amato and D. Previti, "People's Reasons for Divorcing: Gender, Social Class, the Life Course, and Adjustment," *Journal of Family Issues* 24 (2003): 602–626.

20 C. T. Hill, Z. Rubin, and L. A. Peplau, "Breakups Before Marriage: The End of 103 Affairs," *Journal of Social Issues* 32 (1976): 147–168.

21 W. R. Cupach and S. Metts, "Accounts of Relational Dissolution: A Comparison of Marital and Nonmarital Relationships," *Communication Monographs* 53 (1986): 328.

22 D. Vaughn, *Uncoupling: How Relationships Come Apart* (New York: Vintage Books, 1987), pp. 169–175, 194–196, 241–244.

23 J. D. Freezel and P. E. Shepherd, "Cross-Generational Coping with Interpersonal Relationship Loss," *Western Journal of Speech Communication* 51 (1987): 317–327.

24 M. Bullock, J. Hackathorn, E. M. Clark, and B A. Mattingly, "Can We Be (and Stay) Friends? Remaining Friends After Dissolution of a Romantic Relationship," *The Journal of social Psychology* 151 (2011): 662–666.

25 J. Simpson, "The Dissolution of Romantic Relationships: Factors Involved in Relationship Stability and Emotional Distress," *Journal of Personality and Social Psychology* 53 (1987): 683–692.

26 D. Davis, P. R. Shaver, and M. L. Vernon, "Physical, Emotional, and Behavioral Reactions to Breaking Up: The Roles of Gender, Age, Emotional Involvement, and Attachment Style," *Personality and Social Psychology Bulletin* 29 (2003): 871–884.

27 P. Perrig-Chiello, S. Hutchinson, and D. Morselli, "Patterns of Psychological Adaptation to Divorce after a Long-Term Marriage," *Journal of Social and Personal Relationships* 32 (2015): 386–405.

28 A. L. Busboom, D. M. Collins, M. D. Givertz, and L. A. Levin, "Can We Still Be Friends? Resources and Barriers to Friendship Quality After Romantic Relationship Dissolution," *Personal Relationships* 9 (2002): 215–223; P. A. Frazier and S. W. Cook, "Correlates of Distress Following Heterosexual Relationship Dissolution," *Journal of Social and Personal Relationships* 10 (1993): 55–67.

29 R. Burnett, P. McGhee, and D. D. Clarke, *Accounting for Relationships: Explanation, Representation, and Knowledge* (London: Methuen, 1987); L. R. Propst and L. Fries, "Problems and Needs of Adults." In M. Textor, ed., *The Divorce and Divorce Therapy Handbook* (Northvale, NJ: Jason Aronson, 1989), pp. 45–60; T. Stephen, "Attribution and Adjustment to Relationship Termination," *Journal of Social and Personal Relationships* 4 (1987): 47–61.

30 L. A. Kurdek, "Adjusting to Relationship Dissolution in Gay, Lesbian, and Heterosexual Partners," *Personal Relationships* 4 (1997): 145–161. Also see L. A. Kurdek, "The Nature and Correlates of Deterrents to Leaving a Relationship," *Personal Relationships* 13 (2006): 521–535.

31 J. J. Ponzetti and R. M. Cate, "The Divorce Process: Toward a Typology of Marital Dissolution," *Journal of Divorce* 11 (1988): 1–20.

32 M. S. Davis, *Intimate Relations* (New York: Free Press, 1973), chapter 8.

33 C. E. Rusbult, S. M. Drigotas, and J. Verette, "The Investment Model: An Interdependence Analysis of Commitment Processes and Relationship Maintenance Phenomena." In D. J. Canary and L. Stafford, eds., *Communication and Relational Maintenance* (San Diego, CA: Academic, 1994), pp. 115–139; C. E. Rusbult, I. M. Zembrodt, and L. K. Gunn, "Exit, Voice, Loyalty, and Neglect: Responses to Dissatisfaction in Romantic Involvements," *Journal of Personality and Social Psychology* 43 (1982): 1230–1242. Also see S. M. Drigotas, C. A. Safstrom, and T. Gentilia, "An Investment Model Prediction of Dating Infidelity," *Journal of Personality and Social Psychology* 77 (1999): 509–524.

34 D. M. Buss, R. J. Larsen, D. Western, and J. Semmelroth, "Sex Differences in Jealousy: Evolution, Physiology, and Psychology," *Psychological Science* 3 (1992): 251–255; D. M. Buss, T. K. Shackelford, L. A. Kirkpatrick, J. C. Choe, H. L. Kim, M. Hasegawa, T. Hasegawa, and K. Bennett, "Jealousy and the Nature of Beliefs about Infidelity: Tests of the Competing Hypothesis about Sex Differences in the United States, Korea, and Japan," *Personal Relationships* 6 (1999): 125–150.

35 D. A. DeSteno and P. Salovey, "Evolutionary Origins of Sex Differences in Jealousy? Questioning the Fitness of the Model," *Psychological Science* 7 (1996): 367–372. For an example of how the double-shot hypothesis applies to gay and lesbian relationships, see P. Dijkstra, H. A. K. Groothof, G. A. Poel, T. T. G. Laverman, M. Schrier, and B. P. Buunk, "Sex Differences in the Events that Elicit Jealousy Among Homosexuals," *Personal Relationships* 8 (2001): 41–54.

36 C. J. Carpenter, "Meta-Analysis of Sex Differences in Response to Sexual Versus Emotional Infidelity: Men and Women are More Similar than Different," *Psychology of Women Quarterly* 36 (2012): 24–37; D. DeSteno, M. Y. Bartlett, P. Salovey, and J. Braverman, "Sex Differences in Jealousy: Evolutionary Mechanism or Artifact of Measurement?" *Journal of Personality and Social Psychology* 83 (2002): 1103–1116. Also see D. DeSteno, "Mismeasuring Jealousy: A Cautionary Note on Levy and Kelly (2010)," *Psychological Science* 21 (2010): 1355–1356.

37 A. Cann and T. R. Baucom, "Former Partners and New Rivals as Threats to a Relationship: Infidelity Type, Gender, and Commitment as Factors Related to Distress and Forgiveness," *Personal Relationships* 11 (2004): 3035–318; B. H. Henline, L, K. Lamke, and M. D. Howard, "Exploring Perceptions of Online Infidelity," *Personal Relationships* 14 (2007): 113–128; J. Sabini and M. C. Green, "Emotional Response to Sexual and Emotional Infidelity: Constants and Differences Across Genders, Samples, and Methods," *Personality and Social Psychology Bulletin* 30 (2004): 1375–1388; B. J. Sagarin and R. E. Guadagno, "Sex Differences in the Contexts of Extreme Jealousy," *Personal Relationships* 11 (2004): 319–328.

38 G. Clanton and L. G. Smith, eds., *Jealousy* (Englewood Cliffs, NJ: Prentice-Hall, 1977), p. 188.

39 C. L. Carson and W. R. Cupach, "Fueling the Flames of the Green-Eyed Monster: The Role of Ruminative Thought in Reaction to Romantic Jealousy," *Western Journal of Communication* 64 (2000): 308–329; L. K. Guerrero, M. R. Trost, and S. M. Yoshimura, "Romantic Jealousy: Emotions and Communicative Responses," *Personal Relationships* 12 (2005): 233–252; for a list of tactics partners may use to "retain" their partners in the face of relational threats, see D. M. Buss and T. K. Shackelford, "From Vigilance to Violence: Mate Retention Tactics in Married Couples," *Journal of Personality and Social Psychology* 72 (1997): 346–361.

40 S. Puente and D. Cohen, "Jealousy and the Meaning (or Nonmeaning) of Violence," *Personality and Social Psychology Bulletin* 29 (2003): 449–460.

41 L. K. Guerrero and W. A. Afifi, "Toward a Goal-Oriented Approach for Understanding Communicative Responses to Jealousy," *Western Journal of Communication* 63 (1999): 216–248.

42 L. K. Guerrero, and P. A. Andersen, "Jealousy Experience and Expression in Romantic Relationships." In P. A. Andersen and L. K. Guerrero, eds., *Handbook of Communication and Emotion: Research, Theory, Applications, and Contexts* (San Diego, CA: Academic Press, 1998) pp. 155–188.

43 See, for example, L. K. Guerrero "Attachment-Style Differences in the Experience and Expression of Romantic Jealousy," *Personal Relationships* 5 (1998): 273–291; D. J. Sharpsteen, "The Effects of Relationship and Self-Esteem Threats on the Likelihood of Romantic Jealousy," *Journal of Social and Personal Relationships* 12 (1995): 89–101.

44 P. Salovey and J. Rodin, "The Heart of Jealousy," *Psychology Today* (September, 1985), pp. 22–29.

45 C. Ellis and E. Weinstein, "Jealousy and the Social Psychology of Emotional Experience," *Journal of Social and Personal Relationships* 3 (1986): 337–357.

46 L. Stafford and J. R. Reske, "Idealization and Communication in Long-Distance Premarital Relationships," *Family Relations* 39 (1990): 274–279. Also see J. L. Borelli, H. F. Rasmussen, M. Burkhart, and D. A. Sbarra, "Relational Savoring in Long-Distance Romantic Relationships," *Journal of Social and Personal Relationships* 32 (2015): 1083–1108.

47 For articles describing variables linked to the success or failure of long distance relationships see K. C. Maguire and T. A. Kinney, "When Distance is Problematic: Communication, Coping, and Relational Satisfaction in Female College Students' Long Distance Dating Relationships," *Journal of Applied Communication Research* 38 (2010): 27–46; M. C. Pistole, A. Roberts, and M. L. Chapman, "Attachment, Relationship Maintenance, and Stress in Long Distance and Geographically Close Romantic Relationships," *Journal of Social and Personal Relationships* 27 (2010): 535–552.

48 D. H. Felmlee, "Fatal Attractions: Affection and Disaffection in Intimate Relationships," *Journal of Social and Personal Relationships* 12 (1995): 295–311; D. H. Felmlee, "'Be Careful What You Wish For . . . ': A Quantitative and Qualitative Investigation of 'Fatal Attractions,'" *Personal Relationships* 5 (1998): 235–253; D. H. Felmlee, "Disenchantment with a Romantic Partner," *Sociological Perspectives* 44 (2001): 263–280.

49 For a meta-analysis of factors predicting the dissolution of nonmarital romantic relationships see B. Le, N. L. Dove, C. R. Agnew, M. S. Korn, and A. A. Mutso, "Predicting nonmarital romantic relationship dissolution: A meta-analytic synthesis. *Personal Relationships* 17 (2010): 377–390.

50 Hill, Rubin, and Peplau, "Breakups Before Marriage," pp. 156–157.

51 W. H. Jones and M. P. Burdette, "Betrayal in Relationships." In A. L. Weber and J. H. Harvey, eds., *Perspectives on Close Relationships* (Boston: Allyn Bacon, 1994), pp. 243–262.

52 D. Vaughn, *Uncoupling*, pp. 132–134.

53 S. Duck, "A Topography of Relationship Disengagement and Dissolution." In S. Duck, ed., *Personal Relationships 4: Dissolving Personal Relationships* (New York: Academic Press, 1982), pp. 1–30.

54 S. S. Rollie and S.W. Duck, "Divorce and Dissolution of Romantic Relationships: Stage Models and their Limitations." In M. A. Fine and J. H. Harvey, eds., *Handbook of Divorce and Relationship Dissolution* (Mahwah, NJ: Lawrence Erlbaum Associates, 2006), pp. 223–240.

55 L. LeFebvre, K. Blackburn, and N. Brody, "Navigating Romantic Relationships on Facebook: Extending the Relationship Dissolution Model to Social Networking Environments," *Journal of Social and Personal Relationships,* 32 (2015): 78–98.

56 J. H. Harvey, A. L. Weber, and T. L. Orbuch, *Interpersonal Accounts: A Social Psychological Perspective* (Oxford: Basil Blackwell, 1990).

57 J. Doering, "Face, Accounts, and Schemes in the Context of Relationship Breakups," *Symbolic Interaction,* 33 (2010): 71–95.

58 J. H. Harvey, T. L. Orbuch, and A. L. Weber, "A Social Psychological Model of Account-Making in Response to Severe Stress," *Journal of Language and Social Psychology* 9 (1990): 191–207.

59 A. L. Weber, J. H., Harvey, and T. L. Orbuch, "What Went Wrong: Communicating Accounts of Relationship Conflict." In M. L. McLaughlin, M. J. Cody, and S. J. Read, eds., *Explaining One's Self to Others: Reason-Giving in a Social Context* (Hillsdale, NJ: Erlbaum, 1992), pp. 261–280.

60 Author Lillian Hellman prefaces her book, *Pentimento,* with the following definition: "Old paint on canvas, as it ages, sometimes becomes transparent. When that happens it is possible, in some pictures, to see the original lines: a tree will show through a woman's dress, a child makes way for a dog, a large boat is no longer on an open sea. That is called pentimento, because the painter 'repented,' changed his mind. Perhaps it would be as well to say that the old conception, replaced by a later choice, is a way of seeing and then seeing again."

61 M. Cody, "A Typology of Disengagement Strategies and an Examination of the Role of Intimacy, Reactions to Inequity and Relational Problems Play in Strategy Selection," *Communication Monographs* 49 (1982): 148–170.

62 S. P. Banks, D. M. Altendorf, J. O. Greene, and M. J. Cody, "An Examination of Relationship Disengagement: Perceptions, Breakup Strategies and Outcomes," *Western Journal of Speech Communication* 51 (1987): 19–41.

63 S. Sprecher, C. Zimmerman, and E. M. Abrahams, "Choosing Compassionate Strategies to End a Relationship: Effects of Compassionate Love for Partner and the Reason For Breakup," *Social Psychology* 51 (2010): 66–75.

64 See, for example: R. Hopper and K. Drummond, "Emergent Goals at a Relational Turning Point: The Case of Gordon and Denise," *Journal of Language and Social Psychology* 9 (1991): 39–65.

65 J. Ayres, "Perceived Use of Evaluative Statements in Developing, Stable, and Deteriorating Relationships with a Person of the Same or Opposite Sex," *Western Journal of Speech Communication* 46 (1982): 20–31.

66 T. M. Emmers and R. D. Hart, "Romantic Relationship Disengagement and Coping Rituals," *Communication Research* 13 (1996): 8–18.

67 Indeed, Metts argued that initiators may increase their use of such "polite" strategies as the loss incurred from ending the relationship increases (see S. Metts, "The Language of Disengagement: A Face-Management Perspective." In T. L. Orbuch, ed., *Close Relationship Loss,* New York: Springer-Verlag, 1992, pp. 111–127).

68 L. A. Baxter, "Strategies for Ending Relationships: Two Studies," *Western Journal of Speech Communication* 46 (1982): 223–241.

69 J. A. Hess, "Distance Regulation in Personal Relationships: The Development of a Conceptual Model and a Test of Representational Validity," *Journal of Social and Personal Relationships* 19 (2002): 663–683.

70 D. R. Peterson, "Assessing Interpersonal Relationships by Means of Interaction Records," *Behavioral Assessment* 1 (1979): 225.

71 R. L. Street and H. Giles, "Speech Accommodation Theory." In M. E. Roloff and C. R Berger, eds., *Social Cognition and Communication* (Beverly Hills, CA: Sage, 1982), pp. 193–226.

72 M. L. Knapp, R. P. Hart, G. W. Friedrich, and G. M. Shulman, "The Rhetoric of Goodbye: Verbal and Nonverbal Correlates of Human Leave-Taking," *Speech Monographs* 40 (1973): 182–198. For additional information on human leave-taking, see A. Adato, "Leave Taking: A Study of

Commonsense Knowledge Social Structure," *Anthropological Quarterly* 48 (1975): 255–271; S. J. Sigman, "Handling the Discontinuous Aspects of Continuous Social Relationships: Toward Research on the Persistence of Social Forms," *Communication Theory* 1 (1991): 106–127.

73 Davis, *Intimate Relations,* p. 271, rightly notes that the term *friends* is often used euphemistically between ex-intimates to connote a relationship that manifests characteristics of acquaintances.

74 See, for example, F. D. Fincham and T. N. Bradbury, "Marital Satisfaction, Depression, and Attributions: A Longitudinal Analysis," *Journal of Personality and Social Psychology* 64 (1993): 442–452. For a review see T. N Bradbury and F. D. Fincham, "Attributions in Marriage: Review and Critique," *Psychological Review* 107 (1990): 3–33.

75 J. P. Forgas, "Sad and Guilty? Affective Influences on the Explanation of Conflict in Close Relationships," *Journal of Personality and Social Psychology* 66 (1994): 56–68.

76 C. A. Anderson, R. S. Miller, A. L. Riger, J. C. Dill, and C. Sedikides, "Behavioral and Characterological Attributional Styles as Predictors of Depression and Loneliness: Review, Refinement, and Test," *Journal of Personality and Social Psychology* 66 (1994): 549–558.

77 E. Goffman, *Relations in Public* (New York: Basic Books, 1971), p. 83.

78 M. S. Davis, *Intimate Relations.* (New York: The Free Press, 1973.

CHAPTER 11

The Dialogue of Distance and De-escalation

Dear Dr. Vangelisti,

This guy and I have been going together for a long time. We both love each other. However, he is a very moody person. He is quick to jump down my throat for stupid things. When I try to defend myself and explain, a bigger disagreement breaks out. When I say I'm sorry (to avoid a fight), he tells me he doesn't like "pansies," and he knows why I'm saying that I'm sorry. He says I should tell him how I feel, but I know he'll ignore me or we'll have a fight. I don't know what to do. He's so good in so many ways, but I feel helpless in situations like this.

Perplexed Pansy

Some patterns of communication are more likely than others to be associated with the deterioration of relationships. The pattern described here may create a momentary distance between the man and woman; but if practiced often enough, it may lead to a more permanent separation. The woman is asked to state how she feels, but when she does, she feels she is punished. This and other potentially troublesome patterns of communication are discussed in this chapter.

There are many ways to express caring for another person—for example, a gift, a telephone call, a back rub. But sometimes one person's perception of what constitutes a display of affection and caring does not match his or her partner's perception. Consider the husband who resents his wife's being late for appointments— "If she cared about me, she wouldn't be late like this." In the husband's family, being on time was a sign of caring, and tardiness required an extended apology. Although the wife is aware of her husband's concern for her being on time, she doesn't associate it with her caring or not caring for him. Her family was chronically late to everything and so is she. In this case, then, the husband's and the wife's rules for sending and receiving messages of affection do not correspond. Similarly, a husband who works long hours may think, "If my wife cares about me, she'll appreciate my working so hard for her." The wife, however, says to herself, "If my husband really loved me, he would want to spend more time with me and not so much time at work."

On other occasions, these messages of caring and affection are communicated in ways agreed to by both relationship partners, but the painful channels involved may ultimately hurt the relationship. For instance, a wife criticizes her husband's behavior to such an extent that it is hard for him to do anything to please her. As a result, he sometimes breaks things or threatens suicide or takes an overdose of drugs. This behavior elicits a great deal of caring and kindly behavior from the wife. Both agree that the wife's behavior during these times is a sign she really loves her husband. When the husband is no longer "out of control," the wife returns to her critical behavior, expressing her resentment for his previous irresponsibility. A related example concerns a husband who can't lose weight because both husband and wife agree that (1) the wife's love for her husband is shown when she cooks rich and big meals, and (2) the husband's love for his wife is shown by the gusto he displays in eating large quantities of her cooking. In each example, the couple was relying on painful channels of communication for sending and receiving messages of caring and affection.[1]

All the preceding examples illustrate patterns of communication that may lead to divisiveness in a relationship. Sometimes our relationship messages are rooted in different rules, and at other times the partners agree on the rules, but these rules reinforce pain in the relationship. These are only two of many communication patterns that tend to precipitate relationship de-escalation. Ruinous communication patterns can be triggered by a variety of stimuli.[2] Sometimes they are precipitated by events that are perceived to be a violation of a relationship covenant, promise, or expectation. Examples of this might involve infidelity; revealing a partner's secret; or being rude, unappreciative, or inconsiderate of one's partner, especially in public. Value differences related to important relationship issues such as fairness or responsibility also may trigger destructive communication patterns. Certain personality characteristics such as paranoia, overly selfish or self-oriented behavior, and dominance also are capable of triggering unproductive interaction. And sometimes it is a particular way of communicating, which is not a problem for the couple as long as it occurs only infrequently; but when it is repeated over a long period of time, it can create the kind of stress and irritation that precipitates even worse patterns of communication. Complaining and not listening carefully are two examples of such behavior. This chapter is devoted to the explication of a variety of these troubling communication patterns.

Some Potentially Destructive Patterns of Communication: An Interpersonal Chamber of Horrors

Even though some people's communication patterns seem to "drive us crazy," we should remind ourselves that *any* communication pattern has the potential for being perceived as destructive. An extremely paranoid person might perceive a hurried "hello" as a negative evaluation of his or her personality. Although we can agree that perceived destructiveness is in the mind of the observer, we also know that some communication patterns elicit reactions such as fear, distrust, hurt, confusion, vengeance, relationship devaluation, and decreased self-worth, which numerous experts and laypersons believe are unproductive for relationship growth. These patterns are the focus for the remainder of this chapter. They are problematic because they represent extremes—either they are extreme behavioral styles or they are practiced extremely often. The extremes we'll be dealing with are *helpful-critical, active-passive, aggressive-evasive, dominating-submissive,* and *certain-provisional.* As we discuss these various patterns, keep in mind that these specific categories are not mutually exclusive; that is, a pattern may be aggressive and also critical or an attempt at domination may be made by being evasive.

Even though a pattern may be destructive for many people, there is always the possibility that a particular configuration of events, time, and personalities will not activate a pattern's destructive potential. For some of the patterns discussed, the question of whether it is toxic rests on the frequency with which it appears. A pattern may be very effective in accomplishing one's goals one day but very ineffective if used repeatedly. Obviously, many other contingencies affect our reactions to various styles of communicating. When we are physically tired or hungry, we may become antagonistic toward statements that ordinarily would not upset us. People who have had a lot of exposure to a given style of communicating will react differently from someone meeting up with it for the first time. The question of whether any given style of communicating will be considered "abnormal," "frustrating," "insane," or whatever also is a function of the climate of the times, a function of what society or a given subculture defines as normal communication. Was the U.S. military spokesman's infamous comment during the Vietnam War—"We had to destroy the village in order to save it"—symptomatic of the climate of the times or an isolated instance of craziness in message sending? Communication patterns can be offensive, confusing, or damaging simply because of individual differences, perhaps the inability of a person to carry off certain styles. For instance, one person we know tries to be sarcastic but can't emphasize the contrast between voice and words sufficiently, so most people simply glare at him, stupefied, not knowing if he is serious or kidding. The issue of communicative effectiveness, or competence, will be discussed more extensively in Chapter 12, but a knowledge of these contingencies (and we've mentioned only a few) should make us less prone to condemn a word, phrase, tactic, game, or pattern as "bad" without placing it in a specific context with specific people.

In spite of the preceding qualifications, some will still have a tendency to see the following patterns of communication as vile and ruinous and therefore in need of eradication. A number of people would argue that eradication is impossible, that antidotes (especially when applied with missionary zeal) will give rise only to a new disease. Penicillin can eradicate some bacteria, but for those who are allergic to it, the cure only brings greater costs. The words of Koestler's fictional revolutionary make the same point:

> All our principles were right, but our results were wrong. This is a diseased century. We diagnosed the disease and its causes with microscopic exactness, but wherever we applied the healing knife a new sore appeared. Our will was hard and pure, we should have been loved by the people. But they hate us.[3]

And some people would argue that eradication of these so-called destructive patterns of communication would be dysfunctional—that the process of learning to cope with life's tragedies is healthy. Our own personal view is that we should approach these potentially destructive patterns of communication as follows:

1. We should recognize and accept the fact that we will probably never communicate perfectly, but that we should continue trying to do so.
2. We should recognize and accept the fact that others (like us) will probably never communicate perfectly, but we should continue to help them in their efforts to do so—for example, by not being a receptive victim to a destructively manipulative strategy or by resisting the temptation to match (or supersede) the destructiveness of messages directed to us.[4]

3. We should, therefore, recognize and accept the idea that the responsibility for interpersonal destruction cannot ever rest entirely with one person— "I criticize you because you won't leave me alone." "I won't leave you alone because you criticize me."

4. We should try to minimize the usage of any communicative strategy that consistently fails to achieve the results we would like.[5]

5. When we are trapped (or go voluntarily) into a destructive spiral, we should try to learn enough about what happened to us so that we can better cope with it next time.

Helpful-Critical Patterns

Helpful. Initially, it may be hard to conceive of a helpful pattern of communication that is potentially divisive. At least two instances, however, might qualify. Both are attempts to "save" or "protect" others by being helpful. One instance occurs when a person does not need or request help, but the other person insists on giving it. The second instance occurs when a person requests help, and the other person agrees to provide the help but does not deliver.

With all the best intentions, our partners in a close relationship sometimes insist on helping us when we don't ask for their help, nor need it. Consider a situation in which one partner always "helps" the other person tell a funny story at parties. The helper definitely makes the story funny, but the other person wants to, and is perfectly capable of, effectively telling the story by him- or herself. "Helpful" intrusions like this tend to rob the other person of the personal satisfactions associated with performing a task and diminish any self-esteem that might be associated with successfully accomplishing a goal.[6]

A popular and often infuriating mechanism necessary to foretell another's need for help is mindreading. **Mindreading** is an attempt by one person to predict and state to another what the other person is feeling or thinking, how he or she will react, what he or she will accept or reject, what his or her motivations are, and so forth. It can be particularly irritating when the mindreader "helps" an individual by publicly stating the person's thoughts or feelings to a third person in a public setting. If the person denies the accuracy of the mindreader or expresses displeasure with the act of mindreading itself, the mindreader can show a bewildered distress at the ungrateful reaction to "a sincere effort to help you." The following comments might come from helpful mindreaders in different situations:

Mindreading: Assuming complete knowledge of the other person's thoughts and motives.

- You can't fool me. I can read you like a book.
- You're not hurt. You're just embarrassed.
- I can tell you're upset and have had a bad day. No? (Patronizing chuckle that dismisses the denial) Oh, now, don't try to hide it … sit down and tell me about it.
- Judging from the way you're acting, your period must be due soon.
- What you need is a drink.
- I know you're trying not to bring it up, but I know you're thinking about it. You're still mad at me for what I said yesterday.

It doesn't really matter whether the mindreader is accurate or not; the act itself can be aggravating and possibly even more aggravating when accurate. It is true that as intimacy grows, our knowledge of the other also grows, and the other will welcome educated guesses sometimes. With less intimacy, we will probably embrace the strategy less. Most of us want to feel that there is some unpredictability and mystery about us. Even if there isn't much, it can be maddening to be told there isn't any. Furthermore, mindreading often is acted out in a patronizing manner, a manner that, when practiced often enough, tends to drain responsibility for self and knowledge of self from the person being "helped."

The other instance of destructively helpful behavior occurs when help is requested and promised but is either withheld or perceived as unusable. The sequence might go like this: (1) A student feels that the class material is understandable, studies diligently, yet scores low on examinations. (2) The student requests help with the problem from the instructor. (3) The instructor indicates a "willingness to help any student having problems." (4) The instructor is unable to make any of the appointments to discuss the matter, or after a lengthy elaboration of the problem by the student, the instructor quickly terminates the conference by telling the student to "study harder." (5) Now the student gets sullen or angry. (6) This prompts the instructor to show indignation and disappointment in the student—"Boy, that's the thanks I get. I was only trying to help."[7]

Critical. The hypercritical pattern is rarely masked by an exterior of helpfulness or protectiveness. It is more often raw negativity. If there is a chance (and there always is) of finding a flaw, it will be found and brought up:

Wanna go out Friday night?

Sure.

What do you want to do?

How about going to a movie?

There's nothin' on except those dumb musicals and horror shows.

There's a basketball game at the stadium.

You want to fight those crowds? Besides, there's no way we'll win.

Why don't we go out to eat?

That'd be great if we had the kind of money they hit you for … and Burger Queen isn't my idea of eating out.

Well, we could stay home and watch TV. I could make some popcorn.

Yeah … but we always do that.

OK. *You* do what you want, and *I'll* go out with somebody else.

A variation on this sequence may occur when the first person's complaint is countered with a complaint by the second person—"Why do we always have to have hamburgers? I'm getting tired of it." "Well, if you'd get a better job and make more money we could afford steak." A second variation occurs when the criticism is frozen in time—"You got a D in college math and now you want to be responsible for paying the bills and keeping the checkbook balanced? Ha!" This pattern uses the past as a weapon to prove "you'll always be who you used to be." Positive things are hard for hypercritical people to see and still maintain their critical stance. If all we learn from the past is what to hold against another, the study of interpersonal histories isn't worth much.

The critical disaster seeker who looks at the world through black-colored glasses is certainly not without impact on those who are on the receiving end. Constant negativity, even if it isn't directed at the other person, can have a dampening, depressing effect. Humor (other than sarcasm) is a rare commodity. Constant negative statements can make the receiver feel so bad, he or she provides even more stimuli for the complainer to latch onto; it can make the receiver begin to feel negative and that the other isn't much fun to be around.

Sometimes people will focus their negativity and criticism on the other person's personality or behavior. Whether it is actually intended to hurt the feelings of the other person or not, if the other person believes it was intentional, it tends to be particularly hurtful.[8] When hurt is the intended goal, the source of the criticism may be trying to see how much criticism, no matter how unreasonable, the other will take in order to avoid giving up the relationship. This is indeed an insidious way of testing another's commitment to the relationship. Ironically, the people who are most critical and negative also may be the very people who need close, positive, and uncritical relationships the most. Examples of especially hurtful criticism directed at another's behavior and personality include the following:

- Accusations: "You're such a hypocrite." "You caused your grandmother's death. She died of a broken heart because you didn't show her how much you loved her."
- Evaluations: "You're going to look like a blimp if you keep eating that stuff." "You're worthless. You never have done anything worthwhile and you never will." "You don't know what it means to love someone."
- Disclosure: "You're mother told me she never loved you."
- Information: "I had sex with Melvin while you were gone."

Active-Passive Patterns

Active. The level of intensity with which two people approach their encounters also may be carried to divisive extremes. At one extreme is what may sometimes amount to the equivalent of a Siamese twin, someone who is always with you. Interpersonal hyperactivity can be characterized by a person who is constantly seeking any interaction with anyone. Being together is an important end in itself. Sometimes it is not enough simply to be together; it is necessary to be friends.[9] In such cases, we would expect a barrage of "getting close" activity very soon after contact—confiding secrets, using nicknames. It is hard to ignore such intensity, and hard for many to adjust to and like for sustained periods of time. Interactions with such people are often characterized by a high degree of talkativeness;

extraversion; a never-ending list of questions; intense involvement in almost every topic, even the most mundane; and an exhibitionistic participation, which at times includes frequent fever-pitched emotional highs and lows. The frequency of questions that probe every minute detail of the other's experience also may be perceived as an interrogation representing a lack of trust rather than as a sincere interest in what, for many people, is unnecessary filler. If this perceived lack of trust develops, the hyperactive strategy elicits just the opposite reaction from what was desired. Even without the element of trust entering the picture, this extremely active style may cause others to recoil and withdraw. Such reactions may be a result of others feeling that the extroverted, hypertalkative person is trying too hard, forcing them to pay attention or listen, and evidencing a certain desperation in seeking attention or affection.[10] Others may fear getting involved with a person whose desperation could reflect instability.

Passive. At the other end of the scale is the passive person, who is withdrawn, uninvolved, and introverted—a regular passenger on the line of least resistance. This behavior may appear only at certain times, such as at the inception of a disagreement or when a sensitive topic is brought up; sometimes it is more characteristic of a person's general communicative (life) style. In either case, it is common for the person exhibiting a passive style to leave the field of interaction. The person may do this by remaining in the same area but adopting strategies that negate his or her presence while simultaneously denying the validity of the other's argument. Examples include responding continually with silence, pseudo-agreement to reduce the length of the other's argument ("Right." "Um-hmm." "Sure."), or indifference and lack of commitment ("Do what you want"; "I don't care"). The passive person may dramatize the need to withdraw or avoid others by announcing departure at an inappropriate juncture—saying "I'm going to bed" in the middle of another's statement. Equally upsetting, but more devious, is the technique of using sullenness and withdrawal as a means of testing the other person's relationship commitment—seeing how long it will take before the other will try to draw him or her back into participation and coldly observing what methods are used.

Keep in mind that we are not condemning the need to withdraw or to be alone or people with a generally quiet, retiring demeanor. We are saying that a chronic pattern of passivity or withdrawal is *one* style that can be troublesome for relationship maintenance.

A related pattern of interaction often reported to counselors and therapists involves this approach-withdrawal sequence. According to therapist Pierre Mornell, most wives who seek his help for marital counseling want "something more" than what their husbands are giving them. A wife may complain about something specific, but the message is really about her wanting more investment from her husband. He hears her demands for more time spent with her, or more help with kids, or more help around the house, and it seems like she is asking for a lot. He may think, "why is she always so demanding? I don't need this." And the more she tries to get him to give more, the more he feels imposed upon or threatened, which makes him withdraw from her. Of course, because the problem in her view is he is not invested enough, his withdrawal just enrages her, and she redoubles her efforts to get him to provide something more to her and their relationship. Not surprisingly, when she tried harder to change him, it often just makes him more determined to avoid her and her demands. As he moves toward a state of near total passivity, this just makes her more and most hostile. Such cycles can last for years, and once they get started, each person's behavior tends to encourage the other's.[11]

Keep in mind that this same sequence can occur with a female withdrawing and a male who wants "something he's not getting." In fact, both members of heterosexual couples who desire to change their partner have been found to exhibit and reciprocate the demand-withdrawal sequence.[12] It also is a pattern that may be seen in same-sexed dyads as well. The important point is to understand the potentially destructive power of the *pattern* if it is practiced too often or at the wrong time.

Aggressive-Evasive Patterns

The primary distinction between the aggressive and the evasive styles of behavior is the degree of directness. The aggressive style is characterized by a straightforward, head-on orientation in which the aggressor takes full responsibility for his or her messages. Hostility and control are the bywords for this pattern.[13] Evasive strategies, on the other hand, are typified by tangents, misdirection, vagueness, and confusion. Message responsibility is often shirked by the sender. You may not like the aggressive pattern, but at least you know where you stand.

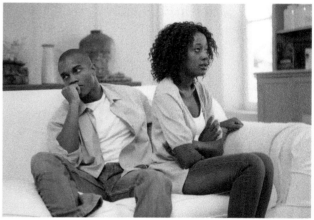

© *wavebreakmedia/Shutterstock.com*

Aggressive. Rosenfield, Hayes, and Frentz have discussed a process they call **hassling**.[14] Hassling isn't the same as aggression, but it involves a five-step sequence that is progressively destructive and aggressive. These five steps associated with hassling vividly remind us how aggressive patterns of communication often manifest themselves. The steps in this sequence are called (1) repartée, (2) cliché, (3) name-calling, (4) provocation, and (5) physiological degeneration.

Hassling: A five-step destructive sequence that demonstrates how aggressive patterns of communication often manifest themselves.

Repartée. The earliest signs of antagonism between combatants appear in the form of witty remarks. These remarks are clever attempts to put the other person down. Like a game of tag, each person is trying to be the last one to touch or hit the other so as not to be "it." Consider, for example, this father-son exchange as the son is leaving the house one evening:

FATHER:	Too bad you can't stay longer. I've got some interesting people for you to meet—your family.
SON:	Oh really? Do you know them?
FATHER:	Yeah, all except one gypsy who doesn't spend much time in any one place.
SON:	Well, sometimes you gotta be quick if you want to catch the best.

Cliché. This stage seems to grow out of the first but differs in the originality of the retorts. The participants are no longer listening very carefully and have to resort to canned or programmed comments.

FATHER:	Is that right?
SON:	You got it, man.
FATHER:	Oh yeah?
SON:	Yeah.
FATHER:	*Very* funny.
SON:	Ha! I'll bet.

Name-Calling. At this point, the assailants begin to use more potent verbiage, trying to humiliate and ridicule with stigmatizing labels. In some cases, this means the use of ethnic slurs. In the conversational sequence we've been following between the father and son, we might hear labels such as hypocrite, child, bum, leech, pig, freak. Name-calling is only one example of destructive labeling. In the process of the deterioration of a relationship, the participants are often prone to look for data to justify their bad feelings and explain their crumbling relationship. It is not uncommon to look for these data in the behavior of the other person. Hence, behavior that may have seemed odd, strange, or atypical during the growth stages may now be labeled as crazy, neurotic, or insane. What was once merely suspicion may now be labeled paranoia. Emotional acts may now be designated as hysteria. If the other person's behavior was "down" or "blue" before, it might now be labeled a state of depression. The same thing happens in the course of one's life span. When you're young, you repeat yourself and forget things, but when you get old, the same behavior may qualify you for the label *senile*. Unfortunately, these labels are often hard to shed, especially when more than one person begins to use the label and when *you* wonder if there might be some validity to it.

Provocation. Even though all the stages mentioned thus far operate on the assumption that "if you can't compete, get out of the interaction," the provocation stage is the strongest test. Both participants know that this is the last chance to designate a "winner" using only words as weapons. This stage is characterized by insults, threats, and accusations. Insults and threats also may follow a progressively assertive sequence. What started out as a nonverbal signal (mock smile, eyes rolled upward and accompanied by an upward spiral gesture made with the index finger) may eventually manifest itself as "That's the dumbest thing I've ever heard, as if it made any difference anyway." Threats also may reflect a developmental pattern: "I'm liable to get mad … really mad … so don't push me … you just try to get away with it—see what it gets you … OK, but I'll remember this." More dramatic appeals are likely to be peppered with what has traditionally been called obscene terminology—"One more crack like that and I'm going to beat the shit out of you." The degree of emphasis applied at this stage is contingent on how effective one's remarks have been at previous stages and to what extent a person has suppressed his or her anger up to this point.

© MicroOne/Shutterstock.com

Physiological Degeneration. At this stage, the participants' faces tighten while their bodies ready for what seems to be the only alternative—a physical fight. Sometimes when the dialogue reaches the fight stage and there is a clear physical inequity, a temper tantrum might result instead of a fight—a husband or lover putting his fist through a door or a child throwing a fit in front of his or her parents. Others who arrive at this stage and feel they can't win a physical encounter may break down, showing they have already been sufficiently abused.

Although the preceding five stages do seem to represent the basic elements of the aggressive pattern, the following should be noted: (1) Even though we often see the aggressive pattern in the sequence presented, the pattern can be entered at any stage in the sequence—for example, an aggression may start with insults and move quickly into physical contact. (2) Even though a certain compelling force is driving the participants toward greater intensity, they can step out of the sequence at any point. Obviously, the ability to step out is sometimes easier in the early stages, but it is not hard to understand why an opponent might be more than willing to allow the other to withdraw at the provocation stage. (3) Stages also may be skipped. But as soon as one person verbalizes thoughts and feelings, the other will usually know where the process was picked up and what is expected in return. (4) Most important, while aggressive tendencies are usually directed at other people, the stimulus for anger is, more often than we may realize or want to admit, something about our own behavior we're displeased with; for example, people who are themselves interested in alternative romantic partners tend to imagine that their partner is attracted to other partners, which often leads them to act negatively toward their partner, even though the source of their anger was really their own "wandering eye."[15]

Couple Violence. Ironically, violence and physical abuse are no strangers to people who profess to have an intimate relationship.[16] It occurs in gay and lesbian relationships as well as heterosexual relationships.[17] In one national survey of about 16,000 American men and women in heterosexual close relationships, 22.1 percent of the women and 7.4 percent of the men indicated their partner had committed at least one violent act against them.[18] One source estimates there are 200,000 people in the United States who are assaulted by their intimate partner each year and that

2,000 of those assaults are fatal.[19] The fact that women engage in violent acts may come as a surprise to some readers, but experts tell us that surveys of the general population reveal women as slightly more likely than men to be initiators of aggression in intimate relationships.[20] The most common forms of assault involved slapping or hitting followed by pushing, grabbing, or shoving. Both men and women may use knives, but women are more likely to bite, kick, and punch whereas men are more likely to choke, strangle, and repeatedly hit their partners. Men typically inflict more damage.

What causes violence in close relationships? There are many reasons. Most relationships have to deal with stressful events—even major ones such as losing a job, going into debt, or an unplanned pregnancy. Not surprisingly, these events can lead to short tempers, conflict, and the exchange of harsh words. When couples do not have the skills to resolve these conflicts and relieve the stress, frustration and violence may erupt. One or both partners may think that the control or domination of their partner will make their problems less stressful, but these actions are more likely to aggravate their partner and create more stress—leading to violence. The use of alcohol and/or drugs also may be viewed as a way to forget one's problems, but drugs and alcohol can make violence a more likely choice to deal with problems. Needless to say, alcohol and drugs are not recommended for effective problem solving. In addition, one or both partners to the relationship may not see violence as an unnatural part of an intimate relationship because it was what they observed while growing up in their own family.[21]

Situational couple violence: Type of couple violence that occurs when typical conflict gets out of control and leads to a violent act.

Coercive controlling violence: Type of couple violence that occurs as part of a pattern in which one partner dominates and controls the other partner's daily life through violence, harassment, threats, and other tactics that invoke fear.

In an effort to further understand the nature of violence in intimate relationships, Johnson and others have found a key distinction based on the extent to which the violence is used by one person to systematically control the other person through coercion.[22] Some violent episodes, referred to as **situational couple violence** (formerly called common couple violence), happen when typical conflict in a couple gets out of control and leads to a violent act. In this case, violence is not used as a way of asserting control or power over one's partner, and bodily harm to the victims is usually less extreme. **Coercive controlling violence** is sometimes called intimate terrorism (or patriarchal terrorism) because it occurs as part of a pattern in which one partner dominates and controls the other partner's daily life through violence, harassment, threats, and other tactics that invoke fear. This pattern nearly always involves violence used by males to exert power over a female partner. The degree of bodily harm is often extreme.

Coercive controlling violence often follows a recurring cycle or pattern.[23] Battered wives, for example, have reported that the cycle of abuse begins with minor battering for which the wife often blames herself. Then more severe battering occurs, causing serious injury. Next, the husband promises to change, gives gifts, acts charming, and in general, plays on her feelings of guilt and sympathy. The wife hopes this temporary behavior will become permanent and remains in the relationship—only to become the victim of another incident of the husband's out-of-control rage. Perhaps one question most frequently asked by people who have not faced this kind of aggression is why the victims stay in the relationship so long after the first beating. Some of the most commonly mentioned reasons include (1) the fear that leaving may only bring on additional violence; (2) the real or perceived lack of support, protection, and safety from friends and community agencies; (3) the feeling of isolation that sometimes keeps the battered woman from gaining knowledge and support; (4) a rock-bottom self-esteem, which argues that she deserves what she gets; and (5) a paradoxical bonding or dependency with the batterer—a person who, when he is good, provides just what she needs—and he is often good following the physical violence. It also should be noted that physical abuse is only one kind of abuse in relationships of this type. Others include restricting freedom to go places and do things; threats to hurt the person financially; making decisions for the other person; requiring sexual behavior against the partner's protestations; intimidation through looks, yelling, smashing things, and physically abusing children or pets. Contrary to what some of these wives believe, this kind of behavior should not be considered typical or tolerable—even though many of these husbands and wives have observed frequent incidents of such violence in other families. There are no doubt many explanations for physically abusing a person you purportedly care about, but the most frequently cited reasons attributed to male abusers are fear of abandonment and fear of rejection.

Evasiveness. Evasiveness, even though it is less direct than the aggressive pattern, can be equally damaging to a relationship if used often enough. Remember that some evasive strategies can be, on any given occasion, the best alternative for communicating—particularly when you perceive all your options for response will elicit negative reactions.[24] This discussion will focus on four general methods of evasiveness: (1) changing the focus of responsibility, (2) changing the direction of the conversation, (3) changing the level of the conversation, and (4) sending incongruous messages.

Changing the Focus of Responsibility. This method uses another person or object to distract or divert attention away from oneself. The purpose of this technique is not simply to change the focus of conversation. Generally, evasive maneuvers have three purposes: (1) avoiding responsibility and control over one's own behavior, (2) giving an excuse to provide a rational explanation for one's behavior, and (3) making someone or something else look like the sole destructive element. Responsibility and control for one's behavior can be dumped on any number of sources—"The boss makes me bring all this work home. I don't want to," or "I know I don't go out much anymore, but Charles is

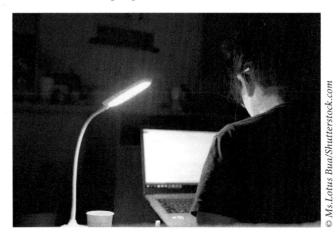

© Ms.Lotus Bua/Shutterstock.com

an alcoholic, you know," or "My parents (wife, boyfriend) won't let me." The model seems to be something like this:

I could be _____	the best lover
	the best husband
	your best friend
	the best salesperson
	and so on
if only _____	men
	my wife
	you
	my manager or my company
	and so on
was (were) (would) _____	stop being so aggressive
	read some books so we'd have
	something to talk about
	not drink so much
	less conservative
	and so on

Berne illustrates the evasive pattern in games he calls "See What You Made Me Do" and "If It Weren't for You."[25] "See What You Made Me Do" has its roots in the familiar situation in which one person is engrossed in some activity and is interrupted. The innocent question of a child to her father, "What are you doing, Daddy?" may precede the father hitting his hand with a hammer. This, then, provides the rationale for "See what you made me do." When such behavior becomes a way of life, it can easily degenerate into other forms of blame ("You got me into this" or "I didn't bring it up, you did") or vengeance ("I told you so" or "See what you've done now"). "If It Weren't for You" is a similar tactic. Let's assume a professional woman architect resigns her job because she wants to have children and stay home and raise them. When the home and child-rearing activities fail to provide the needed professional stimulation, the woman moans, "If it weren't for my kids, I'd go back to work."

Changing the Direction of the Conversation. Numerous strategies can be used to avoid threatening conversations by shifting topics or focus. Washburne, in a delightful piece, outlines several methods for not answering questions.[26] Even though there are overtones of humor in the following strategies, there are serious consequences for relationships characterized by frequent incomplete and tangential transactions. Washburne says there are three basic methods for giving answers that are not answers: (1) "not answering at all," (2) "managing the question," and (3) "managing the questioner." Such answers give the appearance of cooperating but never seem to address the question directly. These tactics,

Washburne says, leave the questioner either satisfied, restrained by politeness from pursuing the matter, or thoroughly confused.

The first method is called "not answering at all." The simplest form is to ignore, or apparently not hear, the question. Watzlawick provides an example of how silence can be used to communicate disagreement without having to be held responsible for it.[27]

THERAPIST: Well, now what kind of weekend did you have after our session Friday evening?

HUSBAND: Oh, I would say, a very good one, wouldn't you, Jean?

WIFE: (remains silent)

What makes this tactic so difficult for the husband to cope with is that the wife has made her point, but if she is questioned about her silence indicating disagreement, she has numerous escape routes—"Oh, was I supposed to say something?" "Did I say that?" or "Oh … I was just trying to remember." She can deny her communicative intent and in turn accuse the questioner of making unwarranted inferences or of mindreading. Watzlawick argued that this is a situation in which agreement cannot be reached, disagreement cannot be tolerated, so a stand is taken without really taking a stand. Engineering a distraction is another way of not responding. Following the question, the receiver may spill a drink, knock over a vase, drop a lighted cigarette into the depths of a sofa, or point out some external event such as "how rough" the kids are playing outside. Pipe smokers have an arsenal of equipment for creating possible distractions and a lengthy lighting ritual for delaying responses—time that can be used to plan one's defense if all else fails.

The second method Washburne calls "**managing the question.**" There are numerous ways to manage a question. Intentionally *misunderstanding* the question is an obvious means to avoid answering—"Is your car paid for?" "You know, I really got a bargain with this car. They were asking … but …" *Limitation* is the process of taking a broad question and answering only that aspect of it with which you feel comfortable—"How did you like my meatloaf?" "I particularly liked the sauce. It must have taken you a long time to make it." The *non sequitur,* as the label implies, is a response that is not logically related to the question. Some people seem to have a mouthful of topics that they can launch into no matter what the question. Usually these monologues are lengthy enough so that the questioner either gives up or forgets the original question. Such monologues might begin with, "This reminds me of … " or "I can best respond to that by recalling a similar situation." A political candidate may be addressing an audience when a heckler yells out, "What are you proposing to do with all the waste from the nuclear plants you propose building?" Using the non sequitur strategy, the candidate may pause, smile, and say, "Today's my birthday and I've vowed not to get mad at anybody." *Restatement* is the act of seeming to restate the question (for the sake of clarity), but converting it to one you find easier to deal with—"Are we going into a depression?" "As I understand your question, you are really asking about the present state of the business cycle.

Managing the question: Appearing to answer a question without really answering it using strategies like intentionally misunderstanding the question, limiting the scope of the question, replying with a non sequitur, restating the question, suggesting there is a more fundamental question, asserting the question is moot, or making an assertion of nothing.

Business income is the highest in history." A similar evasive maneuver is the *more fundamental question*—"Are you a liberal?" "Well, before we can deal with my own personal stance, we need to consider the more fundamental question, what does *liberal* mean?" Professors are often cited for a technique Washburne calls the *hypothetical answer*. When asked a question, a direct answer is avoided by explaining all the various alternative perspectives without identifying with any one of them. *Is this really a question*? is an approach that attempts to annihilate the question itself by pointing out that it is actually several questions, that there are false premises, and so forth. Once the question has been sufficiently dissected, the respondent can discuss any subquestion desired. The *moot question approach* asserts that the question is almost impossible to answer and that there is no sense pondering the imponderable. For example, a mother says, "Why do you suppose our son gets so upset and runs to his room every time you start to talk to him?" The father replies, "Look, you're asking a question the best minds of the world can't answer—what makes kids tick. There's no sense spending a lot of time trying to figure out what causes people to act the way they do—it's so complex and there are so many factors involved we'd only get into more trouble by considering it." The last method of managing the question is called the *assertion of nothing*. A friend is asked to comment on a new outfit that the wearer obviously likes but the friend doesn't: "Boy, that is *some* outfit!" The voice emphasis makes otherwise empty words seem full of meaning. It should be remembered that some of these methods we use to deliberately avoid answering questions are the same methods we use when we are trying to answer questions.[28] For example, when someone asks, "Are you going to Bob's party?" you may reply, "Does a submarine have screen doors?" Although most of us would assume the person isn't going to Bob's party, the reply certainly qualifies as a non sequitur and does not directly answer the question. Other indirect responses are more closely related to the question but still avoid clearly and unambiguously affirming or negating the question—for example, "Are you going to Bob's party?" "Bob and I are best friends" or "Are you going to Bob's party?" "I have a really important test to take in the morning." The receiver is expected to infer the answer through an understanding of how the reply connects back to the question.

Bavelas and her colleagues have found that people's evasive, indirect, or ambiguous messages are the result of a person who believes he or she is facing an avoidance-avoidance conflict.[29] In short, the communicator is faced with a situation in which any direct message, whether it is a lie or the truth, will get negative consequences. As a result, the communicator engages in what Bavelas calls, "**equivocal communication**." Let's say a husband has found some old letters that reveal his wife had an affair several years ago and, on the basis of the evidence, says. "You must have really loved him." The wife knows the content of the letters, so she wants to avoid saying no because she knows the husband will then point to various sentences. On the other hand, she wants to avoid saying yes because she knows how much that would hurt her husband and she wants their relationship to remain intact. She chooses instead to equivocate by saying, "I hardly knew him." The implication is that no matter what the letters say, the only kind of love that would be threatening would be one that involved

Equivocal communication: Messages that are indirect and can be interpreted in multiple ways.

knowing the other person well and this was not the case. The husband may still feel rotten, but he also may be secretly happy he didn't get a direct, straightforward, unequivocal response. As this example illustrates, evasive or equivocal responses can be appropriate and useful in avoidance-avoidance conflict situations. When they are overused or used repeatedly in situations in which one's partner wants a direct response, they are likely to precipitate further problems with the relationship.

Washburne's third method to change the direction of the conversation is to "**manage the questioner.**" One effective way to do this is to put the questioner on the defensive. This can be done by a rather direct insult such as "The very fact that you'd ask that question shows how uninformed you are on this topic," or in a friendly tone, you might say, "You probably didn't mean to ask that ... what you really want to know is ... " Another maneuver that Chapman calls "Whine and Decline" is an effort to bring up a topic you know will irritate your partner in order to stimulate a climate of conflict.[30] This, then, provides the rationale for avoiding any subjects or behavior the partner may have wished to initiate. Specifically, one spouse who wants to avoid sexual intercourse begins the pre-bedtime preparations with something like, "I know you don't like to discuss it, but I think we really must decide something about. ... " After the ensuing battle, the initiator can then not only justifiably decline the sexual advances, but feign previous interest—"Every time I feel affectionate, you seem to figure out some way to blow up and ruin it." Another way to manage the questioner is to relieve the questioner of his or her role so that you can become the questioner. Such a sequence might go something like this: "What happened at the convention?" "Oh, it was very dull. I wish I'd stayed home. What did you and the kids do?" The last, but far from the least effective way to manage your fellow interactant, is to use compliments or praise. Sometimes it can be disarming. Your partner may forget the original topic or question, and the whole tone of the conversation can dramatically change with comments such as "Where did you learn to argue so effectively?" or "You always seem to hit the nail right on the head. How did you develop this ability?"

> **Manage the questioner:** Avoiding answering a question by redirecting the conversation toward the questioner using strategies such as putting the questioner on the defensive, bringing up another topic that will irritate the questioner, or complimenting the questioner.

Changing the Level of the Conversation. Conversational smoke screens also can develop when people shift the level of discussion on a concrete-abstract continuum. One variation is to bring a high level, philosophical discussion down to the "but what would happen if we actually put this into practice" level. The more frequent occurrence is shifting from a specific analysis to a more general, abstract one. A student wants to know why a professor can't spend more time helping him or her, and the professor launches into a discussion of criteria for promotion, various perspectives on student-teacher relations, and how this all relates to the philosophy of education.

Conversational level also can be varied on a serious-joking continuum. A person can camouflage an inability to deal with humor or light conversational banter by shifting from a nonserious to a serious dimension—an example is a person who gives an oral sociological or historical treatise on the use of obscene language during a "bull session." On an occasional basis, such behavior may gain one the label of "conversational boor"; frequent practice will likely breed impatience, frustration, and eventual avoidance on the part of receivers who dislike being sobered up during a humor binge. Sometimes we find people replying to a serious comment or question in a way that indicates their refusal to respond seriously—"Son, do you use marijuana?" "Gee, Dad, how did you know? I've been hooked since I was thirteen. My habit is up to $100 a day. I wanna quit, but I just can't. I'll probably be on the hard stuff in no time."[31] If the father takes the son's comment seriously, he risks the charge of naiveté; if he retorts with anger at the mockery, the son can protest unfair punishment—"Hey, whatdya want? I admitted it, didn't I?"

Sending Incongruous Messages. When a speaker sends two simultaneous messages that communicate vastly different things, he or she is sending incongruous or discrepant messages. *Sarcasm,* for instance, relies on one's ability to contrast a message sent in nonverbal channels (voice, face, hands) with the words used—saying "This is a great book, Professors Knapp, Vangelisti, and Caughlin" accompanied by nonverbal signals that leave considerable doubt about the veracity of the words alone. Contradictory messages also are sent when the speaker has no intention of being cutting or sarcastic. Consider the parent who, with clenched fists, a reddened and strained face, and a harsh vocal tone, towers over his or her child and screams threateningly, "Damn it, Lester, don't you know that I love you!" The parent's verbalization may have been very sincere, and the contradictory nonverbal signals may have been unconsciously added; nonetheless, the child gets two very different messages. The game Berne calls "Rapo" is built on contradictory messages of approach-avoidance or acceptance-rejection or both. In the case of Rapo, however, the contradictory messages are not communicated simultaneously, even though they may coexist in the mind of the perpetrator. An example is one person who flirts with another until the target begins to respond fully and positively to what is perceived as an amorous set of messages. Then the game player abruptly changes the message and rejects the responder with a "How dare you!" or "I just don't understand men (women)." Gratification for the game player may come not only from the discomfort caused the victim, but also from perpetrating an act that further confirms his or her low estimation of the opposite sex. Laing has identified several other instances of these double-edged messages, which, he says, given the right conditions, can produce enough confusion in another person to make that person doubt his or her sanity.[32] The right conditions include a high frequency of occurrence, an intimate relationship between the communicators, and the presence of no other people to whom the receiver can turn for discussion and possible clarification of the confusion.

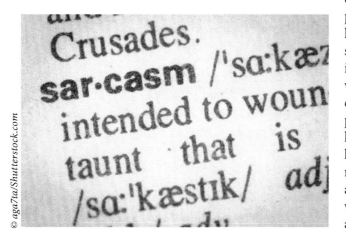

Some methods Laing described for sending inconsistent messages include (1) communicating on two unrelated levels at the same time—intellectually and sexually; (2) constantly switching from one emotional wavelength to another while on the same topic; and (3) switching from one topic to another while remaining on the same emotional wavelength—for example, discussing the death of a loved one in an automobile accident in the same emotional tone you would discuss what you had for breakfast.

Thus far we've been talking primarily about the construction of the incongruous messages. We haven't said much about the receiver's options following the confusing presentation. Some messages might be incongruous, but at least there is a choice of possible responses; other messages, however, are constructed so that the receiver is left without a legitimate choice. The receiver is faced with a **double bind**—damned if you do, damned if you don't.[33] The double bind occurs when person A puts person B in such a position that regardless of what person B says or does, sanctioning will be the result.[34] The enormity of the dilemma is seen when we consider that no matter what we do, we cannot keep from communicating—and to communicate is to be punished. Consider these examples:

Double bind: A conversational dilemma when regardless of what a person says, sanctioning will be the result.

Injunctions	Response Choices	Punitive Reactions to Choices
You should be less obedient.	OK, I will.	See? You obey my every whim.
	No, I won't.	You do what I tell you to do! or You must not care much for me if you won't do as I ask.
You ought to love me more.	OK, I will.	You can't just turn love off and on like that. You're just saying that because I asked you to.
	I'm sorry, I can't.	Then you'd better learn! or If that's all you think of me, then let's forget it.

You can think of other choices "open" to the respondent, but since the injunction is paradoxical, there will be something wrong with these choices too. "Be spontaneous" and "I want you to dominate me" are familiar injunctions that are well within the genre of the examples given. Notice how the plea for domination defines the relationship as complementary and symmetrical at the same time. (See pages 77–78 for a discussion of complementary and symmetrical relationships.) This is the nature of a paradox. A final illustration of how double binds manifest themselves in everyday conversation is presented by the following hypothetical situation. "Red" Doyle is the coach of a football team, the Boone Bombers. He is discussing a just-completed play with one of his players, Bill "Concrete" Connolly. Connolly, according to his instructions for the play, blocked an opponent named Greene. An opposing linebacker, named Jenkins, rushed past Connolly and tackled Connolly's quarterback for a fifteen-yard loss. Notice how Coach Doyle is able to create double binds that cover Connolly's thinking, feeling, and acting.[35]

"Jenkins really murdered us on that last play. We've got to stop him. Were you trying to block him?"

Connolly might legitimately assume, at this point, that blocking Jenkins would have been rewarded and not blocking him would have been punished. Since he hadn't blocked Jenkins, Connolly tries to alibi.

"Yeah, Coach," said Connolly meekly. "I was going to, but ..." he began in a slow, uncertain voice.

Only to find out his assumption was totally wrong, Connolly is punished for his actions.

Coach Doyle forcefully threw his cap on the ground, and while looking Connolly straight in the eyes, said in a firm, punitive tone: "Going to? You can't block every man on the field, superman. This is a game of discipline and of following orders. Since when do you decide who to block? Are you the new coach?"

"No, Coach, I only thought ..."

This is the opening Coach Doyle uses to punish his player for thinking. He frightens Connolly into not thinking for himself, but intimates that the player should think about how to protect his quarterback.

"You only thought! How nice! I'll thank you not to think. I can do all the thinking around here."

After having communicated the seriousness of this matter—a matter in which fear of authority, guilt, and remorse are appropriate emotions—Coach Doyle shifts gears again and punishes his player for being frightened and discouraged.

As Connolly lowered his head, turned, and looked hurt, Coach Doyle began to laugh. "Look at you. Just look at you. Has my concrete turned to marshmallow?"

Given the nature of the double bind in the context of a relationship that is important to the person put in the double bind, it is not hard to see how many believe it can lead to schizophrenia and other pathologies. Some try to reduce the inconsistency of double binds and paradoxical messages by increasing their own consistency of response. A person, for instance, might interpret all messages received as suspicious, untrustworthy, and filled with hidden meanings. If this behavior is continued, it will eventually gain that person the label of paranoid. Another person might react to all messages as unimportant, irrelevant, and laughable. This may cause others to diagnose that person's behavior as a disorder called hebephrenia. Still another person may simply withdraw into himself or herself, a process which in its extreme form is known as catatonia.

Some believe that constant exposure to a learning context in which the goal is to escape punishment rather than to seek rewards is more damaging than the confusion caused by the double bind itself. Suffice to say, the combination of negativity, confusion, and punishment can be lethal. Fortunately, most of us will arrest the process before it becomes pathological. This can be done by invalidating some of the conditions prerequisite to driving one crazy—for example, by reducing the amount of exposure by leaving the environment that produces the double binds and talking to others about one's confusion in an effort to see the process more objectively.

© fizkes/Shutterstock.com

Therapists have reported an interesting twist in coping with double binds, something like a reverse double bind. Watzlawick, Beavin, and Jackson report a couple who came to therapy because they argued too much.[36] The couple were told by the therapist that they argued so much because they loved each other so much. To disprove this "absurd" and "ridiculous" theory, the couple stopped arguing—only to find they got along much better. Watzlawick gives this example of how a double-bind situation was reversed by "schizophrenic communication":

> [T]ake the example of an alcoholic father who demands that he be seen as a loving, respectable parent and not as the violent drunkard which he is—and, of course, knows himself to be. When this man threatens his children with punishment if they show fear when he comes home drunk, the children are placed in a particular dilemma which requires a denial of their perceptions in order to support Father's deception. Suppose further that this father, after having terrorized his children into going along with his make-believe, suddenly does an about-face and accuses them of trying to deceive him about their fear. Now they are faced with two alternatives, both of which entail punishment. If they betray their fear, they will be punished for implying that he is a dangerous drunk. If they conceal their fear, they will be punished for their "insincerity." And, of course, if they were capable of protesting and saying, "Look what you are doing to us," they would again be punished. … What possible adaptive reaction, short of a catatonic stupor, is there to the paradox posed by a double bind? … One of the children could conceivably run away from home, claiming that he had actually seen a "huge black gorilla breathing fire" in the house. … The child's message, i.e., his symptom, denies that it is a communication about Father and it further denies that it is a denial. In other words, the child's fear now has a reason, but of a kind which implies that it is not a real reason. After all, there are no black gorillas at large. … Now paradox is countered with paradox and Father is himself in a double bind, as he can no longer coerce his child into concealing his fear. After all, the child is not afraid of him and who can argue with a child's fantasy? Nor can the father label the metaphor, as this would be tantamount to admitting that he looks like a dangerous beast—which is the very thing that Father demands be overlooked.[37]

Dominating-Submissive Patterns

In most relationships, behaviors that show dominance or submission fluctuate with the topic being discussed, who has the expertise or experience, the roles required for a given task, interpersonal needs of the participants, amount of energy, and many other factors. However, when either dominance or submission becomes a habitual response—an inflexible communicative pattern—it can easily tear a relationship apart.

Dominating. The dominant extreme is composed of a person who plays a constant game of winning and losing. Life is a continual parade of competitive events in which one person wins power and another loses it. In order to hold power over others (or a particular other), a person will try to become the primary source of important rewards and punishments; try to assert his or her "expertise" on a wide variety of topics; and generally try to maintain control over resources that directly affect the relationship, such as, money, information, or ability to perform certain asks. For the person seeking dominance, differences between people often are evaluated not simply as differences, but as marks of superiority or inferiority, strengths and weaknesses. The downside of treating a relationship as a competition, of course, is that it can take an extremely negative emotional toll on the partner; being in a relationship with an overly dominant person is dissatisfying.[38]

Encounters with a dominant partner often are more like contests or jousting matches. Many times the dominance-prone individual is unaware of the behavior he or she manifests. There may be such a predominant concern for oneself that others are seen only as props. A person exhibiting this pattern may even believe he or she is doing things for others when he or she is not—for example, buying expensive tickets to a concert featuring a performer the dominator really likes, but the partner could easily live without seeing. Many times the driving force behind this need for dominance and power is insecurity—"Since nobody thinks I'm a good decision maker, I'll show them."

A number of communication patterns are characteristic of the dominant style, but the implicit assumption behind all of them is that the other person is somehow not quite adequate. The other person is either dumb, childish, inexperienced, unsophisticated, tasteless, uninformed, or possessed of some other inferior quality. With such an assumption, it is easy to predict communicative manifestations. All the important decisions need the "superior" person's input; sometimes the benevolent dictator will allow the partner to make some "unimportant" decisions in order to keep him or her happy and to let the partner feel that he or she has a role in determining things. Commands and ultimatums often are the order of the day, usually framed around two polarized alternatives—"Do this and not that" or "I don't care what you want, we're going to … " or "It's either my way or not at all." Since life is seen as a competitive arena, we also might expect to hear an abundance of trade-offs if the authoritarian edicts don't work—"OK, you can do that, but if you do, you're going to have to … " or "I'll let you get away with it, but in turn I'm going to … "

Dominance often requires control. In a romantic relationship, for example, the dominating person may seek to (1) control information—that is, wanting a lot of information about his or her partner while offering little about him- or herself; (2) control social contacts—that is, seeking to isolate his or her partner from family, friends, and coworkers after the couple has achieved emotional closeness in order to reduce any influence of "outsiders" on his or her dominance; (3) control of time—that is, wanting to know details of where his or her partner will be, when, and for how long (frequent phone calls and attempts to monopolize the partner's time may initially be perceived as pleasant romantic attentions but eventually be seen as overly controlling); (4) control of the relationship—for example, threatening suicide if the partner hints at ending the relationship or engaging in reckless behavior that makes his or her partner afraid of what might happen if he or she should want to terminate the relationship.[39] Naturally any analysis of specific communication behaviors associated with dominance should recognize that dominance can be exhibited in many ways. Dominance displays that involve talking loud and fast often may subside as the partner shows acceptance of the other's dominant role. Dominance may appear differently as different issues are discussed, and some dominance patterns may be highly idiosyncratic and known only to the interacting pair—for example, "When he sits up in his chair and speaks very slowly, I know I'd better give him what he wants."

Sometimes dominance displayed in rather straightforward, stereotypical ways is rebuffed and more indirect methods are tried. It is the interpersonal equivalent of guerrilla warfare. Strategies Chapman calls "You Can Never Repay Me" and "Torture Rack" are two of these indirect methods at domination.[40] The key to domination in "You Can Never Repay Me" is some basis for the dominator to claim he or she has made great sacrifices for the other and the only way to be repaid is by an endless deference to demands. These demands often are accompanied by whimpering resignation, which attempts to produce feelings of guilt and eventual submission in the other—"Go ahead and enjoy yourself; after all, your happiness is what I've worked and slaved for all these years." "Torture Rack" uses some form of physical ailment (headaches, backaches) to induce submission by the other person. Submission is forced because the ailment always seems to intensify when the dominant person's wishes are thwarted in the least—"Don't let my suffering change your plans."

It should be clear by now that the ideal situation for the autocrat is one in which he or she speaks and the other listens and obeys. However, there are instances in which the dominator must cope with a partner who does not conform through subservience. These situations are not unlike those confronting authorities in organizations who wish to discourage individuals from seeking reform. O'Day outlined what he called a series of intimidation rituals in organizational settings.[41] O'Day's paradigm seems to be just as useful for analyzing any interpersonal situation in which an uncooperative person must be dealt with by someone who wants to maintain his or her dominance. Generally, the communicative goals of the authoritarian are (1) to keep the other person from getting any additional support, (2) to make it look as if the authoritarian is blameless, and (3) to neutralize the other person without letting him or her become a martyr. O'Day says such efforts usually follow four escalating phases: (1) nullification, (2) isolation, (3) defamation, and (4) expulsion.

Nullification. Here the reformer, or person to be dominated, is expected to give up simply on the word of the authority—"Take my word for it, you're wrong" or "Do as you're told and you'll be OK." If necessary, the dominant person might resort to something like, "Ok, I'll look into it" in order to defuse the other person's request and, if necessary, cover up anything that might support the other's contention.

Isolation. If the dominator's authority continues to be questioned, attempts are made to isolate the questioner. This might be difficult if the stage of the relationship does not permit opportunities for such isolation. A husband might try to keep his wife from talking to the neighbors, her mother, friends. A mother might try to keep her daughter from talking to her peers about an issue that might challenge the mother's knowledge and authority. Even children who dominate their parents learn how to "divide and rule"—"Dad is always picking on me, Mom" may start a process that ends up with Mom and Dad fighting and Junior triumphantly looking on from the sidelines.

Defamation. Continued persistence by the person challenging the authoritarian in the face of these indirect attempts at suppression may bring about more direct efforts. This phase, for instance, calls for the dominator to question the motives of the challenger, to point out various problems that have caused the person to "act this way" recently, to find every instance of an error on the part of the other person and blow it up to show a lack of competence.

Expulsion. Although this might be a ready alternative for less intimate relationships that manifest this situation, expulsion comes only as a last resort in more intimate relationships. The problem with expulsion is that other people are often brought in for observations of the situation. If the authoritarian can terminate a relationship without the possibility of anything approaching a formal review, then expulsion would be a more desirable alternative.

Submissive. In direct opposition, but with no less potential for relationship destruction, is the perpetually submissive response type. Exaggeration of dependency, abdication of responsibility, and self-deprecating remarks characterize this communicative style. Wanting to be led by others is a common manifestation in which submissive types seek subordinate positions rather than positions in which some responsibility might be involved. When it isn't possible to seek such positions, the submissive person might complain, "I didn't ask to be promoted to this higher-level position. I knew I couldn't do it." Comments that reflect one's inadequacies abound in the talk of the submissive person: "How stupid I am" or "What an idiot I was for. ..." Since a person using this pattern has a low self-concept and has little confidence in his or her abilities, it is common to give in to the slightest request from another. In short, the behavior seems to be the archetype of "I'm Not OK, You're OK."[42]

Speakers who are reticent to talk, whose speech rate literally invites interruptions, who express themselves tentatively by using qualifiers and hedges, who are unassertive and uncertain, are manifesting the characteristics of what some have called "powerless speech." Generally, women's speech is not, as some used to believe, characterized by these features. And men do not generally exemplify "powerful speech" either.[43] Language choices and speech styles that characterize power or the lack of power are usually a function of the situation, your role in that situation, your interaction history, your interpersonal needs, and the nature of your partner's speech. On the other hand, when one relationship partner *consistently* exhibits submissiveness through powerless speech, relationship stress is an expected result.

Initially it might seem strangely attractive to some to be in a relationship with a submissive other. After all, wouldn't it be nice to be paired up with a slave? Most people we've known, however, who have found themselves in this position don't agree. Consider that if you want to build an intimate relationship, you must fuse with and become part of the other—absorbing some of your slave. But the slave provides little in the way of challenges or stimulation and relinquishes responsibilities. It is ironic that the dominating pattern previously discussed may be so effectively instituted by a dominator that a helpless follower develops. Then, if the dominant person wants the pattern to change ("Why don't you get out on your own and take some responsibility for yourself?"), he or she may find the slave unwilling or unable to change. This sets up a pattern in which the parasitic monster created by domination now begins to burden rather than please the creator.

Certain-Provisional Patterns

The last extreme and potentially destructive communication patterns we will discuss revolve around the issue of predictability. At one extreme, the communicator consistently expresses a certainty about the way things are; at the other extreme, the communicator sees the world and the people in it as an ever-changing, unfathomable web of interconnections.

Certain. The certainty pattern is so much a part of our everyday experience that we have a familiar label for a person exhibiting this behavior—a know-it-all. Some people believe that the less we know about something, the more certain we seem to feel and act. Know-it-alls believe, or at least act as if they believe, that it is possible to know and say everything about something. It probably is impossible to know everything about something. Try this simple experiment with a friend or acquaintance. To make it easier, don't pick something complex like a human being;

© adriaticfoto/Shutterstock.com

pick something very concrete and structurally simple such as a pencil or a door. Now try to say or write everything that could be said about the object you chose. Were you able to say everything about it—atomic structure, evolutionary origins, uses, and so on? As noted in Chapter 5, we perceive only a portion of what is out there. Further, we communicate about an even smaller portion than what we have perceived. For this reason, it can be especially annoying when someone selects an occasional behavior we perform and turns it into an unqualified, stable personality trait. Let's assume person A and person B are friends and have exchanged constructive criticism on numerous occasions previously. Now we find person A, on this occasion, to be hot, tired, and particularly sensitive to criticism about body odor. Person B makes a derogatory remark about person A's body odor. Person A explodes. Now, person B says, "You know, one of your big problems is you can't take criticism." The unqualified, nonspecific nature of this comment and A's current disposition will probably turn this molehill into Mount Everest in a very short while.

Other variations on the know-it-all style include the person who behaves, not as if he or she were saying everything on the subject, but at least everything important on the subject. This, of course, denies the importance of other people's perceptions. Then there is the "nothing new under the sun" approach—everything has been thought of and/or done before in some form. Usually, the person exhibiting this style will find so much predictability in life (often on a post hoc basis) that he or she may manifest a slow, methodical unexciting, and possibly uninteresting demeanor. There are other variations of the know-it-all style, but the preceding should provide a broad sampling.

We tend to be on guard when we encounter this pattern of extreme certainty because outward appearances suggest that the other person has THE answer. If that is the case, if no further data are needed, of what value is our input? However, the outward manifestations of certainty and assuredness may only mask an insecurity and a deeply felt need to be right.

An interesting twist on this certainty mechanism is the ability of our certain attitudes to bring about confirming evidence. This, of course, only provides further testimony to our skills at accurately perceiving and predicting life around us. This situation, in which the process of predicting an outcome brings about that outcome, is an example of a *self-fulfilling prophecy*.[44] This process begins with a false definition of a situation: A father believes that parents and teenagers cannot get along, that war is inevitable. The next step is for the father to begin behaving as if this assumption were a fact—looking for things that show hostility on the part of his son and preparing his defenses. The third step is the impact the father's behavior has on the son—the son notices what he thinks is an increased hostility on the part of his father and responds with what he considers defensive maneuvers. The final step is the proof for the father. Now that the father can interpret his son's behavior as hostile, he can pat himself on the back for the accuracy of his initial prediction, little realizing that his own behavior is closely linked to his son's. In short, a faulty assumption triggered a new behavior that made the original faulty assumption appear to come true.

Thus, many of the "facts" we are so certain about (and which support our prejudices) may be largely a consequence of our behavior reflecting our own attitudes. There is even evidence that people who believe that loneliness is an inevitable part of getting older actually become more lonely as they age, probably because their expectations about aging lead them to expect that their relationships will deteriorate and that it is pointless to invest in new ones.[45] The way expectations can undermine a relationship is illustrated below; although the dialogue was designed originally to be humorous, it aptly illustrates how, sadly, we can initiate our own destruction:

YOU: Well, our first big fight.

MATE: Yes.

YOU: (Pause) Do you think we have anything left?

MATE: What do you mean?

YOU: I mean do you think we still have a relationship?

MATE: Of course. (Pause) Why—don't you think so?

YOU: Well, I thought so before, at any rate.

MATE: What's that supposed to mean?

YOU: That I thought so before.

MATE: And you don't think so now?

YOU: (Pause) I don't know. What do you think?

MATE: (Pause) I don't know. I thought so before.

YOU: But now you're maybe not so sure, is that it?

MATE: (Pause) I don't know. Maybe not.

YOU: Well, since you're obviously planning to break up with me sooner or later, you might as well do it sooner and not prolong the agony.[46]

Provisional. The antithesis of the overly certain pattern is found in the person who expresses constant uncertainty, provisionalism, and qualification. Life, and the everyday decisions that need to be made, is so complex and unpredictable, the provisional person won't do or say anything "for sure." We've all had fascinating (and frustrating) discussions about what we know "for certain" or what is the "truth" of any particular observation; furthermore, if most of us err on this certainty-provisional continuum it is probably on the side of too much certainty. However, there are those who become almost inactive because they feel there are so many contingencies that need consideration before any given decision can be made. Closure is a rare commodity. Tasks and decisions are more often left up in the air. The inability to make decision based on all the alternatives considered can lead to an inaction, which others will find hard to cope with over a long period of time. Partners can become frustrated with this style of communication if they rarely hear the provisional person say something definite or unqualified.

An extremely provisional orientation is particularly problematic when the doubts expressed are about the relationship itself. Being very uncertain about the relationship can impede the healthy planning for the future in a relationship. Instead of acting confident in the future of the relationship, someone who is very uncertain about the relationship is likely to frequently seek reassurances from the partner.[47] Although some reassurance is characteristic of maintaining any relationship, asking the partner for reassurance too often may immobilize the relationship. Having to focus so much on the simple question of whether the relationship will enduring and remain vital, the couple will have less energy to focus on other, more invigorating conversations and activities. Moreover, if a person is asked too frequently for reassurance that everything in the relationship is okay, it may lead that person to wonder why the partner doesn't seem to believe the reassurances, perhaps suggesting that something is, in fact, wrong. This may help explain why partners in dating relationships tend to have similar levels of relational uncertainty.[48] When partners' expressions of provisionalism begin to feed off each other's doubts, it may begin cycle of ever increasing uncertainty that is only alleviated once the partners become certain that the relationship is ending.

Summary

This chapter detailed some specific extreme communication patterns that past experience and professional testimony suggest are common sources of relationship destruction. Obviously, any pattern has the potential to build or destroy, but the following, because they represent extremes or because they are applied extremely often, are especially suited to elicit unproductive responses—fear, distrust, defensiveness, confusion, vengeance, decreased self-worth, and hurt. We should, however, be careful not to condemn these patterns as inherently and consistently "bad." *On any given occasion, using one of these patterns may be the best rhetorical choice an individual could make.*

First we discussed the *helpful-critical patterns.* The "helpful" pattern was analyzed from two perspectives: (1) that of a person not requesting help but having another try to give it by "reading the other's mind" and (2) that of a person requesting help, which another person consents to give but then does not provide. The critical pattern concerned the fault-finder or complainer.

Other extremes were represented by the *active-passive patterns.* A person who is oversocial—who forces himself or herself on you—can be just as destructive to a relationship as the person who represents the antithesis—someone who is frequently withdrawn, indifferent, and silent.

The *aggressive-evasive patterns* were discussed. Aggressiveness can be divisive and provoke an individual to physical violence. The aggressive counterpart may be less direct, but evasiveness can be equally damaging. There are many manifestations of evasion in interactions. We discussed four major methods: (1) the process of changing the focus of responsibility away from oneself and onto another or others; (2) the process of changing the direction of the conversation by either not answering, managing the question, or managing the questioner; (3) the process of changing the level of conversation by treating a serious response lightheartedly or vice versa, or by trying to bring a very abstract discussion down to a concrete level or vice versa; and (4) the process of sending incongruous messages and putting people in double binds.

In discussing the *dominant-submissive patterns,* we noted that the dominant style assumes that the other is somehow not quite adequate in some area or areas and therefore needs to be shown THE way. Domination can be sought directly through commands and ultimatums or indirectly by such games as "Torture Rack" or "You Can Never Repay Me." We suggested a process through which a dominant individual may seek to squelch "insubordination"—nullification, isolation, defamation, and expulsion. The submissive style can elicit undesirable responses in a relationship because of its exaggeration of dependency, avoidance of responsibility, and self-deprecating remarks.

The last pair of extremes presented varied on the amount of predictability felt—*certain and provisional patterns.* The certain approach may overgeneralize, exhibit absolutism in verbal behavior, avoid qualifications, or be characterized by feeling that one is saying all that is important to say. In some cases, this know-it-all approach manifests itself in a self-fulfilling prophecy. For the provisional pattern, life is far too unpredictable to ever know or say anything "for sure." Hence, a decisionless state of limbo is maintained.

Throughout this chapter we've tried to emphasize the fact that relationships crumble through the efforts of two people—not one. There will always be those issues that give rise to relationship crises (tardiness, sloppiness, impoliteness, or some personal hygiene issue). We need to realize and accept our own communicative imperfections and those of others, minimize the use of strategies that consistently get poor results for us, and try to learn from our mistakes.

Selected Readings

Problematic Patterns and Schemes

Berne, E. *Games People Play*. New York: Grove Press, 1964.

Canary, D. J., and H. E. Canary. "Conflict in Close Relationships." In C. R. Berger, ed., *Interpersonal Communication,* pp. 177–199. Boston, MA: de Gruyter, 2014.

Caughlin, J. P., and Scott, A. M. "Toward a Communication Theory of the Demand/Withdraw Pattern of Interaction in Interpersonal Relationships. In S. W. Smith and S. R. Wilson, eds., *New Directions in Interpersonal Communication Research*, pp. 180–200. Los Angeles, CA: Sage, 2010.

Coupland, N., Giles, H., and Wiemann, J. M. eds., *"Miscommunication" and Problematic Talk*. Newbury Park, CA: Sage, 1991.

Kowalski, R. M., ed. *Behaving Badly: Aversive Behaviors in Interpersonal Relationships*. Washington, DC: American Psychological Association, 2001.

Lederer, W. J., and Jackson, D. D. *The Mirages of Marriage*. New York: W. W. Norton, 1968.

Roberts, L. J. "Fire and Ice in Marital Communication: Hostile and Distancing Behaviors and Predictors of Marital Distress." *Journal of Marriage and the Family* 62 (2000): 693–707.

Segrin, C., and Flora, J. "Marital Communication." In C. R. Berger, ed., *Interpersonal Communication: Handbooks of Communication Science: Vol 6*, pp. 433–466. Berlin, Germany: De Gruyter Mouton, 2014.

Spitzberg, B. H., and Cupach, W. R., eds., *The Dark Side of Interpersonal Communication* 2nd ed. Mahwah, NJ: Erlbaum, 2007.

Stamp, G. H., Vangelisti, A. L., and Daly, J. A. "The Creation of Defensiveness in Social Interaction." *Communication Quarterly* 40 (1992): 177–190.

Vangelisti, A. L., Maguire, K., Alexander, A., and Clark, G. "Hurtful Family Environments: Links with Individual, Relationship, and Perceptual Variables. *Communication Monographs* 74 (2007): 357–385.

Vangelisti, A. L., and Young, S. L. "When Words Hurt: The Effects of Perceived Intentionality on Interpersonal Relationships." *Journal of Social and Personal Relationships* 17 (2000): 393–424.

Weger, Jr., H. "Disconfirming Communication and Self-Verification in Marriage: Associations among the Demand/Withdraw Interaction Pattern, Feeling Understood, and Marital Satisfaction. *Journal of Social and Personal Relationships* 22 (2005): 19–31.

Double Binds and Incongruous Messages

Edwards, M. R. "The Role of Husbands' Supportive Communication Practices in the Lives of Employed Mothers." *Marriage & Family Review* 40 (2006): 23–46.

Fleming, J., and Darley, J. "Mixed Messages: The Multiple Avoidance Problem and Strategic Communication." *Social Cognition* 9 (1991): 25–46.

Hamilton, L., and Armstrong, E. A. "Gendered Sexuality in Young Adulthood: Double Binds and Flawed Options." *Gender & Society* 23 (2009): 589–616.

Hawes, L. C. "Double Binds as Structures in Dominance and of Feelings: Problematics of Dialogue." In R. Anderson, L. A. Baxter, and K. N. Cissna, eds., *Dialogue: Theorizing Difference in Communication Studies*, pp. 175–207. Thousand Oaks, CA: Sage, 2004.

Heller, J. *Catch 22*. New York: Simon & Schuster, 1961.

Knickmeyer, N., Levitt, H. M., Horne, S. G., and Bayer, G. "Responding to Mixed Messages and Double Binds: Religious Oriented Coping Strategies of Christian Battered Women." *Journal of Religion and Abuse* 5 (2004): 29–53.

Leathers, D. G. "The Impact of Multichannel Message Inconsistency on Verbal and Nonverbal Decoding Behaviors." *Communication Monographs* 46 (1979): 88–100.

Schuham, A. "The Double Bind Hypothesis a Decade Later." *Psychological Bulletin* 68 (1967): 409–416.

Sluzki, C. E., and Ransom, D. C., eds. *Double Bind: The Foundation of the Communicational Approach to the Family*. New York: Grune & Stratton, 1976.

Watzlawick, P., Beavin, J. H., and Jackson, D. D. *Pragmatics of Human Communication*. New York: W. W. Norton, 1967.

Wilder, C., and Collins, S. "Patterns of Interactional Paradoxes." In W. R. Cupach and B. H. Spitzberg, eds., *The Dark Side of Interpersonal Communication*, pp. 83–103. Hillsdale, NJ: Erlbaum, 1994.

Physical Abuse and Aggression

Arriaga, X. B., Cobb, R. J., and Daly, C. A. "Aggression and Violence in Romantic Relationships." In A. L. Vangelisti and D. Perlman, eds., *The Cambridge Handbook of Personal Relationships* 2nd ed., pp. 365–377. New York: Cambridge University Press, 2018.

Dailey, R. M., Lee, C. M., and Spitzberg, B. H. "Charting Dangerous Territory: The Family as a Context of Violence and Aggression." In A. L. Vangelisti, ed., *The Routledge Handbook of Family Communication* 2nd ed., pp. 479–495. New York: Routledge, 2013

deTurck, M. A. "When Communication Fails: Physical Aggression in Marriage as a Compliance Gaining Strategy." *Communication Monographs* 53 (1987): 106–112.

Hardesty, J. L., Crossman, K. A., Haselschwerdt, M. L., Raffaeilli, M., Ogolsky, B. G., and Johnson, M. P. "Toward a Standard Approach to Operationalizing Coercive Control and Classifying Violence Types." *Journal of Marriage and Family* 77 (2015): 833–843.

Johnson, M. P. *A Typology of Domestic Violence: Intimate Terrorism, Violence Resistance, and Situational Couple Violence.* Boston, MA: Northeastern University Press, 2008.

Khaw, L., and Hardesty, J. L. "Leaving an Abusive Partner: Exploring Boundary Ambiguity Using the Stages of Change Model. *Journal of Family Theory and Review* 1 (2009): 38–53.

Olson, L. N. "Relational Control-Motivated Aggression: A Theoretical Framework for Identifying Various Types of Violent Couples." In D. D. Cahn, ed., *Family Violence: Communication Processes*, pp. 27–48. New Paltz, NY: SUNY Press, *2009.*

Stamp, G. H., and Sabourin, T. C. "Accounting for Violence: An Analysis of Male Spousal Abuse Narratives." *Journal of Applied Communication Research* 23 (1995): 284–307.

Dominance and Power

Berger, C. R. "Power, Dominance, and Social Interaction." In W. Donsbach, ed., *The International Encyclopedia of Communication.* Hoboken, NJ: Wiley Online, 2008.

Blau, P. M. *Exchange and Power in Social Life.* New York: Wiley, 1964.

Burgoon, J. K., Johnson, M. L., and Koch, P. T. "The Nature and Measurement of Interpersonal Dominance." *Communication Monographs* 65 (1998): 308–335.

Dunbar, N. E., and Abra, G. "Observations of Dyadic Power in Interpersonal Interaction." *Communication Monographs* 77 (2010): 657–684.

Dunbar, N. E., Jensen, M. L., Bessarabova, E., Burgoon, J. K., Bernard, D. R., Harrison, K. J., Kelley, K. M., Adame, B. J., and Ecksteinm, J. M. "Empowered by Persuasive Deception: The Effects of Power and Deception on Dominance, Credibility, and Decision Making." *Communication Research* 41 (2014): 852–876.

Falbo, T., and Peplau, L. A. "Power Strategies in Intimate Relationships." *Journal of Personality and Social Psychology* 38 (1980): 618–628.

Huston, T. L. "Power." In H. H. Kelley et al., eds., *Close Relationships*, pp. 173–219. New York: Freeman, 1983.

Rogers-Millar, L. E., and Millar, F. E. "Domineeringness and Dominance: A Transactional View." *Human Communication Research* 5 (1979): 238–246.

Sadikaj, G., Moskowitz, D. S., and Zuroff, D. C. "Negative Affective Reaction to Partner's Dominant Behavior Influences Satisfaction with Romantic Relationship." *Journal of Social and Personal Relationships* 34 (2017): 1324–1346.

Simpson, J. A., Farrell, A. K., Oriña, M. M., and Rothman, A. J. "Power and Social Influence in Relationships. In M. Mikulincer, P. R. Shaver, J. A. Simpson, & J. F. Dovidio, eds., *APA handbooks in psychology. APA handbook of personality and social psychology, Vol. 3. Interpersonal relations,* pp. 393–420. Washington, DC: American Psychological Association, 2015.

Notes

1 J. Strayhorn, "Social-Exchange Theory: Cognitive Restructuring in Marital Therapy," *Family Process* 17 (1978): 437–448.

2 R. M. Kowalski, "Aversive Interpersonal Behaviors: On Being Annoying, Thoughtless, and Mean." In R. M. Kowalski, ed., *Behaving Badly: Aversive Behaviors in*

Interpersonal Relationships (Washington, DC: American Psychological Assn., 2001), pp. 3–25; W. H. Jones, D. S. Moore, A. Schratter, and L. A. Negel, "Interpersonal Transgressions and Betrayals." In R. M. Kowalski, ed., *Behaving Badly: Aversive Behaviors in Interpersonal Relationships* (Washington, DC: American Psychological Assn., 2001), pp. 233–256; S. Metts, "Relational Transgressions." In W. R. Cupach and B. H. Spitzberg, eds., *The Dark Side of Interpersonal Communication* (Hillsdale, NJ: Erlbaum, 1994), pp. 217–239; R. A. Reynolds, "Discouraging Messages," *Communication Reports* 19 (2006): 16–30.

3   A. Koestler, *Darkness at Noon* (New York: Modern Library, 1941), p. 58.

4   X. B. Arriaga and C. E. Rusbult, "Standing in My Partner's Shoes: Partner Perspective Taking and Reactions to Accomodative Dilemmas," *Personality and Social Psychology Bulletin* 24 (1998): 927–948.

5   The "results we would like" are often hard to determine, since in the rapid give and take of daily interpersonal communication, we desire multiple goals, any one of which may drift in and out of our conscious awareness at any given time. For instance, I want to "win" this argument and I want to maintain your friendship. I may realize how important my friendship goal was only after I have verbally decimated my former friend and the current loser. In Chapter 8 a similar problem was discussed—a person wanting to be open and to disclose something critical about another's behavior, but not wanting to hurt them … or be hurt by them.

6   D. Gilbert and D. H. Silvera, "Overhelping," *Journal of Personality and Social Psychology* 70 (1966): 678–690.

7   For an elaboration of this interpersonal sequence and other "games people play," see E. Berne, *Games People Play* (New York: Grove Press, 1964).

8   J. A. Theiss, L. K. Knobloch, M. G. Checton, and K. Magsamen-Conrad, "Relationship Characteristics Associated with the Experience of Hurt in Romantic Relationships: A Test of the Relational Turbulence Model," *Human Communication Research* 35 (2009): 588–615; A. L. Vangelisti and S. L. Young, "When Words Hurt: The Effects of Perceived Intentionality on Interpersonal Relationships," *Journal of Social and Personal Relationships* 17 (2000): 393–424.

9   What we are describing here is closely aligned with what Schutz calls the *oversocial* and *overpersonal* types; this assessment is based on these people's interpersonal needs. *Undersocial* and *underpersonal* types merge with

what we've called *passive*. Schutz's description of the Abdicrat and Autocrat will be integrated in the Domination-Submission category. See W. C. Schutz, *The Interpersonal Underworld* (Palo Alto, CA: Science & Behavior Books, 1966).

10   C. Derber, *The Pursuit of Attention: Power and Individualism in Everyday Life* (Boston: G. K. Hall, 1979). Also see A. L. Vangelisti, M. L. Knapp, and J. A. Daly, "Conversational Narcissism," *Communication Monographs* 57 (1990): 251–274.

11   P. Mornell, *Passive Men, Wild Women* (New York: Ballantine, 1979). See also A. Christensen and C. L. Heavey, "Gender and Social Structure in the Demand/Withdrawal Pattern of Marital Conflict," *Journal of Personality and Social Psychology* 59 (1990): 73–81.

12   J. P. Caughlin and A. M. Scott, A. M., "Toward a Communication Theory of the Demand/Withdraw Pattern of Interaction in Interpersonal Relationships." In S. Smith and S. R. Wilson, eds., *New Directions in Interpersonal Communication* (Thousand Oaks, CA: Sage, 2010), pp. 180–200; J. P. Caughlin and A. L. Vangelisti, "Desire for Change in One's Partner as a Predictor of the Demand/Withdrawal Pattern of Marital Communication." *Communication Monographs* 66 (1999): 66–89.

13   J. E. Stets and M. A. Pirog-Good, "Interpersonal Control and Courtship Aggression," *Journal of Social and Personal Relationships* 7 (1990): 371–394.

14   L. W. Rosenfield, L. S. Hayes, and T. S. Frentz, *The Communicative Experience* (Boston: Allyn & Bacon, 1976), pp. 167–170.

15   A. M. Neal and E. P. Lemay. "The Wandering Eye Perceives More Threats: Projection of Attraction to Alternative Partners Predicts Anger and Negative Behavior in Romantic Relationships." *Journal of Social and Personal Relationships* 36 (2019): 450–68.

16   M. P. Johnson, "Violence and Abuse in Personal Relationships: Conflict, Terror, and Resistance in Intimate Partnerships." In A. L. Vangelisti and D. Perlman, eds., *The Cambridge Handbook of Personal Relationships*, pp. 557–576. New York: Cambridge University Press, 2006.

17   L. K. Burke and D. R. Follingstad, "Violence in Lesbian and Gay Relationships: Theory, Prevalence, and Correlational Factors." *Clinical Psychology Review* 19 (1999): 487–512.

18   P. Tjaden and N. Thoennes, *Extent, Nature, and Consequences of Intimate Partner Violence: Findings from the National Violence Against Women Survey* (Washington,

DC: National Institute of Justice/Centers for Disease Control and Prevention, 1999).

19 O. W. Barnett, C. L. Miller-Perrin, and R. D. Perrin, *Family Violence Across the Lifespan* (Thousand Oaks, CA.: Sage, 1997).

20 J. Archer, "Sex Differences in Aggression Between Heterosexual Partners: A Meta-analytic Review." *Psychological Bulletin* 126 (2000): 651–680; M. A. Straus, "Trends in Cultural Norms and Rates of Partner Violence: An Update to 1992." In S. M. Stith and M. A. Straus, eds., *Understanding Partner Violence: Prevalence, Causes, Consequences, and Solutions* (Minneapolis: National Council on Family Relations, 1995), pp. 30–33.

21 Foley, M. K., "Locating 'Difficulty': A Multi-Site Model of Intimate Terrorism." In D. C. Kirkpatrick, S. Duck, and M. K. Foley, eds., *Relating Difficulty* (Mahwah, NJ: Erlbaum, 2006) pp. 43–59.

22 Hardesty, J. L., Crossman, K. A., Haselschwerdt, M. L., Raffaelli, M., Ogolsky, B. G., and Johnson, M. P. "Toward a Standard Approach to Operationalizing Coercive Control and Classifying Violence Types." *Journal of Marriage and Family* 77 (2015): 833–843; Johnson, M. P. A *Typology of Domestic Violence: Intimate Terrorism, Violence Resistance, and Situational Couple Violence.* (Boston, MA: Northeastern University Press, 2008).

23 L. E. A. Walker, *The Battered Woman* (New York: Harper & Row, 1979); G. H. Stamp and T. C. Sabourin, "Accounting for Violence: An Analysis of Male Spousal Abuse Narratives," *Journal of Applied Communication Research* 23 (1995): 284–307; F. S. Christopher and T. S. Kisler, "Sexual Aggression in Romantic Relationships." In J. H. Harvey, A. Wenzel, and S. Sprecher, eds., *The Handbook of Sexuality in Close relationships* (Mahwah, NJ: Erlbaum, 2004) pp. 287–309.

24 When politicians are evasive with listeners who are very "issue involved," the ambiguity allows these listeners to read their own beliefs into the statement. If the ambiguous statement is presented with great intensity, firmness, and certainty to uninvolved listeners, the listeners may feel the speaker "really knows her (or his) subject." See C. J. Orr and K. E. Burkins, "The Endorsement of Evasive Leaders: An Exploratory Study," *Central States Speech Journal* 27 (1976): 230–239. Nofsinger points out that in everyday conversation we expect others to cooperate in helping make sense out of our utterances. Hence, what might seem like an indirect or evasive response is sometimes generously interpreted by the receiver as an answer that follows logically—Q: "Are notebooks allowed during the final exam?" A: "Are porcupines allowed in balloon factories?" See R. E. Nofsinger Jr., "On Answering Questions Indirectly: Some Rules in the Grammar of Doing Conversation," *Human Communication Research* 2 (1976): 172–181. Also see T. Holtgraves, "Interpersonal Foundations of Conversational Indirectness." In S. R. Fussell and R. J. Kreuz, eds., *Social and Cognitive Approaches to Interpersonal Communication* (Mahwah, NJ: Erlbaum, 1998), pp. 71–89. Bavelas has shown that indirect and evasive messages are most likely to be produced when the communicator perceives the situation as one in which other message choices have negative aspects to them. See J. B. Bavelas, "Situations That Lead to Disqualification," *Human Communication Research* 9 (1983): 130–145.

25 Berne, "Games."

26 C. Washburne, "Retortmanship: How to Avoid Answering Questions," *ETC: A Review of General Semantics* 26 (1969): 69–75.

27 P. Watzlawick, *An Anthology of Human Communication: Text and Two-Hour Tape* (Palo Alto, CA: Science & Behavior Books, 1964), p. 18.

28 J. W. Bowers, N. D. Elliott, and R. J. Desmond, "Exploiting Pragmatic Rules: Devious Messages," *Human Communication Research* 3 (1977): 235–242.

29 J. B. Bavelas, A. Black, N. Chovil, and J. Mullett, *Equivocal Communication* (Newbury Park, CA: Sage, 1990); N. Chovil, "Equivocation as an Interactional Event." In W. R. Cupach and B. H. Spitzberg, eds., *The Dark Side of Interpersonal Communication* (Hillsdale, NJ: Erlbaum, 1994), pp. 105–123.

30 A. H. Chapman, *Put-Offs and Come-Ons* (New York: G. P. Putnam's Sons, 1968), pp. 14–16. This book outlines many games that reflect put-off forces—fear, anger, and competitive hostility. The come-on forces (forces which draw people together) also are discussed extensively.

31 For an elaboration of various kinds of put-ons like this one, see R. A. Stebbins, "Putting People On: Deception of Our Fellowman in Everyday Life," *Sociology and Social Research* 59 (1975): 189–200.

32 R. D. Laing, *The Self and Others* (Chicago: Quadrangle Press, 1962), p. 131.

33 P. Watzlawick, J. H. Beavin, and D. D. Jackson, *Pragmatics of Human Communication* (New York: W. W. Norton, 1967), pp. 194–229. Today the double bind is sometimes referred to as *catch-22* after the novel by the same name. The novel deals with a person who tries to avoid flying

missions by showing how he is afraid—even "crazy." He is told that people who fly these missions are indeed crazy and it would be abnormal not to be afraid. Hence, he must be sane and must fly the missions.

34 For further perspectives on the double bind, see also L. Hamilton and E. A. Armstrong, "Gendered Sexuality in Young Adulthood: Double Binds and Flawed Options." *Gender & Society* 23 (2009): 589–616; C. E. Sluzki and D. C. Ransom, eds., *Double Bind: The Foundation of the Communicational Approach to the Family* (New York: Grune & Stratton, 1976); A. Mehrabian, "Inconsistent Messages and Sarcasm," in *Nonverbal Communication* (Chicago: Aldine Publishing, 1972), pp. 104–132; A. Schuham, "The Double-Bind Hypothesis a Decade Later," *Psychological Bulletin* 68 (1967): 409–416; and C. Wilder and S. Collins, "Patterns of Interactional Paradoxes." In W. R. Cupach and B. H. Spitzberg, eds., *The Dark Side of Interpersonal Communication* (Hillsdale, NJ: Erlbaum, 1994), pp. 83–103.

35 P. Watzlawick presents a similar analysis in *An Anthology of Human Communication: Text and Two-Hour Tape* (Palo Alto, CA: Science & Behavior Books, 1964), pp. 41–42.

36 Watzlawick, et al., *Pragmatics of Human Communication,* pp. 251–252.

37 Watzlawick, et al., *An Anthology of Human Communication,* pp. 39–40.

38 Sadikaj, G. Moskowitz, D. S., and Zuroff, D. C. "Negative Affective Reaction to Partner's Dominant Behavior Influences Satisfaction with Romantic Relationship." *Journal of Social and Personal Relationships* 34 (2017): 1324–1346.

39 Campbell discusses these and other methods of control used in relationships based on deception. See S. Campbell, *Romantic Deception: The Six Signs He's Lying* (Holbrook, MA: Adams Media Corp., 2000).

40 Chapman, *Put-Offs and Come-Ons,* pp. 17–18; 28–32.

41 R. O'Day, "Intimidation Rituals: Reactions to Reform," *Journal of Applied Behavioral Science* 10 (1974): 373–386.

42 T. Harris, *I'm O.K., You're O.K.* (New York: Harper & Row, 1967).

43 S. H. Ng and J. J. Bradac, *Language and Power* (Beverly Hills, CA: Sage, 1993).

44 R. Merton, "The Self-Fulfilling Prophecy," *Antioch Review* 8 (1948): 193–210. For an analysis of how this process works in the classroom, see also R. Rosenthal and L. Jacobson, *Pygmalion in the Classroom* (New York: Holt, Rinehart and Winston, 1968); also see P. D. Blanck, ed., *Interpersonal Expectations: Theory, Research, and Applications* (New York: Cambridge University Press, 1993).

45 J. Pikhartova, A. Bowling, and C. Victor, "Is Loneliness in Later Life a Self-fulfilling Prophecy?" *Aging and Mental Health* 20 (2016): 543–549.

46 D. Greenberg, *How to Make Yourself Miserable* (New York: Random House, 1968).

47 L. K. Knobloch, L. M. Knobloch-Fedders, and C. E. Durbin, "Depressive Symptoms and Relational Uncertainty as Predictors of Reassurance-Seeking and Negative Feedback-Seeking in Conversation," *Communication Monographs* 78 (2011): 437–462.

48 L. K, Knobloch and J. A. Theiss, "Relational Uncertainty and Relationship Talk within Courtship: A Longitudinal Actor–Partner Interdependence Model," *Communication Monographs* 78 (2011): 3–26.

PART VI

Toward More Effective Communication in Relationships

CHAPTER 12
Evaluating and Developing Effective Communication in Relationships

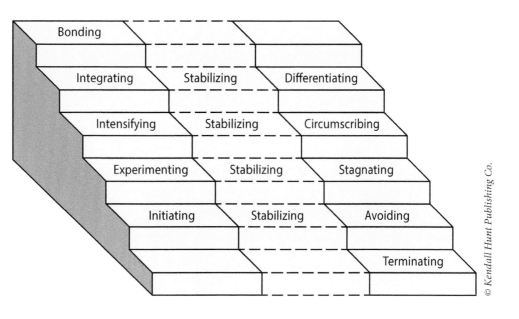

© Kendall Hunt Publishing Co.

CHAPTER 12

LEARNING OUTCOMES

After reading this chapter, students will be able to . . .

. . . explain three reasons why evaluations of communication success may depend on who is doing the evaluations.

. . . identify and describe the four time-related considerations that may affect evaluations of communication success.

. . . describe why evaluating communication success depends on what is being evaluated.

. . . recognize how the reasons for evaluating communication success might affect the evaluations.

. . . recognize the four dimensions that underlie perceptions of interpersonal relationships.

. . . know the six statement that tend to clearly discriminate effective from ineffective communication.

. . . describe four pathways to miscommunication.

. . . explain the four ingredients for developing effective communication in relationships.

KEY TERMS

accurately detecting

commitment

multiple goals

profit

quality

relational standards

tangibility

unrealistic expectations

Evaluating and Developing Effective Communication in Relationships

Dear Dr. Caughlin,

I have difficulty talking to people I really care about. I get along fine with most people and have lots of "friends" at work. But when it comes to someone I love, I just can't say what I really feel. It doesn't matter whether the person is female or male. If I'm upset with someone I care about, I never confront the person. When I want to say, "I love you," I freeze up. Sometimes I deal with this by writing people notes. Most of the time though, I'll sit there quietly when I would really like to express my feelings. How can I be the life of the party with people I barely know but a social reject with people I care about the most?

Caring but Clumsy

The standards for a communicator's success or failure may not be the same from situation to situation. The people who make the evaluations, the reasons for making the evaluations, and the things that are evaluated all may vary greatly from the school environment to the home environment. These and other factors that form the basis of our judgments about effective communication in relationships are covered in the first part of this chapter. Then the link between our perceptions of communication and our perceptions of relationships is discussed. A number of suggestions for improving our communication abilities in the context of our relationships are noted. In addition, because becoming an effective communicator is a very complex, never-ending process, the ingredients necessary for developing effective communication skills are covered. The chapter concludes with several ways we can strive for more communicative successes in our relationships.

Making a judicious evaluation requires that the critic be aware of the intricacies of human communication and cognizant that he can never know everything about the communication situation.

—Robert Cathcart

Let's begin with some statements about the behavior of effective communicators, statements with which many of you will no doubt agree:

1. An effective communicator avoids ambiguity and abstract words; he or she addresses issues clearly.

2. An effective communicator would not throw a childish temper tantrum and deliberately yell abuses at another person.

3. An effective communicator knows that the best way to get people to do something is to praise them, make them feel important, and tell them what they want to hear.

On the surface, the foregoing statements seem sound and reasonable. After all, most introductory communication textbooks tell you to speak clearly, sometimes supporting their contention with footnotes from ancient, revered rhetoricians such as Aristotle or Quintilian. (Effective sales texts frequently make the same point without the footnotes.) The second statement might seem to some to be so obviously and intuitively true that evidence to support it would be superfluous. The last statement reflects a key thread in the communicative philosophy of Dale Carnegie, whose influence on American communicators was—and is—immense.

Let's look at the statements again. Since none of them is qualified by phrases such as *most of the time* or *usually* or *often* or *probably,* we need find only one exception to the statement's contention to disagree with it. You can probably find other exceptions, but let's look at these:

1. It's generally good advice to make messages clear, but there are times when people might need to be deliberately vague in order to accomplish their objectives.[1] A politician who speaks to several different constituencies may find too much specificity antithetical to getting elected; a fiancée may wish to spare her future husband the unambiguous and "gory" details of her previous love affairs; an adult son may not want to disclose the specifics of his financial affairs to his parents. Too much clarity in initiating labor-management negotiations may create a polarization that is difficult to undo. Sometimes people are more likely to agree with a proposition stated in a fairly abstract way and disagree when the specifics of that proposition are made known. And, strange as it seems, sometimes people even attribute greater credibility to those who communicate messages they don't understand—thinking the communicator is so much more intelligent and that is the reason they are unable to grasp what he or she is saying. Some people get a lot of

mileage out of this phenomenon until it becomes clear that other so-called intelligent people can't even sort through the vagueness and jargon used by this person.

© ASDF_MEDIA/Shutterstock.com

2. Of course, we wouldn't suggest the rigidity and imprudent behavior associated with a temper tantrum for everyday communicative fare. It can, however, be an effective strategy for accomplishing one's goal—for the person who continually seeks compromise and conciliation through sensitivity and understanding from another person who stiffly rejects any of the responses. The first person may "give up" and "blow up," a stimulus that can then elicit the same spirit of conciliation earlier sought. It is a dangerous, risky, and seldom recommended ploy, however, because it can just as easily (if not more easily) result in further antagonism and polarization. But it has worked. In abbreviated form it might look like this:

HE: Please . . . (reaches to touch)
SHE: No. (pulls away)
HE: I'm sorry.
SHE: Ha! Forget it.
HE: I want to help.
SHE: You can't.
(etc. and eventually)
HE: ALL RIGHT! . . . GOD DAMN IT! . . . I'VE HAD IT! . . . YOU CAN COUNT ME OUT! . . . (throws magazine across room) I'M TIRED OF TRYING! (kicks coffee table and heads for the door)
SHE: C'mon, now. I didn't mean for you to get so upset . . . I'm sorry I was so nasty (reaches to touch) sit down and let's talk.

3. For the third statement, we might look at a long-term marital relationship. Suppose the wife was seeking a promotion at work and asked her husband for feedback on her resume. A number of things could go wrong—the wife may see the praise as excessive and may, as a result, mistrust her husband's feedback; if she receives only praise from her husband and receives a more critical response from her boss, she may lose respect for her husband's opinions in this area.

The point of this find-the-exception-to-the-rule exercise is that almost any advice that purports to be a key to success in relational communication will—with some person, in some situation, at some time—be impotent or ineffective. We've already noted that even patterns normally considered pathological may sometimes be effective strategies when all other avenues are blocked (see Chapter 11). The only reason the so-called temper tantrum succeeded in the dialogue just discussed was because of the particular relationship between the parties and the messages that preceded it. Any pattern of relational communication can be successful or unsuccessful, effective or ineffective. Yes, sometimes effective communication will be threatening, withdrawing, and inflexible. To be sure, some patterns are better suited than others for more frequent successes in a wider variety of situations; they'll be discussed later. For now, let's take a closer look at the concept of communicative success, or effectiveness in our relationships.

The Relativity of Effective Communication

Success is not an absolute concept. That is, we don't all use the same standards to evaluate our successes in any endeavor.[2] Some feel that they are successful in their careers if they are able to attain the job or position they want. Some feel they are successful if they earn a lot of money. Still others feel successful if they work for a prestigious organization—regardless of position or salary. Evaluating the success or effectiveness of the communication that occurs in our relationships is also relative; a judgment that any individual is communicating effectively (or is an effective communicator) is dependent on who is doing the evaluating, when it is done, what is evaluated, and how and why it is done.

Success can eliminate as many options as failure.

—*Tom Robbins*

Who Is Evaluating Communicative Success?

Montgomery notes that different criteria for effective communication are established and maintained by different societies, relationships, and individuals.[3] For example, a society's beliefs and values affect the standards its people use to judge communication. Research comparing evaluations made by those who live in the United States and those who live in other countries (e.g., Colombia, Korea) suggests that there are differences in the ways members of these societies judge interaction.[4] Furthermore, within the United States, various ethnic groups evaluate certain aspects of verbal and nonverbal communication in different ways.[5] Montgomery argues that many of today's Western societies tend to value positive communication over negative communication, that they see intimacy and openness as central components of close relationships, and that they believe that individuals should have control over what happens in their relationships. These assumptions may not always be accurate. There are times when negative communication is important to relationships, when openness can create relational discord, and when individuals are simply unable to "work" hard enough to control their relational outcomes. Even so, criteria such as these sometimes affect the ways members of a particular society evaluate relational communication.

The criteria used to assess effective communication also may differ from one relationship to the next. Relational partners often negotiate standards for communication that are both unique to their relationship and different from those held by their society. Some couples value conflict; others view conflict as a destructive form of communication.[6] Some families believe that members should all have similar values; others place a high premium on individuality.[7] Some people think that humor and sarcasm are an important part of good family interaction; others see the same sort of communication as detrimental to family relationships.[8] Because they are unique, these shared relational standards can serve to reinforce intimacy between relational partners. (Recall, in Chapter 9, our discussion of personal idioms.) It also is possible, however, for partners to develop destructive relational standards. Research has demonstrated, for example, that negative communication within the marital dyad often predicts later dissatisfaction in the relationship.[9] Similarly, couples who have unrealistic expectations for their relationship (e.g., "We should never argue with each other") tend to be less satisfied.[10] Although it is difficult to determine whether standards such as these actually *cause* dissatisfaction in the relationship, we can conclude that they are not usually associated with "healthy" or "satisfying" relationships.

© Tong_stocker/Shutterstock.com

Finally, individuals often develop and maintain their own idiosyncratic criteria for quality communication. Different standards for effective communication may be used by people with different interests, priorities, values, and experiences. Furthermore, perceptual differences can arise even when people have agreed to use the same criteria—coworkers may view behavior differently than do best friends or lovers. When individuals themselves are the evaluators, they may be able to consider their own abilities and past accomplishments and arrive at an evaluation emphasizing effectiveness because "it was the best I could have done." Often, this is a perceptual luxury that may not be afforded an outside observer—or even an intimate relational partner. Our acceptance and receptivity to judgments of our effectiveness also are colored by the person(s) doing the evaluating. We sometimes look at evaluative feedback differently when it is sought from a specific person than when it is not sought but volunteered by the evaluator. Whether we consider the people evaluating our effectiveness as better or worse at communicating than ourselves also may make a difference in how we receive or accept the evaluation.

When Is Communicative Success Evaluated?

Several time-related considerations also can affect our judgment of effective communication. These include (1) the specific situation(s) or circumstances involved, (2) the stage of the relationship under consideration, (3) the life stage of the communicator, and (4) the time in history.

In examining any communication situation, a number of questions must be addressed. Am I to evaluate your ability as a communicator during our interaction, immediately after the interaction, or six months from now? And if I do all three, will the judgments be similar? Should they be? Some research methodology is based on the assumption that these measures at different times should be similar in order to be considered accurate. Anyone who subscribes to the view that people and things are in a process of continual change would probably find such a belief problematic. The question, however, remains, "Will I evaluate your effectiveness at one point in time or at many points?" If I select only one point, I might evaluate you following a personal tragedy or while enacting a new role that you may feel is not representative of your usual behavior. Sometimes people do use a single instance to generalize a person's overall effectiveness—"Did you hear what she said to her boyfriend? I can't imagine even associating with someone who is so insensitive!" Sometimes the reverse is true; people use the frequency with which a pattern or outcome occurs as a standard of success or failure. This latter point of view leads to another question, "Can we communicate effectively in every situation and every relationship?" If not, how often do we have to demonstrate effectiveness to be considered generally successful?

Implicit in the preceding chapters is the assumption that any consideration of effective relational communication must take into account the stage of one's relationship with the other person. To be judged effective with a stranger, I might have to conform more closely to accepted cultural norms; with my friends, however, there may be tacit agreement to break certain of these norms to indicate our closeness. Thus, if we communicate differently at different stages of our relationship with another, judgments of communicative competence must consider the expectations for communicative behavior at that stage in the relationship. Suppose, for instance, both participants to a relationship want to terminate it. Both parties are reflecting on their differences. Can we say this is "ineffective communication" or a "communication breakdown"—or just a natural and expected pattern for ending a relationship? If one or both parties do not want the relationship to deteriorate, we will have to determine whether our judgment of effectiveness will be based on the behavior of both parties or on the behavior of either one individually.

Another consideration for the timing of evaluations focuses on our life stages. Most people don't hold children to the same standards for effectiveness as they hold adults. Although, admittedly, some do. Traditionally, most of the standards for communicative competence in children have focused on mastery of the rules of language—grammar, syntax, sentence construction. Rarely are such concerns the focus for measuring communicative competence in adults. Standards for competence in adults more often focus on the speed and fluency of their performance and the speed with which they are able to acquire new skills.[11] Suffice to say, people's stage of life will influence the criteria used to evaluate the effectiveness of their communication.

When discussing the communication skills that are acquired at different life stages, it is important to note that skill differences can be seen within life stages, as well as between them. For example, Delia and Clark identified five periods of development that boys experience as they develop proficiency in listener-adapted communication skills.[12] At first the child is unable to perceive that listeners have certain characteristics that play an important role in their efforts to accomplish certain communicative tasks. Gradually, the child perceives the communication-relevant characteristics in listeners but still does not connect these characteristics with specific communication tasks. Then the child learns to associate listener characteristics with his or her communicative efforts, but the knowledge of how to control and alter messages to offset or support certain listener characteristics is not yet available. In time the child tries to adapt to different kinds of listeners and situations through the use of very general adaptation strategies—for example, altering tone of voice or including a phrase to show deference. The final stage is one of refinement in which more control over the communication situation is manifested in the use of specific listener-adapted strategies based on inferences about the attitudes, qualities, and possible reactions of the listener. Given these different developmental skills, it would seem most appropriate to apply different standards for communicative success at different periods in the life of the child. Although we don't have comparable information for middle-aged and older adults, it seems reasonable to assume that listener-adapted communication skills may show changes at other life periods as well.

There also seem to be different priorities given to various communication styles at different times in history[13]—the formal, grandiose eloquence of yesteryear would seem strangely out of place today; the dictum that "good marital communication is devoid of conflict" is a standard of bygone days; and although Harry Truman's proclivity to be open and "tell it like it is" can now be admired, it was often considered a tragic mistake during his presidency. Some periods in history have emphasized (some would say overemphasized) either the rational–calculating–task-oriented style or the affective-feeling oriented style. In short, the climate of the times also influences our judgments of what is "good" and "bad" communication.

What Is Evaluated for Communicative Success?

By far, the most common approach currently used for assessing communicative effectiveness in relationships is the correspondence between what relational partners set out to accomplish and the extent to which they accomplish it—did they get the response they desired? For example, if you wanted to have somebody understand something, how well did he or she seem to understand it? If you wanted to influence somebody or make that person do something, did he or she do it? If you wanted someone to evaluate you in a certain way, was it done? If you wanted to entertain somebody, was he or she entertained?

Aside from the obvious difficulty in verifying each desired response through ordinary feedback, there are other sources of potential variation in this "response sought–response obtained" paradigm: (1) Communicators may have **multiple goals**.[14] Is the accomplishment of any one or all of them considered successful? Can communicators partially accomplish each goal and still be successful? Must successful communicators be able to select strategies that

Multiple goals: More than one objective or aim.

can accommodate incompatible goals?[15] If communicators obtain a response from themselves (relief) by "getting something off my chest," is that effective communication? Can communicators fail to achieve their objective but achieve an unexpected goal and still be successful? This last question raises the issue of whether we are always aware of what we want to accomplish with our communications. How can we know what another knew or didn't know as he or she entered an encounter? Does anyone's overt behavior accurately reflect what he or she knew or didn't know? (2) Some feel there is an ethical or moral dimension to effective communication. A communicator may accomplish a goal, but if that goal is not one that is considered ethical or moral, success is obviated. For example, if someone wanted to hurt you, lie to you, decrease your self-worth, or confuse you, that person might do so and still be considered an ineffective communicator by some. (3) Some feel that one's own effectiveness is inextricably linked to the goal attainment of the other person—*you* can't be considered effective unless the *other person* has attained his or her interaction goals. You may think you did "a great job." The other person felt rotten. Under these conditions, you would not be considered successful. In fact, researchers have found that people's sensitivity to their partners' goals affects the degree to which they are perceived as competent communicators. People who are seen as more sensitive to their partners' goals tend to be judged as more competent.[16]

Of course, not all communicative goals are self-serving; you may have as one of your goals "not to make the other person feel rotten." Listeners may sometimes seem to be dissatisfied and still be accomplishing their goals—you may not like to "give in" to your relational partner during a disagreement, but in a public setting it may be the most appropriate (and least hurtful) thing to do. Sometimes listeners feel completely satisfied, but no other observer of the interaction would agree. Listeners also change or modify their goals during the interaction. Someone might be so uncompromisingly dogmatic that you, as listener, will adjust your original goals and feel "lucky" to have accomplished what little you did—given the other person's behavior. (4) In well-established relationships, another situation adds a different hue to the response sought–response obtained paradigm. Perhaps the speaker wants to communicate the message, "Allow me an opportunity to be an ineffective communicator." For example, without verbalizing it, a person might get across this message, "I've had a rotten day; a rotten week; I'm tired and frustrated; I'm going to be ranting and raving, using obscene language, making outlandish claims, saying things I don't mean . . . and all I want from you is agreement and support!" If this communication sequence is understood by the listener and acted out by the communicator—if one person wants to vent his or her emotions under a rhetorical guise and another is party to it—is this communicator effective or ineffective?

Sometimes criteria for effectiveness are based on quantity of response—frequent eye contact or frequent verbalizations indicating supportiveness. The quantitative criteria for effectiveness seem to ignore the possibility that more may not always be better; too much eye contact may be negatively perceived as staring or too much indiscriminate supportiveness may eventually be perceived as insincerity. Most of us have encountered the person we felt was just "too smooth." Thus, we're faced with the fact that on some occasions we can't give enough of a particular behavior; on other occasions a small amount may be too much.

The size and diversity of a communicator's repertoire may distinguish more effective from less effective communicators. Indeed, the greater the number of alternative strategies at your disposal, the greater your chances of accomplishing your goal. But some people on some occasions will get the communicative job done because they keep hammering away with a limited range of strategies. These people will predictably have less overall success in a variety of situations and relationships, though.

Another judgment within the province of what is to be evaluated for communicative success comes from the twofold process of diagnosing, or analyzing, a situation versus executing, or carrying out, the behaviors deemed appropriate from the analysis. Some people are perceptive analysts or critics but find it difficult to enact the called-for behaviors. Even if a person knows the truth and tries to speak the truth, it can come out sounding like a falsehood.[17] Others manifest behaviors that are judged effective but diagnose the situation in seemingly superficial terms. Part of the process of diagnosis is the ability to predict responses: Miller points out that when we make predictions about the consequences of our messages, we deal with information on three levels:

1. **a cultural level**—judging our predictions against culture-specific norms (e.g., anticipating little political success in the United States by running on a Marxist ticket)
2. **a sociological level**—basing our predictions on what we know about a person's reference groups (e.g., thinking that most accountants like math)
3. **a psychological level**—making predictions based on a specific individual and how that individual differs from the cultural norms and the general characteristics of his or her reference groups.[18]

These levels lead to still other questions: "Must we be proficient at all levels of prediction before we are considered effective?" Indeed, since knowledge at each level of prediction has some presuppositions for the next level, is it even possible to be a better predictor at level one (the cultural level) than at level three (the psychological level)?

Research on the decoding abilities of married couples underlines the notion that being able to accurately diagnose or analyze a situation is only part of what it takes to be a successful communicator. Although **accurately detecting** a partner's feelings and intentions certainly can be helpful to relationships, studies show that accuracy is not always associated with relational satisfaction.[19] Indeed, Sillars notes that there are several conditions when accuracy might even be harmful to relationships.[20] These include:

Accurately detecting: When a person's beliefs about a partner's feelings or intentions match the partner's actual feelings or intentions.

1. **irreconcilable differences**—when clarifying partners' views on an issue will not help to resolve the differences between them

2. **benevolent misconceptions**—when maintaining certain misconceptions helps facilitate relational satisfaction and stability[21]
3. **blunt, unpleasant truths**—when being completely "truthful" or "honest" creates pain or distress for one or both partners.

Under each of these three conditions, increased accuracy may lead partners to feel more dissatisfied and less secure about their relationship. Knowing how to communicate about issues that are particularly distressing or that make one or both partners feel insecure may be a more important criterion than accuracy for effective communication when couples find themselves in situations such as these.

There seems to be an almost interminable list of dimensions upon which to seek a judgment of effectiveness. For instance, we might look at pronunciation, vocabulary, nonverbal behavior, effective verbal content, message organization, use of logic, written messages, or public speeches. Clearly, a communicator can be judged effective in one mode, level, or type of communication and less effective in another. President Lyndon Johnson was said to be very persuasive in private settings and with one or two other people but much less effective when he addressed large groups. Some of our most effective novelists and poets manifest considerably less eloquence when speaking orally. Some communication skills appear to transcend modes and levels, whereas others are mode or level specific.

Finally, as we consider what to evaluate, we should account for individual differences. Certainly, known differences in an individual's physical or mental capabilities should contribute to an alteration of our criteria for communicative success. Further, as adults, all of us have developed a style of communicating based on past interaction rewards and models. This does not mean a style is an inflexible response pattern; instead, it designates the boundaries around which we typically operate. As we consider which communicative adaptations we need to make to another person, we also need to realize that not all the behaviors we feel will be effective will fit our style. We recall a rather dull, puritanical professor who tried to "identify" and become more "relevant" with his students. He chose to increase the use of *damn* and *hell* in his lectures—a feature alien to his normal style. Instead of enhancing his credibility, he succeeded only in arousing sympathy from some students and outright laughter from others at the disharmony produced by the two contrasting styles. Similarly, in the context of a close relationship, if one partner tries to modify his or her communicative style in a way that is unnatural (perhaps as a last-ditch effort to "save" a relationship), the efforts may be perceived by his or her partner as awkward or even irritating.

How Is the Evaluation of Communicative Success Performed?

There are just about as many ways to gather data on communicative success as there are ways to evaluate those data.[22] Criteria and standards for effectiveness will influence and be influenced by how we gather data on communicative success. If, for instance, you are a participant observer, part of your evaluation of another is colored by your own behavior. Would you be inclined to say your behavior contributed to another's *ineffectiveness*? Will you obtain only audio, only video, only written, or some combination of these types of messages to analyze effectiveness? Will you obtain evaluations from other people, paper-and-pencil tests, or physiological measures? Will your standards of effectiveness change if the only location for gathering the data you need also is heavily saturated with communication "noise"? Such questions are nearly endless. We've raised them only to show that the methods for gathering

the corpus for communicative evaluations also impinge on our ultimate judgments of effectiveness.

Why Is the Evaluation of Communicative Success Performed?

People perform evaluations of others' communication for a variety of reasons. The motivation for performing the evaluation and the uses to which that evaluation will be put certainly affect what will be evaluated. The behavior of the person being observed may be altered if he or she is aware of the evaluation and its consequences. If an individual is aware of the evaluation only after it is finished, his or her acceptance of that evaluation may be influenced by a knowledge of why it took place. Sometimes evaluations are conducted for a reason not apparent to the person evaluated—for example, researchers who fail to report the results of their evaluations back to those who provided the information to the researchers. Sometimes assessments of communicative success are closely linked to the success in work or the mental well-being of the person being evaluated—performance reviews for promotion, firing, grading, or self-help evaluations in therapy or evaluations for a politician who wants to improve his or her ability to communicate with various constituencies. Other times, relational partners may do their own, personal evaluation to decide whether they want to increase relational intimacy ("Would she really be supportive of me if I were to have a crisis?") or to end a relationship ("If he would just pay more attention to me when I need to talk, I'd be happier"). In most cases, these sorts of evaluations are done without consulting the partner for his or her input. As a result, important relational decisions can be made based on incomplete information and without the other partner even knowing about them.

Is Evaluation of Communicative Success Possible?

The preceding contingencies for judging communicative effectiveness in relationships were not designed to show that legitimate judgments of effectiveness can't be made, but only to reiterate the difficulty, relativity, and complexity resident in such judgments. Once we agree to (or are subjected to) a set of standards—with all their strengths, shortcomings, and arbitrary rules—we then know better (still not for sure) what to expect and how to achieve effectiveness. This should not suggest that these standards or evaluative criteria are the "best." Surely we will operate with many sets of standards as we go about our lives; we will have to adapt to each of these standards and none of them will be exactly the same. It should be clear that absolutes are hard to come by in this business of communicating. We've discussed success in terms of listener satisfaction, speaker goals, and a priori standards among other things.[23] We've suggested that your success as a communicator in your relationships will depend on how you adapt to each moment-to-moment change in people, places, topics, and events. You'll read websites and books that purport to give easy answers to extremely complex problems with, we hope, a new appreciation for what was left unanalyzed, what was analyzed superficially, and what might have been analyzed using standards for communicative success different from those discussed here.

Although the following summary definition of effective communication may not satisfy everyone in every situation, it seems to be the composite that encompasses the major perspectives we've discussed:

> Communication behavior is evaluated as effective when a person (or persons) is perceived as having appropriately adapted to the self-other-topic-situation interface in order to achieve a desired response or responses.

Scholars note that communication competence involves control (an ability to put forth and achieve goals), adaptation (an ability to respond to the social environment), and collaboration (an ability to sustain interaction with others).[24] If a person is perceived to exhibit effective communication behavior in a variety of situations involving different people, topics, and goals, he or she is likely to be called an "effective communicator"—without reference to a specific situation.

Since the act of perceiving is so critical to understanding what constitutes effective communication, the next section will address the following question, "How do we perceive effective communication?"

Perceptions of Effective Communication

Our judgments of communicative effectiveness are intertwined with our judgments of interpersonal relationships in general. For example, it is hard to make a judgment about the communication between a guard and a prisoner apart from our perceptions of the relationship between guards and prisoners in general. Wish, Deutsch, and Kaplan conducted a study that provides some information on the dimensions underlying perceptions of interpersonal relationships.[25] They asked people to make some judgments: (1) about their own relationships—between themselves and their close friends; (2) about what typical role relations might be like—between husband and wife, parent and young child, teammates (during a game), nurse and patient; and (3) about their own relationships as a child—between themselves and their mothers. When all the responses were analyzed, it seemed that these subjects tended to view interpersonal relationships along four major dimensions: (1) cooperative-friendly versus competitive-hostile, (2) equal versus unequal; (3) intense versus superficial, and (4) socioemotional-informal versus task-oriented–formal.

To show how these dimensions combine, here are some sample relationship ratings:

Competitive-hostile and unequal	guard and prisoner
Competitive-hostile and equal	political opponents
Cooperative-friendly and equal	close friends; husband and wife
Cooperative-friendly and unequal	teacher and student; nurse and patient
Superficial and task-formal	salesperson and regular customer
Superficial and socioemotional-informal	second cousins; spouse's parents
Intense and socioemotional-informal	husband and wife; close friends
Intense and task-formal	teacher and student; business partners

As might be expected, not all the participants in the study seemed to interpret each dimension in the same way, nor did they attach the same importance to each dimension. Some felt that people in a hostile relationship avoided each other and that occasional interactions were marked by formality and superficiality. Others felt that a hostile relationship meant clashing head-on with intense and emotional interactions. Returning to the paradigm outlining various stages of interaction in a relationship (see Chapter 2), we can see that these different perceptions were simply recalling different stages in a deteriorating relationship. Younger and single respondents tended to attach more importance to the socioemotional-informal versus task oriented–formal dimension, whereas older and married subjects attached more importance to the cooperative-friendly versus competitive-hostile dimension. Further, respondents felt the intense versus superficial dimension was more important in evaluating their own relationships, but the cooperative-friendly versus competitive-hostile dimension was more important in viewing others. Finally, as we suggested earlier, our perceptions of which dimensions are important will change as we move through different stages of life. We may, at some points in life, emphasize the intense or superficial qualities of relationships; but as certain events affect our lives, we may perceive the friendly or hostile dimensions as most critical in evaluating our own relationships or the relationships of others.

COMMUNICATION

Relational standards: Beliefs about the qualities relationships should have.

Unrealistic expectations: Beliefs or anticipations that are overly idealistic and improbable.

At any life stage, our perceptions of communication effectiveness are going to be influenced by our expectations for, and beliefs about, our relationships. For example, a number of researchers have studied people's beliefs about the qualities their relationships should have. These beliefs, or **relational standards**, play a role in how individuals evaluate their relationships.[26] When their relational standards are met or exceeded, people tend to be relatively satisfied. By contrast, when their standards are not fulfilled, people are likely to be dissatisfied or disillusioned with their relationship and may try to change their partners.[27] Researchers also have noted that **unrealistic expectations** are associated with relational dissatisfaction.[28] When a partner strongly holds beliefs such as, "Spouses should be able to sense each other's needs and thoughts as if they could read each other's mind" or "Spouses should be completely supportive of all of each other's ideas and actions," it is inevitable that he or she will be disappointed. Any communication behavior that does not comply with these very strict standards will fall short of what a partner "should" be communicating. Perceptions of the communication will, therefore, be negative and perhaps even detrimental to the relationship—regardless of the intentions of the speaker.

Although relational contingencies have a strong influence on what we perceive to be effective and appropriate communication, it also is possible to discuss our perceptions of communication on a more general level. Feingold, for instance, tried to identify the general characteristics of an effective communicator.[29] After an extensive review of typical prescriptions for effective communication behavior, he developed a questionnaire that was administered to more than 600 people from various walks of life. Some were asked to fill out the questionnaire about a person they felt was generally an effective communicator; others were asked to complete the form with a specific *in*effective communicator in mind. The dimensions along which these respondents tended to judge communicative ability included (1) other versus self-orientation, (2) similarity versus dissimilarity to receiver, (3) clarity versus vagueness, and (4) message vigilance–attention versus message neglect–inattention.[30]

The following six statements, taken from Feingold's questionnaire, tended to discriminate most clearly between the effective and ineffective communicators being judged. According to this study, then, we would be most likely to report that people we know who demonstrate effective communication in their relationships do the following things frequently and that those we classify as ineffective relational communicators seldom do them:

1. This person says the right thing at the right time.
2. This person adapts his or her communication to others.
3. This person avoids using language that might be offensive.
4. This person reveals something about his or her feelings when he or she is talking.
5. This person is aware of the effect of his or her communication on his or her partner.
6. This person is not difficult to understand.

Rx for Effective Communication

What is the best advice we can give to people who want to improve their ability to communicate in their relationships? Scholars and laypeople alike have addressed this question in various ways for the past 2000 years. There seems to be an almost inexhaustible supply of lists that give advice on how to improve communicative behavior. Some of this advice has been excellent; some of it has been just shy of inane. Sometimes these prescriptive statements contain a kernel of sound advice but suffer from inflexibility ("A good communicator *never* criticizes"), vagueness ("A good communicator uses self-disclosure"), or incomplete explanations ("Use facts instead of inferences").

© Ivan Marjanovic/Shutterstock.com

One way to reduce our tendency to make these overly simple prescriptions is to appreciate what a complex task we accomplish when we communicate with another person. It is very easy for two people to misunderstand each other. And unfortunately, many relational problems begin with misunderstandings. A wife who comes home from work every day in a bad mood may not clearly explain to her husband that the source of her moodiness is work-related stress. Even though she would like to talk about her problems, her husband may avoid interacting with her. He may reason that her moodiness is a signal that she "needs space" at the end of the work day. She, in turn, may see his avoidance not as consideration, but as a sign that he doesn't care. This interpretation is likely to increase her stress level and her moodiness. Over time, when the husband sees that his efforts to reduce his wife's stress are not effective, he may begin to assume that her moodiness is directed at him—and by this time, some of it is.

Obviously, in trying to remedy this case, a simple prescription (e.g., "A good communicator is expressive") is not very useful. It may be more helpful to describe the misunderstanding and then to discuss some of the ways misunderstandings such as this one can be prevented—or at least minimized. Fincham, Fernades, and Humphreys define four pathways to miscommunication:[31]

1. The speaker's intent and the message do not correspond. Imagine if in our previous example, the husband had asked his wife what was bothering her. Although sincere, his message would likely be misunderstood if he used a sarcastic or disinterested tone in his voice. This sort of miscommunication can create problems for couples even though the speaker has very positive intentions.

2. The listener infers the wrong intent from the message even though the speaker encodes it properly. Now visualize the husband asking his wife what was bothering her, while using all of the appropriate nonverbal signals.

A misunderstanding would still occur if the wife inferred that her husband was acting concerned only because he wanted something—money, sex, or an uninterrupted evening of quiet television watching.

3. Both the speaker and the listener make errors. This is probably a good description of the miscommunication that happened between the couple in our initial example. The wife did not send a clear message to her husband about the source of her stress or about her desire to discuss her problems. The husband did not check his assumptions about what was bothering his wife or about her desire to be left alone at the end of the work day. As a consequence, both partners ended up feeling unheard or uncared for.

4. Both the speaker and the listener perform their task adequately and neither makes an error. Although counterintuitive, it is possible for misunderstandings to occur when both partners clearly communicate what they intend. This is often due to some external factor encroaching upon the interaction. For example, it is possible that the husband in our example asked his wife what was bothering her and the wife in our example communicated her need to talk about her problems at work, but a phone call, a knock at the door, or crying child interrupted their efforts to connect with each other. If something like this were to take place, the husband might not realize how important his wife's need was and the wife might infer that her husband doesn't care as much about her needs as he does about answering the phone, going to the door, or attending to the crying child. Another way this can happen is when partners have different rules or beliefs about communication. For instance, the husband in our example may have had one belief about how to interpret moodiness ("When people act moody, they are sending the message that they want to be left alone"), and the wife may have had another ("When people act moody, they are sending the message that they want attention"). If partners are unaware of such differences, it may be difficult for them to unravel their miscommunications.

Even though you could probably think of some additional pathways to miscommunication, the four presented here help illustrate why it is problematic to make overly simple prescriptions for improving the way we interact. Many misunderstandings are too complex to be addressed by such prescriptions. Does this mean that all advice about effective communication is useless? Certainly not. A number of scholars have made concerted attempts to study effective (and ineffective) communication. Although their findings may not apply to all situations, they provide us with tools we can use to diagnose our communication problems and improve our communication skills. For instance, Wiemann's research on initial interactions found that effective communicators were perceived as (1) other-oriented—empathic, affiliative, supportive, and relaxed; (2) flexible—capable of adapting during an encounter or across different types of encounters; and (3) interaction-oriented—capable of managing "procedural" aspects of the encounter so that it flows smoothly.[32] Effective interaction management refers to the ease with which speaking turns are exchanged and the appropriate degree of control or responsibility over topics initiated and discussed. The fascinating contribution of Wiemann's research to our understanding of communicative competence is his finding that management of the interaction can be extremely important. Relatively minute changes in management behaviors (interruptions, pauses longer than three seconds, unilateral topic changes) resulted in large variations in evaluations of competence by participants tested. As listeners and relational partners, then, we are apparently attending to and evaluating a host of fleeting, subtle, habitual, and noncontent features of another's communicative behavior. Unless, for some reason, these behaviors are magnified (making it a content issue, "Why don't you ever let me finish without interrupting me?"), neither listener nor speaker is very much aware of these actions.[33]

Hart's approach to effective communication also emphasizes the complex interplay between listener judgements and speaker behaviors.[34] As listeners, we come away from our encounters with evaluations—many of them unspoken— "She's really weird. . . . I have no idea what she means"; "I got the impression all he wanted to do was get the conversation over with as soon as possible"; "He's a pretty slick salesperson, but I have this nagging feeling that he really doesn't give a damn about *my* needs"; or "She didn't sound like she believed what she was saying, so why should I?" As a result of weighing and analyzing reactions just like these, Hart developed five principles that he believes need to be enacted for effective communication to occur. These principles, of course, are not instilled in listeners simply because a speaker states them—just because you tell me you're interested in my welfare doesn't necessarily make me feel it. So, Hart also proposed *some* of the possible ways to demonstrate these principles. Obviously, as we've said so many times before, different relationships, different people, different topics, and different situations will dictate which ways are best for making a relational partner feel that a principle has been enacted. The methods that work for one situation may fail miserably in the next. Of the five principles, Hart says, each principle should be given approximately equal attention in any given encounter. However, there will be exceptions—the unfaithful husband or wife who must stress the relationship principle above all others or the job interviewee who must stress his or her expertise before showing how it will help the company. See Table 12.1.

Looking at Hart's effective communication principles another way, they seem to address themselves to the matters of **profit** (for the speaker and the listener), **commitment** (to the message and the listener), **quality** (of the interaction and the relationship), and **tangibility** (of the message). We might perceive each dimension as present or absent, high or low. For instance, the ultimate speaker profit may be seen as exploitative, whereas the absence of any perceived speaker profit might be viewed as altruistic. A speaker "loss" might elicit perceptions of sympathy, pity, or stupidity. Listener profits may be seen as beneficial, useful, absent, or even injurious. Listeners' commitment may be identified by examining attentiveness, interest, and sensitivity. Extreme message commitment may be seen in a person who is perceived as certain and obstinate or uncertain and changeable. When we perceive the quality of our interaction, we usually are looking at questions of whether it was effortless and refreshing or laborious and draining. Relationship quality, in this context, seems to deal with not only an accepting-rejecting dimension, but also a time dimension—lasting

Profit: Reward, gain, or benefit.

Commitment: Sense of obligation, responsibility, or dedication.

Quality: Characterstics or attributes

Tangibility: Concreteness or presence.

Table 12.1 Hart's Principles for Achieving Effective Communication

Principle	Some Ways to Show It	Samples	If Principle Is Violated, Speaker Is Seen as:
I am committed to you and will try to deal with your immediate existence. (i.e., "I'm going to talk *with* you, not at you.")	• use audience involvement • adjust to feedback • use analogies to connect your "worlds" • attach yourself to their values • use familiar, practical examples • show immediate benefits to be derived from the interaction • adapt to situational changes, etc.	• "Well, son, majority rule is like if you and I want to go for ice cream and Mommy doesn't. We'd go because we outnumber her." • I think my stand on consumer protection proves I'm the person for the job." • "I get the feeling you're still not convinced. What do you think we ought to do about the problem?"	• *Paternalistic* (e.g., true believer or authoritarian parent) • *Ego-tripper* (e.g., a braggart or know-it-all) • *Irrelevant* (e.g., a required course in Latin)
I am committed to my message. (i.e., "I mean what I say, and I know what I'm talking about.")	• cite personal experiences • take a firm stand on the issue • appear factually knowledgeable • show your stake in the interaction • show you've made an investment in the subject, etc.	• "Now listen, I've been to Ethiopia and I've seen those people starving." • "The average giraffe is usually mute and has 12,000 bones in its neck." • "You may not vote for me, but I'm in this race 'til the bitter end."	• *Phony* (e.g., all talk, no action) • *Wishy-washy* (e.g., a sycophant) • *Ignorant* (e.g., doesn't know what he or she is talking about)
I hope that both of us will profit from this interaction. (i.e., "I'm talking to you for our mutual benefit.")	• teach them something they hadn't known • detail the *concrete* benefits to be derived from listening to you • establish common ground • depict interaction as profitable or entertaining for you, etc.	• "Hey, it's been great talking to you." • "Just think, honey, a whole week by ourselves at the beach with nobody else around." • "If you don't heed my warnings about pollution, your very lives will be in danger."	• *Boring* (e.g., a lecture on East Indian toothpicks) • *Suspicious* (e.g., a "free" giveaway from a used car dealer)

I want to interact with you and hope that our relationship will continue. (i.e., "We will communicate and, perhaps, form a relationship.")	• dialogue with audience • show that they can affect you • link your proposal to their future well-being • don't rush through the interaction • specify your future intentions, etc.	• "As you go to college, John, remember that we'll miss you and that you can count on us." • "Hey, let's get together again soon. Next week?" • "If you have trouble with the radio, Mr. Smith, bring it back. We've been in business for fifty years and will be here for another fifty."	• *Parasitic* (e.g., a fly-by-night salesperson) • *Dogmatic* (e.g., chair of the board with 51% of the stock)
I want you to understand fully the practical implications of my message. (i.e., "I'm talking about things that can be understood and utilized.")	• don't overload the listener with more information than he or she can handle • avoid difficult abstractions • summarize; reorient the listener when necessary • move from easily understood information to complex information • use details to vivify your thoughts, etc.	• "If you remember nothing else, just remember that I love you." • "As Linus says, 'Happiness is a warm puppy.'" • "And so, folks, remember our motto: 'If you're looking for safety, dependability, and style, buy an Acura.'"	• *Incomprehensible* (e.g., explaining "responsibility" to a two-year-old) • *Confused* (e.g., a bumbling professor lecturing on perfect communication)

Reproduced and adapted from R. P. Hart (lecture notes, University of Texas, Department of Speech Communication) 1991.

versus transient. Indeed, researchers have found that relational commitment—the dedication to continue the relationship even in the face of difficulties—is an important factor in determining long-term relational quality.[35] Further, many efforts to rejuvenate and repair distressed relationships focus on enhancing each partner's commitment to the other's communication messages.[36] One survey of marital and relational counselors found that one of the most common problems of distressed couples involves a lack of commitment to one another's message—partners are unwilling and/or unable to take the other's perspective when listening.[37] For this reason, most forms of couples' therapy involve, at least to some extent, training in skills such as diagnosing the partner's feelings; summarizing and restating those feelings; and demonstrating acceptance through vocal tone, facial expression, and posture.[38] These types of communication skills not only enable partners to express their commitment to one another's messages, but also help them make their own messages more clear and tangible.

By now it should be apparent that we can (carefully) make some prescriptive statements about how to improve the way we communicate with our relational partners. Granted, some partners may establish rules or norms that render these statements inappropriate for their relationships. For many of us, though, the statements will provide a guideline as to how to enhance the quality of our interactions and decrease misunderstanding.

One of the most common recommendations made by researchers and clinicians involves validating our relational partners. Validation, according to Gottman, is letting your partner know that you understand him or her.[39] In Hart's words (see Table 12.1), validation touches on your commitment to your partner ("I am committed to you and will try to deal with your immediate existence") as well as your commitment to the interaction ("I want to interact with you and hope that our relationship will continue"). By validating the other, you demonstrate that you care about his or her message—that you are willing to attend to the message and put time and effort into understanding it. Validation may be composed of small, seemingly unimportant behaviors such as nodding or making eye contact with your partner when he or she speaks (rather than reading or checking your phone). However, it may also involve more global behaviors such as expressing appreciation to your partner when he or she does something you enjoy (e.g., makes a nice meal, gives you a massage). In the latter case, your partner's message is often an unspoken one (e.g., "I did something for you to make you happy"), reflected in behavior rather than in words. Validating something your partner does, though, can be just as important as validating something your partner says. When we fail to validate the other, we create a context in which he or she may very well feel unheard and unloved.

Of course, showing the other person that you understand him or her is only one part of the equation. You also want to speak so that your partner understands what you say. As noted at the beginning of this chapter, though, sending a clear, unambiguous message is not always the most effective way to get someone to understand you. Many times, in the midst of conflict, partners send very clear messages (e.g., "You are such a selfish pig!") that they later regret. Furthermore, some messages that sound clear to listeners actually don't say what the speaker intended them to say (e.g., "We never go out anymore" might actually mean "I'd like to spend some quiet time alone with you"). If your goal is to speak so that your partner understands you, you need to formulate your messages with an awareness of how they may be interpreted. For instance, when couples discuss "touchy topics" (e.g., a desire for change in their sexual interaction or dissatisfaction with the way household tasks are divided), both partners are typically ready to defend themselves. As a consequence, messages often are interpreted in a more negative way than they were intended. It also is very easy during these types of conversations to send messages that place blame or responsibility on the other.

Researchers and clinicians make several recommendations to minimize partners' feelings of defensiveness and increase the likelihood that they will understand each other. One of the most common recommendations is that partners "take responsibility" for their feelings when they communicate. Rather than blame the other person for how you feel (e.g., "You make me feel so stupid!"), this means that you express your feelings using "I statements" (e.g., "I feel really stupid when . . ."). Another common recommendation is that partners make an attempt to place statements that may be interpreted as negative (e.g., "I wish you'd spend more time with my family") in a positive relational context (e.g., "I really liked it when you went out to dinner with my family the other night and I wish you'd do that more often"). People generally expect their relational partners to communicate with them in ways that demonstrate positive regard.[40] Couching what might be seen as a negative message in positive terms is one way to show your partner that you see him or her in a positive (rather than a negative) light. Similarly, "balancing" negative messages with positive messages often helps your partner be more receptive to what you say.[41]

Some people may object to the idea of modifying their messages so that their partner will understand them. They may feel if their partner really cared about them, they wouldn't have to watch what they say—that if they really had an "intimate" relationship they would be able to express themselves without worrying about the way their partner would react. The problem with this perspective is that (1) it assumes that our partner will always understand our intentions; (2) it fails to recognize the fact that our communication influences others—that what we say has an effect on our listeners; and (3) it does not attend to the feelings, needs, and experiences that our partner brings to the interaction.

Markman and his colleagues argue that it is critical for each partner to recognize the impact his or her messages have on the other.[42] From the speaker's perspective, this means that messages sometimes need to be "edited" in order to be understood. From the listener's perspective, it means that assumptions about the meaning of a message sometimes need to be checked (e.g., "Did you have a bad day at school, or did I do something to upset you?"). In short, both partners need to adjust their communication behaviors to the other in order to communicate effectively. In Hart's terms, these adjustments not only make the speaker's messages tangible (understandable) to the listener, but they bring the speaker's desire for a quality relationship (one that is rewarding to both participants) to the forefront.

Becoming an Effective Communicator

Communicators are born. We humans seem to be brought into this world with the capacity to learn and use language. People who are effective communicators in their relationships, however, are made, not born. How? The following four ingredients—knowledge, experiences, motivation, and attitudes—seem to adequately cover the necessities for developing social competence and/or effective communication in relationships.

Knowledge

To become an effective communicator, it seems reasonable to expect that a person should develop a sizable, well-rounded knowledge base. Part of this knowledge is *content knowledge* ("knowing what" or "knowing that") and can be obtained from books, lectures, the internet, and the experiences of others. Another part of any well-rounded knowledge base is *procedural knowledge* ("knowing how"), which involves an understanding of what effective communicators do.[43] For many of our interactions with others, a broad liberal arts education seems to be extremely helpful. An extensive and intensive educational base helps build a knowledge of people's behavior, our environmental surroundings, group behavior, cultural norms, history, and the arts. This knowledge, in turn, certainly assists in developing much needed predictive ability concerning cultural and sociological expectations; it also helps build expertise and confidence in message sending. In our close relationships, however, we also need an extensive knowledge of our relational partners—their usual responses to certain situations, their assumptions about relationships, their family histories, and so on. Without this intimate, individualized knowledge, we really don't have an intimate relationship. With this knowledge (and, perhaps more important, a conscious awareness of this knowledge), we are better able to respond and adapt to the daily events that make up a close relationship. Since much of our message sending in our relationships is preceded and/or followed by reflection on why we did or did not behave in a certain way, it is important to build a mental reference library of information that may help clarify why we interact as we do. This book was designed for that purpose. Vicarious learning through books, lectures, the internet, and the experiences of others is indeed an important source of knowledge, but for optimum development, it should be supplemented with knowledge obtained from actual experiences in life's laboratory.

Experiences

Communicative experiences may be obtained by observing others (building diagnosis skills) and by participating with others (building performance skills). From early childhood throughout life, we imitate communicative responses and model our behavior after that of others. Some of this behavior is so subtle we learn it with little conscious effort—for example, using eye behavior to signal one's desire for a speaking turn. Mostly, however, learning effective relational communication, like developing proficiency at any skill, is hard work. The most effective communicators probably expose themselves to many different communicative situations and are not afraid to try novel experiences and challenges.

> *It is not doing things, but understanding what you do that brings real excitement and lasting pleasure.*
>
> —*Robertson Davies*

There are many reasons why a wide variety of communicative experiences can be helpful in building one's effectiveness. For instance, without the knowledge of different people and different situations, flexibility and adaptation are impaired. You may learn how to interact with one type of person, perhaps the type who agrees with you, but you may be extremely ineffective when cast in a role outside this limited group. Children, because of limited experiences, do not have the same predictive abilities as some adults—but adults who constrict their experiences may find similar limitations. More experience may mean the possibility of some initial communicative and relational failures, but ultimately these failures can be turned into a far greater success than that enjoyed by the person who safely sticks with only easy communicative experiences and easy relationships. The person with a greater experiential base will increase his or her chances of learning realistic expectations for communicative success. Accuracy in person perception should increase. There also should be an increase in understanding one's own interaction needs and goals in various relationships and ways that can and cannot achieve these goals.

Bochner identified five ways in which communication functions in relationships: (1) to foster favorable impressions, (2) to organize relationships—negotiating and living by certain rules, (3) to validate and support a view of reality common to you and your partner, (4) to express your feelings and thoughts, and (5) to protect yourself—those areas in which you are most subject to being hurt.[44] Since the specific ways in which we use communication to accomplish these goals change with different types of relationships and different people, a broad base of experiences with many types of relationships and different types of people may be helpful in preparing for effective communication in any one relationship.

The widely experienced person should have an appreciation for the complexity of the process of communication and the complexity of people in general. If it is true that we tend to fear the things we know the least about, perhaps we should get to know other people better—and get to know ourselves better at the same time through those people. It may mean that our appreciation for our fellow human beings' shortcomings and strengths (and our own) will help us reduce maladaptive behaviors.

It should be clear that a broad-based set of experiences needs a great deal of self-motivated practice and helpful feedback to be useful. Becoming an effective communicator in any relationship is a never-ending process—a constant process of analysis that continues as long as (and sometimes longer than) the relationship does. Seeking and analyzing feedback on our communicative behavior from our relational partners, from experts, and from diagnostic tests (including videotaped interactions) will surely help us develop more realistic expectations of our own skills. Learning how to communicate more effectively should become somewhat like driving a car—behavior that is largely habitual and that contributes to a smooth operation, but with constant vigilance for that ever-present possibility that will require adaptation to changing relational circumstances.

Motivation

The desire to communicate effectively is probably as important, if not more important, than all the behavioral prescriptions we might employ. If we strongly desire to have a person or a group of persons understand something, believe something, or do something, it is not at all unlikely that the necessary behavioral techniques will follow.[45] Also, on a more general level, our desire to approach and engage ourselves in social situations (rather than to avoid or extricate ourselves) will influence the type and quality of communication behaviors we employ.[46] For example, when relational partners withdraw from a situation involving conflict, certain sorts of messages may be sent—"I don't care enough about this relationship to continue the discussion," "I don't see the issue as an important one," or "I want you to work harder on this relationship than I do so that I know you really love me." In many cases, the lack of willingness to engage in dialogue with one's partner results in misunderstanding about what each partner wants and needs from the relationship. Over time, these sorts of misunderstandings can redefine the relationship in ways that neither partner originally intended.

If a lack of motivation to communicate with one's relational partner potentially creates feelings of distance, the motivation to succeed in our relational communication should, in most cases, enhance relational closeness. Recall Hart's approach to effective communication: demonstrating to our partner that we are motivated and we *want* to interact with him or her is one factor in determining how effective we are. Suffice to say, when we are sufficiently motivated to succeed, when we are able to visualize ourselves succeeding, when we get an inner feeling of pleasure out of communicating effectively with our relational partners, we have taken a giant step toward becoming an effective communicator.

Attitudes

Attitudes, too, can be critical to effectiveness in communicating with others. Certainly we could predict potential differences in effectiveness between communicators who enter a relational situation with these different attitudes:

A My communicative behavior is going to be important in this situation.

A_1 I have so much to be concerned with I can't worry about something as abstract as "communication."

B This is going to be a tough situation, so I'd better be on guard and watch carefully what they say and what I say.

B_1 This is going to be a tough situation. I know I'll goof it up.

C I'm not anxious to go, but I may learn something.

C_1 There's nothing I can get out of this situation.

Furthermore, if we believe that being able to communicate effectively with others is closely linked to becoming a "better person," we might expect to see an increasing security in our own identity as our communicative efforts are rewarded. Security in our own identity will, in turn, contribute positively to our communicative efforts.

Becoming an effective communicator in our relationships involves continual efforts to improve our understanding, analytical skills, and performance skills. Some skills are easier to learn than others. Irving Lee, a noted teacher and scholar of human communication, said that the development of communication skills involved the following five activities.[47] They are listed according to how difficult they are to master—*with the easiest activities listed first and the most difficult last.*

1. We have to acquaint ourselves with what is known about the subject of our communication—theories, facts, and so on.

2. We have to learn to recognize proficiencies as well as shortcomings and defects in the communication behavior of others.

3. We have to learn to recognize proficiencies as well as shortcomings and defects in our own communication behavior.

4. We have to learn to develop skills in prescribing methods for improving our own communication.

5. We have to learn to develop skills in prescribing methods for improving the communication behavior of others.

Writing Your Own Story

You, the reader, are about to finish a book on how people communicate during the various twists and turns that their relationships take. Some of you will remember a lot from this book; some won't remember much. Some of you will sell your book, whereas others will use it as a future resource. Two things, however, will be the same for everyone who has read this book: (1) all of you will continue to have communication experiences in your relationships that you want to understand and analyze and (2) everyone's ability to analyze those experiences and to recall information will be greatly assisted with a simple memory jogging device. Journalists, novelists, and anyone who has had a high school English

© DGLimages/Shutterstock.com

course is familiar with a set of questions—"who," "what," "where," "when," "how," and "why"—that is designed to uncover key information for telling and understanding a story.

We think these same questions will be useful in understanding the communication in your own relationship story. They will help you explain why you feel especially good or bad at a particular time and clarify puzzling communicative transactions. Notice how many familiar comments people make about the communication in their relationships can be categorized in this simple system. Although this system will not provide ready solutions to problems, it should be very helpful in the first stage of problem-solving—identifying the nature of the problem. A final note concerns the absence of "why" questions. We feel that a focus on the other aspects of the communicative experience will naturally stimulate "why" questions.

Who initiated the communication?

"I am always the one who says 'I love you' first. How come you never think to say it first?"

"You brought it up, not me."

"It's not my fault we don't talk about it. You never bring it up."

"I like it when you start talking about what happened to you during the day because then I feel more like talking about my day."

What was or was not said/done?

"You never respond when I talk to you."

"You always have something positive to say and I like that."

"You never tell me I look nice."

Where was something said/done?

"Why did you have to say it in front of my mother?"

"You can't expect me to talk about that here."

"Let's wait to talk about this until we're alone."

When was or was not something said/done?

"Getting flowers from you when there was no special occasion was the last thing I expected."

"You seem to know when I need comforting."

"You didn't have to bring that up; you know I'm incredibly stressed out right now."

"You knew I was expecting you to ask me about that when I said . . ."

"It's too late for apologies now; you should have contacted me earlier."

How was it said/done?

"The way you said it—so abruptly—I just didn't believe you."

"The intensity in the way you expressed yourself overwhelmed me."

"I feel accepted and understood when you focus on me like that."

How often was something said/done?

"Saying you love me every day really makes me feel good."

"You used to want a lot of sex; now you don't seem interested as much."

Communicating Effectively Together

What is the "bottom line" for effective communication in relationships? It should be clear to you, by this point, that we are not going to provide you with a specific formula for relational success (and that you should be wary of anyone who does offer such a formula).[48] There are, however, several principles of effective communication in relationships that can be gleaned from the material presented in this chapter as well as other literature on couples' therapy and counseling. We offer these principles not as an "answer" to relational problems but as a guideline or tool that you can use to help you through the difficulties (and the rewards) that relationships bring.

© Phovoir/Shutterstock.com

1. Be both flexible and stubborn. Combine a willingness to adapt with a basic, gut-level refusal to give up on the relationship. As we've repeatedly noted in this book, people change, situations change, and values change. These changes and others often will require modifications in how and what individuals communicate to their relational partners. Without an ability (and a willingness) to adapt to the changing communicative needs of their relationships, people may be unable to maintain close and satisfying romantic partnerships. The flexibility we are talking about here is not weak or submissive (e.g., "Of course I'll change dear—whatever you want."). Instead, it is coupled with a stubborn determination to make the relationship work (e.g., "I'm willing to do what it takes to keep us together.").

2. Talk about your feelings, attitudes, and opinions. In any relationship, both partners will decide to keep some things to themselves. When we advise you to talk with your relational partner, we are not saying that you need to express every feeling, all the time, in every situation (e.g., it's probably not a good idea to initiate a discussion about the state of your relationship right after your partner has flunked an exam). Nor are we suggesting that you should express yourself without considering the effect of what you say on your partner (e.g., "You really look fat in that outfit!"). Expressing your feelings, alone, will not solve all of your relationship problems. When we advise you to talk with your partner, we hope to remind you that communication is the "life-blood" of romantic relationships. If you want another person to love you, you must allow that person to know you and to respond to your wants and needs.

3. Respond to your partner in ways that show respect, value, and caring.
One of the quickest ways to silence relational talk is to be unresponsive. Even when discussing "routine" issues, such as how the day went or what needs to get done tomorrow, people usually feel bad if their relational partner does not act interested in what they are saying. When the topics of discussion are more intimate (e.g., feelings about the relationship, sexual desires), we are even more sensitive to our partner's responses. It is important to note here that romantic partners may "listen" to each other without acting responsively. Responsiveness involves more than just hearing a relational partner's words. It also involves showing that you value your partner and what he or she is saying. Responsive behaviors may include eye contact, paraphrasing, head nodding, or touch. Regardless of the specific behaviors you demonstrate, the important thing is that your partner feels like you care enough to listen.

4. Attend to the important.
Even the most responsive people will encounter difficulties if they fail to respond to the things their partner feels are important. In most cases, it is easy to respond to the things that we, ourselves, feel are important to the relationship. Since we usually know what these things are, we can attend to and prioritize them as central aspects of the relationship. It is more difficult, however, to identify the things our partner feels are important. At the beginning of relationships, partners may be so eager to please one another that they fail to express their wants and needs. Later, when their needs have not been met, they may become resentful—assuming that "If she really loved me, she would know that this is important to me!" "Attending to the important" involves taking the time and effort necessary to discover what both you and your partner feel are central aspects of your relationship. It also involves letting go of things that are unimportant. Sometimes partners spend a great deal of energy on parts of their relationship that don't mean very much to either one of them. Other times, they fix their attention on "little things" about their relationship that they find annoying. When partners focus on aspects of their relationship that they feel are unimportant or trivial, they have less time and fewer resources to devote to the things they really care about. Also, in many cases, seemingly trivial issues mask more important concerns. A heated argument about who drank the last soda or who left the toilet seat up actually may represent partners' worries about whether they are receiving the respect or consideration that they need. Focusing on seemingly trivial issues may prevent partners from uncovering and attending to their more significant concerns. Those more important concerns may involve affection, an ability to self-disclose, sexuality, or even career aspirations. What do you and your partner believe are the important components of a "good" relationship? What do the two of you define as "good" relational communication? What do you want out of your relationship? These are questions that you and your partner need to answer (and continue answering) together.

5. Work at the relationship but remember to have fun.
Generous amounts of both serious effort and silliness are often needed to create a close, satisfying romantic relationship. After reading this book, it should be clear to you that intimate relationships usually require a great deal of time and effort. But "all

work and no play" can make almost any relationship tiring. Create space in your life to enjoy your relationship. Find activities that you both like and take the time to do them. Laugh together. Remind yourselves of what initially made you fall in love. Talk about your dreams. One of the main reasons people come together in romantic relationships is because they enjoy each other. Allow that sense of fun and enjoyment to be one of the reasons you stay together.

Summary

This chapter was deliberately designed to follow the chapters outlining communicative behavior at various stages of a relationship. Our hope was that an understanding of messages produced at different points in a relationship would provide a framework within which effective relational communication could be viewed. As we so frequently stated, no pattern, no style, or no word is always going to guarantee that a communicator will effectively communicate. The only "sure-fire, never-fail, key to success" is to analyze sufficiently each situation so that messages can be adapted accordingly. Success in relational communication ventures depends on a number of factors. Some of these are (1) who makes the judgment of effectiveness; (2) at what point or points in time (relationship, life, history, conversation) the judgment is made; (3) what the judge(s) chooses to evaluate—obtaining a desired response, being ethically sound, helping the other to achieve his or her goals, certain verbal and/or nonverbal behavior, quantity of cues produced, number and diversity of strategies employed, ability across different modes, and so on; (4) how the judgment is made—the conditions for testing or observation; and (5) why the judgment was made and whether the subject is aware of the evaluation.

In the belief that people cannot completely separate their judgments of relationships from their judgments of people's communication within relationships, we reviewed the Wish et al. study, which provided a look at broad categories often used to examine relationships. We also discussed the notion that people's assumptions and expectations of their relationships affect the way they perceive their partners' communication. In addition, a study by Feingold examined perceptions of communicative behavior. Almost every one of six statements found in his study to discriminate reliably between the behavior of effective communicators and the behavior of ineffective communicators focused in one form or another on proper adaptation.

Another part of this chapter presented statements of advice for those interested in improving their communicative abilities. This was an effort to identify those suggestions that, although subject to variation in any given situation and/or relationship, seem to be generalizable across situations more than are other suggestions. We made a concerted attempt to get a variety of approaches without sacrificing intellectual quality and usefulness. To provide a context for the discussion, we presented Fincham et al.'s pathways to miscommunication. Then we looked at Wiemann's research, which reiterated the fact that effective communicators seem to be other-oriented and flexible but added a dimension, interaction-oriented—one's ability to manage the "administrative" aspects of the conversation (turn taking, topic initiation) as well as the substantive aspects. In addition, we examined Hart's work, which suggested five principles to guide the effective communicator. These principles were grounded in the communicators' ability to make partners feel that they (1) are committed to them and are trying to deal with their immediate existence, (2) are committed to their own message, (3) hope both participants will profit from the interaction, (4) want to interact with the other and hope that the relationship will continue, and (5) want the listeners to understand fully the practical implications of the message. Finally, the section concluded with an application of some of these ideas about effective communication to the context of personal relationships. Some of the common communication difficulties faced by couples were discussed and suggestions as to how partners might effectively deal with those difficulties were provided.

After developing a better understanding of what an effective relational communicator is (from research and credible prescriptions), we sought some explanation of how a person might achieve this status. We suggested that one needed a firm knowledge base, a continuous variety of experiences, strong intrinsic motivation, and a set of positive attitudes regarding oneself and one's communicative acts.

We also provided a set of questions that we hope will serve as a memory jogging device for people who are interested in analyzing and understanding their own communication. Journalists and novelists often use the questions, "who," "what," "where," "when," "how," and "why" to help them understand a story. We believe that these same questions will help you analyze and explain the communication in your own relationship story.

We concluded the chapter with a discussion of what might be termed the "bottom line" for effective communication in relationships. Although we recognize that it is impossible to provide "ten easy steps" to competent relational communication, we hope that some of these comments will provide a clearer understanding of how your communication influences the quality of your close relationships.

Evaluating Communication

Asher, S. R. "Children's Ability to Appraise Their Own and Another Person's Communication Performance." *Developmental Psychology* 12 (1976): 24–32.

Burleson, B. R., and Denton, W. H. "The Relationship Between Communication Skill and Marital Satisfaction: Some Moderating Effects." *Journal of Marriage and the Family* 59 (1997): 884–902.

Delia, J. G., and Clark, R. A. "Cognitive Complexity, Social Perception and the Development of Listener-Adapted Communication in Six-, Eight-, and Twelve-Year Old Boys." *Communication Monographs* 44 (1977): 326–345.

Feingold, P. C. "Toward a Paradigm of Effective Communication: An Empirical Study of Perceived Communicative Effectiveness." Ph.D. dissertation, Purdue University, 1976.

Habermas, J. "Toward a Theory of Communicative Competence." In H. P. Dreitzel, ed., *Recent Sociology.* No. 2. New York: Macmillan, 1970.

Hymes, D. *On Communicative Competence.* Philadelphia: University of Pennsylvania Press, 1970.

Ickes, W., ed. *Empathic Accuracy.* New York: Guilford, 1997.

Krauss, R. M., and Glucksberg, S. "The Development of Communication: Competence as a Function of Age." *Child Development* 40 (1969): 255–266.

Longabaugh, R. "The Structure of Interpersonal Behavior." *Sociometry* 29 (1966): 441–460.

Mehrabian, A., and Ksionzky, S. "Categories of Social Behavior." *Comparative Group Studies* 3 (1972): 425–436.

Montgomery, B. M. "Quality Communication in Personal Relationships." In S. W. Duck, ed., *Handbook of Personal Relationships,* pp. 343–359. New York: Wiley, 1988.

Mortensen, C. D. *Miscommunication.* Thousand Oaks, CA: Sage, 1997.

Pearson, J. C., and Daniels, T. D. "'Oh, What Tangled Webs We Weave': Concerns About Current Conceptions of Communication Competence." *Communication Reports* 1 (1988): 95–100.

Spitzberg, B. H. "The Dialectics of (In)competence." *Journal of Social and Personal Relationships* 10 (1993): 137–158.

Weinstein, E. A. "The Development of Interpersonal Competence." In D. A. Goslin, ed., *Handbook of Socialization Theory and Research.* Chicago: Rand McNally, 1969.

Wish, M., Deutsch, M., and Kaplan, S. J. "Perceived Dimensions of Interpersonal Relations." *Journal of Personality and Social Psychology* 33 (1976): 409–420.

Developing Communication Skills

Allen, R. R., and Brown, K. L., eds. *Developing Communication Competence in Children.* Skokie, IL: National Textbook, 1976.

Argyris, C. "Explorations in Interpersonal Competence—I." *Journal of Applied Behavioral Science* 1 (1965): 58–83.

Bochner, A. P., and Kelly, C. W. "Interpersonal Competence: Rationale, Philosophy, and Implementation of a Conceptual Framework." *Speech Teacher* 23 (1974): 279–301.

Fincham, F. D., Fernades, L. O. L., and Humphreys, K. *Communicating in Relationships: A Guide for Couples and Professionals.* Champaign, IL: Research Press, 1993.

Gottman, J. M. *Why Marriages Succeed or Fail.* New York: Simon & Schuster, 1994.

Greene, J. O., and Burleson, B. R., eds. *Handbook of Communication and Social Interaction Skills.* Mahwah, NJ: Erlbaum, 2003.

Hart, R. P., and Burks, D. M. "Rhetorical Sensitivity and Social Interaction." *Speech Monographs* 39 (1972): 75–91.

Kelly, A. B., Fincham, F. D., and Beach, S. R. H. "Communication Skills in Couples: A Review and Discussion of Emerging Perspectives." In J. O. Greene and B. R. Burleson, eds., *Handbook of Communication and Social Interaction Skills,* pp. 723–751. Mahwah, NJ: Erlbaum, 2003.

Markman, H. J., Stanley, S. M., and Blumberg, S. L. *Fighting for Your Marriage: A Deluxe Revised Edition of the Classic Best Seller for Enhancing Marriage and Preventing Divorce.* San Francisco, CA: Jossey-Bass, 2010.

Notarius, C., and Markman, H. J. *We Can Work It Out: Making Sense of Marital Conflict.* New York: Putnam, 1993.

Parks, M. R. "Communicative Competence and Interpersonal Control." In M. L. Knapp and G. R. Miller, eds., *Handbook of Interpersonal Communication,* pp. 589–617. Thousand Oaks, CA: Sage, 1994.

Rosenthal, R., ed. *Skill in Nonverbal Communication: Individual Differences.* Cambridge, MA: Oelgeschalger, Gunn & Hain, 1979.

Segrin, C., and Flora, J. "Poor Social Skills Are a Vulnerability Factor in the Development of Psychosocial Problems." *Human Communication Research* 26 (2000): 489–514.

Spitzberg, B. H., and Cupach, W. R. *Interpersonal Communication Competence.* Beverly Hills, CA: Sage, 1984.

_____. *Handbook in Interpersonal Communication Competence.* New York: Springer-Verlag, 1989.

_____, "Interpersonal Skills." In M. L. Knapp and J. A. Daly, eds., *The Sage Handbook of Interpersonal Communication,* 4th ed., pp. 481–524. Thousand Oaks, CA: Sage, 2011.

Wiemann, J. M. "Explication and Test of a Model of Communicative Competence." *Human Communication Research* 3 (1977): 195–213.

Notes

[1] M. L. Williams and B. Goss, "Equivocation: Character Insurance," *Human Communication Research* 1 (1975): 265–270; See also C. J. Orr and K. E. Burkins, "The Endorsement of Evasive Leaders: An Exploratory Study," *Central States Speech Journal* 27 (1976): 230–239; M. L. Williams, "The Effect of Deliberate Vagueness on Receiver Recall and Agreement," *Central States Speech Journal* 31 (1980): 30–41; J. B. Bavelas, A. Black, N. Chovil, J. Mullett, *Equivocal Communication* (Newbury Park, CA: Sage, 1990).

[2] J. C. Pearson, *Lasting Love: What Keeps Couples Together* (Dubuque, IA: W. C. Brown, 1992).

[3] B. M. Montgomery, "Quality Communication in Personal Relationships." In S. W. Duck, ed., *Handbook of Personal Relationships* (New York: Wiley, 1988), pp. 343–359; B. M. Montgomery, "Communication in Close Relationships." In A. L. Weber and J. H. Harvey, eds., *Perspectives on Close Relationships* (Boston: Allyn Bacon, 1994), pp. 67–87.

[4] L. C. Chung, "Crossing Boundaries: Cross-Cultural Communication." In K. D. Keith, ed., *Cross-Cultural Psychology: Contemporary Themes and Perspectives* (New York: Wiley, 2019), pp. 375–398.

[5] See, for example, T. R. Tili and G. G. Barker, "Communication in Intercultural Marriages: Managing Cultural Differences and Conflicts," *Southern Communication Journal* 80 (2015): 189–210.

[6] M. A. Fitzpatrick "A Typological Examination of Communication in Relationships." In R. B. Rubin, ed., *Communication Yearbook 1* (New Brunswick, NJ: Transaction, 1977), pp. 263–275; J. M. Gottman, "The Roles of Conflict Engagement, Escalation, and Avoidance in Marital Interaction: A Longitudinal View of Five Types of Couples," *Journal of Consulting and Clinical Psychology* 61 (1993): 6–15.

[7] M. A. Fitzpatrick and L. D. Ritchie, "Communication Schemata within the Family: Multiple Perspectives on Family Interaction," *Human Communication Research* 20 (1994): 275–301. For a review see A. F. Koerner, "Relationship Typologies." In A. L. Vangelisti and D. Perlman, eds., *The Cambridge Handbook of Personal Relationships,* 2nd ed. (New York: Cambridge University Press, 2018), pp. 65–76.

[8] See, for example, J. P. Caughlin, "Family Communication Standards: What Counts as Excellent Family Communication and How Are Such Standards Associated with Satisfaction," *Human Communication Research* 29 (2003): 5–40.

[9] J. M. Gottman, J. Coan, S. Carrere, and C. Swanson, "Predicting Marital Happiness and Stability from Newlywed Interactions," *Journal of Marriage and the Family* 60 (1998): 5–22; J. M. Gottman and L. J. Krokoff, "Marital Interaction and Satisfaction: A Longitudinal View," *Journal of Consulting and Clinical Psychology* 57 (1989): 47–52; T. L. Huston and A. L. Vangelisti, "Socioemotional Behavior and Satisfaction in Marital Relationships: A Longitudinal Study," *Journal of Personality and Social Psychology* 41 (1991): 721–733.

[10] J. Epstein and R. J. Eidelson, "Unrealistic Beliefs of Clinical Couples: Their Relationship to Expectations, Goals, and Satisfaction," *American Journal of Family Therapy* 9 (1981): 13–22.

[11] See, for example, S. E. Caplan and J. O. Greene, "Acquisition of Message-Production Skill by Younger and Older Adults: Effects of Age, Task Complexity, and Practice," *Communication Monographs* 66 (1999): 31–48; M. Dragojevic and H. Giles, "I Don't Like You Because You're Hard to Understand: The Role of Processing Fluency in the Language Attitudes Process," *Human Communication Research* 42 (2016): 396–420.

[12] J. G. Delia and R. A. Clark, "Cognitive Complexity, Social Perception and the Development of Listener-Adapted Communication in Six-, Eight-, Ten-, and Twelve-Year-Old Boys," *Communication Monographs* 44 (1977): 326–345. For a review of children's social competencies see

L. Stafford, "Parent and Sibling Interactions during Middle Childhood." In A. L. Vangelisti, ed., *The Routledge Handbook of Family Communication,* 2ⁿᵈ ed. (New York: Routledge, 2013), pp. 256–270.

13 T. Stephen, "Communication in the Shifting Context of Intimacy: Marriage, Meaning, and Modernity," *Communication Theory* 4 (1994): 191–218.

14 J. P. Caughlin, "A Multiple Goals Theory of Personal Relationships: Conceptual Integration and Program Overview," *Journal of Social and Personal Relationships,* 27 (2010) 824–828.

15 For a commentary on this and other similar issues, see B. H. Spitzberg, "The Dialectics of (In)Competence," *Journal of Social and Personal Relationships* 10 (1993): 137–158.

16 S. G. Lakey and D. J. Canary, "Actor Goal Achievement and Sensitivity to Partner as Critical Factors in Understanding Interpersonal Communication Competence and Conflict Strategies," *Communication Monographs* 69 (2002): 217–235.

17 A. Koestler, *Darkness at Noon* (New York: Modern Library, 1941), p. 58.

18 G. R. Miller. "Interpersonal Communication: A Conceptual Perspective," *Communication* 2 (1975): 93–105. For further elaboration of this material, see G. R. Miller and M. Steinberg, *Between People* (Stanford, CA: Science Research Associates, 1975).

19 B. R. Burleson and W. H. Denton, "The Relationship Between Communication Skill and Marital Satisfaction: Some Moderating Effects," *Journal of Marriage and the Family* 59 (1997): 884–902; W. Ickes, *Empathic Accuracy* (New York: Guilford, 1997); G. Thomas, G. J. O. Fletcher, and C. Lange, "On-Line Empathic Accuracy in Marital Interaction," *Journal of Personality and Social Psychology* 72 (1997): 839–850.

20 A. L. Sillars, "Interpersonal Perception in Relationships." In W. Ickes, ed., *Compatible and Incompatible Relationships* (New York: Springer-Verlag, 1985), pp. 277–305.

21 See also S. L. Murray and J. G. Holmes, "A Leap of Faith? Positive Illusions in Romantic Relationships," *Personality and Social Psychology Bulletin* 23 (1997): 586–604; S. L. Murray, J. G. Holmes, and D. W. Griffin, "The Benefits of Positive Illusions: Idealization and the Construction of Satisfaction in Close Relationships," *Journal of Personality and Social Psychology* 70 (1996): 79–98.

22 See, for example, G. D. Bodie, S. M. Jones, A. J. Vickery, L. Hatcher, and K. Cannava, "Examining the Construct Validity of Enacted Support: A Multitrait-Multimethod Analysis of Three Perspectives for Judging Immediacy and Listening Behaviors," *Communication Monographs* 81 (2014): 495–523; J. N. Martin, "Revisiting Intercultural Communication Competence: Where to Go From Here," *Journal of Intercultural Relations* 48 (2015): 6–8.

23 For a review of criteria that are used to evaluate communicative success, see B. H. Spitzberg and W. R. Cupach, "Interpersonal Skills." In M. L. Knapp and J. A. Daly, eds., *The Sage Handbook of Interpersonal Communication*, 4ᵗʰ ed. (Thousand Oaks, CA: Sage, 2011), pp. 481–524.

24 B. H. Spitzberg and W. R. Cupach, *Handbook of Interpersonal Competence Research* (New York: Springer-Verlag, 1989); for an example of how social competence plays out in an online context, see M. W. Savage and R. S. Tokunaga, "Moving Toward a Theory: Testing an Integrated Model of Cyberbullying Perpetration, Aggression, Social Skills, and Internet Self-Efficacy," *Computers in Human Behavior* 71 (2017): 353–371.

25 M. Wish, M. Deutsch, and S. J. Kaplan, "Perceived Dimensions of Interpersonal Relations," *Journal of Personality and Social Psychology* 33 (1976): 409–420. For similar research, see also R. Longabaugh, "The Structure of Interpersonal Behavior," *Sociometry* 29 (1966): 441–460; and C. E. Osgood, "Speculations on the Structure of Interpersonal Intentions," *Behavioral Science* 15 (1970): 237–254.

26 L. Campbell, J. A. Simpson, D. A. Kashy, and G. J. O. Fletcher, "Ideal Standards, the Self, and Flexibility of Ideals in Close Relationships," *Personality and Social Psychology Bulletin* 27 (2001): 447–462; G. J. O. Fletcher, J. A. Simpson, and G. Thomas, "Ideals, Perceptions, and Evaluations in Early Relationship Development," *Journal of Personality and Social Psychology* 79 (2000): 933–940; A. L. Vangelisti and J. A. Daly, "Gender Differences in Standards for Romantic Relationships," *Personal Relationships* 4 (1997): 203–219.

27 N. C. Overall, G. J. O. Fletcher, and J. A. Simpson, "Regulation Processes in Intimate Relationships: The Role of Ideal Standards," *Journal of Personality and Social Psychology* 91 (2006): 662–685.

28 D. H. Baucom and N. Epstein, *Cognitive-Behavioral Marital Therapy* (New York: Brunner/Mazel, 1990); N. Epstein and R. J. Eidelson, "Unrealistic Beliefs of Clinical Couples: Their Relationship to Expectation, Goals,

and Satisfaction," *American Journal of Family Therapy* 9 (1981): 13–22; S. Metts and W. R. Cupach, "The Influence of Relationship Beliefs and Problem-Solving Responses on Satisfaction in Romantic Relationships," *Human Communication Research* 17 (1990): 170–185.

29 P. C. Feingold, "Toward a Paradigm of Effective Communication: An Empirical Study of Perceived Communicative Effectiveness" (Ph.D. diss., Purdue University 1976).

30 This does not mean, of course, that effective communicators are always found in one category. For instance, effective communicators seem to be generally perceived as other-oriented. Like any orientation, however, it can be overdone. If communicators consistently send you-oriented messages or verbal stares, it may create some of the discomfort engendered by nonverbal staring. See R. J. Cline and B. M. Johnson, "The Verbal Stare: Focus of Attention in Conversation," *Communication Monographs* 43 (1976): 1–10.

31 F. D. Fincham, L. O. L. Fernades, and K. Humphreys, *Communicating in Relationships: A Guide for Couples and Professionals* (Champaign, IL: Research Press, 1993).

32 J. M. Wiemann, "Explication and Test of a Model of Communicative Competence," *Human Communication Research* 3 (1977): 195–213.

33 Research by Street and Murphy has detailed a related, but distinct ability called Interpersonal Orientation. See R. L. Street, Jr., and T. L. Murphy, "Interpersonal Orientation and Speech Behavior," *Communication Monographs* 54 (1987): 42–62.

34 Some of these ideas can be found in R. P. Hart, G. W. Friedrich, and B. Brummett, *Public Communication,* 2nd ed. (New York: Harper & Row, 1983).

35 For a review, see C. R. Agnew and L. E. Vanderdrift, "Commitment Processes in Personal Relationships." In A. L. Vangelisti and D. Perlman, eds., *The Cambridge Handbook of Personal Relationships* (New York: Cambridge University Press, 2018), pp. 437–448.

36 M. L. Knapp and E. H. Taylor, "Commitment and Its Communication in Romantic Relationships." In A. L. Weber and J. H. Harvey, eds., *Perspectives on Close Relationships* (Boston: Allyn & Bacon, 1994), pp. 153–175; W. W. Wilmot, "Relationship Rejuvenation." In D. J. Canary and L. Stafford, eds., *Communication and Relational Maintenance* (San Diego, CA: Academic, 1994), pp. 255–273.

37 A. L. Vangelisti, "Couples' Communication Problems: The Counselor's Perspective," *Journal of Applied Communication Research* 22 (1994): 106–126.

38 G. Bodenmann, P. Hilpert, F. W. Nussbeck, and T. N. Bradbury, "Enhancement of Couple's Communication and Dyadic Coping by a Self-Directed Approach: A Randomized Controlled Trial," *Journal of Consulting and Clinical Psychology* 82 (2014): 580–591; G. R. Childs and S. F. Duncan, "Marriage Preparation Education Programs: An Assessment of Their Components," *Marriage and Family Review,* 48 (2012): 59–81; W. K. Halford, R. H. Rahimullah, K. L., Wilson, S. Occhipinti, D. M. Busby, and J. Larson, "Four Year Effects of Couple Relationship Education on Low and High Satisfaction Couples: A Randomized Clinical Trial," *Journal of Consulting and Clinical Psychology,* 85 (2017), 495–507; J. Owen, G. K. Rhoades, S. M. Stanley, H. J. Markman, and E. S. Allen, "Treatment-as-Usual for Couples: Trajectories Before and After Beginning Couple Therapy," *Family Process* 58 (2019): 273–286.

39 J. M. Gottman, *Why Marriages Succeed or Fail* (New York: Simon & Schuster, 1994).

40 See, for example, H. T. Reis, S. M. Smith, F. Tsai, C. L. Charmichael, P. A. Caprariello, A. Rodrigues, et al., "Are You Happy for Me? How Sharing Positive Events with Others Provides Personal and Interpersonal Benefits," *Journal of Personality and Social Psychology,* 38 (2010): 311–329.

41 F. D. Fincham et al., *Communicating in Relationships,* 1993.

42 H. J. Markman, S. M. Stanley, and S. L. Blumberg, *Fighting for Your Marriage: A Deluxe Revised Edition of the Classic Best Seller for Enhancing Marriage and Preventing Divorce* (San Francisco, CA: Jossey-Bass, 2010).

43 B. H. Spitzberg and W. R. Cupach, Interpersonal Skills." In M. L. Knapp and J. A. Daly, eds., *The Sage Handbook of Interpersonal Communication,* 4th ed. (Thousand Oaks, CA: Sage, 2011), pp. 481–524.

44 A. Bochner, "Functions of Communication in Interpersonal Bonding." In C. Arnold and J. W. Bowers, eds., *Handbook of Rhetoric and Communication* (Boston: Allyn & Bacon, 1984).

45 For instance, Ickes and his colleagues argue that differences in the accuracy with which women and men decode messages are not due to women's greater empathic ability, but rather to their greater motivation. See W. Ickes,

P. R. Gesn, and T. Graham, "Gender Differences in Empathic Accuracy: Differential Ability or Differential Motivation?" *Personal Relationships* 7 (2000): 95–109.

[46] M. Kuster, K, Bernecker, S. Backes, V. Brandstätter, F. W. Nussbeck, T. N. Bradbury, M. L. González Martín, D. Sutter-Stickel, and G. Bodenmann, "Avoidance Orientation and the Escalation of Negative Communication in Intimate Relationships," *Journal of Personality and Social Psychology* 109 (2015): 262–275.

[47] Reported in: W. V. Haney, *Communication: Patterns and Incidents* (Homewood, IL: Richard D. Irwin, 1960), p. viii..

[48] Hendrick provides a very interesting critique of the notion that researchers should generate prescriptions for how couples can encourage "good" interpersonal outcomes and prevent "bad" ones. See C. Hendrick, "A New Age of Prevention?" *Journal of Social and Personal Relationships* 19 (2002): 621–627.

GLOSSARY

Acceptance: Seeing another person as favorable; embracing or approving of another person.

Accurately detecting: When a person's beliefs about a partner's feelings or intentions match the partner's actual feelings or intentions.

Affection: The feeling of liking or caring for someone or something.

Affinity-seeking strategies: Communication strategies that individuals use to get others to like and feel positively toward them.

Altruistic love: Style of love that is unselfish, patient, caring, and kind.

Anxiety responses: Cluster of behaviors resulting from guilt or psychological distress, such as blushing, shaking, or perspiring.

Anxious/ambivalent lovers: Attachment pattern in which people experience emotional extremes, obsession, jealousy, and extreme sexual attraction.

Assurances: Showing and telling your partner how much he or she means to you and stressing your commitment.

Asynchronicity: A situation when objects or events exist or happen at two differnet times.

Attenuation rule: A conversational rule suggesting that the expansiveness of a greeting will gradually subside with each subsequent greeting.

Attitudes: The orientations that you enter an encounter with.

Attribution theory: A theory that suggests people are motivated to explain others' behavior, particularly when the behavior is unexpected and/or negative.

Avoidant lovers: Attachment pattern in which people fear intimacy and experience emotional extremes and jealousy.

Avoiding: Stage at which communication is specifically designed to avoid the possibility of face-to-face or voice-to-voice interaction.

Bases for prediction: Different levels of information from which people can make predictions about others in interpersonal encounters.

Blending social networks: Spending time with common friends.

Bonding: Stage in which a public ritual announces to the world that commitments have been formally contracted.

Breadth of interaction: The range of topics discussed and how much information about these topics is revealed.

Catharsis: Communicative release or unburdening that can occur with self-disclosure.

Chain of reciprocal events: A series of behaviors that are elicited and returned mutually by partners.

Challenge: Calling another person to engage in a competition or test.

Chilling effect: Avoiding revealing certain information due to fears that its revelation will result in ridicule, rejection, or conflict.

Circumscribing: Stage in relationships during which information exchange markedly decreases in both breadth and depth.

Codified: (Codification of commitment)—a lasting symbol of partners' intentions for relationship over the long-term.

Coercive controlling violence: Type of couple violence that occurs as part of a pattern in which one partner dominates and controls the other partner's daily life through violence, harassment, threats, and other tactics that invoke fear.

Commitment talk: Communication that implicity or explicitly reflects and demonstrates relational commitment.

Commitment: Involves the short-term decision to love another and the longer-term determination to maintain it.

Communal themes: Factors in relationships that stress the joint or mutual relationship.

Communication interdependence theory: A theory that suggests that different means of communicating, such as mobile phones and face-to-face interactions, become more intertwined as dyads become closer.

Communication norm: An accepted way of communicating that most people agree with.

Communication rule: A followable prescription that indicates what communication behaviour (or range of communication behaviour) is obligatory, preferred, or prohibited in certain social situations.

Companionate love: Style of love based on friendship and companionship.

Complementary relationships: Relationships based on different and complementary behaviors; for instance, one person controls while the other submits, one person leads and the other follows.

Computer dating type: Compatibility is examined and sought on the basis of practicality.

Constraint: A feeling of being limited or restricted.

Consummate love: Type of love that combines all three of Sternberg's dimensions: Passion, intimacy, and commitment.

Content level: The specific information or references that a message conveys.

Control: The power to direct other people's behavior or the course of actions.

Costs: Factors that reduce the enjoyment of being in a relationship and interacting with one's relational partner.

Coupling: Coupling involves giving another person your self-symbols and/or bringing the other's self-symbols into alignment with your own.

Critical talk: Focusing on your and your partner's flaws.

Cross-complaining: Conflict pattern in which complaints are reciprocated between partners.

Cross-sex friendships: Ostensibly non-romantic friendships between a heterosexual man and heterosexual woman.

Dependability: The knowledge that you can rely on your partner when it counts.

Depth of social interaction: Describes the extent to which the conversation includes information that is private or personal.

Dialectical theory: Theory for which the primary tenet is relational change takes place as the result of trying to resolve the inevitable tensions of relationship life.

Differentiating: Stage involing a process of disengaging or uncoupling.

Difficult communication: Involves interactions in which participants experience strain, difficulty, and awkwardness.

Disassociation: Messages of Disassociation—messages that prepare one or both individuals for their continued life without the other—increasing concern for one's own self-interests and emphasizing differences.

Disclaimer: Communication strategies that acknowledge that a rule is going to be broken.

Distance: A reflection of detachment, remoteness, or a lack of intimacy.

Double bind: A conversational dilemma when regardless of what a person says, sanctioning will be the result.

Double-shot hypothesis: Suggests that men will be more distressed by their female partner's sexual infidelity because they believe that women who are sexually unfaithful probably will also be emotionally unfaithful.

Dyad-locus problem: A problem linked to qualities or characteristics of the couple.

Dyadic phase: A phase or stage of relationship dissolution during which partners discuss the perceived problems associated with the relationship.

Editability: A state of being correctable, changeable, or modifiable.

Effective conflict management: Proper and timely use of apologies, listening, cooperation, and forgiveness.

Ego depletion: The idea that self-control draws on limited mental resources that can be used up.

Emotional contagion: Largely unconscious tendency for people who interact to be affected by each other's emotions in such a way that their emotions converge.

Empty love: Type of love that is high in commitment but low in passion and intimacy.

Equality rule: The idea that relational satisfaction is highest when each partner is perceived as contributing equally and benefiting equally.

Equity: The notion that relationships progress in the most satisfying manner when the the ratio of benefits to contributions is similar for both of partners.

Equivocal communication: Messages that are indirect and can be interpreted in multiple ways.

Escalation: Conflict pattern that develops when both parties want to fight rather than flee

Excessive responses: Potential indicator of lying in which a response goes beyond the boundaries of normal behavior for the individual being observed.

Experimenting: The stage during which we being interacting with another person to find out more.

Explicitness: A message for which there can be little misinterpretation.

External legitimizer: A communication strategy that focuses on external forces such as the situation or the environment.

External problem: A problem caused by the situation or context.

Eyebrow flash: A distinct up-and-down movement of the eyebrows which is barely detectable.

Faith: The belief that your partner will continue to be responsive and caring in the future.

Familiarity: Being well-known, recognizable, or understood.

Fatuous love: Type of love that combines commitment and passion but lacks intimacy.

Forgiveness: Expresses the desire to avoid retaliation, put the hurtful act away, and move on to more constructive acts for the relationship.

Formality: A relatively strict adherence to rules or conventions.

Fundamental attribution error: The tendency to overestimate the influence of dispositional factors in one's own behavior and underestimate the role of situational factors in other people's behavior.

Giving advice: Making recommendations for your partner's behavior.

Grave-dressing phase: A phase or stage of relationship dissolution during which partners focus on physically, psychologically, and socially ending the relationship.

Hassling: A five-step destructive sequence that demonstrates how aggressive patterns of communication often manifest themselves.

Have to commitment: Type of commitment based on obstacles to leaving the relationship.

Imitation: Specific type of reciprocated response that follows soon after the initial response and closely mimics the initial behaviour.

Immediacy: The degree of liking between communicators; the verbal linkage of the speaker with the content of his or her communication.

Impersonal themes: Factors/forces outside a relationship that are believed responsible for shaping it.

Implicit personality theory: A theory that suggests people believe that certain personality traits are likely to co-occur.

Impulses: Factors that push people together into relationships.

Inclusion: The state or condition of being part of a whole.

Incongruous responses: Potential indicator of lying involving an inconsistencies in one's statements or between the verbal and nonverbal messages.

Indirect responses: Potential indicator of lying involving evasiveness, vague responses, or few verifiable factual assertions.

Individual themes: Emphasizes separate identities and roles.

Infatuation: Type of love with high passion but no intimacy or commitment.

Initiating: The stage that incorporates all those processes enacted when we first come together with other people.

Integrating: Stage when relationships reach a point at which the two individual personalities begin to fuse or coalesce.

Intensifying: Stage of development in which partners have become "close friends" and the relationship becomes intensified.

Interdependency: Among the communication dimensions means that changes on one dimension will prompt changes on others.

Internal legitimizer: A communication strategy that focuses on individuals' responsibility for a particular behavior.

Internet compulsion: An irresistible urge to have access to and use the Internet.

Intimacy: Feelings of closeness, sharing, communication, and support.

Intra-psychic phase: A phase or stage or relationship dissolution during which individuals assess their partner's behavior and evaluate the extent to which that behavior provides a justification for terminating the relationship.

Joint identity: The blending of two individuals to create a new shared identity as a dyad or couple.

Liking: An attraction that is a result of positive reinforcement received from another person.

Listening talk: Talk that shows you have heard and understood your partner's message.

Love of beauty: Style of love that is passionate, intense, and rooted in a powerful attraction to physical beauty.

Maintenance: Sets of skills that require keeping a relationship from disappearing through possibly making it satisfying to both parties.

Manage the questioner: Avoiding answering a question by redirecting the conversation toward the questioner using strategies such as putting the questioner on the defensive, bringing up another topic that will irritate the questioner, or complimenting the questioner.

Managing the question: Appearing to answer a question without really answering it using strategies like intentionally misunderstanding the question, limiting the scope of the question, replying with a non sequitur, restating the question, suggesting there is a more fundamental question, asserting the question is moot, or making an assertion of nothing.

Matching hypothesis: The tendency of individuals to select a partner who is similar to them with regard to physical attractiveness.

Meshing: When mutual knowledge results in smooth, complementary interaction.

Mindreading: Assuming complete knowledge of the other person's thoughts and motives.

Multiple exposure: Characteristic of close relationships recognizing that interacting with the same person repeatedly can influence communicative outcomes (e.g., the ability to detect lies).

Multiple goals: More than one objective or aim.

Mutual influence: Describes how people's behaviors in a relationship (e.g., lying and lie detection) are influenced by both themselves and their partner.

Need-based rule: The idea that equity is not as important as exchanging resources according to the respective needs of the partners.

Negative affect: Expressions of hostility or other negative emotions.

Negative problem talk: Expressing problems in a way that the negative tone overshadows the problem itself.

Negative solution talk: Presenting unreasonable, unrealistic, or impractical solutions.

Negativity effect: The tendency to place greater emphasis or weight on negative information or events than positive ones.

Nonimmediacy: Distance as communicated by the communication content; not liking.

Nonlove: Relational state that lacks intimacy, passion, and commitment.

Nonverbal messages: The use of means other than words to convey meanings.

Norm of reciprocity: The strong tendency on the part of human beings to respond in kind to the behavior they receive.

Obsessive love: Style of love that is possessive, consuming, and somewhat like an addiction.

On-again/off-again relationships: Relationships in which the partners cycle between periods of being together and being broken up.

Ought to commitment: Type of commitment based on a sense of moral obligation to stay in the relationship.

Overhelping: Occurs when individuals explicitly help another person achieve some goal so that observers will attribute the person's success to the help he or she was given.

Partner-locus problem: A problem stemming from a quality or characteristic of the partner.

Passion: Psychological arousal and an intense desire to be united with the loved one.

Passive strategies: Strategies that are indirect; strategies that involves watching, listening, and observing.

Pentimento: An underlying image that reappears in a painting over time after it has been painted over.

Perceptual anesthesia: A distortion in what individuals sense due to their inner drives.

Personal idioms: Distinct names and phrases in intimate relationships that allow people to convey a great deal of information with few words.

Personalized communication: Involves revealing information that most people do not know, the use of multiple channels for communication, and the exchange of unique or private meanings.

Phantom-other technique: Technique in which researcher asks subjects to evaluate people they think are real but are actually made up to vary in key ways (e.g., being very similar or very dissimilar to research participants).

Playful love: Style of love in which individuals consider love a game.

Pollyanna Principle: The tendency to perceive and remember good, positive, pleasant objects and events more accurately than bad, negative, unpleasant ones.

Positive demeanor: Enacting an upbeat, cheerful style.

Positive problem talk: Attempting to provide information about the problem in a focused, specific, and relatively neutral manner.

Predictability: The expectation that your partner will act consistently in positive ways toward you.

Presence: The sense that relational partners are still together in a relationship, even when they are not physically co-present.

Primacy: The state of being first or primary.

Principle of Least Interest: The person with less interest in a relationship tends to have more control over it and typically determines the outcomes of the relationship, including whether it endures.

Privacy: Confidentiality; a freedom from being observed or disturbed by others.

Profit: Reward, gain, or benefit.

Quality: Characterstics or attributes.

Realistic love: Style of love based on practicality and logic.

Reassurance rituals: Attempts to reestablish the unity of the pair after a conflict has suggested differentiation.

Recency: The state of being most current or proximate.

Relational standards: Beliefs about the qualities relationships should have.

Relationship assurances: Relationship maintenance strategy involving showing or telling partners how much they mean to the person trying to maintain the relationship.

Relationship level: The message about the message, which tells us how to interpret the content and tells us what kind of relationship the two people have in this situation.

Relationship maintenance: The various things people do to try to keep their relationship functioning at the desired level, countering other forces that may contribute to undesirable changes in the relationship.

Response matching: A tendency for people to react to others' communication behaviors with similar behaviors.

Responsiveness: A core characteristic of intimate relationships marked by individuals doing things out of consideration for the other person that they would not otherwise do.

Resurrection: A phase or stage of relationship dissolution during which partners consider lessons they have learned from the previous relationship as they get ready for future relationships.

Rewards: The pleasures, satisfactions, and gratifications that people enjoy due to their relationship.

Romantic love: Type of love that combines passion and intimacy but lacks commitment.

Sandbagging: Occurs when people display weakness or low ability so that an opponent will reduce his or her effort.

Save face: Attempts to minimize the importance of the conflict to each other's identity.

Script: Sequences of actions that we carry out automatically, with very little thought.

Secure lovers: Attachment pattern associated with being happy, friendly, trusting, and accepting of one's partner despite known faults.

Selective perception: Sensing (e.g., seeing or hearing) only a portion of available information, often due to cognitive or emotional biases.

Self-disclosure: Revealing personal or private information about oneself to another person.

Self-fulfilling prophecy: When an individual's expectations or predictions become true simply because the individual believes they are true and behaves as if they are true.

Self-serving bias: The tendency to interpret one's own behavior in more positive, generous ways than others' behavior.

Self-surrender: Process in which people put the needs and feelings of the other person ahead of their own.

Sex talk: Discussions about sex, including the ways that people negotiate the initiation, acceptance, and refusal of sexual activity.

Sharing tasks: Relationship maintenance strategy of taking a fair amount of responsibility for tasks, offering to help.

Situational couple violence: Type of couple violence that occurs when typical conflict gets out of control and leads to a violent act.

Small talk: Polite conversation about unimportant or uncontroversial issues.

Social exchange theories: Theories contending that (1) in social relationships, we are constantly exchanging resources (e.g., love and status); (2) these resources are evaluated by us as rewarding or not; and (3) people have a tendency to seek those things that will be rewarding to them.

Social phase: A phase or stage of relationship dissolution during which partners concern themselves with the public acknowledgment to the social networks associated with the relationship that the relationship is being dissolved.

Spiral of reciprocal perceptions: A concept suggesting that individuals simultaneously observe others, are observed by others, and are influenced by both sets of observations.

Spring fever: Attributes one's feelings of intimacy to environmental changes associated with a new season of the year.

Stages of relationship development: Periods in which the communicative and perceptual changes associated with relational development become relatively stable.

Stagnating: Stage at which relational counterparts stop trying to talk about many topics of conversation because they "know" how the interaction will go.

Statement labeling: The identification of a statement as a fact, feeling, or inference.

Stereotype deductively: Inferring individuals' specific features based on their personality or group membership.

Stereotype inductively: Inferring individuals' personality or group membership based on their specific features.

Stereotyping: Formulating an overgeneralized belief about a particular category or group of people.

Stylized behavior: Communication practices or behaviors that are conventional and acceptable to many people.

Surveillance: Being well-known, recognizable, or understood.

Symmetrical Relationships: Characterized by each participant exchanging the same sort of behavior; an equal relationship.

Synchronized communication: Involves conversations that are smooth flowing, effortless, spontaneous, relaxed, informal, and well coordinated.

Tangibility: Concreteness or presence.

Terminating: Stage at which relational partners recognize that they are no longer part of a distinct relational unit.

Tie signs: Public displays that demonstrate the existence and importance of one's relationship.

Triangulating: Verifying data or information with several different methods or sources of data.

Trust: The degree of confidence people feel when they think about their relationship.

Unrealistic expectations: Beliefs or anticipations that are overly idealistic and improbable.

Want to commitment: Type of commitment based on attraction to the relationship.

Warmth: A sense of comfort, affability, or hospitality.

Withdrawal: Conflict pattern that arises when both parties want to flee the conflict

INDEX

formality, perceptions of, 127–128
freedom, need of, 260–261
friendships
    characteristics of, 244
    cross-sex, 245
    evolution of, 24
    love *versus*, 244–245
    role of, 88
fundamental attribution error, 164
future encounters, analysis of, 60–61

G

Garfinkel, Harold, 196
gay and lesbian relationships, 405
gender-marked titles, 206
"getting close" activity, 401
getting together, in relationship, 154–158
    conditions that facilitate or impede initial interactions, 157–158
    impulse to
        assert oneself, 155–156
        enhance enjoyment of certain activities, 157
        express experiences, 155
        receive stimulation, 155
Gilley, Mickey, 180–181
goodbye, in face-to-face transactions, 384
Greene, Graham, 258
greetings and relationships, 201–205
grooming talk, 214

H

Hart, Roderick P., 194
hassling, process of, 403
hebephrenia, 414
hedging, 198

hello, rhetoric of, 200–205
heterosexual relationships, 367, 405
honesty, 285
hookup, 36
human communication, 4, 110
    factors affecting, 7
    patterns of, 34
human intimacy. *See* intimate relationship
humor, sense of, 285

I

"ideal" relationship, 9
idiosyncratic communication system, 18
imagined interactions, 48
imitation, phenomenon of, 61
immediacy, concept of, 78–79
immediate physical environment, influence of, 123–131
implicit personality theory, 162–163
inclusion, of interpersonal needs, 75–77
ineffective communication, 438
infancy and childhood, interpersonal needs in, 84–87
infatuation, 241, 258
informal communication, 207
initial interactions, conditions that facilitate or impede, 157–158
initiating, of relationship, 40–41
initiation and reciprocity, importance of, 319
in-law/spouse relationship, quality of, 38
instant intimacy, 282
integrating, of relationship, 44–45
intelligence, need of, 261
intensifying, of relationship, 42–44

interaction stages, model of, 35
interaction, synchronization of, 19
internet
    chat rooms, 212–213
    compulsion, 132
    infidelity, 132
interpersonal
    communication, 12
    forms of, 115
interpersonal destruction, 399
interpersonal needs
    across the lifespan
        adolescence, 87–89
        adulthood, 89–91
        infancy and childhood, 84–87
        older adult, 91–94
    influence of, 74–80
        affection, 78–80
        control, 77–78
        inclusion, 75–77
        our own needs and those of others, 82–84
        plotting of, 80
        role of, 80–82
            complementary relationships, 81–82
            symmetrical relationships, 81
        in romantic relationships, 89
        satisfaction of, 200
        self-analysis of, 83
        of women and men, 95–99
interpersonal relationships, 4, 63, 94–95, 98, 110, 113, 116–118, 120, 122, 444
interpersonal skills, 84, 261
intimacy, 244, 276, 342
    and close relationships, 247–250
    commitment to, 251
    communication of, 346
    foundations of, 249, 265

persuasion, 333–336
    in abusive
        relationships, 333
    advantages of, 335
    goals of, 336
    strategies for, 333, 334
        effectiveness of, 335
    used to get
        cooperation, 334
Peters, Thelma Z., 208
phantom-other technique, 176
phatic communion, 214
phenylethylamine (PEA), 256
physical attraction, 241
physical attractiveness, 172,
    180–181, 241
physical fight, 405
physical inequity, 405
physiological degeneration, 405
playful love, 236
pleasant experiences, enjoyment
    of, 155
Pollyanna Principle, 169
poor physical health, 77
popular literature, visions of,
    118–120
pornography, 234
positive problem talk, 302
powerless speech, 419
power, sense of, 206
presence in one's life, sense
    of, 275
primacy (first impressions), 172
Principle of Least Interest, 318
privacy, perceptions of, 128–129
private communication, 128
problem solving, 295, 302,
    340, 458
procedural knowledge, 454
provocation, stage of, 404–405
pseudo-apologies, 304
psychological and physical
    development, processes of,
    369–370
psychological distress, 77, 291
psychological information, 42

psychological well-being, 180
public personality, 17–18, 40
public social performances, 47

Q

quality of life, 154

R

Reader's Digest, 118
realistic love, 236
reassurance rituals, 303
recency (last impressions), 172
relational communication, 132–
    133, 136–137, 275, 435–436,
    438, 454, 456, 460
    effective, 462
    evaluation of, 436
    features of, 134
relational contingencies, 446
relational intimacy, 443
relationship assurances, 274
relationship commitment,
    responsibility for, 318–325
relationship decay,
    communication during,
    375–384
        distance between
            interacting
            communicators and,
            378–379
        dyad-locus problem, 377
        external problem, 377
        nonimmediacy of, 378
        nonverbal behaviors
            and, 379
        partner-locus
            problem, 377
relationship development, stages
    of, 34
        identification of, 36
        interaction stages
            avoiding, 48–49
            bonding, 45
            circumscribing, 46–47

            differentiating, 46
            experimenting, 36,
                41–42
            initiating, 40–41
            integrating, 36, 44–45
            intensifying, 36, 42–44
            stagnating, 47–48
            terminating, 49–50
    movement stages
        dialectical theory of,
            55–57
        directions available for,
            50–53
        rate of, 53–55
        social exchange
            theories, 57–63
relationship disengagement,
    process of, 359–360
    cognitive dissociation, 379
    communication during,
        375–384
    farewell addresses,
        382–384
    strategies of, 376
    terminating relationships,
        360–375
relationship maintenance,
    273–276
    affects on health, 296–297
    constructive conflict,
        292–305
    lying, issue of, 285–291
    self-disclosure,
        confidentiality, and
        trust in, 276–285
relationship messages, 5–9
    commitment associated
        with, 8
    communal themes, 8
    content level, 5
    impersonal themes, 8
    individual theme, 8
    involvement theme, 8
    misconceptions about,
        9–15
    nature of, 9